T0384183

SEVEN SOCIAL MOVEMENTS THAT CHANGED AMERICA

OTHER BOOKS BY LINDA GORDON

The Second Coming of the KKK:
The Ku Klux Klan of the 1920s and the American Political Tradition

Feminism Unfinished:
A Short, Surprising History of American Women's Movements
(with Dorothy Sue Cobble and Astrid Henry)

Dorothea Lange: A Life Beyond Limits

Impounded: Dorothea Lange and the Censored Images of
Japanese American Internment (coedited with Gary Y. Okihiro)

The Moral Property of Women:
A History of Birth Control Politics in America

The Great Arizona Orphan Abduction

Pitied But Not Entitled: Single Mothers and the History of Welfare

Heroes of Their Own Lives:
The Politics and History of Family Violence

Cossack Rebellions: Social Turmoil in the Sixteenth-Century Ukraine

SEVEN SOCIAL MOVEMENTS THAT CHANGED AMERICA

LINDA GORDON

Liveright Publishing Corporation

A Division of W. W. Norton & Company

Independent Publishers Since 1923

For information about permission to reproduce selections from this book,
write to Permissions, Liveright Publishing Corporation, a division of
W. W. Norton & Company, Inc., 500 Fifth Avenue, New York, NY 10110

For information about special discounts for bulk purchases, please contact
W. W. Norton Special Sales at specialsales@wwnorton.com
or 800-233-4830

Manufacturing by Lakeside Book Company
Book design by Brooke Koven
Production manager: Anna Oler

ISBN 978-1-631-49371-3

Liveright Publishing Corporation, 500 Fifth Avenue, New York, N.Y. 10110
www.wwnorton.com

W. W. Norton & Company Ltd., 15 Carlisle Street, London W1D 3BS

1 0 9 8 7 6 5 4 3 2 1

CONTENTS

SEVEN SOCIAL
MOVEMENTS
THAT CHANGED
AMERICA

INTRODUCTION

Social movements have changed the world as often and as profoundly as wars, natural disasters, and elections have done. A relatively new feature in history, appearing first in the eighteenth century, social movements have been a means by which the common people—as opposed to elites—could impact public politics. Arising when the great majority of the world's populations was disfranchised, social movements spread as suffrage spread, both a product of democratization and a key factor in the spread of democracy. In the twentieth-century United States, they have been not only valuable but vital to progress in countless ways—from civil rights to Social Security, from support for the disabled to women's rights, from freedom of speech to expanding higher education. Not all social movements are admirable, of course, and those promoting antidemocratic and repressive policies have also exerted great influence.

As in all history writing, this study arose in the context of contemporary developments. Today news and images of social movements are ubiquitous and inescapable. Me Too, Black Lives Matter, and gay rights on one side, QAnon, the Aryan Brotherhood, and "incels" on the other; peace signs and pink triangles on one side, nooses and MAGA hats on the other. It would be impossible and probably undesirable to study social movements in a value-free manner. That is not a problem: understanding how social movements operate is more valuable, and far more interesting, than cheering or reviling them. This book aims to advance that understanding. The past will never yield formulas, typologies, or predictions that can be applied directly to the present. But examining social movements historically can reveal their common dynamics. As

Mark Twain is said to have noticed, history does not repeat itself, but sometimes it rhymes.[1] Although social movements do share characteristics, they are never merely the sum of their participants' values and actions; each becomes a living creature with its own complex behaviors. That is why individual narratives can often best capture their workings. Still, I am telling these stories in a way designed to reveal their commonalities as well as their distinctiveness.

This book examines seven social movements that arose in the United States between the 1890s and the 1980s. I admire six of them and abhor one, the Ku Klux Klan. In all seven I concentrate not on ideologies but on the experience of participants, focusing on what the movements did more than on what they believed, and on less-well-known participants more than on publicly recognized leaders.

Settlement houses, the subject of chapter 1, transformed social work approaches to combating poverty and discrimination. The chapter examines two vastly different settlements: Hull-House, the most studied and arguably the most elite and influential American settlement, whose residents were upscale women reformers, and the Phillis Wheatley Home, created by a poor African American woman to house other poor African American women. Both settlements sought to improve the lives of poor immigrants and migrants, but both also faced resistance from their intended beneficiaries whose view of their needs and priorities did not always match those of the "settlers."

The 1920s multimillion-member northern Ku Klux Klan, introduced in chapter 2, built a massive panic among white Protestants, especially evangelicals, that Catholics and Jews were undermining the nation's destiny. Then in the 1930s the KKK spawned fascist groups that adulated European fascist parties and governments and that followed Nazi Germany in directing their hatred—and violence—onto Jews and labor organizers. This two-decade history shows that the Klan's bigotry was flexible enough to change its targets while retaining its emotional and ideological structures. By placing the 1920s Klan and the 1930s fascists side by side, the chapter sheds light on the threat from white nationalists today.

Chapters 3 and 4 examine two movements engendered by the disastrous economic depression of the 1930s. The Townsend movement for old-age pensions made the elderly into an activist political force for the first time in history, and its pressure led to including old-age pensions in the Social Security Act of 1935. Though its members admired their national leader, the beating heart of the movement—and the source of its spread—was its local chapters and the sociability and support they provided. Townsend resembled the Ku Klux Klan in some ways, notably in its domination by white evangelical Protestants, even as its objective was progressive and secular. In the same decade, the unemployed movement, the subject of chapter 4, helped millions survive by pressuring government to provide emergency financial aid and longer-term relief and jobs programs. The unemployed movement was led by left parties, notably Communists and Socialists, whose energetic and altruistic work helped millions. But leftist hopes to build a socialist movement were foiled by the unemployed themselves, who compelled the Left leaders to focus on meeting immediate survival needs, strengthening capitalism rather than building a socialist movement.

Chapters 5 and 6 examine relations between leaders and followers in social movements, showing how followers often exerted vital but less-often-recognized leadership. The Montgomery, Alabama, bus boycott of 1955–56, discussed in chapter 5, arguably the founding inspiration for the civil rights movement, provides a particularly vivid example. This local struggle catapulted the young Martin Luther King, Jr., into national renown, and its victory in maintaining Montgomery Blacks' morale through a thirteen-month refusal to ride the buses owed much to his eloquence and courage. But it was the Montgomery laity—the followers—whose sacrifices, labor, and skills made the victory possible, and they are the protagonists of this chapter. So too the followers who built the United Farm Workers union in the 1960s and '70s, discussed in chapter 6. United Farm Workers (UFW) union founder Cesar Chavez resembled King in his charismatic ability to inspire, but he differed from King in functioning as strategist as well as inspirer.[*] He turned many followers into leaders by requiring them to lead. But

---

[*] In proper Spanish his name is César Chávez, but he used it without accents—quite possibly because so many Anglo publications didn't get it right—so in this book I use his spelling.

after about a decade, Chavez's extraordinary abilities became a liability: the second-tier leaders he helped develop became so dependent on him that they feared challenging him and allowed the union to shrivel beneath his increasingly paranoid and dysfunctional decisions.

Chapter 7 examines the women's liberation movement of the late 1960s and '70s—the largest social movement in American history—through a close look at two Boston-area organizations, Bread and Roses and the Combahee River Collective. Both were part of a socialist-feminist stream within feminism, the first an organization of several hundred mainly white middle-class women, the second a group of about a dozen mainly African American middle-class and working-class lesbians. Decades before the word *intersectionality* was coined, referring to the interconnection and interaction among seemingly different identities and causes, the two groups tried to put it into practice in their campaigns against sex, race, and class discrimination. Their considerable immediate impact was dwarfed by their long-term influence in advancing a feminism that merged with antiracist, antihomophobic and pro-working-class politics. Combahee's 1977 manifesto became the leading articulation of intersectional feminist politics, reprinted in hundreds of leaflets, newspapers, and anthologies throughout the world. Like many other social movement groups, however, these two organizations found it difficult to create effective democratic, accountable leadership.

SOCIAL MOVEMENTS have no standard or "classic" form, and the term remains imprecise. I am comfortable with an imprecise definition—large-scale, participatory activism, beyond electoral politics, aimed at social and political change—because social movements display immeasurable variety. They may involve hundreds, thousands, or millions of "members," and can be local, national or even global. They can represent particular population groups—say, women or disabled people—or a whole population, as in anti-colonial independence movements. They may be tightly organized or disorganized. They may have publicly visible leaders or seemingly anonymous leadership. They may or may not include formal organizations. Their bases of support may be elites or commoners. They can be progressive or conservative, inclusive or exclusionary, unruly or law-abiding. In democracies, social movements provide not an alternative to voting but a muscular supplement to it—informing voters about what is at stake in their choices, bringing voters to the polls, and expanding the range of electoral options. While some movements aim at specific policy changes, they can also stimulate a citizenly imagination, challenging the population to think "outside the box," generating new policy ideas, and disrupting assumptions that the status quo is preordained and insuperable.

However varied, social movements do share characteristics, and they will be evident in the narratives that follow. I want to introduce a few of the more important commonalities here. Beginning with the most basic, social movements bring people together, including those who were once strangers. Though they sometimes engender organizations, the movements themselves are typically larger and less bounded. They are evanescent, sometimes because they face discouraging failures, sometimes because they win what they were asking for, sometimes because they demand more time and energy than their participants can provide. Social movements may be defeated by the oppositions they arouse, but their influence rarely disappears entirely.

Because social movements have often been so influential, many scholars have tried to evaluate their impacts, as measured in legislation, judicial decisions, and numbers—data about wage rates, health indicators, and educational gains, for example. But their major effects may lie in matters unquantifiable, notably the climate of political debate and the universe of political possibilities—effects often visible only over protracted periods of time. They generate their influence by challenging what appears as natural, or common sense. New words have exemplified new ideas created by social movements. *Racism*, for example, was a relatively new word in the 1930s, imported from Nazi assertions of the superiority of the "Aryan race," then reversed in meaning by the civil rights movement. The women's movement made *sexism* a common noun. The act of naming something denaturalizes it, challenging its appearance as inevitable and suggesting its impermanence and instability.

That social movements are almost always short-lived is not in itself a sign of failure. Nor are limited goals. The Montgomery bus boycott, for example, succeeded in desegregating only one site of racism—buses—but it bequeathed inspiration, strategies, leadership, and determination to later civil rights campaigns. Short-lived movements have occasionally engendered lasting organizations, such as the thirty-eight-million-member American Association of Retired People (AARP), which arose from the Depression-era Townsend movement for old-age pensions. Destructive movements also leave legacies. The 1920s northern Ku Klux Klan imploded after only five years, but its influence continued long afterward: its anti-Semitism consolidated support for discriminatory immigration restriction that lasted for forty years, and it spawned American fascist groups in the 1930s.

Most social movements are by their nature nonviolent, because their power comes from reaching a broad public through peaceful and legal activism. The extremely violent southern Ku Klux Klan had to be, ostensibly, secret, but its progeny, the northern Klan, became a behemoth by adhering mainly to nonviolent tactics. Its successors, the 1930s American fascist groups, achieved less, in large part because they promoted violence, which of course required secrecy. Activists' commitment to nonviolence could be fragile, however, especially when opponents used violence against them. In the civil rights and farm-worker movements, for example, Martin Luther King, Jr., and Cesar Chavez had to use their charisma, eloquence, and the respect they had earned to stop members from retaliating in kind, and their success in doing so proved crucial to their movements' successes.

Many social movements try to be prefigurative—that is, they seek to make their movement or organization a microcosm of the society they want to create. Prefigurative movements reject "ends justify the means" strategies, recognizing that an authoritarian movement cannot yield a democratic result. As the poet Audre Lorde put it, "The master's tools will never dismantle the master's house." The Hull-House settlement modeled free discussion and debate over its dinner tables. Chavez began his organizing by initiating a cooperative welfare state for farmworkers, including a health clinic, a credit union, life insurance, even an auto repair cooperative. Montgomery's bus boycott built unity among African Americans, making it possible for each of them to share in the work and the deprivation and thereby take pride in their contribution. Even Ku Klux Klan chapters were prefigurative: their rituals and public events modeled their goal, a homogeneous white Protestant society "cleansed" of Catholics, Jews, and people of color; and it operated as a for-profit business, replicating the capitalist ideal it honored. At a time when the dominant culture was increasingly disrespectful of the elderly, the Townsend movement for old-age pensions advanced a culture of respect for the elderly. Prefigurative goals are ideals, imaginings, often implausible, almost never fully realized. But even failed campaigns serve to keep their ideals alive.

Relations between leaders and those I am calling "followers" are crucial to how social movements work. Those who acknowledge and support formally recognized leaders—that is, followers—often include subordinate, less publicly visible leaders. In the Montgomery bus boycott, for example, it was followers who designed a complex alternative transportation system and operated it for over a year, leaving King and other ministers free to raise money and to concentrate on inspirational, morale-building sermons and rallies. Social movement victories often depend on synergy between leaders and followers. In the farmworker movement, Chavez systematically cultivated leaders from among his followers by entrusting them with responsibility for major projects—in other words, he created leaders by requiring them to lead. Followers at times resisted, even defied their leaders' plans. Although the KKK succeeded in weaponizing its ideology, winning major electoral and legislative contests, its corrupt leaders' incessant demands for money, and their increasingly evident immorality—womanizing and drinking heavily despite Prohibition—produced disaffection and high turnover among followers, which led to a precipitous collapse after a few years. Dr. Townsend was adored by participants in the movement he began, yet they rejected his choice of presidential candidate. Left-wing organizers hoped to win over the unemployed to socialism, but they failed because their followers forced them to concentrate on their immediate survival needs.

Leader/follower synergy often foundered in movements and organizations committed to "participatory democracy." The 1960s New Left coined that phrase in reaction to the Old Left's undemocratic, top-down leadership: it described an ideal in which all members participate in developing goals and strategies. Practicing it, however, was a demanding proposition, possible in small groups but unlikely in large ones like SDS with its hundreds of thousands of members. Still, a degree of participatory democracy has been common among social movement chapters, smaller groups where followers can debate strategy and work together, doing more than, say, contributing money. Yet the participatory democracy ideal itself has been at times self-sabotaging. It has led, for example, to replacing official leadership with informal and unaccountable leadership, as happened to some degree in feminist organizations. That problem was mitigated, even overcome, in decentralized organizations like Bread and Roses that allowed small groups to take initiatives without seeking formal approval from organization or leaders.

Social movements require resources, and in this respect they are as unequal as the societies in which they arise. Chicago's Hull-House founders used their connections with the wealthy and influential to support their settlement, but the African American founder of Cleveland's Phillis Wheatley Home had to work as a maid, beg for money from wealthy white philanthropists, and accept their humiliating supervision. The Klan became a national force by extracting millions of dollars in dues and purchases from its members. Farmworkers' poverty meant that even those most committed to their union campaign could not afford to strike, and sometimes had to scab. Cultural resources mattered also. Hull-House's influence owed much to its highly educated residents, as did the women's liberation movement decades later. The Montgomery, Ku Klux Klan, and farmworker struggles benefited from shared religious practices, and the unemployed movement from networks of left-party organizers.

Time, another crucial social movement resource, has been plentiful for some movements and scarce for others. Townsend grew so large primarily because its base constituency was retired. Hull-House residents could do survey research and organize activities for their neighbors because they did not need to earn a living. Unemployment in the 1930s spread poverty and emotional depression, but it also left many of the unemployed with more time for organized protest. But reliance on members' disposable time could also be limiting: in some groups, for example, the influence of those with flexible schedules led to overly lengthy meetings, forcing those with children and/or demanding jobs to leave before they ended. As a result, those with fewer obligations were disproportionately influential.

Yet another important resource for social movements is space where people can come together. Creating physical space was the very definition of the settlement movement, but all the movements profiled here needed spaces large enough to hold hundreds of people. While the Townsend movement could hold meetings in public libraries, and the KKK could use public fairgrounds for their spectacular rallies, Montgomery's African Americans had no access to public facilities and relied instead on their churches. The farmworker movement's first headquarters, though very small, became a vital site where newcomers and supporters could "find" the movement, and the movement weakened when its staff moved into a remote area. Some social movements also need spaces private enough to allow participants to speak freely without fear of repression or punishment. Cesar Chavez's organizing began in farmworkers' homes where they could listen, share experiences, and discuss strategies without fear of growers' retaliation; women's liberation consciousness-raising groups thrived because meeting in private homes made participants feel safe in expressing intense emotions and revealing aspects of their private lives.

Social movements always educate their participants, for better and for worse. By bringing people together in the unemployed movement, members could see that their predicament had arisen neither as a personal failing or from bad luck but was shared among them, while Communist and Socialist organizers explained how the capitalist economy produced economic depressions. Women's liberationists learned to recognize the myriad and often taken-for-granted structures that maintained male supremacy. Even in the Ku Klux Klan, despite its speeches, reading material, and chapter conversations promoting bigotry and false tales of conspiracy, electoral and legislative work made members more sophisticated about how American politics worked.

Successful social movements create sociability, camaraderie, enjoyment, and mutual support for their participants. These benefits multiply when members work together in small groups. People may join a campaign because of its goals, but they remain when participation is itself rewarding. True, movements of the disadvantaged often arouse pain and anger, as participants confront discrimination and insults that had been psychologically buried, socially hidden, or bitterly tolerated. Misery loves company, but even so, social movements make the pain more bearable by bringing people together in enjoyable and supportive company. And sociability itself, the strength of numbers, evokes optimism and resists fatalism.

Social movements that seek to change the world simultaneously change their participants, who become less deferential toward the powerful and less likely to accept conventional stereotypes about their capabilities. They transform passive into active citizenship and encourage people to take responsibility for the society and polity in which they live. So members come to see themselves as politically potent, a process visible in every movement discussed in this book. Personal transformations are particularly vivid among the Townsend movement's elderly, California farmworkers, and women's liberation activists. While the Ku Klux Klan attracted people who were already bigots, it also created them, promoting its members' pride in being the only "true Americans," by which they meant white Protestants. Klanspeople came to view their whiteness and Protestantism as a more prominent, more valuable, but also more fragile core of their identities.

Social movements are unpredictable. Some seem to explode suddenly, others arise from years of organizing. They can be unruly because they intensify emotions, both anger and exhilaration. A protracted social movement becomes a qualitatively new entity, and its momentum may be destructive as well as constructive. In other words, social movements are risky. Their shortcomings will be evident throughout this book, but they remain crucial to democracy. They are especially vital when elections are unfair, but even fair elections usually do not introduce new values and initiatives—those require discussions beyond choosing among preformulated alternatives, whether candidates or referendum questions. American social movements have been responsible for some of our society's best features and a few of its worst. The best ones have nurtured democracy and freedom and made their participants more active citizens.

CREATING FREE SPACES

The Settlement House Movement and Two Janes

Jane Adams.   Edna Hunter.

We fatuously hoped that we might pluck from human tragedy itself a consciousness of a common destiny which should
bring its own healing.

—JANE ADDAMS, 1913

A home for all the other poor motherless daughters of our
race . . . the expression of the faith of a group of poor Negro
women and their devotion to the poor and homeless of their
own people.

—JANE EDNA HUNTER, 1941

This is the story of two settlement houses. One of great fame, the subject of hundreds of books, founded in the 1890s, was funded by wealthy donors and operated by upper-middle-class, well-educated white women—Hull-House in Chicago. Its renowned leader, Jane Addams, was the best-known American woman of her time. The other, mainly unknown, was established three decades later as a residence for poor young African American women—the Phillis Wheatley Home in Cleveland. Its founder, Jane Edna Hunter, born to a formerly enslaved mother and deprived of decent education, began her project while cleaning houses for a living. Both "houses" were part of a social movement that created residences as bases from which to work at improving the lives of the poor. They designed their spaces to meet the different needs of those they sought to help. Hull-House worked to help poor immigrant families struggling in an unfamiliar environment. The Phillis Wheatley Home provided a safe space to migrant Black women also struggling in an unfamiliar environment, weighed down not only by poverty and racism but also by the physical dangers—assault, harassment—facing young women far from families.

Both projects were part of a social movement racially segregated and unequal. The two projects might seem different species, but they shared the fundamental strategy of the settlement movement: creating a residential space from which to help the needy. Access to space was vital to all social movements (until social media provided virtual space late in the twentieth century), including those discussed in this book. But in this chapter, creating new spaces was the core of a social movement.

The two Janes' biographies were as different as their projects. Born in 1860, the daughter of a Republican state senator, Jane Addams graduated from the Rockford Seminary. Her stepmother tried to marry her off to her stepbrother, which would have made Jane doubly a dutiful daughter. She successfully resisted this marriage but remained stuck at her parental home, and that literally made her sick. Ordered to observe a "rest cure," which meant lying abed and doing nothing, she only got

worse.* She escaped at age twenty-seven when her college friend—
and romantic partner for a time—the adventurous Ellen Starr, then a
Chicago schoolteacher, initiated a European trip for the two of them.
Such European tours were then an acceptable means of ladylike accul-
turation. Less acceptably, once in London, they ventured beyond the
path expected of lady tourists and discovered a settlement house, Toynbee Hall, created a few years earlier by a radical minister and his wife.
Toynbee arose from the conviction that individualized charity work
could never eliminate poverty; only organized social action could do
so. Inspired, Addams and Starr decided to create a settlement in the
United States. The two women moved to Chicago with a plan and created a settlement within a year, using first Addams's family money, then
gifts made possible by her ability to reach wealthy donors. Jane Addams
was never sick again and became an American heroine.

Jane Edna Hunter, the African American daughter of poor sharecroppers in South Carolina, faced a life far more imprisoning than
Addams's. Born in 1882 to a violent father who beat her mother, she
was sent at age ten to do cleaning, laundering, and childcare for a family of six while also working in the fields. Working full time as a live-in
domestic, she first attended school at fourteen, thanks to being discovered by Black missionaries. Then her mother forced her to marry a
man forty years her senior, a man she came to detest.[1] She deserted
him—a poor woman's version of Jane Addams's refusal of an arranged
marriage—and became a live-in domestic in Charleston. Displaying
the same mettle with which she left a miserable marriage, she managed to enroll in a Black nurse-training school, even while remaining
a domestic servant. She achieved enough there to go on to the more
elite Hampton Institute in Virginia. After graduating in 1905 with a
nursing degree, she fled to Cleveland with $1.75 in her pocket, an early
member of the Great Migration of southern African Americans to the
North that would take off in the 1920s. Finding that hospital nursing

---

* This postcollege depression-caused ailment—labeled neurasthenia in the nineteenth century—afflicted other women in her cohort, notably Julia Lathrop and
Charlotte Perkins Gilman, whose short story "The Yellow Wallpaper" provided a
painful picture of the domestic imprisonment called a rest cure.

jobs were not open to Blacks, she supported herself by cleaning houses, until a connection made through her church brought her some private, live-in nursing jobs. She soon met other working-class Black women who longed for homes of their own and began to plan creating one. After six years, she got the financial support she needed.

CREATING SETTLEMENT houses became an influential social movement at the turn of the twentieth century—in 1891 there were six settlements, seventy-four by 1897.[2] Understanding settlements as part of a social movement requires, of course, a capacious understanding of social movements. The rapid spread of settlements, like the spread of the women's liberation movement (discussed in chapter 7), reflected a new understanding of social problems and a new approach to solving them. The settlement movement encompassed great variety, not least because it was segregated: for decades, white settlements did not invite, even excluded, people of color. African Americans responded to the new big-city problems by developing their own settlements, sometimes in response to that exclusion, sometimes independently. Some arose even before white ones. But the movement shared a single common tactic: developing homes as bases from which to offer help to those who were often facing danger. Welcoming strangers into their spaces was not only a settlement tactic but its raison d'etre.

Though settlement founders ranged from the wealthy and well connected to others as poor as those they sought to help, they were all women. This was fundamental to their project: creating homes as bases of operation. Across vast differences of class and race, women were accustomed to the work often called domestic. Yet settlements were most uncustomary: they were homes not of conventional families but of groups of unrelated women. I call them queer households— not in today's sexual and gendered sense—because I can find no other term that captures their implications. First appearing in English about 1513, the word *queer* meant "not normal," or "peculiar," and in some ways it has recently returned to that meaning. It began to signal homosexuality in the United States about 1914; it was originally derogatory, but as sometimes happens with people resisting stigmatizing terms, gays began using it, defiantly, in a positive way. The settlement movement's queerness arose less from unconventional sexual or gender relationships than from its nonfamily living arrangements. The geography scholar Kevin Hetherington calls settlements an "alternate mode of social ordering."³ In this meaning, settlements could be "queer" while being entirely respectable, even to conservative gatekeepers of respectability.

Consider also the meanings of *settlement*. To settle is to create residency; in colonial America, having a "settlement" in a colony was a proof of residence that carried certain entitlements. A settlement is also a place of multiple residents, a community or village. A settlement can refer to conflict resolution: settling a strike, a suit, or an international dispute. A town resident is a "settler" only if they have just arrived, perhaps a pioneer or a newcomer. We also speak of "settler colonialism," a form of imperialism in which a foreign conquering power sends its nationals in to settle in the colony. The settlers of this chapter were in some ways settler colonialists, claiming to uplift the "natives," as both Hull-House and the Phillis Wheatley Home sought to raise the cultural level of the poor. Some settlers, including those at Hull-House, even called their residences colonies.⁴

Settlers offered both material help and tutelage, aiming to bring a higher culture to their neighbors.* Using white settlements as the model, scholars have not always recognized Black projects like the Phillis Wheatley as settlements. They were indeed different: many were religious in origin and purpose, and Black settlers, even if they were middle class, also contended with the racism that surrounded their clients. All settlers believed that their constituents needed guidance.†

---

* It is illuminating to compare this tutelage to that offered by SNCC (discussed in chapter 6) and by the women's liberation movement (chapter 7).

† Of course, the term *constituents* is usually applied to those represented by politicians. Settlements did at times have constituents in this sense, as when they lobbied politicians to act to improve the public welfare. One could also call those to be helped "clients," a term that signals their freedom to reject what settlements offered, and the settlers' ability to learn and respect what their constituents needed. No single term does all this work, and I will use whichever carries the connotations appropriate to different contexts.

But unlike conservatives, they knew that their constituents suffered not from innate inferiority but rather from poverty and discrimination. In this regard, settlements were democratic projects. Many settlers developed a critique of the economic and political system that created the inequality they hoped to ameliorate, but for many that critique was moral rather than political: they blamed greedy and exploitive employers and politicians rather than systemic race and class inequities.

All settlers, Black and white, approached their projects with confidence in their view of right living, and typically assumed that their benighted constituents could do better if they changed their habits. Critics have named this approach "social control." The New Left of the 1960s and '70s criticized social control, labeling it a means of counterinsurgency, of repressing radical activism. They argued that social control turned courtesy into deference, civility into suppression of protest, cooperation into acceptance of illegitimate authority. But in the early twentieth century, *social control* had a positive meaning among even the most progressive activists. Addams, for example, believed that some restraints on individual action were necessary if people were to live in peace with others, and Jane Hunter would have agreed. Social control was for them a vital social good.[5]

Yet a crucial race difference structured their approaches. White settlers sought to transcend a negative model, to avoid behaving like the "lady bountifuls" of traditional charities.[6] They often called the objects of their efforts "neighbors," a term of equality, signaling their intention to avoid or at least minimize hierarchical relations. Addams was at first somewhat surprised by the generosity of the poor to each other. She sought to emulate "the emotional kindness with which relief is given by one poor neighbor to another poor neighbor" and to avoid "the guarded care with which relief is given by a charity visitor."[7] Black settlers felt no need to distinguish their work from that of condescending charity agents because they typically came from the same class and suffered the same racism as those they sought to help.

Social movements frequently use and develop expertise, but much depends on what counts as expertise. Subordinated people often develop skill at understanding the dominant culture. For some, it is a survival skill, while elites are often ignorant of the cultures of the disadvantaged.* The well-educated, worldly Hull-House women used state-of-the-art social-scientific research to learn about their constituents' deprivations and needs, and their findings were accepted and relied on by prestigious academics. Nevertheless they made mistakes in their understanding of their constituents. By contrast, Jane Hunter conducted equally serious research into her constituents' needs. (Today it might be called participant-observer research.) While most academics would not have considered it research or respected its findings, Hunter may have made fewer mistakes than did Hull-House.

JANE ADDAMS wrote of the "subjective necessity" of settlements, and her settlement arose also from her own "subjective necessity." She and other Hull-House women intended to use their privilege and ambition to do something of social value, but at the same time they were seeking freedom from the constraints imposed on women of their class. Their escape depended on a resource of the privileged: disposable time. Few women from prosperous families worked for wages. They were expected to leave their parental homes only through marriage, after which they were to be supported by husbands and would remain in their husbands' homes. Arrival at Hull-House freed women from these aspects of a Victorian gender culture. As Addams later realized, "There was not one 'needy' class in the city . . . but two." In identifying a need to escape these gendered constraints, she saw, in the words of Vida Scudder, that the settlers had "received far more than we gave."[8] Their vision of Hull-House involved creating simultaneously a base from which to help the poor and an unconventional, "queer" home for themselves.

Arriving in Chicago in 1889, Addams and Starr rented the former mansion of real estate magnate Charles Hull, built near his extensive landholdings. She described it as "a fine old house standing well back

* Alice Hamilton of Hull-House provides a good example. Hard-rock miners knew that the dust from drilling was making them sick, while experts denied it, until she proved the miners right. Other examples: migrant farmworkers in California knew that pesticides were making them sick while experts denied it; soldiers in Vietnam knew that Agent Orange made them sick while experts denied it.

from the street, surrounded on three sides by a broad piazza . . . supported by wooden pillars of exceptionally pure Corinthian design and proportion." She thought it "hospitable"—a word that hints at her intentions.⁹ Located in what was once the outskirts of the city, it had become surrounded by slums, with a mortuary on one side and a saloon on the other. The neighbors were mostly immigrants, as were nearly three-quarters of the one million Chicagoans, and many residents were extremely impoverished. The older Irish and German artisans who had built the neighborhood had been replaced by Italian, Greek, Polish, Russian Jewish, and Bohemian immigrants.* (A few decades later Mexican immigrants would join them.) The Italians and Jews tended to work in sweatshops, often in the garment industry. The houses were mostly wooden, originally built for single families but now routinely occupied by many; there were also tenements with additional shanties put up in their backyards, with no direct street access. Dwellings frequently had little or no ventilation. Most had neither running water nor sewage/garbage disposal facilities and used backyard privies; extremely high levels of illness and infant mortality resulted. There were no fire escapes. The neighborhood was just what the two young women wanted, but it was entirely unfamiliar: both had grown up in semirural towns, and Addams had never lived in a city, much less a slum.

Focusing on a small neighborhood as a method of social reform resembled what is today called community organizing. The neighbors were at first bewildered about what these women were about, or even hostile. It was not always easy to explain this new and strange enterprise to the uninitiated. When one visitor asked a tram conductor how to get to Hull-House, the latter asked, "What is it? Is it a theayter or what?" Were these women slumming? Perhaps. Consider Hull-House resident Edith Abbott's first impression of the neighborhood as a "vast city wilderness . . . conditions more primitive than the prairie frontier . . . indescribably filthy."¹⁰ Or were they spying for employers? Boys threw garbage onto the Hull-House porch and broke windows with

* *Bohemian* was then a rather catch-all term referring to immigrants from the Austro-Hungarian Empire; Chicago was then the third-largest "Bohemian" city in the world.

stones. It took patience and hard work to win acceptance among their neighbors—as well as among more influential Chicagoans.

Hull-House depended on the resources of privileged women. They had free time because they were unburdened by employment or family. Their social status helped them raise funds, and Addams's money gave them a head start. As Ellen Starr wrote, "Of course our great advantage lies in not being obliged to begin by asking for money."[11] Addams used her elite connections to generate news coverage, which helped the settlers find the donors they needed to renovate the house. She soon proved a masterful fundraiser. Her style and confidence show in this letter to Nettie Fowler McCormick, whose family owned International Harvester, one of the country's wealthiest corporations:

> *You have always been so generous to us that I find myself hesitating when I write to make an appointment about still another matter, lest I may be imposing upon you. You have seen our old house, so you know that while it is large and commodious in many respects, the number of bed rooms is limited . . . and we are obliged to take rooms outside of the House. This is not very comfortable for the young ladies themselves and their parents seriously object to their crossing the street late at night. To obviate this we are planning to add a third floor to our house. Mrs. Nancy Foster has given us $2500.00 toward this project but we still lack about $800.00 according to the architects estimate. I am now writing for permission to come to see you to talk over these plans and our needs, and of course while I shall be most grateful if you can help us out, I will certainly understand if you are too burdened with other things to do it.*[12]

A different strategy showed in her approach to Louise de Koven Bowen, the daughter and wife of bankers, whose grandfather owned much of the property now in Chicago's Loop.[13] Addams asked her if she "would come over there and do some work."[14] By soliciting not just donation but participation—a key tactic of successful social movement organizers—Addams recruited a lifelong funder of Hull-House who would go on to pay for several whole buildings. Addams soon broke up with Ellen Starr and found a new partner, Mary Rozet Smith, daughter of a large paper company owner; she not only helped fund Hull–House but also used her connections to bring in more benefactors. Smith and Addams became partners both in a lifelong romantic relationship and in exploiting their social capital. One example: Smith enterprisingly complained to the wealthy owner of some nearby houses that they were being used by prostitutes and got him to agree to donate the properties to Hull–House. Addams refused to take the gift until he agreed to pay to tear them down, then she got him to pay the taxes for fifteen years and turned the lot into a playground.[15] As immigrant neighbor Hilda Polacheck wrote, "Whenever Jane Addams felt that Hull–house needed an addition . . . the addition miraculously came."[16]

Most settlements reflected their female origins. Settlements founded by college graduates often sought to duplicate the small "cottage" dormitories in upscale women's colleges such as Smith and Wellesley.[17] Though Addams and Starr had no college experience, they aimed for a similar environment in a single large house. Free of the constraints of conventional family life, they constructed a living space that was simultaneously a work site. Hull–House became a family for a core group of women who stayed for many years, and an extended family for the many who stayed more briefly and for nonresident visitors who joined in their mission. It also resembled a religious order,[18] another unconventional family form. Like both orders and families, Hull–House imposed on its residents rituals, rules, and the sacrifice of a degree of privacy. Also like both orders and families of the time, it had a head: Jane Addams. No one ever doubted her position. She always sat at the head of the head table at meals, and among the residents there was jealousy over who could sit next to her.[19] Once when Alice Hamilton had to share a room with Addams— temporarily, in order to clear space for a visitor—she experienced it "as if she had been told to room with her housemother at boarding school."[20]

Over time Hull–House grew into an entire city block of buildings with a variety of purposes: day nursery, music studio, textile museum, gymnasium, coffeehouse, residence for working girls, and more. Addams wanted to make it a "Cathedral of Humanity," in which the buildings "made visible to the world that which we were trying to do."[21] This is an example of the prefigurative paradigm found in many social movements that sought to embody and model members' vision of a good society. (The women's liberation movement, discussed in chapter 7, offers an example.) Taken together, the Hull-House buildings created both open and closed spaces: there were numerous entrances from the street, but as a quadrangular block, it designated a space distinct from the neighborhood outside, like an Oxford college or a monastic cloister. Resident Francis Hackett saw Hull-House as "plumb in the middle of the neighborhood" even as its "grave, deep, spacious reception hall . . . declared you were out of the world. We . . . could hardly help feeling it was a sort of withdrawn community."[22] This spatial duality was fundamental to its purpose, as simultaneously home and community center. The duality was also gendered: when someone referred to settlements as clubs, settlement leader Vida Scudder retorted that men formed clubs while women formed homes.[23]

WITH JUST a touch of derision, we could say that the Hull-House residents were playing house, since without marriage they would normally never have had a residence of their own. Still, they brought one of the Addams family servants, Mary Keyser, to care for them—it simply would not have occurred to them to do housework or cook for themselves. The later resident Florence Kelley, a socialist, referred to Keyser as a "full-time professional" and her wage as a fellowship, trying to suggest an egalitarian relationship that did not actually exist.

Even as they escaped conventional family life, Addams and Starr created a decor that replicated the tastes of their gender and class. They filled their new home with fine Victorian furniture and art: "the photographs and other impedimenta we had collected in Europe, and . . . a few bits of family mahogany." They chose furnishings and decorations that complemented the marble fireplaces, leaded-glass windows, and high ceilings, such as fine vases, glass-doored bookcases, small carved mahogany side tables with silk-shaded lamps, luxurious rugs, leather-bound books, and marble statuary. By 1891 they had spent $1,800 on furniture.*[24] Brocade

---

* To estimate the current value of numbers like these, throughout the text, go to an inflation calculator such as the one at https://westegg.com/inflation. For example, this $1,800 is equivalent to about $62,000 in 2023—the latest year for which these figures are available.

curtains framed the windows, brass fixtures lit the house, and Addams's silver service rested on an elegant sideboard. Reproductions of Raphael paintings and casts of Donatello sculptures further adorned the house. At the same time, the residents were admirers of John Ruskin, a Victorian intellectual who urged rejection of the tyranny of highbrow taste, urging artists to ignore hidebound rules of composition. So they placed hand-crafted things next to the high Victorian ones. Addams wrote, "Probably no young matron* ever placed her own things in her own house with more pleasure than that with which we first furnished Hull-house."[25]

This elegance raises the question, how did the neighbors respond? I suspect they felt more curiosity, appreciation, and pleasure than resentment in gaining entry to Hull-House. Still, one settler's claim that Hull-House's luxuries generated "elevation by contact" for the neighbors seems both dubious and a bit dishonest.[26]

The bedrooms—on the second floor, to separate them from the public spaces—were more Spartan, each containing a bed, dresser, desk, chair, and bookcase, although long-term residents added furniture. Addams's bedroom also had two rocking chairs, several extra chairs, and a sofa, and she used it not only for sleeping and writing—voluminously—but also for receiving private visitors.[27] Making Hull-House both open and closed, a neighborhood project and a home, required some discipline and forbearance. Though residents had private quarters, they had to put up with noise, crowds, and seeming chaos—quite a change from the homes in which these privileged women had grown up.[28] There were rules, but there was also an ad hoc, makeshift spontaneity.

They were creating a queer domesticity, symbolically refusing the nuclear family as the only right way to live. Though men and married couples sometimes stayed at Hull-House, no man was head of household.[29] This was noticed: one neighbor who took advantage of Hull-House programs reported that people frequently asked her, why weren't these women married?[30] True, female households were not unknown, often multigenerational ones; but in Hull-House the female head was not acting in the place of an absent male, as a widow or single mother might. Because the residents were not economically dependent on men, they could create a domestic-

* *Matron* here means "married woman."

ity not only man-less but also somewhat egalitarian. Addams's unquestioned headship was not the same as that of a male head of household; the other residents might be deferential but they were also independent. Such a household might seem dangerously anarchic, even ideologically anarchist to conventional outsiders. We should not underestimate its radicalism.

Within the space there were same-sex liaisons; sexual or not, they were often romantic. At the time, passionate female friendships, known as "Boston marriages," and flowery declarations of love between women were not uncommon.* Over time Hull-House housed both same- and opposite-sex couples. Mary Rozet Smith, Addams's partner for decades in a relationship that would today be called lesbian, functioned not only as a financier of Hull-House but also as a wife, habitually following Addams around carrying a "shawl, pocket handkerchiefs, crackers . . . or anything she might want."[31]

This probably seemed normal to residents, given their adoration of Addams. It was not these romantic relationships that were unconventional but rather the household in which they lived. Hull-House's intensity and sisterhood—and they often used familial titles for each other, for example, "Sister Kelley"—created pleasure and inspiration. By bringing together women of charisma, enthusiasm, and adventurousness, the settlement facilitated sexual attractions and relationships, although typically behind closed doors. Early Hull-House residents exhibited anxiety about "illicit indulgence," as did most feminists of the time. Addams insisted that "platonic love" was "much higher than what is generally implied in the word 'love,'" and she thought sex education should focus on encouraging sexual restraint, which she considered necessary for a civilized society. (So did Jane Hunter, as we will

---

* The term *Boston marriage* came from Henry James's *The Bostonians* (1886), which featured a long-term co-habiting relationship between two unmarried women. Likely some of these relationships were sexual, some not. The term was particularly associated with well-to-do women; while women of all classes had romantic relationships with other women, the majority could not avoid heterosexual marriage because they needed the support of a male wage. When lesbianism became more publicly acknowledged, many women who "came out" were in couples with men for that reason. A good discussion can be found in the work of my former student Lauren Jae Gutterman, *Her Neighbor's Wife: A History of Lesbian Desire Within Marriage* (Philadelphia: University of Pennsylvania Press, 2019).

see.) But she also cautioned against "'damming up' this 'sweet fountain.'"[32] (This anxiety about sexuality relaxed over the next decades, and in the 1920s Hull-House residents campaigned for birth control and even opened a clinic at the settlement.)[33]

HULL-HOUSE WAS unconventional not only in personal relationships but also in the conversations it nurtured, which often resembled seminars. Most residents intended to practice careers in reform and/ or social science, their political/social perspective shaped by progressive female college faculty. The dining room hummed with talk about everything from tuberculosis and alcoholism to who could run for office and how to amend the Constitution. Six o'clock dinner was "the meeting ground of the day," a resident wrote in 1897. In the words of one Hull-House visitor, "Here the generalizations of the over young are discouraged with kindness and qualifying facts; here are the all-experienced induced to reconsider and admit another fact of the great truth. . . . Thus the social consciousness of the living house grows."[34] The conversations could be subversive, introducing new perspectives and challenging older ones. The residents were a family, yes, but as Edith Abbott put it, "a very argumentative" one.[35]

Conversation remained always respectful, even formal in tone— "always a fair field and fair play"[36]—so it built solidarity and independent thinking simultaneously. Addams welcomed initiative, even criticism, and fostered mutual respect. As a result, the female residents gained the freedom and challenges they craved without losing familial security. They were indeed, as the neighbors had suspected, slumming, but they turned slumming into a project of sociological research and reform. As the historian Kathryn Kish Sklar put it, Hull-House "collectivized their talents," making the fertility of the community greater than the sum of its individuals.[37] Though Addams was the head of household, she was by no means always a leader in its myriad activities. When new settlers arrived, she might suggest projects, and it was clear that everyone was expected to do some of the community outreach work, but she did not make assignments. She neither preached nor ordered.

Hull-House attracted so many prospective residents that it had to establish application procedures and reviews to select from among them. House meetings lengthened as the number of applicants grew. With so many newcomers, formal initiation into the culture of the houses became necessary. Still, when someone turned up who seemed perfectly suited to the group, immediate acceptance was possible. One was Florence Kelley, who would later become arguably the country's most important progressive reform leader. Like Addams, she was the daughter of a Republican politician, but she had escaped her family at a younger age. She enrolled first at Cornell and then at the University of Zurich; there she took in the theory and passion of European revolutionary socialism. She became a suffragist and a socialist, studied Marxism, corresponded with Engels and translated his work into English, and married a revolutionary Russian Polish Jew, Lazar Wishnevetsky. They immigrated to New York City. Wishnevetsky turned out to be a violent man. To escape his abuse, Kelley fled to Chicago with her three children and two trunks of clothes. She went first to the only women's place she knew of—the Women's Christian Temperance Union (hardly a comfort zone for a European Marxist). A WCTU worker told her about Hull-House, and she showed up there very early on a snowy morning in late December 1891.[38]

Immediately recognizing Kelley as of their kind, both in social class and in political perspective, the residents invited her to join them at breakfast, and she stayed for seven years. At first, Hull-House also took in her children, but the residents soon registered that the disease-ridden neighborhood and totally inadequate schools would not do for these children. They did not consider denying Kelley's children the upbringing and opportunities appropriate to their class. Besides, Kelley feared that her husband would seize the children, and under most state laws at the time, he was legally entitled to their custody. They solved these problems by placing the three children with the family of upper-class reform journalist Henry Demarest Lloyd, who had "just added a new children's wing to their home, Wayside, in the woods of Winnetka."[39] Later the children were placed with Frank Lloyd Wright's mother. Connections with such wealthy and renowned people, and the confidence to ask them for help, solved Kelley's childcare problem just as they had made Hull-House viable.

Hull-House's growth required rearrangements of time and space. All social movements do, but in a residential project, organizing space was fundamental to the residents' activism. Some came for long-term stays, some for shorter visits, which created a bedroom problem. A third floor of bedrooms was added, but it was not adequate. Long-term residents usually had private rooms, and thus a space of retreat from socializing, but they were often required to bunk with someone else in order to free up a room for a shorter-term guest.[40] This lessened a sense of owning or even renting a particular space, and while it probably produced some irritation and loss of privacy, it surely increased the aura of family. Sharing bathing and toileting facilities required flexibility, and one never knew who would be at supper. One resident referred to Hull-House space as "plastic," by which she meant flexible.[41] Shannon Jackson provides examples: "Residents learned to write up urban reports in the middle of a house filled with children's social clubs. Bedroom spaces became receiving spaces with the addition of extra chairs . . . storage spaces when the settlement's theater director housed all of her costumes and props in her room . . . adapting or retreating when the disruption was too much . . . 'we were trying to sweep back the tide with a broom.' "[42] Yet another aspect of their unconventional domesticity.

Soon the old dining room could no longer accommodate the swelling attendance at the meals that cemented Hull-House solidarity. So the residents fundraised and built a grand new dining room: two stories high and thirty by forty-five feet, connected by a walkway to the original building. Elegant but not ostentatious, the addition featured nine first-floor windows capped by arches and six second-floor windows, all mullioned with square panes below and a diamond-shaped pane above; it was lit by six frosted-glass and wrought-iron hanging light fixtures.[43]

As Hull-House's reputation spread, people of influence—academics, politicians, reformers, other VIPs, and potential supporters—came to visit. They were beginning to see settlements as the most advanced, most progressive, and most effective model for "social work," which at the time meant social reform. They wanted to see everything. They stayed to supper. They included intellectual luminaries. Although women could not get professorships until 1909, when the University of Chicago started hiring women to teach social work, Hull-House influenced several distinguished academics. John R. Commons and Richard Ely, economics professors at the University of Wisconsin and progressive social reformers, came often. The philosopher John Dewey, leading proponent of "progressive education"—calling for curriculum based on children's actual lives as opposed to study of the "classics"—came by frequently and influenced Hull-House's own programs for children. The muckraking journalist and Democratic gubernatorial candidate Upton Sinclair lived at Hull-House while doing the research for his enormously influential novel *The Jungle*, an exposé of the appalling conditions at the Chicago stockyards, conditions that sickened and killed both workers and meat consumers. Financier philanthropist Julius Rosenwald, owner of Sears Roebuck and endower of many Black colleges, also contributed to Hull-House.

These stars couldn't be slighted. They had to be welcomed whenever they came. But as Hull-House became well known it drew in many reform-minded visitors, and they disrupted the comfort of this intimate community, making residents feel their control of space and time eroded. The doorbell seemed to ring incessantly. When John Dewey visited in 1894, he thought that "the irritation of hearing the doorbell ring, & never doing one thing without being interrupted to tend to half a dozen others would drive them crazy."[44] Residents had to conduct guided tours of Hull-House's numerous rooms and buildings. Florence Kelley branded these tasks "toting," and referred to visitors as "totees," and the labels caught on. As these responsibilities multiplied, the residents established a rota of four-to-five-hour toting shifts, during which one was required to stay by the front door.[45] Weekly residents' meetings became longer as they negotiated schedules. People traded and split shifts, creating ever more complicated schedules, and tried to be excused from shifts with various excuses.

Some visitors complained about the constant hubbub. Beatrice Webb, a British socialist reformer and author, founder of the London School of Economics, who visited in the 1890s, thought Hull-House all "higgledy-piggledy" and disliked its seeming disorder. She found there a "stream of persons, labour, municipal, philanthropic, university, all those queer, well-intentioned or cranky individuals, who habitually centre round. . . . Every individual among them must needs to be introduced to us (a diabolical custom from which we suffered greatly in America)"[46] She erroneously concluded—with some disapproval—that the house's bustle was somehow an American fashion: "There are no doors, or, more exactly, no *shut* doors: the residents wander from room to room, visitors wander here, there and everywhere; the whole ground floor is, in fact, one continuous passage leading nowhere in particular."[47]

Amid the apparent chaos, Hull-House remained a headquarters for the residents' "social work." They began with research, studying the neighborhood, the neighbors, and their needs. They listened, thereby accumulating "facts obtainable in no other way," as settlement leader Lillian Wald put it.[48] (Listening as a key research method was practiced not only by Jane Edna Hunter but also by Cesar Chavez, discussed in chapter 6.) Their research implemented a relatively new Progressive-era method, designing and carrying out social surveys that yielded quantitative data. They proved master quantifiers. Though excluded from academic positions, several Hull-House residents were expert social scientists.[49] They approached their research, as did many other Progressive intellectuals, not as value-free or "objective" but as reformers. In this era, social science, like social work, was ethically driven, concerned, as Marx put it, not merely to interpret but to change society. Most social scientists of the time considered their research part of a responsibility to create social progress.[50] In fact, up until World War I, most quantitative social science was developed outside universities, by reformer-intellectuals. For Hull-House residents, social knowledge had value only when it facilitated reform.[51]

To some extent, Hull-House women benefited from their exclusion from universities. Even without academic credentials and support, they pioneered the application of quantitative knowledge to society, and their expertise confirmed the common view that social science was the feminine side of political economy. As Franklin Sanborn, founder of the American Social Science Association, had remarked, "The work of social science is literally woman's work." This fit the gendering of Hull-House, of course—quite a few men resided there, but they had to be comfortable in a women's community and with female leadership or co-leadership.

Hull-House provided "a means of bypassing the control of male associations and institutions," as Kathryn Kish Sklar put it.[52]

HULL-HOUSE RESIDENTS had the time and the freedom to explore worlds that would have been inaccessible to them without the home they had created. Their observations often clashed with their naïve preconceptions. Examining their immediate neighborhood, Chicago's nineteenth ward, they first counted buildings. Along with butchers and grocers, they found 255 saloons, seven churches, no public schools, and ten parochial schools for fifty thousand people. Walking the filthy and noisome streets, they found children unsupervised and often not in school. They talked to exhausted and unhealthy women. They found that their neighbors rarely connected with those outside their ethnic groups and that few adults spoke English. And they were shocked to find the neighborhood inhabitants resigned to their narrow and difficult lives.

When Florence Kelley arrived in 1891, straight from European Marxism and a "man's" formal education, she nevertheless considered social reform a path to socialism; only socialism could counter "the brutalizing of us all by capitalism," as she wrote to Richard Ely.[53] Still, she was at first naïve about what to do. She first tried setting up an employment agency for women, for which she used space in the next-door funeral home's morgue. This failed, because the city had neither a labor market that could provide decent jobs for women nor the child care to enable them to take jobs.[54] (One might wonder if locating the project in a morgue also discouraged takers.)

This failure showed Kelley how much she needed to learn, so she put her academic skills to work, organized a house-to-house survey of the neighborhood, and produced the extraordinary book, *Hull-house Maps and Papers*. Though influenced by Charles Booth's 1891 *Life and Labour of the People of London*, Kelley's survey covered a smaller area in greater depth and produced results quickly.[55] Hull-House volunteers visited every flat in every building of the ward and created a map that showed each one. Placed over the map was a series of transparencies, color-coded and hand-colored,[56] which allowed the reader to see one variable at a time—a device that foreshadowed today's digital mappings. The survey detailed its own methods of investigation, defined its variables, and reprinted the schedules it used. It produced an extraordinary amount of information, including the eighteen nationalities present in the ward; the earnings, family size, facilities, health status, and ventilation of every household; and the location of every brothel, saloon, sweatshop, and employed child. The survey counted the number of bathtubs (few) and found that many tenement apartments lacked even a kitchen sink.[57] *Maps and Papers* had considerable influence. It corrected the 1890 census on several counts. Moreover, it influenced the pioneering sociological studies of W. E. B. Du Bois, the leading Black intellectual of the period and frequent Hull-House visitor.[58]

The survey revealed immediately why Kelley's job bureau failed: women's earnings derived primarily from industrial home work under the "sweating system,"* and women doing this work also had children to care for. The poorest workers in Chicago, their earnings were so low that they had to put their children to work. Kelley saw children as young as eighteen months, sitting in high chairs, required to pull out basting threads, adding eighty cents a week to the family income. The impoverishment was such that when the 1893 depression laid off 20 percent of the workforce in one winter alone, it put 10 percent of Chicago's population near starvation.[59]

Armed with this data and connections made through Hull-House, Kelley aggressively lobbied politicians and officials. With Addams's help, she got herself appointed a special agent of the Illinois Bureau of Labor Statistics, then began a study of sweatshops. She visited nine hundred to a thousand homes, working from nine a.m. till seven p.m. Hull-House even got the Department of Agriculture, the most conservative of federal agencies, to fund a study of the diet of the Italians in the district.[60] Nothing symbolizes Kelley's transformation of Hull-House as well as her feet: Ellen Starr wrote that when Kelley

---

* Sweating was a system in which garment manufacturers subcontracted work to others who in turn hired their own workers, paying them a piece rate at very low levels. They worked in their own homes, which created pressure to put every possible family member to work at very long hours.

returned to Hull-House in the evenings, her feet were "so swollen despite wearing extra large shoes that she sits with her feet in the washtub all the time that she is not in the street."[61]

As Hull-House activities multiplied, it became clear that its greatest gift to its neighbors was space for the astonishing number and range of its activities, but equally important, Hull-House residents invited hundreds of neighbors into their "home." (Accustomed to families living in one or two rooms, one working-class visitor to a settlement remarked that its rooms without beds were a waste of space.)[62] The flow of visitors required them to expand and reconfigure their space and to raise the money to do so. By 1896 one resident wrote, "The old home is almost submerged."[63]

By its second anniversary in 1891, nearly a thousand neighbors came into this space every week. Its program was packed. Mondays and Tuesdays alone looked like this:

Every weekday 9 AM–noon, kindergarten
Mondays 3:30–5 PM, calisthenics; sewing for Italian speakers
Mondays 7:30–9:30 PM, art-history, math, drawing and cooking
     classes; Girls' and Embroidery Clubs; reading party for young
     men; library hours for working girls
Tuesdays 3:30–5 PM, Fairy Story, Jolly Boys and Hero Clubs;
     Knights of the Round Table; Red Stars; piano class; library
     hours for schoolboys
Tuesdays 7:30–9:30 PM, Latin, drawing, and English literature
     classes; Travelers' and Young Citizens' Clubs; library hours for
     working boys[64]

By 1894, as Hull-House entered its fifth year, the number and range of activities it offered was hardly short of amazing. In addition to the many classes and clubs, it hosted a debating society, a dispensary of medications, a gymnasium, free concerts every Sunday afternoon, an art gallery, a reading room, several choral groups, a playground, a free nursery for thirty to forty infants and toddlers, a kindergarten for thirty

kids, summer picnic outings for children, and baths and laundry facilities. (Typically, Hull-House residents saw the neighbors' lack of hygiene
as a problem of poverty, not of character. While providing baths, they
also lobbied the city to build a public bathhouse, which opened in 1893.)
Its clubs now included more sophisticated and directly reform-related
gatherings. The Arnold Toynbee Club focused on economics, the Chicago Question Club on the problems of the city, the Nineteenth Ward
Improvement Club on the neighborhood, the Women's Club and the
Working People's Social Science Club on a wide range of political questions such as woman suffrage and labor unions. There were weekly
"receptions" for German-speaking neighbors. Similar receptions for
the Italian-speaking were less successful, largely because the Italian
Catholic hierarchy disapproved of the place.[65]

The neighbors who participated in these activities were not only
beneficiaries but also agents, however little they realized it. Those
who used the settlement's programs reshaped and redesigned them,
responding to some, ignoring others, and introducing still others. Consider the Hull-House coffeehouse, set up in 1893 behind the kitchen.
Hull-House investigators had found that many women who did piece-
rate sewing in their kitchens found it difficult to feed their children
well. To serve the neighbors' needs, the coffeehouse was open from
six a.m. to ten p.m. It was intended "to combine the convenience of a
lunch-room, where well-cooked food can be sold at a reasonable rate,
with coziness and attractiveness." It also offered takeout, foods sold by
the quart or the pound. It would even deliver coffee, soups, and stews
at lunchtime to nearby workplaces and found that an indurated (coated)
fiber container made it possible to deliver the food hot. "Employees"—
their term was meant to signal a status higher than *workers*—"could
purchase a pint of soup or coffee with two rolls for five cents, and the
plan of noon factory delivery is daily growing in popularity."[66]

For the settlers, the coffeehouse also had a second purpose. They
considered the foodways of their neighbors inferior, notably their love
for "highly seasoned" dishes, and they wanted to reform their neighbors' diets, to introduce them to the "simple fare known as New
England," Jane Addams wrote.[67] The coffeehouse was even designed
in New England style: "an attractive copy of an English inn, with low,

dark rafters, diamond windows, and large fireplace."[68] But the neighbors resisted the "reforming" of their tastes. Progressive household efficiency expert Ellen Swallow taught Hull-House residents how to prepare healthy food for neighbors, but they wouldn't eat it. The coffeehouse/restaurant was used more by visiting academics and middle-class reformers than by working-class people. The settlers tried to compete with the saloons by experimenting with every soft drink they could imagine, including grape juice, to no avail. One man who tried the coffeehouse remarked, "This would be a nice place to sit in all day, if one could only have beer."[69] One woman told Addams that "she likes to eat 'what she'd ruther.'"[70] So cooking classes failed to attract students.[71] Decades later, at Hull-House's fortieth-anniversary event, a speaker admitted that the Hull-House women were often wrong: she had "come to the conclusion that the immigrant mothers knew much more about feeding children that we specialists did."[72]

One group of neighbors was particularly influential: children. Florence Kelley's first glimpse of Hull-House in 1891 showed her the need for child care vividly. As she later recalled, Addams opened the door, "holding on her left arm a singularly unattractive, fat, pudgy baby belonging to the cook, who was behind-hand with breakfast." Addams was further "hindered in her movements by a super-energetic kindergarten child, left by its mother while she went to a sweatshop for a bundle of cloaks to be finished."[73] In other words, the Hull-House nursery was created in part to keep the children from running helter-skelter through the house. How did the children get there? The answer illuminates part of Hull-House's success. The first child came in late 1889 when a neighbor *asked* to leave her baby at Hull-House while she did some errands. I suspect that this request for babysitting was a way of testing what Hull-House was willing to offer. The settlers had by then learned how much and how often neighbors traded help and goods, treating children as a collective responsibility to some extent. Children, for these working-class people, were a central part of these exchanges.

The young children directly, and their mothers and older siblings indirectly, generated a major Hull-House initiative—organized childcare. This is an example of a social movement in which leaders' tactics were led by those they sought to help (a phenomenon that will be visible in later chapters). Many neighboring women worked in sweat-shops, factories, and at home, doing garment manufacture in particular, and the work imposed deadlines and required out-of-home errands. Their babysitting requests—that is, their agency—shaped Hull-House's agenda, and it responded. By the end of their first year, the residents were caring for fifteen children. They soon rented other space, found a volunteer director to run the nursery, and charged five cents per child per day.[74] By 1895 Hull-House had a separate children's building, designed by an elite architectural firm. It must have daylight on three sides, the residents insisted. Four stories high, it cost $12,000 and contained a crèche, kindergarten rooms, clubrooms for older children, a music room, and an art studio. The rooms were painted in pastels—pink, green, blue, and yellow—and the wooden furniture was also brightly painted. The babies wore matching pinafores and took naps in rows of white-enameled cots.[75]

In organizing the nursery, the residents were influenced by German childhood education theorist Friedrich Fröbel. An early advocate of what came to be called progressive education, he argued that play is the principal means of learning in early childhood. This was radical—the dominant child-raising ethos of the period included rigid scheduling, requiring obedience and sitting still, allowing only "educational" play organized by adults. By contrast, at Hull-House children were often to be found exploring, running, and playing all over the House—reflecting an emphasis on children's free expression that would be anathema to those who ran the Phillis Wheatley Home (as we will see below). When Ellen Starr organized groups of children to decorate the Hull-House Christmas tree, she undecorated it after each group finished, so the next group could design it with their own preferences.[76] Meanwhile the uninhibited younger children brought older ones into Hull-House, or as a visitor from another settlement put it, "residents began to be accredited to older brothers and sisters [who] were ready to storm the house as they became conscious of welcome."[77] The older children took up yet more space and moved at a higher velocity. In an effort to limit their dominion, the residents worked to organize them into clubs for boys and girls.

Neighborhood boys and young men turned a piece of Hull-House into a male space. Responding to their requests, Hull-House created a gymnasium. When it became too small for the demand, a new, larger one was built. As one Hull-House regular recalled, "Hundreds of boys, who had no other means of recreation could go to the gymnasium and play basketball until they were so worn out that they could only go home and go to bed."[78]

The most famous Hull-House response to neighbors' needs, perhaps, was the Jane Club.* In 1898 a group of young single women, on strike against a shoe factory, were searching for a place to live while they were without wages. They appealed to Hull-House. Addams helped them collectively rent an apartment, and Hull-House donated furniture and the first month's rent for two apartments. This was a radical step, at a time when unmarried women were expected to board with families. In their apartments, these young women workers created a working-class version of Hull-House's own female dominion. This ad hoc response soon became a permanent Hull-House institution: yet another Hull-House building, a YWCA-like boardinghouse offering thirty rooms plus a library, dining room, kitchen, and a parlor with a piano. The women who moved in wrote their own rules, elected officers, and paid three dollars a week for room and board. They ran the home as a cooperative, writing a constitution, reviewing the applications of those who sought to join, and electing officers with the proviso that no one could be elected for more than one half-year term. (This regime contrasted sharply with that in the Phillis Wheatley Home, as we will see.) The officers included a "stewardess" who received complaints and suggestions. Visitors could eat there for fifteen cents a meal, and overnight visitors could stay for four dollars a week, though these charges increased when they hired a cook and two maids in order to make the Jane Club self-supporting.[79]

MANY HULL-HOUSE settlers, including Addams, believed that class harmony between workers and employers was not only desirable but possible. Though not hostile to labor unions in principle, she held to

---

* Though there was no connection, it is striking that some seventy years later Chicago women's "Jane" project offered abortions before they were legalized. The spirit and premise of both "Janes" was similar—women relying on each other for help.

the belief that understanding and cooperation would be the best solution to the sufferings of working-class people.* She tried to mediate strikes and denounced the greed of employers—seeing the problem as one of morality rather than exploitation.† By contrast, Florence Kelley thought capitalism depended on exploitation and that the working class needed labor unions to fight back.[80] Remarkably, these differences did not produce conflict. Addams's comfort with disagreement and respect for diverse perspectives allowed Hull-House to become a valuable space for radical ideas and organizing. When labor unions began requesting meeting space, Hull-House obliged, another example of how space was one of the most valuable resources it offered. Women workers were prominent in several garment strikes but could not use the meeting places used by men, which were typically saloons. So ultimately three unions and the Chicago branch of the Women's Trade Union League were born at Hull-House.[81]

Several unions held regular meetings at Hull-House, and workers met there during several strikes, though this was a time of severe repression of labor organizing. (A bomb thrown at an 1886 labor rally in Chicago's Haymarket Square had unleashed ruthless repression of anarchists and labor unions.) The organizer of the Bindery Girls Union, Mary Kenney, had lived at Hull-House for several months, and her cause no doubt profited from connections she made there.[82] Soon some Hull-House settlers began writing and speaking on behalf of workers.[83]

Hull-House took further risks in the meetings and lectures it hosted. The anticlerical Giordano Bruno Club met there, bringing down the wrath of the neighborhood's priests. The Working People's Social Science Club met at Hull-House weekly for seven years and became one of Chicago's major sites of socialist debate. W. E. B. Du Bois lectured there. Hull-House also displayed courage in its fundraising. Although

---

* Sarah Hart, a Hull-House donor and wife of a large manufacturer, felt betrayed by Addams's support for garment strikers. Thanks to Felice Batlan for this point.
† The strikes included the 1894 Pullman strike pitted railroad workers against the Pullman corporation, when marshals and the army charged into picketers, leaving dozens dead and scores wounded.

reliant on the very wealthy for support, it refused to accept a big donation from an employer notorious for underpaying the girls he hired.

Hull-House and other settlements were regularly attacked as un-American, unpatriotic sites of immorality and, later, as promoters of Bolshevism. A Chicago newspaper grumbled that Hull-House was "a socialistic labor union center. . . . The only matter of surprise is that . . . the grand jury does not indict its members for conspiring to injure the company's business." The reporter thought, with some accuracy, that Hull-House got away with it because it was a women's operation, but "when women act like men they must expect to be treated like men," he threatened.[84]

Attempts to introduce high culture to the poor were at best a mixed success. The effort expressed a democratic confidence that the poor were not intellectually deficient. Rejecting the Americanization agenda typical of other Progressives, Hull-House did not emphasize vocational education intended to prepare neighbors for low-wage jobs. Instead it sponsored "uplift" programming, some of it resembling a college humanities education. It created a Shakespeare Club; offered classes in various European literatures and languages, math, and history; and held concerts and lectures on literature, music, and art. Residents also sought to encourage their immigrant neighbors' pride in their national cultures. Having observed that Italians and Greeks knew nothing of the great arts of their homelands, Hull-House displayed reproductions of Renaissance art, established a lending library of reproductions, and put on Greek plays.[85] A Woman's Club drew hundreds who listened to lectures and soon got its own building, paid for by Louise de Koven Bowen. Hilda Polacheck recalls women of wealth and women who barely had enough to eat, educated women and illiterate women, sitting side by side, listening.[86]

A Hull-House art gallery became a popular attraction. The *Chicago Herald* described it as "Art for Poor People" and as a "New Educational Home Where Pictures and Books May Be Enjoyed by Those Who Are Not Accorded the Privileges of More Pretentious Institutions." Hull-House donors loaned paintings by Corot, Inness, G. W. Watts, Alberto Pasini, and Jean-Charles Cazin for display in the gallery.[87] The exhibits also functioned to let people wander through Hull-House, taking in its fine furnishings and decoration, perhaps seeing such luxury for the first time. And of course Hull-House used the gallery to build support from elites. The gallery's opening gala brought millionaire donors along with distinguished guests from the settlement movement, notably Reverend and Mrs. Barnett, Toynbee Hall's founders. The *Chicago Herald* reported that "Miss Adams [*sic*] looked her best in violet crepe with velvet trimmings. Her hat was a gracefully poised bunch of wood violets."[88]

Some neighbors seized upon these opportunities and were changed by them. Greek neighbors' blossoming nationalism led some to attend classical plays presented in modern Greek and lectures on the greatness of Greek civilization.[89] But most neighbors did not respond to these high-culture efforts. The Italian journalist Alessandro Mastro-Valerio became a short-term Hull-House resident and was able to attract some of his countrymen to events he promoted, but he soon left, and the events for Italian speakers were discontinued.[90] We know about these less successful projects partly because of Jane Addams's willingness to declare her mistakes publicly. "There was in the earliest undertakings at Hull-house a touch of the artist's enthusiasm when he translates *his inner vision* [my emphasis]. . . . We fatuously hoped that we might pluck from human tragedy itself a consciousness of a common destiny which should bring its own healing."[91]

Some of the failures resulted from the misleading findings that occur when one asks the wrong questions or doesn't listen. Consider Kelley's survey category "Italian." The immigrants she classified that way actually had little if any Italian identity; their identities were Neapolitan, Sicilian, Calabrian, and so on, which may partly explain their apparent lack of interest in events that celebrated Italian culture. A Denison House settler described these as an effort to "Italianize Italians."[92] Some Hull-House residents blamed the failures of its high-culture offering on the passivity of immigrants who were not energetically seeking to better their lives, and this assumption kept the settlers from relating to, partnering in, or aiding immigrants' own initiatives, such as the mutual benefit societies they had created—which numbered over a hundred.

Hull-House residents thought their Jewish neighbors unresponsive to local political campaigns, perhaps unaware of their protest activity against the pogroms occurring in the Russian and Austro-Hungarian empires. True, the Jews had a dense network of their own institutions, including literary and radical political societies, and they probably associated Hull-House with Christian missionaries. But Hull-House did not reach out to Jews.[93] A disconnect between Hull-House's and their neighbors' values and economic assumptions showed in the failure of a coal-buying cooperative it initiated. The idea was to buy in bulk so as to get a lower price. But the cooperative's managers were not capitalists, and when approached by destitute neighbors, they gave away free coal so often as to bankrupt the project, which then closed.[94]

Hull-House did better when it responded to its neighbors' own desires. Boys thronged to the gymnasium and sports teams. Neighbors used the showers and baths. Mothers took advantage of the nursery, kindergarten, and after-school clubs for children. The most popular men's activity was an "electrical" club with lab and machine shop, training men in this new technology and perhaps preparing them for future jobs. Women came in large numbers to classes in dressmaking, also a bankable skill.[95]

Despite taking pride in service to the community, Hull-House residents did not always find their neighbors' intrusions easy. Providing space for a larger community inevitably inhibited residents' space. A Boston settlement leader noted a reaction undoubtedly present in Hull-House as well, remarking that residents sought with "jealous watchfulness to keep the house as far as possible like a family residence."[96] Residents also wanted to preserve Hull-House's elegance. So rather than permanently making their space more institutional, residents accommodated events by shifting rooms and furniture temporarily. They turned parlors into meeting rooms by setting up folding chairs and tables, then removing them.[97] These near-constant shifts created annoyance and tensions.

Time as well as space had to be fluid. Except for short-term guests who came to observe, Hull-House residents all worked—depending, of course, on the definition of *work*. Many worked outside the house, but when they returned, they were working still. Leisure time and work time were not easily distinguished. Although residents had few housekeeping duties, the staff could not do the hostessing. No doubt some longed to retreat to bedrooms when they were obliged instead to attend meetings and welcome guests. Mainly from prosperous families, a few senior residents spent summers away from Hull-House to escape settlement bustle.[98] Addams discovered Bar Harbor, Maine, when one of Hull-House's benefactors invited her; in 1904 she and her partner Mary Rozet Smith bought a house and spent every summer there.[99] Yet for Addams, leisure and work were almost indistinguishable. She said she could raise more money in a single month in Bar Harbor than all the rest of the year in Chicago. Still, the greatest privilege of many Hull-House residents was their ability to devote themselves to Hull-House without families or jobs to support them.

SETTLEMENTS THROUGHOUT the nation influenced state and local politics and legislation, and Hull-House did so particularly successfully. With her formidable energy, Florence Kelley chalked up substantial gains for the working class and poor of Chicago and Illinois. She made Hull-House a major force in city and state politics, mixing expert research with aggressive lobbying. She led, for example, an investigation of the smallpox epidemic of 1881–82, which killed almost 2,500, showing its origin in garment sweatshops, spread by infected clothing. She persuaded the Progressive governor John Peter Altgeld, whose election Hull-House had actively supported, to appoint her the state's factory inspector. She pressured municipal authorities, sometimes successfully, to inspect and regulate the sweatshops. A Hull-House exhibit on substandard housing got the city council to pass a housing ordinance requiring at least minimally safe conditions. It contributed to legislation raising the minimum age for full-time child workers to fourteen and providing compensation to workers who contracted industrial diseases. By documenting the lack of bathtubs, Hull-House pressure yielded more municipal bathhouses. Similar pressure produced better garbage collection, more schools, public playgrounds, Chicago's first public swimming pool, and the first juvenile court.

Although unable to vote for several decades after founding Hull-House, these settlers won governmental and institutional positions,

Factory inspectors past and present. From left to right: Ella Haas, state factory inspector, Ohio; Mary Malone, state inspector ten-hour law, Delaware; Florence Kelley; Jean Gordon, factories inspector, New Orleans; Madge Nave, factory inspector, Kentucky; Martha D. Gould, factories inspector, New Orleans, Louisiana.

both official and unofficial. Jane Addams got herself appointed Chicago's garbage inspector, a job she invented with the aim of improving public health. She followed garbage collection vehicles so as to document the poor service in the working-class neighborhoods. (She received a salary of $1,000 a year, thereby pulling municipal funds into Hull-House.) An eight-hour-day law pushed by Hull-House, with union support, was in effect for a year before the state supreme court overturned it. The physician Alice Hamilton, one of Hull-House's most stellar researchers, pioneered the study of occupational diseases and accidents. She became a member and de facto head of the Occupational Diseases Commission of Illinois and later the first woman appointed to the Harvard faculty. Kelley went on to organize the famous Brandeis brief, which pioneered the use of social science research in legal argument; she got her settlement allies Josephine and Pauline Goldmark to write it and Supreme Court justice Brandeis to use it in the 1908 *Muller v. Oregon* Supreme Court decision. The first time the Court approved a protective labor law, the case set the precedent for marshaling social science data to support legal arguments.[100] In short, Hull-House leaders became power brokers, able to compel officials to reckon with them and seek their approval.

But except for Kelley, Ellen Starr, and a few others, Hull-House women did not work to increase the political power of their working-class neighbors. Their achievements were typically gains *for* the people rather than victories *of* the people. While residents often responded to the initiatives of their neighbors, they did not ask the neighbors to help design the projects they created. Like most women reformers at the time, they often framed their goals in maternalist terms, extending the expectation that women nurture children to argue that women have a responsibility for nurturing a safer, healthier society.* Some labeled this work "civic housekeeping." That framing authorized women to talk to mayors, senators, governors, lawyers, professors, and capitalists without challenging the gender order. Combined with their class confidence, the maternalist stance enabled them to practice as experts in worlds of men. But the reverse face of this maternalist sense of responsibility showed in attempts to reform their constituents' private lives, and in those attempts the Progressive-era women reformers engaged in forms of social control that have been criticized as undemocratic.

Hull-House settlers, blessed with Addams's capacity for openness, even humility, rarely focused on reforming their neighbors' morals. They did try to reform the diet and health practices of their constituents, and those efforts reveal a paradox: women who did not sew or cook established classes in sewing and cooking; women without children sought to improve child-raising methods.[101] An Italian mothers' club never succeeded—perhaps because Progressive expertise about child-raising clashed with the immigrants' standards, or simply because its target membership didn't think they needed to learn how to raise children.[102]

---

* *Maternalism* is a historians' concept referring to the widespread belief in this period that women, as "natural" mothers, could and should extend this "instinct" toward building a more nurturing society, and that elite women could and should nurture less advantaged people as mothers nurture their children.

The residents' greatest contribution to their neighbors ultimately came from their ability to influence politicians and policy makers.

Hull-House fundraising inevitably reinforced the position of the neighbors as objects of charity, because donors responded best to appeals on behalf of victims needing rescue. When Addams spoke about Hull-House to Chicago organizations, she often took a working-class neighbor along. She called this person an "auditor." I am not sure how she meant this—perhaps to suggest that one of her constituents authenticated her presentation? In any case, the role of the auditor was to listen, not to speak. The settlements offered many classes but none on the skills of political organizing: calling on politicians, talking to the media, convening and chairing meetings. No settler suggested inviting neighbors to participate in Hull-House's governance or to conduct their own surveys of working and living conditions. Hull-House programs did respond to neighbors' appeals, but their research priorities did not come from asking their neighbors for their priorities. Their visits to neighbors' homes produced information that they used to benefit those neighbors, but those visits also reinforced their authority. They did not encourage their neighbors to develop organized political action groups of their own. That would come later in Hull-House history.

IT SHOULD not lessen admiration for Hull-House to see that it was a class and a racial project. Its neighbors were not only working class but also, to the settlers, a different "race." At the turn of the twentieth century, the word *race* was widely used when today we would use *ethnicity*, and it often meant "not quite white." Moreover, in the powerful anti-immigration lobby of the period (of which more in chapter 2, on the 1920s Ku Klux Klan), whiteness almost required Protestantism. Hull-House residents were probably less racist than the white American norm.[103] They attributed to Blacks the same potential they saw in immigrants: the capacity to move up—economically, socially, culturally. In 1913 Addams articulated, presciently, a global analysis of racism similar to that of the New Left of the 1960s: that racism was produced by "the so-called 'superior' races who exact labor and taxes from Black and yellow men with the easy explanation of 'manifest destiny.'"[104] In 1902 she unsuccessfully urged the Federation of Women's Clubs to accept a Black women's organization. Moreover, she observed that some of her "ethnic" neighbors *learned* racism as they became Americanized.[105]

Still, most settlers did not object to separate programs and facilities for Blacks—that is, to segregation.[106] At the turn of the twentieth century, every settlement begun by whites was segregated; the more liberal among them chose to encourage or even sponsor separate Black settlements rather than integrate. As late as 1934, the National Federation of Settlements held its annual conference at a Christian conference center that refused to allow African Americans to occupy rooms, even when several white attendees offered to share their rooms with Black attendees. The federation declined to protest this policy.[107] Even Jane Addams harbored some embedded racist assumptions. Although she understood that Blacks suffered from segregation, although she strongly opposed lynching, and although she was a founding member of the NAACP, her attitude toward Blacks contained some ignorant ideas. For example, she opposed housing segregation, but on the grounds that it removed Black people from the social-control influences of white neighbors. She contrasted the supervision of daughters in Italian families with what she thought about African American families. Black daughters, she wrote, "have not been brought under social control. . . . If they yield more easily to the temptations of a city . . . who shall say how far the lack of social restraint is responsible for their downfall?"*[108]

Distinguished Black activists such as Ida B. Wells-Barnett, Isabel Eaton, Mary Church Terrell, Fannie Barrier Williams, and W. E. B. Du Bois were welcomed and respected at Hull-House. Black groups held meetings at Hull-House. But faith in the potential of ordinary African Americans did not mean encouraging them to join in Hull-House activities. It was decades before Hull-House reached out to Black Chicagoans. This was partly a demographic matter—in 1890 only fourteen thousand African Americans lived in Chicago, forming 1.3 percent of the population, while immigrants constituted 40 percent—and partly a

---

* Addams's belief was shared by several major African American scholars of her time and later, such as Du Bois and Franklin Frazier, who considered a deformed Black family structure partly responsible for Black poverty and "vice."

geographic matter, since few Blacks lived in the Hull-House neighbor-hood.[109] But well into the 1920s, Hull-House's activities and clubs were segregated. It did not include African American women in its Moth-ers' Club but established a separate Black Mothers' Club. Its summer camp and Jane Club were for whites only.[110] The Jewish leftist artist Morris Topchevsky, once close to Addams—even traveling in Mex-ico with her—left Hull-House because of its seeming indifference to Black Chicagoans.[111]

One personal conflict illustrates the limits of Hull-House's welcome to African Americans.[112] The physician Harriett Rice,* Hull-House's first Black resident, arrived there in 1893 at age twenty-seven, accepted because of a recommendation from her mentor, Alice Freeman, the president of Wellesley College. The daughter of a steamship steward, Rice was the first African American to graduate from Wellesley. She roomed for a time with Florence Kelley. She offered medical care to the residents, though many of them distrusted her ability and did not attempt to hide that distrust. Unlike most white residents, she did not have private wealth, so a "fellowship" paid her room and board (and that of a few other nonelite residents), while she sought paid work. Addams and Julia Lathrop, a Hull-House resident who would go on to be the director of the federal Children's Bureau, thought she should take a position at the city's "colored" hospital, but Rice resisted practicing in a segregated facility. It was no doubt inferior to white hospitals, but it was the only one in Chicago that hired Black doctors—in the whole city there were only forty-five Black physicians—so her refusal appeared to them unreasonable.

Addams concluded that Rice lacked the "settlement spirit" and accused her of refusing to "do anything for the sick neighbors." Rice's problem in finding work derived, of course, from structures of racism and segregation, structures that influenced Hull-House leaders' failure to understand the predicament of a lone Black woman. They did not include Rice in Hull-House's inner circle, as evidenced in the fact that she was not referred to as "Sister" as were the other residents; nor did

---

* The name is spelled Harriet in some sources, Harriett in others.

they help her find a position she deserved.[113] She left Hull-House for good in 1904.*

Nor did Hull-House support African American women's attempts to work with other settlements. An initiative by Sophonisba Breckinridge, a leading reform intellectual close to Hull-House and the first woman to hold a professorship at the University of Chicago—although in its low-status, woman-dominated social work school—shows that even the best intentions did not transcend embedded racism. She persuaded Julius Rosenwald to pay the tuition for Birdye Haynes and Sophia Boaz to study social work at the University. Both had graduated from Fisk, one of the historically Black colleges, but settlement leaders did not think that that diploma qualified the two to lead a settlement. After completing their social work qualification, Haynes became head resident at Chicago's Black settlement, the Wendell Phillips, and Boaz became her assistant. But Haynes was obliged not only to defer to a board dominated by Chicago's wealthy and influential white men, but also to get approval from Breckinridge and Grace Abbott for any programs she wanted to initiate. Haynes appears to have done as much as was possible given her poor funding and lack of authority, but she was fired after a few years.[114]

EVALUATING HULL-HOUSE'S achievements and failures, and those of the whole white settlement movement, needs context. Its failures to nurture African Americans and to bring its working-class neighbors into decisions about what Hull-House did were but a mild reflection of the country's racism, prejudice against immigrants, and class privilege. But its achievements were valuable. It broke with traditional charities' disdain for those they helped, and it found ways to help the needy in a more democratic fashion, an approach that influenced other settlements. It contributed to major progressive reforms, providing a

* Rice went on to medical practice of unusual bravery, working on the front lines of World War I in a French hospital, for which she was awarded a Reconnaissance Française medal. But she continued to experience discrimination in the United States and ended her career working in a Columbia University laboratory.

vivid example of social movements' potential power. Hull-House was unique, however, in basing its agitation for reform on research. True, that research, and the ability to make powerful men listen, were made possible by the residents' formal education and class confidence. But at least equally important were Hull-House women's hard work and commitment to social justice. Moreover, the whole was greater than the sum of its parts; Hull-House was a core of energy that traveled ever outward, a centrifugal force, and its influence continued for many decades afterward.

While Hull-House influenced scores of other settlements, African American settlements had different origins and trajectories. Black settlements, like white, were built by women and were responding to large-scale migration. But this migration, domestic as opposed to global, brought African Americans from the South to large northern cities. (Their experience was vividly painted by Jacob Lawrence in images that continue to resound today). This mass exodus, known as the Great Migration, was often compared to the flight of the Jews from ancient Egypt; like that flight, this migration was an escape—from Jim Crow, proliferating lynchings, and the impoverishment of sharecroppers. For migrants, it was also a quest—for jobs, education, and freedom, as a grapevine sent reports from the North to the South. In one respect, the migrants' paths resembled those of immigrants: both populations moved from rural to big-city environments. Their differences were great, however: immigrants often lived as families, while most African American migrants arrived singly. Among them, women often came alone, typically seeking work as domestic servants.[115]

So when Black women organized settlements, they served different populations with different needs. These settlements thus arose not only because of white exclusion but also to address the specific needs of African American women. Among those needs were protection from violence and prostitution, as well as housing, jobs, and education.

Unlike white settlements, Black ones often arose out of Protestant missions, some of them established in the South by well-meaning whites after emancipation. Often evangelical in spirit and aims, they sought to strengthen the religious commitment of African Americans and make their behavior "respectable." Along with proselytizing they encouraged literacy, created schools, and later provided some medical services and meals. Missions like this appeared in northern cities as early as the 1860s.[116]

Yet one of the most important, the White Rose Mission, was only peripherally religious. Founded in New York City in 1897 by Victoria Earle Matthews, it was an ancestor of the Phillis Wheatley Home, created fourteen years later. Matthews was born enslaved in 1861 in Fort Valley, Georgia, fathered by her mother's owner. That mother, a woman of uncommon determination and talent, escaped to the North, then returned after emancipation, fought a long but ultimately successful court case to secure custody of her children and moved them to New York City. To enable the family's survival, Victoria Matthews left school at seven or eight to work as a domestic servant. Remarkably, she managed nevertheless to become well educated. Her achievements were nothing short of extraordinary: she became a journalist, writing a political affairs column for Frederick Douglass's paper; she founded an Inquiry Club for New York City African Americans to debate race matters; she wrote short stories about "miscegenation" and a play that was produced on Broadway.[117] In short, she became a major intellectual and reformer.

Observing the flow of lone Black women into New York City, Matthews began by conducting research into migrants' problems, just as Hull-House settlers began by studying their neighborhood and Jane Edna Hunter would begin by studying lone Black women in Cleveland. Matthews saw in New York City what Hunter would see in Cleveland a few years later—the many moral and physical dangers confronting migrant women. Excluded by the "pink-collar" boardinghouses that served young white women, Black female migrants faced a housing shortage and rents often higher than those for whites, and these problems made them prey for pimps. Moreover, the housing available typically had no running water or bathing facilities, forcing women to use unsanitary public bathhouses.[118]

Matthews's research soon uncovered predatory trafficking. After attending the 1895 Congress of Colored Women of the United States in Atlanta, she traveled through the southern Black belt and learned how girls were seduced into migration. Rapacious employment agents recruited women by promising good jobs, sometimes even marriage, advancing the cost of their transportation to the North, for which they charged exorbitant rates. The women thus incurred debts that often forced them to work for months without pay; some traffickers appropriated the women's belongings until the debt was paid off.[119] These women were essentially indentured. Many became sex workers. The historian Sarah Deutsch has called these patterns a new "urban sexual geography."[120] Even those who managed to secure "respectable" employment—typically, as low-wage domestic servants—could be assaulted by men in the homes they cleaned, as Hull-House women Sophonisba Breckinridge and Edith Abbott observed in Chicago.[121] As Matthews saw the problem, speaking at the Hampton Institute in 1898, "Many of the dangers confronting our girls from the South in the great cities of the North are so perfectly planned, so overwhelming in their power to subjugate and destroy, that no woman's daughter is safe away from home."[122]

For "the young and unfriended (women) of other races, there are all sorts of institutions," Matthews observed, but for Black girls and women "there is nothing."[123] She organized a group of women who shared her concern. One, a Brooklyn public schoolteacher and then an assistant school principal, Maritcha Remond Lyons, had earlier organized an antilynching campaign with Matthews, raising the money to publish Ida B. Wells-Barnett's antilynching pamphlet, *Southern Horrors.** The Harlem renaissance poet Alice Dunbar Nelson joined Matthews's project.[124] In 1897 they created a settlement that they called the White Rose Mission—a white rose was the symbol of hope and new beginnings but also of purity, reflecting their concern with the sexual safety of Black women. Located near today's Lincoln Center, it provided temporary housing, education, and job placement services for new women migrants from the South and the Caribbean.

Meanwhile Black women's clubs were proliferating.[125] In 1896 they federated into the prestigious National Association of Colored Women (NACW). Its founders were luminaries of African American reform,

* A passionate feminist, Lyons also fought for voting rights for women with the Colored Women's Equal Suffrage League of Brooklyn.

professional-class, often relatively light-skinned women.* (That Matthews was light-skinned enough to pass for white probably helped her gain support.) The NACW motto, "Lifting as we Climb," however, illustrates the precariousness of their privilege: prosperous, well-educated elite Black women faced the same racism that working-class Black women did. This Black women's movement encompassed competing strategies. Many activists, including those in the North, endorsed the strategy of southern leader Booker T. Washington: rather than attacking racism directly, he advocated building Black businesses, strengthening Black farming, and training Blacks to become skilled and educated workers, in the hopes of demonstrating that they were both competent and unthreatening. Other activists presaged what would become northerner W. E. B. Du Bois's more militant strategy. He urged direct challenges to segregation and denounced the assumption that African Americans had to prove their entitlement to equal rights through exemplary achievement and behavior.† Focusing on the Washington–Du Bois dichotomy, however, obscures the complexity of their perspectives and their variety of strategies.

This was the context from which grew the Phillis Wheatley Home in Cleveland, which would gain a fame among African American activists similar to that of Hull-House. Its origin in the dreams of a young girl sharecropper in South Carolina might have seemed miraculous to those who didn't know Jane Edna Hunter. Many Black migrants headed to cities where they had connections, part of a "chain migration," but

* The NACW was the first national civil rights organization, preceding by a decade the establishment of the NAACP. (Dorothy Height, feminist head of the NACW in the 1960s, will appear in chapter 7.) Its founders included Harriet Tubman, Margaret Murray (Mrs. Booker T.) Washington, poet and author Frances E. W. Harper, anti-lynching heroine Ida B. Wells-Barnett (wife of the owner of Chicago's leading Black newspaper), Josephine St. Pierre Ruffin (wife of the first Black graduate of Harvard Law School), Lugenia Burns Hope (wife of the president of Atlanta University), and Mary Church Terrell (first Black woman to earn a college degree from Oberlin, the wife of the first Black federal judge). I have listed their husbands' positions in order to underscore their privileged-class status among the African American population.
† Du Bois publicly articulated his challenge in the 1905 meeting of Black intellectuals at Niagara Falls, Canada, but NACW women had been defying segregation long before.

Hunter arrived in Cleveland in 1905, having probably heard of opportunities in Cleveland through a grapevine. Without friends or kinfolk to take her in, she later recalled her "despairing search for decent lodgings—up one dingy street and down another, ending with . . . the least disreputable room." Though she was a trained nurse, she found no work in that field available to Blacks, so she did house cleaning and laundering. Her first opportunity for a better job came from the connections she made through an African Methodist Episcopal church—private nursing in the homes of wealthy white families. She began to meet other Black servants whose long-buried dreams of homes of their own became her own . . . and she began to act on them.

Hunter faced a Cleveland that was changing, and for African Americans, the change was not in a positive direction. The Black population was growing—from 8,500 in 1910 to 34,000 in 1920—and so was segregation.[126] In decades past, Cleveland's white elites had been influenced by a liberal abolitionist heritage that had mitigated race discrimination.[127] African Americans had once lived scattered about the city and attended integrated schools and churches; many were professionals and business people. But as Hunter arrived, Jim Crow was intensifying in all northern cities, particularly in Cleveland, and it was intensifying class distinctions among Blacks. No longer would members of the Black elite take in lodgers, which had once been a common form of housing for newcomers. An attempt to create a Black YMCA in 1911 failed because middle-class Black women refused to support a segregated institution.[128] Black fraternal organizations—notably Masons and Odd Fellows—provided their members with networking opportunities and insurance, but they did not offer help to the poor.[129]

Accustomed to the southern political economy of racism, in which whites depended on Black live-in domestic servants and private nurses, Hunter found a different color line in Cleveland. Black newcomers were being driven into a ghettoized neighborhood, and many lost jobs to white immigrants.[130] Restaurants and hotels began excluding them; recreational facilities created separate days and/or separate areas for Blacks. That there were no "whites only" signs created greater difficulties and humiliation for Blacks who didn't know the city's unwritten segregation rules.

Many Black elites struggled to ignore the growing Jim Crow by avoiding segregated areas and worked to distinguish themselves from the southern newcomers. Conceiving of themselves as part of what Du Bois called the "talented tenth" of African Americans, they believed, in a willful denial of these changes, that they had earned the respect of whites. Their defensive position only increased their disdain for those they saw as uncouth. Still, ignoring segregation and insult became more difficult even for middle-class Blacks. In 1908, when the National Education Association held its convention in Cleveland, its African American members were turned away by hotels. In 1919 the NAACP chose Cleveland for its convention because of its earlier reputation for racial liberalism, but once there, its officers could not get served in restaurants. In 1923 when Robert Moton, Booker T. Washington's successor as head of the Tuskegee Institute, was invited to address Cleveland's Chamber of Commerce, he was first denied a hotel room, then was finally offered one provided he would take his meals in his room. Well after Hunter had become an honored public figure, she was invited to speak at a 1926 Cleveland Community Chest conference but was refused entry to the main elevator—she was told to take the freight elevator. Fifteen years previously, while courting donations for her Phillis Wheatley Home, she would have gritted her teeth and complied. Now she was able to stand her ground and refused to comply, arriving at the meeting late and in tears—a humiliation that must have cut deeply.[131]

The *Crisis*, organ of Du Bois's NAACP, reported that young single women were "literally pouring into Cleveland."[132] There they faced the same dangers that Victoria Matthews had documented in New York. Unable to get decent housing and jobs, many "fell" into "sin." Hunter's rural, conservative family values left her shocked by what she saw: an underworld of drinking and gambling, a virtual industry of pimps using women for profit, and poverty that pushed women into sex work. In her first lodgings, she was horrified to find women beer drinkers and a young part-time prostitute. When she went to a dance hall—a common site of working-class entertainment at the time—she was repelled by "women with heavily painted faces and indecently short skirts; men slightly intoxicated and somewhat noisy." This revulsion was not limited to African American reformers: Jane Addams similarly feared that dance halls created "over-stimulation of the senses" that opened young women to "dangerous exploitation." She condemned the "great temptations that beset a young woman in a large city" as a primary problem.[133] *Temptations* is a crucial word here. While Hunter knew well the economic discrimination that Black women faced, she focused on morality. "At home on the plantation, I knew that some girls had been seduced. . . . In Charleston I was sent by the hospital to give emergency treatments to prostitutes, but they were white women. Until my arrival in Cleveland I was ignorant of the wholesale organized traffic in Black flesh."[134] She had not previously confronted large-scale trafficking.

Hunter's anxiety was not entirely a prudish obsession. Nor was "policing the Black woman's body," as Hazel Carby put it, always a repressive and/or racist project.[135] True, Hunter shared with many other progressive reformers of the period, white and Black, an anxiety about sex and unease with women's sexual agency. But such agency was largely an illusion, in the face of the exploitation and brutalization of young women by predatory men. Premarital sex and motherhood did not ostracize single women in rural Black southern communities, where they had family support, but became dangerous in the urban north. African American reformers of all political stripes were worrying over the fate of young Black women in northern cities. As the *Crisis* described it in 1929, "The problem of the colored girl in a Northern great city is . . . more pressing than that of the young man. . . . They are open to insult and even attack from the irresponsible elements of both races. . . . It is peculiarly easy for them to drift into questionable company and into social surroundings which might ultimately prove fatal."[136] True, Black activists often shared a religious Christian abhorrence of "promiscuity"; they were Victorians in this sense. But it was the exploitation and sexual abuse of young single women that motivated their protective orientation, a maternalist but also feminist impulse.

Hull-House women were also concerned with immorality and supported prohibiting both prostitution and alcohol. They were particularly concerned with the sexual trafficking and victimization of young women. As Jane Addams put it in 1909, "Let us know the modern city in its weakness and wickedness, and then seek to rectify and purify it until it shall be free at least from the grosser temptations."[137] But sexual immorality was not her greatest concern. What most shocked the Hull-House women and spurred their reform attempts was poverty, filth, and contagious disease. Perhaps Matthews and Hunter were more accustomed to those conditions. (These contrasting emphases offer a gloss on expertise and social science research: one sees, and counts, that which is surprising.) Equally important, Hull-House's European immigrant neighbors lived in families that protected young women. Those Hunter wanted to help faced not only a racial wall but also a gendered racism that smeared Black women's sexual morality.[138] The campaign for respectability common among Black reformers at the time, especially women, was simultaneously an attempt to protect these women victims.

Like Matthews and Hull-House women, Hunter began her campaign with research.[139] Today we might call her method ethnographic, in a form now known as participant-observer research.[140] Discussions with other Black servants gave her intimate, bodily, first-hand knowledge of Black women's working conditions. From this research, Matthews and Hunter drew an identical conclusion: the only way to protect Black women was to offer them a safe space—a home that could provide protection spiritual as well as physical. The safety they envisioned would protect young women not only from fraudulent recruitment, economic thievery, and sexual exploitation but equally from immorality itself—from the devilish temptations that the big city brought.

Hunter's strategy differed from Matthews's in one important way, however: Matthews gathered middle-class Black women to help their sisters, while Hunter began by gathering working-class Black women. Hers was an effort not only *for* but also *of* working-class women—the reverse of most Hull-House initiatives with the exception of its Jane Clubs. In her six years in Cleveland, Hunter had developed a friendship and support group of Black working women; they were maids, laundresses, and the single other Black nurse in Cleveland. She brought seven of them together in the home of a friend from church, Hattie Harper. In a conversation—an early example of what would later be called consciousness-raising—they shared grievances: surly landladies, dark and dingy rooms, weak gaslights that had to be turned off at ten o'clock, bans on visitors, lack of access to kitchens, dangerous nearby streets, predatory men.* Black women needed a room of their own, a space that they controlled themselves, not just a room but a household of their own, as opposed to that of an employer. They shared with Hull-House's privileged white settlers the desire to escape living as dependents in households headed by others. Still, living as a maiden aunt with prosperous kinfolk could not be compared to life as a live-in domestic servant.

The young "women adrift," as they were sometimes called, were not just vulnerable but also lonely. Far from family, having grown up in dense kinship networks, they were perhaps even more forlorn living under the roof of a white employer family than they would have been living alone. So Hunter proposed creating a "home for all the other poor motherless daughters of our race." It would be "the expression of the faith of a group of poor Negro women and their devotion to the poor and homeless of their own people," as she put it. The seven women she had gathered formed a club and agreed that each member would contribute a nickel a week to a fund for creating such a home. Hence the title of her autobiography, *A Nickel and a Prayer*.

Hunter's method for inspiring and organizing was telling her own story. As a narrative of determination and uplift, nothing could have been more optimistic. (Some fifty years later, as we will see in chapter 6, master organizer Cesar Chavez would also begin his appeals by telling his personal story.) Decades later Hunter wrote a personal narrative of her struggles, sacrifices, and achievements. It was saturated with scripture, in a manner characteristic of southern African American reform writings. Self-published and self-distributed, it reads like a sermon. "Yet, even then, I knew that we should have to make our path uphill through thorny country; that rocks would sometimes block our way; that we might stand on the brink of a great chasm, over which only faith could build a bridge."[141] The text reflects, of course, a deep religiosity, as

---

* They may well have complained about employers, and not only for sex abuse. Some female employers cursed at and even beat domestic servants. In her memoir, Hunter does not mention those grievances, perhaps because she considered those problems irremediable or less urgent, perhaps also because she would later require financial support from these employers of maids.

well as a biblically based education, and her command of this language would have made her a fine preacher. Perhaps it is not disrespectful to suggest that her discourse belonged to the tradition that Martin Luther King, Jr., inherited as well (examples of which we will see in chapter 5). Her aims, like King's, were worldly as well as spiritual. She was writing to inspire and encourage younger African Americans, to convince them that change was possible, while presenting herself as leader in the prophetic tradition.[142] Her discourse resounded with the classic tropes of African American women's autobiography: unlike Addams, whose class confidence allowed her to admit her mistakes freely, Black activists frequently used autobiography to illustrate heroism, stimulate confidence, and create role models. As a rule, these writings reveal self-doubt only rarely, and never despair, only triumph over adversity.

Fifteen months after beginning the project, however, the nickel-a-week group had raised only $500, even though two cooks had contributed their entire life savings—$100 and $250 respectively.[143] Discouraged, one women protested that at that rate it would take a hundred years to buy a home. Hunter responded, "It is for us to let our light shine before men and leave the rest to God."[144]

But Hunter did not count on God. Despite her Bible-quoting facade of confidence, the five-cent contributors were right—domestic servants could not raise enough money to purchase a home. With her charisma and boldness, she became a big-time fundraiser, an entrepreneur for her cause, a responsibility that falls on many social movement leaders. One scholar described her style as "aggressive but non-abrasive."[145] Her method involved strategic duplicity, telling different potential funders what they wanted to hear, an approach forced on many fundraisers. The racial structures in which she was working required her to squeeze money out of both Black and white potential donors, who had differing motivations and values.

In searching for support, she found herself caught in a Cleveland version of the Washington–Du Bois debate, a debate that reflected opposing class interests. Cleveland's Black middle-class women, those who had lived in the city for decades, were angry about the city's increasing segregation and feared that Hunter's project would serve to confirm and justify it. In that sense, they were in the Du Bois camp. Their perspective was shared by many in the National Association of Colored Women. The African American *Cleveland Gazette* consistently denounced segregated facilities.[146] When the NACW women had asked to join the YWCA, its board of trustees made its segregationist policy explicit for the first time and offered to support a Black branch.[147] Humiliated and outraged, they refused the offer. Fearful of losing the small measure of integration they had experienced in earlier decades, Cleveland's Black elite refused to support Hunter's project when they learned that it was for Black women only, and some denounced it angrily. To them, Hunter's plan was a step backward. The snobbishness of the "old guard," as Hunter called them, rested on the delusion that they had earned white respect and that integration would come sooner or later.[148]

By contrast, Hunter was an admirer of Booker T. Washington, whose strategy for advancing African Americans involved accepting and excelling in humble, low-wage work as a step toward moving up economically. In accusing the NACW women of snobbery, she was right. Their disregard for the needs of poor Blacks, especially poor Black women, often extended to disdain for the "unrefined" manners and dress of these southern rural immigrants. As an editorial in the *Cleveland Gazette* charged,

> *Those Negroes who insist on "flocking to themselves" . . . have given greater impetus to "Jimcrowing" our people . . . than our enemies. . . . Shall we sit supinely by and let a few selfish cowardly "Jim Crow" Negroes whose life in the South . . . makes it impossible for them to appreciate what the older Afro-Americans of Cleveland . . . have enjoyed . . . wipe out all the remaining advances our parents and their true white friends fought so long and so hard to secure?*[149]

This scorn was not confined to Cleveland. Frances R. Bartholomew, head worker at a Philadelphia Black settlement, wrote in 1903 that "the weaker element in the Negro race that comes drifting into the Northern cities" constituted "the most serious menace to the progress of the Negro race."[150] Sarah Collins Fernandis, a Baltimore social and public health worker, considered Black couples who were not legally married to be a major obstacle to the progress of the race, and she rejoiced that "a marriage certificate is now held among its [the family's] most valued possessions."[151]

UP TO this point, in her approaches to potential Black donors, Hunter had not announced another part of her plan: to train Black women for domestic service jobs, understanding that many of these jobs required living in the homes of employers. She rejected the distaste for servility among Cleveland's middle-class African Americans because she had concluded that "for many years to come, the great mass of Negro girls must carve out of the domestic field a livelihood for themselves and [their] families."[152] (African American families in the South often depended on the wages of a distant wage-earner, as immigrant and migrant families often do.) Responding to the "old guard's" criticism that her "undertaking is degrading to the Negro girl, because it deprives her of ambitions to reach a higher economic status," Hunter replied that Black women would be unable to do better, "even if they received help from others."[153] What appeared Uncle Tom-ish to Black elites was, to Hunter, simply realism about the limited job and educational opportunities for African American women.

At the same time Hunter shared the Cleveland's Black elite's assumption of the superiority of middle-class culture. She argued that living and working in white homes would enable Black domestics to absorb a higher domestic and familial culture, just as Jane Addams believed that immigrants needed to learn from Americans. Hunter also argued that Black servants working in white homes could promote interracial understanding and harmony. But before that could happen, it was necessary to "elevate" standards of domestic service in order to meet the standards of cleanliness in northern middle-class homes.[154] So when the Phillis Wheatley Home opened in 1913, Hunter immediately set up an employment bureau providing domestics to upscale families.

While Hunter continued to work toward a home for Black women only, she offered a form of compromise with the Black clubwomen's rejection of segregation, supporting their refusal to accept a separate Black YWCA.[155] This gesture failed to moderate the old guard's opposition, which became an open clash when Hunter met with them. The middle-class women took complete charge of the meeting. "Our girls must go to the YWCA along with the white girls." "We have never had segregation," they claimed.[156] This was not true: the Cleveland Home for Aged Colored People had opened in 1896 without objection to its segregation. Their claim expressed a not uncommon lack of historical memory, or a memory reconstructed from wishful thinking. It also reflected a self-deluding refusal to reckon with the city's increasing color bar.[157] Distinguishing themselves from southern (read: backward) African Americans, one of the clubwomen said (in Hunter's memory), "Why should you . . . come up from the South and tell us what to do? . . . Now that the more intelligent of us have broken down the barriers between the races, you are trying to build them up again with your absurd Southern ideas for working girls."[158] A male ally of the clubwomen, the prominent Black Ohio Republican George A. Myers, wrote that Hunter "has no standing among our better class of women."[159]

Hunter was shocked and angry, convinced that her opponents were maintaining a head-in-the-sand obliviousness. She characterized her opponents as "a small group of club women who, blessed with prosperity, had risen from the servant class and now regarded themselves as the arbiters and guardians of colored society." She saw clearly that the integration that the clubwomen demanded was a class privilege and that domestic servants could not reasonably expect equal treatment in the near future.

She had no choice, then, but to approach wealthy white contacts for donations, and she did not hesitate to promise them that the Phillis Wheatley Home could provide more efficient and better-behaved servants. The home thus offered well-to-do white women a double reward: disciplined servants and a way to appease the Black women angry at their exclusion from the YWCA. Mrs. Levi Scofield, president of the YWCA and wife of a prominent architect, would become the head of the Phillis Wheatley Home's board of trustees.[160] She accepted this position on the condition that she could choose the other board members. Hunter agreed. In other words, she accepted the appearance of independence without the reality.[161] (Hunter was replicating the experience of Hull-House's Dr. Harriett Rice. Contrast this with Jane Addams's fundraising: she too shaped her appeals to match donors' interests, but she would never have shared decision-making power with them.) Overriding the Black board that Hunter had already established, Scofield created a new board, all white with a few token Blacks who would be selected by the white members.[162] Moreover, since the board members were allowed to cast votes by proxy, the whites could, if they desired, avoid sitting in a meeting with African Americans.[163] Hunter became the board's executive secretary. She accepted this disrespect as the price of an institution that would protect and elevate Black women newcomers.

Thus when Hunter was able to buy a house to serve as a home for Black working women, she was relying mainly on white money. Mrs. Scofield solicited funds from Henry Sherwin, president of Sherwin Williams Paint, who also conditioned his support on a white governing board for the home. Hunter kept her "executive secretary" title and received a salary of seventy-five dollars a month, so for the first time she could give up her other jobs and devote herself to the project.

Just three years later Hunter accepted an offer to affiliate what was now called the Phillis Wheatley with the *national* YWCA. The deal remained insultingly discriminatory, because this Black "affiliate" had none of the rights of full membership. Nevertheless, Hunter saw advantages in this connection. In 1914 and 1915 she attended the YWCA's National Training School, which helped her obtain resources. In later

Residents in training at Phillis Wheatley House.

years, she refused to join formally, because doing so would have meant that she could not continue as the head of the Phillis Wheatley—YWCA leaders were required to have college degrees.

Undeterred, Hunter soon managed to dredge up support from some Black leaders—notably John P. Green, the first African American to be elected to the Ohio legislature. He became a Phillis Wheatley board member, though even he was a token member without influence. Meanwhile, newer and younger Black elites in Cleveland came to support the Phillis Wheatley Home. They were businessmen and professionals who drew their clients and customers from African Americans, including the first Black city councilman and his wife. This generation of middle-class Blacks had grown up with segregation and succeeded within it.[164] By the 1920s, even ardent advocates of integration made their peace with the Phillis Wheatley and other Black settlements, acknowledging that young Black women's safety was a matter too urgent to be postponed while struggling for principle.[165]

Hunter had accepted insult after insult—a steep personal price paid for helping African American women. A decade later, however, she may well have felt a degree of satisfaction, possibly even spite. In 1925 she earned a law degree from Cleveland Law School, then affiliated with Baldwin-Wallace College in nearby Berea, Ohio. She eventually received four honorary degrees. More important, she joined the NACW, the prestigious alliance of many upscale clubwomen, including some who would have disrespected her. This membership brought her nationwide connections, and she became for a time the chairwoman of its settlement department.[166] She had beome a nationally known and admired Black leader, though never free from racist humiliations.

THE PHILLIS WHEATLEY HOME opened in 1911, a three-floor Victorian frame house, right next to the AME church that had been Hunter's first source of support in Cleveland. This location made its Blackness highly visible and assured white donors that it would not bring Black women into their neighborhoods. Whites had contributed most of the money, and some came from missionary societies, but the Black working-class women with whom Hunter began did the work: they scrubbed it, repaired it, and furnished it with their labor. I don't know if any of this original group came to live there, but I think not: they were serving the race, not themselves, providing for young newcomers to Cleveland.

In 1915 the Wheatley Home's yearly budget was $1,500. It had rooms for a "matron," for Hunter herself, and for fifteen boarders, who paid $1.25 a week for rent and two dollars a week for two meals a day.[167] It contained a kitchen, a laundry room, and a parlor in which to entertain guests. Soon it added a dining room, which Hunter considered essential, because she saw public cafés as places where women could be accosted by rapacious men. The home was immediately so popular with "working girls" that it had to turn away dozen of applicants. Within three years, twenty-three residents crammed into the Phillis Wheatley, which offered them a considerable improvement over their previous accommodations—the shelter was clean, orderly, and safe. That it offered the companionship of other women made it even more attractive.[168]

The Phillis Wheatley grew rapidly, in size and in functions, much as Hull-House did. Hunter's prowess as fundraiser became apparent, achieved without Hull-House's upper-class connections. In 1915 eighty-nine young women lived there for a month or more, forty-one for under a month. In 1919 it added an adjoining building that provided more bedrooms and meeting rooms. In 1921 it gained yet another building, next door to the first, with seventy-two rooms. The staff then numbered twenty. In 1925, after a major capital campaign, the Phillis Wheatley took over a nine-story building, providing rooms for one hundred residents on the top six floors; it was funded in part by the Rockefeller Foundation. A brick rectangle, with an imposing doorway, it lacked the charm of the original house, but it was designed for multiple activities beyond its function as dormitory. It featured an elevator, numerous parlors and club rooms, and hot and cold running water on every floor. Residents paid between $2.75 and seven dollars per week. Its 1928 annual budget was $84,000, about a third coming from the Cleveland Welfare Federation.[169]

The Phillis Wheatley's ambiance was that of a college dorm, though its residents had shorter stays. Once they got jobs and a church to belong to—an essential part of Hunter's vision of a protected, disciplined life—they were expected to leave and make room for others. In

1915 the Wheatley's employment bureau reported having made 549 job applications and placed 403 workers. In 1928, the ratio was even better: 1,455 women applied for work and 1,270 were placed.[170] But young residents at the Phillis Wheatley were students as well as employees. With no qualms about providing white women with servants, Hunter wrote with pride about the efficiency of those she trained. Residents took classes in "domestic science," nutrition and hygiene, and "superior" cleaning methods. They wore proper maid's uniforms with starched white aprons and took turns cooking for and serving each other. Eventually the training course extended to six months. The range of training expanded to include laundry work, ironing, sewing and beautician skills.[171] Wheatley "graduates" were employed as seamstresses, cooks, waitresses, even elevator operators and clerks. The home even offered some practical nursing training, established a nurses' registry, and got nursing jobs for some.[172]

To Phillis Wheatley residents, the accommodations were heavenly. The safe and clean shelter offered apartment-style amenities—hot running water, lounge spaces, a clean kitchen, and meals. It developed a country camp on Lake Erie near Lorain, Ohio, offering some 570 poor Black women the luxury of a vacation. It commanded city services—garbage collection, police and fire protection—not typically afforded in poor Black neighborhoods. It gave its residents a respectable address. By obviating newcomers' need to find food and shelter immediately, it protected its residents from having to accept undesirable or dangerous work.[173] A free space, it offered residents the luxury of community in a large and alienating city, a community that they could retain once they moved out. The Phillis Wheatley's popularity suggests how much its residents enjoyed this refuge from the stress of living and working amid whites who frequently treated them with disrespect and abuse.

The Phillis Wheatley also gave its residents a base of support from which they went about exploring a big city. Living together made for conversations about past lives and imagining better lives. These benefits became known through a grapevine that reached into the Deep South, where ever more young women became northbound migrants. This not only made the Phillis Wheatley ever more desirable but also contributed to the development of similar homes for young single women. As to its women-only rule, the resultant calm and safety made these con-versations freer. But the rule did not keep residents from socializing with men, any more than a college dorm did; nor did it mean that all residents accepted its rules without protest (as we will see below).

The home began to offer activities that resembled those of Hull-House: sewing, art, music, and dramatics. It created a restaurant that became a favorite lunch-time meeting place among Cleveland's middle-class and elite Blacks. Adjoining it were a very large dining room and two smaller rooms for special occasions, often used by nonresidents whose rental fees helped support the whole institution. It hosted events that drew in many outsiders, claiming a yearly attendance of almost ten thousand.[174] With so many residents and activities, its public space benefited all of Black Cleveland: the spread of segregation had made it difficult for Blacks to find large spaces for meetings and social activi-ties, even middle-class Blacks who had once spurned the project.[175] In time its space became less homelike, less familial. Like Hull-House two decades earlier, it was becoming a community center. Unlike Hull-House residents, who often disliked the endless bustle created by visitors and neighbors, Phillis Wheatley residents probably benefited from the variety of clubs and community organizations that met and held special events there, gaining opportunity-expanding knowledge of the city.

HUNTER'S EMPHASIS on protecting young women exemplified the maternalist feminism that was characteristic of Progressive era woman-led reform campaigns, including many Hull-House programs. This was a feminism, sometimes called social feminism, that used mother-hood as a model for helping the poor. Through direct contact as in settlements and through campaigns for social welfare programs, mater-nalist feminists sought to help immigrants and migrants adjust to urban America, to improve their health, and to "uplift" their culture. Still, maternalist feminist reform strategies varied across class, race, and cul-tural differences. The Phillis Wheatley's maternalism was more literal than Hull-House's, because its residents were young, single newcomers; Hunter and the other "matrons" operated like house mothers at a college, although more strictly. Hunter's certainty that these young women needed parental discipline reflected her religiosity and conservative morality, and it was above all a response to racism. Her emphasis on maintaining—and displaying—the moral respectability of her wards reflected the need to battle the ugly racist smears commonly applied to Black women. Her motives might seem prudish today, but they were above all protective, focused on preventing Black women's victimization by pimps and traffickers, not to mention rapists and seducers. This protection, however, involved attempting to squelch young women's own agency—particularly their newcomers' eagerness to explore the entertainments and thrills that the big city offered.

Anxiety about Black women's respectability characterized much of the Black uplift movement in this period, but Hunter employed an unusually authoritarian approach to assuaging this concern. She and her staff assumed a responsibility to ensure that their wards conducted themselves at all times with unimpeachable propriety. Hunter required her staff to set and enforce severe rules and procedures to control the Phillis Wheatley's residents. Fearing the natural unruliness of young women, the matrons saw their job as insulating the residents from temptation. They gave daily moralistic lectures. They treated residents like minors: curfews, no men allowed, rooms inspected for neatness, a dress code. Staff conducted surprise inspections of residents' rooms. Dancing was forbidden; the "unsavory atmosphere" of dance halls drew in "lewd men and wretched women" and lured young people into the wrong "channels." "The use of intoxicants in any form or the bringing of them into the building . . . will be sufficient cause for immediate cancellation of all privileges." The reference to "privileges" of course positioned the residents as wards. The penalty for noncompliance could be eviction.[176]

White YWCA residences also applied some rules, but they were much less stringent than Hunter's. She was a well-meaning tyrant, driven by her knowledge that her wards might be preyed on and that their behavior—even their victimization by predators—would bring shame upon the race. She supervised residents' contacts by listening to their conversations through the switchboard, keeping, she wrote, "a vigilant ear to the switchboard in my office to catch conversations of a

doubtful character, and to intercept assignations." If she learned of residents' immoral behavior, she would, astoundingly, call the police and
together with the officer "sometimes follow couples to places of assigna-
tion, rescue the girl, and assist in the arrest of her would-be seducer."[177]
In many colonial situations—say, in a Presbyterian mission in Africa or
an American boarding school for Native Americans—whites imposed
this kind of repression. But here was a Black woman imposing it on
other Black women.

Hunter's goal was to produce exemplary African American
women—in the double sense of exemplary, as virtuous in itself and
as an example for others to aspire to. Equally important, she aimed to
produce exemplary *servants*. She believed rigorous restrictions necessary because of what she deemed the currently inferior state of Black
character and morality. (A perspective not entirely different than Jane
Addams's view that African Americans needed to learn restraint.)
As the historian Adrienne Lash Jones points out, Hunter frequently
wrote sentences like these in the Phillis Wheatley newsletter: "So
many Negroes are inefficient, restless, unwilling to sacrifice for the
convenience of their employers and to stay on the premises. . . . The
Negro race as a whole has somehow lost ambition."[178] The home never
counseled women to expect, let alone demand, respectful treatment. It
emphasized not just respectability, not just "character building," but
also "the ability to endure and to bear with dignity and courage, poverty and insult and discrimination" and to appreciate "the generosity
of white folk."[179]

We must, of course, consider the context of these statements. The
newsletters and annual reports were fundraising tools, and Hunter—
like Addams—was an expert fundraiser. This required reassuring
donors, especially white donors, recognizing and allaying their anxieties about Black women's behavior. Though we do not know to what
extent the Phillis Wheatley's white board exerted control over its day-
to-day operation, we can surmise that the newsletters had to please
both the board and the donors.

Not all residents of Phillis Wheatley Home accepted its rules without resistance. This is hardly surprising. How could scores of young
women living together, nervous but also thrilled to be in a big city,

not find ways around the rules? How could they live, work and study together without forming collective gripes and a will of their own as well as friendships? One historian, Virginia R. Boynton, has examined the Phillis Wheatley Home records with these questions in mind, and I rely heavily on her work.

The Phillis Wheatley's rent policies had contradictory effects on residents. Despite the appallingly low wages of domestic servants, they were required to pay in advance. That demand aimed to inculcate thrift and prevent "frivolous" expenditures. The matrons complained that residents were profligate in their spending.[180] They may have been right, because the city offered attractive commodities not widely found in poor southern Black communities: stylish clothes, impractical shoes, perfumes, and makeup. The house occasionally lowered rents but then treated the beneficiaries with increased surveillance. The lack of privacy and freedom made some residents eager to "graduate."

The Phillis Wheatley actually faced contradictory imperatives: to keep residents from danger and immorality, but also to move them out. Minutes of a Phillis Wheatley board meeting acknowledged these clashing goals: it was their hope that residents "would be encouraged to earn more and would *want* [my emphasis] to get [out] from under the supervision."[181] Behind this contradiction lay yet another: by offering young women comfortable accommodations, the Phillis Wheatley had fostered their obstinate holding out for attractive employment. Residents sometimes rejected jobs they considered undesirable—jobs with poor working conditions, particularly expectations to be available at any hour and to work seven days a week. They also refused offers when the wages were even lower than the already paltry norm for domestic servants. One staff meeting discussed a woman who was refusing most of the jobs offered her, and the residence secretary was tasked with criticizing her for her "attitude."[182] Residents also accepted but then left jobs with unacceptable working conditions. "Quitting was the domestic worker's ultimate form of protest," Boynton found. The residents' stubbornness arose because Phillis Wheatley had raised their expectations.

The most common and most overt resistance took the form of refusing live-in domestic service jobs. Well into the 1930s, Hunter insisted that live-in situations were preferable, because the women would be protected from vice (a dubious claim, given widespread sexual assault by male household members) and because, she continued to believe, the more "refined" culture in employers' families would rub off onto the servants. The majority of Phillis Wheatley residents, by contrast, wanted day work. Live-in servants were typically required to be available to serve their employers at all times, every minute, with one day off at best; the Wheatley's young women wanted leisure time that they could count on, time "to do what we will."[183] Maids' rooms in prosperous homes were often tiny, dark, and located right next to kitchens—underscoring the fact that their responsibilities were endless. Employers might limit their access to bathing and often created separate, inferior bathrooms for servants. They might expect maids not to eat the family's food but to rely on cruder fare, a practice often justified with the claim that that was what poor Blacks liked. Many Phillis Wheatley women working as live-in maids complained. They objected to being "deprived of their social life" and feeling "lonesome without companionship." They "insisted on going home at night" and needed to "get away from their employers."[184] Domestic workers' preference for living in their own homes has a long historical record, as the historian Tera Hunter has documented, and this wish went along with a rejection of uniforms and a preference for their own clothes—even when uniforms were supplied by employers.[185]

Unsurprisingly, Phillis Wheatley–trained domestics sometimes encountered unreasonably demanding, rude, even abusive employers. In a contradictory phenomenon, the very pride in being a Wheatley "graduate," which Hunter and her staff cultivated, could sometimes lead to declining deference toward white employers. One wonders whether the graduates' training led employers to treat them with greater respect and better treatment, or whether the training made no difference. The communal living conditions at the Phillis Wheatley meant that reviews of employers circulated quickly among residents. Hunter, however, seemed to accept employers' complaints about their servants without question. She would remark that her students were "privileged to serve in the homes of others." One of the required virtues, for her, was humility.

Some residents displayed a lack of enthusiasm for domestic service training altogether and dreamed of better employment. Some of those already working as domestics had no interest in further training because they hoped to find different work.[186] Nevertheless, the Phillis Wheatley staff apparently did not explore alternative job options.

But the residents' resistance to the terms of the domestic service jobs threatened to undercut the home's finances. The Phillis Wheatley's main attraction to donors was its promise to supply domestic servants who would be grateful as well as efficient and hardworking. Hull-House also depended on philanthropy, but when whites contributed to Hull-House, it could retain its absolute independence, while when they donated to the Phillis Wheatley, they claimed the right to exercise control.

Residents' resistance to oppressive jobs flowed into resistance to the Phillis Wheatley's rules. Flouting the rules was widespread, sometimes surreptitious but occasionally overt. The residents did drink, and the staff did find beer bottles in the rooms. Drinking could make them jolly but also disorderly, and staff meetings discussed how to deal with "drunk, loud, boisterous" women. A matron complained of one resident who "goes out and . . . returns at three, four and five o'clock in the morning so drunk that we wish she had not returned." Dance halls were so popular that the Phillis Wheatley was forced to compromise and hosted supervised dances in the home itself. But then the residents rolled out their own ideas about what made for an enjoyable dance evening—the hours, the music, the lighting (which they wanted dim). They asserted their preferences strongly, and the result was frequent conflict. Disciplinary action did not end the mischief. The power struggle did not abate.[187]

Curfew was a major object of conflict. Residents were supposed to be in by midnight, and those who came late were listed in matrons' reports with the time they arrived. In just one month in 1933, twenty-four different women, who constituted 30 percent of the residents, defied the curfew or stayed out all night. The night matrons tried to discourage this behavior by cutting off elevator service late at night, a considerable source of annoyance in the nine-story building. If the woman was young, the staff also tried reporting the infraction to her parents. But the staff essentially caved on the matter of curfew. "It is rather unfortunate for young people to stay out late," one set of minutes remarked, but "all young people stay out late."[188]

Paradoxically, these conflicts were a perverse consequence of Jane Hunter's own strategy. By providing a shelter, by creating a community that was, among the residents, egalitarian, she had given these women not only a home but also produced solidarity—a resistant collective will, spread through a peer culture, that undercut her own preachings.*

Jane Hunter was certain about what her working girls needed, an opinion that rested on both research and her own experience. Unlike the Hull-House mistakes that reflected ignorance of their neighbors' needs and desires, Hunter's policies arose from intimate knowledge of her wards' conditions. She was far more authoritarian than anyone at Hull-House, but her wards were more vulnerable, and her staff knew it. The conflicts at the Phillis Wheatley took the form they did precisely because African American service providers were trying to help African American service receivers. In other words, it was similarity that motivated the stringent rules. Moreover, Phillis Wheatley residents almost certainly shared many of Hunter's perspectives: they were religious, southern, lonely, not well educated, and hardworking; some were likely children of sharecroppers, as was Hunter. Even the most rebellious residents knew that Hunter's motives were altruistic. They might even have forgiven her capitulation to the racist demands of wealthy whites.

Two distinguished African American feminist scholars, Adrienne Lash Jones and Hazel Carby, disagree. Writing in the Du Boisian tradition of militant demand for equality, they have criticized Hunter's repressive rule, her defense of segregated institutions, and her acquiescence to white funders. Carby writes with respect for Hunter but also suggests that she was motivated by her personal longing to be "part of the emergent black bourgeoisie." She argues that Hunter's approach stemmed in part from a desire to secure "her personal autonomy in . . . claiming the right to circumscribe the rights of young black working-class women and

---

* In writing this chapter, I often wished that someone had interviewed Phillis Wheatley residents, not only while they were residents but also years or decades later so as to examine the home's influence.

to transform their behavior on the grounds of nurturing the progress of the race as a whole." Carby also psychologized her critique, suggesting that Hunter transmuted her early loss of a mother into an over-the-top matriarchal repression "on behalf of the black women she designated as helpless."[189] That Hunter was ambitious for herself is clear, but her tenacious work on behalf of young Black women migrants was motivated by more than personal ambition. She was not wrong in her focus on the dangers lone Black women migrants faced. In fact, the Phillis Wheatley resembled many colleges that used the principle of *in loco parentis* to restrict far less vulnerable young women. But thanks to Virginia Boynton, we now know something of how Hunter's wards fought back against the rules, evidence that the Phillis Wheatley's repressiveness was by no means omnipotent. In bringing single women under one roof, Hunter paradoxically made their rebelliousness possible.

Another line of criticism of the Phillis Wheatley Home continued Cleveland middle-class Blacks' earlier condemnation of Hunter's acceptance of segregation. In 1929 Du Bois's paper the *Crisis* praised the "astonishing" achievement of Jane Hunter but also expressed unease with her accomplishment:

> *Phillis Wheatley House is a monument to American Negro womanhood: to its ability to endure and to bear with dignity and courage, poverty and insult and discrimination. . . . And yet and again Phillis Wheatley House is a monument to American Prejudice: to its inability to rise above alms-giving, into human brotherhood and a desire for the full and free development of every human being to its greatest capacity.*[190]

While it was of course white racism that had forced Hunter to create a segregated institution, she also saw value in temporary segregation. Recent scholarly discussion of Booker T. Washington's strategic ideas offer a more nuanced, less critical view of his approach than that of earlier decades. A simple binary contrasting Du Bois, rendered as more radical and more principled, to Washington, rendered as accommodationist, is an interpretation removed from the imperatives and opportunities of location and local racial structures. Washington, situated in a totalitarian southern racism enforced by violence and law, was not entirely wrong in refusing to view integration as the only path to combating racism, and in concentrating on the upward mobility that Blacks could achieve among their own people. Black-only and Black-women-only spaces had and continue to have considerable attraction for African Americans when they are voluntary. (We will see this preference again in chapter 7, on the women's liberation movement.)

But Booker Washington's preferred strategy avoided the fact that segregation was never voluntary. Hunter's northern environment, where the abuse of single women migrants was widespread, presented different and immediate imperatives. Though many immigrant wives and mothers in the Hull-House neighborhood had to earn, they often did so in their own homes, doing the hand sewing needed in garment production. No doubt some of these women suffered domestic violence, and Hull-House research did not ask about that.* To Jane Hunter, campaigning for racial integration did not seem likely to address the needs of the women she sought to help, so her choices seemed to her the best possible. She thus avoided, or ignored, a dilemma common in social movements, one that will appear repeatedly in this book: that urgent needs make it difficult to focus on long-term goals, and that achievable reforms become the goal.

HULL-HOUSE AND the whole white settlement house movement were part of an early twentieth-century social democratic feminism, sometimes called simply social feminism. This orientation differed from, say, that of the suffrage movement, by concentrating on economic and social reform, though settlers of course supported enfranchising women. But Hull-House's strategy for helping the poor relied on the connections, resources, education, leisure time, and self-confidence of the privileged, which enabled its residents to engage with campaigns for legislation, elections, and labor unions. The Phillis Wheatley Home did not and could not do this; its constituency, even more disadvantaged than poor white immigrants, kept it from political engagement. So did

---

* Hull-House did address the vulnerability of single women migrants at a later date.

its dependence on white donors. Nor did white settlements address the needs of African Americans. Hunter's approach represented, for better or worse, another variant of feminism and one possibly of equal value for young African American women migrants in the North at the time.

And yet Hull-House and the Phillis Wheatley Home shared a method for helping poor migrants and immigrants: offering them spaces away from their daily struggles. Settlements provide a perfect example of the fertility of social movement spaces. They are typically both enclosed and open, they enhance solidarity while also intersecting with the outside world, and they bring people together over stretches of time that allow for protracted interaction. The safety, comfort, and companionship that the Phillis Wheatley provided allowed the residents space from which they could explore in relative safety the city they had just entered, acquire training and employment opportunities, and not least, create friendships with others in the same situation. Hull-House's space benefited both its residents and its constituents, while the Phillis Wheatley's constituents *were* its residents. Both settlements contributed to forming communities of support that likely continued over decades to come.

These communities were female. The settlement movement was a female form of activism, not only in personnel but in style and substance, and this was central to its achievements. To repeat Vida Scudder's pithy view, men form clubs while women form homes.[191] Both Hull-House and the Phillis Wheatley Home were unconventional, non-family, woman-dominated residences. In this sense, they were "queer." Hull-House women used their freedom from "the family claim" to devote themselves to social activism. Despite Jane Hunter's authoritarian rule—and it was probably no more repressive than that in many male-headed families of the time—the space she created was as unconventional and fruitful as Hull-House's. In neither project did leaders criticize conventional, male-headed, nuclear families.[192] Nevertheless they offered comfortable and secure alternatives to them, alternatives that contributed to democratizing them.

Both settlements capitulated to the dominant racism of their time. While some scholars have criticized Hunter's emphasis on training domestic servants for the wealthy, this was a strategic decision, and one for which there was some justification. By contrast, Hull-House's capitulation was less justifiable, because it had the resources to bring more people of color into its sphere of activity and influence. Lone Black women in northern cities needed immediate support and shelter, and the Phillis Wheatley provided it for them. While Hull-House was a project *for* subordinated groups, the Phillis Wheatley was a project *of* them.

Some social movements have distinct moments of success. The Ku Klux Klan's victory in the passage of the 1924 immigration restriction law was one; Montgomery's 1956 victory over bus segregation was another. On a larger scale, however, all the movements profiled in this book succeeded by changing public opinion. The settlement movement's success was less measurable but no less impressive. Hull-House and the Phillis Wheatley Home were part of a national settlement movement that enhanced the safety and health of their constituents— all migrants—and that enabled them to explore the possibilities that their new environment offered. Hull-House became a powerful base of reform activism, and the Phillis Wheatley Home did not, but by helping young Black women survive and enter an urban labor force, it contributed to democratizing the city. All social movements create virtual space, but the settlement movement shows the particular value of physical space, especially nonfamily spaces that helped migrants both immediately and in their future aspirations.

2

FROM KU KLUX KLAN TO AMERICAN FASCISTS, 1920s–1930s

KKK burning cross.

Hundreds of German Americans give the Nazi salute to young men marching in Nazi uniforms. The event was a German Day celebration sponsored by German American Bund, a Nazi organization in the United States, at Camp Sigfried on Long Island.

Our capacity to maintain our cherished institutions stands
diluted by a stream of alien blood.

—WASHINGTON STATE CONGRESSMAN
ALBERT JOHNSON, KKK SUPPORTER, 1927[1]

I take the road of fascism.

—CATHOLIC PRIEST CHARLES COUGHLIN,
HEAD OF THE CHRISTIAN FRONT, 1936[2]

A rising in the South after the Civil War, the Ku Klux Klan
was a terrorist group in the precise meaning of that term—it
used torture and murder, notably thousands of lynchings, as
well as economic and social coercion, to terrorize the whole African
American population and squelch their efforts to gain political rights
or economic opportunity. The Klan's revival in the 1920s is less well
known. Often called the second Klan,* it was a different beast: a mass
movement of some three to five million members, not counting 1.5
million in the women's Klan (WKKK). It was strongest in the North
and Northwest, it was not at all secret, and it was primarily nonviolent.† Like other movements in this book, the Klan's career demonstrates that electoral and social movement strategies are not alternatives
but are often mutually reinforcing. By exploiting and promoting fears
of immigrants, especially Catholics and Jews, it put thousands of its

---

* In fact there have been four avatars of the Ku Klux Klan. A third arose in opposition to the civil rights movement, focused on defending school segregation and
thwarting Black voting rights; the White Citizens' Councils were essentially cousins
of the Klan. A fourth appeared in the last few decades in what is now called "white
nationalism" or white supremacists, but now it is just one small group among hundreds of others.

† Reliable figures on the second Klan's membership are unavailable. Estimates of its
size ranged from 1 to 9 million members. Both pro- and anti-Klan people exaggerated its size, and members left the Klan as often as new people joined. Yet focusing
on membership lists has the effect of minimizing the degree of support for its views
among nonmembers.

candidates into office and helped create discriminatory immigration restriction legislation.[3]

As the second Klan was the progeny of the first, so the hundred-plus American fascist groups that flourished in the 1930s were the offspring of the second Klan. Narrowing and intensifying KKK bigotry, the fascist groups welcomed Catholics as "true Americans" and targeted Jews and labor leaders, often violently, while preserving venomous racism against people of color. With an ideology simultaneously adroit and incoherent, the American fascists wrapped themselves in patriotism while claiming Hitler and Franco as their heroes. Though minuscule in membership in contrast to the massive Klan, the fascist grups perpetrated considerable violence, murdering and assaulting thousands of labor organizers and Jews.

The second Klan's bigotry was by no means marginal in the 1920s. It was then a respectable public organization, and it is quite possible that a majority of white Americans shared its views. It lasted less than a decade as a mass organization, but during that time it elected hundreds of Klansmen to public office, stopped the Democratic Party from nominating its strongest candidate for the presidency, and greatly influenced the passage of the 1924 immigration restriction law, a model of legislative bigotry that remained law for forty years. By contrast, the fascist groups had no electoral or legislative agenda. Their propaganda focused on condemning democracy and exalting European fascist leaders. Had it not been for Nazi territorial aggression, the American fascists might have become a lasting party in American politics. Instead, they became understood as traitors, while the Klan's nonviolent bigotry, promoted through propaganda and electoral campaigns, imbricated itself into the American fabric. One might conclude that racists did better by sticking to nonviolence. But examining the two movements together shows how a nonviolent program of bigotry can give birth to a violent movement, whose impact was limited only by global events.

This chapter grew from my book *The Second Coming of the KKK.**

---

* This chapter includes material from that book, *The Second Coming of the KKK: The Ku Klux Klan of the 1920s and the American Political Tradition* (New York: Liveright, 2017), which provides a fuller picture of the 1920s KKK, including discussions

As loathsome as the Klan was, my concern there was nevertheless to examine it as a social movement—how it became so large, what it offered its members, how it went about influencing American politics. The American fascists did not constitute a social movement in its usual meaning, because they comprised scores of small groups, most of which kept their membership secret. I include them here because they illuminate where Klannish ideas can lead and because today fascism, both domestic and global, is an increasing concern.

IN THE 1920s a renewed, remodeled KKK burst onto the national scene with amazing speed. Its ancestral lineage was familial as well as organizational: General Nathan Bedford Forrest, head of the first Klan, was the grandfather of Nathan Bedford Forrest II, Grand Dragon of the Georgia realm of the second Klan. This renovated Klan maintained its parent's racism with a twist: it blamed Jews for stirring up Black resistance.* The second KKK attacked other people of color where they were numerous—for example, Asian immigrants in the Northwest—but in the 1920s a campaign focused against African Americans would have had less traction in the northern states where the Black population was relatively small.[4]

Like its southern parent, the northern KKK had distinguished ancestors, primarily nineteenth-century nativists, who feared that immigrants threatened the political and economic dominance of white Protestants. The nativists, and then the KKK, were arguing what today

of Klan women, Klan economic warfare, the attack on Catholic schools, Klan chapters in universities, finances, ideology, and membership—along with new material on the KKK. The material on fascist groups is entirely new.

* In an eerie sort of prefiguring, the Klan's belief that Jews colluded with Blacks was not true in the 1920s but would become true years later when Jews numbered disproportionately among white civil rights activists and supporters. Decades later the dystopian novel *The Turner Diaries*, a bible for white nationalists, described a near-future in which Jews have unleashed Blacks and other undesirables into the center of American public life. One of the fascist organizations, the German American Bund, seeking constitutional support for its anti-Semitism, claimed that its demand for "racial separation" between Jews and Christians was allowable under the Supreme Court's 1896 *Plessy v. Ferguson* decision.

has been called a "replacement" theory, that "true" or "real" Americans were in danger of being replaced by undesirable groups. (Today's white nationalists shouted "You will not replace us" in the 2017 Charlottesville terrorist attack.)[5] An early nativist group, the "Know Nothings" (formally the Native American Party), arose in New England in the 1850s, charging that "Romanists"—a label for Catholics also used by the Klan—were conspiring to subvert American freedom. They briefly controlled dozens of congressmen.

Far more influential were the upper-class nativists who formed the anti-immigration American Protective Association in 1887. Consider a few of the distinguished scholars and lawyers who spoke for the cause: Charles Benedict Davenport, Harvard professor, descendant of Puritans; Robert DeCourcy Ward, whose ancestors arrived with John Winthrop; the historian Henry Cabot Lodge, who claimed descent from William the Conqueror; Prescott Farnsworth Hall, who claimed descent from Charlemagne (!); and H. Fairfield Osborn, son of a railroad tycoon, president of the American Museum of Natural History. Nativist scholars produced a blizzard of numbers to build their case. Scholar Henry Goddard tested arrivals at Ellis Island and "found" that 83 percent of the Jews, 80 percent of the Hungarians, and 79 percent of the Italians were either morons or imbeciles. The superior "Nordic race" (a label they handed down to the KKK) was in danger of extinction; turning Darwinism on its head, they were saying that the fittest were being replaced by the unfit.[6]

To rescue the nation, the nativists promoted, first, a eugenics program to reduce reproduction by the "unfit" and to increase reproduction by the "fit" so as to breed a "superior" people. Eugenics theory assumed the heritability of characteristics that we now know are primarily shaped by environment, but it passed as good science in the early twentieth century.[7] Secondly, the nativists sought to stop the immigration of alleged "inferiors," who from the 1880s to the early 1920s were mainly Catholics, Jews, and in the West, Asians.*

---

* Because recent decades have seen another anti-immigrant alarm in the United States, it is worth comparing contemporary immigration to that of a century ago: Immigrants arriving between 2000 and 2010 constituted 3 percent of the U.S.

The Klan updated these views on the basis of three pillars: patriotism, bigotry, and evangelical Protestantism.* Each of the three required the others: for the KKK, you couldn't be a patriot unless you were a white Protestant and believed that America must reclaim an identity as a white Protestant nation. Klan patriotism, promoted as a unifying principle, was actually a disunifying principle. "True" or 100 percent Americans had to be "white," or "Nordic." Catholics and Jews—not to mention smaller groups such as Muslims and Greeks—allegedly worshipped false gods and owed primary allegiance to foreign leaders, such as the pope or an imaginary Jewish cabal of financiers. The Klan sought to make these disloyal Americans second-class citizens, so as to keep them from contesting white Protestant political and economic power. The Klan's explosive growth magnified the fearmongering of elite conservatives, claiming that America's destiny was being subverted by aliens, supported by its claim that sixty to 90 percent of government employees were illiterate Catholics, while the army and navy had been "Romanized." Klan patriotism aimed to build a sense of dread through its massive media empire.

Prohibition helped the Ku Klux Klan harvest massive support from white evangelical Protestant conservatives. (Mainline Protestants, such as Episcopalians and Lutherans, found the KKK less attractive.) Some Klanspeople called their organization an "extreme militant wing of the temperance movement."[8] They fulminated against sexual immorality and blamed it on Hollywood and big-city cosmopolitanism. They campaigned for religious education in public schools. It is not just that evangelicals provided the Klan's base; in fact, the Klan *was* an evangelical revival. As Klan propaganda put it, God had chosen the KKK to rescue the nation from the menace of the ungodly: if Jesus were alive today, he would be a Klansman. It boasted that forty thousand evangelical ministers were among its members; they praised the Klan in sermons

---

population, while those arriving between 1900 and 1910 constituted 8.9 percent of the population.

* I use the term *bigotry* because the term *racism* is usually applied to discrimination against people of color, and today Jews and Catholics, at least, are typically considered white. In the 1920s, however, what counted as a "race" was fuzzy; moreover *race* and *ethnicity* were used interchangeably.

and many served as traveling lecturers and recruiters for the Klan.* To the Klan, the battle against "untrue" Americans was a battle against sinfulness. (This was the official ideology, but not always the practice, because Klanspeople, like everyone else, sinned, compromised, dissembled, and drank.)

All social movements thrive by creating a social as well as a political community, and the Klan was no exception. Its chapters offered conviviality, its mass outdoor rallies a larger camaraderie, and both provided riveting entertainment. Klaverns—Klanspeak for "chapters"—offered arcane oaths, eerie rituals, and esoteric ceremonies and codes; known only to members, they provided the pleasure of being entrusted with secrets. Members could climb ladders of status, as in scouting, with fanciful, military titles—Field Marshal, Most Excellent Commander, Sublime Augustus, Dictator, Grand Knight, and Chancellor Commander. The Klan produced a rich variety of organized activities for men, women, and children: sports teams, bands and choruses, picnics, youth groups; ceremonies marking births, christenings, marriages, funerals. It staged large outdoor events that combined the spirit of evangelical rallies with the games and contests of traditional fairs. Its klaverns provided opportunities for networking, leading to economic opportunities.

In these activities, the KKK resembled fraternal and sororal orders, and many members regarded it as one more of the same. Americans were accustomed to them: in 1897, some 5.4 million Americans belonged to fraternal orders, 10.2 million by 1926, with half a million children in affiliated youth groups. One Klan advertisement described it as "a Standard Fraternal Order."[9] A Wisconsin recruiter promoted the Klan as "a high, close, mystic, social, patriotic, benevolent association having a perfected lodge system." As Maine fisherman Charlie York explained, "I never enjoyed any Lodge so much as I did the Klan at first. It had the principle of brotherly love for feller members and they [*sic*] was a high moral tone to it." A former Klanswoman recalled that

---

* Such numbers, like those of the overall membership, cannot be regarded as even approximately accurate. Like many groups seeking more members, the Klan always exaggerated its size, calculating a bandwagon effect. And scholars have no way of identifying national membership.

it became your whole family.[10] Klan members often belonged to other fraternal orders, especially the Masons: when Klan recruiters arrived in a new location, they frequently began by contacting the local Masonic Order. Women hoping to start a klavern often recruited from among Daughters of the American Revolution.[11] The 1920s Klan, it must be repeated, was entirely mainstream.

IN KLAN ideology, the threat to "true" Americanism was diversity. Only a homogeneous nation could be strong, the Klan assumed. Congressman Albert Johnson, chair of the House Committee on Immigration and a Klan supporter, put it this way:

> *Today, instead of a nation descended from generations of free men bred to a knowledge of the principles and practice of self-government, of liberty under law, we have a heterogeneous population no small proportion of which is sprung from races that, throughout the centuries, have known no liberty at all. . . . Our capacity to maintain our cherished institutions stands diluted by a stream of alien blood with all its inherited misconceptions respecting the relationships of the governing power to the governed. . . . The United States is our land. We intend to maintain it so.[12]*

The Klan spoke of the "Babel of voices" that arose from the immigrant enclaves in big cities and industrial or mining towns; such a hodgepodge led to chaos. Order required uniformity.

The Klan argued that Catholics were incapable of patriotism because the pope and his subordinates demanded their exclusive allegiance. Catholics brainwashed children through parochial schools, while Catholic teachers in the public schools taught disguised Catholic ideas. Moreover, subordination to the pope made Catholics subservient, unfit for the manly independence that democracy required. Jews served an international cabal of financiers, the charge repeating the centuries-old libel that Jews were by nature ruthless and dishonest swindlers.

These "aliens" operated through conspiracies. With circular logic, Klan spokesmen explained the lack of evidence for these allegations by pointing out that conspiracies are secret. Sometimes the KKK manufactured "evidence" by using a "black psywar" method (an abbreviation of "psychological warfare," used by the United States during the Vietnam War, when it distributed material disguised as emanating from the National Liberation Front). For example, the Klan circulated a counterfeit oath attributed to the Catholic Knights of Columbus that called on members to "wage relentless war, secretly and openly, against all heretics, Protestants, and Masons. . . . Burn, waste, boil, flay, strangle and bury alive . . . rip open the stomachs and wombs of their women and crash their infants' heads against the walls in order to annihilate their execrable race."[13] The most famous piece of anti-Semitic black psywar was the *Protocols of the Elders of Zion*, a foundational text for fascists. A Russian forgery, it purported to be the minutes of a meeting of Jewish bankers discussing their conspiracy to achieve world economic domination.[14]

The KKK promoted its conspiracy charges through a media network that included more than one hundred print publications, two radio stations, and scores of traveling lecturers. Catholic immigrants, they explained, came to the United States because the pope had ordered them to come, even told them where to settle, so that they could take over schools, government, and police forces. Local Klan chapters concocted their own conspiracy stories: in Dubois County, Indiana, for example, speakers claimed that the assassinations of Lincoln, James Garfield, and William McKinley had been committed by Catholics on the pope's orders. Jews planned to take over the American economy through its financial institutions—or even to establish a secret government within our government, called the "deep state" by today's inheritors of Klan ideology.[15]

The Klan blamed sexual immorality on Jews, who promoted women's immodest dress, makeup, and recreation through their control of department stores, garment manufacture, and the media—and above all Hollywood. "Jew Movies urging sex vice" was typical. Jews fed their immoral urges by kidnapping women for their "white-slave dens." "What happens to the army of young girls who are lost every year? From 60,000 to 75,000 of them disappear annually. . . . The Jews get them and sell them as white slaves. They have a regular price list."[16]

The KKK condemned Charlie Chaplin after his appearance in the 1923 film *The Pilgrim*, in which he offered a burlesque version of a hypocritical minister—this "proved" that he was Jewish—a falsehood but one he honorably declined to deny.[17] Defiance of Prohibition was also a conspiracy between Catholics, who did the drinking, and Jewish bootleggers, who supplied them. This map of sin was not only incorrect, since many Protestants manufactured, wholesaled, retailed, and drank liquor and the majority of Americans opposed Prohibition, but also hypocritical, because Klansmen were often caught drinking, a fact that contributed to the Klan's decline.

THE KLAN'S 1920s critics made some mistaken assumptions that displayed their own prejudices. They diagnosed the Klan as an inane hysteria of uneducated, lowbrow hicks, a "booboisie." The liberal *New Republic* magazine suggested in 1925 that people joined the Klan because of the monotony and boredom of small-town life.[18] Novelist Sinclair Lewis made fun of a Klan "type" in his 1922 novel *Babbitt*, and that name soon came to mean someone closed-minded, narrow-minded, and conformist, though at least middle class in economic status. Other derogatory epithets included *insane, busybodies, believers in ghosts, gullible, shabby of mind, social deviants.* More accurately but equally disdainfully, the renowned liberal southern historian Francis Butler Simkins called the KKK "an authentic folk movement."[19]

Klanspeople simply ricocheted that disdain, condemning the snobbery, lack of moral values, and lack of patriotism among their critics. A few decades later some scholars, notably the eminent mid-twentieth-century historian Richard Hofstadter, branded the KKK an example of the irrationality and paranoia of the "crowd." These criticisms equated fear and anger with irrationality. But mass emotion, and fomenting mass emotion, can be rational even if it is based on false beliefs. In yet another mistaken analysis, the Klan's contemporary critics such as Frank Bohn, Clarence Darrow, Frank Tannenbaum, and William Allen White branded it an aberration, an outlier in the national political culture. In that understanding they shared, ironically, a key Klannish idea: that one and only one culture was truly American.[20]

These contemptuous descriptions were debunked by the first serious historical studies. Charles Alexander in 1965 and Kenneth Jackson in 1967 showed that the KKK was primarily an urban phenomenon. By correlating names on membership lists with census records, they found that Klanspeople were no less educated that most Americans, were not primarily rural and small-town people, and were not poor.[21] In fact, Klan members were primarily "middling" people—lower middle class, white collar, lower professionals.[22] The most common occupational categories in the northern Klan were small businesspeople, white-collar workers, lower-level professionals, and police. It had few very wealthy members, although there were some, while working-class people could not afford its dues.

Critics also misunderstood the Klan's hooded uniforms. Assuming that they were intended to conceal their identities, some cities and towns prohibited group appearances by masked men, only to find that Klanspeople were entirely comfortable marching without hoods.[23] The robes served primarily to create visual drama and a link to the first KKK. Other critics thought that merely exposing the Klan would shrink it. That folly became clear when in 1921 the *New York World* newspaper published reports of odious Klan activity by a disaffected former Klansman; the articles generated a large increase in its membership.[24] Similarly, opponents expected 1921 congressional hearings about the KKK to reveal its shady practices. The second Klan's founder, William Simmons, testified, with pride, that he headed a benign fraternalist, nativist organization, one that was not just respectable but, more important, patriotic. It promoted, he said, an "uncompromising standard of pure Americanism," dedicated to maintaining "the distinctive institutions, rights, privileges, principles, traditions and ideals of a pure Americanism." He did not hesitate to acknowledge its campaign for white supremacy but assured the congressmen that it "would be done in a patriotic and just way."[25] The hearings actually grew the Klan— Simmons told a journalist that "calls began pouring in from . . . all over America for the right to organize Klans. . . . We worked twenty-four hours a day trying to meet the demand."[26] Before the newspaper stories and hearings, Klan membership was about 125,000, but afterward it reported five thousand new members per day. It was featured on newspaper front pages all over the country, even in *Variety*, alongside gossip about movie stars.[27]

Perhaps the most definitive disproof that the KKK represented unsophisticated bumpkins lay in its state-of-the-art recruitment techniques. In addition to advertising in newspapers and on the radio, paying commissions to recruiters and selling trinkets, it showed the film *Birth of a Nation* throughout the country—possibly the first time a film helped build a social movement. Released in 1915, based on Thomas Dixon's 1905 novel *The Clansman*, it showed newly freed slaves rampaging, threatening to rape white women, aided by northern "carpet-baggers," and brave Klansmen rescuing "white womanhood." Masses of Americans regarded the film as documentary. President Woodrow Wilson—who famously refused to meet with African American leaders—showed it at the White House—the first time any movie was shown there—and praised it effusively: "It is like writing history with lightning. And my only regret is that it is all so terribly true."[28] For many viewers, the film was their first experience of a movie, and it brought in both recruits and money.

Nothing could have been more modern than the Klan's recruitment-through-commission system, built by the Atlanta PR firm of Elizabeth Tyler and Edward Young Clarke. To the best of my knowledge, this was the first time that a social movement hired professional publicists. The PR team realized that to grow the Klan outside the South, they had to ditch southern whites' fear of Black power and appeal to northern bigotry against Catholics and Jews. Their approach represented a new "science" of salesmanship. They registered the new Klan as a for-profit enterprise and marketed it as if they were selling insurance. A contemporary journalist thought they had "brought recruiting to a point of efficiency . . . beyond any similar system." A recruit paid an initiation fee, labeled a Klecktoken, of ten dollars (a reminder that it was not poor, small farm or working-class people who rushed to join). Of that ten dollars, the recruiter, known as a Kleagle, would keep four; the remaining six dollars would be forwarded to the Atlanta head office, of which Clarke and Tyler took 80 percent.

With such financial incentives, Clarke and Tyler's "Propagation Department" had recruited eleven hundred active Kleagles within a year, working in thirty-five states plus the District of Columbia. Each new member could in theory become a Kleagle himself, recruit members, and keep 40 percent of their initiation fee. As the organization expanded, regional leaders would get a cut as well. Why should selling something for profit not be patriotic? This understanding showed in KKK support for personal enrichment. Despite some populist rhetoric and its claim to represent the "common man," the 1920s Klan never evinced anything but respect for the very wealthy. Any faults in the American economic system stemmed from Jews' and Catholics' corruption.[29] A classic pyramid scheme, its recruiters would ultimately exhaust the available buyers in their community, leading to high turnover in membership.

Beyond the initiation fee, members were to pay dues ranging from eight to fifteen cents a month, and Kleagles and higher officers took commissions from these as well. Each Klavern had to pay an Imperial Tax to the national headquarters and a Realm Tax to the region. The Atlanta team also instituted a ladder that members could climb, with rungs called "degrees" as in Masonic groups: You started out at K-Uno, then could advance to K-Duo, K-Trio, and K-Quad; the higher degrees allegedly brought prestige but required an initial payment and higher dues.

The Klan also profiteered by selling paraphernalia. Klan leaders ran many side businesses—notably a recording company and a realty enterprise that bought lots in bulk and sold them singly. Klan-friendly merchants marketed all sorts of Klan-marked trinkets and memorabilia. A "Kluxer's Knifty Knife," a "real 100% percent knife for 100% Americans," could be bought for $1.25. For five dollars you could get, allegedly, a fourteen-karat gold-filled ring with a ten-karat solid gold Klan emblem on a fiery red stone, and for $2.90 a cross on a watch chain. Also for sale were phonograph records and player-piano rolls with favorite Klan songs. Advertisements for this merchandise appeared in newspapers across the country and in flyers at large Klonvocations. The KKK tried to sell for-profit burial and life insurance, claiming to have written $3 million worth of policies in 1924, but it is not clear that the insurance ever materialized.[30]

Sales of Klan costumes brought in big profits, and the garments were elaborate enough that women were unlikely to be able to sew them by hand. Produced industrially at the cost of four dollars each, later only two dollars each, they were sold for $6.50. The white robe sported a red, white, and black insignia over the left breast. The insignias varied slightly, but all contained a cross (typically a Prussian cross) within a circle—sometimes called a crosswheel; a diamond in the center that sometimes contained a red mark in the shape of a drop of water (the blood drop). A sash was to be tied around the waist. The hat, called a helmet, was lined with a stiffened material to create and stabilize its cone shape, and a regulation red tassel hung from the top. Over the helmet went two "aprons": one hung from the back bottom of the conical hat to the shoulders; another in front had eyeholes.

So the cost of joining the Klan might total $23.30 for the first year—a ten-dollar initiation fee, $6.50 for the costume, annual dues of about five dollars, and a yearly $1.80 tax to the national headquarters. In addition, members were dunned for contributions to political candidates, gifts to churches, and assessments for special projects, such as an $80,000 auditorium with four thousand seats in Fort Worth. According to one recent estimate, the Klan took in at least $25 million annually. This is likely an exaggeration: at any one time, as much as one-third of the membership never paid, fell behind, or just quit paying dues.[31] But even allowing for exaggeration, Klan profiteers did very well by soaking their members.

To many recruits, joining the Klan seemed a productive investment. Klaverns often functioned much like Rotary Clubs, where contacts could lead to jobs or promotions and, for businessmen, customers—opportunities for upward economic mobility. The Klan was not just respectable but often prestigious. It allowed members to socialize with the "best" citizens, including many businessmen, managers, and political officials. One Klan leader explained it as a recruitment strategy:

> The majority of reputable citizens are going into [the Klan,] and the bad ones are kept out. . . . You see the Klan is a select crowd. You can't join unless someone asks you. . . . None but good men are asked.[32]

When sociologist Kathleen Blee interviewed elderly former Klanspeople three decades ago, some told her that "all the better people" had belonged. A study of Portland, Oregon, where the Klan was exceptionally strong, found that working-class people felt they could become middle class by associating with middle-class people in a proudly middle-class fraternity. The Klan's emphasis on patriotism, church affiliation, temperance, and sexual morality also contributed to the implicit promise that membership could bring upward mobility.[33]

To identify Klan-friendly stores or services, the Klan produced placards to display in windows. Its slogan, "100% American," was by then so well known that placards often read only "100%." Some used the code TWK, Klanspeak for "Trade With Klansmen." (Plans to publish a national TWK directory of Klan businesses did not materialize.) Its attempts to create a boycott of Jewish-owned establishments probably drove some small Jewish-owned stores out of business, but when the KKK targeted large department stores, many of which were Jewish-owned, it failed. So did the Klan's attempt to keep people away from Hollywood movies, as crowds continued to pour into theaters, eager to see the fruits of this new invention.

With so much money pouring in, Klan leaders' corruption became hard to hide. Simmons got a $33,000 home in Atlanta, known as Klankrest, two expensive cars, and a bonus of $25,000. He purchased the Peachtree Creek Civil War battleground, sacred to the Confederacy, and planned to build a university there—one of many unrealized fantasies. His immorality also became apparent; he liked horse races and prizefights, and his partying was making him a noticeable drunkard.[34] Tyler and Clarke, who had taken in more than $850,000 in their first fifteen months on the job, also became a moral liability when Atlanta police literally rousted them out of bed and arrested them for disorderly conduct—that is, adultery. (Both were married to other people.) Newspaper coverage of the arrest revealed that they used false names and were in possession of whiskey. The scandal was big news, covered even in the *New York Times*.[35]

If the organization was to thrive, national leaders believed, this moral and financial bleeding had to stop. In 1922 two of them—Hiram Evans from Texas and David Stephenson from Indiana—executed a coup. They bought off Simmons by anointing him an "emperor" and paying him $140,000. (The Klan was legally his wholly owned business.) Hiram Evans became the Imperial Wizard. A man of vision, ambition, and confidence, he was well born, the son of a judge, educated at Vanderbilt. He fired Clarke and Tyler. He had no further need for their services—now that the Klan's membership had exploded, he saw no reason to give away 80 percent of Klan revenue. Hoping to cleanse the Klan of corruption, Evans put recruiters on salary rather than commission, but allowed his supporters in Klan leadership to continue earning commissions, in a somewhat feudal arrangement that cemented their loyalty and his control.[36]

Evans envisaged the Klan becoming a political party—this did not happen, but he did make electoral politics his top priority. He hired professional speechwriters and attorneys and deployed Klan lobbyists. He established more publications, notably a stealth magazine, *Fellowship Forum*, designed to promote "pure Americanism" among those who "shy away from the mention of the Ku Klux Klan."[37] He tried to combat drinking and other moral infractions among members, threatening sinners with expulsion. Although in his first years with the Klan he had organized "black squads" that kidnapped and tortured at least one black man,[38] he now denounced violence and revised the oath to make recruits swear to uphold the law. He urged members to avoid using their masks when not participating in formal rituals. He was determined to make the Klan a major national political force, and for a time he succeeded.

MEANWHILE THE Klan developed a wholesale recruitment method that normalized it to a larger public: producing elaborate patriotic events with entertainments for whole families. These Klonvocations or Klantauquas, often held on Independence Day, fit an American tradition of picnics and parades. Carefully choreographed, they presented the Klan as simultaneously pleasurable, nonthreatening, and patriotic. Klan leaders became impresarios of patriotism, boasting that "The Klan is the peace-time Army of Americanism serving the nation as the United States Army does in war time."[39]

Carnivals but never carnivalesque, these events were wildly popular.[40] Located in fairgrounds, in public parks, in rented or loaned private fields, they were announced in church sermons, newspapers, handbills, and posters tied to trees. People came from miles away by the thousands, sometimes tens of thousands. These were family events, offering "wholesome" entertainment and activities for people of every age and interest: music, rides, ballgames, races, contests with prizes, lots of food to sell or buy, even hot-air balloon rides. Huge tag sales offered bargains. Physicians staffed first-aid stations. Concerts featured youth groups, drum and bugle corps, and of course minstrel shows, white performers singing and dancing in blackface. There were beauty contests and team sports. A Minnesota event featured a "fat man's race" for those over 225 pounds. A Nebraska event featured a "water pageant" at which displays floated around a lake on pontoons. There were thrilling spectacles. In a 1924 Indianapolis event, a daredevil leaped from a hundred-foot tower into a net.[41] Airplane stunts were particularly exciting. Parachutists jumped from planes. One plane arrived at a Klonvocation in Jackson, Michigan, "with the black sky as a background, a flaming red cross streaked across the heavens . . . when the aviator turned on a red electrically lighted cross" on the bottom of its fuselage.[42] This was superb entertainment, free to all comers.

Klanswomen did much of the work to mount these events, replicating their domestic labor on a colossal scale. KKK publications offered women fashion and cooking tips, as did all publications of the time, but as in many conservative movements, past and present, what women did in reality did not always align with their conservative gender ideology. Some resisted male control, to the extent that they could be considered feminists of a sort.[43] Women's klaverns often claimed autonomy from Klan leadership, appointed their own leaders, and devised their own projects. One Klanswoman went public in condemning her husband's control of the family's money, writing in a KKK newspaper, "I have a right to know where it goes. . . . I have brains and know how to use them."[44] Many had supported woman suffrage, because they believed that women voters, determined to rid the country of sin and corruption, would strengthen white Protestant supremacy and the Klan in particular. They sometimes appeared more tolerant than the KKK norm—one official document alleged that the "restrictions" they sought were "not intended to cast aspersions upon the Patriotism and other great and noble qualities of women of other faiths and other nationalities."[45] But there is no evidence that they were more open to diversity than their male colleagues.

The KKK's tactics allowed it to benefit both from secrecy and lack of secrecy.[46] It published openly, prominently featuring its distinguished members, and invited the public to its grand pageants, while its secret mystic rituals attracted members like a magnet.[47] Thus its secrets contributed to its desirability and public influence. A recruit entered a mystical world known only to initiates, enforced by fearsome oaths of initiation, threatening "direful things" should a member breach this trust. Those entrusted with its codes and rituals not only received a gift of high value but also built solidarity among others who knew the secrets. That so many were excluded added to the prestige of being an insider.

A new vocabulary symbolized entry into the privileged community.* Officers, beneath the Imperial Wizard, included three Great Klaliffs, the Great Klabee, the Great Kligrapp, the Great Kludd, and the Great Nighthawk, together forming the Furies. An Exalted Cyclops headed each Klavern.[48] The twelve officers of a klavern, or local chapter, each of whom had his own K title, formed the Terrors. This profusion of official posts allowed many members to hold offices, thereby increasing their investment in the organization. Several dozen secret acronyms, composed of the first letters of words in a phrase, allowed Klanspeople to recognize each other.† For those who could not commit all these secrets to memory, the Klan sold manuals, providing yet another source of cash intake. The codes, titles, costumes, and rituals gave members the pleasures of participation in a dramatic performance.

Klavern meetings followed a script laid out in the "Kloran." Unlike

---

* For example, days of the week, weeks of the month, and months of the year had new names, almost all of them intended to frighten. The days of the week were Dark, Deadly, Dismal, Doleful, Desolate, Dreadful, and Desperate. The months began with Bloody and ended with Appalling, in one version; in another, from Dismal to Dying. Even the hours were renamed, from one o'clock, Fearful, through Startling, Awful, Woeful, to Appalling and Last. What fun it must have been to coin these names.

† Thus one might ask, *Ayak?*, meaning, "Are you a Klansman?" To which one would answer, *Akia*, "A Klansman I am," or *Itsub*, "in the secret unfailing bond." Particularly important was *san bog*, or "strangers are near, be on guard."

its namesake the Koran, or the Bible, this secret document had to be "rigidly guarded" to prevent "aliens" from learning its contents. A few examples from the script: The Exalted Cyclops orders the Kladd to "ascertain with care if all present are Klansmen worthy to sit in the Klavern during the deliberations of this Klonvocation." The Kladd then approaches each member, who must make a countersign and whisper the password directly into his ear. In addition to these Orientalisms, as the sociologist Kathleen Blee pointed out, many Klan verbal rituals resembled Catholic catechisms. Like Protestant services, however, members joined in singing hymns and patriotic songs at prescribed moments. Military titles also abounded: "the Klaliff (vice Cyclops) must appoint as his assistant a Lieutenant Colonel . . . one Corporal to serve each eight Klansmen."[49]

Meetings followed elaborate spatial choreography, and this too invited members into a theatrical event.[50] Members took up assigned posts, thereby forming symbolic shapes with their bodies—a square, within which was a circle, within which was another square, within which was an altar. The Kladd moved counterclockwise to verify the membership of each attendee, who must provide a password and the "sign of God," called *tsog*. (If they forgot it, they could not be seated until the Kligrapp gave them permission.) The others all stood, and the Exalted Cyclops rapped twice with his gavel and said, "My Terrors, you will take your respective stations." As a grand finale, the Exalted Cyclops would pour a few drops of "dedication fluid" (the purchased Klan water) on each candidate's back, then on his own head, then toss some drops upward and finally move his hand horizontally in a circle around each candidate's head. (These four locations symbolize body, mind, spirit, and life.) It was a virtual baptism.

Held in darkness, these ceremonies must have been electrically charged, possibly even eerie, as was their intent. Participants entered a fantasy world, unlike workaday life. The weirdness, the out-of-the-ordinariness, made the Klan thrilling. At a time when movies and radio were still new, Americans spent more time in participatory activities than they do today. They sang in church and at home, played pianos and guitars, gathered for card games and ballgames and quilting sessions. So they understood that in a club you *did something*. As sociol-

etc

ogist Francesca Polletta wrote, in the tradition of Emile Durkheim, rituals can strengthen group solidarity "by taking people out of the routine of daily life and reenacting their essential groupness."[51]

Producing mass outdoor rallies was a key element in building this movement. Carefully designed, the mass choreography constituted a visual demagoguery that resembled, in miniature, the European fascist and Nazi rallies in which acres of supporters, soldiers, children, and performers of calisthenics moved in unison. Studies of mass unison movement find that participation leads to stronger bonding.[52] Alice Yaeger Kaplan calls such performances "binding machines."[53] KKK choreography constituted a visual expression of the order and homogeneity so basic to its political ideology and aspiration. Unison movement reenacted organizational unity, the homogeneity of the imagined "pure" nation, and the rejection of diversity.[54] The visual drama created by a mass wearing identical costumes not only intensified the impact of the choreography but also signified and promoted a lie fundamental to its success: that the organization transcended, even erased, inequalities of status and class. The choreography also functioned as a faux militarism, allowing Klanspeople to see themselves as soldiers defending the threatened white "race," nation, and cross.

Particularly impressive choreography appeared at mass public "naturalizations," the term for induction of "aliens," a language that positioned the Klan as a nation.[55] Naturalizations turned "aliens" into "citizens." The spatial optics typically presented an inner core of white-robed Klanspeople, standing in front of kneeling "aliens" and surrounded by spectators in varied clothing. One dramatic nighttime orchestration featured a circle of automobiles facing inward, headlights focused on a central platform on which leaders stood. The spatial arrangements thus displayed magnitude but also enclosure, replicating the insider-outsider distinction, making the organization visible but also exclusive, thus escalating its desirability.

In the evenings at these large events, tall crosses, some fifty feet high, were burned, intensifying the impact of the choreography. They were the equivalent of fireworks, thrilling entertainment. And those thrills were of great political value. Susan Sontag, referring to fascist mass rallies in Europe, wrote of "the dissolution of alienation in ecstatic feelings of community."[56] Anyone who has ever sung with a choir, danced with a company, played in a band, or marched with demonstrators knows the satisfactions of participating in a group activity. This is one of the often-unnoticed, even hidden satisfactions of participation in a social movement. Though there may be major and minor roles, soloists and corps de ballet, the movement's overall impact depends on every participant's individual performance.

BEYOND ATTENDING Klavern meetings and public events, what were rank-and-file Klanspeople doing? Many of them, very little. Unlike other social movements, in this one only a small proportion of members were "activists." The outdoor spectacles, of course, required extensive logistical planning: reserving trains, parking cars, bringing in entertainers, organizing games, providing food, and more, but these tasks were sporadic. Of many members, the Klan asked only that they bring in money, by recruiting new members, paying dues, and buying and promoting Klan paraphernalia. (Members increasingly complained of being soaked, and that discontent contributed to the Klan's decline, as we will see.)

The grandiose KKK productions, open to all, served not only to recruit new members but also to build electoral clout. By making its mass following visible, the rallies intimidated politicians and candidates into seeking Klan support or at least not defying it. Members were expected to work in election campaigns. Like a political party, the KKK secured nominations for friendly candidates, circulated slates of approved candidates and lists of those it sought to defeat, brought supporters to the polls, lobbied politicians in office, and scored positive newspaper coverage.[57] In Indiana, its campaign literature was distributed in Sunday schools. It called on ministers to sermonize on the duty to vote for approved candidates. It even assigned topics for sermons: the topics for October 26 were "Christian Citizenship" and "The Need of Revival of Pure Protestantism"; for November 2, "Moral Civic Forces Seen and Unseen" and "The Duty of the Protestant Citizen."[58]

Nationally the Klan elected sixteen senators, scores of congressmen, and eleven governors. (Of course the Klan exaggerated, claiming twenty-six governors and seventy-five congressmen; at another time it claimed to have elected 62 percent of Congress.)[59] Klan candidates ran mostly as Democrats but occasionally as Republicans, Progressives, even Farmer-Labor supporters—attitudes toward the Klan did not divide along party lines.* In their youth, Supreme Court justices Hugo Black and Edward Douglass White were Klansmen. (Black was "naturalized" into the Klan in one of its megaevents, along with fifteen hundred recruits, but resigned later in his career.)[60] The Klan claimed President Warren G. Harding as a member, and President Harry S. Truman joined when he thought it was "just" a patriotic group. (He quit when he learned that he would have to break off his relations with Catholics.)[61] With this kind of support, the Klan was able to thwart numerous attempts by its opponents to put together support for anti-Klan resolutions. Neither major political party and none of the presidents—Wilson, Harding, Coolidge, and Hoover—could be persuaded to condemn the Ku Klux Klan.[62]

No one has been able to count the Klan candidates elected to state and local offices, and the exercise would probably not be worthwhile, since so many nonmembers shared Klan ideology. As the Illinois Grand Dragon Charles G. Palmer bragged, "We know we're the balance of power in the state." The KKK wielded decisive political influence in several states—Indiana, Oklahoma, Oregon, Colorado, and Texas.[63] For ten years, from 1922 to 1932, most of Oregon's elected officials were Klansmen, and opposition was so weak that Klansmen ran against one another. Between 1924 and 1928, for example, Tillamook, Oregon, elected Klansmen as county sheriff, state representative, superintendent of schools, schools director, city attorney, the majority of city councilmen, county clerk, chief clerks of the post offices, and principals of both the elementary and high schools. In contrast to its contemporary critics' claims that Klan strength lay in rural and small-town America, the Klan won control of city governments in Dallas, Fort Worth, and both Portlands—Maine and Oregon.[64]

In Indiana, Klan electoral achievements were stunning: eleven of

---

* In the 1920s the Democratic Party was the voice of white southerners, devoted to defending racial segregation, Prohibition, and evangelical Protestantism.

the thirteen men elected to the U.S. House of Representatives between 1924 and 1926 were Klansmen.[65] This success resulted from a strategy referred to as the "Military Machine." Every Klan member was supplied with a list of names, addresses, and vocations of every "alien" of voting age and was to get ten nonmembers to vote for Klan candidates. Stephenson loaned candidate Ed Jackson his Cadillac for campaigning around the state, and the Indiana Klan spent at least $73,000 to get him elected governor.[66]

Klan-friendly candidates often dog-whistled, adjusting their appeals strategically, avoiding religion-based attacks where they might hurt, focusing on cleaning up immorality when that would help. Muncie, Indiana, business and civic leaders supported the KKK because, they claimed, its Prohibitionist and patriotic campaigns would raise moral standards.[67] Where they deemed it safe, however, some spoke in plain English. In Oakland, California, a Klan leader argued that electing its candidate was "imperative if we are to remove the Jews, Catholics and Negroes from public life in California." He won with an overwhelming majority.[68]

Klanswomen often proved equally adept at politicking. In Indiana, Imperial Empress Daisy Barr benefited from a host of organizational connections. (In that respect, she could be compared to some of the Hull-House women.) She was president of the Indiana Humane Society, creator of the Muncie YWCA, and founder of a "refuge," the Friendly Inn, for "fallen women." After World War I, she became president of Indiana War Mothers. A Quaker, she got support from the Friends.* After the woman suffrage amendment passed, she became vice-chair of the Republican state committee. She was a traveling Klan lecturer. As head of the WKKK, she arranged for the naturalization of two hundred women in one ceremony and claimed that an additional thousand would-be members attended but couldn't be naturalized because they didn't yet have the Klan regalia.[69] Indiana Klanswomen staffed an army of activists that could serve as a model for effective campaigning even today. It selected point people in every county, each of whom organized a group whose members were to organize other groups, forming a lad-

---

* The association of Quakers with progressive politics was a later development.

der that pushed information rapidly through the state. These "skirted lieutenants"—no doubt purposely using a military metaphor—called their groups "poison squads." Leaders bragged that they could communicate anything Klan-related throughout the state within twelve hours. This "phone chain" was all the more impressive because not everyone had phones in the mid-1920s.[70]

The Klan spent much of its electoral power promoting state legislation prohibiting Catholic schools.[71] It alleged that these schools brainwashed children with Catholic authoritarianism. Scandalously, Catholic schools even taught foreign languages! Couching the campaign in patriotism, the Klan harped on the need for unity—that is, conformity—in promoting Americanism. It introduced bills to ban Catholic schools in many states, but it succeeded only in Oregon. Ultimately the Oregon law was overturned by the Supreme Court, but its legal reasoning is significant: the Court expressed no concern about religious discrimination but objected to the law because it deprived "parents of their rights, private school teachers of their livelihood, and private schools of their property" without due process.[72]

Despite this loss, the Klan continued efforts to "cleanse" schools of people and material that did not promote its version of white Protestant patriotism.[73] In various locations it called for requiring loyalty oaths of teachers, disallowing teachers who had been educated in Catholic schools, firing teachers who wore religious dress in the schools (about twenty nuns taught in the Oregon public schools), establishing textbook commissions to scrutinize educational materials and license acceptable ones, and mandating exclusive use of approved textbooks.* While bloviating about the separation of church and state, the KKK flooded state legislatures with bills mandating daily reading from the Protestant Bible *without commentary*, giving pupils release time for religious study, requiring weekly meetings between schools and churches to coordinate religious education, and compelling colleges and universities to grant credit for religious study in authorized churches.[74]

A major legislative victory in 1924 demonstrated the KKK's national clout. The Johnson-Reed immigration restriction law built on seventy-

---

* Eerily similar to right-wing demands to censor, or "cleanse," textbooks today.

five years of nativist agitation, but its final passage owed much to the Klan's electoral strength and lobbying expertise. In 1923 the Imperial Wizard Hiram Evans had called for an "Imperial [*sic*] Immigration and Naturalization Commission" to draft an anti-immigration law.[75] The notion that the Klan could author legislation was grandiose but not necessarily naïve, given its extensive lobbying. Afterward, Evans repeatedly claimed credit for getting the bill passed—an exaggeration no doubt intended to build deference to Klan legislative priorities.[76]

The congressional manager of the immigration restriction bill was Republican Albert Johnson, chair of the House Committee on Immigration and Naturalization. Whether he was a Klan member is uncertain but immaterial; his congressional opponents labeled him a tool of "undercover Ku Klux Klan dictators." His history suggests his allegiances. Elected to Congress in 1913 on an anti-immigration platform, he was an outspoken anti-Semite and a Mason, as were many Klansmen. Johnson had served as president of the Eugenics Research Association. No single-issue politician, he had fought conservationists, socialists, and those who supported divorce and "free love."[77] He had joined vigilante actions against the IWW, socialists, and immigrants; one such mob, in 1907, forced hundreds of South Asians out of Bellingham, Washington, and into Canada.[78] During the mass deportation of political dissidents in 1919, Johnson, as chairman of the Immigration and Naturalization Committee, showed a flair for the dramatic: he escorted deportees as they were transported from Ellis Island to the Brooklyn waterfront, where they were marched onto an old troopship, the *Buford*, to be returned to Europe. Accompanying him on this stunt was J. Edgar Hoover, then head of the Department of Justice's new "Radical Division."[79]

Guiding the Johnson-Reed bill into enactment would become the high point of Johnson's career and proof of his ability to manage Congress.[80] The law culminated decades of anti-Japanese exclusions by banning all Japanese immigration. (The Japanese government called it "National Humiliation Day.") In order to assure that "Nordics" and "Aryans" would continue to dominate the country, it installed a quota system for other immigrants. The quotas constituted a major victory for the KKK and its nativist ancestors. A few examples:

Germany	51,227
Great Britain and North Ireland	34,007
Russia	2,248
Greece	100
Asians	0
All Africa except Egypt	1,100*

This law remained in effect until 1965. Its quotas contributed to the mass murder of Jews by providing legal cover for the government's refusal to accept Jewish refugees. The law not only embodied Klan values and made them operational but also shaped public opinion; it not only resulted from decades of bigotry but reinforced it.† Wrapping immigration restriction in patriotism, it prefigured American fascists' claim to be patriots (as we will see below).

A few months later the Klan scored another political victory. At the 1924 Democratic Party convention in New York City, Klan supporters were so numerous and aggressive that the convention got labeled the "Klanbake" (referring also to the blistering summer heat in Madison Square Garden).‡ Al Smith, the charismatic Democratic governor of New York, entered the convention as the leading candidate for the presidential nomination. A classic Progressive, he had put through New York State welfare policies such as mothers' pensions and workmen's compensation, and worked closely with the social democratic feminist Frances Perkins, later to be FDR's secretary of labor. But Smith was

---

* Restrictions on immigrants from East Asia—Chinese, Japanese, Filipinos—had been growing piecemeal for decades; this law placed a total ban on immigration from Asia. It would last until World War II, when the restrictions on Chinese ended, and other exclusions gradually lifted. There was no restriction of immigration from Latin America, largely because the big growers of California and southwest states insisted on access to low-wage farm labor; by the 1920s Mexicans constituted the largest population of farmworkers. See chapter 6.

† Author John Steinbeck felt it necessary to denounce bigotry against Italian immigrants as late as 1961 in his novel *The Winter of Our Discontent*. Thanks to my extremely erudite editor Bob Weil for calling this point to my attention.

‡ The Klan's clout and stubbornness, refusing to accept one candidate after another, made this the longest convention in U.S. history, lasting from June 24 to July 9, requiring 103 ballots to settle on a candidate.

a Catholic, and what's more, three of his top advisers were Jews.* He opposed Prohibition—the Klan called him "Al(cohol) Smith."[81]

The Klan promoted William McAdoo, a popular Georgia Democrat and son-in-law of Woodrow Wilson, but a corruption scandal and his open support for the KKK lost him some support.† The convention was raucous. Klan supporters chanted "Mac, Mac, McAdoo" while opponents shouted "Ku Ku, McAdoo." Fistfights among delegates broke out. After an exhausting 103 ballots, both Smith and McAdoo were defeated, and John W. Davis of West Virginia was nominated. (He went on to lose the election to Calvin Coolidge.)‡ Smith also tried to get a denunciation of the KKK into the party platform; Klan opponents created compromise language that denounced "intolerance" generally, but even that was defeated, though by a tiny margin. This vote indicated, even more than Smith's defeat, that it was not only southern and evangelical delegates who feared the Klan. (At the Republican convention, an anti-Klan resolution never made it to a vote.) Though it could not get McAdoo nominated, the KKK was now a national force.

THE NORTHERN Klan was mainly nonviolent, but that judgment depends on one's definition of violence. Consider its attack on the family of Malcolm Little, who later became Malcolm X. The Littles lived in Omaha, where his father was a Baptist minister and an organizer for Marcus Garvey's "Back to Africa" movement, the Universal Negro Improvement Association.§ While he was away preaching, a group of

---

* Abram Elkus, Belle Moskowitz, and Joseph Proskauer.
† He had accepted a $25,000 contribution from Edward L. Doheny, an oil tycoon implicated in 1922 in the Teapot Dome scandal.
‡ Smith received just one vote from southern delegations and scarcely more than twenty votes from states west of the Mississippi. Surprisingly, the speaker most outspoken against the Klan was Senator Oscar Underwood of Alabama.
§ Had the perpetrators known anything about Garvey's campaign to get African Americans to leave the United States, might they have supported him? Perhaps not: they no doubt sensed that any organizing among African Americans was dangerous to white supremacy.

Klansmen on horseback arrived at their house, demanded to see him, threatening that "the good Christian white people" would not stand for "spreading trouble" among the "good Negroes" of Omaha. They galloped several times around the house, carrying burning torches, whooping and yelling, shattering the windows. Mrs. Little, pregnant with the future Malcolm X, alone with three small children, was terrified. Had her husband been there, she was sure they would have lynched him. With some 45,000 fellow Klansmen in Nebraska, the attackers knew that no jury would ever convict them. They succeeded in driving out the Littles, who moved to Lansing, Michigan. A decade later a fascist group, the Black Legion (which we will meet later in this chapter), took up what the Klan began, burning the Littles' home to the ground.[82]

The attack on the Littles was typical of northern Klan vigilantism. Unlike southern Klan lynchings, northern Klansmen usually stopped short of physical assault, but nevertheless communicated serious threats. "If you do not endorse the above principles," an Oregon Kleagle warned, "you would be a fit subject for a Vigilance Committee."[83] Some threats relied on fear of the murderous southern Klan; a warning to a Vermont journalist read, "Unless certain newspaper reporters . . . stop attacking the Klan, they will be taught the same lesson that some editors in the south have learned."[84]

The Klan exploited an increase in crime to justify vigilantism.[85] Although the KKK exaggerated, the crime rate did rise 24 percent in the early 1920s, largely as a result of charges against violators of Prohibition—who the Klan insisted were Catholics and Jews. Police, who constituted the most common occupation, per capita, among KKK members, shared its complaint that criminals were going free due to petty legal loopholes. As one Klansman put it, vigilante justice allowed "a law breaker or a moral or social degenerate" to get what they deserved without "a bunch of lawyers [who] construct testimony to free criminals." Moreover the KKK often provoked anti-Klan violence in order to frame their own as defensive, by marching through hostile neighborhoods and pasting placards announcing their meetings on the walls of synagogues and Catholic churches.[86]

But another justification for vigilantism—that the police were not doing their job—risked antagonizing police officers. So Imperial Wizard Evans astutely promoted Klan collaboration with lawmen: police frequently paraded with Klansmen and made them formal or informal deputies.[87] The Portland, Oregon, Klan announced that 150 members of the police department had become "citizens" of the KKK. The mayor there formed a hundred-man vigilante squad to augment the police force: they got guns and badges and could make arrests, but their names would remain secret—and the Klan would "advise him" in selecting them.[88] In Madison, Wisconsin, a police chief recalled later that "pretty near all" of his men were members. They joined civilian Klansmen to form the Klavaliers, a "military unit trained to fight crime, fires, floods, riots, and strikes"; deputized under the police department, its members helped "clean up" the neighborhood known as Little Italy, arresting its "most noted characters." The local Women's Christian Temperance Union—to which many Klanswomen belonged—expressed approval, a reminder that Klanswomen had no objection to vigilantism.[89] In Anaheim, California—a city so controlled by the Klan that its nickname was Klanaheim—the town government allowed its police officers to patrol in Klan robes and symbols as they raided saloons, gambling parlors, dance halls, and houses of prostitution.[90]

Although Imperial Wizard Hiram Evans believed that remaining legal was the best route to power, he nevertheless recognized that vigilantism was attractive to some men.[91] He could dodge this contradiction at times because Klan rhetoric and secret rites enabled members to imagine themselves warriors even as they behaved peaceably. But he also dog-whistled, hinting that the Klan offered vigilante opportunities when his audience seemed receptive. Klan media regularly fused bigotry with appeals to aggressive masculinity, appealing to "real Men" and employing feminine labels to discipline members. "Remember when you come to lodge that this is not an old maid's convention," the minutes of an Oregon chapter read.[92] A Klan political candidate called an anti-Klan newspaper a "poor old female . . . busy feathering its nest," while a Klan minister spoke of his contempt for "mollycoddle Masons" and "softshell" preachers who urged ecumenism.[93] These gendered sneers could be multiplied by the hundreds. Klan fraternities arose at numerous universities, and most were officially accepted alongside the "Greek" fraternities.[94] At Madison's University of Wisconsin, the Ku Klux Klan fraternity required pledges to parade around the capitol pushing baby carriages as part of their hazing.[95]

Occasionally local Klans ignored Evans's caution. In Lewiston, Maine, they set off a "dynamite bomb" to announce their campaign against Catholic French Canadians.[96] In Arkansas City, Kansas, they invaded "Darktown" and kidnapped a Black man who, they claimed, stole suitcases from the train station, hung him until he "confessed," then forced him to leave town forever. A few near-lynchings in Oregon became national news, known as the "Oregon outrages." The Klan threatened Sam Johnson, described as "part-Mexican," accused of stealing chickens and being an "idler," and drove him out of town. A white piano salesman, targeted because he allegedly did not pay a debt to a Klansman, was threatened and accused of illicit sexual affairs. Arthur Burr, an African American bootblack accused of bootlegging, received the worst treatment. Klansmen abducted him, took him to the crest of the Siskiyou Mountains, noosed him, strung him up, and let him down three times. Releasing him, they fired revolvers near his feet, demanding that he leave the area permanently, yelling, "Can you run, nigger?" Though charges were brought against the culprits, in each case juries acquitted them, on the grounds that the vigilante actions benefited the community because the victims were morally bad.[97]

At the northern edges of the South, notably Oklahoma, Indiana, Kansas, and southern Illinois, the Klan morphed from a social movement to violent vigilantism, employing whippings, tar-and-featherings, and lynchings. Oklahoma law officers handed suspects over to Klan whipping parties and even participated in the beatings. This violence became so widespread, with reports of "one flogging for every night of the year," that the governor placed parts of the state under martial law—until Klan efforts got him impeached in 1923.[98] In Kansas, Klansmen abducted an anti-Klan mayor, tied him to a tree, and "laid thirty stripes on his bare back." In "Bloody Williamson," as one southern Illinois county became known, the local Klan allied with the Anti-Saloon League to attack Prohibition violators, resulting in twenty murders, then forced the anti-Klan sheriff out of office.[99] In several locations, Klan membership was automatically suspended for any man called for jury duty, so that he could not be excluded for bias.[100]

Klansmen attacked both union men and strikebreakers, depending on the context, because bigotry was always the deciding factor. (By contrast, the 1930s fascists, as we will see, always fought on the side of corporate interests.) In Maine, the Klan fought for big lumber companies against Catholic French Canadian loggers who had been organized by the radical union IWW, aka the "Wobblies." After KKK cross-burnings and bombings failed to intimidate the loggers, the lumber companies brought criminal conspiracy charges against the IWW but not against the violent Klansmen.[101] At other times, workers' bigotry and fear of having wages undercut led them to side with the Klan. When in 1923 a southern Indiana mine boss hired some Slavic workers, a thousand United Mine Workers members, faces concealed, joined the Klan in attacking the immigrant workers, beating some of them badly, and within forty-eight hours drove them out.[102] But Klan candidates sometimes promised "to advance the rights of the workingmen," and in one Oregon town they even denounced Klansmen who scabbed. More than a few socialists supported or even joined the Klan, though its anti-immigrant and anti-Catholic agitation often drained support for socialism.[103]

These were isolated skirmishes, however, in comparison to Klan violence in the Pacific Northwest. Already fertile ground for anti-Asian racism, Oregon and Washington had been legislating against Asians since the mid-nineteenth century.* An Anti-Chinese People's Alliance (which included the anarchist International Working People's Association) organized mobs that drove "Chinamen" hired as railway builders from Tacoma, Seattle, and the state of Idaho. These attacks escalated when Filipino and Japanese immigrants began arriving. White farmers, fearing the greater productivity of Japanese farms, supported alien land laws that prohibited people ineligible for citizenship—Chinese and Japanese—from owning and leasing land; these laws were then incorporated into the Oregon, Washington, and California state constitutions.[104] (Law constructs as well as reflects social

---

* Nineteenth-century Oregon laws also prohibited African Americans from entering the state and from living, voting, or owning property there. Oregon did not ratify the Fourteenth and Fifteenth amendments until the mid-twentieth century.

values: these laws "taught" the white public that Asians were dangerous and expanded support for discrimination against them.) Filipinos, hired on farms and in canneries at wages lower than white men's,
were establishing particularly militant labor unions in the canneries.[105]
Later, Filipino men would become leaders in organizing farmworkers.
(Their role is discussed in chapter 7.)

Some of the anti-Asian hysteria was delusional: the president of
Washington's Anti-Japanese League claimed that Japanese in the
United States regarded the Pacific coast as a colony of Japan and whites
as a subject race—another early version of "replacement" allegations.[106]
Klan-inspired mobs terrorized Filipino, Japanese, and African American workers in several locations in the 1920s, and in 1927 and 1928 forced
all the Filipino farmworkers out of Wapato, Toppenish, and Wenatchee
in Washington State. Armed gangs broke into Filipino homes, beating
their residents, smashing furniture, then rounding them up and forcing them onto trains leaving the valley, threatening them with hanging should they ever return. This kind of violence continued into the
1930s, when the Klan and its supporters bombed and set fire to several
Japanese-owned farms.[107]

In California's Central Valley the Klan's major targets were Mexicans and Mexican Americans, who by the 1920s dominated the farm
labor force. Here the Klan's opportunism created a de facto alliance
with white Catholics against Mexican Catholics, when the state's Catholic hierarchy, largely Irish, refused to defend Mexicans against Klan
attacks (just as it refused to support farmworker organizing, discussed
in chapter 6). Misunderstanding California's agricultural economy,
Hiram Evans sought support from the big growers, charging that many
of the Mexicans and Mexican Americans were Communists; but the
growers depended on cheap Mexican labor and even sent squads into
the fields to protect their farmworkers from the Klan.[108]

KKK BIGOTRY and occasional violence did not go unanswered, but
large-scale organized resistance was rare, while spontaneous local resistance left few records.[109] Some cities and states took legal action: banning Klan parades, prohibiting mask-wearing in public, requiring the

release of membership lists, even attempting to levy fines on the KKK for promoting hatred.* Organized Catholic and Jewish protest was limited, no doubt because the KKK was less visible where Catholics and Jews were numerous. Catholic universities, by contrast, could not afford such passivity. When forty carloads of Klansmen arrived at the Catholic University of Dayton, the football coach "called out all my big football players" and encouraged them to "take off after them . . . tear their shirts off or anything else." The invaders quickly fled. When Klanspeople paraded in South Bend, Indiana (one of the KKK's strongest states), a "raucous band" of Notre Dame University students disrupted a Klan march, then threw potatoes through Klan headquarters windows.[110]

A few anti-Klan coalitions arose. Chicago's American Unity League, led by a combative Catholic lawyer, produced a national newsletter, *Tolerance*, challenging the Klan's claim to patriotism. When the Klan arrived in Atlantic City, New Jersey, African Americans and Knights of Columbus members cooperated to spread warnings. In Los Angeles, the NAACP and one Catholic bishop jointly raised funds for victims of Klan racism.[111] Some Black leaders called for injunctions restricting the Klan, but most—including W. E. B. Du Bois—minimized the Klan's threat in the North, perhaps because of the group's low profile in cities with high proportions of non-Protestant immigrants and few white evangelicals. Some of that perspective reflected bitterness at a racial double standard—many who condemned the Klan's religious bigotry remained silent about lynchings of African Americans.

A few anti-Klan groups took violent action. In Waukesha, Wis-

---

* The Cleveland City Council set a $500 fine for anyone belonging to a society "tending to promote racial hatred and religious bigotry," and the mayor vowed to "use all of my power" to keep the Klan from getting a "foothold" in the city. Kansas's governor made a similar vow. So did James Curley, mayor of heavily Catholic Boston, though what that meant in practice is unclear. In Chicago, the police chief prohibited Klan parades, the mayor ordered police to push it out of town, and two judges refused to seat Klansmen in juries. A New York state law required "oath bound" organizations to produce lists of members and bylaws and banned circulating anonymous documents; everyone knew that its target was the Klan, and this move may have intensified the Klan's determination to defeat Al Smith. The ACLU, arguing that many of these edicts were unconstitutional, came to the Klan's defense, just as it defended, fifty years later, the American Nazi Party's right to march through a Jewish neighborhood in Chicago.

consin, a crowd burst into a Klan meeting and beat several Klansmen badly. New Jersey saw several instances: in Bloomfield a crowd tore the robes off a parade of 250 Klansmen; in Bound Brook and Perth Amboy, crowds attacked and forced some five hundred Klansmen to seek refuge in a church and an Odd Fellows Hall.[112] In New Castle, Delaware, one thousand men forced the Klan off a field and destroyed its cross.[113] One attack was lethal: in Carnegie, Pennsylvania, miners—many of them Catholic or Orthodox—met a Klan parade with rocks and bottles thrown from rooftops and shot one Klansman to death. Thus in a very few cases, the Klan could honestly complain of victimization.

The scarcity of collective opposition shows the effectiveness of Hiram Evans's nonviolent, legal strategy. Despite the size of the Klan media empire, it was ignored by potential opponents. The Klan's impunity derived mainly from its respectability, its anti-Catholicism, and the anti-Semitism common among white Protestants, including upperclass men of influence. Had there been large-scale opinion polling in the 1920s, it might well have shown widespread agreement with core KKK principles: that the United States had been and should remain primarily a white Protestant country, that immigration was disturbing this essence of Americanness, that patriotism and "true"—that is, Protestant—Christianity should be promoted.[114]

BY THE mid-1920s, that KKK was shrinking, but it nevertheless produced a major spectacle. Its dramatic denouement, on August 8, 1925, was a march in the nation's capital that brought in 25,000 to 30,000 Klanspeople—though not the 50,000 promised by Klan publicity. "The roads leading to D.C. turned into a parade of automobiles decorated with extravagant Klan signs and symbols," one newspaper reported, with signs such as "100% American." One vehicle had "a big fiery cross, emblazoned with tiny electric bulbs, attached to the radiator cap of their motor."[115] Rumors that African Americans were arming themselves to "combat the parade" were probably started by Klan publicists to create a buzz.

Some 150,000 came to watch. They saw a choreographed parade of unmasked men and women, many carrying American flags, walk-

KKK Parade in Washington, D.C., August 8, 1925.

ing in formation from the Capitol along Pennsylvania Avenue to the Washington Monument.[116] Klanswomen did not wear full-length robes but shorter ones, with white stockings and white shoes—some wore brightly colored capes—uniforms clearly made specially for the event. The leaders at the front of the march wore bright-colored robes. A few rode horseback. In order to occupy the wide avenue, marchers maintained wide spaces within each row. Equally generous spaces between rows made the march many blocks long. The marchers formed the letter K at one point, a cross at another. (Here too KKK choreography anticipated that of the mass rallies staged by the Nazi regime.) On the east steps of the Capitol, they draped a giant American flag that extended from the base of the steps to the entrance.[117]

The march finished dramatically, and symbolically, as if nature were endorsing the Klan's decline. Just as the thousands gathered around the Washington Monument, as a *New York Sun* reporter wrote,

At 7 PM *"one might say karma struck. There was to be a massive pageant where the "eloquence of Klan orators," was to "have poured forth to stimulate and perhaps electrify the multitude." Instead, dark clouds gathered overhead. District Dragon L. A. Mueller attempted to reassure the crowd, "I have faith enough in the Lord that He is with every Klansman . . . You ought to have as much faith in Him as I have. We have never had a drop of rain in Washington when we got on our knees." Right about then, the heavens opened up. As the crowd hurriedly dispersed, Mueller cried out for them to stick around long enough to hear the details of the following day's events. In half an hour the . . . assembled Klansmen had dissolved from view.*[118]

To emphasize the Klan's patriotism, the next day a contingent crossed the Potomac to Arlington, Virginia, where they placed wreaths on the Tomb of the Unknown Soldier. They also honored the grave of Klan hero William Jennings Bryan, who had been the prosecutor in the Scopes trial, then died the previous month. That evening they "burned" an electrically lit cross eighty feet high and thirty feet wide at the Arlington Horse Showgrounds and "naturalized" two hundred initiates.

But KKK membership was shriveling precipitously, from an estimated five million in 1925 to only 350,000 in 1927. The Klan's decline owed less to a rejection of its ideology, however, than to disgust with its incessant demands for money and its leaders' corruption. A Delaware Klaliff explained that he quit because the Klan was a "gigantic swindle."[119] Merchants complained that the Klan did not pay its bills. Its hypocrisy became evident as Klansmen were frequently caught drinking and engaging in illicit sex. Oregon Klansman Ellis O. Willson, a dentist, was twice convicted for raping and killing his secretary while attempting to perform an abortion. Philip Fox, editor of the *Imperial Night-Hawk*, was sentenced to life imprisonment for killing his rival, William S. Coburn.[120] In Indiana, Klan member Governor Ed Jackson was indicted for bribery, the officers of the state's major Klan bank were indicted for embezzlement and grand larceny, and a Klan minister was accused of crimes "so sensational that persons who heard the sordid details were loath to believe they were true."[121]

Beyond the corruption, the Klan's arcane secret rituals seemed to be losing their appeal. Its array of entertainments and public rituals—the monster rallies with their burning crosses, air shows, family activities, and semi-professional baseball teams—drew thousands, but everyone could enjoy these, whether or not they were members. Klaverns' promise of profitable networking and prestige was rarely realized. Besides, not all Klanspeople were ideological zealots. They may have remained bigoted, but they did not feel a need to dedicate themselves to bigotry. Prohibition, once a major KKK cause, was proving ineffective and unpopular.

The Indiana Grand Dragon Stephenson would soon deliver a lethal blow—literally. His corruption and immorality were no secret: he used Klan money to buy a luxurious yacht on which he entertained lavishly, sailing on Lake Erie accompanied by senators, congressmen, and state-level politicians. He drank heavily and often went directly from Klan functions to "private orgies of dissipation." A habitual sexual predator—one victim described him as "a beast"—he was once caught with his pants down in his Cadillac with a young woman. During a party at his house, he locked a woman in a room, knocked her down, bit her all over, and attempted to rape her. Imperial Wizard Hiram Evans, alarmed and anxious to avoid negative publicity, convened a tribunal that called for his expulsion. But Stephenson's Indiana power base apparently made that impossible—within the somewhat feudal structure of the KKK, Stephenson had transformed the Indiana Klan into an autonomous organization.

Stephenson delivered a fatal wound to the Klan when he kidnapped, tortured, raped, and murdered his twenty-two-year-old secretary, Madge Oberholtzer, a crime so sensational and bizarre that it was covered widely in the national press.[122] On the night of March 15, 1925, he sent his chauffeur to pick her up, forced her onto a train to Chicago, and attacked her in a closed compartment. He bit her so violently that she was literally chewed all over her body. (His repeated biting suggests that he was seriously and sadistically deranged.) He dragged the bleeding woman into a hotel, refusing to get her medical help. When she said she needed rouge, he let her go to a drugstore, but instead she bought bichloride of mercury tablets (used to treat syphilis despite their extreme toxicity) and swallowed six of them. She became deathly ill. Still refusing to seek medical treatment for her, he delivered her to her mother's house in Indianapolis, where she died, slowly and in agony. Stephenson was convicted of second-degree murder. (This conviction reflected a bitter contemporary standard: her violation made her permanently "ruined" and thus caused her suicide.)[123] Furious at national leaders' refusal to defend him, he took revenge by releasing documents detailing an extensive web of graft inside the Klan.[124]

THE KU KLUX KLAN'S shrinkage, however, left a vacuum into which its most zealous members entered, building a new set of Far Right organizations: American fascist groups, many of them in thrall to European fascist leaders. *Fascisti* began appearing in 1920s New York City among Italian supporters of Mussolini. (*Fascism* was not yet a generic, transnational term.) Other early fascist groups appeared uniquely German.

The spread of these groups required a major reorientation of Klan ideology.[125] The ACLU estimates that at least a hundred groups formed between 1933 and 1941, most of them initiatives of Klansmen.[126] Unlike the Klan, the fascist groups were violent. Luckily their groups were mainly small and local, only one of them with a membership in the thousands.

Many of these groups arose among former Klansmen, on the basis of a major reorientation of Klan ideology. Simultaneously intensifying and narrowing Klan bigotry, the fascist groups made anti-Semitism their sole cause. Like the Klan, they referred to Jews as a race—"Jewish blood"—rather than a religion. Also like the Klan, they considered people of color an inferior species, but it was the Jews who they deemed a threat. Their anti-Semitism had ancient roots, of course, but it became more virulent through identifying Communism as a Jewish plot. This fusion of anti-Semitism and anti-Communism performed a marvelous sleight-of-hand for the fascist groups, because it allowed them to stand for American patriotism while openly supporting European fascist leaders. They defended this contradictory allegiance by arguing that democracy was draining the nation's strength and that only strongmen, *Führers*, could create and sustain a great nation.

The fascists entirely abandoned the Klan's respectability and legal-ity. Instead of attempting to build a mass movement, they resolved that only violence could bring the country to fascism. That required secrecy. One fascist group, the German American Bund (Deutsche-Amerikanische Berufsgemeinschaft), maintained a benign public presence, but most of the fascists longed to fight and relished militarist fantasies. Their plots, luckily, were mainly delusional, but not all of them. Members committed murders, arson, and bombings; harassed and beat Jews on the streets; and served as anti–labor union thugs for powerful corporations. As a contemporary antifascist put it, "the country swarms with these miscellaneous hick Führers who walk the streets of big business offering their wares." Their violence was limited only by their relatively small size.[127]

Among the fascist groups, four were particularly newsworthy: the Silver and Black Legions, the German American Bund, and the Christian Front, this last created by the pro-fascist radio personality Father Charles Coughlin.[128] Since they were secret, an accurate count of their followers was impossible, and both the fascists and their opponents had reason to exaggerate their size. The House Committee on Un-American Activities estimated the Bund's membership at 480,000, while its leader, the *Bundesführer*, claimed only 200,000, the American Legion estimated 25,000, the FBI 6,000 to 8,000. Examining what the groups *did* will provide a better sense of their threat.

The Black Legion's founder, physician William Shepard, was Grand Cyclops of the Bellaire, Ohio, KKK. (Bellaire, located on the West Virginia border, remains today among the Ohio cities with the largest Ku Klux Klans.)[129] By the mid-1920s he found his group dormant because, he thought, it had become commonplace. Seeking to revitalize it, he shed the white-as-godly symbolism of the robes and designed more edgy costumes—black robes, trimmed in red, decorated with a skull-and-crossbones insignia. He introduced a new, more terrifying initiation ritual. "You have to have mystery in a fraternal thing to keep it alive," he said; "the folks eat it up." At an Ohio Klan convention, the new robes were a hit, and many attendees wanted them. New recruits were told that they were joining "a link of the old Ku Klux Klan," and the group retained Klan anti-Catholicism for a time, once planting explosives in Coughlin's Shrine of the Little Flower.[130]

Choosing the color black gestured to Italian fascist Blackshirts, and at first the color symbolized fascism internationally: Blackshirts fought unemployed demonstrators in London, marched in Kenya, and patrolled the streets of Cordoba, Argentina. Soon, however, there were fascist "shirts" of many colors: grey in New York, Johannesburg, and Cape Town, blue in China, green in Cuba, gold in Mexico City, and white in Tennessee. Whatever the color, these groups understood themselves as part of a rising global movement.[131]

Long attracted to violence, Shepard had led a Klan vigilante group in raiding moonshine stills (though he himself was known to be a drunkard), so he knew the draw of vigilantism. He first created an elite unit within the local Klan, the Black Guards, intended to prepare for battle. He soon divorced the Klan, considering it too tame, and named his new organization the Black Legion. A surreptitious method for identifying other members added to the mystique and symbolized their intentions: members carried a bullet and signaled their membership to others by casually flipping it.[132]

Members had to swear to support lynch laws, to procure guns—like several fascist groups, they collaborated with the NRA—and to perjure themselves when necessary for the sake of the organization. They took bloodthirsty but inconsistent oaths that swore them to "work unceasingly toward the extermination of the Jewish people," "to drive the Jews out of this country," "to bury 'em here." The majority of Klansmen might have considered this too extreme, but it attracted the kind of men Shepard wanted. When another renegade Klansman, Ohio's former Grand Titan Virgil "Bert" Effinger, seized the helm of the Black Legion, he escalated its militarism. Declaring his intent to become dictator of a fascist America, he created military ranks among his men, setting up "death squads" to massacre Jews. They amassed arms and ammunition and prepared to take over government agencies and arsenals when they heard the code word *Lixto*.[133]

The Silver Legion founder, William Dudley Pelley, was so weird that he would not have been welcome in the evangelical Protestant Klan. A devotee of spiritualist fads, he reported that he had died and gone to heaven where he remained for seven minutes, during which the rise of the *Führer* was prophesied, and he "acquired the ability to 'unlock hidden powers within myself.'" He claimed to have been a "secret courier" sent to the U.S. ambassador in Moscow, where he "learned" that the "Jewish race" had created the Bolshevik revolution and installed the alleged "half Jew" Lenin to lead it.[134] Bringing together his heavenly and earthly experience, Pelley announced that he had been chosen by God to lead the fight against Jewish Communism, and he established the Silver Legion the day after Hitler came to power. He designed uniforms imitating those of the European fascists: riding breeches with leggings and high black riding boots, adding a silver shirt with a scarlet *L* (for *Lixto*) on the shoulder and sold them for ten dollars. As with the Black Legion, dramatic, militarist uniforms attracted recruits.[135]

Pelley's anti-Semitism caught the attention of an experienced Klan organizer who did not share his occult interests but seized the opportunity to promote fascism: Luther Ivan Powell, the recruiter who had introduced the KKK to Oregon. His connections made the Silvers particularly strong in the Northwest and in Portland in particular, where they collaborated with some remnant local Klans and worked jointly with the police (as did most of the fascist groups).[136] By the spring of 1933, the Silver Legion claimed chapters in twelve states and fifteen thousand members, probably an exaggeration. Powell installed a "Field Marshal," Roy Zachary, a Seattle restaurant owner, who became the most warlike Silver Legion leader.[137]

The Silver Legion forged a document known as "The Franklin Prophecy," no doubt inspired by the *Protocols of the Elders of Zion*; it "exposed" a Jewish plot to "strangle" and "devour" the United States.[138] In the Silver leaders' plan for a fascist government, the United States would become a for-profit corporation, issue each adult citizen a share of common stock, and pay each a dividend of eighty dollars per month. Jews and bankers—the same thing in fascist talk—would be required to register as resident aliens and would be stripped of civil rights unless they forswore their Judaism. (This was unusual among American fascists, most of whom labeled Jews a race who could not, therefore, become un-Jewish.) One version of the plan moved the Jews onto Indian reservations, perhaps emulating an early Nazi proposal to move Jews to Madagascar. An alternative Silver plan would allow them to live in one city in each state. Negroes would become "wards of the state."[139] Like most fascists, they referred to President "Rosenfeld" and the "Jew Deal." They accused Secretary of Labor Frances Perkins of being a Jew (she was not) and not American (she was). Foreshadowing a demand made of Barack Obama in the next century, Pelley offered a reward of $1,000 to "the person who will bring me her American birth certificate."[140]

However delusional, the group was by no means timid. "Every red blooded American citizen should have a good gun and ammunition," Zachary told an "enraptured crowd" in Portland, anticipating the NRA's similar call a century later; "put up a target and have your wife practice shooting it if you want to keep a free government."[141] Like other fascist leaders, he sought dominance, hoping to become an " 'American white king' and the 'American Hitler.' "[142]

In 1934 the Silvers scheduled an armed uprising against the Roosevelt administration for May 1, a labor and Communist holiday. A hundred-man subgroup, called Storm Troopers—a translation from the German—would lead, and local army units would join. They promised that U.S. Marines would train the insurgents, and while that was nonsense, they managed to "buy" rifles from the Marines and "obtain" pistols and shotguns from the San Diego armory. They would use these weapons not only for the coup they planned but also to recruit men who wanted to own guns. When no attack materialized, the Silvers talked of taking over the National Guard in all forty-eight states, then fell back on the less ambitious fantasy to seize the San Diego City Hall. Several aborted plots could have been particularly murderous. They planned to release cyanide gas in local synagogues during Chanukah or Yom Kippur, and to inject typhoid germs into a dairy that served Jewish neighborhoods.[143]

The Black and Silver Legions' implausible plots can be laughed off, but when they got corporate sponsorship, they were capable of real violence.[144] Ford Motors tried to entice workers into anti-union organizations, such as the Knights of Dearborn, which met jointly with the Friends of New Germany and the Veterans of Foreign Wars.[145] Ford and General Motors hired Legionnaires, like the mining companies that hired Pinkertons, to suppress the union organizing drives that would lead to the United Auto Workers.[146] "I may be exceptionally blood-thirsty," Pelley threatened, "but I feel that the late winter snows will be tinged scarlet in the streets of Detroit."[147]

The legions created a mini-reign of terror, bombing and setting fires at union offices and meetings with highly concentrated naphtha. They committed multiple murders, beatings, lynchings, and floggings. The head of the Michigan State Police believed that at least fifty unexplained "suicides" were the Black Legion's work.[148] In Cleveland, the Legionnaires served as strikebreakers and shared their stock of weapons with other strikebreakers.[149] In Minneapolis, they harassed, threatened, and attacked Teamsters Union strikers, in collaboration with the police.[150] Eric Sevareid, the future CBS war correspondent, then a university student there, reported seeing police "massacre" union picketers: "Suddenly . . . I understood deep in my bones and blood what Fascism was." Between threats, armed demonstrations and actual attacks, the whole city was on edge. The Communist feminist novelist Meridel Le Sueur, equally frightened, wrote that fascism seemed to pervade "the whole social anatomy" of Minneapolis.[151] The Teamsters, however, armed themselves in defense, so when Zachary led his troops against the union headquarters, they met an armed guard and quickly retreated.

The legion's fraternal relations with police and the U.S. Army, and the presence of legion members within them, induced those forces to facilitate or at least protect fascist violence. A congressional investigation revealed that the two legions and some Klansmen, working together, had acquired army horses to serve as a cavalry for their planned coup.[152] In Detroit, the many law-enforcement officers in the legions included the police commissioner and the prosecutor who was assigned to charge the attackers. As a result, it was difficult, usually impossible, to convict them. Zachary of the Silvers claimed that "the police know that some day they'll need our support and that's why they're supporting us now."[153]

That was true nationally as well. FBI head J. Edgar Hoover refused to investigate the legion despite being ordered to do so by President Roosevelt. Several mainstream organizations also supported the legions' violence: the American Legion worked to get charges dismissed and provided meeting space in its offices; Detroit's Wolverine Republican Club was a front for the legions; the Hearst newspapers supported them by red-baiting labor unions.[154] Dabbling in electoral politics, three Detroit Black Legion members ran for public office, including the U.S.

Congress; journalists held them responsible for defeating a Jewish candidate for mayor of Highland Park, a Detroit suburb. But unlike the Klan, they plotted to kill rather than to outvote political opponents. They targeted a town mayor who had hired African Americans, a Jewish civil rights and labor lawyer, the publisher of a community newspaper, and Homer Martin, the president of what would become the UAW. Happily these schemes did not materialize.[155]

ONLY ONE of these fascist groups continued the Klan's dependence on religious authority, but with a twist: abandoning anti-Catholicism. Catholic priest Charles Coughlin had become a national radio star. One of the most famous men in the United States in the 1930s, his listenership reached tens of millions, and he received some eighty thousand letters a week, a million on occasion. His speaking style was histrionic, hammering the pulpit, gesturing with a fist, "sweat streaming down his face."[156] He came to fascism with a sudden and opportunist reversal. Once an FDR supporter, he had spoken for Roosevelt at the 1932 Democratic Party convention. "I am with you to the end," he wired the president. "Say the word and I will follow." He denounced the Ku Klux Klan because of its anti-Catholicism, even claiming—probably falsely—to have personally "helped beat out the fire" started by a Klan cross-burning at his church.[157]

But soon the Klan and the Catholic Christian Front became allies. The basis of this new alliance was of course anti-Semitism, and Coughlin blamed Jews for everything evil. Moreover, to Coughlinites, anyone who criticized their leader must be a Jew. Opposing FDR's attempt to bring the United States into the World Court, Coughlin described its advocates with the classic labels for Jews: "international plutocrats," "international bankers." This Jewish cabal had caused the Depression, he charged, even as he also charged that Jews were all Communists—the classic, contradictory anti-Semitic trope.[158] The Christian Front assimilated its racism against African Americans, as strong as that of the KKK, to anti-Communism, once claiming that a delegation of Negroes had been sent to Russia to learn how to organize a Communist revolution. Like the Klan, Coughlin rooted some of his prejudice in eugenics: FDR leaned left because doing so was in "Jewish blood." He drew his arguments and most of his "facts" about Jews directly from Nazi publications, and the *New York Times* Berlin correspondent reported that Coughlin was "the new hero of Nazi Germany."[159] Asked about his plans, he responded, "I take the road of fascism."[160]

Coughlin took the name "Christian Front" from the Spanish fascist leader Generalissimo Francisco Franco, for whom it signaled Catholic determination to battle the antifascist Popular Front. Inspired by the Catholic-fascist alliance in Spain, Coughlin urged his followers to fight "in the Franco way" and publicly celebrated Franco's final victory in March 1939. Franco's support from the Spanish Catholic hierarchy allowed Coughlin to claim that Hitler and fascists were "the champions of Christian social order against the forces of anti–Christian chaos."[161] He claimed that Pope Pius XI had called on Catholics to join such an organization. A few Catholic leaders distanced themselves from the Christian Front, including Cardinal Mundelein, an FDR ally, but most of them remained silent, if not supportive.[162]

Until 1938 Coughlin stuck mainly to broadcasting, but soon thereafter he decided that more aggressive action was needed to head off the alleged Jewish threat. "Our people have passed beyond the point of being satisfied with a mere study club. . . . We are ripe for action clubs," he announced.[163] From its outset he had conceived the Christian Front in military terms, envisaging twenty-five-man "platoons" and "riflemen's groups," and it soon began building a militia, training young men in military discipline. (Some "platoons" fudged their identity by calling themselves sporting or rifle clubs.)[164]

In the Detroit area, the Christian Front joined the Black and Silver Legions in attacks on union supporters, but it was strongest and most violent in two cities with many Catholics, particularly Irish Catholics—Boston and New York. (The organization had little success in enlisting Protestants and had only a "sprinkling" of German and Italian Catholics.) The Boston and New York police, many of them Catholic, protected Christian Front vigilantes from prosecution. While the Christian Front's claim that six thousand police officers were members is dubious, an investigation by New York City's police chief reported that over a thousand of his men admitted membership, and several hundred refused to answer.[165] In the Dorchester, Roxbury, and Mattapan neighborhoods of Boston, Christian Fronters beat and stabbed Jews on the streets, "some girls having their clothes ripped off." Jewish Girl Scout troops and other clubs had to stop meeting, and residents said they were living in "mortal fear."[166] Nat Hentoff, who grew up in a Boston Jewish neighborhood, remembered of his family, "We felt hunted . . . None of us had the slightest doubt . . . that pogroms could happen here too." Boston's mayor Jim Curley dubbed Boston "the most Coughlinite city."[167]

Curley was wrong: New York City came in first with its alleged twelve thousand members. Ninety years later, in a city where Jewish food, slang, performers, and politicians are so plentiful, Christian Front violence against Jews may seem startling, but in 1930s New York City, Jews were poorer and less assimilated. The Christian Front staged some forty street meetings a week, typically in early evenings, often drawing audiences of four hundred, up to nine hundred in summer months, and many led to verbal and physical attacks on Jews. Members would run through subway cars, taunting and abusing passengers who looked Jewish.[168] At a Bronx meeting, a Christian Front speaker "had his hoodlum audience yelling for a pogrom."[169]

A super-aggressive subgroup, the Christian Mobilizers, armed with pickax handles, brass knuckles, and lead pipes, engaged in daily street assaults and desecrations of synagogues. An FBI informer uncovered a cache of bombs, rifles, and thousands of rounds of ammunition, intended for destroying Jewish-owned newspapers and stores, blowing up bridges, utilities, docks, and railroad stations in New York, and assassinating unfriendly New York congressmen. "Headquarters has passed on orders," a Christian Front organizer told a meeting, "that you are to train yourselves in smashing up stores—Jewish stores—and beating the brains out of Jews that put up a fight." New York City police did not usually intervene, and some were openly sympathetic, though at least once the Mobilizers attacked policemen.[170]

The Christian Front attacked City College in particular, as a hotbed of Communists and Jews—a charge not entirely false. Some universities allowed lectures by prominent fascists and Nazi propagandists while banning antifascist speakers.[171] Once the European war began,

Christian Front violence tapered off, but its stalwarts turned to promoting the idea that the Jews were dragging the United States into an unnecessary war.[172]

The fascist movement also encompassed a variety of women's groups, with an estimated aggregate membership of 1 to 1.5 million. The Christian Front's religiosity made it more comfortable for women than other groups, but some women's organizations had no religious facade, such as the Women's National Association for the Preservation of the White Race.[173] As it seemed that the United States might go to the defense of European countries against Nazi aggression, women became particularly active in attempting to prevent that. Campaigning for American neutrality and against Lend-Lease, the Front used its Mothers Movement to agitate for a negotiated settlement with the Third Reich. By speaking in a maternalist voice—a trope used by feminists and other progressives as well as the Far Right—the fascist groups could recruit women who were not openly fascist. One was Elizabeth Dilling, whose virulent anti-Semitism and anti-Communism made her an ally of the fascists. Among her work was cataloging thirteen hundred "subversives," published as *The Red Network—A Who's Who and Handbook of Radicalism for Patriots*.[174]

The largest and least violent of the fascist groups was the German American Bund, and it illustrates some of the paradoxes of the American fascist movement. It emphasized patriotism but took orders directly from Nazi Germany and worked to make German Americans identify with Nazi Germany. It specialized in uniformed military drills, in which men carried rifles and boys carried wooden replicas of rifles. Its large female membership made it a family organization, hosting summer picnics, organizing children's Bund groups, and creating activities for children.

Unlike the other fascist groups profiled here, the Bund was an ethnic organization and the only group large enough to organize typical social movement activities. Many American "ethnics" felt loyal to their heritage, but the Bund racialized this feeling: "Every person of German ancestry . . . is a racial comrade."[175] These German loyalties created a discursive contradiction: while one leader also called the German *Volk* an "expression of . . . the most sublime form of true democracy," Chicago Bund leader Fritz Gissibl declared, "We will not be fooled by your sugar-coated democracy." Anti-Communism helped obscure the contradiction, and Gissibl argued that Americans had to choose either the Soviet star or the swastika.[176] The Bund attempted to resolve this inconsistency by drafting the greatest American hero, George Washington. Calling him the "first fascist" and "a realist" who knew that democracy could not work, a Bund spokesman transformed the KKK slogan "if Jesus were alive today he would be a Klansman" into "if Washington were alive today, he would be a friend of Adolf Hitler."[177]

The Bund arose from an ethnic fraternal order, the Teutonia Association (Nationalsozialistische Vereinigung Teutonia), a club of German Americans and German nationals living in the United States. For a time, the Teutonia remained a beer-drinking club, its members attracted by the opportunity to socialize with other German Americans and German speakers. It also called itself a socialist club, just as the Nazi Party named itself a socialist and a workers' party, the NSDAP (Nationalsozialistische Deutsche Arbeiterpartei). It promoted grievances against the punitive reparations payments imposed on Germany after its defeat in World War I. As early as 1931, portraits of Hitler shared wall space with flags of the pre–World War I German Empire, and *Heil Hitler* rang out from the audience.

Then the Nazi seizure of power in 1933 led the Teutonians to rename themselves, proudly, Friends of the Hitler Movement. From that moment the organization became directly subordinated to the German Nazi Party.[178] This relationship was not always smooth. Fearful of alienating the U.S. government, deputy *Führer* Rudolf Hess ordered the name changed to Friends of the New Germany (Bund der Freunde des Neuen Deutschland) and appointed a new, less aggressive and more American head of the organization, Heinrich "Heinz" Spanknöbel. He was an administrative employee of Ford Motors, and the Bund became particularly strong in Detroit-area enclaves of German Americans, many of whom also worked for Henry Ford and were thus familiar with the anti–Semitic screeds he circulated among his employees.[179] For his service, in 1938 on his seventy-fifth birthday, the German consul in Detroit honored him by ceremonially awarding him the Grand Cross of the German Eagle, the highest honor bestowed upon foreigners.

Ironically, the Nazi regime tried to get the Friends group to tone down its identification with the Third Reich. Alarmed when these American fascists began circulating German Nazi materials and demanding that the German-language newspaper *New Yorker Staats-Zeitung* publish pro-Nazi material, Berlin's foreign office (Deutsches Ausland-Institut, DAI) tried to protect the Bund from appearing disloyal by further Americanizing it.[180] Hess replaced Spanknöbel with the upper-class American "colonel" Edwin Emerson. A Harvard graduate, member of the National Press Club, and U.S. correspondent for some thirty-six German newspapers controlled by the Nazi government, he called himself "colonel" in reference to his previous membership in President Theodore Roosevelt's Rough Riders.[181]

Still uneasy, the DAI ordered the group to be renamed the German American Bund, to present it as an ethnic fraternal order, but even that did not solve the problem. "Nothing has resulted in so much hostility toward us in the last few months as the stupid and noisy activities of . . . the German-American Bund," wrote the Third Reich's ambassador to Washington.[182] The DAI ordered German nationals and Nazi Party members not to join the Bund, and threatened to cancel the passports of those who did, but this was never enforced. German consuls often attended Bund meetings, and the Bund often used the address of the German consulate in New York.[183] German shipping lines offered free passage to Germany for Bund members.[184] Like the Third Reich, the Bund harped on Communism as the main enemy: "So long as there's a swastika, there'll be no hammer and sickle in this country."[185]

But German policy was inconsistent. As the ambassador put it, "I am not so sure that all the agencies in Berlin . . . are observing . . . restraint" in its sponsorship of the Bund. The Third Reich poured material support into the Bund. It provided books and teachers to Bund youth groups studying the German language and German philosophy, arranged for the students to listen to Hitler's speeches on shortwave radio, and set up "pen pal" relationships with Hitler Youth members to develop "the courage and strength to fight for their racial existence."[186]

Berlin appointed yet another Bund *Führer*, Fritz Kuhn, a naturalized U.S. citizen born in Munich and, again, a previous employee of

Henry Ford.* It ordered that the American flag always appear along with swastikas. (Bundists sometimes insisted that the swastika was an American Indian symbol and thereby proved their group's American-ness.) The Bund briefly replaced *Sieg Heil* with "Free America" (though the Bundists understood that slogan to mean "free it from the Jews"), but *Sieg Heil* soon returned.[187] Well into World War II, the Third Reich hoped to prevent the United States from entering the war, but finally, in 1939, it gave up the pretense. Gustav Moshack, head of the *Ameri-kaabteilung* of the DAI, wrote that the Bund "must recognize itself as the go-between for Germany and the U.S."[188]

The DAI promoted nonviolent tactics similar to the Klan's, such as boycotting and picketing Jewish stores,[189] but Bundists continued dreaming up violent schemes—to sabotage defense industries that were ramping up production, for example. None were realized. Instead the Bund gave its members a chance to perform a theatrical militarism. It created a subgroup, the Ordnungsdienst (Order of Service or OD), the optics of their uniforms, training and marches designed to suggest a "steely . . . menacing and highly ordered human machine." (In prac-tice, however, it served only as a personal honor guard to Kuhn.)[190] The Bund did, however, engage in provocations: chanting ugly anti-Semitic slurs in outdoor rallies in Jewish neighborhoods,† plastering Jewish homes with anti-Semitic material on Yom Kippur. With strategic cyni-cism, the Philadelphia Bund mobilized anti-Black racism in support of anti-Semitism. It distributed anti-Semitic literature promising that lib-erating the country from Jews would end African Americans' protests, since they were cooked up by Jewish Communists.[191]

The Bund stood out among the fascist groups by developing social-movement-style activities for children and families, much like the KKK's. Its women's division, the *Frauenschaft*, assumed major responsibility for running these doings. Those not in Nazi uniform

---

* Kuhn turned out to be a loose cannon. Inaugurating his new job, he took a group of fifty Bundists to Germany, expecting to be granted a meeting with the *Führer*. But the Third Reich, still focused on keeping the United States neutral, snubbed him, and he got to meet only with an aide. On his return, Kuhn claimed, falsely, that Hitler had appointed him the American *Führer*, which no doubt enraged Berlin.
† One of its slurs—"Jewish dadaists"—merits a laugh, but it also makes a connection between Jews and modernism which was not wrong.

often wore Teutonic peasant garb, including lederhosen and dirndl skirts. The Bund purchased several campgrounds and built recreational facilities. With these it could stage events that also resembled the Klan's: marriage, birth, and funeral ceremonies as well as large outdoor Fourth of July celebrations at its Camp Siegfried in Yaphank, Long Island.* At one event, eighteen thousand showed up. Bund events featured bands, singing, games, gymnastics, and contests, even children's camps, including a summer camp at Windham in the Catskills. The camps offered political education to the children, including eugenics, and published a magazine for children, *Junges Volk*. Also like the Klan, the Bund financed these activities through members' dues and purchases: on top of twenty-five-cent monthly dues, members paid twenty cents for a membership card and $1.50 for promotional material; they were expected to buy uniforms and a wide variety of Nazi insignias, accessories, and paraphernalia. Open to any "patriotic Aryan American," the camps served to recruit new members, to soften the Bund's reputation, and—as in most social movements—to bond members into a familial community.[192] The National Rifle Association contributed to Americanizing the Bund by recruiting at Bund events and providing guns and ammunition.[193] I find myself wondering if the American fascists could have stabilized and grown their organizations had they refrained from violence and followed the Bund's strategy.

But allegiance to fascist leaders and militarist performances never ceased. Members greeted each other with *Heil Hitler* and *Heil Mussolini* salutes, and a huge swastika usually topped their stages. Events began with singing "Deutschland über Alles" and ceremonially raising a Nazi flag. Men in fascist uniforms goose-stepped; children in brown uniforms practiced marching in perfect unison; boys received weapons training. The official camp song included the words

> *Youth, Youth—We are the future soldiers*
> *Youth, Youth—We are the ones to carry out future deeds*
> *Yes; by our fists will be smashed whoever stands in our way.*[194]

---

* As if continuing its fascist legacy, Yaphank continues today as a conservative island in a largely Democratic New York region.

Paradoxically, providing men and boys a chance to march and use weapons may have served to keep violence in check, giving them a proxy for actual armed combat.

The Bund's peak visibility came from a massive "Pro American Rally" on February 20, 1939, celebrating Washington's birthday, in Madison Square Garden.[195] It was a wakeup call for the many who had not registered the growth of fascist groups. Some 22,000 attended; tickets were $1.10 for the main floor, forty cents for the balcony. First the audience recited the Pledge of Allegiance. Then three thousand Ordnungsdienst men in gray shirts, black pants, Sam Browne military cross straps, and swastika insignia entered marching in perfect lines.[196] Demonstrating its *Ameri-*

On February 20, 1939, some 22,000 supporters attend a Nazi rally at Madison Square Garden as two thousand police keep protesters outside.

can fascism, a thirty-foot-high image of George Washington, flanked by American flags and swastika banners, hung behind the podium. His picture was vital because he was "America's first fascist." The keynote speaker quoted Washington's farewell address and proclaimed that he spoke for "A Nation of true Americans . . . Patriotic . . . the true Christian Americans," the last phrase reflecting the influence of the Christian Front. Bund leader Kuhn called out, "Wake up! You, Aryan, Nordic and Christians, to demand that our government be returned to the people who founded it!"[197]

The loudest and most repeated theme was Jews. The Garden's manager had allowed the rental on the condition that there would be no anti-Semitic content, but the rally organizers completely disregarded this promise. Ringing the hall were large signs with slogans such as "Stop Jewish Domination of Christian America." Speakers competed to offer the most fanatical slurs—"the Jew is an Alien . . . a thousand times more dangerous to us than all others by reason of his parasitic nature," "the grip of the palsied hand of Jewish Communism in our schools, our universities, our very home," "conniving sorcerers," "money-mad leeches"—and a promise to create a "Jew-free America!" They denounced "job-taking Jewish refugees." (In fact the 1924 immigration restriction law barred all but a small number of Jewish refugees.) Rousing cheers greeted each slur, along with boos for President "Rosenfeld" and Manhattan district attorney Thomas Dewey, aka "Thomas Jewey." To further Americanize the bigotry, speakers praised anti-miscegenation laws, immigration restriction, and racial segregation.[198]

Meanwhile thousands of protesters massed outside the Garden, some claim 100,000, with many affiliations: New Dealers, B'nai Brithers, Communists, Trotskyists, union members, and unaffiliated Jews determined to make the fascists unwelcome. Two thousand police cordoned off a two-block square, turning the Garden into a virtual fortress.[199] Protesters received exhilarating support when the orchestra from a Broadway musical came out and played "The Star-Spangled Banner" for the crowd. Someone had set up a record player and loudspeaker in a building nearby that broadcast over and over, "Be American, Stay at Home."[200]

Despite the security, some opponents made it inside. The intrepid journalist Dorothy Thompson, who had interviewed Hitler himself, got in with her press pass and made a point to laugh and catcall as loudly as she could. An audacious Brooklyn plumber, Isadore Greenbaum, made his way into the Garden, jumped onto the stage, "yanked on the cables so Kuhn's microphone fell over and yelled 'Down with Hitler.'" Bund security men tackled and beat him badly, "even ripped his pants off, to the delight of the crowd," until the police pulled him to safety. He had a black eye and broken nose and was fined twenty-five dollars for his disruption, but said he would do it again. Soon he joined the war against fascism by serving in the U.S. Navy.[201]

THE FASCIST groups faced more organized opposition than had the Klan. An earlier Madison Square Garden rally, held in 1934, organized by the American Jewish Congress and headed by Rabbi Stephen Wise, was attended by twenty thousand. It enacted a trial of Hitler, with the verdict delivered by carefully chosen Protestants, Judge Samuel Seabury and John Haynes Holmes.[202] A coalition of two hundred Jewish women's groups initiated a campaign against "intolerance." Many labor unions denounced fascist activity; members of the ILGWU, with its many Jewish members, called for creating an Anti-Fascist Union Guard.[203]

Organizations including veterans' associations and women's clubs promoted boycotts of German goods. Catholics, worried that the Christian Front's outrages would escalate anti-Catholicism, spawned several antifascist groups. Catholics for Human Rights issued a strong statement: "if allowed to go unchallenged . . . [they] will create pogroms, split the labor movement, endanger . . . American . . . democracy, and bring the fire of persecution down upon the Catholic Church of America."[204] One Catholic group refused to mince words, calling itself Catholics Against Anti-Semitism.[205]

Several municipal governments, notably in New Jersey and New York, banned Nazi uniforms, salutes, and swastikas in public parades, and the New Jersey legislature extended the ban statewide. As war drew near, the Selective Service prohibited replacing defense industry workers who were inducted into the military with Bund members, who were also barred from WPA employment (along with Communists, of course).[206] After the mass pogrom known as *Kristallnacht* in November 1938—which the Bund declared a justifiable retribution for Jewish crimes[207]—anti-Nazi public opinion finally forced the justice system to act. Three years after the worst violence in Detroit, nearly fifty Black Legionnaires were imprisoned for murder or assault; thirteen received life terms.[208] The Department of Justice threatened to charge Coughlin with sedition unless the Catholic hierarchy put an end to his incitement.[209]

A few antifascist protests turned violent. Jewish American war veterans slipped into one of the Bund's rallies, and during a particularly virulent speech, they stood up, put on their Jewish American war veteran caps, and "started swinging."[210] Unionizing workers, accustomed to battles with strikebreakers and police, brawled with fascists. At an indoor fascist rally in Chicago, several hundred men seized the podium and attacked the Silver Legion's Zachary, putting an end to legion appearances in that city. When the Friends of New Germany arrived in buses for a rally in the New York City suburb of Irvington, which had a considerable Jewish population, they were attacked with bricks and bats, and the bus drivers fled, leaving them stranded; they sought refuge in the police department.[211] Jewish gangsters including Meyer Lansky, Bugsy Siegel, and Mickey Cohen broke up Bund meetings.[212]

No resistance came from Congress. A House Special Committee on Un-American Activities, chaired by progressive Democrats, had begun to investigate the fascists, but in 1938 Congressman Martin Dies, Jr., of Texas took over the committee and changed the focus to "Reds." His committee repeated fascist claims that Black resistance to segregation was a Communist plot—i.e., that without Communist agitation, Blacks would be content; that Communism was a Jewish plot and that the Depression was caused by "conspiratorial elements"— a widely recognized code for Jews. It suggested that suppressing them "would quickly restore the nation to a 'normal condition.'"[213]

Like the Klan's 1925 march on Washington, the 1939 Madison Square Garden rally marked the beginning of the decline of American fascist groups. Whether because of protests, ennui, distaste, or hesitation to identify with the German conquests—first Poland, then Denmark and Norway, then western Europe—the groups shrank by the end of the 1930s.* A Bund recruitment drive in Chicago flopped:

---

* The impact of German aggression on the American fascists resembled the impact of Stephenson's violence on the KKK in setting off a sharp desertion, but in different

of the 700,000 Chicagoans of German descent, and the 40,000 in German fraternal organizations, only 450 joined the Bund.[214] Salesmen peddling Coughlin's *Social Justice* newspaper found few buyers. Christian Front attempts to generate a boycott of Jewish-owned department stores had no discernible impact (like the KKK's attempt to boycott Jewish department store chain Meier and Frank). Its planned "Gentile Day" event had to be cancelled because of "aroused public opinion."[215] Even the Klan drew back. Declaring the fascists too extreme, Imperial Wizard Hiram Evans called on the federal government to "stamp out" the Black Legion.[216] Still, as with the Ku Klux Klan, no national opposition movement arose.

MY FORAY into discussing the fascist offspring of the KKK is motivated, unsurprisingly, by the growth of similar groups today, generically known as white nationalists. Allowing for the differences that arise from one hundred years of history, the movements share ideology, strategy, and some tactics. They aim to "cleanse" America of dangerous alien influences that are trying to "replace" real Americans with dangerous outsiders; they recruit by inciting fear and then anger. But the 1930s context was radically different—the American fascists faced burgeoning leftist and labor movements and a social democratic national government, while today's white nationalists are increasingly comfortable within a burgeoning Far Right.

Today the f-word has taken on new life. Many scholars have defined *fascism* generically—displaying what one scholar called a "mania for formulas"—a focus I do not consider useful.[217] No universal definition, not even a universal description, fits all cases. My understanding of American fascism was influenced by Italian culture critic Umberto Eco, who argued that "fascism had no quintessence" but is rather "a fuzzy totalitarianism, a collage . . . a beehive of contradictions. . . . The fas-

---

ways and for different reasons. The Stephenson case was a "last straw" in a movement whose members overwhelmingly disapproved of violence; by contrast, the fascists were not repelled by Nazi violence but feared condemnation by the growing American antifascist sentiment.

cist game can be played in many forms." The historian Robert Paxton agrees, warning against identifying fascism "by its plumage."[218] Equally helpful is the historian Joseph Fronczak's treatment of fascism as a form of political behavior.[219] In that behavior, violence is central, even when it is only a threat or a fantasy. Violence and planning violence were the main activities of the Black and Silver Legions and the Christian Front; although forced by German pressure to remain comparatively nonviolent, the Bund glorified fascist violence through its militarized drills and weapons training for men and boys.

In any attempt at defining it, *fascism* has to be a cluster concept, in which its various instances share many but not all characteristics.[220] One might speak of a family resemblance among these fascisms, and considering the KKK alongside the fascist groups helps to clarify their commonalities. Ku Klux Klan discourse included an extreme nationalism, which the Klan called patriotism, directed at a nation it defined as white Protestants. It also included allegations that "aliens" threatened the national "destiny;" distrust of secular experts and professionals; demagoguery and hypermasculinism in sensationalist and aggressive gestures and words (as opposed to the "polite language" of elite conservatism); and affinity with law enforcement officers. The 1930s American fascists shared those characteristics, but what they added was of great significance: the rejection of democracy on the grounds that it weakens the nation; devotion to authoritarian leaders; repudiation of civil liberties, the protection of minorities, and the rule of law; support from and solidarity with foreign fascist movements and states; and perhaps most important, the justification, encouragement, and often the practice of violence.

Yet despite their considerable differences, the Klan and the fascists groups shared an emotional infrastructure, if in varying intensity. Both constructed fear that the wrong racial, ethnic, or religious groups were conspiring to "replace" "true" Americans and that diversity led to chaos and national weakness. These are emotional as much as cognitive matters. The British social and cultural critic Raymond Williams wrote of a "structure of feeling" that undergirds and sustains ideology.[221] Shedding the Klan's anti-Catholicism, for example, did not require an emotional change, only a redefinition of the target. These angry emotions were not only a cause but equally an effect of Klan and fascist propaganda. Both not only ratcheted up these emotions, but also created them among people who had not previously felt them. Certain personalities may be particularly prone to fear and anger, but social movements can weaken, strengthen, redirect, and manufacture such feelings. Emotions are no more fixed than ideas.

The Ku Klux Klan was a large social movement; the fascist groups were not. Crucially, the Klan gave its members something to do, notably participation in dramatic events both large and small—a fundamental source of social movement success. European Nazis and fascists offered members the participatory drama of huge rallies, but the American fascists did not and could not. They offered members only delusional plots and violence, often in the service of corporations that considered union organizers rather than Catholics and Jews as their primary enemy. The fascist groups spread anti-Semitism, but Klan bigotry made deeper inroads into the culture and convinced more people. (The Left theorist Antonio Gramsci would have called it hegemonic.) The Klan made bigotry respectable, an achievement the fascist groups could not duplicate. The Klan put bigotry in office through electoral work. It influenced passage of the 1924 immigration restriction law that closed the door to millions of would-be immigrants for forty years. The fascists achieved none of this.

That the *northern* Klan—unlike its southern parent—remained relatively nonviolent was also key to its success as a social movement. Its nonviolence made secrecy unnecessary, except as a device manufactured to make its rituals more enticing. Its nonviolence made it a family movement. By contrast, the Bund's attempts to make itself a family organization were limited—its events were occasional. Klanspeople met regularly and could surround its members with the sociability of klavern meetings and mass rallies. The Bund's family events could not rival the size and drama of the Klan's public celebrations. Klanswomen created autonomous groups, became leaders, and took responsibility for many Klan public events, while women never became full members of the fascist groups.

The Klan gave its members something nonviolent to *do*. Klan rituals, ceremonies, and spectacular public events required hours of volunteer labor. Electoral and legislative work kept members busy, while the fascist groups' argument that fascism was the best way to organize the nation had no substantive content. The KKK benefited from both secrecy and openness: it was centralized enough to enforce nonviolence on most of its members and to operate political campaigns, but decentralized enough to let members adapt to local conditions and to allow some vigilantism, protected by collusion from police, prosecutors, judges, and juries. It gave men opportunities to perform masculinity nonviolently, through uniforms, parades, rituals, and hierarchical military ranks and titles. The German American Bund did that also, but the other fascist groups had no nonviolent projects to keep its members busy. They offered only violence, planning violence, and delusional fantasies of violence.

Similarly, few if any of today's white nationalist groups create large-scale nonviolent community activities. Like the 1930s fascists, they have no authoritative national organization that can impose strategic and tactical discipline, so small groups feel no restraint on their beatings, bombings, and murders. A 1930s journalist could have been describing 2020s fascists when she noted the fascists' inability to persuade "all of the warring little Hitlers that the train would carry plenty of gravy for everybody. . . . Each one of the big boys has a pretty good opinion of himself and feels that he was just naturally meant to be the man."[222]

In one respect, the fascists had an advantage that the KKK did not— they felt themselves part of a global movement that seemed unstoppable. But that advantage rested on a contradiction: For a time they appeared able to make American patriotism and adulation of foreign dictators compatible, but these dual loyalties became increasingly untenable due to the growth of fascist military aggression abroad. Moreover, most powerful conservatives in the United States, beyond the corporate leaders who used fascists as thugs, maintained a qualified allegiance to democracy and refrained from supporting the fascist groups.

Still, we should not imagine that the United States is immune to fascism; its core values—racism, nationalism, violence, and authoritarian leadership—retain their appeal to some Americans. No warning is as apropos as that of journalist Dorothy Thompson, who lived through the 1920s heyday of the Klan, spent years covering Nazi Germany, and jeered loudly at the Madison Square Garden fascist rally: "No people ever recognize their dictator in advance. He never stands for election on the platform of dictatorship. He always represents himself as the instrument [of] the Incorporated National Will. . . . When our dictator turns up you can depend on it that he will be one of the boys, and he will stand for everything traditionally American."[223]

As I write this conclusion, I am concerned that discussing the fascist groups may serve to understate the Klan's malign influence. Observers in the 1930s noticed this effect: a Detroit newspaper headlined "THE BLACK LEGION MAKES KLAN LOOK LIKE CREAM PUFF."[224] I hope that is not what readers will conclude, but I stand by my view that violence is worse than what is now called "hate speech." Beating up Jews on the streets is worse than shouting anti-Semitic slurs; murdering union organizers is worse than slandering Catholics. Calling for exiling or even eradicating whole populations, as the fascists did, is worse than attempting to disempower those populations politically and economically, as the KKK did.

Still, the KKK's hate speech surely encouraged violence. Moreover, the Klan's greatest accomplishment was not to elect officials or promote legislation but to normalize bigotry. Though many white Americans had long shared its prejudices, it mattered when bigotry expressed in private became bigotry shouted, by an organization with 150 print publications, two radio stations, and as many as five million adherents. The Klan built on America's long history of racism, anti-Catholicism, and anti-Semitism, and it spread and intensified that bigotry. Its impact on American society was broad and deep. Toni Morrison made an astute comment about fascism some eighteen years ago: "Before there is a final solution, there must be a first solution, a second one, even a third. The move toward a final solution is not a jump. It takes one step, then another, then another."[225]

3

TRUSTEES OF THE NATION

The Campaign for Old-Age Pensions

On the way to Townsend conference from Lawrence, Kansas.

[Social Security] would take all the romance out of life. We
might as well take a child from the nursery, give him a nurse,
and protect him from every experience that life affords.

—DEMOCRATIC NEW JERSEY GOVERNOR
ARTHUR HARRY MOORE, 1935[1]

No such crusade as ours had been seen on this earth in 2,000
years. No such ardent army has ever enlisted in any cause
in all the world. Where Christianity numbered its hundreds,
in its beginning years, our cause numbered its millions. And
without sacrilege we can see that the effects already apparent from our movement . . . may bring some of the deep and
mighty changes upon civilization which Christianity sought.

—DR. FRANCIS TOWNSEND[2]

It was California's sun that created old-age pensions, or so it could be argued. An eccentric physician in Long Beach had joined a large westward migration of older, often retired Americans in search of good weather—weather that would not only end their struggles with snow and ice but also, it was believed, make them healthier and live longer. Some might say that old-age pensions became inevitable due to the aging of the American population, the increase in nuclear family households that left elders living on their own, and the massive unemployment of the 1930s—but that is speculation; many other social and economic changes do not produce results. In fact, a mass social movement of the elderly was arguably the major force behind Social Security old-age pensions: the Townsend movement, named after its founder, Francis Townsend, M.D.

Townsend was by far the largest social movement of the 1930s—larger than the protests of the unemployed and labor union organizing taken together. Never before had the elderly organized to advance their interests as old people. Yet despite its size and originality, it is the least studied social movement in American history. Scholars and policy wonks of its time focused almost exclusively on debunking the Townsend plan, pointing out its economic fallacies and labeling its supporters naïve and crackpot. Very few contemporary scholars have studied it.[3] I find myself wondering, is this a sign of disdain for old people, precisely what the movement was challenging?

The Townsend movement's influence continued even after the 1935 passage of the Social Security Act. It created a "senior citizen" political identity, now a powerful voting bloc.[*] Through their activism, elderly people came to see themselves as *deserving* of government-guaranteed economic security. Their lifetimes of labor had earned it, they felt, and their pensions would serve as an economic stimulus during the Depression. Moreover, their pensions would enable them to contribute to their communities and the nation through volunteer work.

---

[*] The powerful American Association of Retired Persons (AARP)—note the avoidance of the terms *elderly* or *older*—was one of Townsend's progeny.

Townsenders insisted that the elderly should become a "guiding force in all things, political, social and moral."[4] This was a claim to wisdom and relevance at a time when the culture was increasingly disrespectful of old people. That claim allowed a single-issue social movement to consider itself a patriotic cause, one that could improve the well-being of the entire nation. Part of the Townsend movement's appeal was that it could be both narrow and wide: its narrowness made it recognizable and straightforward, its message stickier; its width made it selfless. Its genius lay in joining its members' material interests with altruism. Townsenders saw themselves as simultaneously beneficiaries of the nation and contributors to it, givers as well as takers.

UNIQUELY AMONG social movements, this one was initiated by a lone visionary: Francis Townsend. Other large social movements have had identifiable founders, such as Cesar Chavez. But this one was known by the founder's name. Sixty-seven years old when he initiated his campaign, Dr. Townsend became a virtual guru to his millions of followers and a dangerous quack to its enemies. His looks—a lean man, his ill-fitting suits hanging loosely—matched his eccentricity and unlikely career. His appearance communicated visually his salt-of-the-earth style and background, which surely did no harm in attracting followers.

He was born in 1867 in a log cabin in Illinois, where his father had homesteaded. The father then took the family to Nebraska, where he invested in a hardware store. Inheriting his father's restlessness, the teenage Francis left home alone and traveled westward, finding work, consecutively, as a cowboy in California, a teamster in Washington, a schoolteacher in Kansas, a miner in Colorado, and a salesman in Kansas. He returned to Nebraska at age thirty-one to attend Omaha Medical College, where, he recalled, his instructor in "eye, ear, nose and throat work" also "held frequent bull sessions on Socialism."[5] He then set up a semirural medical practice in South Dakota where he became active in the Socialist Party, which at that time and place emerged as an extension of the 1890s Populist Party: commonsensical, not ideological. In 1917 he answered the army's wartime call for "medical men" and enlisted—at fifty! After the war, he developed peritonitis and nearly died, so he moved his family to warmer weather in Long Beach, California.

One scholar called him "rootless," but I see him rather as adventurous, improvisatory, and impatient with routine. Although his socialist beliefs were fuzzy, even contradictory (as we will soon see), he initiated a campaign for pensions out of a sense of social responsibility. In Long Beach he worked for fourteen years at a public medical clinic, where he saw old people both poor and in desperate need of medical care. He was infuriated when the Depression closed the clinic in 1933. (Later, when Townsend supporters were asked how they would spend a pension, their top three items were medical care, warm clothing, and self-improvement, in that order.)[6] Among his own varied accounts of the inspiration for his proposal, Townsend described his horror at seeing old women, bent with age, scrounging food from garbage cans. "A torrent of invectives tore out of me," he wrote later. When his wife told him to quiet down, he replied, "I want all the neighbors to hear me! I want God Almighty to hear me."[7] Now unemployed, his savings rapidly shrinking, he was moved to write letters to the local newspaper proposing a pension plan. Rarely if ever have letters to the editor been so consequential.

Dr. Townsend was aware that the United States was alone among developed countries in providing no government old-age pensions. Still, he was surprised by the firestorm his letters kindled and its rapid spread. He published eight letters in the Long Beach *Press Telegram* between September 30, 1933 and February 20, 1934, and in those five months found he had jump-started a social movement. He soon sketched out an actual pension plan. Recruiting two partners—his brother Walter L. Townsend and real estate broker Robert Earle Clements—he created Old Age Revolving Pensions, Limited (OARP).[8] The organization thus acquired two sorts of leaders: the doctor who led the social movement and the shrewd commission-earning businessmen who built the organization. This division of labor made the movement a juggernaut, but it also produced conflicts and allegations of corruption. (By contrast, the 1920s KKK managed to fuse inspiration and profit.)

From early on it was clear that a social movement was arising. OARP's newsletter, *The Modern Crusader*, soon sold 100,000 copies—granted, it cost only two cents.[9] The proposal generated excitement throughout California, and OARP chapters appeared so fast that the headquarters could not keep track. Every small-town newspaper covered it, and some journalists calculated how much money elders would get. San Diego chapters urged boycotting businesses that would not advance credit on the forthcoming pensions. By 1935, San Francisco's Immigration and Naturalization office reported a "record-breaking rush of aged foreigners seeking naturalization" so as to get a pension. Widespread support also came from younger people—petition signers had to provide their age. San Diego's Rotary Club membership exploded because younger supporters expected that the plan would boost the economy. (Pensions would also lessen their burden of caring for elderly relatives.) Within months, Townsend claimed that in some California towns, signers numbered more than 50 percent of residents. Kathleen Norris, one the most widely read and highest-paid woman writers of the day, whose fiction promoted family values and the nobility of motherhood, endorsed it—an early indication that many women would become ardent Townsenders.[10]

Oregon soon became second—after California—in enthusiasm. The *Oregonian* newspaper reported that Townsend support in the state was "40 percent greater than the combined strength of all other parties." Radio station KWJJ broadcast fifteen-minute "Townsend flashes" every morning at nine a.m., while also granting time to socialists and labor unions. In Klamath Falls, the first Townsend club was organized by the mayor. Portland was a key bastion, as it had been for the 1920s KKK. Townsenders there threatened anti-Townsend newspapers with boycotts, and after a socialist member of the city council denounced the plan's funding as regressive, they disrupted the city council by loudly singing "America."[11]

A committee, allegedly including statisticians, began drafting legislation, and within a year John McGroarty, the seventy-three-year-old poet laureate of California, got himself elected to Congress, where he introduced the first Townsend bill, HR 3977.[12] (The plan would be revised several times.) Its major provisions were: Every American citizen* aged sixty or older would receive a monthly pension of $200,

---

* Some renditions of the proposal restricted beneficiaries to citizens, and some did not.

provided that they retired and refrained from wage-earning.* Younger people who were "hopelessly invalided or crippled" would receive the same pension. Originally the plan proposed funding the pensions through a 2 percent sales tax—a regressive tax that would have disproportionately burdened low-income people. Later the plan substituted a tax on transactions, which continued to be regressive, would have raised commodity prices exponentially, and would have provided an incentive for vertical integration.[13] (More on the flaws of the plan later.)

When McGroarty first introduced the bill, he presented it not as a pension proposal but as a plan for economic recovery, a claim often repeated by its supporters, one of whom called it a "big business" plan.[14] It would work because the legislation would require each stipend to be spent within a month.[15] The plan thus called itself "revolving" pensions on the theory that, after the first month, what was paid out would be recompensed by taxes, as if the same money would be cycling through the economy. The pensions would thus stimulate an economy in deep depression by boosting consumer spending. In practice, the requirement that stipends—whether distributed as scrip or as checks—would be worthless after a month was probably unnecessary, because the plan soon had to lower its proposed monthly pension, and most beneficiaries would spend it all on monthly living expenses.

Even better, Representative McGroarty argued that freeing up jobs held by older people would open jobs for younger people—four million jobs would allegedly become available.[16] Retirement would then allow elders to become a "service class" of volunteers doing charitable work; this would allow government to operate at a "high standard," as a supportive newspaper put it.[17] To the criticism that government stipends would encourage passivity and dependence, Dr. Townsend responded

---

* The plan originally called for $150 a month. As its leaders tried to meet objections, they compromised by promising pensions that would vary depending on availability of funds, and they expanded eligibility to include only those who earned less than $2,400 a year. The stipends were only enough to bring the yearly earnings to that level. The means-testing also meant that there need be no requirement to spend the pension stipend within a month, because recipients were poor enough that they would have to spend it all on living expenses. So a Wisconsin Progressive Party representative introduced an amendment to remove the monthly spending requirement.

that volunteerism should be a fundamental aspect of active citizenship. As he put it, the "secondary purpose of Townsend clubs is a desperate fight to continue the democratic spirit and form of government in these United States."[18] He argued that his plan would end child labor and reduce or even do away with crime, which resulted, in Townsend ideology, from poverty and unemployment. It would end war, which was also the result of poverty and inequality.[19] Dr. Townsend's arguments became ever more utopian and less realistic—an unusual trajectory, as over time most social movements make compromises, and their goals become more modest.

As the movement grew, its supporters' metaphors multiplied. One compared the body politic to the human body so as to explain why a physician was a good leader: "A physician knows . . . that for a human, or any animal, to live, the circulatory system must continue to function normally." The body politic was suffering from "acute anemia." Another analogized the fiscal stimulus to a water pump: to start it, one had to pour in enough to seal the valve.[20] The metaphors were homey, even corny, but no more naïve than most Americans' understanding of a complex capitalist economy.

DESPITE DR. TOWNSEND'S claims of originality, welfare "experts" had been devising plans for old-age pensions since the Progressive era. Before that, their efforts had been constrained by a deeply embedded assumption in the charity and social work establishment that "indoor relief" was better than "outdoor." This quaint language distinguished institutional care for the indigent in asylums ("indoor relief") from cash payments allowing recipients to live independently ("outdoor relief"). The traditional preference for the institutional care was both punitive and stingy. The charity establishment believed that outdoor relief would encourage improvidence and penalize thrift, a process then called "pauperization," more recently called "dependency." They also believed that institutional care was cheaper. Both beliefs were wrong: there is no evidence that welfare assistance makes recipients lazy, and institutional care is far more expensive than grants to people living in their own homes.[21]

The first exceptions to the stigma of "outdoor relief" were the small "mothers' pension" programs, established by thirty-nine state governments in the Progressive era. These very small pensions aimed to support only white widowed mothers, who could hardly be accused of laziness. Mothers' pensions aimed to keep recipients out of the labor force, as respectable white mothers belonged at home. This standard was of course based on class and race privilege, as the majority of American mothers had to contribute in some way to their families' income, and the pensions were far too small to relieve most mothers of that responsibility altogether. Single or divorced mothers were not eligible. Excluding immigrants and people of color was so standard that it did not need to be specified. Not all states offered these pensions, and those that did appropriated very limited funds to the programs. Thus the program benefited only a tiny fraction of lone mothers.

When the Depression hit in 1929, mass unemployment finally forced acceptance of "outdoor relief." Impoverishment was affecting middle-class people who had a stronger sense of entitlement and more political leverage than did working-class and poor people. Another "deserving" group, the elderly, were particularly hard hit, the crash having destroyed savings and investments. People over sixty-five were at the time the poorest age cohort in the country, and two-fifths of them could not support themselves. Many had no children to help, and those that did increasingly found their children unable to support them. The country's geographic mobility meant that many adult children no longer lived near their parents, while the nuclear family—husband, wife, children, but no other relatives—became increasingly the gold standard. As the number of extended-family households declined, fewer old people could rely on their children for support.

The predicament of the elderly was particularly pronounced in California, where the elderly population had almost doubled since 1920. In Long Beach, sometimes called the geriatric capital of the United States, the elderly constituted a third of the population, a ratio 1.7 times that of the national average.[22] So California organizations, such as the Fraternal Order of Eagles with its forty-thousand-plus members, had been proposing old-age pensions even before the Depression hit. In the 1920s the Eagles joined with the American Association for Labor Legislation, a national group of policy wonks, to promote a model state pension bill. In 1929 California created a pension program, and by 1934 twenty-eight states plus Alaska and Hawaii had done so. The average California grant, however, was a mere twenty-two dollars a month and far lower where need was greatest.[23] Many state pension plans were punitive, requiring that recipients turn over all their property to the state.[24] When the Depression bankrupted or forced retrenchment on the states, state officials begged for federal aid.[25]

Depression conditions had haltingly strengthened the influence of the approach we today call Keynesian: government spending to stimulate the economy.[26] Dr. Townsend was right in claiming that pensions for older people could boost the economy doubly: by providing a stimulus and by opening up jobs for younger people. Experts in groups such as the American Association for Old Age Security, the American Association for Labor Legislation, and the National Conference of Social Work had been discussing possible welfare programs since the 1920s. Some of them would participate in writing the Social Security Act of 1935, including lions of social reform Edwin Witte, John R. Commons and Arthur Altmeyer, and social democratic feminists Grace Abbott, Sophonisba Breckenridge, Florence Kelley, Julia Lathrop, and Mary van Kleeck (many of them part of the Hull-House network).[27] They had promoted the 1933 Dill-Connery bill, which would have provided federal grants-in-aid for the elderly, to be matched by the states, in amounts up to fifteen dollars a month per person. It passed the House in 1933 and 1934, but failed both times in the Senate. President Roosevelt did not support it, and Massachusetts sued the Treasury Department, arguing that the program was an attack on the constitutionally reserved powers of the states. Though that argument was rejected by the conservative Supreme Court, the bill's failure suggests the strength of resistance to such welfare expenditure—and the difficulty of overcoming opposition to the Social Security Act a few years later.

Dill-Connery's stipends would have been too minuscule to help low-income people, and they would have been controlled by state governments, which almost guaranteed that nonwhites would be excluded. The Social Security Act to come would have equally great limitations. It excluded the majority of Americans—farmworkers, domestic workers, and most other employed women—who worked mainly for small employers who were not required to participate. Unemployed women were expected to share a husband's stipend. Divorced women would have no entitlement to an ex-husband's pension, and other unmarried women would get nothing.[28]

The Townsend plan was better. True, it relied on discriminatory funding, like Social Security. Townsend proposed funding by sales taxes, while Social Security was funded by a percentage of earnings, so the poor who needed help most would get least. But the universality and the size of Townsend plan pensions would have mitigated inequality, by providing the same level of support to all Americans. Moreover, it would include people of both sexes and all races, a nondiscriminatory policy that might have set a precedent for future programs. The Townsend plan might also have ideological influence, contributing to a positive view of government responsibility for the public welfare. Put simply, the Townsend plan was advancing a democratic understanding of citizens' entitlements. By contrast, most New Deal programs were discriminatory, offering more to those who needed less, by excluding the great majority of people of color and white women.

Although the Townsend plan would have been redistributive across class, sex, and race lines and could thus be categorized as a left or progressive plan, it was also redistributive along age lines, and this was problematic. It called for transferring massive resources from young and middle-aged adults to older ones. One opponent calculated that it would give half the national income to one-eleventh of the population.[29] A historian recently estimated that a quarter of U.S. GDP would move from those under sixty to the elderly.[30] Either figure confirms the plan's unfairness toward younger people and their needs. Townsenders countered with a moral argument: "We supported our children in youth, is it not right and just that in old age we shall be taken care of by youth?"[31] This sentiment, consistent with traditional family values, brought in socially conservative supporters.

Dr. Townsend's Socialist Party history, during a period of the party's strength, must surely have influenced his concern to help the needy. Nevertheless he took care to dissociate his plan from socialism. He frequently insisted that the plan did not undercut the profit system "or any part of the present administration of business."[32] In fact, he argued that the program would prevent a popular turn toward socialism or communism by making capitalism less vulnerable to challenge during this and future economic depressions. And despite his rhetorical identification with down-home people of modest means, Townsend, like the Klan, expressed no criticism of corporate or financial wealth.[33] Nevertheless, the Townsend movement implicitly rejected hegemonic laissez-faire understandings of how an economy should function and maintained an older, historical view of what an ethical capitalism should be and do: offer help to economic victims, especially a fragile cohort with a disproportionate need for medical help.[34] Movement propaganda defended capitalism as a bulwark against socialism and communism, but its pension plan looked, however inadvertently, toward a social democratic form of capitalism.

This political ambiguity made the plan seem inconsistent, even incoherent to its opponents. Yet it was a "masterly synthesis of conservatism and radicalism," in the words of one scholar.[35] Townsend supporters were not naïvely "falling for" this political fusion of left and right, as their opponents charged. While Townsenders were supporting an impossible means of financing the pensions, as opponents pointed out repeatedly in every conceivable medium, they might be classified as intuitive social democrats—believing, and hoping, that a rich capitalist country could become a welfare state. For some, that belief was more emotional than political, and few of them had a broad conception of a welfare state. But the critics' disdainful appraisal of Townsenders as fools was itself foolish. They were as educated and informed as any middle-class Americans.

ONCE DR. TOWNSEND saw the mass enthusiasm his venture had evoked, he began traveling widely to promote it. The movement spread exponentially throughout the country except in the southeastern states. The *New York Times* called its growth "spectacular." Politicians were dumbfounded.[36] By the end of 1934, Townsend headquarters claimed that the movement had over a thousand local clubs, three million active club members and fifteen million supporters. Those numbers were no doubt exaggerated; as with the KKK and many other movements, inflating the number of members served to create a bandwagon effect. By appearing powerful they increased their power. Contemporary journalists, both friendly and hostile, offered numbers more modest than those Townsend claimed but gigantic nonetheless: one thousand clubs with 150,000 members in 1934, four thousand clubs and half a million members in 1935, eight thousand clubs and two million active members in 1936. Cleveland alone had ninety clubs, Los Angeles two hundred.[37] The district around industrial Jamestown, New York, for example, had one hundred clubs by the fall of 1936.[38] And these figures do not include supporters who hadn't joined.

While anyone could join and everyone would be entitled to a pension in the Townsend plan, the movement's racial and religious composition was extremely homogeneous and almost identical with that of the Klan—white and Protestant, particularly evangelical. One writer commented that "one sees no foreign-looking faces."[39] There were a few exceptions. In one upstate New York industrial county, most votes for the Townsend/Democratic Party candidate came from immigrant voters, and one organizer pleaded for literature in Yiddish, Polish, and Italian.[40] But the national Townsend organization never crafted appeals

Townsend headquarters, Hardwick, Vermont, September 1936.

to immigrants, "ethnics," or Black Americans. There were a few African American clubs and a few integrated clubs, mostly in California—Los Angeles, Long Beach, Oakland, Stockton—but the overwhelming majority of clubs were 100 percent white.[41]

Townsend national leaders probably had little concern for elderly Black people or people of color in general. The demographics of southern California may have played a role here: in 1930 African Americans constituted only 1.4 percent of the state population. On the other hand, the state's population included tens of thousands of people of color who rarely appear in material by or about Townsend: 415,000 people of Hispanic origin, about 7 percent, and 169,000 of Asian origin, just under 3 percent.[42] No doubt the whole movement had not only a white but a Protestant evangelical appearance and discourse, and most nonwhite people in the western states had learned caution about entering unknown "white" spaces. Certainly the Townsend movement and its clubs did not attempt to recruit them.

As with the Klan, many Townsend movement members were businessmen and white-collar workers, with some professionals. Its demographics contrasted with the Klan's in several ways however—it had more big-city dwellers, more women, of course more gray hair, and fewer young and middle-aged people.[43] But while most active Townsenders were middle class, conceived broadly, that label meant something very different in the midst of an economic depression: the majority had probably experienced a sudden economic collapse rather than chronic deprivation.[44] Some West Coast members, especially the poorest ones, were refugees from the "dust bowl." But regions of chronic poverty, such as the southern states, did not produce many Townsend clubs. The universality of proposed pensions, which threatened to include African Americans, no doubt repelled many white southerners.[45] As a Jackson, Mississippi, newspaper editorialized, "The average Mississippian can't imagine himself chipping in to pay for able-bodied Negroes to sit around in idleness."[46]

Like the Ku Klux Klan in the previous decade, the Townsend movement produced large-scale events to demonstrate its size and draw in recruits. The doctor called on local organizers to hold simultaneous meetings throughout the country on Sunday, October 28, 1934, at one p.m. Pacific time. He seems to have intended the rallies to be held outdoors, because he specified a "sunny Sunday afternoon." (He could count on "sunny," I assume, because he lived in southern California.) Soon realizing, however, that the weather might not cooperate in colder climates, he instructed organizers to seek free use of a church or large auditorium.[47] Townsend and Clements boasted that these rallies would constitute "THE BIGGEST MASS MEETING EVER HELD IN ALL THE WORLD" and later claimed that 500,000 people attended seven hundred of the events[48]—likely exaggerated. The rallies built enthusiasm, solidarity, and optimism about the power of their movement, though they lacked the dramatic choreography of Ku Klux Klan spectacles.

The life of the movement, however, lay in its chapters. Dr. Townsend's Socialist Party experience had taught him that local groups where people connected personally would keep members involved. He also knew that movements thrive when members are asked to *do* something. (This understanding was basic also to Cesar Chavez's organizing, as we will see in chapter 6.). He created a system for forming local chapters, which he called "clubs," a word with connotations of enjoyment and friendly relations. Clubs would make coming to meetings attractive and enable recruiting new members through friendship networks; they were also an efficient way for headquarters to communicate with members. Often social movement activisms devolved over time into staff organizations—that is, organizations whose "members" are expected only to donate money and to learn about the organizations' doings through newsletters.* The Townsend movement never took that path, despite its large expenditures on staff.

But while members worked to recruit, to circulate petitions, and even to speak on behalf of the plan, they were not invited to participate in developing strategies or tactics. The organization was not democratic in any of its operations. Clubs received "constitutions" from Clements; headquarters appointed state managers, who then appointed nominating and credentialing committees. Headquarters sent agents to supervise, advise, and "trouble shoot" local groups. All tactical and strategic

---

* There are thousands of nonprofit staff organizations, but the key "successor" of the Townsend movement, AARP, can serve as exhibit A.

decisions came from headquarters. Members and clubs never received an accounting of the movement's revenues and expenditures. After Clements broke with Townsend in 1936, no other leader arose who might have been privy to the doctor's use of the movement's resources. At its best, the OARP corporation never established a stable chain of command or clarity about the authority of regional leaders.[49]

The Townsend movement's national convention in Chicago, on October 14, 1935, sought to present an image of democratic control of the movement but did not create even a facsimile. It drew seven thousand delegates from around the country, who traveled there by "hitchhiking, riding in trains, under trains." (I don't know if "under trains" was supposed to be humorous, or if some Townsend members did ride the rails, like hoboes, because they were broke and homeless.) The doctor arrived by air. Except for some singing, the delegates mainly listened to him, worshipfully, as if he were a California version of the wildly popular evangelist Aimee Semple McPherson (who was, by the way, a Klan supporter). The leadership sought to use the event to imply that members controlled the movement, but the conventions were no more democratic than the movement as a whole. They were tightly scripted, the credentialing committee could reject delegates it didn't approve, and there was no path for ideas to move from the rank-and-file to the leadership, no room for nominations or even suggestions from the floor. Attendees were limited to listening and testifying to the doctor's leadership. They unanimously endorsed every resolution presented.[50]

Townsend supporters' willingness to accept this undemocratic arrangement resulted in good part from his persona and style. He was nothing like academic economists, policy wonks, or Washington pols. His self-presentation was downright cornpone, with small-town charm. He liked to project himself as "simple," just as the KKK Imperial Wizard Hiram Evans liked to call himself "ordinary." The doctor's ideas were in some ways simple, but he was no simpleton as a movement builder. Without talking down to his audiences, he nevertheless presented his ideas and proposals clearly—a capacity that was part of his genius—though without nuance or mathematical accuracy. It would be absurd to suggest that Francis Townsend was a great moral leader at the level of Martin Luther King, Jr., but he was able to enunciate a vision of a good society that was appealing, however unrealistic and incoherent its content.

If the plan leaned left, the doctor's hopes for the clubs leaned right. Dr. Townsend imagined that clubs would replicate the community ambiance of early New England town meetings, reflecting his nostalgia for family farms and small towns.[51] The movement's texture and the atmosphere of the clubs were similarly conservative. That contradiction captures the ambiguity of his politics, ahistorical nostalgia combined with commitment to a welfare state.

ALSO LIKE the Ku Klux Klan, the Townsend movement was a business. Millions flocked to it because of the pension plan and the doctor's hokey charisma, but also because it offered them a chance to make a bit of money. Clements introduced the same recruitment-by-commission arrangement that had so ballooned the KKK. Previously an organizer for the Anti-Saloon League (like quite a few Klan organizers), he "hired" some three hundred organizers, aka recruiters, many of them also former Anti-Saloon League employees, some of them ministers.[52] There were no wages, only commissions: they earned 20 percent, or 2.5 cents, from every twelve cents that new members paid. One early organizer claimed that the doctor promised him "handfuls" of money from the work.[53]

At first the doctor worried about the opportunities for embezzlement created by the commission system, but his staff clung to the system because it was so cheap. Understandably, Townsenders appreciated the opportunity to earn in the midst of the still worsening Depression. Members felt even better because they were earning by bringing people into a just cause. Dr. Townsend defended the system by arguing that it freed the organization from having to solicit large donations from the rich. Recruitment by commission was more democratic, he said—it meant that the needy supported the movement themselves and would not be beholden to big money.[54] Yet the doctor also defended this approach with an argument that justified and flattered his personal leadership: "Townsend . . . is a Program of Proxy. . . . Thousands of the world's best people do not possess the high qualifications for personal leadership . . . yet they can partake in the program by letting their money become proxy for them. . . . Your dollars can become *you*."[55]

As the movement grew and multiplied its publications, staff, and mass events, its leaders continually sought more income, again using methods that resembled those of the KKK. Headquarters coordinated the clubs and formalized membership through procedures connected to its finances. Organizers responsible for particular congressional districts, known as "live wires," would initiate clubs. "Minor" clubs were to have a minimum of fifty members and pay $12.50 for a charter, while "major" clubs had to have a hundred members and pay twenty-five dollars for a charter. Dues, or "contributions" as they were called, seem to have varied not only over time but among different clubs, and this may account for the fact that different sources provide different figures. Yearly "memberships" cost ten to twelve cents a year early on, gradually increasing to fifty cents, and members had to purchase copies of the Townsend plan booklet. To this clubs added their own levies; in Wisconsin, for example, yearly dues began at twenty-five cents in 1934 and rose to fifty cents in 1937, then went up to two dollars toward the end of the decade. Clubs were supposed to send an additional ten cents per member per month to national headquarters "as a gift." Still, Townsend was much cheaper than the KKK: its dues were far lower, its members were not required to purchase uniforms, and its leaders' profiteering was minimal compared to what went on in the Klan.

Acknowledging that unemployed and "penniless" people could not pay, a category of "associates" allowed them to participate without paying dues, and within the clubs they were likely treated as full members. Some clubs established sliding scales through which employed members paid more than the unemployed,[56] an indication of group solidarity, club intimacy, and/or collectivist political leanings. But headquarters' search for ever more income led away from solidarity, establishing a hierarchy of membership, as the Klan had done. Membership in a Townsend National Legion of Honor cost one dollar a month. These "Legionnaires," who numbered eleven thousand by 1936, got their names printed in an honor roll in the *Townsend National Weekly*.[57] An even more prestigious membership category cost twenty-five dollars.

A Friend In Need

Like the KKK, the Townsend organization also profited by sell-ing things and giving members a chance to earn money as salespeople. Members could sell movement literature and paraphernalia on com-mission, earning a penny for each book, pamphlet, or button sold; they could buy Townsend newspapers for two cents each and sell them for five cents. Soon there were Townsend buttons, badges, banners, post-ers, pictures and busts of Dr. Townsend, office supplies, calendars, even tire covers. The *Townsend National Weekly* brought in money by selling ads for tonics, balms, and other products that might attract the elderly.[58] Merchants were asked, or coerced, to buy and display Townsend plac-ards in their windows. Then headquarters imposed monetary quotas on individual clubs, requiring an additional ten-cent contribution per member. They even tried demanding one dollar from every attendee at a mass meeting.[59] Townsend lecturers also brought in money. They had to be licensed by the leadership and were allowed keep a percentage of the fees, but a significant proportion went to the OARP treasury. Head-quarters announced revenue of $686,803 as of the end of 1935.[60]

Townsend's fundraising practices appeared unseemly to critics who thought devotion to a "cause" should require volunteering. Liberals denounced the commission system on the grounds that it created members who were unprincipled, often with little understanding of the project, let alone commitment to it. This was true enough, but the charges ignored the problems of grassroots fundraising. Townsend was not a movement of the privileged aiming to help the nonprivileged, like Hull-House, for example. It was a self-help movement, in all senses of that word.

With this massive flow of money, allegations of corruption arose amid intraleadership conflict. Townsend's publicity director alleged that the doctor, who was broke when he began the movement, now lived in a luxurious apartment, owned "a beautiful Lincoln Car," wore clothes of "the finest weave," and stayed "at the finest hotels and uses airplanes almost exclusively." He also charged that fees for lectures and radio talks, often $150 to $400 apiece, went not into the OARP treasury but into Dr. Townsend's safe-deposit box in a Washington, D.C., hotel. He called the whole movement a "pocket-lining scheme."

The doctor called the allegations a libel and blamed Clements, who had never been strongly committed to the cause, for whatever profiteering was going on.[61] Although the doctor took a relatively small salary, it was sweetened by unlimited reimbursement for "personal and family expenses." Four relatives of Clements and Townsend also drew salaries.[62] At least one arrangement was completely dishonest: members were led to believe that the *Townsend Weekly*—a sixteen-page tabloid that netted $2,000 a week by late 1935[63]—was owned by the OARP nonprofit when in fact it was the property of Prosperity Publishing, a for-profit business incorporated by the doctor, Clements, and one other man. Whatever the truth, Townsend movement money was doubtless collected and spent with a complete lack of transparency and accountability. It was a corporation in which members were not stockholders.

THE DOCTOR'S original plan for pressuring Congress was amateurish. Elderly people would be invited, through the press and radio, to polling places where they would sign petitions; meanwhile a census of people over sixty would be taken. Dr. Townsend boasted that such a campaign would convince Congress to act before its next session. But another distinctly nonamateur tactic reflected his Socialist Party lessons: requiring members to do more than sign petitions, attend rallies, pay dues, and buy the newsletters and trinkets.[64] The most experienced organizers consider this foundational.

Several requirements kept club members active. A club was to field four officers (president, vice-president, secretary, and treasurer), an advisory committee, and multiple other committees and committee chairs, so that each club could have as many as twenty-four elected leaders. This proliferation of offices enlarged the number of members with titles and responsibilities, which in turn increased their investment in the movement. (With the same intent, the Klan also prescribed numerous titled positions in each klavern.) Officers often had or developed connections to other organizations and thus attracted members. Above the club level, members could be elected to district boards or councils, state and regional councils, and the national advisory council. One scholar noted that these arrangements could build grassroots leadership, "an opportunity for thousands of people to give vent to leadership abilities that had been lying dormant."[65]

Once there were clubs, there had to be meetings, and historian Steven Burg's close study of a small-town Wisconsin club illuminates how they operated. Meetings required places to hold them. These locations had to be available frequently, because weekly meetings were an important aspect of the movement's success. When the clubs attracted large numbers, finding space was not easy, producing a circular effect: meeting discussions often consisted of brainstorming about places to hold future meetings. Few Townsend clubs could afford their own. Los Angeles was one exception—with fifteen thousand in its "club" and *daily* meetings that attracted hundreds, it rented an old opera house. A few other large southern California clubs purchased halls, which required raising money beyond standard dues. In La Habra, a town in Orange County, California, the club bought a building on the installment plan for $6,000, paying forty dollars per month. Some clubs were able to use public spaces for lectures and larger meetings while others had to rent them, which also required raising money.[66]

Public spaces had an additional advantage: they probably made it easier to attract new people, who might have been hesitant to come to the home of a stranger. This problem could also become an advantage, however, because the need for money and space required reaching out to neighbors and community organizations. The search for spaces served simultaneously to publicize the movement through churches, schools, public libraries, Labor Temples, and fraternal orders. A Portland, Oregon, club, for example, met in the Odd Fellows Hall.[67]

Furnishing a space also took work, but it built the movement in other ways. In the La Habra space, the furniture reflected the members' desire for sociability: they brought in not only dozens of folding chairs but also overstuffed upholstered chairs, rockers, a davenport, and a piano.[68] Members did not conceive of the clubs' purpose as limited to official Townsend business. Clubs typically came together out of existing social networks—friends, relatives, neighbors, workmates, and networks among members of the same church, for example—but also brought in loners. Club socializing was particularly valuable to the many elderly people who lived alone. Once they joined and experienced discussions of the pension plan and its progress in amassing support, they could enjoy feeling politically engaged and efficacious.

That Townsend chapters were called "clubs"—quite possibly a conscious decision by the doctor—signaled a welcome to those unaccustomed to political activism. A "club" was less intimidating than a "chapter" or an "organization" might have been. Still, Townsenders were already involved in churches, fraternal or sororal societies, temperance organizations, and other groups. It is of course possible that reading or hearing about the campaign for pensions would be enough to make someone seek out a local club and arrive at a small meeting without knowing anyone else there. But for the most part, Townsend, like most social movements, spread through preexisting social connections. Recruitment often follows the sinews of friendships.

A club meeting could easily be mistaken for an evangelical revivalist gathering. Many Los Angeles members were accustomed to this style of performance, having thrilled to the fervid preaching of Aimee Semple McPherson, arguably the most charismatic evangelical preacher of the period. Evangelicals, as in the Ku Klux Klan, were disproportionately numerous in the Townsend movement, especially in smaller towns.*

---

* No scholar has found enough Townsend membership lists to show the religious identification of rank-and-file Townsenders, so we have no accurate count on this question.

156 / SEVEN SOCIAL MOVEMENTS

The doctor described his constituency as those who "believe in the Bible, believe in God, cheer when the flag passes by, the Bible Belt solid Americans."[69] Arthur Schlesinger, Jr., viewed the whole movement less as political than as a revival of "old time religion."[70] Many Townsend members had conservative, illiberal views on issues other than pensions. In Los Angeles, many listened to radio evangelist Robert Shuler's sensationalist talks about how vice was threatening American values. He condemned blacks, Catholics, and Jews, as well as the president of the University of Southern California for permitting the teaching of evolution. He also frequently lauded the Klan—"as sweet music as my ears have ever heard"—and called it the only hope to save the city from liberals and blacks.[71]

Townsend club meetings and large gatherings were often evangelical in style and content.[72] Although racial or ethnic identity was never a prominent theme in Townsend literature, the Prohibitionist, hymn-singing culture of the movement conveyed the message that this was a movement of white native-born "real" Americans, or "100% Americans" as the KKK called them. As the historian William Leuchtenburg put it vividly, the "meetings featured frequent denunciations of cigarettes, lipstick, necking, and other signs of urban depravity." After all, Townsend propaganda promised that the pensions would stop young people from "spending their time in profligate pursuit of sex and liquor."[73] The *Townsend National Weekly* often promoted Prohibition, and Townsend supporters continued to support Prohibition well after its repeal. Townsend social functions were in theory dry, though we should not assume that all the clubs observed this rule. The evangelical culture was also a function of how often news of the movement spread through white Protestant churches and fraternal orders. Meetings began and ended with Protestant prayers and hymn singing. A Townsend convention "was interrupted," a *Harper's* article reported, "by frequent outbursts of song, and speakers were continually drowned out by 'amens,'" after which they all sang "Onward Christian Soldiers."[74]

Townsend clubs were supposed to follow a script prescribed by the national headquarters, though Steve Burg's research suggests that they were less rigorous in sticking to the script and rituals than were KKK klaverns. Here is a description of one meeting in Holcombe, a small town in northern Wisconsin: The club met at first in the Odd Fellows Hall, which charged them fifty cents per meeting. Later, they secured the town hall for meetings, rent free except for a one-dollar cleaning fee after a large event.[75] (The use of a town facility suggests that a Townsend club could be a recognized town activity and could communicate that the movement was open to all.) Several dozen showed up, and the meeting began by the singing of the first and last verses of "America the Beautiful," then reciting the Pledge of Allegiance. Then everyone recited the Townsend pledge, swearing allegiance not only to Townsend goals but also to "Dr. Francis E. Townsend, to its leaders, and to all loyal coworkers; and [I] rededicate myself to maintain the democratic spirit and form of government in America."[76] The secretary-treasurer then read the minutes of the previous meeting and gave a financial report; the club president, a sixty-seven-year-old retired railroad night watchman, read aloud from the *Townsend Weekly*; typically, it carried articles about the plan and the movement's activities, though it included occasional comments on Prohibition, Communism, or another contemporary issue. (Reading aloud might suggest that not everyone present had paid for their own copy of the newsletter.)

Singing continued at various points in a meeting, often of traditional Protestant hymns with new words. For example: "Onward Townsend Soldiers / Forward to the Fight / Into Bloodless battle / For our Human right." (Associating his campaign with the concept of human rights was characteristic of the doctor's rhetoric and his progressive political background.) Finally an "orchestra"—perhaps what we would call a band—played as the members socialized and danced. Most meetings featured at least one performance and/or participatory activity—a sing-along, a dramatic reading, a skit, a piano recital, a minstrel show, even tap dancing. In Eugene, Oregon, for example, ten women formed the Townsend High-Headed Harmonica Band and performed wearing "ornate plumed fezzes." Some elderly people seemed to harbor desires to perform, and the conviviality of meetings overcame whatever bashfulness members retained. Some Townsend performers, individuals or groups, gained enough confidence and reputation that they began performing for other clubs or on public occasions. In Cleveland, a Townsend leader reported that he had so many requests to perform, he could not find venues for them.[77] At a time of such economic deprivation, this cheap entertainment was a gift.

Townsend headquarters provided scripts for funerals, which were more frequent than those of the Klan, for obvious reasons. The *Townsend Song Book* published a detailed script for a memorial service, also like the Klan. It prescribed placing a sprig of evergreen and a white carnation on the body, symbolizing "purity of thought and purpose," and concluded with this prayer: "And grant, we pray thee, that we may be inspired with renewed courage and hope to press onward, doing the things s/he would have done, until we meet with her/him again in the Great Beyond."[78] (It is striking that the songbook did not use the male pronoun as universal, perhaps because women were typically the majority of the elderly members.)

Much of a Holcombe club meeting was freewheeling and ad hoc— the group was not only called a "club" but behaved like a club. After the Pledge of Allegiance, the meeting was turned over to the chair of the entertainment committee who was, as one might expect, a woman—a fifty-nine-year-old housewife and mother of four. She introduced, first, the club's "Kitchen Band," who made music with kitchen utensils (probably including washboards, but the minutes did not list them). Then it was time for a "silent wedding," a political skit, marrying Mr. Townsend Plan to Miss New Deal.* This gendered language—unlikely to have been unique to this club—associates the doctor with masculinity, with a feminine New Deal wife. The Holcombe club clearly did not conform to the doctor's hostility to the New Deal, suggesting a degree of club autonomy, or perhaps they did not pay close attention to his political views.

Women seem to have orchestrated much of the meetings' content, which may have increased their creativity. Married couples typically joined together, but the clubs also included more single women than single men, in part because women's life expectancies exceeded men's.[79] At the national level, women were relatively invisible, as they were rarely elected officers or even mentioned in Townsend publications. Only later, in a gendered pattern common within organizations, as the movement declined and lost influence, did women gain more authority within it, to the extent that the editor of the *Townsend National Weekly* complained that it has become a "pie baking movement."[80]

---

* The Townsend–New Deal wedding happened at other clubs as well.

In the clubs, however, women were always active contributors, and some chapters developed women's "auxiliaries" which afforded them autonomy in their activities. Townsend women often promoted the cause through traditional female skills. Women's auxiliaries created knitting and sewing circles. Women of the Mitchell, South Dakota, club produced a large quilt of eighty-one squares—probably contributed by eighty-one women—honoring the plan.[81] One Oregon auxiliary created uniforms for themselves and wore them in separate women's marches. Women baked, made candy, and crafted needlework items to sell. They maintained informal lending libraries and kept scrapbooks of clippings. Clubs typically assumed that women would organize fundraising events, such as bazaars, and do clerical work, such as maintaining files.[82] As in the Klan, clubs also provided neighborly support, organized primarily by women. They collected money to help members with medical and burial expenses. They visited the sick and the disabled, and they cooked and delivered food to those in need, practices common in churches and other organizations that included women. Larger clubs, where members did not all know each other, often took responsibility for integrating people, holding "mixers" and playing get-acquainted games, entertainments likely produced by women. But there were also less conventional women's activities, such as a Women's Drill Corps, whose marches in striking uniforms contributed color to the national conventions—and resembled the Women's KKK.

Many clubs considered whole families to be members. In Washington State, a campaign provided members with "Every Family a Townsend Family" window signs.[83] Like the Klan, Oregon Townsenders created a youth association and held a picnic every few weeks—when weather allowed, this being rainy Oregon—organized and staffed by women. Their Fourth of July patriotic parades and celebrations often featured speakers along with fun and games. An August 1935 Chautauqua lasted three days and filled the local papers for several days.* These events typically featured dance bands, skits, horseshoe pitching, boxing

---

* Chautauquas arose from an adult education movement that began when Sunday school teachers organized family summer camps, combining entertainment and celebration with educational speeches.

and wrestling contests, and races for children and elders—again, like KKK affairs. There were races for children and for those "over sixty," suggesting the presence of supporters in between those ages.* The festivals always featured plentiful food.

Events like these could easily attract five thousand people or more. A picnic at Jantzen Beach amusement park in Portland drew 35,000, and a fifteen-year-old girl, said to be the youngest Townsender, was crowned "Goddess of Liberty" and led a parade through downtown Portland.[84] An Oregon Chautauqua chose a "Townsendite queen" from among forty-five contestants.[85] To a May 1935 extravaganza at Ben Lomond state park, just north of Santa Cruz, an estimated eight thousand automobiles and specially chartered excursion trains from a number of cities brought in some 42,000 celebrants. For thirty-five cents, you could get barbecued beef, salad, beans, and a "bottomless" cup of coffee. As there was no alcohol, one observer noted, there was "no rowdyism, no vulgarity."[86]

Townsend clubs also offered education, which often stimulated action. Steve Burg called the clubs "schoolrooms."[87] Reading aloud from Townsend publications might lead to reports on political developments and serious discussion.† Portland club members heard reports on conditions at an old-age home, on various New Deal officials, and once on Bernard Baruch.[88] Discussions improved members' articulateness and confidence, though older people, especially women, are often less timid than the young about speaking, even in a large gathering. Like consciousness-raising in the women's liberation movement, individual stories of how people had fallen on hard times, sharing the difficulties and insults of old age and meager budgets, might engender discussions of the cause of these problems. (Such discussions were standard in unemployed movement groups, as we will see in chapter 4.)

Discussions might lead to proposals. One observer found that "rarely was there a meeting when a resolution to support or censure

---

* Specifying "over 60" points to the fact that life expectancy was shorter and good health uncommon in the 1930s.

† In this respect, Townsend differed entirely from the Klan, while it resembled the unemployed movement meetings discussed in chapter 4.

something or somebody was not passed."[89] Members received petitions for collecting signatures, and in 1936 a "Townsend Caravan," consisting of thirty-seven cars and ten trucks, carried an alleged ten million petitions to Congress. The petitions came not only with detailed instructions but also with scripts for defending the plan to potential signers: "Much effort will be put forth by the opposition to confuse, to discourage and to put fear in the minds of the people. . . . Our plan is equitable, practical, American ideals. . . . [It] creates full employment . . . protects all citizens, including war veterans." Headquarters assigned to each club quotas for letters to the editor, so members might also have developed writing skills.[90] Because Townsend members were mostly not employed, they could do more work for their movement than could younger people.

Training lecturers was not only an educational project but also a central recruitment tactic. They had to be "licensed" by national headquarters, but there were hundreds despite this requirement. By February 1935, for example, a Cleveland club had produced sixteen speakers who were busy every day of the week; a Minneapolis bureau offered forty speakers. Some Townsend lecturers were ministers, experienced in delivering sermon, as in the KKK, but many gave speeches for the first time in their lives. So headquarters provided help. A Townsend speakers' manual provided detailed instructions about how to draw an audience, even about how the ushers should collect contributions.[91] But a speaker also had to be able to answer questions and counter opponents' arguments. The manual contained scripts, graphs, and charts showing the concentration of wealth, average per capita income, and statistics demonstrating what the Townsend plan would accomplish. The speaker's manual, one historian wrote, was "adroit enough to arouse the professional envy of the most experienced propagandists. . . . [It was] the last word in high-pressure salesmanship."[92]

Despite the adulation of the doctor, dissent appeared in the clubs. Some questioned how leaders were using members' dues. Some clubs fought for and even won considerable autonomy from the national leadership. Oregon clubs hired their own lobbyist to work at the state capitol and published their own paper, the *Educator*. A man sent by headquarters to discipline the Oregon clubs—for example, by trying to control who could be a Townsend speaker—failed totally; the *Oregonian* newspaper condemned him as a dictator. Large clubs were more likely to aim for autonomy, but the national headquarters was more dependent on revenue from these larger clubs and was therefore more determined to squelch these mini-rebellions. In Oregon, for example, a wealthy local leader led dissenters into a new group, labeled, significantly, Townsendites Inc.[93]

In 1938–39 the California clubs succeeded in forcing headquarters to allow clubs to elect councils, which in turn chose a district advisory council, which in turn elected a state advisory council, and so on up to a national council. Yet these sparks of independence remained local, never coalescing into a national challenge, and they never challenged Dr. Townsend himself. He addressed a letter to all Townsend members claiming "the authority vested in me at the Third National Convention . . . to interpret the Townsend Club Manual, and to *waive any of its provisions*" (emphasis in the original).[94] None of this seemed to tarnish his status as sage.

LIKE MANY social movements seeking legislation, the Townsend movement engaged in lobbying. Like the KKK of the previous decade, it could threaten politicians who understood the size of its popular support, and many politicians in both parties feared Townsenders' displeasure.* When the U.S. House of Representatives considered a Townsend bill in 1934, nearly two hundred congressmen declined to cast a vote.[95] Many who expressed support for the plan did so out of fear that not doing so could get them defeated. The *New York Times* estimated that the Townsend movement was powerful enough to unseat seventy-three congressmen.[96] Members flooded politicians with resolutions, often presented in person by delegations, and in a few states they got results. In 1935 the California State Assembly urged Congress to pass the Townsend plan by a vote of 58 to 17, though it barely squeaked

---

* This support from politicians in both parties was unsurprising at the time, when party realignment was still in process; and this bipartisan support recapitulated that for the KKK in the previous decade.

by the California Senate with a vote of 21 to 19. Townsend electoral strength in California was overwhelming: from 1936 to 1950, eighty percent of Townsend-endorsed candidates won their seats.[97] Nationally, 147 Townsend-endorsed candidates won public office in 1938, including ninety Republicans and many "dry" candidates angry at the repeal of Prohibition—thus constituting a direct threat to FDR.

Still, many other factors may have had equal or greater influence on politicians, and fear of Townsend did not necessarily translate into action.[98] But politicians often have incentives to deny being influenced by social movements. Although politics operate in a universe of many influences, difficult to disentangle, a useful indicator of a social movement's significance is the response of its opponents. The Townsend movement drew condemnations so strong that, in hindsight, they appear panicky.

Most of the mainstream press, even in California, issued strident denunciations. The *San Francisco Chronicle* protested "the vulgar plane of figures, the whole occult mystery of the scheme." The *Los Angeles Times*: "High taxes and new taxes never have done other than act as a brake on business." In a front-page story, *Newsweek* warned that "radical schemes" could jeopardize more moderate social insurance. Other periodicals offered the standard conservative claim that handouts make people lazy. The *New York Times* asked, "Why should anybody work?"[99] Relatedly, right-wing critics charged that the plan would destroy business and property.[100] Major corporations and business interests—the Chambers of Commerce, the railroads, the California Manufacturers Association, and Associated Farmers (the group that would go all out, three decades later, to destroy farmworker organizing efforts)—funded attacks on Townsend. So did most academic economists.

Alarm over the Townsend movement saturated the Roosevelt administration, and its policy planners went all out all to fight it. University of Wisconsin economist Edwin Witte, often called the father of the Social Security Act, feared that "Townsendites will decide the next [1936] presidential election." He kept a running log of congressional support for the Townsend plan and other "radical pension proposals." His notebook on the plan recorded every conceivable argument that could be used against it and encouraged a letter-writing campaign against it. Pulling strings, he tried to convince the U.S. Postal Service to indict Townsend leaders for fraud because they solicited donations and charged for their literature.[101] This did not happen, but others asked the Post Office to monitor and count the thousands of letters to Congress and the president, and the FBI to dig up any dirt it could find on Dr. Townsend himself.[102] Congress organized multiple hearings on old-age pensions with an agenda and a slew of witnesses designed to undercut Townsend's popularity.[103] By droning on about the cost of the plan, they were operating a sleight-of-hand maneuver, hoping to draw the public eye away from the stipends it promised.

Progressives also condemned, and feared, the movement. The Twentieth Century Fund and the future Oregon senator Richard L. Neuberger rushed into print denouncing it, as did the well-known writer and editor of the socialist journal *Common Sense* Selden Rodman.[104] Social work leaders organized "Golden Age" clubs for the express purpose of countering the Townsend clubs.[105] The left-wing Workers Alliance (discussed in chapter 4) produced its own "$60 at 60" plan to compete with both the Townsend plan and Social Security and warned that "the drive for adequate social security . . . is so tremendous, that, unless the Congress can meet this demand in a responsible manner, this movement may lead into unhealthy channels."[106]

The AFL, for its part, called the plan a hoax.[107] Writing for the Socialist Party, Harry Laidler laid out a detailed analysis and critique of the plan.[108] Norman Thomas, speaking to 4,500 delegates and ten thousand onlookers at the Townsend movement's 1936 national convention, called it a quack remedy, "the hallucination of simpletons," and warned that it would "divert the masses and waste their energy in seeking the pot of gold at the end of the rainbow instead of organizing for the capture of power." (When the audience heckled him, he responded graciously, with the skill of an experienced outsider to mainstream politics: "All right . . . I am glad to know what you think . . . I have no reproaches. . . . I am talking frankly and you are talking back.")[109] The Communist Party pushed its own Lundeen bill, a far superior alternative not only to the Townsend plan but also to the Social Security Act. Not only denouncing the regressive nature of the sales tax, the party called Dr. Townsend a quack and a fakir, then went on—in its tone-deaf approach—to insist that Townsend's goals could be achieved only with the end of capitalism.[110]

The doctor, however, made the criticism serve his cause with Populist rhetoric that matched his ill-fitting suits. Political and academic critics of the plan failed to register that the plan's simplicity, by contrast with economists' complex calculations, was to its supporters its best defense. The doctor drolly explained that economists could not accept the plan because it was "too simple for them."[111] " 'Experts' and 'economists' should be discounted in favor of common sense."[112] (Note the quotation marks around *experts* and *economists*.) The doctor condemned the policy wonks with heavy sarcasm:

> *You, in all your almighty power and wisdom . . . proclaiming to the world . . . that Dr. Townsend is a lunatic. . . . Being that you are all-wise and profound, would you mind telling the thirty million Townsend Club Members and also the thirty million potential Club Members just how you reach your super-intelligent conclusion?*[113]

He liked to call his supporters "the little people." Townsend literature railed against "college professors, economists, and newspaper writers," as well as "stock-market operators."[114] In playing the part of a "simple" man, he even insisted that he had never been a "top-flight" doctor.[115]

AND YET: politicians and experts on pensions also understood that Townsend pressure would help get their Social Security bill passed. Roosevelt himself warned that "the Congress can't stand the Pressure . . . nor can I face the country . . . unless we have a real old-age insurance system."[116] At Senate Finance Committee hearings in 1935, Dr. Townsend's testimony revealed his economic incompetence. Senators shredded his attempts to justify or even explain his proposal and his naïve equation likening the national economy to a family economy.[117] Yet senators were so afraid to let the plan be heard that they constantly interrupted him, and that led to a foolish mistake. Angry at the interruptions, he grew so angry that he walked out. The committee charged him with contempt of Congress. FDR, who understood Townsend's appeal far better than the legislators, sent him an *unsolicited* pardon, afraid that the charge would make him a martyr and energize the movement.[118]

Alarm within the Roosevelt administration continued even after passage of the Social Security Act in 1935. The law's old-age pensions produced no groundswell of approval because the stipends were puny compared to Townsend's and in any case would not begin until 1942.[119] In early 1936 the House voted again to investigate the movement in response to allegations of fraud. Initiated by Congressman Jasper Bell of Missouri—hardly disinterested since he had been repeatedly targeted for defeat by the Townsend organization—the investigation never proved fraud but did demonstrate the lack of transparency.[120] The hearings stigmatized the plan as atheistic and Communist, prefiguring the McCarthyist "investigations" of the next decade.[121]

Dr. Townsend counterattacked. Appealing to fiscal conservatives, he boasted that the plan was to be financed through a pay-as-you-go system; Social Security, by contrast, would collect taxes for several years before issuing any pensions.[122] And of course Social Security did little to relieve unemployment—it provided no economic stimulus. As one Townsend supporter wrote, "No doubt that security bill will help a man out of work but it will not help men to get employment. I doubt it will help mothers and children but hurt children's chances for work when older."[123] The anti-Roosevelt, anti–New Deal sentiment of many Townsenders extended beyond pension concerns. One Oregon speaker remarked, "Some people believe that recovery comes from destroying our basic crops. Well, I believe in the Townsend Plan." Called a "sucker" by an opponent, he replied, "A lot of suckers will hear about this if you don't vote for the Plan." Another asked sarcastically, "I suppose the system we've been under is a howling success."

Yet conservatives associated the Townsend plan *with* the New Deal. An editorial in Portland's conservative *Oregonian* newspaper charged that the plan was "founded on exactly the same error as that of the New Dealers when they began pumping government funds into the body politic."[124] Others lumped together Townsend and the New Deal as "Handout Statists."[125]

The opposition was both right and wrong. The plan was unworkable.

The pension was larger than the average family income; the transaction taxes wouldn't pay for the pension; the taxes would be regressive, like all sales taxes; the spend-within-a-month requirement would be impossible to enforce. These criticisms and many more were entirely justified. The plan was naïve and slapdash. But these critics avoided attacking its premises—that the elderly deserved a pension big enough to live on and that the pensions should be universal. Administratively, a universal grant would have lowered administrative costs radically, thus allowing pensions more generous than the Social Security system could afford. More important, the democratic nature of the Townsend plan, its inclusion of all Americans, would have avoided the discrimination against people of color and white women that was built into all the New Deal welfare state programs. It would have eroded the subjugation of African Americans. It would have improved the leverage of low-wage workers, including farmworkers. By providing older women with individual pensions, it would have undercut their financial dependence on husbands, with its attendant implications for gender and family structure. Similarly the impact on the low-wage labor market, providing pensions for the poor and, notably, people of color, would have been massive.

Moreover, Townsend was calling for a Keynesian approach to economic depression. The plan aligned, in principle, with what some New Deal economists advocated: reject austerity policy and instead increase government spending, which would boost consumer spending. The doctor's first Long Beach letter to the editor spoke of what is today called stimulus.[126] His diagnosis of the Depression—"a lack of buying power"—was not wrong. And despite his hostility to the New Deal, he was a proponent of public employment, arguing that government should "provide a job for every college graduate as soon as he steps out of school."[127] (Note the appeal here to the well-educated.)

But a Keynesian approach never consistently dominated in the Roosevelt administration, and its policies flip-flopped between spending and cutting (as chapter 4 will illustrate). This incoherent policy deserves at least part of the blame for the administration's failure to end the Depression (until wartime spending did so). The Townsend plan was unrealistic in its financing, in the initial organizational work it would require, and possibly in the size of the stipend it proposed. But its aim and its basic economic approach were reasonable, and a stimulus of this size might well have ameliorated the Depression.

THE TOWNSEND movement exemplifies the difficulty in categorizing ideas and strategies as left or right. Labeling it "populist" can be equally ambiguous, especially given today's application of the label to Far Right causes. The doctor was an 1890s Populist, member of a large movement protesting the exploitation of small grain and cotton farmers, coal miners, railroad workers, industrial workers, even of small businessmen by big financiers and corporations. His early letters to the editor denounced Wall Street's "total disregard for the public interests." In listing the benefits of old-age pensions, he argued that they would further the "socialistic attainments" of the United States.

Whatever *socialistic* meant to him at this time, however, it did not mean "anticapitalist." If the "human race is not to retrograde," he argued, only "adequate monetary reward" could guarantee individual effort and progress.[128] The country needed to revive capitalism, not restrain it.[129] He rejected criticism that the sales tax he was promoting was regressive, and he found no difficulty in allying with some extremely right-wing politicians. When he listed his American patriotic heroes, he often included Susan Anthony, possibly to appeal to women, who were probably a majority in the movement. But his gender politics were as conservative as the Roosevelt administration's. Townsend literature asserted, erroneously, that single women and divorced couples were products of the Depression and would disappear when prosperity returned; so did the Social Security Act's designers. Like the New Deal, the Townsend movement promoted old-age pensions as a way to help men reassume their rightful role as family heads.[130]

True, the Townsend plan promised unparalleled economic independence to women over sixty. But younger women were to remain, implicitly, the economic dependents of husbands, and single women would leave their jobs after marriage. The doctor assumed that the Depression had frustrated women's natural desire for full-time domesticity, motherhood, or grandmotherhood. The Townsend press featured expressions of heartache on behalf of women who were denied marriage because potential husbands could not support them. These were the hegemonic ideals at the time, and Townsend women likely shared them.

CRITICS' CONDESCENSION toward elders who supported the plan replicated just what the Townsenders were challenging. Intellectuals and experts constantly insulted them, calling them old coots, over the hill, too old to think straight, "poor dears" with "quavering hands," possessing a "total absence of knowledge of arithmetic."[131] The distinguished historian Arthur Schlesinger, Jr., called them "pathetic."[132] The diplomat Nicholas Roosevelt, a distant cousin of Theodore Roosevelt, accused them of believing in Santa Claus.[133] Both Left and Right argued that old people were "fodder for the devious, fantastic, and dangerous schemes of demagogues."[134] (Surely most of those taken in by demagogues were not elderly.) These claims resembled attacks on the 1920s KKK that relied on disparaging its adherents but not its bigotry. And the attacks may have had similar results, intensifying resentment of the arrogant belittlers of their movement. "As we were 'cock-eyed' and 'crazy' and 'fantastic' and 'impossible,'" Dr. Townsend wrote in his autobiography, "we also became more militant and more ardent in our effort."[135]

The insults were intended to malign the Townsend plan, but they also represented an ongoing cultural shift toward disdaining the elderly. From at least the beginning of the twentieth century, older people were increasingly represented as dependent, foolish, and frail mentally as well as physically. (The Townsend style might seem hokey to younger, big-city sophisticates, but whatever the proportion of dementia among its supporters, it was overstated.) Townsenders countered that the elderly were wise and judicious and that everyone would benefit from their experience.[136] They would be a force against corruption, would "break up the coercion of political machines whose object is excessive government expense for personal profit," and they would be the "distributor custodians" of the nation's wealth, trustees of the nation.[137] The Townsend plan would turn old age into a virtual honorary society. Many supporters envisioned, nostalgically, a return to a time of deference to the aged. Instead of being supported by their children, they were endowing the young. The movement was attempting to reverse assumptions about old age.

While the Townsend movement did not deny that the elderly were dependent, its message challenged the negative connotations of dependence.[138] Doing so was perhaps particularly important for men ashamed at their inability to support themselves and families. Few had entirely escaped the view that accepting "handouts" was a sign of personal failure. This problem became exponentially greater in the Depression, and it continues today. Women suffered less from this problem because they were not expected to earn, but both men and women wanted to be respected.[139] In attempting to make "dependence" on a pension honorable, the Townsend movement promoted, however inadvertently, a social democratic notion of citizenship and entitlement. Interviewers found that the title old people most liked was "retired citizens."[140]

Just as the Townsend threat pushed its left, liberal, and conservative opponents into a de facto alliance, the plan merged progressive and conservative values. This was possible because at root Dr. Townsend and many of his followers saw the world through moral and religious rather than political categories. As one supporter wrote in a Townsend propaganda book, "There are just two classes of people NOT working for the Townsend plan. One class is all those that do not know the plan . . . the other class is all those that are so ignorant, greedy, miserly, cussedly mean and ornery." Opponents were "potential murderers, whether they know it or not . . . killing thousands of poor, innocent babies . . . besides keeping millions in a half-starved, frozen and sickly condition."[141] But once "destitution and want" disappeared, the "sharp practices and greedy accumulation will disappear. Benevolence and kindly consideration for others will displace suspicion and avarice, brotherly love and tolerance will blossom into full flower and the genial sun of human happiness will dissipate the dark clouds of distrust and gloom and despair."[142]

Dr. Townsend was not above selling himself as a savior, sometimes with biblical language. For example, "God planted the seed of a divine thought in the soul of this humble and kindly man."[143] He also associated himself with patriotism, speaking of America's heroes from Washington and Jefferson through Lincoln and Theodore Roosevelt. It is not impossible that he thought to join them through a political campaign.

THE TOWNSEND movement had always combined social movement activism with electoral politics, and in 1936 the doctor joined a third-party presidential campaign. The decision had major negative consequences for the movement: it revealed his complete lack of accountability to his followers, diluted the movement's strength by sidelining the cause that had attracted millions, and allied him with racist demagogues.

The popular Huey Long, governor and then senator from Louisiana, began the campaign. His Share Our Wealth (SOW) program resembled Townsend's in fusing pensions with economic stimulus, and he thought to ride this program into the presidency. Roosevelt called him the second most dangerous man in America. (The first was General Douglas MacArthur.) H. L. Mencken described Long as "the gutsiest and goriest, loudest and lustiest, the deadliest and damndest orator ever heard on this or any other earth."[144] But Long was assassinated in 1935, and his assistant, Reverend Gerald L. K. Smith, later labeled "America's No. 1 Fascist," inherited Long's loyal base. He too could speak with preacher-like fervor, demanding "not a little old sow-belly, black-eyed pea job but a . . . beefsteak and gravy, Chevrolet, Ford in the garage . . . Thomas Jefferson, Jesus Christ, red, white and blue job for every man!"[145]

Smith then brought the Catholic radio star Father Charles Coughlin into his third-party venture, hoping to capture his following, estimated at 30 to 45 million. To those, Smith thought to add the millions of Townsend supporters, calculating that the doctor's naiveté would allow him to do so "at a cheap price."[146] The doctor calculated that the campaign would yield new supporters of the Townsend plan, but he was also motivated by his fury at Roosevelt and his mortifying treatment in the congressional hearing. That personal insult became a political one when the 1935 Social Security Act threatened to steal his mass support. His rage was intensified by the fact that Social Security offered elders so much less than his plan. (His anger at FDR had become so consuming that he refused to endorse a single

Democratic candidate in the elections, causing twelve members of his headquarters staff to resign in protest.)[147] He was gratified, even flattered, that Smith and Coughlin wanted him, so he joined the campaign, without consulting the membership or leaders of his movement. The *Townsend National Weekly* never even mentioned his support for the campaign.

The group of three formed the National Union Party (NUP), aiming to challenge both FDR and the Republican candidate Alf Landon in the 1936 election. They persuaded Long's friend William Lemke, a Republican congressman from North Dakota, to run on their ticket. Lemke and Dr. Townsend shared backgrounds in the upper midwestern Populist Party. Lemke had launched a Farmer-Labor party in North Dakota, continuing in that tradition: for example, the Frazier-Lemke Farm Bankruptcy Act of 1934 restricted banks' ability to foreclose on small farmers unable to make mortgage payments. But he soon soured on the New Deal in general and on Secretary of Agriculture Henry Wallace in particular, calling him "the greatest vandal in history" when he started a policy of destroying crops in order to support farmers' income.[148]

To win the doctor's support, the new party included the Townsend plan in its platform, and it was probably the biggest attraction. All three attended the second Townsend convention in 1936. Lemke drew only a small audience and was applauded only when he pledged support for the Townsend plan.[149] Smith delivered a fevered harangue, an indication of the organizers' poor political judgment, alleging that Roosevelt planned to rid the country of Santa Claus, Christmas trees, and the Easter bunny. This evoked ecstatic *amens!* but so did the cheers for a speaker who lauded FDR as a "golden-hearted patriot," an indication of Townsenders' overall political inconsistency.[150] The more "Hate Roosevelt" became the essence of the campaign, the more doomed it was.[151] In November, the vote was 882,000 for Lemke and twenty-eight million for Roosevelt.

The doctor proved to be a sheep among wolves. Smith and Coughlin cheered the growth of European fascism, and Coughlin would soon create his violently anti-Semitic Christian Front (discussed in chapter 2). The two were "populists" only in today's pejorative usage of that term, pasting a thin gloss of concern for the "little guy" onto Far Right politics. The doctor's decision to ally with them energized his critics' scorn, recapitulating their disdain for the elders who could become "fodder" for America's fascists; some even equated Dr. Townsend with Hitler and Mussolini. That was an exaggeration. Dr. Townsend did not anticipate and did not support Smith's and Coughlin's turn to fascism. In fact, he supported Henry Wallace's 1948 campaign for the presidency on the Progressive Party ticket, usually described as Communist-dominated.[152] The doctor was inconsistent and given to delusional hyperbole, but he was not a fascist. Rather, his willingness to join Smith and Coughlin points to the incoherent mix of progressive and conservative values that had characterized the movement all along. If his Protestant evangelical leanings made him comfortable—or at least not uncomfortable—with the virulent anti-Semitism of Coughlin and Smith, that fact matched the campaign's inability to put forward a consistently progressive politics.

The doctor's decision also reflected his failure to grasp the source of his own movement's strength: its ability to pressure politicians from outside the electoral system. Many members relished being political outsiders. Without ideological coherence, the movement was held together only by its support for pensions. Many clubs refused to endorse Lemke and insisted that the movement should remain nonpartisan, as the doctor had once promised. Oregon officers went so far as to hold a "high Townsend court" to try some club officers for acting as "tools of politicians" of poor repute.[153] Two Oregon clubs formed an internal group, "Townsend Minutemen"—named for the eighteenth-century elite militia prominent in the Revolutionary War—with the goal of democratizing the movement; even worrying, "Is the Townsend movement going fascist?"[154] But this overt opposition was the exception. The movement's heart and energy lay in the clubs, not the national organization. Accustomed to the doctor's eccentricity, Townsenders could ignore this decision and continue to be loyal to him—and to a movement they saw as theirs. He was by this time as much a figurehead as a leader.

Still, the Townsend movement was shrinking even before the doctor's Faustian alliance with Smith and Coughlin. As it became clear that the Townsend pension's chances of success were minuscule had convinced many members to support FDR and Social Security.[155] Simultaneously the movement's corruption was becoming evident, and members were restive about headquarters' unending demand for revenue. A few years later defense production produced an economic stimulus that "trickled down" to some extent. In 1942, as Social Security programs began to pay off, many more lost their passion for the Townsend movement.

SOCIAL WELFARE scholars attacked the Townsend plan and denied that it influenced Social Security, but they failed to see that the *plan* was not the source of influence. The influence came from the social movement, which transformed consciousness, spread the sense of entitlement to a pension, and activated the elderly. For the first time, old age became a *political* identity that continues to influence American politics.

Opponents sensitive to the country's political temperature, including President Roosevelt's closest advisers, granted that the Townsend movement helped pass the Social Security Act. Secretary of Labor Frances Perkins, a member of the committee drafting the Social Security bill, concluded that Townsend had made creating old-age insurance "politically almost essential" and forced a reluctant FDR to support adding old-age pensions to the bill. "One hardly realizes nowadays," she wrote, "how strong was the sentiment in favour of the Townsend Plan and other exotic schemes for giving the aged a weekly income. In some districts the Townsend Plan was the chief political issue, and men supporting it were elected to Congress. The pressure from its advocates was intense." Addressing a 1934 national conference of experts planning the legislation, Roosevelt had said "I do not know whether this is the time for any Federal legislation on old-age security." To this the Townsend organization reacted massively, inundating the White House with calls, letters, and telegrams. Perkins then phoned the president in Warm Springs and got him to issue a press release strongly supporting old-age pensions.[156]

The plan did have another sort of influence: the outlandish size of its promised pensions made initiatives that had once been considered unacceptable seem moderate.* Townsend made Social Security acceptable. Social Security could well have been defeated in Congress until Townsend made it a "safer" alternative. Moreover, by persuading millions that the government aid was honorable, Townsend strengthened support for other social welfare programs that would be included in the Social Security Act.

Moreover, radical proposals can improve "moderate" ones, and the Townsend plan did that for Social Security. Social Security's original stipends did not reach those who were eligible until several years after its passage, so it did nothing to aid recovery, and it excluded most people of color and most women—a majority of Americans—from benefits.[157] After Social Security passed, Townsend pressure forced Congress to accelerate the timetable to begin paying benefits in 1940 instead of 1942, extend benefits to individuals who had only recently retired and thus had not paid minimum contributions, cover additional categories of workers, and provide pensions to the widows and children of covered workers. The poor sister of Social Security old-age pensions, Old Age Assistance (OAA), also benefited from Townsend activism. OAA was and remains an inferior program: it requires states to match federal funding, so many received little or nothing at all due to states' stinginess and discrimination. But in 1939, in a move that journalists attributed to Townsend pressure, Congress increased the federal share of OAA stipends, even as Republicans were able to block much of FDR's agenda.

TRUE, THE movement that motivated these gains was deeply flawed. It was not democratic, and its autocratic leadership was by no means astute. Its finances were corrupt, though on a relatively petty scale, and most of its revenue did go to campaigning for pensions. Its proposal was economically and administratively impossible, even absurd. Its criticisms of Social Security did not include objections to its discriminatory

---

* That trajectory has been labeled the Overton Window, referring to the insight from libertarian thinker Joseph Overton that more radical proposals "drag" more modest ones toward greater ambition as to what is possible.

provisions. The movement never produced a clear answer to its critics or a more practicable version of the pension plan, let alone a coherent vision of a welfare state. Worse, Dr. Townsend tried to pull his movement into alliance with fascistic, racist demagogues. Most Townsenders did not follow these demagogues, but they did not rebuff their leader. This has often been a weakness in social movements in which a leader is so charismatic that followers become reluctant to challenge him (a phenomenon we will see again in chapter 6 on farmworker organizing).

That Townsend members did not denounce their leader's poor decisions, however, resulted not only from his status as guru but also because other aspects of the movement brought immediate rewards. Their participation brought them a pleasurable sociability, a sociability all the more enjoyable because members were campaigning to create a more equitable society. Townsend had created a way for them to be both beneficiaries and contributors, because they understood that old-age pensions would simultaneously strengthen the economy. Melding self-interest and altruism, they gained confidence and pride. They challenged the growing disdain for the elderly and constructed old age as a collective political identity and interest group. In crafting this new political identity they were becoming more active citizens. No doubt the elderly could never reclaim the respect they received in some traditional societies, but for a time they reveled in their political clout.[158]

The best part of the Townsend plan—its universality—was decisively defeated.[159] That defeat haunts the United States today. Social provision in the United States is both regressive (in that it provides more help to those who need it least) and stigmatizing (as in the negative connotations of "welfare" that arose after World War II). Today social provision—medical care, child welfare, education, for example—is under threat. It divides rather than unifies Americans.

Many Townsend members lived long enough to witness its impact on the politics of old age and the welfare of elderly Americans. Through a series of intermediate moves and organizations, the Depression-era movements for old-age pensions became AARP, formally established in 1958. Claiming thirty-eight million members as of 2021, it is the largest public-interest organization in the United States, the "800 pound gorilla" lobby.[160] (As I was writing this chapter, a huge AARP ad on the side of Washington, D.C., buses showed an older person looking through binoculars; it read, ELDERS ARE WATCHING.) These "elders" created a reversal in poverty demographics: during the Depression, the elderly were the poorest cohort; today the poorest by far are children.[161]

Townsend's achievements, like those of most social movements, transcend material gains. The clubs provided members with entertainment, companionship, support for those suffering the pains and ill health of old age, and political education. Conversations took on some of the features of 1970s feminist consciousness-raising: as members discussed their personal problems, they also discussed the socially constructed problems of aging—poverty, loneliness, disrespect—and found them remediable, just as women's movements showed that male dominance was remediable. Offering some of what houses of worship do, their rituals—the hymns, the pledges, the recitations—could be heartening and reassuring in the face of a cruel economic depression. The rituals created and cemented communities larger than families. Despite the hero-worshipping of Dr. Townsend, the clubs were relatively democratic. Without direction from above, members designed activities and programs—replicated today in senior centers—that made old age more enjoyable and healthier.

Members also "networked," sharing information about illness, medications, recipes, bargains, vacations, and events—topics vital to survival and social connection, despite the mockery of Townsend's enemies. They built camaraderie and provided mutual help. They turned even their money-raising into activities that fostered connection, organizing picnics, bake sales, yard sales, and more. These activities illustrate something important about social movements: that they command allegiance not only because members seek material benefits or social justice but also because they offer sociability, solidarity, and fun. They also raise participants' self-esteem, show them the potential power of social movement activism, and thereby make them better citizens.

4

SHAREHOLDERS IN RELIEF

The Unemployed Movement in the 1930s

Men lining up to register immediately after unemployment benefits begin, San Francisco, 1937. Photograph and caption by Dorothea Lange.

A new "institution" has arisen in America—the organization of the unemployed. These organizations ... have permeated the poorest and most amorphous groups in the American masses. ... A group two years ago nonexistent now plays a significant role in influencing the relief policy of municipality and state.

—NATHANIEL WEYL, ECONOMIST, AGRICULTURAL
ADJUSTMENT ADMINISTRATION, 1932[1]

We are talking to you, you men who have come here to throw out the furniture of unemployed workers. . . . You, too, are unemployed men who have had to take this job in order to eat. We don't blame you. You are one of us. We represent the Unemployed Council and last night we made a collection among the unemployed. We have enough money to pay you off. How much are you going to get for evicting an unemployed worker? Five dollars? Six dollars?

—ROSE CHERNIN, AT AN EVICTION PROTEST, BRONX, 1930S[2]

The black crowd swarmed around the officers and their cars. . . . One officer lost his head and drew his gun, leveling it at the crowd. Then a young fellow stepped out of the crowd and said, "You can't shoot all of us and I might as well die now as any time. All we want is to see that these people, our people, get back into their homes. We have no money, no jobs, and sometimes no food. We've got to live some place. . . ." The officer looked at the boy, at the crowd, and the crowd looked at him. No threats, no murmurs, no disorder; the crowd just looked at him. . . . The officer replaced his gun in his holster.

—SOCIOLOGIST HORACE CAYTON,
AT AN EVICTION PROTEST, CHICAGO, 1931[3]

The near-total collapse of the American economy in the 1930s left tens of millions of unemployed Americans facing hunger, homelessness, cold, social isolation, emotional depression, and relentless anxiety. By 1933 the national income had halved.* A quarter of the nation's labor force was unemployed, and in industries the figure was far worse—it was 90 percent in New York's garment industry. Ford Motor laid off two-thirds of its employees and cut wages for the rest by 50 percent. Millions who had once worked full

---

* A quick comparison: the GDP fell fifteen times further in the 1930s than in the 2008 recession.

time were now, at best, finding only part-time and occasional jobs. The value of stocks fell by 80 percent, so those who might have lived on savings or investments, such as retired people, often lost everything.[4] Millions of evictions—200,000 in New York City alone in 1930—made more millions homeless.[5] There is a romanticized and misleading literature about the two million "hobos," but it was no fun to sleep under bridges, in freight cars, haystacks, and ditches, to eat Johnson grass stalks and roots, wild onions, mustard greens, crawfish tails, and sour duckweed, and to beg grocery stores for overripe and damaged food. "Have you seen grown men cry?" one recalled.[6] Even less attention was paid to the many homeless women hidden behind the ranks of homeless men.

At the same time, the 1930s saw an explosion of social movement activism, most of it (excluding that of the fascist groups discussed in chapter 2) aimed not only at surviving but also at helping future generations gain a secure standard of living. Labor organizing almost doubled union membership, from 3.5 to 6 million. Less well known is the social movement of the unemployed. Ranging from local community barter projects to campaigns for emergency relief, unemployed activism made realistic what once seemed a utopian dream—long-term government support.

Some might assume that calamities like the Depression would inevitably produce mass protests. But the historical evidence shows the opposite: more often economic crises produce despair, passivity, and individual isolation.[7] The 1930s unemployed movement grew and became influential because of the devoted organizers who built it. There had been protests about unemployment earlier in the United States, but none had approached the two million participants in this one. That number represented at most only some 10 percent of the unemployed, but it is a big number for a protest movement (surpassed, of course, by the Ku Klux Klan's three to five million).[8]

Three leftist political parties led the unemployed movement: the Communist Party, the Socialist Party, and a group led by the radical minister A. J. Muste that morphed into a Trotskyist organization. It is the only movement discussed in this book that was led by the ideological left, and as such, it offers a look at how that leadership affected a social movement. Examining it yields surprises. The three Left parties insulted each other, disrupted each other's events, and condemned each other's ideologies—yet used the same strategies and tactics. All three hoped to guide this activism into a movement toward socialism, and all three found these hopes quashed. That failure arose, of course, from Americans' deeply individualist orientation, but also from a problem common in many social movements: the tension between helping people whose needs were urgent and building a movement for fundamental political and economic change.

This dilemma intersected with another—the tension between social movement activism and labor unions. When the federal government, especially through the Works Progress Administration (WPA), provided emergency relief in the form of jobs, the unemployed groups merged, forming the Workers Alliance. The Alliance soon functioned as a labor union, representing WPA workers in their dealings with their new employer, the government. As Alliance leaders focused on negotiating wages and working conditions, they neglected those who remained unemployed, a population far larger than that of WPA workers. The explosive growth of labor unions confirmed leaders' hope that an organized working class could lead the way to socialism, thereby confirming their focus on the employed.

Even before the WPA, the desperation of the unemployed forced organizers to prioritize assistance for the unemployed rather than structural change. As the German playwright Bertolt Brecht once wrote, "First feed the stomach, then talk right and wrong." Steve Nelson, a Communist Party (CP) organizer, summarized this shift away from trying to build a socialist movement "to what might be called a grievance approach . . . to raise demands for immediate federal assistance . . . a moratorium on mortgages . . . the need for national unemployment insurance." Even the most ideological leftists were helpless to alter that trajectory; they deserted anticapitalist organizing for "shepherding clients through red tape" in order to get food and rent money.[9] They could not focus on long-term goals because people joined the movement *in order* to get immediate help. One might say that the movement's leaders were overruled by its members, much as Hull-House's and the Phillis Wheatley Home's programs were refashioned by those they sought to help.

The movement's shift toward representing WPA workers disadvantaged not only the unemployed but all people of color and white women. Concerned that unemployment undercut men's self-esteem as breadwinners and family heads, federal aid sought to restore men to their "proper" place in the society and economy through massive jobs programs for men. Most women supported that goal, and many women benefited from jobs provided to their husbands, sons, and fathers; prioritizing jobs for men arose not from misogyny or "sexism"—a concept that did not exist at the time—but from hegemonic family values. People of color, both men and women, lost doubly: they suffered most from the Depression while they were disproportionately shortchanged by both unemployment relief and WPA jobs, especially in the South, where racism was most extreme. These inequalities weakened not only the unemployed movement but also the permanent welfare programs that emerged from the New Deal.

Another casualty of the Depression, inevitable but nevertheless regrettable, was the failure of cooperatives—community programs of barter, exchanging goods and services. Unable to provide for their members, most cooperatives disappeared once the Roosevelt administration created federal emergency relief in 1933. The cooperatives' vision of mutual help with democratic, grassroots control might have worked in smaller communities but could not provide for large and desperate populations.[10] Coop organizers had no choice but to join the unemployed organizations in agitating for federal help, which came with top-down, bureaucratic, and undemocratic management. A democratic approach to mutual aid was lost.

The unemployed movement ended when mass production of military matériel for World War II created millions of jobs. It might well have declined anyway. Most social movements are short-lived. The strongest movements, those with the largest constituencies, may be particularly fleeting because members are so dispersed. But the unemployed movement was by no means a failure. It helped millions of Americans when they most needed it. Moreover, through bringing the unemployed together, it dissipated, at least temporarily, the shame of poverty and contributed to an understanding that it was the economic system, not its victims, that needed fixing. Most important, unemployed activism built a more expansive understanding of government responsibility. These achievements were not permanent, and today's threats to drain the social safety net of resources remind us of the fluidity of political culture. But this new consciousness, like that engendered by the Townsend movement (discussed in chapter 3), helped bring about permanent New Deal programs, especially those in the Social Security Act.

COOPERATIVE "SELF-HELP"

Cooperative attempts to meet the crisis eventually involved as many as 1.3 million people in thirty states, the most numerous in California. Out of the "Hoovervilles"* of Oakland, for example, arose a fifteen-hundred-member mini-economy that operated a machine shop, a woodshop, a garage, a soap factory, a print shop, lumber mills, ranches, and more, distributing forty tons of food a week at peak. Santa Monica coop members worked at dairies in exchange for milk and cheese. Compton's forty-five different projects served 150,000 people. Los Angeles members, who included Japanese American farmers as well as other people of color, tended UCLA's experimental farm in exchange for fruit.[11]

Seattle hosted a particularly ambitious project. A network of unemployed men with backgrounds in the Communist Party (CP), the Socialist Party (SP), the Industrial Workers of the World union (IWW), and even the nineteenth-century Knights of Labor organized the Unemployed Citizens' League (UCL). With strong support from Seattle's labor unions, the UCL saw its membership grow to as many as 50,000, constituting a third of the voters in this city of about 365,000. Most UCL participants were far from radical. One observer described them as "staunch standpatters, established householders, flag wavers"—a

---

* *Hooverville* was a pejorative nickname for sites where homeless people lived, like today's proliferating tent encampments. The name reflected anger at President Herbert Hoover for doing so little to help Depression suffering, while indicating the growing belief that government had a responsibility to help.

sign that its program made sense to a large swath of the population. The majority were of the skilled working class, averaging an eighth-grade education, married with children.[12]

The UCL operated a complex barter system through which members could exchange goods and labor through neighborhood warehouses and accounting systems. It obtained 450 acres of farmland and set members to work growing fruits and vegetables for the community. Members also engaged in "chiseling," the polite term for begging, through a regularized system of requesting donations from merchants.[13]

Realizing that barter alone could not meet its members' needs, the UCL simultaneously sought municipal aid. It asked the city council for $1 million for public jobs, paying a minimum wage at the prevailing unskilled-labor rate, and with a rotating workforce so that each family head would be guaranteed one week's work per month. The city and county together provided only a small fraction of that—$50,000 for direct relief and $144,000 for jobs.[14] The city did, however, provide some seeds, sugar, canning supplies, and transportation for donated goods. The municipal utility, Seattle City Light, promised to continue electricity and gas service to those who could not pay their bills. The city also provided meeting places, such as public libraries, a valuable resource for any social movement. In those spaces, UCL locals could hold not only business and educational meetings but also dances, games, and other social activities. UCL locals became informal neighborhood centers, prefiguring those that soon developed in all the unemployed organizations.[15]

The UCL also moved into politics and endorsed a slate of candidates for the city council, all of whom won election. Gaining unprecedented political power, the UCL persuaded the mayor to create a district relief administration and to *let the UCL operate it.* The city turned over its community fund to the UCL, and its officers took the place of administrators in distributing help to the unemployed, both as straight cash relief and as jobs. If you needed help in Seattle in 1932, you went to the UCL.[16]

It was a radical experiment in democracy. First, it amounted to a *dual power* situation. A term usually applied to revolutionary situations, such as France in 1789 and Russia in 1917, it describes a situation in which a civic organization takes on some of the legitimacy and functions usually attached only to government. The UCL thus foreshadowed the San Francisco general strike of 1934, in which a labor union briefly took on governmental powers. The Socialist UCL leader Carl Brannin said, somewhat overoptimistically, that they were "building a society within a state [proving] that bankers and bosses are not needed."[17]

Second, the UCL was engaging in *prefigurative politics;* that is, it tried to be a microcosm of an ideal democratic society and economy. The cooperatives made giving and taking personal and visible, creating a we're-all-in-this-together sensibility that encouraged a democratic, communitarian vision of government. One leader called their group "the republic of the penniless."[18]

Third, the UCL aimed to be a *participatory democracy.* An ideal of the 1955–80 New Left (as we will see in chapter 7), the phrase describes an organizational structure in which every member participates in making decisions. In the UCL, this meant participating not only in making decisions about principles and policies but also in day-to-day administration of policies, so that members rather than professionals were dispensing relief.

These were experiments, their goals utopian. Providing help without insult or stigma required transforming *how* aid was delivered. Today, for example, some government aid programs, like Social Security old-age pensions and Medicare, are not stigmatizing, because they do not require proving one's worthiness. In the UCL's case, however, despite its democratic promise, conservative ideologies about who was "deserving" continued their hold. The age-old fear of "pauperism" resurfaced, with its charge that those receiving economic aid would lose the incentive to work and become "dependent," a precursor of the stigmatizing phrase "on welfare." UCL managers could not transcend the old "poor law" approach that began by insisting that the "deserving" must be not only destitute and without relatives who could support them, but also of "good character," not drinkers or sexually immoral. As a result, moralistic screening of those asking for aid reinforced assumptions that individual failings were responsible for their need. Invasive assessments also stripped potential recipients of privacy. As one recipient argued, " 'Home Visitors' or snoopers . . . are picked for their ability as snoopers and stool pigeons only. They ask you so damn many questions that there is nothing personal left to you anyway."[19] These moralistic standards not only led inevitably to biased decisions but also deepened the emotional depression and humiliation that the Depression was creating.[20]

The old stigmatizing charge of dependence was fundamentally gendered, expressed in the perspective that "dependence" was appropriate, natural, and not shameful for women, while it was stigmatizing for men.[21] That stigma would ultimately prove damaging to the struggles of the unemployed.

The UCL's participatory approach to public welfare was not practicable for larger populations; cooperatives could not meet the needs of the unemployed, and nearby farms could not produce enough to maintain urban populations. Cities and towns became bankrupt—by 1933 a thousand local governments had defaulted on their debts.[22] Only the federal government could meet the need. Luckily, in March 1933, the new president, Franklin Roosevelt, initiated federal relief. But it ended the promise of democratic control. The federal government relied on state, county, and municipal governments to administer relief, and their administrators engaged in victim-blaming, worsened by racial, ethnic, and gender bias and by vulnerability to pressure from powerful politicians and business leaders. So the unemployed organizations often had to face relief administrators in an adversarial manner in order to get help.

COMMUNISTS: UNEMPLOYED COUNCILS IN NEW YORK CITY AND THE SOUTH

American Communists created the first organizations of the unemployed. They believed that their strategy could both combat the Depression and build a socialist movement. A few had tried unemployed organizing well before the "crash," starting in 1921, when "most Americans were still celebrating Republican prosperity," in the historian Roy Rosenzweig's words.[23] In 1928, however, the American CP became captive to a Soviet-dictated Communist International (Comintern) strategy known as the "Third Period," in the hopes that it would be followed by the end of capitalism.* Demonstrating its ignorance of American conditions and consciousness, the Comintern ordered national CPs to denounce any organization or government policy that accommodated itself to capitalist relations.

This approach was hardly likely to gain support from workers. Communists heckled and disrupted meetings of other groups and, with staggering obliviousness, condemned demands that government help the needy—on the grounds that it would shore up capitalism! Relief programs, the CP insisted, were mere Band-Aids aimed at saving capitalism. The American CP established the Trade Union Unity League (TUUL) to rival existing unions; it might more accurately have been named the Disunity League. Only workers were worth organizing, it insisted, so it declined to organize women and the unemployed (whom it derogatively labeled *lumpen* proletarians).[24] In 1930 one New York City Communist group led a protest *against* a free employment agency that was operated by Tammany Hall.[25] The CP even condemned cooperatives as "collective picking in garbage cans"[26]—quite an insult, given that many people at the time *were* raiding garbage cans for food. In CP logic, alleviating people's distress deradicalized them, preventing them from recognizing that a capitalist government served only the ruling class. It labeled Seattle's UCL and other leftist groups "social fascist."[27]

Not all Communists followed orders, however. Many led or joined demonstrations demanding economic relief. Thousands stormed Cleveland's, Philadelphia's, and Los Angeles's relief agencies, where they were attacked with tear gas.[28] Soon a most unusual Communist leader emerged. Herbert Benjamin, once influenced by anarchism, now a Communist, had been organizing the unemployed since 1928, ignoring Comintern directives. Born Benjamin Grefenson into a working-class family in a small town in Illinois, he, like many Communists, took a new name to protect his family (and no doubt to make him appear

---

* In the Comintern's analysis, the "First Period," following World War I, was a time of a revolutionary upsurge and then defeat, leading to a "Second Period" of capitalist consolidation in the 1920s. The 1930s "Third Period" was to see the collapse of capitalism and mass working class radicalization.

more "American"). Now he was himself unemployed. "I came into the unemployed movement by reason of undernourishment," he wrote with droll humor.[29] His organizing prowess helped grow the CP—6,000 joined in 1930, and by 1935 it had 31,000 members, 90,000 in 1939. In 1932 a stunning 90 percent of new CP members and 60 percent of all members—were unemployed.[30] That proportion points to the party's weakness among employed workers.

CP organizers named their new organization the Unemployed Councils. "Councils" was a translation of the "soviets" of the 1917 Russian revolution, an indication of the CP's tone-deaf approach to American workers; when party leaders spoke at council demonstrations, they argued that defense of the USSR must be the top priority.[31] But in the three areas where the party organized most vigorously— New York, Chicago, and Alabama—ideology became a secondary concern.[32] While party rhetoric denounced the state as a tool of the ruling class, the councils were asking the state to provide federal unemployment insurance, a moratorium on evictions, and emergency relief. In his reports, Benjamin deployed the Communist jargon necessary to please his superiors, referring to "the toiling masses" and the "arrogant master class."[33] But read further, and one would encounter heterodox, even heretical thinking and practical suggestions for meeting people's survival needs.

Benjamin tried to create democratic practices within the Unemployed Councils, specifying that leaders must not impose policies on members, and that officers must be elected democratically among members. He produced a handbook that showed his detailed knowledge of the conditions of homelessness. About "flop houses"—an early version of today's homeless shelters—it emphasized the need for more aisle space between beds, as well as clean linen and towels, and condemned the insulting requirement that the sheltered population must awaken and hit the streets in the very early morning. (This requirement continues today in many big cities.) Following Benjamin's lead, many Communists encouraged demonstrations demanding government action. By rejecting Comintern instructions, they created greater legitimacy and respect for the Communist Party among the unemployed.

Local CP chapters set very low dues, initially five cents a month, and often skipped collecting dues altogether. At demonstrations they often solicited contributions of one penny. By 1932 there were Unemployed Councils in 340 cities and towns, Benjamin claimed; in 1933 he cited a membership of 250,000.[34] (He likely exaggerated those numbers, as did the KKK and Townsend movements, in part because of high turnover—many left as others joined.)

Benjamin finally succeeded in winning over the party leadership. The CP organized an International Unemployment Day demonstration for March 6, 1930, which attracted, they claimed, 1.25 million participants across the country, 50,000 in New York.[35] Party head William Z. Foster walked with the protesters and was arrested. The demonstrations' size alarmed government and business leaders. The New York City police force, including mounted cops, attacked the crowd in Union Square swinging nightsticks and blackjacks, pummeling men who had fallen, chasing and beating even those who were running away. (This account comes not from a leftist source but from the then-conservative *New York Times*.) The

Demonstrators from the Unemployed Councils gather in front of the White House, March 6, 1930.

demonstration brought results: the city government appropriated $1 million for relief jobs.[36]

Despite Benjamin's guidelines, Communist leadership in the Unemployed Councils was rarely democratic. He and his fellow organizer Israel Amter complained that CP organizers felt "responsible to the Party but have no responsibility to the masses."[37] Council organizers often made decisions without consulting members and maneuvered to win members' approval of what they had already decided—practices shared with the Townsend movement and likely with many centrally organized social movements. Party members assumed leadership positions without identifying themselves as Communists—in part an understandable adaptation to the much-exaggerated fear of Communism. True, these practices may have mattered less to the unemployed than did the material benefits that CP organizers could extract from relief administrators. But when the party exerted control, the result could be destructive. When the Harlem council elected leaders who were unacceptable to the CP hierarchy, it replaced them with orthodox party apparatchiks, leading to high turnover of those who joined the councils but could not tolerate authoritarian leadership.

Just as the Communists did not always obey Comintern orders, the Unemployed Councils did not always behave as the Communists wanted. The party's frequent denunciations of unauthorized demonstrations and slogans were largely fruitless.[38] Councils often cooperated with groups condemned by the CP, such as Seattle's UCL.[39] Everywhere the councils called for government action, particularly a jobs program and a moratorium on evictions. Local councils undermined CP control, even if unintentionally, by creating and fostering rank-and-file leaders. An organizer in southern Ohio reported apologetically to the party bigwigs that no Communists were elected to the executive committee.[40]

NEW YORK City's Unemployed Councils drew their largest following from African Americans and Jews of East European background, groups characterized by what the historian Robin D. G. Kelley has called "cultures of opposition."[41] The two populations typically organized separately—by preference and by working through preexisting community networks. This separation was so complete that some New York Council meetings were held in Yiddish! New York's sheer size and housing segregation meant that its councils were often community organizations. In fact, councils did best when they were neighborhood groups. Racial/religious homogeneity was not only a comfort factor but also an organizing asset: for example, many Jewish immigrant women saw the councils as an instance of the women's charitable associations they knew in the old country, just as African American councils built on traditions of civil rights and on community and church organizations. One can be sure, however, that Jewish council members were not free of racist assumptions about Blacks, who claimed that Harlem's Jewish store owners treated them disrespectfully.

Among both Jews and African Americans, women dominated the Unemployed Councils. A decade earlier, in 1923, Jewish women in or close to the Communist Party had organized the United Council of Working Class Women, mainly supporting men's activism by turning out picketers, preparing food for gatherings, and cleaning up after them. The Depression changed that. Interviewed decades later, Rose Nelson Raynes recalled that the Depression experience stimulated women to challenge the male dominance in progressive activism. "We felt we wanted to express ourselves, to learn to speak and act and the only way was through a women's council."[42]

Women's council members were soon confidently addressing crowds in demonstrations or picket lines. They organized boycotting and picketing of grocers they accused of overcharging.[43] Demanding that butchers lower their prices by 25 percent, they threatened those who did not comply. Women sometimes "jumped up on the tables in front of stores and tore down old price signs and put up new ones. . . . No store held out for more than five minutes after the picketers arrived." The CP's *Daily Worker* crowed that all the "stores between 129th street and 145th street, with the exception of L. Oppenheimer's . . . reduced prices 25%."[44]

The charismatic West Indian Bonita Williams took a key leadership role among Blacks. A poet, published often in the *Harlem Liberator*, she created a Harlem "flying squad" that created instant demonstrations, targeting evictions and price inflation. She had been drawn to the Communist Party by its energetic defense of the Scottsboro "boys," African Americans who had been framed in 1931 on rape charges.* The CP was the only white organization to do so, as plenty of African Americans knew. As Williams put it, "If they've got a movement like that . . . then this may be a good thing for me to get into to free my people."[45] Police charged into their demonstrations, including one protesting the Scottsboro frame-up that drew several thousand. The historian Mark Naison found that white Communists' willingness "to endure arrests and beatings to protect a black comrade gave Communist arguments in behalf of interracial solidarity a new . . . concreteness." Communist militancy also functioned as an act of masculine redemption at a time of severe blows to men's status as breadwinners. During the Popular Front period, Harlem's Black membership in the party grew rapidly, up to two thousand. Although the average membership at any one time was closer to one thousand, triple that number participated in the unemployed groups.[46]

All the unemployed groups experienced high turnover. Paradoxically, their very successes created turnover, as participants often quit when the organizations brought them aid. But African Americans' turnover also reflected the racism they experienced within the unemployed groups. Though the CP made civil rights a strategic priority, its overwhelmingly white (and male) national leaders could be arrogant and dismissive toward members of color. Between the spring of 1936 and the spring of 1938, 2,320 Blacks joined the party and 1,518 quit. Many complained that they did not receive an equal share of party resources, leading to what Frank Wilderson has called Afro-pessimism.†

The high turnover was a class and cultural as well as a race problem: African Americans who remained in the CP tended to be intellectuals and professionals, while the party had difficulty retaining white Chris-

---

* These nine Alabama teenagers were falsely accused of raping two young white women. They were convicted, even though one of the women admitted that they had fabricated the rape story.

† Frank B. Wilderson III, *Afropessimism* (New York: Liveright, 2020); Solomon, 139–140, 161; Mark Naison, "Harlem Communists and the Politics of Black Protest," in *Community Organization for Urban Social Change*, ed. Robert Fisher and Peter Romanofsky (Westport, CT: Greenwood Press, 1981), pp. 13, 34, 43, 46–49, 69, 264, 280–81.

tian working-class members, who often lacked the activist traditions of Jews and African Americans.[47] The CP acknowledged "white chauvinism" among its members and even expelled some whites for racist behavior, but its efforts focused only on overt discrimination and language, and the party did not usually work to draw members of color into making decisions about tactics. Black men dated white women they met through the party, which stirred considerable resentment among Black women (a problem that reappeared in southern civil rights activity three decades later). Few Harlem Blacks participated in the CP's racially integrated social activities, preferring Black-only events, just as other ethnic/racial groups preferred socializing among their own.

Still, throughout the Depression, African Americans, like Jews, were disproportionately represented within the national Communist Party. One Harlem CP local, headquartered in a vacant store but meeting in a church, soon had a membership of over six hundred. Moreover, leaving the CP did not mean leaving unemployed activism, which continued strong, supported by Black Harlem's preexisting community structure, its networks of communication, and its experienced leadership.

Because so many of the unemployed could not pay rent, evictions grew exponentially—185,794 in New York City in the first half of 1932 alone.[48] This despite the fact that many landlords held back from evicting tenants because they doubted they could find other paying renters, because they had to pay marshals for evictions, because they accepted IOUs or even labor in exchange for rent, or because they sympathized with unemployed tenants.[49] The Unemployed Councils led eviction resistance, quickly gathering people at eviction sites, and hundreds often showed up. When eight evictions were in process at one Bronx apartment building, a crowd of fifteen hundred massed outside. Protesters sometimes threatened or even attacked police, throwing stones and bottles. Women were particularly aggressive: barricading themselves in apartments, they cursed marshals loudly from windows and wielded kettles of boiling water, threatening to scald anyone who dared move furniture into the street. If an eviction could not be stopped, Rose Chernin recalled, they would cover the furniture with a tarpaulin until the police left, then "break the lock, put back the furniture, install a new lock" so "the landlord would have to go through the whole procedure another time.">⁵⁰ In Brownsville, Brooklyn, police had to create "a virtual martial law situation" to regain control. Eviction protests provided platforms for Communist and other radical speakers.⁵¹

New York's Unemployed Councils successfully prevented many evictions. Of those receiving eviction notices in early 1932, protests stopped an estimated 41 percent and enabled 77,000 families to move back into their homes (although for how long we don't know).⁵² In 1933 the protests got Mayor O'Brien to instruct city marshals to inform the city relief agency upon issuance of a dispossess order, to give the bureau time to provide aid before an eviction; when evictions occurred, officials were to guard tenants' furniture until a relief worker arrived. City and state relief agencies were required to find housing for those evicted, though whether they did so remains unknown.⁵³

Evictions sometimes produced violence. Once when police tried to protect the marshals who were moving people's furniture onto the street, people in a crowd of some four thousand attacked with fists, stones, and sticks. This kind of large-scale, militant protest, including standing up to police, did not work every time, but the protests' visibility led renters to rely on the unemployed movement for help. One protest won two-to-three-dollar monthly rent reductions for each apartment—in Depression deflation, a major saving—and the return of evicted families to their apartments.

The Unemployed Councils also led and supported rent strikes. A 1932 protest known as the Great Rent Strike War erupted in a quiet section of the Bronx, just east of Bronx Park, where many East European Jews had moved "up" from the Lower East Side. Their middle-class status had been gutted by the Depression. Many had family legacies of socialist and labor union activism, so the neighborhood contained one of the largest concentrations of Communists in New York City. They supplied the early leadership for the "epidemic" of rent strikes that spread into more than two hundred buildings in Brooklyn and the Lower East Side.

The councils' strategy also included pressuring New York City relief offices to provide rent money. In the process council leaders gained considerable expertise about relief procedures and staff: "We learned the rules and where they might be bent."⁵⁴ (Communist organizers were also beginning to learn how to speak American English as opposed to CP jargon.) Council chapters gathered groups of tenants to make demands of relief bureaus; if the demands were refused, the tenants would return in larger groups, even camp out in the offices until they got rent money—or were arrested. Almost all of the forty-two New York City emergency relief offices reported "frequent dealings" with unemployed groups asking for rent money.[55] While individual appeals could be ignored, delegations of ten or more often produced action. One Harlem woman "stood in the rain for three days and the Home Relief Bureau paid no attention to me. Then I found out about the Unemployed Council. . . . We went in there as a body and they came across right quick."[56] Some delegations became so large they were themselves demonstrations, and their arrival would disrupt routine procedures at relief offices. They succeeded in forcing New York City Home Relief Bureaus to discard their policy of not paying rents.

News of their successes grew the Unemployed Councils. Moreover, those who sought help were soon helping others, thereby gaining in skills and confidence—and strengthening their local organizations. Investigators sent by the New Deal administration reported that their meetings became sites where unemployed people shared tips: which arguments would persuade relief officials, which officials were more generous, and which officials to avoid.[57]

UNEMPLOYED ORGANIZING in the South faced obstacles exponentially greater than elsewhere and, unsurprisingly, achieved very little. Even when organizers focused exclusively on unemployment relief, they could not avoid implicitly challenging white supremacy, or "Jim Crow" as it was then known.* "Advocating social equality" was a crime synonymous with advocating Communism. (For decades afterward, civil rights activists were automatically labeled Communists, as a means of revving up white anxiety, as we will see in chapter 5.) Council organizers—some northern whites, some southern Blacks—plunged

---

* The "Jim Crow" phrase seems to have come from the early-nineteenth-century performances of a white actor, Thomas Dartmouth, who initiated the minstrelsy cliché by blackening his face to present an insulting imitation of African Americans. By the late 1830s, "Jim Crow" had become a pejorative epithet for African Americans.

in nevertheless. At first the northerners insisted on integrated meetings, but soon learned that any gathering of whites and Blacks together
would lead to arrests, even violent attacks. Accepting segregation was a
survival necessity. In Greenville, South Carolina, the site of five neighborhood councils with several hundred members, the Ku Klux Klan in
full regalia busted up a council meeting—at the mayor's request.[58]

The Birmingham CP drew in ninety to one hundred members and may
have reached a thousand at its peak in 1934. The Communists' bravery
and willingness to adapt to local cultures earned them respect from African Americans and attracted thousands of sympathizers, the vast majority Black.[59] The Communists, in turn, were often awed by the bravery
of southern African Americans, as when Mrs. Fanny Herbert spoke her
mind to the Greenville City Councilors, all white of course: "I've worked
in every cotton mill in Greenville since I was eight years old. . . . When
you gentlemen in your nice clothes sit down at your table and have plenty
to eat, I wonder if you ever think of the half-naked children of Greenville
who have nothing to eat. Something must be done and done quickly."[60]

The CP discovered and nurtured organizing talent among African
Americans. Hosea Hudson found the Communists when he was a Birmingham steel worker. Noticing that he was a quick learner, the party
brought him to New York City, where he studied Marxism—and learned
to read and write.[61] As he described his approach to Depression organizing:

> If someone got out of food and been down to the welfare two or three
> times and still ain't got no grocery order . . . we'd . . . let her tell her
> story. Then we'd ask all the people, "What do you all think could be
> done about it?" We wouldn't just jump and say what to do. We let the
> neighbors talk about it for a while, and then it would be some of us in
> the crowd, we going to say, "If the lady wants to go back down to the
> welfare, if she wants, I suggest we have a little committee to go with her
> and find out what the condition is."[62]

Hudson was of course maneuvering to get approval for a tactic he had
already planned. But these people were not dupes—what Hudson
wanted was what they wanted, to shake loose immediate material aid
while avoiding the existential risks of a public demonstration. As much

as the CP "used" the Unemployed Councils, the unemployed "used" the energy and commitment of Communists—and occasionally benefited. Ohio-born Angelo Herndon began working in the mines at age fourteen. In Birmingham in 1930 a white council member gave him a copy of *The Communist Manifesto*, which showed him that working-class whites as well as Blacks could be exploited. When he saw a leaflet announcing an Unemployed Council meeting, he went, and met people who, he recalled, gave him a new life.[63] The CP soon recognized his gifts and sent him to Atlanta, where he became the state's most effective organizer.

Atlanta had a distinguished branch of the NAACP, but as in many locations, its constituency was mainly middle class. Supported by ministers, reluctant to challenge segregation, and terrified of red-baiting, the branch condemned demonstrations, even demands for relief, insisting that "the dole" had "paralyzed our people." It railed against the councils and women's participation in particular. NAACP national head Walter White called women joiners "ignorant and uncouth victims . . . led to the slaughter by dangerously bold radicals." By contrast, the Communists addressed the poor majority, who had less to lose. Herndon soon recruited some three hundred to the councils—a membership far larger than the NAACP's. His team made home visits in the Black neighborhoods, door to door, street by street (as Cesar Chavez did in the 1960s; see chapter 6). A clandestine "telegraph" system transmitted news of protests not only throughout the state but across state lines. They won a small victory. When Atlanta's Fulton County cut relief by a third, Herndon, together with his white partner-in-organizing Nannie Leah Washburn—an association dangerous in itself—organized a march to the county commission office, and an interracial crowd of a thousand or more showed up. The commission approved an emergency relief appropriation.[64]

Council leaders encountered something that civil rights activists would experience three decades later: when organizers arrived, people yearning for action and leadership sought them out.[65] In Winston-Salem, North Carolina, where tobacco farmers were hard hit, a few of them approached CP organizers who helped them form an integrated unemployed group. As a member recalled,

They would go down to city hall or to the county commissioners and put pressure on them. My mother along with a few others were able to get some food and clothes, a ton of coal or a load of wood every now and then, and sometimes six or eight dollars to help pay the rent. Now it was nothing but just the roughest food, pinto beans and fatback, but it was something to keep you from starving.[66]

Southern union and unemployed organizers faced great violence. The ACLU reported that attacks in Birmingham, the South's largest industrial city, were "continuous, not incidental."[67] The unemployed sometimes fought back. Hosea Hudson reported that landlords hesitated to evict tenants "because if they put a family out, the unemployed workers would wreck the house and take it away for fuel." This was "a share-the-wealth situation," he added drolly, quoting Louisiana governor Huey Long.[68] Women were prominent in these risky protests. When, for example, a group of Black women were ordered to dig a ditch—an assignment that would never have been given to white women—they refused, went directly to the relief office, and refused to leave until they were granted a meeting with the Georgia relief administrator.[69]

Unsurprisingly, the ferocious repression, both legal and extralegal, almost shut down unemployed organizing in the South. The southern brand of anti-Communism gave rise to a new group—American Fascisti, Order of the Black Shirts. Its application form read, "If you are opposed to social equality . . . and if you are in favor of white supremacy . . . then you are by nature and principle a Black Shirt." Its propaganda focused on "niggers taking our jobs," convincing white workers that Blacks were responsible for their unemployment.[70] In contrast to the CP's view that economic crisis would strengthen a socialist movement, the southern experience showed that it could empower the Right. It also showed, in an American version of European fascism, that racism could beat class unity even in an economically desperate moment.

Still, as historian Glenda Gilmore pointed out, the unemployed organizing in the South was not entirely wasted, because the rank-and-file leadership that developed in these bitter struggles would reemerge in the civil rights movement a few decades later. Before that, however, the federal response to unemployment was also weakened by racism, as we will see.

SOCIALISTS AND COMMUNISTS IN CHICAGO

Until 1932, the Communist-led Unemployed Councils were the uncontested leaders of the activist unemployed. As Len De Caux, later publicity director for the CIO, wrote of the Communists, "If they didn't start things themselves, they were Johnnies-on-the-spot.[71] Soon, however, the economic crisis energized and grew the Socialist Party, and by July 1933 the SP's national convention drew some eight hundred delegates from thirteen states.[72] This was small compared to the numbers at KKK and Townsend gatherings but a considerable achievement for a socialist political party. Together with its college affiliate, the Intercollegiate Socialist Society, the SP claimed to have 8,000 to 15,000 members before the stock market crash and 25,000 by 1935.

The great industrial city of Chicago was the site of the Socialists' greatest success. With a 40 percent unemployment rate in 1931, its threadbare relief agencies could not even begin to provide help. Moreover, big businesses blocked city efforts to help by mounting a "tax strike," withholding millions in taxes; a group of them actually incorporated an association for the express purpose of conducting a tax boycott. Its impact was so great that the media referred to a "super-government" as the real power in the city.[73] In response, the SP successfully organized Unemployed Leagues. Spreading quickly, they took over abandoned stores for meetings and for emergency shelters, appropriated chairs from deserted movie theaters, persuaded employed friends to pilfer office supplies, and found old mimeograph machines. Some members became expert at stealing electricity from streetlights and tapping gas lines without setting off the meters.

As with fraternal orders, chapters were often ethnically homogeneous, unsurprising in a city of many immigrants. So meetings were sometimes conducted in foreign languages (Polish, Rumanian, etc.) and used the spaces of ethnic organizations (the Ukrainian Hall, the Polish Library, a Slovak Catholic *sokol*) as meeting rooms.[74] Integrated into ethnic communities, the meetings featured dances, pot-luck meals, children's outings, and team sports. Women, unsurprisingly, were key organizers of this recreation.[75] One observer, though hostile to unemployed activism, nevertheless acknowledged that members participated actively in these meetings, speaking from the floor "with readiness and ease." She noted that every committee drew plenty of volunteers. "A sense of solidarity and social unity is very strong in the group."[76] Nor did sociability exclude education. Members seemed hesitant to go home when a meeting ended, she reported.

> *Little groups gathered . . . to discuss and gossip. The most common topic was the exchange of grudges against case workers. The entertainment planned for the next week in order to raise money for the organization was also the subject of conversation, while gossip of the neighborhood wound its way in and out of the talk. One group . . . engaged in a heated argument about the subject matter to be included in the workers' courses that were being inaugurated. . . . Loath to leave, this informal meeting went on till the lights in the church were turned out.*

This observer affords us a detailed inside view of one meeting, attended by about seventy-five, in a Congregational church basement. Colored by her snobbish disdain, her report is nonetheless illuminating.

> *The Congregational minister is model 1933 [a snide reference to Depression-era activists] . . . rather shabby. . . . But like his brethren peddlers of less liquid assets, his sales methods are strictly up to date. . . . The speaker of the evening . . . is droning monotonously on the subject "Bankers and Breadlines." He used to be a Republican, used in fact to belong to the American Legion. He relates that when Debs was put in jail during the war, he thought that was the place Debs belonged.* He is proud of his emancipation from these ideas. . . . He says we have to build the American brand of Socialism.*

---

* Eugene V. Debs was the renowned founder of the Socialist Party. His successor, Norman Thomas, played a small role in criticizing the Townsend movement, the subject of chapter 3.

The questions [from the floor] are surprisingly intelligent and reveal unusual interest, obviously coming from two sorts of questioners, one, those under the educational influence of Socialism, their questions being of an academic nature; the other, from people who vigorously nod their heads in approval when the speaker mentions solidarity, or fighting the authorities. . . . They even more than the other . . . want a fight and are ready to sacrifice. This is especially true of the women. All the women [are] chewing gum in unison; all have frizzed hair, strong capable bodies, and a rough and coarse sense of humor. . . . Examples of how the "big boys" run things for their own ends are exchanged with relish among the audience. . . . The banking system is no longer as awe inspiring as it was in the hands of the nervous speaker.[77]

If we bracket the snideness ("surprisingly intelligent," "frizzed hair," etc.), this description offers a vivid if partial picture of an Unemployed League meeting. Her observation that "the personal is thus brought into the discussion and the audience gets very intimate with each other, and everyone feels at home" actually describes a vital feature of many social movements. There's a speaker, clearly inexperienced; noisy working-class women; people expressing anger and discussing politics; and evidence that they feel comfortable in participating. This chapter's representative to the Chicago Socialist Party's central committee was "by trade a painter, an ardent union man," the guy who "gets the boys fixed up when the cops pull them in for selling the *New Frontier* [an SP newspaper] or putting out handbills," and he is treated with "a great deal of respect."[78]

Because the Socialist groups could attract support from liberals and liberal institutions, notably Hull-House in Chicago and Greenwich House in New York City, they were better funded than the Unemployed Councils. The Chicago Unemployed League was able to field grievance committees in every chapter, a central grievance committee, and an office staffed full time by volunteers. Unlike members of the councils, many League members could provide middle-class skills. They set up a speakers bureau and sent out more than three hundred discussion leaders to chapter meetings. League members also used their skills to help the unemployed navigate city bureaucracies.[79] They were able to devote time to needy individuals as well as to groups. In 1933, for example, twenty members of the Chicago league spent a day beseeching officials to find a hospital admission for two old ladies. They successfully procured coal for twelve families who had been caught in a double bind: the relief office had refused to provide money for heat because the fire department had declared their tenement unsafe for habitation, but they had nowhere else to go.[80]

Meanwhile the CP's Unemployed Councils—one study counted eighty chapters in Chicago—reached out to new populations. At least sixteen ethnic fraternal organizations, seven of them Slavic, worked cooperatively with the councils. White ethnics constituted half the circulation of the party's daily newsletters. Unusually, an interethnic coalition developed in "Packingtown," as the stockyards were known, where wages were so low that workers were typically poor even when they were employed, while unemployment made them desperate. The stockyards council included Poles and Lithuanians but also Mexicans.[81] It called for ousting anti-union company spies in the yards and asked for weekly supplies of meat for unemployed workers. (Consider the irony that workers who slaughtered and butchered animals could not afford to buy meat.)

Council demonstrations drew people from across the city, providing visual evidence of common interests among ethnic and Black populations. In an unprecedented interracial "hunger march" of six thousand, African Americans marched along with whites—"the first time that Black workers had marched into the white territory around the Yards."[82] The historian Lizabeth Cohen found that even those who at first watched from the sidelines, "because they were employed or wary of joining a 'radical' cause," soon joined in many of these actions.[83]

SP ideology did not acknowledge the autonomous force of racism, insisting that it was a product of class exploitation and would disappear under socialism—let alone denounce it strongly.[84] By contrast, the CP put fighting racism at the top of its agenda and prioritized reaching African Americans. Even a vehemently anti-Communist observer acknowledged that the "CP made sure that all of its agitation in the unemployed councils included protests against racial discrimination by relief agencies, landlords, and local and federal government."[85] Although

African Americans were by no means influential in the party, its official antiracism "created space in which Blacks could interpret Communism . . . through the lens of race consciousness" and could equate the
class struggle with the Black struggle.[86]

But in winning the trust of African Americans, the CP's ideology
was less important than its track record. The benefits were mutual—
the Unemployed Councils gained from Black militancy, and Blacks
benefited from Communist energy. Once reluctant to attend white-
dominated meetings, African Americans started to show up. One who
joined a council, Lowell Washington, recalled that he had "never really
talked to a white man before . . . and here I was being treated with
respect and speakin' my mind. . . . It changed the way I thought about
things."[87] The Socialist Party was caught in a circular problem, unable
to recruit Blacks because it had so few Black members.[88] The difference
between the two parties was striking: Blacks comprised 25 percent of
council members and 21 percent of council leadership, while the figures
for the Socialist Unemployed League were 6 and 5 percent respectively.[89]

African Americans were no more unanimous in their political views
than any other group, and the councils' militancy alarmed old-guard
Black leaders. George Edmund Haynes, a founder of the Urban League
and executive secretary of the Race Relations Department of the Federal
Council of Churches, worried that Negroes were "loosening their contact with the usual avenues of guidance and help," namely the churches
and the Black "intelligentsia"—an attitude similar to that of many
white settlement workers. He criticized their call for "social equality," clinging to an "uplift" strategy. The best traditions of Negroes,
he argued, rested on understanding "the deep-lying urge of democracy that has uprooted chattel slavery and has tardily given the freemen
and their children a chance for education and advancement."[90] This
advice reflected the distance between poor and working-class Blacks
and middle-class leaders, especially ministers. Still, when council leaders reached out to Black ministers and spoke in their churches, many
were supportive, disregarding the anti-Communism of the more conservative clergy. Pilgrim Baptist Church, for example, invited Angelo
Herndon to speak, pulling in a cheering audience of three thousand.
The best-selling author and Communist Mike Gold thought that Black

religious enthusiasm was being transmuted into protest enthusiasm, shouting agreement with their "Amens."[91] Council members did "soap-box" speaking regularly in Washington Park, a major gathering place (and often the starting place for protests) on Chicago's South Side.

Sometimes Unemployed Council leaders found themselves respond-ing to demands from their organizees. Interrupting a council speaker, an elderly black man shouted, "What you folks figure on doing about that colored family that was thrown out of their house today?"[92] The Communist Steve Nelson later recalled, self-critically, that bottom-up initiatives were sometimes better than those of official leaders. He had once begun a meeting by emphasizing that the bourgeoisie makes the workers pay for depressions, an approach that "demonstrated just how isolated we were from most workers." He considered it lucky that his ideological discourse was swept aside after someone called out, "the first thing we have to do is set up a committee that can deal with griev-ances. Let's have some volunteers."[93]

The Unemployed Councils responded to evictions by demanding rental assistance from relief agencies, but with only a few modest suc-cesses, they began to resist evictions more aggressively. Both white eth-nics and African Americans joined in. One woman recalled, "I hurried over to the Greek Workers Club and got a whole number of people to help break down the door, put in the furniture." No doubt council lead-ers contributed, but eviction-resistance squads were also organized by residents. The unemployed often hung out at council meeting places, so they could respond quickly to evictions and meanwhile enjoy the fellowship. Some chapters kept an eviction-response squad on standby. When tenants could not pay the rent, landlords sometimes tried to force them out by making apartments unlivable. Council men responded by doing repair work. When the marshals removed doors, carpenters put up new ones; when a kitchen was flooded, thanks to a hole chiseled in a water pipe, an eviction squad plumber put in a new pipe; when electric lines were disconnected, they were reconnected.[94]

Men in Chicago's largely Black South Side formed a particularly fearless rapid-response squad, calling themselves "black bugs," also known in a pun as the "black reds."[95] They moved furniture from the pavement back inside apartments, breaking locks when necessary.

Renowned sociologist Horace Cayton, who later published the influential *Black Metropolis* about Chicago, encountered one such event by chance. While sitting in a restaurant in the Black Belt, he saw a long line of "serious and determined" Black men headed to "put in a family." He followed them. At the eviction site, a woman was "intermittently crying and thanking God" for the arrival of the "black bugs." After moving her furniture back inside, someone shouted that a family in the next street had been "put out," and the squad hurried there.

Cayton described what happened when the police arrived—a quotation from his report stands at the beginning of this chapter. The conflict did not end well. A siren rang out, four cars and a paddy wagon arrived, and the police came out swinging. As Cayton reported, "Clubs came down in a sickening rain of blows on the woolly head of one of the boys who was holding her [the woman speaker] up. Blood spurted from his mouth and nose." Cayton ended his vignette bitterly: "Tomorrow I will perhaps read in the paper that a 'red riot' was stopped only with the intervention of a number of officers; that 'red' agitation among the Negroes is on the increase; that Mr. Fish, Mr. Hearst, and Mr. Jimmie Walker were right—American institutions really are in danger."[96]

The risks of protest in Chicago were dwarfed by those in the South, but they were by no means absent. Police often attacked Black demonstrators even when they had obtained permits, and leaders could not always control council members' responses. Angry crowds, especially from the predominantly Black South Side and the predominantly immigrant Packingtown, baited and attacked the cops. The worst happened when police killed three African American men at a peaceful parade. The councils organized a mass funeral in the Odd Fellows Hall, with an open casket—under an image of black and white clasped hands (and a portrait of Lenin!). Over two days some 25,000 people paid their respects. After the funeral the South Side councils, largely Black, received 5,500 new applicants for membership.[97] The episode brought some positive change: Mayor Anton Cermak ordered a renters' court to suspend evictions for a period, which lasted several months. It was a small victory, achieved at great cost.[98]

Unemployed activism made Chicago officials fearful, and they made feeble attempts to provide help. Cermak threatened the millionaires behind the tax strike, saying "money now or troops later. . . . They should be glad to pay for it, for it is the best way of ensuring that they keep that property."[99] But these threats had no teeth and produced no help, while violence against protesters surged. Chicago's Red Squad labeled the protesters Communists—a tactic later employed by J. Edgar Hoover against civil rights activists—and boasted that he knew "how to manage them." Protesters were beaten not only at demonstrations but in jail cells. More than twenty participants in a demonstration on Michigan Avenue needed "surgical attention," a local journalist reported. Protesters sometimes fought back: a protest in Humboldt Park, an immigrant neighborhood, sent three policemen and three demonstrators to the hospital.[100]

Finally, a Communist-Socialist coalition formed—an instance of local CP chapters defying the party line—and developed a joint strategy, with some success. The Socialists used their establishment connections to procure newspaper and radio coverage of the crisis and persuaded local bankers to fund relief offices for two more months. When municipal relief funds were cut by 50 percent in 1932, the coalition organized dozens of demonstrations, including one of 25,000, the biggest in years. In the pouring rain, the demonstrators walked silently through the Loop holding signs asking for food and work. A large demonstration stopped an attempt to cut food allowances by 10 percent in November 1934. Mayor Cermak again appealed for federal help with a threat: send $150 million or federal troops. Though he got only a fraction of that sum—$6.3 million from the Reconstruction Finance Corporation—he was one of many mayors pressured into becoming lobbyists for the unemployed.[101] The gains were small, but all were produced by unemployed activism.

A. J. MUSTE AND THE NATIONAL UNEMPLOYED LEAGUE

The leader of the third Left group, Abraham Johannes Muste, liked to repeat a pithy aphorism: students "did not know anything but knew how to say it"; workers "knew a great deal but did not know how to say it."[102] He was promoting a socialist movement that was more democratic than that of the other Left parties. A tall, lean man with an angular face, Muste shared with Dr. Townsend a somewhat ascetic appearance. Born in the Netherlands in 1885, he was brought to the United States at age six. His organizational history, again similar to Dr. Townsend's, constitutes a long list. He was first a Congregationalist pastor, then a Quaker minister. He joined other ministers in supporting a 1919 textile workers strike and helped found a textile workers union. He headed the faculty at the Brookwood Labor College. He formed the Conference for Progressive Labor Action (CPLA), which became the National Unemployed League, then the American Workers Party.[103] But he was no dilettante; influenced by the social gospel and by renowned educator and philosopher John Dewey, he was always seeking the best route to a just society. Muste entered the unemployed movement as a Marxist but one fiercely critical of both CP and SP. (His antagonism to the CP was returned: William Z. Foster of the CP called Muste's group "The Little Brothers of the Big Labor Fakers.")[104] Muste's strategy was to build and educate grassroots leadership through helping the unemployed.[105]

Responding to the economic crisis, Muste established the National Unemployed League (NUL). His rejection of Communist and Socialist ideology showed in its inaugural event—an outdoor Independence Day rally on July 4, 1933, staged with patriotic fanfare on the state fairgrounds in Columbus, Ohio, a site previously used for Ku Klux Klan rallies. The event symbolized NUL's attempt to steep unemployed protests in American patriotism. A superb orator, Muste's call for the unemployed to rise up drew cheers from the audience of some fifteen thousand. Repeating the two-channel strategy of the Seattle UCL, he announced a plan to develop cooperatives and to campaign for government relief. Then some seven thousand of those gathered marched to the state capitol to present their demands.

NUL's "Declaration of Workers and Farmers Rights," modeled on the Declaration of Independence, further articulated its patriotic organizing strategy:

When, in a nation possessing unlimited resources, along with the greatest industrial and transportation equipment the world has ever known, there develops a condition wherein millions of citizens are forced into dire destitution . . .[106]

Emphasizing "Americanism" to distinguish it from the "foreign ideologies" of the CP and SP, Muste's group deployed patriotic symbols such as the American Revolution's Gadsden flag (a rattlesnake image with the slogan "Don't Tread on Me"). Its rhetoric was so ultrapatriotic that it drew in some KKK members.[107] Thus the group resembled the Townsend movement in its appeal to white working-class conservatism and in positioning Muste as a guru. However opportunist, NUL's strategy was to build a broad-based movement by appealing to the values of its constituents.*

The patriotic tropes operated in tension, however, with other principles of NUL's parent, the Conference for Progressive Labor Action—notably its denunciation of racism, including racism in labor unions. The CPLA proudly announced its commitment to an "organic, specifically American path to black liberation."[108] It is not clear what that meant and the Muste organizers may well have preferred this ambiguity. In any case Muste's movement attracted few African Americans. Remarkably for the time, NUL emphasized outreach to working women, especially in southern textile mills. This goal might seem to conflict with another of its ideological principles: that women belonged at home. But in the context of trying to build a working-class constituency, it represented the demand for a family wage for men so that women would not need to earn.[109] Like the Ku Klux Klan, NUL appealed to native-born whites with conservative race and gender values, but unlike the Klan's largely middle-class membership, NUL's base consisted of working-class whites, notably from rural areas and small towns where neither the CP nor SP was organizing. In the segregated, religiously fundamentalist-leaning textile mill towns of North Carolina, Muste's rousing oratory

---

* The Muste vision was in some respects more democratic than that of the SP or CP, but on the other hand, his organization depended more on a single charismatic leader than did the others. Moreover, none of the organizations were able to control the behavior of their locals—a reminder that this was a social movement, not a set of centralized organizations.

resembled evangelical Protestant sermons.[110] In the mining towns of Ohio, NUL claimed 100,000 members, and in Pennsylvania, 50,000.

Muste's followers could be militant and inventive, unafraid to use disruption to pressure relief offices. When members discovered a hoard of flour stashed in a Pittsburgh warehouse, they marched in, seized it, and distributed it according to recipients' level of poverty. In Glouster, Ohio, NUL unemployed miners appeared at relief offices with empty gunny sacks and announced that if they got no relief funds, they would return one week later and fill them from store shelves; they got the funds.[111] A Pittsburgh group of women drew up a list of 4,400 children unable to attend school because they didn't have shoes. They got the city council to appropriate $40,000 to meet the need, and when the mayor vetoed it, NUL women picketed for six weeks and got the money. An Ohio group badgered relief administrators so much that it forced a reorganization of the local relief system, making it friendlier to its clients. At least one NUL chapter, in Allegheny County, Pennsylvania, took on some of the recordkeeping that relief authorities usually did, setting up a small "dual power" situation: tracking weekly food prices, they presented a "fair prices" list and a biweekly report to the county's relief administrators, demanding that the relief board meet with NUL officers monthly.[112] Like those in the CP and SP networks, these victories were typically small and local, but they demonstrated the determination and creativity of Muste's followers.

The NUL tried to generate labor union support for the unemployed and made some progress to that end despite the disapproval of the AFL. In San Francisco, it developed an informal alliance with the left-wing International Longshore and Warehouse Union, and in 1934 supported the longshoremen's strike that briefly became a general strike.[113] The apogee of this strategy was its participation in the famous 1934 Auto-Lite strike, which became known, with Napoleonic grandeur, as the "Battle of Toledo."* All three unemployed organizations vowed

---

* Auto-Lites were spark plugs and ignition wire sets. When an injunction against strikers did not deter them, the National Guard was called in for what became the largest peacetime military action in Ohio history. In weeks of pitched battles, two union activists were killed and scores were wounded. The settlement gave the union much, though not all, of what it had asked for.

not to scab, but the Musteites did much more, deploying hundreds on the picket lines; this was a principled act, considering that a strike victory would not immediately benefit the unemployed. Ultimately some ten thousand strike supporters surrounded the plant in an attempt to prevent strikebreakers from entering. When sheriff's deputies began arresting demonstrators, including Muste himself and his second-in-command, Louis Budenz,* the crowd began hurling stones, bricks, and bottles at the law-and-order men. A five-day struggle ensued, ending with two dead and more than two hundred injured. The union won a great deal: a 5 percent wage increase, a minimum wage of thirty-five cents an hour, reemployment of all the strikers, a grievance system, and, most important, recognition of the union, thereby obliterating a company union that the Electric Auto-Lite corporation had attempted to create.[114]

Despite NUL members' willingness to fight, their leaders killed off the organization, betraying their democratic rhetoric. This would seem an irrational decision because NUL had accomplished a great deal. It had mobilized thousands outside of big cities and spawned creative grassroots activism and leadership; because of its role in the Auto-Lite strike, it won the respect of the more militant side of the growing labor movement. But instead of building the existing organization, Muste and a few other NUL leaders became persuaded that the "masses" required a vanguard party to lead them, a move consistent with Muste's history of changing commitments. Influenced by the fact that followers of Leon Trotsky shared his implacable hatred for the CP, in late 1933 NUL leaders folded their movement into what became the Trotskyist American Workers' Party.† Ironically, and paradoxically, it was the independent and relatively democratic NUL rather than the hierarchical Left parties that turned to this most undemocratic vanguardism.

---

* As a Communist, Budenz was an editor of the *Daily Worker*, and a Soviet spy. He later became a professional anti-Communist—and a leading light of the McCarthyist persecution of his former comrades.

† Trotskyists, followers of Russian revolutionary hero Leon Trotsky, were Marxist-Leninists who considered the Stalinist Communist Party an enemy almost worse than the capitalist parties.

Reversing the appeal to American patriotism, the American Workers' Party quit organizing the unemployed and became a miniature replica of the CP in its most doctrinaire period, following Trotsky as slavishly as the Comintern followed Stalin.[115] After less than two years with the Workers' Party, Muste parted from the organized Left and returned to his Christian pacifist roots.*

THE UNEMPLOYED MOVEMENT AS A WHOLE

Though the three parties leading unemployed organizing condemned each other bitterly, their tactics showed few differences among them. All three generated impressive grassroots initiatives—agitating for more relief, stopping evictions, organizing protest marches—that marginalized their socialist agendas. All three drew in members who were so desperate that all three had to focus on meeting urgent needs for food and shelter. All three won small victories in prying more relief out of local offices, and all three contributed to the pressure that forced the federal government to fund relief measures.

Importantly, the community and sociability generated in local unemployed chapters helped members reject or at least temporarily escape their despondency. As in many social movements, chapters often functioned as mini-community centers, entering the fabric of neighborhood life alongside saloons, churches, and fraternal orders. Like the Ku Klux Klan, they organized dances, picnics, sewing clubs, bands, children's outings, drama groups, team sports, and holiday parties as well as educational programs—speakers and classes, including English-language classes.[116] Meetings strengthened neighborliness and provided emotional support. The journalist Martha Gellhorn observed that "jobless men, tired of tramping the streets in search of work, came to rest and talk . . . establishing mutual relations of identification on the

---

* Presenting Christianity as a revolutionary doctrine, Muste went on to direct the Fellowship of Reconciliation, to mentor Bayard Rustin—who played a significant role in the Montgomery bus boycott, treated in chapter 5—and to lead pacifist opposition to the U.S. invasion of Vietnam.

basis of their common misfortune."[117] One Unemployed Council member recalled, "There was always something to eat"[118]—characteristic of social movements that included women.

Offering material as well as emotional support, members "networked," trading tips about which merchants were generous, which restaurants and bakeries discarded old food, which relief administrators were most sympathetic, and where medical care could be found. All three unemployed organizations provided political education, especially about the causes of unemployment. The lessons were as much personal as ideological; by sharing experiences, participants learned that their predicaments were not individual but were produced by social and economic structures. Second-wave feminism would call it consciousness-raising. One sociologist calls it "cognitive liberation,"[119] but it is not only cognitive. It could also be emotional liberation.

All the unemployed groups spent most of their time and energy addressing members' immediate crises. The stigma that had long been attached to receiving public help worsened these crises by preventing the unemployed from asking for relief until they were desperate, facing homelessness and hunger. Men especially delayed in seeking help, their self-esteem undermined by their inability to provide for a family.[120] Having to beg a relief office for help could deepen the humiliation of unemployment. The muscular, confrontational activity of the unemployed movement gave unemployed men something to do, thereby bolstering a threatened masculinity.

Gendered constraints also affected women, but in contradictory ways. Women experienced poverty particularly keenly because they were responsible for family budgeting and children's needs, but wifely and maternal responsibilities made it more difficult for them to find the time for activism. None of the three unemployed organizations encouraged women to become leaders or to speak up in meetings. None challenged the assumption that domestic labor was an exclusively female responsibility. The CP condemned "male chauvinism" in theory but never made it a prominent issue. Men assumed that women would staff relief kitchens, mimeograph leaflets, and organize food and entertainment for meetings.[121]

Yet in confrontations, some women were as assertive, even as belligerent, as men. During evictions one New York City woman reported, "When the police went for the men, the women rushed to protect them. . . . We would tell all the men to leave the building. It was the women who remained in the apartments," calculating that authorities would be less aggressive toward them.[122] When the Chicago police Red Squad drove motorcycles into a demonstration and pulled down a speaker, women rescued him and helped him escape. A Polish woman threw cayenne pepper into the cops' eyes at an eviction protest, while another, extremely fat woman used her bulk to block them from entering a home to carry out an eviction order. At a march in an Illinois coal-mining community, the men found that their efforts to keep their wives from the front ranks were futile.[123] Women in Michigan "liberated" food supplies from relief stations. (Early in the Depression, relief was sometimes given "in kind.")[124] Many women did not feel comfortable in male-dominated meetings and chose to create auxiliary groups, but these were not always less aggressive than the male-dominated groups. One such "auxiliary" held relief officials hostage for several hours until food orders were issued.[125] Moreover, women sometimes manipulated gendered conventions, exhorting their male comrades to "act like men" when attacked.

Women also developed some of the movement's most creative tactics. In Chicago's Unemployed Councils, women formed some twenty committees that pestered relief offices demanding aid to purchase items men did not often think about, such as diapers and baby formula. In several small towns where NUL thrived, women established Mothers' Leagues and Mother-Save-Your-Child clubs, focused on finding shelter for the homeless and relief for the hungry.[126] In Harlem, women broadened the unemployed movement to address other survival issues: unemployed organizer Ella Baker—later a founder of the civil rights movement's most radical organization, the Student Nonviolent Coordinating Committee—worked with the Young Negroes Cooperative League to set up cooperatives and to agitate for Harlem's "Don't Buy Where You Can't Work" campaign.[127]

Although most female activists were wives and mothers, we should not assume that they followed their husbands into the unemployed groups; as in the KKK, some wives probably brought in husbands.

Seventy percent of Harlem's Communists were women, and they were concentrated in the unemployed movement.[128] In Chicago, women constituted only 15 percent of CP members but a much higher percentage of activists, and they generated some twenty women's committees in the Unemployed Councils, coordinated by a citywide executive committee. Yet Communist Party newspapers continued to feature beauty and housekeeping tips as their strategy to recruit women.[129] And no matter how numerous or assertive women were, they rarely became official leaders.*

Precisely because the unemployed movement often succeeded in securing economic help for its members, it experienced three problems common to all social movements: free ridership, high turnover, and an inability to focus on long-term social change, let alone build a socialist movement. Free riders were those who used the organization to get help without contributing to the movement—thus taking but not giving. Many "members" participated briefly, then dropped away, because they got the help they needed, or because they cycled between unemployment and occasional part-time jobs, or because many, especially single men, were on the road looking for work.[130] The high turnover thus arose not from individuals' flightiness but from life itself. Turnover then led to inconsistent decisions, a continual need to orient new people, and a lack of collective experience, all of which created obstacles to internal democracy. (Self-help projects, because they were cooperatives, experienced less turnover because the barter system was by definition one of give-and-take.)

The last problem—how to work toward permanent social change in the face of immediate survival needs—dogged the unemployed movement constantly. All three Left parties challenged the "common sense" of the capitalist economy, which assumed that deprivation was an exceptional problem rather than an integral part of the system. Though focusing on the unemployed, they sought to develop a class consciousness uniting all those who had to sell their labor. They worried that

---

* The proceedings of the second annual conference of the Illinois Workers Alliance, for example, lists just one woman among the sixteen delegates from Chicago and one woman on its executive board.

helping the unemployed get food and shelter served to keep an unjust economy afloat. Socialists all, they wanted to create an anticapitalist movement. They were all disappointed.

Even if unemployed organizers sometimes convinced members of the fundamental unfairness of the economy, they could not get them to focus on structural change when they could not pay their rent. The democracy of the unemployed movement, however imperfect, made itself felt as the members compelled leaders to focus on their survival needs. The very altruism of the Left organizers undermined their hopes for socialist transformation. In a spiral they could not alter, the stronger the unemployed organization, the more quickly the needy came to it for help, forcing it to concentrate on activity that could produce quick results. Harry Hopkins, head of the New Deal's relief administration, faced the criticism that he was giving away money without a long-term plan. "People don't eat in the long run," he responded. "They eat every day." He could have been speaking as an unemployed organizer.[131]

THE WORKERS ALLIANCE

Rank-and-file members of the three unemployed organizations had been cooperating at the local level for some time.[132] That pattern became the ideal by late 1934, when the threat of fascism led European Socialists and Communists to create Popular Fronts, alliances among antifascist parties.[133] The Comintern finally gave "permission" for Communists to formalize their informal cooperation into a new organization, the Workers Alliance.[134] Unlike European Popular Fronts, however, the Alliance was not an electoral coalition but a social movement organization focused on unemployment.

At first the three groups that formed the Alliance were leery, suspicious of the others' ulterior motives and "incorrect" politics, but the advantages of the merger overcame their doubts.[135] It meant that money and organizers could move from the center to regions with fewer resources, and that activities and achievements in one place could encourage others. Meanwhile, permanent social welfare legislation—particularly the Social Security Act and the National Labor Relations

Act, which protected workers' rights to unionize—actually grew the movement rather than undercut it, by creating optimism that progressive change was possible.[136] The Alliance became a considerable national force, claiming a membership of 600,000, half of it with dues paid up, with sixteen hundred locals in forty-three states.[137]

Alliance organizers knew that Communists were vulnerable to right-wing attacks, so Communist Herbert Benjamin ceded the presidency to a less controversial and most atypical activist, David Lasser of the SP. The son of working-class Russian Jewish immigrants, he had dropped out of high school to help support his parents, then enlisted in World War I. After the war, he talked his way into MIT and graduated with a degree in engineering in 1924. In 1929 he became managing editor at the magazine *Science Wonder Stories*, where he promoted a form of science fiction that rested on good science. NASA considers him the originator of the plan to use rockets to propel space ships.[138] His 1931 book, *The Conquest of Space*, was the first English-language explanation of why space travel was possible. It inspired a generation of science fiction writers, including Arthur C. Clarke, author of the screenplay for the film *2001: A Space Odyssey*. Ridiculed and regarded as a kook at the time—one congressman called him a lunatic—Lasser is now considered the father of space flight.[139]

The Alliance started strong. Although not an experienced movement leader, Lasser was energetic and personable, able to translate its aims into popular language, as opposed to the deadening Communist jargon. Alliance locals demanded help for the unemployed with greater systematization and national communication. Alliance publications reported on national and state legislative actions and on changes in administrative policies regarding, for example, allowances for rent, gas, electricity, clothing, medical care, and the like. The New York City Alliance published a regular newsletter, with a page in Italian (at a time when Italian Americans were widely regarded as slovenly but potentially dangerous anarchists).[140] Local bulletins let members know when particular resources were available, as in this Chicago bulletin of September 1936:

Certain articles of clothing are in stock at the Surplus Commodities Distribution Center. A list of such articles follows. . . . There are,

however, no overcoats and no shoes, and also no heavy underwear.
Local grievance chairmen are asked to assist clients to get what can
be obtained.[141]

Local initiatives continued—the Illinois Alliance, for example,
attempted to create á consumers' cooperative, much like the self-help
projects of the early Depression years.[142] Alliance chapters continued
to send delegations to relief offices, often supported by crowds standing outside, but now these local groups could speak for a large national
organization—and this of course made them less likely to be ignored
or to give up.

Many relief workers were stressed by enormous caseloads—a single
worker might be handling four to five hundred cases—and found the
protests irritating. But some responded sympathetically, well aware of
the desperation behind the delegations.[143] An assistant director of relief
in Lancaster County, Pennsylvania, wrote from this perspective:

> *Relief is a tyranny not only because of its pitiful inadequacy, but more*
> *truly because it is a* we to *them proposition. . . . not a democratic prop-*
> *osition. . . . That the activities of the pressure groups are often mis-*
> *directed, that their requests and threats are often more annoying than*
> *intelligent, cannot be denied. The local group goes to the local supervi-*
> *sor or director because of his accessibility. . . . It is hard to see anything*
> *but simple justice in allowing these people the privilege to which their*
> *heritage entitles them—a voice in their own affairs.*[144]

Meanwhile, an expanding progressive caucus within social work,
known as the Rank and File movement, emboldened some caseworkers
to side with their clients and to realize that pressure from relief clients
would leverage more funds from relief administrators.[145]

Though most protests remained locally initiated, they nevertheless helped the Alliance grow. In Kentucky, for example, Don West,
a Congregationalist minister and a Communist, sermonized for the it.
His talk of a class-conscious Jesus, a workers' Jesus, may have been
opportunist, but it worked: he made Kentucky an Alliance stronghold.
When he was jailed, a crowd of more than three hundred WPA workers

and miners forced a local judge and sheriff to free him.[146] In Escanaba County, at the northern tip of Michigan, an Alliance chapter developed a Good Government Forum that got rid of corrupt politicians, endorsed candidates, and forced the city council to hire a Socialist city manager sympathetic to the unemployed—this while led by Communist Carl Anderson.[147] At the same time, CP influence pushed the Alliance into passing resolutions on international issues, such as censuring Italian aggression against Ethiopia in 1935–36, and condemning the persecution of radicals like the IWW's Tom Mooney, imprisoned for twenty years based on falsified evidence of participating in a 1916 bombing.[148]

Then in 1935 the landscape of New Deal relief worsened radically: the Roosevelt administration ended emergency relief, turning the responsibility over to state and local authorities, whose resources had shrunk just as the unemployed needed their help. Unsurprisingly, protests grew larger and more disruptive. Several Alliance chapters conducted "deathwatches," packing the galleries of state legislatures and municipal councils when relief appropriations were debated. In eight states—Colorado, Minnesota, Missouri, New Jersey, New York, Ohio, Pennsylvania, and Wisconsin—protesters occupied government offices and legislatures. A group from the New Jersey Alliance took over the state assembly chamber in Trenton, calling themselves the "Army of No-Occupation." They stayed for eight days, ostentatiously "reading newspapers and smoking cigars to portray the indifference" of the legislators. While there they "legislated" a progressive income tax, a steep tax on corporate income, a thirty-hour workweek, and minimum wage requirements. In St. Louis, a group occupied city hall demanding $1 million for relief. In Colorado, mobs stormed the state legislature and drove frightened legislators out.[149]

The Alliance's national leadership tried to limit these local actions, convinced that they were unproductive, but did not always succeed. Moreover, the leadership may have been wrong. Disruptions can produce results. The civil rights leader Bayard Rustin (whom we will meet in chapter 5) believed that "our power is in our ability to make things unworkable," truth of which became clear in 1960s civil rights struggles.[150]

Alliance pressure contributed to the creation of a massive federal jobs program in 1935, the Works Progress Administration (WPA), intended to compensate for the end of federal emergency relief. It did not compensate, however. Abandoning the millions who could not get WPA jobs, the end of emergency relief constituted a 50 percent cut in aid for the unemployed.[151] Those who were hired were extremely positive about the WPA, preferring work to straight relief. But jobs programs were far more expensive than straight relief, because they required expenditures on tools, materials, supervisors, transportation, and more. So over its seven years, the WPA hired only eight million people, 2.5 million at any one time, while the unemployed at any one time numbered three to four times that.[152]

The Alliance showed its muscle vividly in congressional debate about the WPA budget for fiscal 1938. Roosevelt asked for $650 million; the Alliance and its congressional supporters demanded $1.04 billion. By the time of the floor fight on appropriations, their demand had gone up to $1.5 billion.* A few months later, when the administration asked for $1.5 billion, the Alliance, represented in Congress by Rep. Gerald Boileau of Wisconsin (where the Progressive Party had elected Phillip La Follette as governor and Bob La Follette as senator) and the progressive caucus, were demanding $3 billion for fiscal 1938. In response, the liberal bloc in Congress[153] raised their request to $2.4 billion. Defending the jobs program against the anti-Roosevelt caucus, the administration got $1.5 billion—which was the Alliance's original proposal.[154] It was a remarkable victory over the powerful southern Democrats in the Senate.

But it was not enough. Despite passage of the Social Security Act in 1935, unemployment rose well into 1938, and Social Security's smaller programs, such as Old Age Assistance and Aid to Dependent Children, were completely inadequate to address it. Relief administrators gave up trying to provide "coverage" and simply parceled out what funds were available. "No one knows how people live," a Washington, D.C., admin-

---

* This proposal included $400 million for the Farm Security Administration—a small progressive program within the Department of Agriculture—to use on behalf of sharecroppers and migrant farmworkers. It was a sign that the Alliance was expanding its concerns and may have been dreaming of organizing farm workers.

istrator remarked. African Americans were typically the first claimants to be rejected.[155]

But the Alliance increasingly focused on representing WPA workers rather than the unemployed. Alliance leaders had to develop new skills—negotiating with job supervisors and administrators and informing workers of their rights, while WPA administrators often did not know the rules themselves. Once again an unemployed organization began to do the work of relief authorities: Herbert Benjamin created a guidebook explaining WPA entitlements to overtime pay, holiday pay, weekly paydays, workplace safety, compensation for accidents and illness, and more.

WPA workers frequently had grievances concerning wages, hours, and layoffs, and learning of their rights from the Alliance led to them to air more grievances.[156] In handling them and often winning, the Alliance repeated what earlier unemployed groups had accomplished: it demonstrated that administrators had the power to change unfair or arbitrary regulations. Equally important, it showed workers that authorities responded to pressure from below. Its reputation grew further when it forced the removal of incompetent or biased local administrators and supervisors.[157] In an upward spiral, the more victories the Alliance achieved, the more WPA workers went to it with their complaints. But the rank-and-file no longer participated in delegations or protests; workers relied on Alliance representatives to frame and handle their complaints because grievances had to be made "through channels."

Alliance experts also worked to protect overall WPA policies. Employers demanded that the WPA pay wages that were lower than low private-sector wages—that is, that the WPA not "steal" their labor force.[158] Left to stand, this policy would have created a downward spiral: private employers could have reduced wages, which in turn would require the WPA to cut its wages. The Alliance challenged the employers' demand and won. Over the objections of Treasury secretary Morgenthau, the WPA agreed to conform to "prevailing" wage rates.[159] This victory then produced grievances about what counted as "prevailing" and about WPA administrators who were not complying, creating yet more reliance on Alliance experts. Alliance representatives were becoming professionalized.

The Alliance's greatest victory, the victory that produced more victories, was forcing Aubrey Williams, assistant to FDR's relief director Harry Hopkins, to recognize the Workers Alliance as "bargaining agent" for WPA workers.[160] This then generated yet another valuable power, the right to appoint job stewards.[161] The Alliance was riding high. It had become a labor union in all but name. Significantly, it won that status just after the National Labor Relations Act guaranteed workers the right to unionize. It was a moment when, as many workers and organizers liked to say, President Roosevelt wanted you to join a union.

Recognition of their "union" did not, however, suppress WPA workers' protests. While it is true, as sociologists Frances Fox Piven and Richard Cloward argued, that organization building and maintenance, such as that needed to run the Workers Alliance, has often drained energy from mass protests, WPA workers were by no means quiescent. Though they never won the legal right to strike, they actually struck frequently. The 288 strikes on record—and many were not on record—involved about 140,000 WPA workers.[162] Employers fought these "folded arms" strikes, as they were called, with lockouts, firings, arrests, and violence. Strikers were called "intractable," "obstructionist," "unadaptable to a work program," and of course, "Communists."[163] The strikes continued nevertheless.

The Alliance's metamorphosis into a government labor union produced conflict with private sector labor unions. Most of them saw WPA workers as relief recipients, not as "real" workers, so they did not belong in labor unions. Because unions understood their very raison d'être as bargaining with employers, they considered a WPA job merely disguised relief. One might think that fear of undercutting wages would have made unionizing the unemployed advantageous. But the unions' refusal arose as much from identity—including gender identity—as from strategy. Union members enjoyed pride and status as workers, an identity they were defending against the stigma of being unemployed, still often seen as "dependent."[164]

Identifying the consequences of the Alliance's shift toward representing workers rather than the unemployed does not mean that it was a mistake, a wrong turn. Not to seize that opportunity would have seemed a strategic failure, even unprincipled, because it would have meant ignoring discriminatory and exploitive working conditions. Moreover, the WPA won nationwide concessions, while the victories of the unemployed had been primarily small and local. And in the late 1930s, the WPA seemed likely to endure for a long period, even become permanent, while unemployment relief was *emergency* relief. Had a program of public jobs continued past World War II, the Alliance might have continued, even grown stronger.

At the same time, the Alliance's shift toward representing WPA workers reflected the optimism generated by the industrial unionizing drives. Those campaigns reinforced the belief shared by all three Alliance partners that workers occupied the position of greatest strategic value for progressive change. This made representing WPA workers part of a long-term strategy. But in practice the Alliance's work, like that of the pre–Alliance unemployed groups, allowed the short term to obstruct the long term.

Representing WPA employees in a virtual labor union strengthened their identity as workers and their frequent strikes served to confirm that identity. Sociologist Chad Goldberg called the strikes "framing devices to establish . . . WPA workers as employees," defining their relation to the state as contractual, not as recipients of the dole.[165] WPA jobs also helped men reclaim identities as breadwinners. One WPA worker spoke for many when he told Martha Gellhorn, soon to become an acclaimed war correspondent, "All we want is . . . the chance to care for our families like a man should."[166] The Alliance's hard bargaining on behalf of WPA workers helped men reclaim a manliness threatened by the Depression. The preponderance of male jobs in the WPA also confirmed that men had an entitlement to work that women did not.

Furthermore, bringing men together in work groups replaced, for many, the mixed-sex unemployed groups. Most WPA workers did construction work, which restored some of the men's pride as wage-earners as well as pride in working to strengthen and beautify the nation. By contrast, being unemployed was a matter of loss, of deprivation, the opposite of pride. Miserly relief funding reinforced the stigma of relying "on the dole," because its recipients continued to be poor, often extremely poor.[167] That meager funding created a downward cycle, deepening the Depression, which prolonged the need for relief, thus

New York women protesting their exclusion from most Depression-era jobs, December 7. 1933.

amplifying the stigma. No wonder it has been difficult to build a social movement of the unemployed.

While men's wages improved the lives of women with male partners, men's breadwinner identity reinforced women's dependent status, whether or not they were actually supported by men. Both unemployment and relief may have demoralized men more than women;[168] WPA employment then made men "independent," while unemployed relief recipients remained "dependent." WPA employment thus replicated the principles of the embryonic American welfare state, which embedded the male/female, independence/dependence binary into its programs. State and local control of WPA jobs and federal aid in general enabled discrimination against people of color as well. Racist administrators disproportionately denied them jobs or gave them the worst jobs. This continued in the New Deal's permanent programs: the premier program, Social Security, excluded the occupations of many people of color, and in many states the inferior programs continued to be discriminatory, particularly because they were administered locally, thus empowering patterns of bigotry.[169]

• • •

THE LEFT parties' hope that they could convince the public that unemployment was a systemic problem was not entirely unfounded—the Depression was changing attitudes. The distinction between honorable and dishonorable sources of help and the shame of "the dole" was fading, while the magnitude, prevalence, and ordinariness of public assistance normalized government responsibility for those in need. As a social worker put it in 1938, "The clients aren't what they used to be. . . . No longer do they supplicate for charity, pleading 'worthiness' . . . they assert their rights."[170]

This change showed in opinion polls. "Big government," a pejorative concept today, then seemed desirable. Gallup polls in 1936 showed that 76 percent of respondents wanted free medical care for the poor, 64 percent a social security program, 88 percent regulation of food and drug advertising, 64 percent control of wartime business profits, 59 percent public takeover of the electric power industry, 42 percent takeover of the banks, and not least, 76.8 percent a guaranteed job for every man. Opinion about the WPA in particular was equally striking: 68 percent thought that WPA workers should not be dropped until they found other jobs, and 46 percent thought they should be able to continue as WPA workers until they found jobs as good.[171]

Qualitative evidence, though anecdotal, matches the quantitative evidence. Harry Hopkins dispatched some fifteen social workers and well-known writers—including Martha Gellhorn, wife of Ernest Hemingway; the popular humorist writer Martha Bruere; and the journalist Lorena Hickok—to travel around the country to take the public "temperature" regarding relief. They found widespread conviction that people felt entitled to government help, a conviction often evidenced by social workers' disapproval. Some representative phrases in the reports to Hopkins: "Relief is regarded as permanent by both clients and relief workers." "The stigma of relief has almost disappeared. . . . The relief client . . . expects relief as his right." Clients were no longer "docile." Relief was a "regular and accepted way of life." "Just a big sucker—that's all Uncle Sam is to them."[172] A local relief administrator reported, "We have made . . . our investigators scared to death of the client. . . .

It would take machine guns to cut off relief."[173] "It is a sad sight to see the attitude . . . changing from . . . a modest request for help temporarily . . . to . . . demanding their share of what the Government has to give." The manager of the Fisher Body plant in Flint, Michigan, used a corporate phrase that, perversely, expressed the new sense of entitlement, telling Hopkins's investigator resentfully that his men "consider themselves shareholders in relief."[174]

Relief recipients were inverting the stigma, insisting that they were taxpayers while their relief supervisors were "parasites."[175] Even African Americans, long excluded from local government benefits, were asserting an entitlement. The Athens, Georgia, Colored Community Association wrote that its members had a "constitutional right" to relief.[176] The "negro advisor" to the WPA, Alfred E. Smith, received seven thousand letters a year asking for federal action against discrimination or exclusion from relief and jobs.[177] President Roosevelt's mail—he received 450,000 letters in the first week of his presidency and an average of eight thousand a day after that (compared to Hoover's average of six hundred a day)—might be expected to consist mainly of complaints or requests for help. Instead they showed that Americans not only supported government welfare programs but also wanted more of them; the majority of the letters offered proposals for initiating or expanding government aid programs.[178] These findings appeared a mere eighteen to twenty-four months after the federal government had gotten into the "business of relief," not much time in which to produce a new political culture.

But that culture had never been safe from right-wing attack. The anti-Communist hysteria that we know as 1950s McCarthyism actually began in the late 1930s, attacking social welfare programs as Communist plots.[179] Red-baiting destroyed the solidarity of the unemployed movement. Locals broke off and formed alternative groups "cleansed" of Reds. Workers Alliance head David Lasser was expelled from the Socialist Party in 1938; two years later, in an attempt to stem the losses, he fired Herbert Benjamin, the Alliance's national secretary. Lasser tried to stake out a middle position, warning against the "tories" who "slander and misrepresent us" as well as the "impure and untrustworthy" members who belonged to "any group not an official body of the Alliance"—that is, the Left. That "middle" position was untenable, and Lasser capitulated, forcing Communists out of the Alliance.[180] So McCarthyism not only victimized leftists but crushed the Alliance, though it staggered on for a few more years. After World War II, red-baiting came roaring back to stigmatize the whole New Deal. This vitriolic anti-Communism went on to smash the whole political Left and made any progressive activism risky for several decades, notably targeting the civil rights movement in the 1950s.

A FINAL APPRAISAL

The unemployed movement not only helped millions survive the Depression but also changed the national political culture, creating a new consensus that government had to take some responsibility for the welfare of the citizenry. The movement bolstered the reputation and legitimacy of the Left organizations that led the unemployed movement. But these gains had been opposed from their outset by conservative politicians, and none were more determined than the southern Democrats who held disproportionate power in Congress due to their seniority: they faced little electoral opposition, having disenfranchised almost all southern African Americans. Their attacks on the New Deal as Communist-inspired functioned as a warm-up for the red-baiting attacks they used against the civil rights movement. These attacks were temporarily curbed because the economic crisis was so severe, the Roosevelt administration so effective, and then military production for World War II so urgent. But neither the Left nor the unemployed social movement could withstand the postwar McCarthyist repression of progressive political ideas.

Anti-Communism was not, however, the only factor in weakening the unemployed movement. Its Achilles' heel was present from the beginning. The movement's leftist leadership had inherited from Marxism the expectation that crises of capitalism would engender a socialist movement. But people's urgent survival needs smothered those hopes. Even the most doctrinaire leftists could not in good faith neglect those who badly needed immediate help. How could any humane social movement offer "pie in the sky" while ignoring suffering on earth?* This is a quandary that has confronted many progressive social movements.

Moreover, the movement faced an enfeebling spiral of its own creation: its very victories in squeezing out aid for the unemployed increased the turnover in its membership. Participants who came to seek help left when they got it, or failed to get it. The movement weakened still further when the WPA moved many of the unemployed into employment, marginalizing those who remained unemployed. Workers Alliance leaders did not *decide* to neglect the unemployed. They were responding to pressure from the workers themselves regarding wages, working conditions, and job discrimination. Their grievances required negotiating with their employer, the federal government, and Alliance leaders understandably focused on what was winnable. In that sense, prioritizing the needs of WPA employees was a democratic move as well as a strategic decision.

There was a note of classic tragedy in these developments: the successes of the unemployed movement weakened that movement, and the government jobs won by unemployed activism further enervated the activism that had brought them about.

Yet the very movement was by no means a failure. It is difficult for historians to evaluate the impact of social movements, all the more difficult because politicians and policy makers are typically reluctant to credit social movements. (To do so would only encourage them!) Just as Townsend movement pressure led to old-age pensions, so the unemployed movement gave rise to federal emergency relief and then made the Social Security Act seem more imperative. Even the capitalist stalwart *Fortune* magazine had to credit the movement: "By mass demonstrations, stubborn, insistent and vociferous protests, the Unemployed Councils . . . have indeed improved the lot of the jobless." It even acknowledged that the size of relief stipends was proportionate to the strength of the movement.[181] Wresting aid from reluctant administrators, case workers, and politicians, the movement helped tens of mil-

---

* The phrase "pie in the sky" was coined by the Swedish American labor activist Joe Hill in his parody of the Salvation Army's song "In the Sweet By and By," which offered heavenly "salvation" rather than worldly help.

lions of Americans survive the Depression. Its activism then led to the WPA, which created jobs with decent wages and working conditions, built some of America's most vital infrastructure, and produced masses of public art, from which all Americans benefited.* The unemployed movement exerted a major influence in the creation of *enduring* social rights programs, not only unemployment insurance but many other welfare programs, including old-age pensions, old-age assistance, aid to poor children and the disabled, and ultimately Medicare and Medicaid.† They remain far from egalitarian and far from adequate, but they continue to offer a lifeline for several hundred million people.

The movement also helped Americans psychologically and spiritually. Sociologists found that the economic depression had produced widespread despair, resignation, and feelings of helplessness. They saw increases in family conflict, including domestic violence, and desertions by husbands shamed by their inability to support their families. Particularly devastating was the social isolation of idled workers. The unemployed movement, like many social movements, mitigated this pain by creating sociability and companionship. And because it was companionship in activism, it engendered hopefulness and a sense of efficacy.

These victories owed much to the Left parties. Their organizers devoted countless hours and skills to building a grassroots social movement that generated unprecedented government action. Once the threat of fascism forced European progressive parties into Popular Front alliances, the American parties constructed an American version of a Popular Front—the Workers Alliance—that united progressives and liberals while lending support to the whole New Deal. The unemployed were indebted to that leadership, whether they knew it or not.

The unemployed movement, however, had some unexpected consequences for that leadership. It engendered rank-and-file initiatives that

---

* The WPA built 40,000 and improved 85,000 buildings, including 5,900 new schools, 9,300 new auditoriums, gyms, and recreational buildings, 1,000 new libraries; 7,000 new dormitories, and 900 new armories. It art programs yielded 2,566 murals, more than 100,000 easel paintings, about 17,700 sculptures, and nearly 300,000 fine prints, along with innumerable posters and objects of craft.

† Chapter 3 considers social movement influence on the creation of Social Security old-age pensions.

often ignored or even defied the Left's agenda. When members of Muste's group expropriated flour stashed in a warehouse, or when Harlemites and Chicagoans resisted evictions, they did not first turn to official leadership for authorization. Grassroots initiatives like these were often original and creative, and at times were more aggressive than organizers envisaged or approved.

These dynamics are by no means unusual in social movements. However efficient their organization, however clear their strategy, however well planned their tactics, social movements can be unpredictable and often uncontrollable by their leaders. Such out-of-control activism can of course be destructive, as when 1920s northern KKK members conducted violent attacks despite their leaders' commitment to a non-violent campaign. But such "wildcat" activism, as it is called in labor unions, can also be heroic and astute. In any case, it is part of what social movements *are*.

5

LEADERSHIP AND FOLLOWERSHIP

The Montgomery Bus Boycott, 1955–1956

Montgomery, Alabama, bus boycotters walking to work.

> Well, my body may be a bit tired, but for many years now my soul has been tired. Now my soul is resting. So I don't mind if my body is tired, because my soul is free.
>
> —"MOTHER" POLLARD, MONTGOMERY, 1955

Fifty thousand people rose up and caught hold to the Cradle of the Confederacy and began to rock it till the Jim Crow rockers began to reel and the segregated slats began to fall out.

——E. D. NIXON

It may be true that the law cannot make a man love me, but it can keep him from lynching me, and I think that's pretty important.

——MARTIN LUTHER KING, JR.

The Montgomery, Alabama, bus boycott of 1955–56 has a strong claim to be considered the founding event of the civil rights movement. African Americans had been protesting and resisting segregation for decades, but what happened in Montgomery was a leap into a new magnitude of resistance: the city's *entire* African American population refused to ride public transportation for over a year, at the cost of considerable sacrifice—and won. Their victory produced oceanic waves even beyond civil rights. One historian concluded that it "radically altered the nature and scope of citizen-based political activism in the US."[1] To Blacks, it emboldened further decades of activism. To whites, it brought the message that African Americans could not only outlast but also outsmart their segregationist opposition. To Montgomery whites, it exploded the self-deluding claim that race relations in their city were "good" and that Black protesters were dupes of white Communists.[2] It launched Martin Luther King, Jr., on his historic career of leadership, meteoric in its brilliance and its brevity.

It also made Rosa Parks into a saintlike heroine, one whom schoolchildren are taught to see as simultaneously brave and perfectly demure. For a time her refusal to move from a "white" bus seat was represented as the naïve, instinctive response of a tired woman, a description that hid her extensive political history.[3] Her mother understood that a Black woman would always have to earn, so she taught Rosa to sew; she perfected her sewing skills at the Industrial School for Girls in Montgomery, founded by northern whites to instill "Christian morals" in their charges while giving them a vocation. Rosa Parks was no stranger to white violence. When the Ku Klux Klan marched past her family's house, her grandfather stood at the front door with a rifle, intent on defending his family. Her husband Raymond Parks was an active member of the NAACP who raised money for the defense of Alabama's Scottsboro "boys," nine African American teenagers framed for the rape of a white woman. Raymond Parks pushed his wife Rosa to complete high school—a rarity among working-class Montgomery Blacks. She soon became active in the NAACP herself, particularly in combating white men's rapes of Black women.[4] She did all this while working full time as a seamstress and dressmaker.

Partly because of the reputations of King and Parks, the Montgomery bus boycott has been the subject of hundreds of accounts. My telling here will repeat just enough of the story to allow examining it as a case study of social movement leadership and "followership." The latter is a word I have invented, to refer to those who are not publicly identified as leaders. I use the term *followership* because it suggests a relationship with leaders that *rank-and-file* and *grassroots* do not. The "followers," however, did not only follow. They designed and organized strategies and tactics. As the longtime Montgomery civil rights activist E. D. Nixon put it, "The leaders were led."[5] Themes that appear elsewhere will reappear in this chapter, notably the often unrecognized work of *women*; the existence of *free spaces* crucial to the protest; the construction of a *community solidarity* that temporarily transcended class differences; and the reconstruction of Montgomery African Americans' collective *identity*.

HERE, FIRST, is the story in a nutshell. Growing Black resentment at the humiliating practices of bus segregation congealed in a test case in December 1955, when Rosa Parks deliberately violated the rules. Montgomery African Americans then decided to boycott the buses. That decision created hardships for the many who had to walk or contrive makeshift transportation to get to their jobs, yet an estimated 98 percent of them stayed off the buses for thirteen months. Despite severe harassment, including bombings, the boycott compelled a Supreme Court decision that declared segregation on urban transportation unconstitutional.

At the beginning of the twentieth century, after the federal government betrayed its promises to guarantee citizenship rights for African Americans, city after city in the South segregated buses. Over the decades, resistance grew more common. In 1940 feminist civil rights lawyer Pauli Murray and a friend were arrested for refusing to sit in the segregated Black section of a Richmond, Virginia, bus. In 1941 Congressman Adam Clayton Powell led a successful boycott of two New York City bus companies that would not hire Blacks except as porters. Between September 1941 and September 1942, there were at least eighty-eight cases of Blacks taking "white" seats and dozens of boycott attempts. Many reflected the fury of World War II veterans who had fought—and seen their brothers die—only to come home to racist insults, discrimination, and disfranchisement. Montgomery's Blacks ultimately won when the Supreme Court outlawed this form of segregation, but only after a year of enduring hardship and violence.

The Montgomery boycott's demand was never about seating alone. It was primarily about disrespect.[6] Bus segregation gave every bus driver—and in Montgomery they were all white—unsupervised police power over every Black passenger. Black passengers were usually expected to enter through the bus's front door, deposit their fare, then exit the bus and reenter through the back door to take a seat, if available, in the back. Many were the tales of drivers who drove off, chortling, before the passenger reached the back door. Women told of being forced off because they had temporarily placed their bags or children on a front seat while fishing out the fare. The slightest comment, sign of resistance, or failure to move fast enough became an excuse for bus driver aggression. Blacks could avoid some sites of white abuse, but working-class Blacks, typically without cars, could not avoid the buses. The seats reserved for whites were often empty, deepening Black passengers' resentment. The drivers were becoming increasingly abusive, no doubt retaliating for their perceived loss in the 1954 *Brown* ruling against school segregation.

IN MONTGOMERY, Black women were the particular targets of abusive bus drivers, and it was their humiliation and anger that led them to instigate the boycott. That abuse was a body blow to men as well, depriving them of a masculinity that included protecting women. Women were more likely than men to ride buses, true, but bus drivers seemed to take particular pleasure in abusing Black women, addressing them as "nigger bitches," "coons," whores, or worse. At least one driver liked to stand up and expose himself when a Black woman was waiting to board; it was intended and understood as a threat of rape—and most Black women knew victims of rapes and attempted rapes. (They also knew that form of violence as a powerful means of enforcing white supremacy.) Some drivers were violent, threatening African American women with blackjacks, throwing them out the door, driving off and dragging a Black passenger caught in the back doors. In 1945 a driver used his blackjack to knock the hats off two Black WACs from the nearby army base, in uniform, then hit them in the breast while uttering profanities. Jo Ann Gibson Robinson, who started the boycott, estimated that 60 percent of all Black bus riders had experienced harassment. Class status was no protection; bus segregation prevented middle-class African American women from enjoying their small bit of class privilege.* Robinson herself, a professor at Alabama State University—an historically Black institution, originally the Normal School for Colored Students, its name changed repeatedly until it became Alabama State University in 1969—had experienced this mortification:

> *I leaped to my feet, afraid he would hit me, and ran to the front door to get off the bus. . . . Tears blinded my vision; waves of humiliation inundated me; and I thanked God that none of my students was on that bus. . . . I could have died from embarrassment. . . . In all these years I have never forgotten the shame, the hurt, of that experience. The memory will not go away.*[7]

---

* As Robinson put it, "Both whites and Blacks were human; both were clean." Her emphasis on cleanliness suggests that she and other middle-class women found it galling to be treated like "low-down," uneducated Black people. Middle-class Black women had been protesting that sort of insult since the late nineteenth century.

Robinson was describing a form of PTSD. The fear remained lodged in the psyche and in the body.

The majority of Montgomery's Black women had long performed stoicism in the face of this abuse. As Mary Burks, founder of the group that planned the boycott, put it, "Their outward indifference was a mask to protect both their psyche and their sanity."[8] The "mask" may have been a reference to a line from one of Paul Laurence Dunbar's poems: "We wear the mask that grins and lies." The "culture of dissemblance," to use Darlene Clark Hine's vivid term, required masking one's rage and pain, before Blacks as well as whites.[9] Burks called their stoicism "hard-faced."[10]

SOCIAL MOVEMENTS often arise less from grievances than from broken promises—the combustible collision of raised aspirations with the frustration of those aspirations. Montgomery had changed politically in the decades before 1955, and these changes kindled the boycott. From 1910 to 1940, an upper-class mayor with paternalist values had managed what by white southern standards was a moderate racism: he was hostile to the KKK, for example, and during the Depression he had initiated a municipal relief program that helped some Blacks as well as whites. Meanwhile the white population of the city grew, so that by 1955 this formerly Black-majority city had a 63 percent white majority.[11] The newcomers largely came from the working class and lower middle class; they were conservative religious people, and white supremacy was crucial to their identities.

Unbeknownst to most Montgomery whites, their dominance was being challenged. While the proportion of Black Montgomery residents had declined, the number of Black *voters* was increasing, thanks especially to the efforts of Rufus Lewis and E. D. Nixon (of whom more later). A new city commissioner, Dave Birmingham, attributed his narrow 1953 victory to these new Black voters, but when they sought to collect on this debt, his only concession was adding four African Americans to the police force. Focusing on children, Black women organized to demand access to Oak Park. Only four of fourteen city parks were open to Black Montgomerians, and the biggest and loveliest, Oak

Park—designed by Fredrick Olmsted, containing the zoo and the only swimming pool in town—was not one of them. (Swimming pools have long been sites of intense racism.) Refused, they brought suit and won in a U.S. district court, but the mayor, militant segregationist "Tacky" Gayle, responded by closing the park. Although Gayle was a segregationist on principle, he also saw that exploiting white racial fears and hostility was his ticket to office. He swore to hold the line against the "horrors" that would allegedly follow from concessions to the "northern integrationist agenda."[12]

For African Americans, the 1950s at first raised, then dashed, hopes. In 1950 the U.S. Supreme Court ruled, in *Henderson v. United States*, that a southern railroad could not force a Black passenger to eat in a separate section behind a curtain in the dining car. Also in 1950 the Court ordered the University of Texas Law School to admit a Black student on the grounds that no Black school offered equal resources, and in still another case, it ruled against the University of Oklahoma for making a Black graduate student sit apart from whites.[13] Then came the Court's historic, unanimous 1954 decision in *Brown v. Board of Education*, holding that segregated schools were unequal and detrimental to Black children. Montgomery Blacks, who considered education crucial to a better future for their children, regarded this decision "as the second Emancipation Proclamation."[14] Moreover, in early 1955, in the context of the Korean War, the Department of Defense desegregated the housing on Maxwell Air Force Base, located just east of the city, where one in seven Montgomerians worked.[15] Rosa Parks's husband worked on the base, and she sometimes experienced its integrated cafeteria and trolley cars, before connecting to a segregated city bus.[16]

But *Brown* sparked "massive resistance" in Montgomery—white defiance of the court order. Mayor Gayle and the school board reaffirmed their commitment to segregated schools, including those on the Maxwell base. Violence in support of segregation was common. In 1955 the Supreme Court ruled in *Lucy v. Adams* that the University of Alabama graduate school must admit Autherine Lucy, but when she came to the campus, a mob prevented her from entering, and the university suspended her on the grounds that she would be unsafe; she sued but lost her case.

Despite such insults, and despite the activism of a few community leaders, there had been little organized protest in Montgomery. As Reverend Ralph Abernathy, a leader of the boycott, wrote in retrospect, "We were an obedient generation."[17] In 1943 Rosa Parks had already defied bus segregation, but when she did so, she heard other Black passengers saying, "She ought to go around the back and get on." As late as 1955, just months before the boycott began, she complained that "the Negroes in Montgomery were timid and would not act."[18] Mrs. Beautie Mae Johnson, later to become a boycott activist, recalled a time when she thought, "I know my place, and since I know my place, I don't have any problem."[19] Erna Dungee Allen, who would become a key boycott leader, thought that "Black people were kind of coasting along, everything was segregated. We had just accepted that."[20]

While racism affected all Montgomery African Americans, it did not create unity among them. Like all populations, they were divided not only by class but also by color, religious denomination, and individual grudges and antipathies. E. D. Nixon complained in 1951 that "the Negroes were all split up . . . and divided into cliques and you couldn't get them together on anything."[21] Methodists and Baptists moved in different circles. Jealousies and resentments divided ministers.[22] Black businesspeople, like the ministers, often depended on powerful whites for small accommodations and were sometimes labeled "Uncle Toms" by less beholden Montgomery Blacks. Those most concerned with respectability—who included both middle- and working-class African Americans, especially women—disdained the disreputable behavior of others.

Several observers attributed Montgomery's absence of protest to the complaisance of the Black middle class. Sociologist E. Franklin Frazier, in his *Black Bourgeoisie* (published, ironically, the year after the bus boycott's victory), denounced the Black middle class who dared not offend whites on whom they relied for patronage. He labeled them "the vulnerables."[23] Black ministers were among them. Jo Ann Robinson agreed, charging that "the ministers would soothe the anger of their congregations" by recommending prayer and promising that God would "make the rough ways smooth."[24] When Martin Luther King, Jr., arrived in Montgomery he thought that its Black community was "crippled by the indifference of educated Blacks, 'expressed . . . in a lack of participation in any move toward better racial conditions and a sort of tacit acceptance of things as they were.' "[25] The "tie and collar" crowd lived in the Centennial Hill neighborhood, near the college and remote from the working class and poor.[26] Fred Gray, the Black lawyer who would defend the boycott in court, observed that Montgomery's Black middle class considered working-class civil rights activist Nixon too aggressive. Nixon, in turn, remarked that "all of the Negroes are yellow."[27] His accusation expressed the frustration of an extraordinary organizer who had been "in the trenches" for decades (as we will see below), but he knew that the reason for inaction was not cowardice. Rather, Montgomery's Blacks were careful appraisers of their chances. The city's Black middle class was not an atomized population. Montgomery boasted some fifty Black organizations, reflecting a long African American tradition of banding together, but their program was mainly one of "uplift," aimed at raising the educational and economic level of African Americans.

Some of these pessimistic appraisals probably reflected men's ignorance of or lack of interest in what African American women were up to. Frazier's disdain for the Black "bourgeoisie" was in part an artifact of sexism, blinding him to the fact that middle-class women's focus on "respectability" in dressing, conversing, and behaving with "manners" was, however inadequate, a strategy.[28] As Charles Payne showed in his study of grassroots civil rights activism, engagement in community service might not appear "political," but in the right circumstances, it could provide the networks and labor force for protest.[29] Montgomery Black women had created eighteen women's clubs. Even in the missionary societies, where members would read the bible and sing hymns, members would report on "what they have done for a whole month for the community."[30] This "uplift" work on the part of middle-class Black women did not directly challenge segregation. But some working-class women were active in labor unions. Beautie Mae Johnson had been politicized, she said, when in 1945 the Amalgamated Clothing Workers organized a local at a small garment factory where she worked. At meetings, she recalled, the union representatives would "tell us . . . that if you were doing the same work, you was supposed to be getting the same pay." She and Amy Harris became two of the six officers of the local. Women organized a "women's auxiliary" to Nixon's union, the Brotherhood of Sleeping Car Porters. The local activist Rufus Lewis saw union members as those most likely to attempt to register to vote—an act requiring considerable courage.[31]

Social movements have often been initiated by the relatively privileged, so it is striking that it was an organization composed mainly of upscale, educated, well-dressed women, many of whom had little contact with Montgomery's working class, who jump-started the boycott. They were women faculty at Montgomery's Alabama State College, a Black institution. Mary Fair Burks, chair of the English department, had tried to join the League of Women Voters, and had even been willing to form a segregated Black chapter, but the leaguers refused her. So in 1946 she created the Women's Political Council (WPC). As one of the founding members put it, "We had no other alternative but to form our own if we wanted to be part of an organization that allowed us *as women* to participate in political life."[32] They acknowledged that they were creating a political organization—they voted down calling themselves the Women's Human Relations Committee.

The WPC was the "largest, best organized and most assertive" of all the African American organizations in Montgomery, not just women's organizations.[33] Their agenda began with voter registration and youth programs—children have historically been a key focus of women's movements, just as campaigns for child health and well-being have almost always been led by women. They worried that teenagers would land in trouble because they lacked recreational spaces, the parks being closed to them, and because police harassment provoked them. They also systematically documented cases of abuse of Black women; they strategized to get the attackers prosecuted, with little success.[34]

Though Burks began the WPC, Jo Ann Gibson Robinson soon became its sparkplug and main risk-taker, and in the end she paid for her leadership by losing her job. Her courage was legendary: "JoAnn could have been fired. . . . JoAnn was something else . . . so determined . . . didn't even seem to be afraid."[35] "She did the work of ten women," Mary Burks recalled, a "Joan of Arc."[36] The youngest of twelve children of Georgia farmers, Jo Ann was six when her father died. Her mother sold the farm and moved them to Macon. Jo Ann stood out even as a child: after becoming her high school's valedictorian, she graduated from Fort Valley State College in Georgia, becoming the first family member to earn a college degree. Founded by fifteen ex-slaves and supported mostly by its neighbors, uneducated African Americans committed to educating the next generation, Fort Valley focused on training teachers. (It also produced Georgia's first Black judge.)

Jo Ann took a job teaching school in Macon; she married Wilbur Robinson, but their only child died in infancy, and the marriage soon dissolved. She then earned a master's degree at Atlanta University and completed a year of doctoral work at Columbia University Teachers College. She moved to Montgomery in 1949 as a faculty member at Alabama State. Her appearance—beautiful, slim, and light-skinned, with "good" hair, that is, not too kinky—won acceptance by Black Montgomery's female elite. Her class status did not, however, protect her from humiliation by bus drivers, and nearly every WPC member had similar experiences.* She soon became active in both the WPC and the Dexter Avenue Baptist Church, where Martin Luther King, Jr., became pastor in 1954. Importantly, she was no snob, and her informal partnership with working-class E. D. Nixon would prove invaluable in initiating the boycott.

The WPC embarked on a voter registration drive, a radical and provocative move in the Montgomery context. It divided the city into four quadrants and assigned a separate committee to cover each; the committee heads were responsible for making "sure everything got done on her side of town." As Amy Harris recalled, "I took from Mobile Drive back to Cavalier Drive . . . and we went door to door."[37] The WPC provided training so that people trying to register knew what they might be asked and how to respond. This does not mean there was no class snobbery in the group. Its leaders seemed to believe that only high-status women could do this organizing and made sure that those in charge of each sector should be "professionals": "We thought this was the best thing."[38] Still, they were probably right that well-

---

* Despite their middle-class status, not all the teachers were prosperous. Many worked as maids on weekends and in summers in order to keep their families afloat.

educated women, already registered to vote, could most effectively coach less-privileged Blacks.

Aware that they could not enfranchise enough Blacks to challenge white rule—in 1956 only 2,058 Black Montgomerians out of at least 34,000 eligible had successfully registered—the WPC supported the white candidates least hostile to Black interests.[39] This strategy allowed the relatively few Black voters to tip the outcome in tight races, forcing some white candidates to seek Black voters. Thus the WPC became a power broker in African American politics and even, occasionally, in overall city politics. Its efforts surely contributed to electing Commissioner Birmingham.

The WPC's voter registration campaign meshed with similar men's efforts, bringing Robinson into a productive alliance with E. D. Nixon. She quickly apprehended the extraordinary leadership capacity of this working-class man with only sixteen months of formal education. Born in 1899 to a Baptist minister father, Nixon was one of seven children. His mother died when he was very young, and the children were scattered among different relatives—no single African American family could support so many. He learned early on that he would be on his own, gained confidence, and developed a reputation as a man who could not be pushed around. His physical presence helped: he was tall, standing six foot four, muscular, and very dark-skinned (Reverend Abernathy called his color "blue-black"), with a "deep commanding voice."[40] In 1923 he found work as a Pullman porter, a position that shaped the rest of his life. Not only did that job command high status among African Americans, but it made him familiar with unsegregated northern cities.

His aspirations grew when he attended a meeting of the Brotherhood of Sleeping Car Porters (BSCP). There he heard A. Philip Randolph, socialist head of the union. "I never heard a man like Randolph talk before," he recalled, calling him "the greatest Black man we had in the last one hundred years."* Nixon's railroad boss learned (through spies) that he had attended the BSCP meeting and warned him that

---

* The BSCP, founded in 1925 by Randolph, was the first labor organization led by African Americans to receive a charter from the AFL.

he would not allow his porters to do that. Nixon retorted that he had joined the union and added, "Of course, before I joined I thought about what lawyer I wanted to handle my case if you started to mess with my job."[41] He had learned the power of audacity as a very young man. During the 1930s Depression, he established the Montgomery Welfare League to support unemployed Blacks and even succeeded in getting them food stamps. Randolph also recognized his acuity and leadership skills—Nixon served as the Alabama president of the BSCP for twenty-five years.

Convinced that winning the right to vote was essential to Black progress, in 1940 Nixon established the Montgomery Voters' League, and taking a leave from his porter job—possible because the porters were now unionized—he traveled through Alabama urging Blacks to register. His reputation for boldness grew after he led 750 African Americans to the Montgomery courthouse to attempt to register. They were refused, but over time, through sheer tenacity, he got several hundred onto the voter rolls.[42] He soon became head of the Montgomery NAACP, then of the Alabama NAACP, where Rosa Parks served as his secretary.* He added twenty-one new branches to the organization, increasing its membership from 478 to 2,256.[43] (Black activists' opinions about the NAACP varied. Parks's husband had not wanted her to join because he considered it too dangerous, while Nixon considered it too cautious—but this was later, when it declined to endorse the boycott.)[44] If Robinson was worth ten women, Nixon, always called E.D., was worth ten men, possibly more, because he was older, he had more community contacts, and his activism more protracted and wide-ranging. He had become a leader with a large reservoir of organizing strategies. Fred Gray called him "Mr. Civil Rights." The Montgomery newspaper called him "the NAACP *mau mau* chief."[45]

The Robinson-Nixon alliance symbolized, and fostered, the cross-class collaboration that made the boycott successful.[46] They com-

---

* In fact, Rosa Parks served as "secretary" to all of Nixon's civil rights activities, answering phones and letters and keeping records on all the various cases of people who came to him for help. Moreover, she did the same for lawyer Fred Gray—she was often in the thick of activism, but always as a helper.

plemented each other. She was the elected leader of a membership organization of elite women, and that, along with her education, academic post, and light-skinned patina, gave her entrée to meetings with the mayor and city commissioners—where she argued hard but got little. E.D. had none of that: he was a rough, working-class guy, expert at creating projects but without a stable constituency. By sheer force of character and persuasiveness, he had won a few skirmishes and produced some benefits for his people, and he commanded the respect of all who knew him. Some of the "tie and collar" crowd were uncomfortable with his uneducated style, but not Jo Ann Robinson—she knew him as "a vital force to be reckoned with."[47] She also knew his integrity and would go on to propose naming him to head the boycott treasury.[48]

SHORTLY AFTER the Supreme Court's 1954 *Brown* decision, Robinson, attempting to use the precedent, wrote the mayor on behalf of the WPC, calling for an end to bus segregation. He refused, so the WPC began discussing a boycott. She later recalled the complex frame of mind among her sister WPC members: "No one was brazen enough" to ask for "integrating those buses. Just to say that minorities wanted 'better seating arrangements' was bad enough. . . . But we knew that deep down in the secret minds of all—teachers, students, and community— Black Americans wanted integration." (That such aspirations existed mainly in "secret minds" points to a racism so embedded that yearnings for equal treatment had to be deeply submerged.) Neighborhood segregation allowed African Americans to enjoy some escape from racism while near home, but the bus company could not afford to run separate buses for Blacks and whites. Middle-class class privilege counted for nothing on the buses: by demeaning all Black passengers, bus segregation strengthened cross-class unity.

Robinson and Nixon began strategizing a lawsuit. They considered several women as potential plaintiffs, but they were rejected for various reasons.* One day fifteen-year-old Claudette Colvin, a straight-A

---

* They did not try to find male plaintiffs. The women were of course brave, but the stakes were higher for men, who stood to lose jobs and were probably somewhat more prone to violence.

244 / SEVEN SOCIAL MOVEMENTS

student, was on the bus coming home from school, where she had read about Harriet Tubman and Sojourner Truth. The driver said "Niggers, move back." Perhaps Tubman and Truth were in her mind when she remained seated and said, "I done paid my dime." As she later explained, "History had me glued to the seat." She also saw her defiance in gendered terms: "Every morning, this male personality used to come out of me. I wanted to fight." "In a few hours every Negro youngster on the streets discussed Colvin's arrest," Jo Ann Robinson recalled. But she became pregnant out of wedlock, so Nixon vetoed making a case around her, considering her vulnerable to being labeled disreputable.[49] Colvin understood this as snobbery: "I didn't represent the middle class . . . because of where I lived."[50] Rosa Parks "took the case very hard" since "the child had been extremely brave . . . and suffered for it."[51]

More potential candidates for the suit soon appeared, all teenage girls. Eighteen-year-old Mary Louise Smith, a maid working for two dollars a day, was also rejected because she lacked respectability: Nixon thought her father was a drunk and her home of "low type" (allegations that she denied in later interviews).[52] He rejected Katie Wingfield because he believed that she "lacked the courage for such a role," and Amelia Browder because she "would not be able to withstand courtroom cross-examination."[53] Nixon was seeking a perfectly blameless but also tough candidate, because he expected the usual racist slurs about their morality and wanted to protect these young women from public shame.

That so many of these challenges to segregation came from teenagers may indicate that young people were restless beneath the quiescence of their elders. Equally striking is the historian Rachel Devlin's finding that girls constituted the great majority of children who tried to integrate schools before *Brown*.[54] Black men and boys were arguably more vulnerable to white retaliation. Johnnie Carr, who would become a leader in the boycott, explained, "If Black men came out, they would have been crucified. The women had more freedom." But she added, "And maybe the women had a little more courage, too. There is something in courage that women are just endowed with."[55]

The teenage girls' defiance was not wasted: it strengthened the community's readiness for action and spurred both Nixon and the WPC to search for the perfect complainant. One journalist called it a "shrewd process of auditioning."[56] So when Rosa Parks was arrested on Thursday, December 1, 1955, Nixon, Robinson, and her cohort knew she was just right. Her arrest was a "trigger event," a concept used by scholars of social movements. But an event becomes a trigger only if people are prepared to take action.[57] Now they were. They understood that Parks was using her body to speak for a community, and her authority to do so came from a community history. In turn, the community honored her by continuing her resistance.

ROSA PARKS was the right person because her virtue was unassailable. The feminine, nonthreatening adjectives applied to her make that clear: *devout, mild-mannered, retiring, soft-spoken*, with "a refined sense of decorum."[58] (By contrast, Claudette Colvin yelled, struggled when they dragged her off the bus, and screamed when they handcuffed her.) Parks was married and also beautiful, middle-aged and light-skinned, unlike the darker Colvin. She was "right" also because she posed no challenge to the ministers' authority.[59] Having worked with her, Nixon knew that she was tough enough not to buckle under a smear campaign. Though she was working class and earned a working-class wage, she was also a class bridger, connecting middle- and working-class Black Montgomerians. Educated at the Montgomery Industrial School for Girls, which was run by white northern women who sought to uplift the Negroes, Parks was an "honorary member of the middle class" and had some middle-class friends.[60]

That Parks was "demure" has long contributed to obscuring her extensive activist experience.[61] She was married to a man whom the Black Communist organizer Esther Cooper Jackson (an inspiration to Black feminists a decade later) considered "one of the more advanced political activists in the union movement." As a speaker at a 1945 NAACP convention in Atlanta Rosa Parks had met and was inspired by Ella Baker, a dynamic organizer who would go on to be a mother-adviser to SNCC. Parks's participation in the campaign to prosecute the particularly vicious rapists of Recy Taylor had already put her at risk.[62] She refused to use segregated drinking fountains and elevators. She was neither naïve nor instinctive in her decisions. African American women close to her knew this, as did at least a few whites. One of the policemen who arrested her whispered to the driver, "NAACP" and "Are you sure you want to press charges?"[63]

A tiny number of whites supported the boycott—certainly fewer than a dozen. Among them the most elite were the Durrs, both native Alabamans. Patrician lawyer Clifford Durr, a former Rhodes scholar, had run a corporate law practice until he left it for a New Deal job (legal counsel to the Reconstruction Finance Corporation). Virginia Durr was of the southern aristocracy, daughter of a Confederate general and then congressman, niece of the governor of Tennessee, and sister-in-law of Supreme Court justice Hugo Black. Born in Birmingham, a descendant of slaveowners and more recently of a KKK member, Virginia Durr began her remarkable journey to leftist views while at Wellesley College.

The Durrs were not Communists, but they refused to join in McCarthyist attacks.[64] They moved to Montgomery in 1951, and in 1954 they were subpoenaed by an un-American activities committee "investigating" whether the Highlander Center (of which more below) had connections with Communists. They refused to testify. Most of Clifford Durr's white clients deserted him, and white friends deserted Virginia. By contrast, at least one Black friend, Johnnie Carr, a cook turned insurance salesperson, supported her: "We are with you and our prayers are with you and we are proud of you."[65] Facing down her white friends' condemnation with her upper-class, sangfroid confidence, Virginia Durr became an active boycott supporter, contributing money and regularly driving workers to their jobs. (Two decades later she became the "unofficial den mother" to SNCC activists.)[66]

Once Clifford Durr arrived in Montgomery, E. D. Nixon pulled him into civil rights lawyering, first by asking him to defend a Black soldier at the Maxwell Air Force Base who was falsely accused of pilfering; Durr proved him innocent.[67] He then became a mentor to Montgomery's leading Black attorney Fred Gray—a former student of Jo Ann Robinson—and would go on to advise him in defending those arrested and preparing the suit against bus segregation. "He more than any other person," Gray wrote later, "taught me how to practice law."[68] (Durr kept his own name out of the litigation for fear that if the case got to the Supreme Court, Justice Black, Virginia's brother-in-law, might have to recuse himself.)

Aubrey Williams, another white antiracist, had been deputy chief of the New Deal's WPA (appearing briefly in chapter 4) and one of the most progressive and outspoken New Dealers. In 1945 he had returned home to Alabama, got a loan from liberal department store magnate Marshall Field, bought the decrepit old monthly newspaper *Southern Farmer*, and transformed it into a fountain of liberal ideas.[69] He invested in affordable housing for Blacks and contributed to the NAACP. After *Brown*, he joined two other activists in shepherding a group of Black children to attempt, without success, to enroll in a new school in a white neighborhood. Like his friends the Durrs, he was a regular target of red-baiting. (The American Legion publication *Firing Line* devoted a whole issue to an attack on him.) He supported the bus boycott by raising money and posting bail. Modestly, he minimized his contribution, but E. D. Nixon insisted that "if it hadn't been for Aubrey Williams, I don't believe we could've ever mustered up courage to do it." This was a wild exaggeration, but Nixon added something that could be said for all the supportive whites: "You don't know what it means to have a white man that negroes can trust."[70]

Several of these few white brave souls became targets of attacks, ranging from obscene phone calls to bombings. The librarian Juliette Hampton Morgan paid with her life. She wrote letters to white newspapers, some of them actually published, denouncing segregation and praising the Supreme Court's decision in *Brown*.[71] During the boycott she transported maids to and from their workplace every day. But she could not withstand the virulent attacks and threats—she committed suicide in July 1957.

The Lutheran minister Robert Graetz was the boycott's most vulnerable white supporter. A white pastor to a Black congregation, he lived in a Black neighborhood—some said he had a "Black heart."

(He had learned about race discrimination while researching a paper on discrimination against Jews.)[72] His house was bombed. He and his family survived only because the largest bomb—eleven sticks of dynamite wrapped around a container of TNT—failed to explode. (Had it exploded, the police claimed, it would have leveled the entire block and killed dozens.) An FBI agent told Graetz not to stay in the house, as your "enemies were still intent on killing [you]." In the crater left in his yard by the smaller bomb, Graetz planted a tree and invited all his neighbors to a dedication ceremony. Seven men were arrested for the attacks, and unsurprisingly, all were acquitted.[73]

Nixon brought Virginia Durr and Rosa Parks together, thereby creating a connection that would prove invaluable to the boycott. Having learned that Mrs. Durr needed a seamstress to help with her daughter's wedding trousseau,[74] he recommended Parks, no doubt with a double agenda—finding more work for Parks and connecting the two politically. As the two women spent time together, Virginia Durr observed that Parks seemed discouraged, then saw an opportunity that might lift her spirits: a school desegregation workshop, to be held in summer 1955 in response to the *Brown* decision, at the Highlander Center in Monteagle, Tennessee. Durr urged Parks to consider attending the workshop as a vacation as well as an educational experience and even bought her a suitcase.[75] She got Aubrey Williams, a member of Highlander's board of governors, to pay Parks's bus fare.[76]

A remarkable white southern institution, the Highlander Center provided a different kind of support. Myles Horton, educator Don West, and Methodist minister James Dombrowski had established it in 1932 as an interracial training school for labor activists. Despite its Christian ideology, it was constantly red-baited and harassed.[77] Parks was worried about being seen going there, so Durr provided some protection by accompanying her part of the way. Parks's two weeks there were simultaneously restful, restorative, and possibly transformative. The workshop was a new experience: forty-eight white and Black people ate together, workshopped together, and joked together about the absurdities of segregation. One of her greatest pleasures, she recalled, was "enjoying the smell of bacon frying and coffee brewing and knowing that the white folks were doing the preparing instead of me."[78]

Beulah Johnson, another Montgomerian who had visited Highlander, said of it, "Democratic living in practice . . . for the first time in my life . . . was mine to observe."[79] In other words, it was prefigurative—a microcosm of a nonracist society. Parks had a white roommate, and they discovered with amusement that each was concentrating on trying to put the other at ease. Septima Clark, who King once called the mother of the civil rights movement, was running workshops there. Parks took copious notes at every session—Clark was an inspiration for her.[80] Nevertheless, at the end of her stay at Highlander, Parks still felt that "nothing would happen [in Montgomery] because Blacks wouldn't stick together."[81] She dreaded returning. Yet a few months later she traveled back to Highlander to tell her story, at a meeting planning school integration workshops, reporting that "Montgomery today . . . it's just a different place altogether since we demonstrated."[82] It is a reminder of how quickly a social movement can turn pessimism into optimism.

Word of Parks's arrest traveled like a lit match in a dry forest. The speed with which it traveled offers a clue to how boycott news would travel. A woman who had been on the bus with Parks called a friend who ran to Nixon's house. He tried to reach Fred Gray, but the lawyer was out of town, so he telephoned Clifford Durr. Nixon put together the $100 bail and picked up the Durrs. The three went to the jail and brought Rosa Parks home.*

Their late-night discussion was tense. Raymond Parks was furious but also fearful for his wife. He had taken great risks himself: while working with Communists on behalf of the Scottsboro defendants, police had killed two members of their group. So he knew just how violent white racists could be, which made him protective of his wife. He thought going after bus segregation a risky provocation, and he did not want her at its center. Virginia Durr recalled that he was in "a state of absolute panic: ' . . . the white folks will kill you.'" Rosa Parks knew her husband's courage, crediting him and his Communist associates with introducing her to a sophisticated analysis of racism, so she respected his warnings.[83] Clifford Durr believed he could get the

---

* The African American lawyer Fred Gray was out of town, but Nixon might have chosen to use Clifford Durr anyway, as a white man would have had more clout.

E. D. Nixon escorting Rosa Parks to the courthouse in Montgomery after her arrest for refusing to give up her seat to whites.

charges dropped, and Raymond Parks tried to talk her into following that path. But Nixon saw the episode as the opportunity he had been waiting for. He knew, he said, that if Rosa Parks gave the word, "hell could freeze but she wouldn't change." Despite her husband's warnings, she gave the word.[84]

A telephone grapevine spread the news. Nixon called Jo Ann Robinson and Johnnie Carr, a former schoolmate of Rosa Parks who had worked with her in the NAACP.* Carr was also a class bridger, connecting middle- and working-class Montgomerians. Someone called another of their classmates, Mrs. Erna Dungee Allen, wife of a local physician, prominent in the upscale Negro Women's Club and secre-

---

* Carr, a former cook and now successful insurance saleswoman, had been active in defending the Scottsboro "boys," which had connected her to the Durrs and with Communist Party members, possibly including Angelo Herndon (profiled in chapter 4).

tary of the WPC. She had inherited and then continued a family activist tradition: her schoolteacher father, an NAACP member, had tried to register to vote; she did so successfully in 1949.[85] Nixon next turned to alerting the ministers, and when it got too late to call them that night, he pulled out a tape recorder and recited into it a list of those he would call in the morning, before he had to leave town for two days for his railroad job. Though he had criticized the ministers' cautiousness and thereby antagonized some of them, he knew that they alone could pull the mass of Montgomery Blacks into solidarity.[86]

THE WPC women made sure that the blaze—the news and the anger—spread throughout Black Montgomery. During the night of December 1–2, Jo Ann Robinson gathered some WPC leaders and two trusted senior students at Alabama State in a college office where she had access to a mimeograph machine. The group wrote and mimeographed leaflets—they printed some 52,000 by cutting each sheet of paper in three—calling for a one-day protest boycott of the buses on Monday, December 5. Between four and seven a.m., they mapped out distribution routes and locations for the leaflets; then they gathered some two hundred volunteers who delivered the leaflets door to door and dropped off bundles at schools, beauty parlors, barber shops, beer halls, and factories, every place where Black people congregated. (Robinson peeled off for a while to teach her eight a.m. class!) They moved through the city quietly, with nonchalant body language so as not to arouse white suspicion. They aimed to confine knowledge of the plan to Black people and to keep the source of the leaflets confidential, because their use of the college's equipment and paper was unauthorized and risky.[87]

The WPC was able to act so quickly because they were prepared. Their leaflet was brief; they did not need to explain the grievances, only state the facts. It read, in part:

Another Negro woman has been arrested and thrown in jail because she refused to get up out of her seat on the bus. . . . This has to be stopped. Negroes have rights, too . . . If we do not do something to stop these arrests, they will continue. The next time it may be you, or your

daughter, or mother. This woman's case will come up Monday. We are,
therefore, asking every Negro to stay off the buses Monday. . . . You
can afford to stay out of school for one day if you have no other way to
go. . . . You can also afford to stay out of town for one day.[88]

It is worth dwelling on the language of the leaflet. The WPC framed
it as an attack on women, who constituted the majority of Black Montgomerians (24,000 women to 19,000 men) and an even greater majority
of bus riders. Everyone, men and women alike, found the humiliations
of women particularly abhorrent. The abuse of women revealed the bar-
barity of whites. What kind of coward would pick on a woman? Since
men were supposed to protect women, the leaflet's gendered appeal
spoke to men as well as women. Robinson gambled that if the women
began a boycott action, the men would go along.

Though middle-class women put out the leaflets, their text addressed
working-class people specifically. The "you can afford to stay out" language spoke directly to the poor. Sixty percent of Black women in
Montgomery worked as domestics, and 75 percent of Black men in
"menial" jobs. The writers understood that what they were asking constituted a considerable sacrifice for some—loss of a day's wages, at best.
These were poor people. Forty percent of the homes, for example, had
no running water or private toilets. The WPC women knew that if a
boycott were to succeed, it would require uniting African Americans
across class, religious, and color lines—a task that many democratic
social movements could not accomplish—and subordinating the personal animosities that divided them. In this respect, the WPC was vital,
even though many of its members had little contact with Montgomery's
poor Blacks. Mary Burks remarked, "Often we not only had to take
time to explain the leaflet, but also to read it to those unable to do so. It
was my first encounter with masses of the truly poor."[89] Constructing
cross-class solidarity in Montgomery would take work; it was not an
automatic by-product of racism.

While Robinson used her professional job and the resources of the
WPC to jump-start the boycott, she did not remove herself from the
boycott's daily labor. Despite her heavy teaching load, she became a
regular driver, ferrying boycotters to and from work. She took min-

utes at boycott meetings and produced its monthly newsletter.[90] But someone told the college president, H. Councill Trenholm, that Robinson had used college resources. He tried to support her but had to ask her to keep a low profile because the college depended for funding on a state that was, at best, skeptical of educating Blacks. After the boycott's success, vengeful state authorities fired seventeen professors, including Robinson.[91]

Robinson's respect for working-class leadership was already apparent on the night before the boycott. At three a.m. she told E.D. what the WPC was doing—the only person outside the WPC she spoke with. She considered him the key male leader. Certainly she regarded the ministers as leaders also, but E.D. knew how to operate politically. She did not, however, telephone Rosa Parks. According to Jeanne Theoharis, in her superb biography of Parks, Robinson did not feel she needed Parks's consent, and unlike Johnnie Carr and those active in the NAACP, she may not even have known of Parks's history of activism—they "moved in very different circles."[92] The WPC assumed their legitimacy as leaders, as representative of middle–class, educated Black Montgomery.

At five a.m., Nixon started calling the ministers. He began with Ralph Abernathy—"Ab," as his friends called him—because Nixon knew him to be the most outspoken of the Montgomery clergy. Three years older than King, he had graduated from Alabama State with a degree in math. Ordained as a Baptist minister in 1948, he also had a radio show—the first African American on Montgomery radio. In 1951 he became the senior pastor at First Baptist, the largest Black church in Montgomery, and his enthralling sermons expanded his congregation; today his eloquence is less remembered only because it was soon overshadowed by King's. Having secured Abernathy's support for the boycott, and for convening a meeting of ministers, Nixon then called the twenty-six-year-old new pastor in town, Martin Luther King, Jr. Because he was new, he didn't owe anything to the "city fathers" and had not yet made enemies among the competitive and often squabbling ministers. Nixon knew this was an advantage.[93]

King had arrived to take over Dexter Avenue Baptist in 1954, at twenty-five years old, looking "more like a boy than a man."[94] During his first year there, the church was often half empty, and many of Montgomery's Black clergymen did not know him. But King had already been quietly initiating action: he joined the NAACP, supported the church's social and political action committee, and even considered making voter registration a precondition for joining the church.[95] Recognizing his gifts and commitment, Abernathy mentored him. Several of those who would become boycott leaders, including Nixon, Johnnie Carr, and Rosa Parks, had heard King speak at an NAACP meeting in August 1955. They were awed. Carr had said, "Listen to that, he's something isn't he?"[96]

When Nixon called him on the night of Parks's arrest, King replied that he'd think about supporting a boycott and asked for time to consider it.[97] Nixon didn't wait long and called back soon, assuming correctly that Abernathy would have phoned King in the interim—a sign that Nixon knew how Montgomery's prominent African Americans operated. King then said yes, to which Nixon responded, "I'm glad of that because I already called 18 other people and . . . told them we were all gonna meet at your church."[98] That Nixon could call a meeting at King's church without King's permission suggests that Montgomery's Blacks regarded churches as belonging to their community. (One scholar called this sense of ownership a "quasi-contractual" relationship "marked by rough forms of accountability to the congregation.")[99]

Forcing King's hand also reflected Nixon's brazenness, which in turn reflected his political assurance. He was accustomed to assuming leadership and to dealing with faint-hearted clergy who preferred to stay out of politics. (Another example of his nerve: at the boycott's first mass meeting, he took in $500 in contributions, then called the police to ask for protection as he took it home. They obliged.)[100] Nixon's audacity also serves as a reminder that it was Montgomery's laity that pushed King into his future career; as Ella Baker put it, "the movement made Martin."[101] Still, some of them sensed, even at this early moment, King's extraordinary gifts. They did not know that he would become a world-historical leader, to whom they would ever after be deeply indebted.

E.D.'s choice of the Dexter Avenue church was doubly strategic: he wanted to bring in the "tie and collar" crowd who attended that church and, through their status, force King's hand.[102] Located directly across from the state capitol, with a view of its Confederate flag, Dex-

ter Avenue served an upscale, fashionable congregation of one thousand, the "cream of Montgomery."[103] The writers understood that what
they were asking constituted a considerable sacrifice for some—loss of
a day's wages at best. In a sign of their political savvy, Jo Ann Robinson
and Nixon both knew they had to bring the city's black elite into action.

Boldness was by now Nixon's modus operandi, a part of his constitution, developed over decades of leadership. With his detailed
knowledge of power relations in Montgomery, he felt he had to be bold
because he understood the ambiguous position of the southern Black
clergy. Their timidity derived in part from their precarious economic
positions, which often depended on white patrons. Most of them had to
work outside jobs to earn a living, as their churches were small (a phenomenon that a historian of Black religion calls "overchurching").[104] At
the same time, the Black laity were closely connected to their churches;
naming the church you attended was a common way to communicate
your identity. The church was the "spiritual home" even of those who
never attended.[105] True, studies of the civil rights movement have sometimes romanticized Black churches and glossed over ministerial conservatism, but their physical spaces were essential to people who had
little access to public places for large gatherings. Churches provided not
just spaces but "free spaces," as theorized by social movement scholars
Sara Evans and Harry Boyte, because they were somewhat sheltered,
authorities were hesitant to invade them, and they therefore allowed
participants to speak out in safety.[106]

THE "BRETHREN," as Abernathy called them, turned out en masse to
a meeting at King's church on Friday evening, December 2. The sixty
ministers, eight women, and some prestigious laymen who attended
found themselves with little decision-making power. They were confronted by a fait accompli: a boycott was going to happen on Monday,
whether they liked it or not. The group did, however, make the crucial
subsidiary decision to call for a mass meeting on Monday evening, after
the boycott, in order "to keep the infuriated masses under control," as
Jo Ann Robinson wrote somewhat sardonically; and to get reports on
the effectiveness of the boycott, so as to make future plans.[107] Some of

those at this Friday evening meeting were already considering more protracted action.

The two women who made the boycott happen—college professor Jo Ann Robinson and seamstress Rosa Parks—were not at this meeting, foreshadowing the imminent exclusion of women from leadership. In retrospect, Robinson identified this meeting as the moment when "the men . . . decided to assume leadership."[108] This development was not controversial, as everyone understood that ministers were formally the Black community's leaders. In retrospect, WPC members had never expected it to be otherwise—the combination of maleness, ministerial status, and/or class position overdetermined the men's leadership status. The women were accustomed to lack of recognition, not only for their work on which churches depended but also for their ideas. Erna Dungee Allen, a member of Montgomery's Black upper class, explained to an interviewer, "Women . . . passed the ideas to men to a great extent. . . . They let the men have the ideas and carry the ball."[109] Black Montgomery women of all classes also understood racism's assault on Black masculinity. Although some of them could offer a lucid critique of male and ministerial leadership, they endorsed, or at least accepted, its necessity—despite the fact that many of these leaders had previously resisted the WPC's call for a boycott.

The women excluded from visible positions would go on to perform indispensable labor, and boycott leaders knew it. Speakers frequently singled out the walking women as heroes, acknowledging that it was the 7,700 "maids and cooks," the "foot soldiers" of the thirteen-month ordeal, who ultimately won the boycott. When it rained for the first time after the boycott began, some whites "said that we'd be back on the buses," Johnnie Carr recalled. Instead, even as she drove as many as could fit in her car, many others just kept walking, "rain just dripping down off of 'em . . . people were willing to do these things, to sacrifice."[110]

Nixon and Abernathy, the primary strategists in this moment, knew that the boycott's effectiveness depended on the participation of lower-class Black Montgomerians. Relying on sermons to spread the word was not enough, Abernathy realized—"the 'saints' would get the message, but what about the 'sinners'?" So he and King visited every club and

nightspot they knew to distribute the leaflets, venues likely unfamiliar to King.[111] Nixon also employed a riskier tactic. He phoned a white
journalist he knew, Joe Azbell of the *Montgomery Advertiser*, the city's
main newspaper, and offered him a story, if "Joe would play it straight,
which Joe agreed to do." That story appeared on the front page of Sunday morning's paper, slanted toward what Clifford Durr paraphrased
as "look what these damn niggers are up to."[112] Nixon's scheme worked
perfectly. The article informed African Americans and simultaneously
panicked the whites, which, paradoxically, strengthened the boycott by
bringing police escorts alongside the buses, making everyone, white
and Black alike, fearful of getting on a bus.[113]

The WPC devised the initial plan to help boycotters get to their
jobs. Starting at 5:30 a.m. Monday, private cars would cruise through
Black neighborhoods, collecting riders. Black-owned taxis would transport many for ten cents each. But these vehicles could transport only
a fraction of the workers. The organizers faced an unknown: would
Blacks stay off the buses in the absence of a transportation alternative?
They did, and the sight of totally empty buses spoke louder than any
pep talk. Coretta King, watching from her front window, saw a bus
passing and shouted out to Martin, "Darling it's empty!"[114] W. E. B. Du
Bois compared it to a general strike.[115]

The Friday-evening meeting of the "Brethren" had been a disaster.
Reverend L. Roy Bennett, president of the Interdenominational Ministerial Alliance, who chaired, pontificated with his well-known "windbag
monologues" and gave no one else a chance to speak.[116] So after the ministers saw the empty buses on Monday morning, they pulled together a
smaller meeting. That group decided, first, that the protests should not
be led by the NAACP—that would be too provocative, and because it
was a national organization, the white "powers that be" could charge
that the protest was led by "outside agitators."[117] So they invented the
Montgomery Improvement Association (MIA) to lead further action.
Nixon made a case for King to head it—"he can talk as good as white
folks and he can talk to white folks,"[118] and after some discussion key figures supported him. That support was not inevitable, and his future was
not yet apparent, as many of the clergy were not yet familiar with him.[119]

The group approved a modest set of demands, probably drafted by

Nixon: that drivers treat Black passengers with courtesy; that the seating plan operate on a first-come-first-serve basis, with Blacks beginning in the rear and whites in the front; and that the bus company employ Black drivers on predominantly Black routes.[120] They postponed a decision about extending the boycott until they could gauge the size and the mood of the evening mass meeting, to be held at Holt Street Baptist, a large, barnlike church. This decision was key: Holt Street was located in the poor side of town, and many working-class African Americans would have hesitated to go to the upscale Dexter Avenue Baptist.[121]

Unusually among social movements, including the later civil rights movement, in Montgomery the clergy played a vital role at first. They were far from fearless, had reason to anticipate white retribution, and had heard rumors that "spies" and "uncle Toms" had infiltrated their group to report on it to powerful whites. So they wanted to keep the identity of the MIA leaders confidential. Nixon was furious. "And how do you expect to run a protest without the whites knowing it?" he thundered. Using language "not in the Sunday school books," he charged them with cowardice. "Here you have been living off the sweat of these washwomen all these years, and you have never done anything for them. Now you have a chance to pay them back. And you're too damn scared to stand on your feet and be counted." He went on to articulate a major theme in civil rights discourse—reclaiming Black masculinity.

> The time has come when you men is going to have to learn to be grown men or be scared boys. . . . We must . . . be men enough to discuss our recommendations in the open. . . . We've worn aprons all our lives. It's time to take the aprons off. . . . If we're gonna be men, nows the time to be mens. . . . If this program isn't . . . brought out into the open tonight . . . I'll take the microphone and tell the people that . . . you are all too cowardly. . . . We ought to be men enough to stand on our feet . . . or admit to ourselves that we are a bunch of scared boys.[122]

His words worked. The ministers agreed to making their leadership public.[123] And yet the other face of protecting women was silencing them. Rosa Parks asked to speak at the Monday evening meeting but was refused the floor. She never spoke at a mass meeting during the boycott—and her public invisibility contributed to making her a symbol of victimhood and ladylike propriety.[124] The historian Jeanne Theoharis imagined, astutely, what Parks might have said: she "might have connected the injustice on the bus to the travesties of Scottsboro, the brutal rapes of Recy Taylor and Gertrude Perkins, the murder of Emmett Till . . . the courageous work of . . . Highlander . . . the actions of her own Youth Council . . . the loneliness of her stand on Thursday and the power of walking together on Monday." Instead, Theoharis concluded, the boycott leaders consciously or unconsciously "obscured" her years of activism in order to make her the symbolic figure they needed.[125] Perhaps they also wanted to silence her because they did not trust her to say what they wanted to hear.

The Monday-night meeting squelched any doubts about the community's eagerness for action. Fifteen thousand jubilant people arrived outside the Holt Street church, five thousand were able to enter, and thousands more stood outside, listening through loudspeakers. Cars were lined up from seven to fifteen blocks in every direction. A *Montgomery Advertiser* reporter wrote that the "clapping seemed to boom through the walls" and compared it to the crowd at an Alabama State–Tuskegee football game. They were cheering, Reverend Abernathy wrote, "for themselves for what they had done that day." King, new not only as a preacher but also as the president of a new organization, the MIA, was making his debut on a large stage. Anticipating that whites would respond to the boycott with violence, he made nonviolence his major theme, one that would resound through his career.

The meeting adopted the moderate demands that leaders had agreed on, and everyone pledged not to ride buses until the demands were met. On their face, these proposed new bus rules could be said to rationalize segregation, to smooth it out by eliminating some of its points of abrasiveness.* Numerous southern cities, such as Mobile, Richmond, Atlanta, and Nashville, already operated with looser bus segregation

---

* This perspective parallels Depression-era leftists' fear (discussed in chapter 4) that small bits of unemployment relief were mere "Band-Aids" designed to save capitalism. Jo Ann Robinson considered the demands too timid but went along for the sake of unity.

rules. But before long, white intransigence moved the MIA from a separate-but-equal to an integrationist demand. Progressive social movements often migrate toward the left as they go along, and often for the same reason: the ignorant bullheadedness of the opposition. The boycotters' demands became more ambitious, more daring, because the city government, the bus company, and Montgomery's elites were so intransigent.[126] Few ideologies have shown more mobilizing power than racism. The protest moved to the left because its opponents moved to the right.

Had the white power structure agreed to a compromise, the protest might have ended. But perhaps not. The 1953 Baton Rouge bus boycott can illustrate. When city leaders made their minor concession, the Reverend Theodore Judson Jemison, assuming authority, unilaterally called off the boycott, and got his decision approved after the fact, enraging many of the rank-and-file boycotters.[127] In Montgomery, by contrast, it soon became clear that no leader or minister could have acted unilaterally, because the followership was in control. When in January 1956 some "white friends" offered a compromise proposal, one of the ministers wanted the MIA to consider it. But King replied, "If we went tonight and asked the people to get back on the bus, we would be ostracized."[128] In February the Men of Montgomery, an elite white club of about one hundred business and professional men, tried to broker a compromise; they met with leaders of the MIA twice, but the MIA would not budge. Once the boycotters saw that they could hold fast for weeks, they were not in the mood for compromise. In other words, the protest was self-strengthening; just seeing the empty buses made participants determined to continue.

On the whole, Montgomery's white "moderates" abdicated and left the field to virulent segregationists who built hysteria about this threat to white supremacy.[129] The Montgomery White Citizens Council (WCC), founded in response to the *Brown* decision, grew from several hundred to fourteen thousand members in just three months. As one reporter put it, "the Montgomery police force is now an arm of the WCC."[130] The KKK, having been quiescent for several decades, regained strength and performed "drive-bys" of leaders' homes to crank up fear.[131] On February 10 the mayor and the city commissioner spoke at a giant WCC rally, keynoted by Senator James Eastland of Mississippi, that filled the Coliseum with eleven thousand people. Speakers called for giving "the niggers a whipping" and a "harsh lesson" to Rosa Parks.[132] The angry discourse of the WCC, like that of the Klan, was as gendered as that of Nixon and the ministers: compromise, even civility, equaled surrender; integration would lead to uncontrolled rapes of white women; defense of white supremacy was the required manly stance.

This poisonous racist discourse produced violence, of course. Whites spat on Blacks as they walked, pelted them with containers of urine, threw bricks at them, and slashed the tires of cars transporting Blacks. Nineteen prominent Blacks had acid thrown at their cars. Two policemen did that to Jo Ann Robinson's car, which was "eaten up," riddled with holes. After crying for a bit, she told others, "Well you know, these are . . . beauty spots."[133] Angry laid-off bus drivers served as deputy police; no longer able to abuse Black passengers, now they harassed, beat, and arrested boycotters. The MIA organized volunteers to guard the churches and kept a rota of night watchmen at the Parks house. Meanwhile the Parkses joined a clean-up crew helping everyone—and they were more than a few—who got bombed or vandalized.[134] Even the Black winos living on the streets helped by guarding the carpool fleets at night.[135] By mid-January 1956, the death threats had become a deluge, some directed at Rosa Parks. (One can only imagine Raymond Parks's anxiety.) King was receiving forty telephone threats a day.[136] On January 30, the King home was bombed, with Coretta and baby Yolanda inside—luckily they were not injured. A furious crowd collected in King's yard, shouting and urging people to grab their weapons; police tried to clear them out, roughly. As Coretta King recalled, "It could have been a riot, a very bloody riot."[137] Their fuse was burning down. In one of his impressive acts of leadership, King rushed home and successfully calmed the crowd with a forceful insistence on nonviolence.*

King's achievement at that moment was all the more impressive because not everyone turned the other cheek.[138] Many Black households, including King's, had guns, and someone had shot at a bus car-

---

* I refer to the importance of this achievement again in chapter 6, comparing it to Cesar Chavez's similar quieting of potential violence.

rying its white passengers.[139] Nonviolence was honored in principle, but in the views of many, nonviolence did not exclude self-defense. Even Abernathy tried to buy a pistol, but no white merchant would sell him one. In the course of the boycott, he saw that nonviolence had to be learned, emotionally as well as tactically: "We had to be willing to suffer and we would have to be emancipated from our fears."[140]

Despite the provocations, Black retaliatory violence remained minimal. Nixon responded to it tactically. He used threats, calculating that the white ruffians were cowards. To one hostile telephone caller, he responded, "I don't intend to go by myself. . . . You can come on out here whenever you get ready." That night there were eighteen people in his house, and "we had all kinds of guns. . . . Nobody could have drove down that street and interfered with anybody. . . . From where I lived to clear down the end of the street, we had people . . . sitting in the hedges with shotguns all down the street." But on other occasions, as when an angry Black crowd assembled around the police station, he urged nonviolence, because he knew the police would use any excuse to attack and arrest people. Don't give them an excuse, he said—"don't even throw a cigarette butt, or don't spit on the sidewalk or nothing." In a later interview, he recalled the difficulty of remaining nonviolent:

> They lifted their feet when they were going to work . . . but they dragged them along the ground when they came home. . . . Some tended to move toward the shot houses for some likker. . . . They got drunked up and swore they'd do bad things to the white so-and-sos. . . . It's hard to do [to remain nonviolent] sometimes, when folks feel downtrodden and whupped up on.[141]

E.D. was not by any means the only African American to issue such threats, nor were they confined to men. One maid told an interviewer, "They think they bad 'cause they got guns, but I sho hope they know how to use 'em, cause if they don't, I'll eat 'em up wid my razor. . . . He'll be in pieces."[142] Others took the risk of talking back, even to police. When a bus driver tried to push Lucille Times's car off the road and shouted "You Black son of a bitch," she yelled back, "You white son of a bitch." A policeman responded and hit her with his flashlight, saying, "Do you know that was a white man you called a white son of a bitch?" She retorted, "Do you know I'm a Black woman that he called a Black son of a bitch?"[143] This was both long-smothered fury and newly intensified fury.

Some of the credit for limiting Black retaliation belongs to an outsider, Bayard Rustin. A middle-class African American from Philadelphia, his parents were activists in the militant days of the NAACP. He knew he was gay early in his youth and was lucky enough to have a supportive grandmother; when he told her he was drawn to men, she replied, "I suppose that's what you need to do."[144] As with Nixon, the influence of A. Philip Randolph led him to his life's work as a social justice activist and sent him to Montgomery, while A. J. Muste (discussed in chapter 4) won him over to pacifism.

Rustin was a risky ally for King: he had been a member of the Young Communist League in the 1930s and had been arrested for homosexual activity in 1953. That King relied on him in spite of these risks suggests the value of his advice. According to Rustin, "Dr. King had very limited notions about how a nonviolent protest should be carried out." Arriving in Montgomery, he found guns lying around in King's house and an "arsenal . . . smuggled in by ministers and porters."[145] While King had a moral and religious leaning toward nonviolence, Rustin won him over to the *strategic* importance of nonviolence. He emphasized that any move away from nonviolence by a leader, even if in self-defense, would authorize followers to stray. Aware that his background could be used to smear the protest, Rustin left Montgomery after eight days, but remained a close adviser to King for the rest of the reverend's life.[146]

Red-baiting has been a staple in attacking twentieth-century progressive social movements. (In this book it appears in the chapters on the KKK, the unemployed, and farmworkers' movement.) The White Citizens' Councils used it heavily, calling the whole civil rights movement a Communist conspiracy to destroy the southern way of life, with Highlander as its center.[147] FBI agents sent daily reports to their leader J. Edgar Hoover, telling him what he wanted to hear: that civil rights activity—like anti–Vietnam War activity later—was a Communist plot, hatched by foreigners intent on destroying the United States.[148] In many cases, red-baiting has been successful, portraying progressive activists as traitors doing the Communists' bidding. But in the Montgomery bus boycott it did not succeed, because its purpose was transparently clear to Montgomery African Americans. As one minister put it sarcastically, "The only 'Red' Negroes . . . were those who did not agree with the philosophy of the White Citizens Council. Calculated from this point of view, there were 50,000 Negroes to be classified as Communists!"[149] In Montgomery, anti-Communism melded with racism to make most whites believe that African Americans were not capable of organizing something as efficient as the boycott, and that Negroes were easily duped, intimidated, or even coerced by clever outsiders. One white Montgomerian remarked that "nine out of ten Negroes don't know what it's about." Some charged that they stayed off the buses only because "Negro toughs" threatened anyone who attempted to board.[150] This underestimation of Black political savvy, competence, and independence contributed to the protesters' victory.

TWO INTERNAL betrayals threatened to divide and weaken the movement, and their failure provides another sign of the followership's clearsightedness. In late January the city commission suddenly announced that it had worked out a settlement with a group of "prominent Negro ministers"—an announcement timed for release on a Saturday night, in order to sow confusion and dissension at Sunday services. Luckily, the news went out on a wire service; Carl Rowan, a Black reporter for the *Minneapolis Tribune* and later a prominent television anchorman, saw it and phoned King. Learning of it in the middle of the night, MIA leaders organized an emergency salvage mission. They woke up every single Black minister, plus Reverend Graetz, so that the clergy could denounce the false rumor to their parishioners as a trick of the opposition. King and other MIA people visited "juke joints" to spread the word that the boycott was still on. The three "turncoat" ministers— one Baptist, one Pentecostal, and one Presbyterian—claiming that they had been "hoodwinked" into this alleged settlement, were compelled to denounce it, and were branded as traitors by Montgomery's Blacks.[151]

It is possible that the city commission actually wanted a compromise. But in their ignorance, the commissioners thought they could achieve this without implicitly acknowledging the real boycott leaders. The terms of the phony settlement resembled the original three MIA demands: courtesy to passengers, a movable border between whites in front and Blacks in back, and a new proposal—separate buses for Negroes during rush hours.[152] But even if the city powers had accepted these terms, it was too late. People were irate, and the three turncoat ministers were scorned for years afterward. This attempt at backroom dealing strengthened the boycotters' determination—it allowed them to vent fury at three people and thereby at the whole tradition of "Uncle Toms," and it sent the message that the boycotters would not tolerate secret negotiations, that MIA policy decisions must be public.[153] The affair also told whites that the movement rank-and-file would decide who its leaders would be. It strengthened the MIA leadership by demonstrating its trustworthiness and positioned it yet more firmly into interdependence with the followership.

In a second act of disloyalty, in June 1956, when both King and Abernathy were away raising money in California, Reverend U. J. Fields of Bell Street Baptist accused MIA leaders of misusing donations, egotism, and self-aggrandizement. The head of the transport operation, Reverend Sims, acknowledged that some of the drivers transporting boycotters apparently cheated a bit, charging people for rides while also taking gas money from the MIA; one sold tires supplied by the MIA; others took money for phony repairs.[154] Nixon later said that ministers who did fundraising speeches, including King, kept some of their take, and he admitted doing this once himself.[155] It is hardly surprising that some among the drivers, garage owners, and ministers, most of them poor, might have done so.[156] Rank-and-file boycotters, however, responded to the allegations with fury. If some knew the allegation was true, they nevertheless joined the irate response.

Fields became "the modern Judas," "a villain with a 'smiling cheek.'" "Look at that devil sitting right next to Rev. King." "All the 'perfumes of Arabia' could not cleanse him of this deed." His church fired him. A domestic servant said, "I just wish I could git my hand on 'im."[157] Right or wrong, the accusations sought to undermine leadership, and the followership wouldn't have it. The followership forced Fields to eat crow publicly. In an evening mass meeting, King entered the church together with Fields, who "recanted." Feeling the need to control people's anger, King then asked the crowd to forgive Reverend Fields, reminding them that Christ had said, "Let he who is without sin cast the first stone."[58]

The day after the bombing of the Kings' home, the MIA filed a suit, challenging bus segregation altogether.[59] Some MIA leaders still hoped for a negotiated solution, but the bombing convinced them to wait no longer—another instance, not uncommon in social movements, in which opponents inadvertently escalate protest demands. The lawyers wanted, of course, to be able to use their own expertise, to do what lawyers do; this was, no doubt, particularly important to the twenty-five-year-old Gray, and it was vital that a Black lawyer argue the case.[160] The lawyers also believed they could win at the Supreme Court. The case would be brought by the NAACP, awoken from the timidity that had previously so angered E. D. Nixon, and Robinson feared that the suit might create a leave-it-to-the-experts passivity and a return to the buses while awaiting the court decision. But in fact the suit had the opposite effect: hope for legal vindication raised spirits and stabilized community commitment to the boycott. There was no serious suggestion to return to the buses.

The suit was risky because it ruled out compromise. Instead of making bus segregation less abusive for African Americans, it was challenging the whole edifice of segregation. As Rufus Lewis put it,

> *The thing is that it was a growth. . . . We wanted to correct this step by step. But as we moved forward the whole horizon seemed to open wider for us. And the wider it is the further you're going to go. That was the type of development.*[161]

He was identifying a pattern that appears frequently in social movements.

WHILE THE community's resolve and pride had grown over the eight weeks of boycotting, so too had the costs, personal hardships, and internal resentments. Working people needed their jobs; the great majority had few savings; many were elderly and already worn down by decades of extremely hard work, especially domestic workers who were on their feet for hours. In the first months of the boycott, the memory of Rosa Parks's arrest was fresh and the attention of the national media was encouraging. But over time both faded. The press had nothing to report, because there were no developments. MIA leaders knew that the community's commitment had to be repeatedly revitalized, and the churches made this possible. Ministers, now responsive to the MIA, led regular mass meetings, twice weekly on Mondays and Thursdays for six months, then weekly, more than a hundred of them over the year. Abernathy called them "pep meetings."[162] People needed to be together. The meetings were rotated among churches, in order to transcend loyalties to a particular congregation.*

Churchgoing is a form of sociability, which is necessary to every social movement. In this era when many had no television, Black church services could be theatrical. They featured entertainment, with high-quality singing and preaching that replicated the power of the music.† People packed the seats and the standing room, so many came early to get themselves a seat. Domestic workers might arrive directly from work, bringing a meal for themselves, sometimes singing as they waited. Some older women laid claim to specific seats. Georgia Gilmore explained that "I would always get there between five and five-thirty. And I had my own special seat where I would sit all the time so if I wasn't early enough to get the seat somebody would save it."[163]

The generic agenda had a fixed sequence: preliminary remarks by the pastor, hymns, prayers, more songs, news and plans, the "pep talk," a collection, more songs. The opening song might be "Onward Christian Soldiers" or "What a Friend We Have in Jesus"—hymns also sung in white churches but with different meanings in Black ones.[164] Then came a scripture reading or responsive reading. Favorites included Corinthians 13 and Isaiah 55. The first dwelled on love, understood here as nonviolence, and also includes the famous "When I was a child, I spoke as a child, I understood as a child, I thought as a child; but when I became a man, I put away childish things"—gendered language in

---

* When the smaller churches hosted, there were often two evening meetings, one at seven p.m., the second often not beginning until ten p.m.

† Compare to the KKK's theatrical rallies, discussed in chapter 2.

which manhood stood for self-respect. The beautiful passage from Isaiah conveyed the message that Black Montgomerians were struggling on behalf of the whole race:

> *I will make an everlasting covenant with you . . . the sure mercies of David. Indeed I have given him as a witness to the people. . . . Surely you shall call, and a nation that did not know you shall run to you, for . the sake of the Lord your God and for the Holy One of Israel, for He glorified you.*[165]

King would report on current developments, not in a matter-of-fact summary but as a sacred quest. He was making social justice integral to Christianity. At the same time, his sermons hinted at his future role as a global leader, speaking of "exploited people . . . rising against their exploiters."[166] His metaphors and cadences were spell-binding. "You had to hold the people to keep them from getting to him," one of the ministers said.[167] One elderly woman told Virginia Durr that while listening to him, she had seen "angels come down and light on his shoulder."[168] While Montgomerians could not have foreseen his future as a national inspirer, they knew that his gifts were extraordinary. But at this early stage in his career he belonged only to Black Montgomery. His spiritual and rhetorical brilliance seemed to be their discovery, even their property, and his individual ability strengthened their collective ability.

Individuals would testify on the theme "Why I am with the Protest." In these personal histories, testifiers left their habitual stoicism to express pain and humiliation. Their testimonies exemplify Cesar Chavez's understanding that organizers' personal narratives mobilize support, but in Montgomery these stories were being told not by organizers but by followers. The mass meetings also served to bond boycotters, at least temporarily, across religious and class lines. "Unity is expressed in words and in the little kindnesses that the people show each other," like car owners providing rides, Lawrence Reddick reported. "The mass meetings . . . engulfed everybody," Rufus Lewis said.[169]

Then Abernathy spoke, his words as organizer a complement to King's as mobilizer: "Now let me tell you what that means for tomorrow morning."[170] He would then then offer a plan and ask for responses.

He usually got them—opinions, suggestions, and criticisms of boycott problems. Then came introductions of visitors, a collection, more
singing, and a closing benediction.[171] The MIA introduced Friday-
night and Saturday workshops in nonviolence (prefiguring what civil
rights groups would do a few years later). Abernathy saw them as "dress
rehearsals," aiming to "drill our people so thoroughly in the philosophy and techniques of nonviolence that when they were attacked their
instinctive reaction would be to protect themselves . . . without lashing
out at the enemy." The theological message, "the power of redemptive
suffering," morphed into instruction in self-protection: elbows guarding
stomachs, hands covering ears and temples. Later he would be proud
of the lessons' success. When people were being attacked with clubs,
bottles and rocks, "Almost without exception they behaved exactly as
we had taught them."[172] This behavior stands as an extraordinary feat
of mass discipline.

FEW HISTORIANS have studied the welfare provision organized by
the MIA. Hundreds of people lost their jobs, including Rosa and Raymond Parks. As Erna Dungee Allen recalled, the MIA took responsibility when possible. "We paid rent. We paid gas bills. We paid water
bills. We bought food. We paid people's doctor bills. We even buried
somebody."[173] Even while the Parkses were struggling economically,
Rosa Parks headed the "welfare" committee. This work has been relatively invisible to many historians. Although she was the detonator and
symbol of the movement, she never spoke at the mass meetings and
worked in a self-effacing manner. Yet no one contributed more labor.
She oversaw the collection and distribution of donations, of food, clothing and above all money for rent, utilities, and medical bills—she even
delivered material herself. She considered cleaning up the destruction
wrought by bombs and vandalism as part of her job description. She
and her committee members sought out new employment for those who
were fired.[174]

Providing alternative transportation was expensive—estimated
at $500 per month (or $5,200 in 2022). The NAACP sponsored some
money-raising events. A speakers bureau brought in contributions

from elsewhere: King was rapidly becoming a sought-after speaker, but Reverends Abernathy and Bennett, Alabama State faculty member J. E. Pierce, E. D. Nixon, and Rosa Parks also traveled to give talks. Parks took her first airplane trip, to Detroit to speak at a union; her brother lived there and she eventually moved there. Then she began traveling widely—to the West Coast, the Midwest, and New York. Nixon's labor contacts brought in resources, including a $35,000 donation from the United Auto Workers. He established out-of-state bank accounts in order to circumvent an injunction secured by the city that froze the MIA's Alabama accounts. The dashing, charismatic Adam Clayton Powell, Jr., minister and congressman from Harlem, helped organize a national prayer day in which more than one thousand churches raised somewhere upward of $100,000.[175] Meanwhile what Black Montgomerians contributed at the church meetings constituted on average 20 percent of their income.[176]

Because the key ministers were so often out of town raising money, their absences strengthened the lay leadership, reducing the rank-and-file's sense of dependence on the ministers and building their confidence in making decisions.[177] Many boycotters served on the MIA's committees, such as banking, finance, welfare, speakers bureau, and newsletter. By the summer, boycotters saw that they were doing something historic, so the MIA formed a "history" committee, "in order that there may be an reliable and orderly record of the bus protest . . . growth and *future development* [my emphasis] of the MIA."[178]

Nothing demonstrates the initiatives of followership as well as the Club from Nowhere. Its founder, Georgia Gilmore, single mother of seven, domestic servant, restaurant cook, and community midwife, had once been arrested on a bus herself.[179] Known both for her "fiery temper" and her barbecue and fish dinners, she "once beat up a white man who had mistreated one of her children. . . . Even the white police officers let her be."[180] Because "what we could do best was cook," she proposed that women prepare and sell food to benefit the movement.[181] The women contributed anonymously—hence the club's name—for fear of retribution. Gilmore lost her cooking job and was blacklisted by other white restaurants, but this did not stop her.

Beginning with fourteen dollars pooled from its members, the Club bought chickens, bread and lettuce, made sandwiches, and sold them at the mass meetings. Soon they were producing full dinners and baked goods. They peddled them at beauty parlors, laundromats, and other gathering places, walking through both Black and white neighborhoods. The boycotters got food as well as the gratification of contributing to the protest. (Later Gilmore opened her own restaurant in her home, where civil rights advocates could meet securely.)

Gilmore made a ritual of presenting the money to the MIA: during collection time at each Monday meeting she would stand, announce herself as representing the Club from Nowhere, and walk ostentatiously to the front bearing the contribution and announcing its amount—typically $150 to $200 each week. She was received with applause, foot stomping, and shouts of "Aaaamen, Amen." Soon Inez Ricks, who lived on the other side of the city from Gilmore, formed another group, the Friendly Club, to compete with Gilmore in how much they collected each week, and the rivalry boosted the size of their gifts. Celebrating these weekly contributions became a favorite part of the meetings.[182]

Because so many Montgomery Black women worked as domestic servants, they were able to provide a more clandestine service to the MIA: intelligence that the middle-class WPC women lacked. White employers of maids would converse in front of them as if unaware that they had ears, reprising the assumptions of slave owners a century earlier. As enslaved people had once done, these modern servants pooled and reported tips about their opponents' tactics to MIA strategists while scrupulously evading employers' frequent questions about MIA affairs.[183]

THE MOST labor-intensive boycott work was building and maintaining an alternative transportation network. It would become one of the most dramatic examples of complex logistics planned and executed by the followers in a social movement. The first day of the boycott had been an overwhelming success. It was "a sight to behold, a parade of humanity never to be forgotten." Hundreds, perhaps thousands walked. Old pickup trucks, bicycles, carts, even mules and one horse-drawn buggy carried people whose jobs were too far away for them to walk.[184] (Seven years later a similar thrill met the hundreds of thousands who came to Washington, D.C., and heard King deliver his "I Have a Dream" speech.) But these improvised solutions could never have survived a protracted struggle. Over the next months, the boycotters would put together a transportation system that carried tens of thousands. It never served all, and many still had to walk—and they did. One man walked fourteen miles a day.[185] But the walkers would see the cars and vans in operation and reported feeling triumphant nevertheless.

At first the MIA relied on some three hundred members' cars. Drivers included retired people, students, teachers, even GIs from Maxwell Air Force Base, anyone with a flexible schedule; others left early for their own jobs in order to provide rides to others.[186] Irene West, the "regal, haughty *grande dame* of Black Montgomery," who "dined at a mahogany table . . . replete with crystal, china, and monogrammed silver napkin rings," drove people in her finned Cadillac for hours every day. Her riders were at first surprised because she usually had a chauffeur driving.[187] Her work was another example of class bridging, bringing Montgomery's working class into direct contact with its middle class. A few white supporters drove, including Reverend Graetz and Virginia Durr, who were both arrested for invented infractions.[188] Hundreds of white housewives who wanted their "help" to arrive promptly picked them up or paid their cab fares. The mayor insisted that they quit doing this, with no success. As Durr characterized the response, the housewives were saying, "Tell the mayor to come and do my work for me, then."[189] As the *Chicago Defender* put it, Black domestics knew that their white employers would "tolerate injustice but never inconvenience."[190]

Boycotters also used taxis from Montgomery's few Black companies, with passengers paying a few cents or nothing at all. The city tried to stop the system: it found an ordinance that set a minimum forty-five-cent fare for taxi rides, a fare well beyond the means of most passengers. Police began arresting the cabbies for not charging the legally set fares and for committing any other infraction they could find or invent.[191] Outmaneuvering them, and in some cases, predicting what they would do—sometimes based on intelligence provided by servants—saved the boycott more than once.

As it became clear that the boycott might continue for a long time, its effectiveness required a long-term, scheduled transportation solution. On Jo Ann Robinson's recommendation, Rufus Lewis took on the responsibility for designing it. He became second only to Nixon among the lay male leaders of the protest. A native Montgomerian, born in 1906, a graduate of Fisk University where he studied business administration, Lewis had spent two years in Cleveland and New York City, experiencing life without legal segregation. He was not only a successful businessman, having inherited a mortuary from his father-in-law, but, equally important to his social standing, he had coached the Alabama State football team for nine years, leading it to two conference championships.

He was a civil rights entrepreneur. In 1947 he had established a club to promote voter registration—he called it the Citizens Club—and built for it a brick building with "fine wood paneling." Cannily, he made it simultaneously a nightclub.[192] He conducted clinics to coach applicants in how to pass the tests specifically designed to stop Black registration. Anyone who succeeded in registering to vote got a celebratory party and a plaque honoring them at the club, thus making a personal success into a community achievement. A member of the Dexter Avenue Baptist Church, he quickly allied himself with King, even as his own work served, quite consciously, to move Montgomery Blacks away from looking exclusively to ministers for leadership.[193]

Working around the clock, Rufus Lewis assembled a committee that met almost daily, creating and maintaining a system that could carry thousands of people a day. Relying largely on King's and Abernathy's national fundraising, the MIA bought thirty vehicles, mostly station wagons. Various churches registered them and, as a defense against city harassment, painted the church names on the vehicles' sides. People enjoyed calling them "rolling churches."[194] They followed regular, prescribed routes several times a day.[195] The system required a central place for communication and meetings, but securing one was not easy—legal harassment forced the office to relocate four times. Forced out of the Alabama Negro Baptist Center, they moved to Rufus Lewis's nightclub until city officials threatened to revoke his license. Then they met in Abernathy's tiny church office, until the Black Bricklayers Union local no. 3 offered to share its larger space.[196] Pharmacist Richard Harris provided a "switchboard" for the system, a telephone at his drugstore located near one of the transfer points. He received and passed on messages and kept the rides flowing. He developed a code—talking "minstrel"—to confuse the police, whom he suspected of tapping his line.[197]

In planning routes, the committee sought advice from postal workers who knew the neighborhoods house by house, resident by resident, job by job.[198] Building on this research, they established fifty morning and forty-one evening pick-up stations where riders could congregate without providing the police with a pretext for arrest. The morning stations operated from five-thirty to ten a.m., spaced so that few had to walk more than a few blocks to a station. From two to eight p.m., workers returning home used pick-up stations in grocery store parking lots, a glass factory, a chemical company, a school, a country club, Black-owned gas stations and garages, even Maxwell Air Force Base. In residential neighborhoods, they relied on churches, so that those waiting for rides had shelter in bad weather. Because not every vehicle could go to every neighborhood, they set up five transfer stations situated downtown, using the Greyhound station, a used car lot, the A&P, the Swift & Co. plant, and the Black-owned farmers' union building. The dispatchers at these stations had to be tough: they could not allow drivers to dawdle, chat, or wait for latecomers, knowing that if they blocked traffic even for a moment, arrests would follow. The system even fielded limited twenty-four-hour service for those on night shifts. Mimeographed carpool schedules were posted on telephone poles, but only the initiated knew what they referred to.

The system relied on a staff of nine coordinators and schedulers, fifteen dispatchers (including Rosa Parks when she was free of her many other responsibilities), twenty full-time drivers, and seventy-four part-time drivers. It provided 15,000 to 20,000 rides a day. Drivers were paid four dollars for a full workday, a boon to some who had lost jobs. Some car owners donated the cost of gas, but others received a chit at the beginning of each driving day that specified the amount of gas that would cover their route. Nine Black-owned gas stations accepted these chits and collected on them from the MIA. Riders paid ten cents per ride, or what they could, not to the driver but to the MIA at the mass meetings. Gas stations contracted with the MIA to supply oil, tires, batteries, servicing, and repair. When Reverend Sims took over management of the system, he initiated daily inspections of all the vehicles, frequently examining them himself. Alabama agencies refused to provide the necessary insurance, so someone connected them with Lloyds of London, which wrote the policies.[199]

The transportation system not only helped people keep their jobs but provided an experience that strengthened solidarity. In some social movements and organizations, people meet in small chapters, but in the Montgomery boycott, the vehicles provided something similar—spaces that allowed sociability more intimate than large church meetings. Riders learned who had been laid off, what employers were secretly a bit sympathetic, and who were the worst police officers.

Anyone who weakened and rode a bus was visible, and the resultant social pressure helped prevent individuals from quitting the boycott. In this sense, white allegations that boycotters were being coerced were not entirely wrong. (Functionally, this coercion resembles strikers' attempts to stop strikebreakers.) But in Montgomery, the typical threat to a quitter was that their conscience would torment them: "Honey, let any of 'em ride who want to. Dey conscious [conscience] will whip 'em."[200] This negative pressure was reinforced by the rewards of camaraderie. The mass meetings created one kind of solidarity, the car rides a more personal kind. Both functioned to turn followers into owners of their social movement.

THE POLICE tried to "cut the legs off" the boycott by arresting drivers for imaginary infractions, passengers for "loud talking," and walkers for stepping on private lawns. Every Black driver seemed to get ticketed two or three times a week. Jo Ann Robinson was stopped once for staying too long at a stop sign and another time for not stopping long enough.[201] These tickets produced fines that added to the fundraising burden. As the tenacity of the boycotters became clear and arrests of individual drivers produced no effect, city officials turned to mass arrests. Using a 1921 statute that banned boycotts in

Birmingham, they got a grand jury to indict approximately one hundred people.[202] They scheduled the arrests for February 22, Washington's birthday and a bank holiday, so the arrestees could not get funds for bail.

The arrests of King and twenty-three other ministers infuriated Black Montgomerians. (By now, the boycott was national news, and the arrests featured on page one of the next day's *New York Times*.) As a list of those charged circulated by word of mouth, those named did not wait to be arrested but presented themselves to the court for arraignment.[203] Singing crowds circled the police station. "Black women with bandannas on, wearing men's hats," Reverend Sims recalled. "Three great big old women with their dresses rolled up over work pants. . . . One of the police hollered 'all right you women get back.' . . . 'We ain't going nowhere. You done arrested us preachers and we ain't moving.' He put his hands on his gun. . . . They said, 'I don't care what you got. If you hit one of us you'll not leave here alive.' "[204]

Voluntarily surrendering to arrest was risky. Every African American knew that those in custody, especially men, faced violence, sometimes deadly. These fears intensified at the first mass meeting, when city police and military police from the Maxwell base identified partic-

Arrest photos of Montgomery bus boycott leaders: (left to right) Jo Ann Robinson, Ralph Abernathy, Martin Luther King, Jr., Rosa Parks.

ipants. "They'd have cameras and recorders there to take it all down," Virginia Durr observed.[205] When King was tried, the prosecution called on several witnesses to name him and a few others as initiators of the boycott. Unsurprisingly, none would do so. Gladys Moore said, "Wasn't no one started it. We all started it over night."[206] Abernathy considered these arrests the moment that "our movement developed into its full maturity."[207]

Intended to intimidate, the arrests actually helped sustain the boycott. Reverend Sims understood, even at the time, that whites most feared working-class Blacks, not the "tie and collar" crowd.[208] Clifford Durr had presumed that after the one-day boycott succeeded, its leaders would say, enough, we've made our point, but the "cooks and the maids" thought, "We ain't showed nothing yet. We ain't going back on those buses until they start treating us right."[209] This may have been a case when the followership—or the "masses," as Marxists had called those in the unemployed movement two decades earlier—were more determined than their official leadership.

On June 4, 1956, a federal district court ruled that bus segregation was unconstitutional. The state appealed, so the boycotters had to continue through four more months of uncertainty, until the Supreme Court upheld the ruling on November 13. Just as the Black bus riders had long found the humiliation worse than the physical abuse, so their victory stirred pride rather than relief. But even after the Supreme Court decision, the boycott had to continue for five more weeks yet, due to slow paperwork. And it did, with no quitters. When the Black riders returned to the buses, they boarded "with poise and dignity, their heads held high . . . their manner stately," as Jo Ann Robinson wrote. Bayard Rustin saw the victory a bit differently: writing to King with generosity and perceptiveness, he pointed out, "It is not only the Negroes' self-respect which was won—but the respect of white people, who though they retain basic prejudice, have lost something that begins their long struggle to genuine understanding."[210]

The segregationists, aware that their way of life was under siege, did not quit either.[211] Forty carloads of KKK members drove through African American neighborhoods on the night of the Supreme Court decision. Refusing to be intimidated, people in the community came out to watch "as if they were watching the advance contingent for the Ringling Bros. Circus," Reverend King remarked. On Christmas Eve, five men beat up a fifteen-year-old girl who was waiting for a ride. Once integrated bus seating became effective, shotguns were fired into buses. One hit a pregnant woman. On January 10, 1957, two homes, including Abernathy's, and four churches were bombed. Bell Street and Mt. Olive Baptist churches were so badly damaged that the buildings were condemned. Two weeks later the King house was bombed again. The explosion crushed the front part of the house and shattered the windows of three taxis, sending the drivers to the hospital. Two Black men denounced the police for their failure to arrest the bombers—and were themselves arrested, and convicted, for inciting a riot.[212]

So the boycotters had to remain disciplined for some time. The MIA organized rigorous preparation for riding the buses. At least a thousand attended weekly classes in churches where they practiced how to respond nonviolently when abused or attacked, using role playing, taking turns acting as racist provocateurs. (The civil rights groups SNCC and CORE would do similar training a decade later.) King himself led one group. When he asked, what would you do if someone not only cursed you but shoved you?, one woman responded, "Well, if someone was to start calling me names . . . I would just sit there and ignore her and let folks see how ignorant she was. But if she were to start pushin' me, maybe I would give her just a little shove." To which other participants cried "No! no!"[213]

THE MONTGOMERY bus boycott worked because it required active, daily, participation—and often sacrifice—from everyone. To be a part of the community, you had to *do* something. This is the essence of a boycott—it forces a protest to be participatory. Boycotting makes defiance compatible with respectability, which was crucial to building widespread support. While boycotting does not always build a social movement, because it can be done privately, in Montgomery it was public, just as not boycotting would have been visible to all. It may seem counterintuitive that the stringent demands on participants strengthened the movement, but in fact that was fundamental, as it was in the farmworkers' struggle (discussed in chapter 6). Every

Montgomery African American could "own" the victory because he or she had not only suffered but contributed. Not all contributions were equal, nor were the burdens borne, nor the subsequent recognition and prestige.[214] But everyone did something and took pride in doing so. Boycotter Gussie Nesbitt explained, "I wanted to be one of them that tried to make it better. I didn't want somebody else to make it better for me. [So] I walked."[215] Montgomery's Blacks saw their project as too valuable to risk losing and therefore worked to transcend divisive developments.[216]

The Montgomery struggle was unique among social movements because its activists included *every* African American in the city. As Rustin pointed out, the community could *see* their solidarity. This left little room for free riders (discussed in chapter 4), that is, people who benefit without helping. Free riders not only increase the burden on others but also stir resentment in those who do help. In many social movements, even civil rights movements, individuals could choose whether to participate—for example, in challenges to school segregation. In Montgomery they had no choice. The boycott provides a paradigmatic case for the impossibility of neutrality—you had to choose a side. In all social movements, social pressure supports solidarity, but in Montgomery the social pressure was so strong as to be compelling. Those who might have capitulated and returned to riding the buses— and surely some must have felt like doing so at times—knew that if they did so, they would face the scorn of others.

In short, the Montgomerians had designed, consciously or not, a self-enforcing social movement; there was no way to leave it. Twenty years earlier, in the midst of a miners' strike in Harlan County, Kentucky, the owners' and Sheriff Blair's thugs had beaten and killed strikers. In response, miner's wife Florence Reece wrote new words to an old melody. Her song, "Which Side Are You On," became a favorite in labor struggles for decades:

> *If you go to Harlan County, there is no neutral there*
> *You'll either be a union man or a thug for J. H. Blair.*

Six years later SNCC created the Freedom Singers and wrote new words to the song:

Come all you Negro people, lift up your voices and sing
Will you join the Ku Klux Klan or Martin Luther King?[*]

In uniting Montgomery Blacks across class lines, women were crucial. Rosa Parks did this in her person and as an emblem of the boycott. Her decision to sit in a "white" seat provided Montgomery with an experienced, courageous activist who was also a perfect protagonist. Even some Montgomery African Americans who thought they knew Rosa Parks were misled by her quiet style. Or perhaps it was just sexism. Reverend French of the AME Zion church referred to her as a "typical American housewife."[217] King not only failed to acknowledge her history of activism but even praised her for not being "a disturbing factor in the community."[218] Moreover, she would not allow herself to become a mere figurehead, instead throwing herself full time into tasks ranging from public speaking to cleaning up bombed homes—in other words, doing both middle-class and working-class work.

Women have often shown a particular capacity, Belinda Robnett theorizes, to bridge social divisions, connecting the political with the personal, leaders with followers, elders with youth, and in Montgomery, professionals and business owners with working class people. Robnett suggests that, paradoxically, women's exclusion from formal leadership helped "develop a strong grassroots tier of leadership that served as a critical bridge between the formal organization . . . and potential constituents."[219] This is what I have called followership. Montgomery women did not get adequate recognition for their bravery, their daring, their strategic and tactical skills, and their labor. To some extent the boycotters' solidarity was enabled by women's willingness to work behind the scenes.

Rosa Parks's willingness to remain in the background was spectacularly unrewarded. In one of the movement's uglier aspects, when she was in dire need (both she and her husband having lost their jobs even

---

[*] In 1962, while visiting Albany State College in Georgia, Pete Seeger was impressed by a Baptist a capella choir and suggested they take their show on the road. The rest is history. The original Freedom Singers consisted of Rutha Mae Harris (soprano), Bernice Johnson Reagon (alto), Cordell Reagon (tenor), and Charles Neblett (bass).

as they were caring for her ill mother), the MIA offered no support, although it paid wages to several other women. Some activists protested the neglect of Parks, including Septima Clark. In Montgomery, Virginia Durr struggled on Parks's behalf, cobbling together a bit of help from Highlander and $300 from the MIA relief fund.[220]

Parks's biographer, Jeanne Theoharis, listed a confluence of factors behind this neglect. Parks's own pride may have hidden her suffering—she raised money for the boycott without keeping a portion for herself. And as a working-class woman, she was socially distant from the WPC network of professional and business women. Theoharis also suggests that there was resentment and jealousy of Rosa Parks—of the fact that she traveled nationally, of the amount of attention she received—and, I would add, the *kind* of attention, constructing her not as an experienced activist but as a saint. Abernathy once called her a "tool," and while he did not mean this disrespectfully, his choice of word did reflect the widespread refusal to recognize and value her extensive political experience.[221]

E. D. Nixon understood the limitations of the boycott's victory. True, he resented that his contribution was not adequately recognized, obscured by King's brilliance and Parks's sanctification.[222] His politics also shaped his view of the boycott. Speaking as a longtime labor organizer, he said in a later interview, "The civil rights movement saw to it that Black people were able to do things legally, like ride on a Pullman car, say. But the labor movement saw to it that Black people had the money to buy the ticket to ride on the Pullman cars, see? What good is it to have the right to do something, if you don't have the money to do it? The labor movement gave Black people the opportunity to do things that the civil rights movement gave the right to do."[223]

No doubt other injustices in the Montgomery struggle have been glossed over because of its victory. And seen from today's vantage point, where racism and race inequality remain devastatingly high, the Montgomery story appears as one of enormous effort and sacrifice for a small gain. It did, however, have offspring. The founders of the 1960 sit-in movement—Joseph McNeil, Ezell Blair, Franklin McCain, and Daniel Richmond—agreed in retrospect that the Montgomery bus boycott was to them a supreme example and inspiration.[224] In 1963, when King and Abernathy were planning their campaign in Birmingham, an unusually violent bastion of racism, their Montgomery experience showed in their plan to combine economic pressure with confrontation, creating a drama and commanding national press coverage that extended northern white support for the civil rights movement. After the victorious Birmingham campaign, 758 civil rights protests took place in 186 American cities.[225]

Moreover, Montgomery's visible, powerful united resistance influenced many other social movements, for peace, environmental protection, sex equality, and much more. The Montgomery struggle was a transformative event, a category defined by some scholars of social movements as one that significantly disrupts, alters, or violates the "taken-for-granted assumptions" that structure political and social relations. The transformation in this sense is less about desegregating buses than about changing the universe of acceptable discourse.

The boycotters achieved this, in King's words, by uniting "self-changing and the changing of circumstances."[226] (His words apply equally to the Townsend and women's liberation movements.) The boycotters' discipline and determination increased their confidence and demonstrated that the powerful can be bested by those with less power. No doubt many churchgoing Montgomerians saw themselves as Davids defeating Goliath. This is a crucial insight: social movements operate by changing their participants who are in the process of attempting to change their world. The Montgomery activist Beulah Johnson quoted Langston Hughes:

I'm comin', I'm comin' but my head ain't bended low
'Cause this is a new Black Joe.[227]

---------- **6** ----------

LEADERSHIP AND FOLLOWERSHIP CONTINUED

The United Farm Workers Union

Cesar Chavez meeting with farmworkers.

It's the kind of organizing that takes a lot of footwork, and especially patience. To go and sit and talk to people in their houses you have to really care for the people.

—PHILIP VERA CRUZ

To make a great dream come true, the first requirement is a great capacity to dream; the second is persistence. . . . I am an organizer, not a union leader. . . . There are no shortcuts. You just keep talking to people, working with them, sharing, exchanging and they come along.

—CESAR CHAVEZ

Just as the Montgomery bus boycott made Martin Luther King, Jr., a national hero, so the struggles of California farmworkers in the 1960s and '70s did the same for Cesar Chavez. Both men offered leadership of the highest order, leadership that included inspirational mobilization, uncommon bravery, and strategic intelligence. Both drew strength from Christian religiosity and communicated with their followers through a shared spiritual vocabulary. Both were committed to nonviolence, and both had to call on their moral authority to enforce it. Both led movements that transformed not only members' material conditions but also the people themselves. Martin Luther King, of course, was assassinated at thirty-eight, at the height of his powers and on the cusp of a decision to move beyond civil rights to challenge broader systemic injustices, foreign as well as domestic, class as well as race. Cesar Chavez lived fifty-six years, including years of great physical hardship, leading a movement that built the United Farm Workers union (UFW) and improved the lives of tens of thousands of farmworkers, one of the poorest groups in the United States. Chavez died with his movement greatly weakened, however, undermined not only by its formidable enemies—corporate agribusiness and conservative politicians—but also by his own slide into paranoia and delusion.

King first became a national leader because of his unmatched eloquence. Chavez was eloquent in a different register—in the colloquial and sometimes profane Spanish and English he shared with the farmworkers he organized. Unlike King, he was also an extraordinary hands-on organizer. While King made no attempt to manage the Montgomery boycott, Chavez, already an experienced organizer when he began to build the UFW, became its key strategist and tactician as well as its spiritual leader. His bravery, self-sacrifice, strategic acumen, and patience were unparalleled. He did not always lead from in front—at times rank-and-file farmworkers impelled him into action that he had not planned. When that happened, however, he quickly grasped the new lay of the land, shifted strategy and tactics nimbly, and found ways to build on these surprises.[1] Accounts of his work read like a textbook for grassroots organizing.

Community organizer and social movement theorist Saul Alinsky liked to say, "If you want drama, get a movement; if you want results, get an organization." Chavez sought to build both. This is sometimes labeled social movement unionism—campaigning not only for better wages and working conditions but also for social justice on a larger scale.[2] As Eliseo Medina—a UFW organizer who went on to become a national union leader—put it, workers don't live in workplaces.[3] Chavez's drive to fuse a Mexican American social movement with a labor union was radical and visionary and, at first, successful, transforming the lives and hopes of farmworkers. But a social movement and a labor union do not always mesh easily, and in this chapter we will revisit the tension between them that appeared in the Depression-era unemployed movement (discussed in chapter 4). There is a paradox here: it was precisely Chavez's inclusive vision of social justice that enabled him to inspire so many to work so hard for their union, but that vision later morphed into a vision of spiritual reawakening that disengaged him from focusing on the welfare of farmworkers. That metamorphosis undermined both union and social movement.

Chavez gathered and mentored a remarkable group of brave, determined, smart farmworker leaders, a major part of his accomplishment. As in chapter 5, I call them followers, though they were also leaders. They constituted a vital second tier of leadership, taking initiatives and devising tactics on which the movement's victory depended, much as in Montgomery. In this chapter they are the protagonists. They are not well known, because to some extent, Chavez's stature hid them from view, so when he grew paranoid and began purging those he considered disloyal, many supporters of the movement were not aware that it weakened disastrously as a result. Challenging him seemed disloyal, not only to farmworkers but also to many outsiders who respected their struggle.

It was not until the early twenty-first century that scholars and journalists—first Frank Bardacke, Matt Garcia, and Miriam Pawel—broke the taboo against criticizing Cesar Chavez.[4] With the greatest respect, they documented how his very strengths as organizer and visionary contributed to undermining his union. At the peak of UFW strength, he began to prioritize spiritual goals over leading a labor union, yet refused to delegate responsibility for operating the union. He became enamored of a charlatan guru who encouraged him to distrust the very farmworker leaders that he had nurtured. Convinced that they were plotting against him, even that they were dupes of Communists, he attacked and fired some of his closest and most effective comrades. Doing this worsened his paranoia because he was depriving himself of the wisdom and skills of his best lieutenants. Attempting to maintain absolute control, more than any other leader discussed in this book, he simultaneously micromanaged and neglected the fundamental but often tedious work of negotiating contracts and serving union members.

Chavez was a tragic figure, in the sense of classic Greek tragedy, a larger-than-life hero who creates his own downfall. His vision and eloquence raised farmworkers' aspirations. His punishingly long hours of work, his personal austerity, his religiosity, and his commitment to nonviolence made him heroic. In several life-threatening fasts, he demonstrated his willingness to suffer for the farmworkers' cause. He was simultaneously a superb strategist and a utopian dreamer, working to create a labor union that was at the same time a social movement, with goals both material and spiritual. He was ambitious for farmworkers, never for himself. The loyalty of his followers and supporters is understandable.

But the followers must share the responsibility for his downfall. Some were already experienced activists. Many others were fast learners. Their collective wisdom was formidable, but they deferred to him, even when they knew he was wrong. Individually, some of them offered criticisms and proposed better strategies, but they never acted collectively. They allowed themselves to be fired, one by one, or they quit, and once they were outside the UFW, they hesitated to voice their criticisms publicly. The union had no loyal opposition.

In retrospect, the seeds of the UFW's decline were visible early on. Chavez won widespread national support by framing the farmworkers' struggle as a moral and religious one. Perhaps he did not intend to present himself as a holy man, but once he saw the advantages of projecting that image, he fostered it. So did some outsiders: Catholic senator Robert Kennedy's visit during one of Chavez's fasts virtually beatified him. Rumors of attempts to assassinate him intensified the protectiveness of his followers. He won the blessing of prominent and influential figures, such as California governors Pat Brown and Jerry Brown, Walter Reuther of the UAW, George Meany of the AFL–CIO, celebrity lawyer Melvin Belli, folk music stars Pete Seeger and Joan Baez, and many more. This made his organizing partners fear that opposing him would alienate supporters. The Mexican farmworker leader closest to Chavez, Gil Padilla, said that when Chavez became a *dictador*, "we let him. Because we needed him."[5]

The problem appears vividly in comparing King's and Chavez's way of enforcing nonviolence in their movements. Both preached nonviolence in Christian terms. Both had to face down constituents whose commitment to nonviolence was challenged by powerful and sometimes violent enemies. Two episodes suggest how differently they did so. When King's home in Montgomery was bombed in January 1956, an angry crowd gathered in his yard, spoiling for a fight, even armed retaliation. King met them in the yard and called on them to honor their Christian duty to love one's enemies. "Don't get your weapons. He who lives by the sword shall die by the sword. Remember that is what God said. . . . I want you to love our enemies."[6] His words were a salve, and the crowd dispersed. In February 1968, some farmworker strikers were retaliating against attacks by growers' hired goons, vandalizing and sabotaging growers' equipment. Chavez got them to stop not with mesmerizing words but with a twenty-five-day water-only fast. Like several fasts that followed, it was a power move, "moral ju jitsu," as labor union organizer Eliseo Medina put it.[7] The fasts brought the movement support from progressive outsiders, but they also intensified the followers' feelings of dependence on him and their resultant fear of losing him—a fear that King's followers did not face.

King and Chavez also differed in their attitudes toward sacrifice. Chavez modeled sacrifice personally through his several fasts, which he presented as penances for sin; a UFW leaflet declared, "He sacrifices for us."[8] For Chavez, suffering was ennobling. "To be a man is to suffer for others," he wrote. By contrast, the Montgomery boycotters sacrificed, but they did not see the sacrifice as itself a virtue, and their sacrifices came from collective decisions. Moreover, while Chavez at times encouraged sacrifice, even among very poor farmworkers, as a test of their commitment, Montgomery leaders worked to minimize the community's sacrifices.

Chavez's emphasis on sacrifice reflected his Mexican religiosity, part of the *mexicanidad* that built the movement. It attracted support that a more secular union campaign could not have done. But to some degree it marginalized non–Mexican farmworkers, particularly Filipinos. Ninety percent of Filipino farmworkers were single, due to immigration restrictions—they lived primarily in labor camps. Their strong bachelor community was more willing to take risks than were many Mexican farmworkers with families. Moreover, Filipino leaders were experienced union organizers, less connected to a religious culture and more connected to a political Left. As the Filipina historian Dawn Mabalon put it, "By erasing Filipinos [from histories of the farmworker movement] you also downplay those radical roots" of the UFW.[9]

AGRIBUSINESS AND ITS LABOR FORCE

In California, the heartland of the UFW, agricultural production derived its unique structure in large part from its climate. The aridity of California's large agricultural valleys made water a key resource, and the large corporate growers had the capital and political clout to get the federal government to provide irrigation at low cost. Family farms had never dominated California agriculture. Chavez likened California to Latin American *latifundia*, where big landowners monopolized huge swaths of farmland. Journalist Carey McWilliams, editor of *The Nation* from 1955 to 1976, called these farms "factories in the field."[10] But unlike most factories, agricultural fields did not need a year-round labor force; they required three to eight times as much labor in August and September as in March. (The ratios varied by the crop.)[11] As a result, though most farmworkers in the Central Valley had more or less permanent homes, a large population of workers moved from job to job, following the crops from south to north. The bracero program, an arrangement negotiated between the U.S. and Mexican governments, subsidized the big growers by providing them with temporary low-wage workers from Mexico who could easily be deported if they protested, let alone tried to organize a labor union. Their presence had made it harder for permanent farmworkers to organize.

Both the migrant and the settled labor force were multiply divided.

Since the 1870s, growers had imported low-wage workers: first Chinese, then Japanese, some Arabs and "Hindus," then Filipinos, then Mexicans, who came to dominate the California farm labor force.* Some were U.S. citizens, others Mexican citizens, who were in turn divided between "legals" and the undocumented. Of the legals, some had green cards and others were braceros. Moreover Mexican citizens often identified primarily with their state or village of origin, and some spoke only Zapotec, Purépecha, Mixtec, or Mayan. Creating a movement or organization that could serve the interests of all these people and unite them despite widespread mutual distrust was no easy task. The big growers, like so many large employers, exploited these tensions by dividing their workers by ethnicity.

On the other hand, racism worked to unite the farmworkers. In Delano, the California Central Valley town that would become the UFW headquarters, railroad tracks divided whites from nonwhites. The larger stores hired only whites and made people of color unwelcome. The movie theater imposed segregated seating. (Cesar and Helen Chavez were once arrested there for violating that policy.) Mexicans ran a few bodegas and cafés but often ate in the yards or patios of homes where farmworker women ran informal eateries. California's Filipinos, known as *manongs*, were colonial subjects—their country was a U.S. colony until 1946—recruited as low-wage labor beginning in the 1920s. They congregated in Delano's "Chinatown" where they could get Filipino food and drink and play pool and cards.[12] As Eliseo Medina described it, "We lived in different worlds—the Latino world, the Filipino world, the African-American world and the Caucasian world."[13]

All these farmworkers endured very low wages and brutal working and living conditions. (They still do: California farmworkers' median annual wage was $28,780 in 2022, about half that of all California workers.)[14] They put in inhumanely long hours in the fields, from "can see to can't see." Because wages were the only expenditures growers could control—unlike seeds, water, pesticides, and the like—they kept them as low as they could get away with.[15] Many growers used subcontrac-

---

* "Okies," migrants driven out of the midwestern plains by drought, poured into California in the 1930s, but by the 1950s Mexicans again dominated the farm labor force.

tors, who competed for contracts by further pushing wages downward. The hourly wage was often as little as one dollar, sometimes as low as sixty-five cents, and piece rates were also common. Women's wages averaged one-third of men's. Twenty-two percent of farmworkers were teenagers or younger, including many who should have been in school.[16]

Migrant workers often camped out under tents or lean-tos or in shanties with no running water. There was little shade in the fields, and growers often provided no drinking water, despite the intense heat of the summer. (Daytime temperatures could reach 100 degrees in the Central Valley and 125 in the Coachella Valley.) Workers often had to bring their own jugs of water. The lunches they carried became overheated and dirty. There were often no toilets, an absence particularly miserable for women. "The women grew weary of perverts watching them from across the vines while they defecated between the rows," farmworker Rey Huerta recalled. Equally if not more offensive to the farmworkers was their insulting treatment by foremen, who would address male workers as "boy" and women with even nastier labels, the equivalent of those that Montgomery bus drivers hurled at Black women.

The pesticides sprayed on fields, sometimes while people were working, made the incidence of cancer and children born with birth defects far greater than that among their urban counterparts.[17] The short-handled hoes, *cortitos*, that workers were required to use kept them bent over for hours at a time and left them with injured backs at young ages. Growers claimed that the *cortitos* did not bother the Mexicans or Filipinos because they were short and thus close to the ground, but one supervisor let slip a more likely reason for this preference: "With the long-handled hoe I can't tell whether they are working or just leaning on their hoes." Farmworkers experienced the *cortito* as a symbol of subordination and disrespect. As farmworker Hector de la Rosa put it, "When you are kneeling, it's showing humility. . . . We weren't going to be on our knees anymore." And he added, "The majority of us are Catholics. We've been kneeling for years. It was time for us to overcome these things."[18]

These conditions had long produced resistance, but the farmworkers' walkouts, slowdowns, strikes, and organizing campaigns had been unable to overcome the power of the big growers and shippers.[19] Their power was virtually totalitarian, as they could force the government to do their bidding. In the 1930s in the Salinas lettuce fields, for example, growers crushed strikes by a massive use of violence—they deployed not only their private armed guards but also police, sheriff's deputies, even the California State Highway Patrol.[20] When John Steinbeck wrote about the ruthless exploitation of Salinas farmworkers (in *The Grapes of Wrath*, *In Dubious Battle*, and many shorter pieces), the big growers and shippers mounted a major campaign against him. They bought up quantities of his books and conducted public book burnings, called him a pornographer and Communist, and commissioned a book to dispute his story.[21]

Occasionally Filipino and Mexican strikes and threats of strikes had won better wages, notably from growers of asparagus, celery, brussels sprouts, and garlic.[22] In the 1930s the Communist-led California Agricultural Workers Industrial Union, with a mainly Mexican membership of some 47,500, conducted some twenty-four strikes and won some wage increases.[23] But the growers always won eventually, firing and blacklisting those they considered troublemakers and using an arsenal of further weapons including injunctions and lawsuits, arrests for trespassing and for conspiracy, and evictions from labor camps. The growers got injunctions requiring that picketers get no closer than fifty feet—which meant they couldn't even picket on a road—and that prohibited even shouting, which meant workers couldn't hear them. Growers hired thugs, mercenaries, to beat and sometimes kill "agitators." Grower violence was so great that the journalist Carey McWilliams labeled the system "fascism in the fields."[24] The many failed unionizing campaigns left farmworkers discouraged and fatalistic, convinced that the California growers' power was invincible.

Chavez knew this history well. Born in 1927 in Yuma, at the southwestern tip of Arizona, he grew up in California's fields, picking peas and lettuce in winter, cherries and beans in spring, corn and grapes in summer, cotton in autumn. He was, put simply, a farmworker. In initiating the movement that became the UFW, he learned from two generations of organizers. Saul Alinsky, son of Russian Jewish immigrant parents, had developed a community organizing approach in the stockyards area of Chicago. Alinsky trained Fred Ross, who worked for the New Deal's Farm Security Administration, offering aid to migrant farmworkers—he was the model for the camp director in John Steinbeck's novel *The Grapes of Wrath*. In 1948 Ross founded the Community Service Organization (CSO) to try Alinsky's methods with California's Mexican Americans. In that work he encountered Chavez, who was at first skeptical about Ross's optimism. But fuller conversations between the two allowed Ross to take the full measure of Chavez's abilities, and in 1952 hired him for the CSO. Ross became his teacher and mentor. Chavez recalled that when he first organized on his own, "I'd call Fred every day to make sure I was on track."[25]

Unlike Alinsky and Ross, Chavez was also inspired by his Catholicism, and he brought these influences together skillfully. As a child, he had breathed in an *abuelita* or folk Catholicism (literally, "granny" Catholicism) learned from his convent-educated grandmother, as well as his mother's many *dichos* and *consejos*. As a young man, he joined a Catholic revival movement, *cursillismo*, which resembled being "born again" among evangelical Protestants. Inspired by arch-conservative Pope Leo XII, *cursillismo* appeared in Spain in 1944 as Catholic revivalism, aimed at bringing apostate young men back into the church. Arriving in the southwestern United States in 1957, American influences reshaped it, attracting young Mexican American men by, for example, bringing folk and popular music into masses.[26]

A young Catholic man could join the *cursillo* movement through a four-day, tightly scripted retreat. Talking or relating to others was prohibited because participants were to meditate on their sinfulness, a process aimed to make the initiate feel helpless and lonely. The candidate's repentance then yielded a symbolic "resurrection," celebrated with music and gifts. Americans began to take *cursillismo* in another direction, encouraging social action. That characterized Chavez's approach to organizing: rejecting a passive, God-will-provide message in favor of a call to engagement. The *cursillo* anthem, *"De Colores,"* became an official UFW song (along with *"Nosotros Venceremos,"* "We Shall Overcome").[27]

When Chavez began organizing Mexican farmworkers for the CSO his approach was secular. He reached people by hanging out at barbershops, bars, and churches, and he offered people rides so that he could talk to them privately and at length. Ever systematic, he mapped all the towns between Arvin and Stockton—eighty-seven of them, including farming camps—and visited them all, listening to workers' concerns, including their fear that organizing would provoke growers' retaliation. Listening was his introductory organizing method. It may well be essential to successful social movements.*

He began by asking potential recruits to allow informal meetings in their homes, because they facilitated fuller, more personal discussions. Chavez recalled being nervous when he began these meetings. "I would get to the meeting early," he recalled later,

> *and drive back and forth past the house, too nervous to go in and face the people. Finally I would force myself to go inside and sit in a corner. I was quite thin then, and young, and most of the people were middle-aged. Someone would say, "Where's the organizer?" And I would pipe up, "Here I am." Then they would say in Spanish—these were very poor people and we hardly spoke anything but Spanish—"Ha! This kid?"*[28]

House meetings meant giving and receiving hospitality, an important aspect of building community, and they could include women, who were vital to the social movement he aimed to build.[29] Philip Vera Cruz, a Filipino leader of the movement, explained Chavez's method this way:

> *When the issues are very controversial and you are dealing with workers who are not sophisticated in the ways of labor unions. . . . You have to first earn their trust. . . . It's the kind of organizing that takes a lot of footwork, and especially patience. To go and sit and talk to people in their houses you have to really care for the people. Fred and Cesar are that way.*[30]

---

* Listening was crucial to Jane Edna Hunter's creation of a settlement (discussed in chapter 1) and to women's liberation consciousness-raising groups and in the formation of the organization 9 to 5 (discussed in chapter 7).

Word of these meetings spread in the small towns of the Central Valley, and gradually even skeptical and defeatist farmworkers began to respond. Their pessimism showed when Chavez began by asking how much the workers thought they should be paid. He was shocked by the timidity of their hopes, how frail their sense of entitlement: their hopes went no higher than $1.25 an hour. These understandably cautious farmworkers could be skeptical, and Chavez often arrived at a promised meeting to find no one home. But he was dogged and patient. Moreover, he knew the importance of asking people to *do* something. At every meeting, he would ask those who came to host another house meeting.[31] He created a file with information about each contact. By the time he left the CSO, he knew "every Mexican community of any size" in California and had created thirty-two chapters with ten thousand paid members.[32]

Crucially, Chavez was *of* those he was organizing. He cursed, he spoke their language. He made himself trustworthy by telling his life story. "A storyteller situates herself and experience in the belongingness of the tribe," writes Olga Davis, speaking of civil rights organizers.[33] He would begin with the familiar, his work in the fields, which in turn demystified the unfamiliar, by showing how his work as an organizer arose from personal experience. Perhaps his physical appearance helped: One future leader in this movement had heard tales of this exceptional man, but when he first came to the movement headquarters, he wondered if this small, unassuming presence, *eso indio pequeño*, could possibly be the fabled organizer.[34]

Chavez left the CSO in 1962 when it refused to support his plan to create a community organization of Mexican farmworker families.[35] He moved with his family to Delano, in the San Joaquin Valley, population 14,500 in 1970. Delano was an early boomtown because the Southern Pacific train from San Francisco stopped there, and it soon became a shipping point for the many agricultural products grown nearby. Without a CSO salary, Chavez now relied on his wife Helen's earnings— Delano was her hometown, and her family could care for their children so she could work in the fields to support them. He initiated an organization: *Asociación de Campesinos*, Farm Workers Association (FWA). In 1963 he rented a converted church building as headquarters: it had a small office, a toilet at the rear, and an all-purpose room where farmworkers could drop by and converse. There was no phone. Chavez explained that he couldn't afford it and that farmworkers had no phones anyway.[36]

Chavez had to work around the California Catholic clergy who, indebted to the big growers, did not share his *cursillo* values. "Here in Delano, the church has been such a stranger to us that our own people tend to put it together with all the powers and institutions that oppose them," he remarked bitterly.[37] Except for one maverick Irish Catholic priest, Donald McDonnell, the church refused even verbal support.[38] Happily the Protestant Migrant Ministry, funded by the National Council of Churches, offered help. Chris Hartmire, head of the ministry, assigned Reverend Jim Drake to work full time for the *chavistas*, and Hartmire soon devoted himself the movement.

To build a *community* organization, Chavez knew it had to include women. Jessie Lopez de la Cruz's husband Arnold had her wait in the car when he first attended a house meeting, but the next meeting was held in her home. Jessie listened from behind the kitchen door until Chavez said to Arnold, "Your wife should be here, she's a farmworker."[39] (She would become a major UFW organizer and later a leader in the League of Mexican American Women—a reminder of what is lost when women are marginalized.) That farmworker families were male-dominated did not mean, however, that women had no power. Maria Saludado Magaña recalled that when Chavez first came by their home, her husband ordered her to stay away. But when he joined, he called on her to pay the dues—she controlled the money. Virginia Rodriguez picked cotton throughout her elementary school years and kept accounts for her uneducated father: "Was it not me he asked to fill out his daily time cards recording day by day what he earned? Was it not my responsibility to calculate his earnings every 15th day of the month, knowing there would never be enough to pay the grocery bill, let alone the other living expenses?"

As women began attending meetings, they often had to bring children, and the children absorbed what they saw and heard, many becoming activists when they grew up. Jessica Govea, later a key UFW organizer, recalled watching "how our parents . . . debated in a respectful way but in a very firm way issues that were important . . . and made decisions by raising their hands and making motions and taking votes."⁴⁰ As Francesca Polletta argues, good organizers are always also teachers, and organizing is partly a tutelary relationship.⁴¹

Though Chavez began constructing a community organization, he considered a labor union an ultimate goal; without it, farmworkers could never have economic power and therefore no political power. "Political power by itself . . . is like having a car that doesn't have any motor in it," he said. "Economic power is like having a generator. . . . we have to develop economic power to assure . . . political power. I'm not advocating black capitalism or brown capitalism . . . [which] gets a black to exploit other blacks, or a brown to exploit others. . . . What I'm suggesting is a cooperative movement."⁴² Aware of the long history of failed unionizing attempts—"suicide strikes," he called them—he wanted time to build something beneath the growers' radar. He believed that only a large community network with a high level of commitment could effectively challenge the growers.

Chavez knew that members would only become reliable members of the Farm Workers Association by taking ownership of it and responsibility for its maintenance. So he insisted that members pay dues, $3.50 a month per family, by no means a small amount for farmworkers. When he sent the first dues-collection notices, the membership dropped from 498 to 160—a decline that might have deterred someone less patient.⁴³ He responded by setting up a "problem clinic," where individuals could get help with, for example, getting a birth certificate or responding to a traffic ticket. Those who received help typically offered to pay something, but Chavez asked instead for work: hold a house meeting, drive another member to a doctor, work in the office. If he had no job for them, he would invent one: once he had volunteers cut up old paper to make raffle tickets that he did not need.⁴⁴ The more people were required to contribute, the more they offered. People too old to do farm work would come to the Delano office to offer help, people with hands "crippled, lumpy, and crooked . . . the result of years of working in the fields." "They'd even bring food that they'd cooked to share with us."⁴⁵

The problem clinic grew into a multiservice center providing benefits to members. In this respect the FWA was a *mutualista*, a traditional Mexican fraternal benefit society, though a more ambitious one. Shrewdly, Chavez used the FWA to provide some of the benefits that labor unions could offer before a union was possible. These came to include a credit union, where farmworkers could get life insurance, so that family members could provide decent burials for their loved ones; savings accounts; small, short-term loans at 1 percent monthly interest, to help them survive seasons without work, while avoiding the loan sharks that preyed on them;[46] and an auto parts cooperative. The FWA's crown jewel began as a medical insurance program, ultimately becoming one of the greatest treasures of the union: an HMO, with clinics open seven days a week in Delano, Calexico, Salinas, Sanger, and Coachella, and later in Mexicali, Mexico. UFW members would pay a flat two dollars for a clinic visit, with no charge for follow-ups. A nurse who worked in the UFW clinics for six years recalled that she never again experienced health care so well delivered. Women in the movement organized day care and summer schools for children. Educating children was an uncompromisable rule; even in crucial strikes, Chavez often pulled children, even teenagers, out of the picket lines except during school vacations. He started a "Huelga school" for adults, recruiting two instructors from the Bay Area to teach reading.[47] Ultimately the problem clinic provided legal aid, a notary, interpreters, assistance with government bureaucracies, and immigration lawyers, all under one roof.[48]

THE FOLLOWERSHIP

As word of the organization spread, farmworkers eager for action sought out Cesar Chavez. Some showed up out of the blue, having heard of Chavez and liking what they heard.* Some felt that they needed to impress Chavez in order to get his support. As Maria Saludado Magaña recalled, "My father told us to invite our aunts and uncles and friends

* This pattern also appeared in the civil rights movement: when organizers came into a town, older people sought them out, often with the attitude, "Where've you been? We've been waiting for you."

[to a house meeting] so that . . . Cesar would see that we were interested in having a union."

Many of these early recruits had imbibed activism from their parents. Alfredo Figueroa's father drilled two lessons into him: "Your boss is your biggest enemy" and "Always share with others."* Jessica Govea's father had been part of a group of braceros who left their jobs and walked thirty-three miles, from Hanford to Fresno, to protest their treatment to the Mexican consul. He later became a leader in the Bakersfield CSO chapter. Helen Serda's father had worked "undercover" signing up workers at DiGiorgio.† Obdulia Flores Rivera's father had pulled his family out of a Richgrove grower's fields and formed his children into a team of organizers and spies; he would wake them before daybreak, drive them to the Schenley Vineyards to talk to workers but also to report on company attempts to intimidate workers. Elizabeth Hernandez knew that her parents would be at any meeting concerning a dispute with growers. One older man had taken part in the Brawley and Holtville strikes of the 1930s: "They'd show us gunshot wounds and jagged knife cuts," she recalled. "They signed the check with their own blood, sweat and tears."

Others carried a family legacy of social responsibility in nonpolitical arenas. Maria Fuentes's grandmother, for example, led the novenas, rosaries, and hymns at their chapel, her mother also dedicated her time to the church, her grandfather was a leader in the Knights of Columbus and the Mexican American Political Association, and her father, active in their church, scrounged for baseball gloves, balls, and bats to give to neighborhood kids.[49]

Immigrants were often particularly militant, having had activist experience in Mexico. Some even had memories of the Mexican Revolution, "of hanging the landlord and dividing up the hacienda." Many remembered the credo of Emiliano Zapata, leader in the Mexican revolution who demanded land reform: "the land, like the air and water,

---

* His father also claimed, proudly, to be a descendant of Joaquin Murieta, a Sonoran miner who became an outlaw and folk hero during the 1848 Gold Rush.

† DiGiorgio Fruit occupied about thirty-three square miles in the San Joaquin Valley. At the time it was the largest grape, plum, and pear grower in the world and the second-largest producer of wine in the United States.

belonged to the people." Hermilo Mojica descended from a Mexican revolutionary general responsible for the nationalization of Mexico's oil industry in 1938. His mother told him revolutionary bedtime stories and his father had been president of his Mexican municipality. Aristeo Zambrano, a school dropout, read the Mexican leftist weekly *Siempre* as well as the Cuban *Granma*; in 1968 he was a young leftist supporting the striking students in Mexico City; in 1976 he was picking broccoli, joined the UFW, and was soon elected to its negotiating team.[50]

Chavez's closest organizing partner, Gil Padilla, had resistance in his blood. His family had been sprayed with DDT when they entered the United States, a humiliation his mother never let him forget. She had been an ardent supporter of the Mexican revolution, later an admirer of FDR. His father and older brothers had participated in a large-scale farmworker strike in 1933. Born in 1927 in a farm labor camp, he picked cotton along with his family, served in the navy, then returned to the fields—a path similar to Chavez's. Wartime experience was an important factor influencing farmworker leaders: veterans, who had been exposed to the military's promise of racial integration and rhetoric of defending democracy, became angrier about racism and exploitive working conditions when they returned to civilian life (a pattern common also among Black civil rights activists). So Padilla arrived already "looking for a fight . . . listening to everybody with a plan."[51] Cesar Chavez had one and hired him onto the CSO staff. Padilla turned out to be a stellar and audacious organizer.[52]

One of the youngest immigrants, Eliseo Medina, became a lead organizer at a very young age. He was born in Huanusco, Zacatecas, where his father was the mayor. His parents brought him to the United States, settling in Delano in 1956 when he was ten. A top student despite working in the fields during weekends and summer, he dropped out when the Delano high school insisted that "Hispanic" students should confine their study to "industrial arts." He worked in the fields until, at nineteen, he saw a copy of *El Malcriado*,* the FWA newspaper. There he read about a struggle that got farmworkers the back wages they were

---

* The name means "The Naughty Boy," an ironic expression meant partly for humor and partly to promote a positive view of militancy.

owed. He sought out the FWA, came to a meeting, and smashed his piggy bank, taking $10.50 out of the fifteen dollars it contained and paying three years of dues up front.[53] Medina later remembered that some college students picketing alongside him "talked about a world I was not familiar with . . . about Berkeley and civil rights and stuff I hadn't even heard about." Yet within a few months, he was a picket captain, and a year later, in 1966, only twenty years old, he was a full-time staff member for the UFW, soon becoming an expert speaker and tactician.[54]

Next to Chavez himself, Dolores Huerta became the most renowned leader of the movement, at times its second-in-command. As I write, she continues her work for social justice at age ninety-three. The only woman in UFW's formal leadership, farmworkers revered her not as a female icon, though she was beautiful and photogenic—a favorite subject of journalist photographers—but because of the magnitude of her contribution and the expertise she lent to the cause. She differed from

Dolores Huerta signs up new members at the founding convention of the National Farm Workers Association, Delano, California, September 30, 1962.

other leaders because she was never a farmworker, though she was the child of an activist, born in 1930 in a New Mexico mining town. Her father, a union activist, was later elected to the state legislature.

Her parents divorced when she was three, and her extraordinary feminist mother became the decisive influence on her life. Fred Ross "discovered" her, mentored her, and brought her into the CSO, where she met Chavez. The three of them divided up the Central Valley towns, going door to door to get farmworkers to register to vote, a priority for the UFW as well. Then Ross hired her as the CSO's lobbyist in Sacramento, and she soon mastered of California's legislative process. Her lobbying won noncitizen farmworkers inclusion in a state pension plan in 1961, a major benefit to thousands. Her allegiance gradually shifted from the CSO to Chavez's project. As Miriam Pawel has put it, Huerta had the three virtues that Chavez most valued: loyalty, fearlessness, and intense commitment to what they were beginning to call *la causa*.

An expert speaker, Huerta was repeatedly called "fiery"—a bit like "feisty," the condescending cliché for a confident and charismatic woman. When she was negotiating contracts, her forceful style took growers by surprise; reflecting their stereotype of Mexican women, one complained that she was a "crazy . . . violent woman . . . Mexican women are usually peaceful and calm."[55] Huerta's familial history also disrupted simplistic assumptions about Mexican American women. Twice married and divorced, she then became the unmarried partner of Chavez's brother Richard, thereby becoming Cesar's sister-in-law.

She gave birth to eleven children. When she joined Chavez's staff, she often had to leave her children, in another departure from conventional expectations of mothers. This was possible because women friends and relatives in Delano cared for her children—often two to a bed—exemplifying a farmworker ethic of community responsibility, similar to that among Hull-House's neighbors (discussed in chapter 1). This arrangement signaled the women's community's acceptance of Huerta's independence, and there is no evidence that other Delano women resented this, exposing the inaccuracy of another assumption about Mexican women's values. Any unease with her unconventional behavior was erased by her hard work, her bravery on picket lines, and her four arrests. She not only inspired admiration from farmworker women but also drew many of them into activism. Rachel Encinas spoke for many in referring to her as the "first lady" of their movement.

Many of the estimated 45,000 Filipino farmworkers on the West Coast had extensive labor union experience,[56] and two of them became part of the UFW leadership team. Philip Vera Cruz arrived in the United States in 1926 at age twenty-two, became active in the IWW, then served as vice-president of International Longshore and Warehouse Union Local 37 (which included farmworkers). He later became president of an AFL-CIO affiliated National Farm Labor Union local. He was still working in the fields at sixty-one, paying for his younger brother in Manila to go to law school. (Many Mexican farmworkers contributed to families across the border too, but among Filipinos this was especially common, since they were usually single men.)

The younger Larry Itliong had a similar activist history: arriving in the United States in 1929 at fourteen, a year later he was in the midst of a lettuce workers' strike. He helped organize a successful strike in Salinas in 1934, and then, with Vera Cruz, a failed asparagus strike near Stockton in 1948.[57] But in personality and skills, Itliong and Vera Cruz differed radically. Extremely flamboyant, a gambler who typically had a cigar in his mouth, nicknamed "seven fingers" because he had lost three in a cannery accident, Itliong's cockiness earned him the nickname "Badass."[58] International in his outlook, his unusual language capacity—fluency in Spanish, Japanese, Cantonese, English, and several Filipino languages—helped him unite workers across national and ethnic differences. By the 1950s, he was widely recognized as the leader of Filipino farmworkers, and before long Huerta recruited him as an organizer. He and Vera Cruz would become members of the FWA executive board.

The most important Anglo among UFW leaders, Marshall Ganz, also arrived as an experienced activist from the African American civil rights movement. He was a young man of contradictions: Harvard-educated, the son of a rabbi, he grew up in Fresno and Bakersfield, so he knew the economy and power structures of the Central Valley economy. He volunteered in the 1964 "Freedom Summer" civil rights project in Mississippi, helped organize the Mississippi Freedom Democratic Party's attempt to have its African American members represent the state at the 1964 Democratic Convention, and joined the Student Nonviolent Coordinating Committee (SNCC), a civil rights organization of great fame. In the fall of 1965 a small SNCC delegation—Stokely Carmichael, Cleveland Sellers, Ralph Featherstone, and Ganz—came to Delano to offer help.[59] Energized by what he saw, Ganz moved back to his home turf, bringing the lessons of civil rights to farmworker organizing. He became one of the last Chavez loyalists, remaining with the UFW until 1981. He is today a scholar of social movement organizing, teaching at Harvard's Kennedy School.

The growers' dozens of lawyers used the courts to stop farmworker organizing, so the union needed its own to face them. By a stroke of good luck, Jerry Cohen, a recent graduate of the University of California Berkeley Law School, and now a legal aid attorney, was hanging out in the People's Bar in Delano in 1966, shooting pool and drinking Mountain Red, a cheap wine. There he met Gil Padilla and learned of the UFW. He became Chavez's personal attorney, then general counsel for the union. A fearless, risk-taking, and creative tactician, he thrived on finding ways to maneuver within a legal system designed to crush the farmworker movement.*

One of the most indispensable followers has been almost entirely unrecognized—Helen Chavez, Cesar's wife. Her parents had immigrated from Mexico and settled in Delano, where Helen started working in the fields at age seven. Her father, Vidal Fabela, was active in the Comisión Mexicana, a community improvement group. When Cesar worked for the CSO, she and their children, who soon numbered eight, followed him from town to town—Madera, Bakersfield, Hanford,

---

* One example of Cohen's creativity: Agricultural workers were not included in the National Labor Relations Act (NLRA) and so should not have been affected by its prohibition on secondary boycotts, as in boycotting stores that sold scab grapes. But a handful of UFW members worked in warehouse jobs that were within the NLRA's jurisdiction, so Cohen set up a fictive organization, the United Peanut Shellers, which freed them from the prohibition. After leaving the UFW, he continued his public interest lawyering; he was the co-lead counsel in the *Exxon Valdez* oil spill case that won $5 billion for the plaintiffs.

Oxnard, Los Angeles—and spent her evenings writing longhand his activity reports and letters.

When Cesar left the CSO and they settled in Delano, she and their older children went back to work in the fields to support his project. She arose before dawn, made breakfasts and lunches for all, went to the fields, and when she returned, cleaned, cooked, and did laundry.[60] She helped care for Dolores Huerta's many children. She lived no better than any other farmworker. One Delano woman recalled that the Chavez family "got their clothes from the same place we all did, the donation bin." Helen Chavez's generosity was legendary. She often invited the community "to bring their own piece of meat to a barbecue," providing "wonderful potato salad and chili beans."* During strikes, the community of women in Delano, including her two sisters, fed a large population of strikers, picketers, and volunteers a main meal at lunchtime, working nine hour days for weeks and weeks.[61] Their work illustrates the movement's lack of separation among home, work, and organizing, which the sociologist Maxine Baca Zinn calls "political familialism."[62]

The movement was of course male-dominated. Unsurprisingly, many farmworker men had imbibed assumptions about Mexican women's quiescence. Women drank beer, cracked jokes, chatted about their kids, and complained about their husbands. Helen Chavez remarked, "He wants to make the babies but he doesn't want to take care of them."[63] A group that also included Rachel Orendain, Gloria Terronez, Esther Uranday, and Josefina Hernandez—wives of FWA leaders—always sat together in FWA meetings. They were labeled the "chewing gum chorus."[64] There were also women's parties: "The women would really let go when there were no men around!" Ida Cousino recalled.

While Mexican women were stereotyped as passive, this was not always the case. An example: Gil Padilla secured a grant from the CSO to run a women's educational project and wanted to include birth control. His co-worker in this project, Reverend Jim Drake of the Migrant Ministry, thought this was a nonstarter because, he thought, the women always accepted Catholic Church dictates. So Padilla set out to disabuse

---

* One Delano woman found it amusing that Chavez was a vegetarian but could never get Helen to become one despite many attempts at persuasion.

him. He took Drake to one of the labor camps, where they quickly signed up a bunch of women eager to take responsibility for distributing free contraceptives to the others. In fact, a nurse in the UFW clinics recalled that although there was an "unwritten policy" not to offer birth control, women demanded contraception, and clinic practitioners obliged. They were defying Chavez's edicts. He denounced birth control, arguing that it was a racist plot to reduce the numbers of nonwhites. He also feared that freeing women from multiple pregnancies and children would encourage them to be employed, thus undercutting men's demands for a family wage.[65]

Male dominance remained. Huerta's example did not bring other women into leadership. Beyond looking after and deferring to husbands, some women suffered from men's heavy drinking and violence. Still, one woman after another described moving from timidity and behind-the-scenes support into public activism.[66] Despite his anxieties about birth control and women's employment, Cesar Chavez fostered women's self-confidence. He would assign women to jobs without telling them how to do them, trusting that they could figure it out. He shifted them from job to job, and as a result they developed a broader knowledge of the union's functioning and went on to train other women, especially volunteers.[67] Hope Lopez Fierro, for example, had it "burned into my brain" never to speak to strangers, but she was soon leading house meetings in six Central Valley towns, driving alone in a 1955 Thunderbird that farmworkers christened the "Huelga Bird."

The women might seem timid in meetings, where they rarely if ever spoke, but on picket lines they could be fearless. They occasionally engaged in hit-and-run protest actions. When the Fresno bishop bowed to grower pressure and withdrew his support for the FWA, a group of women arrived at his office, marched right past a receptionist trying to keep them out, and occupied it. Helen Chavez sat in the bishop's chair. They changed their babies' diapers in his office, and when they got hungry, they used his desk as a surface on which to cut up candy bars for them to eat.[68] So much for deferring to a Catholic bishop.

When negotiations with Gallo, a major grape and wine producer, were getting nowhere, a group of about a hundred women and children piled into whatever old cars they could find and drove the twenty-five miles from Delano to Modesto, planning to call on *Mrs.* Gallo. Their parade of "old clunker cars" arrived at the estate, which contained several mansions, and the women sat down in a tile piazza near a swimming pool with peacocks walking around. When the police arrived, they refused to leave; the police were uncertain and took no action, so the women spent a few hours, singing aloud, and then gradually wandered back to their cars and drove off. The workers won the wage increase they demanded that day.*

MEANWHILE MANY farmworkers, especially those in different regions, were less patient than Cesar Chavez. Farmworkers had long initiated spontaneous walkouts, but now they came to Delano to ask for support. In Texas, some melon workers declared themselves an FWA affiliate without consulting the organization. Wildcat strikes in asparagus, lemon, grape, and garlic fields were no longer simply expressive outbursts but calculated risks, resting on the hope that the FWA would support them.†

Among those looking for support was a group led by Epifanio Camacho, who was less deferential than many Chavez loyalists; he would go on to be a troublemaker in Chavez's opinion. Born in Tamaulipas, Mexico, Camacho was already in his thirties when he came to the United States. He had become a rose grafter, a job requiring a delicate skill. (Rose grafters were called the watchmakers of agriculture.) His group worked for a grower in McFarland, a town just south of Delano, and they were furious about the prevalent wage theft: grafters had been promised ten dollars per thousand plants, but due to hidden "fees," they were getting as little as $6.50. Rejecting Chavez's call for patience, the rose workers sent a delegation of forty to Delano. Arriving not as supplicants but with an attitude resting on confidence in their skills, they told Chavez that they planned to strike and that he ought to sup-

---

* Aggie Rose Chavez credits Gil Padilla with this idea. Today Gallo's operation controls 23,000 acres.

† They came from across California—Imperial Valley, Ventura County, the Sacramento delta, and the Salinas valley.

port them. (They had already gotten a majority of the workers to sign cards expressing their desire to be represented by the FWA.)

Gil Padilla was impressed, but Chavez resisted, considering a walk-out premature. Camacho, however, knew that the timing was right, because rose grafting could be done only at a particular point in the growing cycle, and was far too difficult to be done by scabs. So despite Chavez's doubts, the grafters struck the state's biggest rose grower.[69] Camacho was right: the scabs could not do the work, so on day four of the strike, the growers capitulated and offered them a raise. The growers did not, however, recognize the group as a union or commit to future bargaining with them. So Chavez was also right: the rose graft-ers' gains did not last. This was a common pattern: wildcat strikes won wage increases that were then retracted.

Chavez thought that it would take five, even ten years, to build a community organization strong enough to defeat the big growers, and he feared that a defeated strike would further demoralize the farmwork-ers.[70] But soon another challenge to his long-term plan emerged, this time from Filipino farmworkers. Despite, or perhaps because of their militancy, Chavez was leery of Filipinos. He disapproved of their drink-ing, of what he considered their sexual immorality, and of their previous alliances with Communists.[71] Besides, his FWA relied on Mexican sol-idarity. Moreover, Filipino farmworkers already had a union—in 1956 they had started the Filipino Farm Labor Union, which became part of an AFL-CIO organizing project, the Agricultural Workers Orga-nizing Committee (AWOC). AFL-CIO bureaucrats, however, offered them little help; ignorant of the economy of agriculture, they clung to strategies designed around the National Labor Relations Act, which did not cover farmworkers.[72]

But the Filipinos had some leverage that the Mexicans did not. They formed their own work crews, selected crew chiefs, and traveled and worked together as a unit—they even owned their cars collectively and operated a common kitchen in their labor camps. Their strategic cal-culation soon forced Chavez's hand. Their Filipino labor union had strength in the Sonoran Desert's Coachella Valley. When the bracero program ended in December 1964, depriving growers of a legally bound cheap workforce, the Coachella Filipinos, known throughout California for their precision in picking and packing grapes, seized the opportunity to exploit the growers' labor shortage. Waiting until just before the very high heat could damage the grapes, they demanded a raise from $1.20 to $1.40 per hour, struck, and won.[73]

That victory spurred their Filipino compatriots around Delano to demand the same wage. They sent registered letters to growers, who insultingly returned the letters unopened. At a meeting, Larry Itliong held the unopened envelopes aloft for all to see. Like the growers' practice of addressing even fifty-year-old men as "boy," the insult infuriated the farmworkers. (Many categories of workers resented such disrespect as much as or more than terrible working conditions.) A tumultuous mass meeting voted unanimously to strike. On September 8, 1965, they walked out, several thousand strong.[74]

Chavez still believed that pulling his members into a strike was pre-

Agricultural Workers Organizing Committee members picketing in front of Filipino Community Hall as part of the Delano grape strike on September 24, 1965.

mature, unlikely to succeed, and potentially demoralizing. He knew the cost of feeding and housing strikers and the necessary transportation and legal aid to support them. He also worried about tension between Filipinos and Mexicans; in the past, Filipino strikes had been broken by Mexican scabs and vice versa.[75] But the Filipino decision left him no choice: his FWA could not countenance allowing its Mexican members to cross a picket line. The firebrand Camacho called upon his Mexican brothers to join the strike. Doug Adair, editor of *El Malcriado*, the somewhat maverick, irreverent FWA newspaper, began promoting a strike, to Chavez's distress. With a circulation of about two thousand, it spread the news of the AWOC strike to "every barrio in the southern San Joaquin Valley," from Arvin to Madera.[76]

The FWA leadership decided to put the issue to a mass meeting. They scheduled it for Mexican Independence Day, September 16, at Our Lady of Guadalupe Church. It succeeded—over a thousand attended. They voted unanimously to strike, while setting three conditions: that AWOC would share strike support commitments with the FWA, which had no funds for it; that it be entirely nonviolent; and that it would demand union recognition, not just wage increases.[77]

The vote transformed a reluctant Chavez from a community organizer to the leader of a union. He had been compelled from below, much as the ministers in Montgomery had been compelled from below to endorse a boycott.

Yet the vote also appropriated and ultimately buried the Filipino union. The very strength of their organization led to its subordination, which presaged the position of Filipinos in the United Farm Workers in the years ahead. The Filipino union merged with the Mexican FWA, forming the United Farm Workers Organizing Committee (UFWOC) and eventually the United Farm Workers. (From now on, so as not to litter the text with initials, I refer to the movement as the UFW, although it was not officially chartered under that name until 1973.)

The merger nearly destroyed Filipino unity. Adrian Cruz, one of the few academics to examine the Filipino role in the UFW, pointed out that an "assumed inevitability" about the merger has worked to block closer investigation of it. In fact, many Filipino leaders were leery. In addition to mutual prejudice and conflicts, many Filipino farmworkers doubted Mexican militancy, considered Mexicans less experienced, and predicted that Mexicans would control the union, even gobble up the jobs. Larry Itliong, their leader, never spoke in favor of the merger, but merely declined to oppose it.[78] The Filipinos' fear that Mexicans could be used as scabs, however, left them little choice.[79]

Thus Chavez was co-opted by activist farmworkers into running a union. That co-optation might seem somewhat comparable to how Martin Luther King became leader of a boycott he had not planned. But the whole black population of Montgomery could refuse to ride buses, while the majority of UFW members could not strike, because there were no funds for strike pay. Chavez's community organization was strapped for cash. Abby Flores Rivera, of the Delano women's community, remembered, "We were dependent on food donations and it was not easy to prepare meals from the odds and ends of canned and dry foods we received each week. . . . We rarely had fresh meat, fruits, or vegetables. Cesar had a kitchen set up for us to eat at lunchtime and that was the only good meal we got for the day."[80]

The UFW met the problem creatively but at a cost. It established a strike zone of four hundred square miles, outside which those who wanted to honor the strike could honorably take jobs. As a result, mass picketing was not possible, and many farmworkers had to continue working for the very growers they were challenging. Chavez, feeling defeated, remarked that the situation temporarily resulted in a movement without members.[81] As he predicted, the Central Valley growers rejected all the farmworkers' demands and spent $10 million (equivalent to $100 million in 2020) on publicity campaigns denouncing the UFW.[82]

A LONG struggle lay ahead. Its story has been told so often that it would make no sense to trace its chronology here. Instead I want to examine four challenges its faced, one at a time: the work of the union, the difficulties of multiethnicity, violence and Chavez's fasts, and the boycott that won what strikes could not.

The UFW soon faced a major attack from the Teamsters union. By 1973 the UFW had negotiated 150 contracts with California growers covering some fifty thousand workers. But as these contracts expired, the Teamsters, already expelled from the AFL-CIO for corruption, became in essence mercenaries working for the growers. In a bargain supported by President Nixon's undersecretary of labor, Laurence Silberman, they negotiated "sweetheart" contracts with growers aimed at destroying the UFW. In contrast to Chavez's principled commitment requiring UFW members to pay dues, so that they continued to feel invested in the union, the Teamsters allowed joiners to postpone paying dues. They threatened farmworkers' health by undoing restrictions on pesticide use won by the UFW.[83] Farmworkers who signed the contracts had neither input nor, in many cases, even knowledge of these terms. The Teamsters justified these contracts with the claim that the UFW was not a real union but a civil rights movement.[84] There was some truth in this claim—UFW leaders remained committed to fighting racism. The UFW was part of a social movement unionism; the Teamsters were not.

The UFW's valiant legal and legislative staff scored a significant victory, the California Agricultural Labor Relations Act (ALRA), a progressive labor law passed despite opposition from corporate interests. It improved workers' ability to unionize by dealing with the unique conditions of farmwork. It required secret-ballot elections within seven days after card signing, making it possible for migrant workers to vote (as compared to the forty-five days allowed under the New Deal's National Labor Relations Act), and it gave organizers the right to contact workers in the fields. The law brought immediate benefits to UFW farmworkers, who gained 30 to 50 percent wage increases, health insurance, paid vacations, and pensions. But a law is only as good as its enforcement, and the legislature, where growers had enormous clout, provided so little funding that the ALRA Board shut down for eight months in its first year. As a legal scholar wrote, "With every firing that went unaddressed, every petition that languished in the ALRB's hands, every organizer denied access," the law's promise to workers was broken. A decade later the law was a dead letter.[85]

Meanwhile the UFW was drawing valuable outside support, including visits to Delano from ministers and priests, academics and labor leaders, and African American civil rights groups. SNCC sent some of its paid staff to California to help, including Marshall Ganz, and the

San Francisco SNCC office became for a few years a virtual center for farmworker support. Accustomed to southern racist violence, SNCC donated two-way radios to protect UFW activists, as when Cesar and Richard Chavez were being chased by growers' heavies one night; the radios also enabled spreading information about where scab labor was being used.[86] Eliseo Medina recalled that "SNCC people were the only ones that really had any kind of concept about what to do," and UFW organizer Wendy Brooks gave them credit for teaching the "not particularly nonviolent" farmworkers the value of nonviolence.[87]

That outside support included the many volunteers, often college students, pouring into Delano. Politicized by the civil rights and anti–Vietnam War movements, they saw the farmworkers' struggle as an integral part of a social justice movement. Though most volunteers were Anglo, some were Mexican American college students. Many of them spoke Spanish and viewed the farmworkers' struggle as part of a growing Chicano/a movement which intensified support for the UFW—but tended to further marginalize its Filipino members. The volunteers had the stamina of youth. They often left home as early as four a.m. to start picketing just as workers arrived, sometimes shaking with fear, then elated when scabs would lay down their boxes of grapes and walk out after *huelgistas* reasoned with them. On the picket lines volunteers typically outnumbered farmworkers.[88] They often slept on the floor of the "pink house," just behind the office, among "wall-to-wall sleeping bags," and they received food and five dollars a week.

But then Chavez made a policy decision that began to undermine UFW unity. In an attempt to treat everyone equally, he insisted on paying the entire staff five dollars a week. The volunteers could make do with five dollars a week because they were typically single, had other sources of support, and had middle-class futures awaiting them. Chavez defended the policy by arguing that this low wage prevented jealousies and weeded out "the opportunists who might want to take advantage of the union and the farmworkers." He worried that UFW staff would see their work as a job rather than a cause; if they hesitated to make this sacrifice, it would mean that money was too important to them.[89] His anxiety about opportunism reflected the centrality of sacrifice to his vision of an ideal community. When he fasted, when he embarked on physically torturous long marches, he articulated these acts not as tactics but as *penitencias*. His willingness to suffer—and for decades he lived no more comfortably than did his constituents—was a Mexican Catholic mortification. This sacramental mystique exerted a mesmerizing hold on many of his Mexican constituents. Chavez was bringing them into a *cursillo* of a sort.

But farmworkers, who had the local knowledge and skills to do these jobs, could not work for room and board and five dollars a week.[90] They were adults, most with families to support, such as José Murguia, who in addition to three small children was supporting his mother in Mexico.[91] They could not live dormitory style—they needed privacy. Those who took time away from the fields to serve the union—by investigating grievances or medical claims or lobbying in Sacramento—were not compensated for lost earnings. The result was a staff increasingly dominated by Anglos, which alienated many farmworkers.[92]

Besides, even the best volunteers could not substitute for farmworkers or union staff. They could not reach out to unorganized workers. They could not negotiate contracts. They could not lobby in Sacramento or speak to the press. Many were not fluent in Spanish, let alone a Filipino language. Chavez's refusal to pay salaries to UFW staff left the union short of staff. There was grousing but no challenge to his decision.

UFW lawyers and paralegals, largely Anglos, were exceptions to the no-salary rule—the lawyers earned $600 a month (equivalent to $3,800 in 2021). This staff grew quite large—at peak, seventeen lawyers, forty-four paralegals, and many volunteer attorneys. Their dedication and creativity were remarkable. They would ask what the cause needed, then find a way to fill the need. Farmworkers did not seem to resent the lawyers' salaries but rather appreciated their work; farmworker poet Salvador Bustamante recalled of Jerry Cohen, "I loved seeing him deal with them [growers], avenging every affront they ever did to me."[93] But the lawyers got little guidance from the UFW leadership. As more contracts had to be negotiated, and as arrests and harassment of UFW organizers increased, the lawyers had to make decisions themselves, often without consultation with union leaders, thereby bringing yet more Anglos into the leadership. They did not always welcome this but did not organize themselves to clarify these relationships and responsibilities.

Though the UFW retained the loyalty of thousands of farmworkers

314 / SEVEN SOCIAL MOVEMENTS

and a staff willing to work day and night, the refusal to compensate the nonlegal staff adequately exposed the inequality and lack of accountability in the movement and stirred resentment. Chavez's preference for keeping personal control over information made it worse. Many staff members, including nurses and physicians at the medical clinics, did not know that some were paid and others not, and they were hurt and angry when they found out.[94]

Although Chavez understood that a union was the only route to decent wages and working conditions for farmworkers, he was increasingly impatient with, even uninterested in, the work of running a union. As Jerry Cohen put it, "Cesar couldn't bear to sit in an office and administer contracts."[95] He aspired to something both greater and smaller: a community organization suffused with Catholic humility and religiosity. Chavez's reasons came, of course, from his ethical—and religious—commitment to sacrifice, but they were by no means democratic. Yet Chavez insisted that only he could make decisions, even on minor bureaucratic matters that could have been delegated.

The damage from these policies might have been lessened had there been active union locals. In Montgomery, where participants were united in a small city with frequent inspirational church meetings, everyone was contributing. The Montgomery struggle fit Chavez's early organizing principle, that everyone had to give something. Ideally, union locals offer rank-and-file workers work to do, meetings to attend, and opportunities for close contact with leaders. UFW locals could have provided a conduit allowing input from farmworkers to reach leaders and thus improve decision making. The union could also have benefited from local initiatives taken quickly, without waiting for approval from headquarters. Locals could have provided a base of power from which to challenge Chavez's decisions. They might even have reduced the exodus of farmworkers to the Teamsters.

But after 1973, the UFW functioned, as Eliseo Medina recalled after decades of experience as a national labor leader, as "one big centralized union."[96] When lawyers negotiated contracts, they sometimes made crucial mistakes because they did not know how farm labor was organized on particular ranches. Those working to administer contracts were repeatedly reassigned to different locations, thereby losing the advantage of local knowledge. Contracts were only as good as their enforcement, and only strong locals could have enforced them. Medina argued for training members of "ranch committees" in how to run a meeting and how to administer contracts, for example—but the fact that everything had to go through Delano slowed the union work and made farmworkers feel increasingly distant from decision making. Medina argued with Chavez about it. "See, we don't enforce the contracts—they [the workers] do." When rank-and-file workers participated in dealings with growers, growers treated them with greater respect, he pointed out, but Chavez would not budge.[97]

Maintaining union members' allegiance required hiring halls.[98] The impermanence and seasonal nature of farmwork meant that only union supervision of hiring could protect members from employer favoritism, blacklisting, and capricious choices, and from growers' widespread practice of advertising for more workers than they hired. Union hiring could protect workers from having to bribe foremen with bottles of tequila in order to get work, or from retaliation if they charged foremen with shortchanging their tally of lugs or bushels. Job security would have allowed some migrant workers to settle in one place, by working different jobs for the same farm. Settled farmworkers could have kept their children in school, eased women's domestic labor, and even benefited growers by providing a stable workforce.

But shortage of staff—that is, of bureaucratic capacity—created problems, some of them due to Chavez's refusal to pay living wages to staff. Recordkeeping was inadequate: Chavez had recorded his early recruits on index cards, but now there was no accurate record of how many union members were current, how many paid dues, whether dues corresponded to hours of work, or who got what jobs. Eliseo Medina, head of contract administration, did his best, but he had to supervise some twenty-five field offices and one hundred staff, and arrange hiring in almost two hundred locations. Unsurprisingly, there was no uniformity in how the hiring halls worked, as field offices made inconsistent decisions.

Centralization led to flawed decision making. Seniority rules appropriate to some unions created unfairness here, because many members had lived and worked in locales where there was no union to join. Denying seniority to workers who were in arrears on dues disadvantaged the lowest-paid workers, who were often migrants. (At times, growers actually paid dues to the UFW in order to get experienced workers.) The seniority system penalized non-Mexican farmworkers, particularly Filipinos who had been members of AWOC rather than the FWA and whose compatriot foremen now lost their positions.[99]

Because the rules ignored seniority with a particular grower, the system split up workers who lived near each other and had previously shared rides. The system might even split up families as well as work groups that had been tight for years. In harvesting broccoli, Frank Bardacke explains, longtime partnerships enabled rhythm and synchronization between, for example, a broccoli cutter and a loader, whose work required "the precision of a handoff in football or the flip of a baseball between two middle infielders at the beginning of a double play." The loader stood on a platform extending out from a truck; the cutter had a full bin on his shoulder, backed up to the loader above him, and at exactly the right moment thrust his shoulder up to give the basket a boost so the loader could lift it. If the loader lifted it too late, he didn't get the help of the boost, and the weight of the basket might come down heavily on the cutter's shoulder. "Loaders who don't get it right," says Bardacke, "don't last long on crews."[100] This kind of cooperation is built over time.

The staff who ran the hiring halls were no longer able to send workers to jobs in line with their particular experience. Contrary to common assumptions, farmwork is by no means unskilled labor—it is often highly specialized. Philip Vera Cruz's description of how to tend grapes provides an example: "in the spring . . . the 'suckers' start coming out. You take care of the vines and tie down the tender ones. . . . The berries are the size of rice when you start girdling. . . . You don't want the berries to pop out too soon. . . . You take out the laterals, maybe for the Cardinals, but not the Thompsons or Emperors."[101]

These hiring practices intersected with the Teamsters' machinations, and many workers who were frustrated by the hiring hall system defected to the Teamsters, who often gave seniority to those who had been denied it by the UFW.[102]

THE FARMWORKERS' union, which grew from a Mexican community organization, had always had some non-Mexican members, but the creation of the UFW added more non-Mexicans. Growers had long exploited ethnic divisions by keeping workers of different ethnicities separated in the fields, but farmworkers harbored their own suspicions of other groups. Some Filipinos felt disrespected by Mexicans. Mexicans sometimes condemned Filipinos for their cockfights—illegal but protected through payoffs to police—for their snappy dressing, and for their taxi-dance halls, where promoters hired local white women to dance with them, a practice that was hardly surprising since there were so few Filipino women.[103] Both ethnic groups distrusted Yemeni farmworkers, although some of them had been early union stalwarts. (One AWOC organizer recalled that the first strike signs appearing in 1965 were in Arabic.)[104]

Because journalists presented the UFW as a Mexican organization, the public came to understand it that way. "When it comes to the news, it's all Mexican; when they see television, it's all Mexican," Philip Vera Cruz observed.[105] Spanish was the dominant language in meetings. There was little effort to translate Ilocano or Tagalog or other languages, so the second language of choice was English, difficult for many farmworkers. UFW materials used Spanish and Mexican cultural referents.[106] The UFW's logo was the Aztec eagle of Tenochtitlan.* Its paper, *El Malcriado*, featured Mexican revolutionary woodcuts, put Emiliano Zapata on a cover, and connected the current struggle to the Mexican revolution. Members called themselves *la raza* and frequently referred to the fact that they worked on land that had been stolen from Mexico. Mexican Catholicism pervaded the union meetings; priests spoke frequently, invoking the Virgin, and the members sang *"De Colores."*[107]

In 1966 the UFW conceived of a dramatic way to pressure Governor Pat Brown to persuade intransigent growers to negotiate. It would organize a march of 355 miles from Delano to Sacramento, timed to arrive on Easter Sunday. Mexican culture and Catholicism saturated its iconography. This "pilgrimage," *peregrinación*, also aimed to capture media attention and give farmworkers a participatory, heroic action that would lift their spirits. At the front, marchers carried a large photo of

---

* The Aztec god of sun and war, Huitzilopochtli, had forced his people to leave their dwelling place and resettle where they saw an eagle, atop a prickly pear cactus, devouring a snake.

Farmworker carrying image of Virgin of Guadalupe on the march from Delano to Sacramento.

Emiliano Zapata, a cross, and an image of the Virgin of Guadalupe, Mexicans' chief national religious figure. (She appeared in almost every UFW demonstration.) At every night's stopping place en route, someone read and distributed the credo of the march, the "Plan of Delano," modeled on Zapata's "Plan de Ayala." The text featured quotes from Pope Leo XII and Benito Juárez and defined the marchers as "sons of the Mexican Revolution." It explained that "we carry LA VIRGEN DE GUADALUPE [capitals in the original] because she is ours, all ours, Patroness of the Mexican people." Each marcher swore allegiance to the plan while holding a crucifix. Huerta sometimes asked the workers to place their hands on a crucifix and swear that they would not scab. Leaders set up masses in front of the homes of strikebreakers "to pray for their repentance."[108] For Chavez, pilgrimage was "in the blood of the Mexican American" and intensely Catholic. So was the fact that the marchers suffered; like his own fasts, the march was a "penance for the sins of the strikers."[109] Newsreels showing Chavez limping with a cane on blistered feet associated the marchers' sacrifices with the sacrifices of Jesus.[110]

True, the march included ecumenical gestures and cooperation. Someone carried a Star of David (possibly Marshall Ganz's idea). SNCC operated communications through the long march. The Plan of Delano included class-conscious language: "We know that the poverty of the Mexican or Filipino worker in California is the same as that of all farm workers across the country, the Negroes and poor whites, the Puerto Ricans, Japanese, and Arabians; in short, all of the races that comprise the oppressed minorities of the United States." Chavez's statements frequently described his union as multiethnic, but that did little to alter the perception, both within and outside the union, that it was a Mexican organization.[111]

The march's drama made it particularly newsworthy and brought extensive publicity. It led Schenley Industries, whose vineyards made it the second-largest grower in the region, to capitulate; Dolores Huerta's negotiations produced a thirty-five-cent-per-hour wage increase and a hiring hall to register and select workers.

Union members often used *mexicanidad* creatively. When DiGiorgio, a major grower, got an injunction against picketing on the roads, thus preventing UFW organizers from contacting workers in the fields, Antonia and Maria Saludado created a solution: "Why don't we build an altar, a small church on the public roadway. . . . We can hold Mass and a prayer vigil every night." So they put the Virgin's image in the back of a pickup truck, transforming it into a shrine, parked it next to the main gate, and held mass there every evening, even as they distributed leaflets, spoke about the union, and got signed union cards.[112] Defending the use of Catholic imagery, Huerta said, "We put the virgin to a motion, and virginity won."[113]

Not all Mexicans in the UFW liked the religious emphasis. Epifanio Camacho and Antonio (Tony) Orendain were among the rare leaders willing to challenge Chavez, criticizing the mixing of politics and religion. Others—even some Catholics—declined to participate in Mexican Mariology. Still others were Baptists or simply anticlerical. Obdulia (Abby) Flores Rivera's father refused not only to join the pilgrimage for that reason but also to attend the masses, even when Chavez was

320 / SEVEN SOCIAL MOVEMENTS

fasting.[114] Orendain and Camacho considered the fasts sanctimonious, manipulative, and "playing God," a futile attempt to win support from the Catholic hierarchy.*[115] By contrast, Montgomery's Blacks unanimously honored their churches, and not only for praying—they were social and political as well as religious institutions, which was not true of most Catholic churches.

The Filipinos, although mainly Catholic, shared neither the Mariology nor the fervor of the Mexicans. But they did make use of Filipino culture. Well before Chavez entered the scene, Larry Itliong and other leaders had used Filipinos' hometown associations and clubs to organize strikes. The audacious Itliong would sneak into a labor camp, crawl under the bunkhouse, and speak to workers through cracks in the floor.[116] But the growers continued to sow distrust among farmworkers of different ethnicities, particularly between Filipinos and Mexicans. Growers created, for example, a Filipino American Society that promoted dissension with claims like "Can't you see that these people [i.e., Mexicans] are using you to form an organization that will give them power and great wealth?"[117] The Teamsters did likewise, leading many Filipinos to leave the UFW and join the Teamsters.[118]

Filipino leaders, in line with their leftist politics, tried to promote working-class unity. The flashy, popular Itliong often referred to Mexican farmworkers as "brothers." Even before the UFW was created, he had pleaded, "Let us forget those abuses we had had in the past. Let us win the friendship of all other groups by showing them our cooperation."[119] Plenty of Filipinos respected Chavez and recognized his extraordinary leadership. Many enjoyed and joined in the Mexicans' boisterous approach to picketing, shouting *"Mag labas cayo, cabayan!"*— Countrymen, bring yourselves out [on strike]. Itliong ran for Delano's city council in 1966, and in his publicity he spoke for all farmworkers, condemning the corporations like DiGiorgio, Schenley, and Giumarra that sent their profits away rather than investing in Delano.[120]

The UFW did not, however, take advantage of the Filipino empha-

---

* Objections to Catholic religiosity were most common among those who immigrated from Mexico, where there was a strong anticlerical consciousness among worker activists.

sis on working-class unity. It did not honor the Filipinos' long history of unionization or bring more Filipinos into the union staff. Larry Itliong resigned in 1971, protesting not only discrimination against Filipinos but also lack of union democracy. It is telling that when he left the UFW, no official announced his resignation to the union members, let alone his criticisms; the UFW just let him disappear.[121] Philip Vera Cruz resigned a few years later.

Meanwhile, the bracero program, intended to hold down wages, angered Mexican farmworkers in the United States, who frequently labeled the braceros "scabs."[122] But they got no relief when the bracero program ended in 1964, because the U.S. Immigration and Naturalization Service (INS), responding to growers' demands for a steady low-wage labor supply, replaced it with tens of thousands of green cards. UFW members understood this, quite correctly, as a strategy for rolling back UFW gains, but hostility to the undocumented was already common in Mexican American organizations.[123] Chavez argued that if the "illegals" had not been present, "we would win the strike overnight," a wild exaggeration.[124]

The result was a shameful moment in UFW history. Unable to impede the growers' influence on immigration authorities, Chavez ordered a campaign to keep the undocumented from crossing the border. "We consider this campaign to be even more important than the strike, second only to the boycott," he announced.[125] Manuel Chavez, Cesar's cousin, organized a "wet line"—short for "wetbacks," a translation of *mojados*, referring to Mexicans who entered the United States by crossing the Rio Grande—sending as many as three hundred patrols to police the border, even using an airplane, to catch the "illegals." Those caught were often beaten, sometimes brutally, and turned over to *la migra*, the INS.[126] The patrols cost the union thousands of dollars a week. Not until the end of the 1970s would the union change its approach to undocumented Mexicans.[127]

LIKE AFRICAN AMERICANS in Montgomery in the 1950s, farmworkers in the 1960s and '70s were subjected to considerable violence. As in Montgomery, the UFW leadership was committed to nonviolence. But in California's vast agricultural fields, the violence was so pervasive and so dispersed that UFW leadership found it difficult to stop farmworkers from responding in kind. That it was mainly able to do so was a considerable achievement.

Farmworker strikes had typically failed because of the ready availability of strikebreakers, and few things enraged farmworkers more than scabs. Yet Chavez, with a generosity born of personal experience of hardship, insisted that the *esquiroles*, scabs, be treated as if "they had been with us all along because it [scabbing] was not their fault."[128] So UFW workers tried to dissuade scabs. Picketers directed them to places they could work without scabbing. Strikers sneaked into the labor camps in the evenings to try to discuss the situation with scabs. They deployed "submarines," members who took work as scabs, then urged workers to walk out when picketers arrived. They orchestrated roving and surprise picketing, so that growers' thugs could not be prepared.[129]

But with inadequate strike funds, the pool of farmworkers available for picketing shrank, and the smaller teams of pickets were vulnerable. Growers' enforcers tried to intimidate them by taking photographs, red-bait them by shouting "go back to Russia," and provoke them by calling the men dirty greasers and the women whores.[130] The enforcers were threatening. An example: A car pulls up and two men—one with a shotgun and another with a metal rod—walk menacingly past the line of pickets. Cars accelerate toward the line, stopping inches from the picketers and spraying them with dust; then the driver yells, "When are you going to take a bath?" "Dozens of large beefy men, covered with tattoos and armed with baseball bats, knives, chains and clubs descended."[131]

Sometimes the growers' enforcers went beyond threats. They smashed union cars and firebombed the Delano UFW headquarters and gas station. Sheriff's men burglarized the Delano office several times, allegedly looking for evidence of Communism.[132] They beat up strikers, even women, and in response the police often arrested the bloodied victims. Trained Doberman pinschers charged the pickets. Much of this violence resembled that directed at Black civil rights demonstrators in Birmingham, for example, but some was unique to the agricultural fields, as when one of the grower's men drove a jeep with a pesticide sprayer mounted on it, spraying picketers with the poisonous mist.[133] When the Teamsters moved in, they escalated the violence. The guns aimed at farmworkers were so plentiful that farmworkers christened several San Joaquin Valley locations "Dodge City."[134] Five UFW people were killed.*

Unsurprisingly, some farmworkers thought violence should be met with violence, considering nonviolence not only unmanly but useless. A few, including Epifanio Camacho, Alfredo Figueroa, and some Filipinos explicitly rejected nonviolence, having observed that violence had been effective at intimidating scabs and potential scabs.[135] Most farmworker violence, however, was vandalism against grower property, *chingaderas*, or "dirty tricks." They spread tacks on roads and entrances to vineyards to puncture tires. They destroyed irrigation pumps and set fires in packing sheds. Manuel Chavez led a team who attacked refrigerator trucks, burned storage sheds, and vandalized train cars carrying scab produce. Rudy Reyes became expert at climbing atop train cars carrying scab produce and cutting their electrical wires. Some even shot at train cars. Labor contractors' buses mysteriously burned. Vines and almond trees—which take years to mature—were cut down. Irrigation pumps stopped working. Numerous police cars were suddenly out of service. Sabotage felt deeply satisfying but was also tactical, a means of "hurting them in the pocketbook."[136]

Former farmworker Frank Bardacke believes that Chavez condoned and possibly encouraged this vandalism. Despite the UFW's official love-thy-enemy credo and Chavez's hope that nonviolence could achieve results, it seems clear that he knew what was happening—his cousin Manuel Chavez was a key saboteur—but asked not to be told, so as to maintain deniability.[137] With his characteristic command of language, Chavez wrote, "How many times we ourselves have felt the need to lash out in anger and bitterness." In one deliciously ironic letter to the growers, he wrote, "I think we've learned how not to hate them [growers], and maybe love comes in stages. . . . Of course, we can learn how to love the growers more easily after they sign contracts."[138]

---

* They were the Anglo volunteer Nan Freeman, the Yemeni farmworker Nagi Daifallah, the Mexican immigrant farmworker Juan de La Cruz, the striker Rufino Contreras, and Rene Lopez, who was leading a UFW attempt to organize a dairy.

Even if he provided clandestine support for vandalism, Chavez knew that farmworkers' violence could never defeat the growers and their obedient police; fearing that it could escalate out of control, he determined to check it. He knew that the fight-back response to violence was in part created by farmworkers' need for a manly identity, so he tried to reconfigure that identity: "the truest act of courage, the strongest act of manliness, is to sacrifice . . . in a totally non-violent struggle . . . God help us to be men."[139] But in early 1968 UFW spirits were low—strikers were losing patience, and picket captains were going AWOL.[140]

So Chavez chose to use his body, embarking on the first of three major fasts on February 15, 1968.[141] He presented his fasting not as a tactic but as a *penitencia* for his own sins as well as those of others, just as he would present the pilgrimage to Sacramento. He insisted that his fast was neither a threat nor a disciplinary measure, but this is not credible. He hoped that his self-sacrifice, and the fear of losing him, would suppress farmworker violence and increase the pressure on growers. UFW lawyer Jerry Cohen never believed the penitence talk and understood the fast as a strategic move.

Chavez entered this new territory with stunning courage and masterful strategic calculation. The fast made him a heroic national celebrity and turned a labor struggle into a moral crusade. It also reconfirmed the devotion of his farmworker constituency and brought in valuable outside support and publicity. Coretta Scott King visited, and Martin Luther King, Jr., who would be murdered in April, telegraphed his support. Robert F. Kennedy, who would be murdered in June, visited and literally fed him—nothing could have more perfectly represented Chavez as a saint. The UFW suspended contract negotiations, as well as picketing and boycotting operations, allowing thousands from all over California to make the trek to Delano to pay homage to Chavez's self-sacrifice. They created a tent city outside the small room in back of a gas station in which Chavez lay—surely recalling for many Mexicans the manger in which Jesus was born. Franciscan priest Mark Day held a daily evening mass, and at times Protestant ministers participated.[142] The fast, suffering, and ensuing risk to Chavez's health functioned as a sacramental rite.

One grower, clearly a lesser strategist, got Chavez cited for contempt—for violating an antipicketing injunction. So in the midst of his fast he limped, leaning on others, into the courthouse as farmworkers filled the courtroom and, in a tableau of biblical dimensions, the paths leading up to it, kneeling, singing softly, and praying. Although UFW lawyers knew that they couldn't often defeat the growers in court, they understood that performances like this one—turning a courtroom into a stage—could work to change the "cultural, political, and moral environment in which legal decisions were made."[143]

The extensive, favorable journalistic coverage raised awareness of and respect for the farmworkers' struggle but also confirmed and intensified farmworkers' fear of losing Chavez, thereby making any challenge to his leadership seem risky at best, treacherous at worst. Not all UFW members were pleased with the fasting tactic. Some saw it as coercive. Some thought the workers should be on the picket lines instead of near his bedside. Itliong, irked that Chavez had acted without consulting the UFW executive board, disliked the theatrics. Some Filipino leftists considered the "hunger strikes, marches and religious pageantry" to be moves that undermined a focus on class struggle. UFW secretary-treasurer Antonio Orendain refused to authorize union money to feed the crowd at the fast site. Others worried about the long-term damage to Chavez's body. Doug Adair, a volunteer who became a farmworker himself and stayed with the union for twenty-five years, looked back at this fast as an ominous turning point: it had "an unhealthy impact . . . the nightly masses were orchestrated so that people were literally worshipping at his feet." Former priest, now UFW staffer John Duggan considered the fast Chavez's escape from the nitty-gritty work of the union, a view confirmed in the following years.[144]

THE UFW's greatest victory happened far from the fields—a national grape boycott. It created a triple win: forcing the growers to capitulate, educating and eliciting support from millions of consumers, and building rank-and-file farmworkers' capacity for autonomous, creative decision making, which in turn boosted their confidence. The most successful boycott in U.S. history, it convinced seventeen million Americans not to buy grapes and drained the growers' pocketbooks enough to force them to the negotiating table.

As social movements in support of labor struggles, consumer boycotts have a proud history. The Knights of Labor used boycotts in the 1880s, and Florence Kelley's National Consumers League of 1899 called on women shoppers to buy only clothing with a union label. In 1907 the AFL published a "We Don't Patronize" list to win a nine-hour working day. Consumer boycotts work by defetishizing commodities—that is, they expose the previously hidden conditions under which products are made. Especially in big cities, few shoppers are familiar with the conditions of food production, and this ignorance contributes to employers' impunity in exploiting and endangering their workers. Boycotts extend labor battlegrounds—in the UFW case, from the fields to the cities, from the West to the whole nation.

In 1967, after two years of strikes, only five thousand of the approximately 250,000 UFW members worked under signed contracts. Growers were paying more for the scabs than they offered the union workers, and were bringing in children as young as six to serve as strikebreakers. Aware that the escalating violence threatened to weaken public sympathy for the farmworkers' struggle, Chavez decided to organize a consumer boycott of grapes.[145] Its announcement to the farmwork community in the UFW's newspaper *El Malcriado* resounded like a Martin Luther King sermon:

> *Our ancestors were among those who founded this land and tamed its natural wilderness. . . . It was four years ago that we threw down our plowshares and pruning hooks. These Biblical symbols of peace and tranquility to us represent too many lifetimes of unprotesting submission to a degrading social system that allows us no dignity. . . . Grapes must remain an unenjoyed luxury for all as long as the barest human needs and basic human rights are still luxuries for farm workers.*[146]

To create the boycott, about one hundred farmworkers traveled afield. They had to overcome significant anxiety—most had never traveled far from home, let alone to the alien environments of big midwestern and eastern cities. Twenty-one-year-old Eliseo Medina was sent on his own to Chicago, flying for the first time, without a winter coat, carrying $100 in cash and the name and phone number of a supporter. For

Jessica Govea, facing white people reawakened frightening encounters with aggressive white men in Bakersfield, but "I made myself strong," she said. They were homesick—"I wanted to see a Mexican so badly my eyes hurt," Lopez Fierro recalled. Marcos Muñoz went to Boston, Jessica Govea and Joe Serda to Detroit, and Rudy Ahumada to Philadelphia. Many of them spoke no English. Sacrificing privacy, they lived communally, slept on army cots, solicited donations of clothing and furniture, and accepted every dinner invitation.[147]

Far from Delano, since long-distance phone calls were expensive, the boycott required independent decision making.[148] Eliseo Medina's trajectory to leadership was particularly steep. It helped that Chicago already had a significant Mexican population, and postal worker union activist John Armendariz met him at the airport. But Medina found his footing quickly. He set up a desk in the Hispanic ministry of a local church. He got himself a speaking slot at an Illinois Federation of Labor convention, "so nervous . . . that they fortified him with a couple of stiff drinks." He electrified the audience, which gave him a standing ovation and a $1,500 contribution. He began speaking at colleges, high schools, churches, synagogues, anywhere he could get a chance. He printed cards with a tear-off pledge that shoppers signed, promising not to buy from stores that sold grapes, then sent them to the chain stores' management. He raised the money to buy 120 shares of stock in a big grocery chain, Jewel; then, as stockholders, his crew disrupted the company's annual meeting. They announced a massive demonstration against Jewel and got Chavez to promise to attend; Jewel capitulated. Mayor Daley anointed Medina as Man of the Year.

Medina's success led Chavez to transfer him to New York. His team of fifty farmworkers drove there in a school bus with almost no heat, sleeping in churches and supporters' homes. But he kept his crew together and insisted that "if anybody was invited anywhere [for meals], the invitation had to be for everybody." Having learned from Chavez, he fostered leadership in others by assigning them responsibility, as when he sent Maria Saludado Magaña from his Chicago crew to open a boycott operation in Indianapolis.[149]

None worked harder than the women. They had to find living quarters and schools for the children. They had to learn how to use public transportation, shop in unfamiliar stores, clean, cook, and find medical care for sick kids, while picketing, making signs, stuffing envelopes, mimeographing, and telephoning. Some had to negotiate all this with faulty English. The five-dollars per week that the UFW provided was far from adequate, Kathy Murguia recalled, so "Lupe and I were accountable for raising enough money to meet our budget."[150]

When they began to picket and leaflet in front of groceries, the farmworkers had several advantages. Most people could do without grapes; a later boycott of lettuce was harder. Their leverage was greater than in an earlier wine boycott because grapes are perishable and had to be sold quickly. They also benefited from the fact that 1960s progressive movements—civil rights, antiwar, women's rights—had increased public awareness of injustice and made activism an honored practice. Local newspapers spread the news of the boycott. A river of media acclaim for Cesar Chavez flowed onto the boycott workers, so that when they spoke to customers outside stores, they were, in a way, recognized. Customers could actually *see* and talk to farmworkers, turning political abstractions into people. The picketers pointed out that pesticides and lack of toilets endangered consumers as well as farmworkers. When women picketed with their children, no words were necessary for customers to imagine the effects of farmworkers' low wages and terrible working conditions.

In New York, a city of immigrants and unionized workers, organizers received support from the Spanish-speaking population, largely Puerto Rican and Dominican. African Americans joined the cause: SNCC and CORE got forty-nine Harlem stores to honor the boycott, and the Black Panther Party also mobilized support.[151] Publicity brought in contributions large and small, from high school kids donating their lunch money to big-dollar gifts from churches and wealthy liberals; these donations often surpassed the farmworker teams' expenses.[152]

First they targeted A&P, the largest grocery chain in the city. After it removed grapes from all 430 of its stores, other chains—Bohack, Walbaum's, Hills, and Finast—all except Gristedes—fell into line. Other locations required different tactics. Boycott picketers directed shoppers to stores that had complied with the boycott and even offered rides to and from these alternative groceries. Faced with an injunction limiting picketing, the Los Angeles crew walked *into* supermarkets and spoke with customers one at a time. In Portland, Oregon, the team placed people on the eleven bridges across the Willamette River, holding huge signs promoting the boycott. So many drivers honked and signaled V with their fingers that this tactic spread to many other locations. Mack Lyons, the only African American on the UFW board, got the San Francisco Board of Supervisors to endorse the boycott. The movement got Canadian support: the mayor of Toronto declared November 23, 1968, Grape Day, announcing that the city would not buy grapes.[153] The boycott spread even in Europe—in Sweden, Finland, Norway, Denmark, the Netherlands, Germany, and England. The Nixon administration found this so worrying that it ordered the American embassy in the UK to promote grapes, with little success.[154]

Two personal anecdotes about children tell the story of the boycott's success: One elementary-school child saw grapes at her grandmother's house and asked, "What are those?" A younger child pointed to grapes on sale and said to his mother, "Look, there are boycotts!"

The boycott accomplished what the strikes had not. As overall grape sales fell by as much as 35 percent, the large growers had to capitulate. In July 1970 the twenty-nine major grape growers, who controlled 85 percent of all California's vineyards, agreed to collective bargaining with the UFW. As a result, six million cartons of grapes were produced under union contracts. Victories in the vineyards spread elsewhere. In the 1973 grape and vegetable contracts, workers got 47 percent hourly and piece-rate wage increases, plus cost-of-living and seniority increases, as well as guarantees against wage theft through hidden (and often illegal) "fees." They won an eight-hour day, instead of beginning at four-thirty a.m.—with light from trucks—and working until dark. They won regular fifteen-minute rest periods, six paid holidays, and a week of vacation time after seven hundred hours of work, time off for funerals, company contributions to the union's medical and pension plans, and tools provided by the growers. After several more years of litigious struggle against growers, the *cortito* (short-handled hoe) was banned. Not least, workers would be paid for their time administering contracts.[155] Abby Flores Rivera recalled that the "boycott was making it possible for us to sit at the table and be heard."[156]

The boycotters also gave something of value to those who agreed not to buy grapes: millions could support a social justice movement with minimal sacrifice and as a result take a bit of pride in their contribution. Yet more, they strengthened other movements for social justice by the connections that they made and by illuminating the connections among other campaigns. The farmworkers' struggle modeled uniting a class with an antiracist struggle. And as city dwellers learned of the boycott's success, they observed the power of organized protest.

The boycotters had also benefited personally. They gained confidence and worldliness, improved their English, and learned to communicate their struggle to a diverse audience. They became comfortable talking to strangers. They saw that thousands of Americans respected their struggle. They began to trust their own ideas about tactics. "To me it was really clear what it meant to have a union, forgetting wages and benefits and everything else. Just seeing the difference in the people," one commented. Chava Bustamante wrote a poem about this feeling of empowerment:

> *Poor fools! Those who think*
> *That power comes from money.*
> *Without contemplating*
> *That real power*
> *That which is real and lasting*
> *That is the one which is given through justice.*[157]

Yet he would be one of those forced out of the UFW for dissenting from Chavez's decisions.

DESPITE THESE benefits, however, farmworkers who remained in the fields soon experienced losses traceable to the boycott. The boycott had diverted energy from basic union functions. Many who could have been administering contracts had been drafted into doing boycott work, which made some farmworkers feel deserted—the union never fully explained the boycott strategy or how boycott victories benefited farmworkers. The backlog of contract administration furthered this problem. To rank-and-file UFW members, the boycott's connection to the union came to seem tenuous.[158]

Those losses soon grew. A year after the boycott victories, Chavez decided on a move, both geographic and spiritual, that initiated a downward trajectory. While thousands of UFW members saw union work not getting done, Chavez was concerned that union work was blocking progress toward his imagined spiritual community. He longed for an escape from the busy-ness and crowdedness of the Delano headquarters, which was of course created by union work.[159]

He envisioned a place where families would work, share, and develop the farmworker movement spiritually as well as materially—in this respect resembling the goals of utopian socialist communes of the previous century. He imagined bringing farmworkers into retreats like the *cursillos*. LeRoy Chatfield, who had withdrawn in 1965 from the Christian Brothers, a Catholic monastic order, in order to serve the UFW, found an abandoned tuberculosis sanatorium on one hundred acres in the Tehachapi Mountains, thirty miles east of Bakersfield. Chavez got a wealthy donor to buy it for the UFW. He christened it *Nuestra Señora Reina de Paz*, once again a name that connoted *mexicanidad*, and moved the union's top leadership there. At first only a few key people, including Helen Chavez, were skeptical about the move. (It is quite possible that she, like other women, would be losing a warm and supportive Delano community of women.) Before long, however, nearly everyone in UFW leadership or staff considered the move a mistake, draining energy from building and sustaining the union.

The staff found La Paz pleasurable in some ways. The housing was rough, but the air was cooler and the pace less frantic than in Delano. It was safer, especially for the women—no bars, no drunken guys on the streets, no cockfights. The children—the kids of the Chavezes, of Dolores Huerta, the Encinas, the Murguias—formed a happy community of their own, riding a bus to school in Tehachapi. But staff members also suffered from isolation: the nearest town was ten miles away, and few had access to cars. Tina Solinas missed the bustle of "strikers and organizers, religious folk, lawyers, paralegals, volunteers from the cities, families of strikers and reporters," with farmworkers coming in and out at all times.[160] Gossip and petty jealousies swarmed at La Paz because, Bonnie Burns Chatfield thought, "There were too many people with not enough real work to do."[161] The shortage of work resulted from the separation of the staff—often numbering 125 or more—from farmworkers.

The move not only removed farmworkers from visibility in the daily activities of UFW leaders, who lost contact with farmworkers' ideas and grievances. It also marginalized farmworkers symbolically. The people to whom Chavez had devoted his life were being edged out of his thoughts. He began to talk about "a national union of the poor dedicated to world peace and to serving the needs of all men who suffer." Worse, he began to see farmworkers' aspirations to improve their material lives as superficial. His increasing emphasis on sacrifice seemed to make it the central value of his movement. While previously he had condemned staff demands for salaries, now he began labeling workers' ambition for higher wages "greedy." He explicitly rejected union democracy. He began denying the intelligence of farmworkers, saying that the best strategies came from those who were not farmworkers. "You don't want farm workers managing the union right now. With the attitude they have on money," Chavez said at a conference, "it would be a total god damn disaster. . . . Unless they're taught the other life, it wouldn't work." They should strive instead to lift their spiritual-religious consciousness through rededication to a communal life of "modest possessions and immodesty in self-sacrifice."[162] He wanted his followers to be born again.

Several outstanding historians and journalists—notably Frank Bardacke, Matt Garcia, and Miriam Pawel—have detailed the disintegration of Chavez's leadership. (I use the compound word *disintegration* literally, to characterize the coming apart of his rationality.) He began to see any disagreement with his decisions as evidence of a conspiracy against him, a plot to derail and deform his movement. Even suggestions for alternative procedures and tactics became evidence of disloyalty.

Paradoxically, he sabotaged the development of a spiritual community by micromanaging UFW business, which soon became micro-*mis*managing. Chavez had always overworked himself. This had paid off when he was organizing, but it now reflected his inability to trust others. In 1973 he was arising at three-thirty a.m., opening each piece of mail, dictating answers, often working until ten p.m. He refused to make appointments, so staff had difficulty getting his attention. He pored over each invoice and check—apparently no one else could sign—and tossed rejected bills angrily to the floor. As his brother Richard put it, he wanted an accounting of every spark plug bought for the union's cars.[163] As the union's operations slowed, Chavez blamed staff inefficiency even as he forced out the most competent workers.[164] He was becoming a tyrant without a movement to tyrannize, firing people that he could not replace.

His identification of his enemies shifted—they were no longer the growers but worldly, materialistic Communists. Later his anti-Communism would slide into anti-Semitism: at a 1982 UFW convention, Chavez's supporters distributed leaflets charging that the dissidents were tools of "the two Jews"—Marshall Ganz, the main Anglo staffer and an indispensable strategist, and Jerry Cohen, the union's top lawyer who had beaten back so many legal attacks.[165]

Chavez's feverish anti-Communism turned his marginalization of Filipino farmworkers into a blatant insult: he made a formal visit to Philippine dictator Ferdinand Marcos. In order to bring in a Filipino who would be less critical than Itliong and Vera Cruz, he appointed small businessman Andy Imutan to the UFW executive board. Imutan arranged a royal visit to Manila, where Chavez stayed in luxurious accommodations, accepted an honorary doctorate from a university there, and on his return, praised the regime. He invited Philippine government officials to speak at the 1977 UFW convention. A shocked Vera Cruz resigned, pointing out that Chavez had "violated a principle of the union, that is, the regard for human rights." It is a measure of Chavez's disconnection from the farmworker movement that he apparently expected the trip to please Filipino farmworkers. Many of them were already defecting from the UFW, but now they grew furious. So were many other farmworkers when they learned that some of California's corporate growers ran similar operations in the Philippines.

Meanwhile Chavez fell under the influence of Synanon, a Santa Monica New Age outfit that morphed from a drug rehabilitation program to a "church" offering "therapy" and finally to an authoritarian cult catering to the wealthy, run by the tyrannical guru Charles Dederich.[166] From Synanon, Chavez imported a "therapy" called the "Game," in an effort to cleanse UFW staff of their sins. In 1977 he called the UFW executive board to a meeting at Synanon, where they would "play" the Game.[167] The "players" would form a circle around an individual who was being "gamed," "indicting" him or her for misdeeds, with accusations increasing in severity and tone until they were screaming obscenities.[168] He brought the Game to La Paz, requiring the staff to "play" it every Wednesday, expecting it to expose those plotting against him. He may well have seen in the Game something of the *cursillo* ritual of meditating on one's sinfulness, but it was far more abusive and destructive.

The harsh personal attacks authorized by the Game then multiplied purges, a word the staff had been using for several years. While an analogy to Stalin's purges was already percolating among his unhappy staff, Chavez used it himself. "You do it [the firings] to save the union," he said, "then every time there's opposition developing, boom, you get them. . . . In other words, I got to pull a Joseph Stalin." The UFW purges, unlike Stalin's, were of course small-scale and nonviolent, but they shared one destructive consequence: expelling the most experienced and capable staff. Dederich actively encouraged Chavez to fire people: "if these old cronies here don't follow you, drop 'em."[169] When La Paz staff were sacked, they were immediately evicted. In an event that came to be called the "Monday Night Massacre," a play on Nixon's Watergate firings, in a Game-like proceeding on April 4, 1977, Chavez fired seven people, then required them to leave that evening and refused them access to telephones to work out transportation.[170] Deirdre Godfrey, a banished volunteer, wrote that she would "never forget the frenzied, hate-filled faces and voices of people who had been warm and friendly with me right through to the hour of the meeting."[171]

Chavez's understanding of his position became *l'état, c'est moi*. Disagreement was treachery. People quit arguing with him.[172] If they did, he threatened to quit. They all feared losing him, and some were not sure he was wrong. Their leader had become indispensable, a danger for any organization and especially for a social movement. Bob Moses, a charismatic leader in the civil rights organization SNCC, saw in

Chavez's behavior a much exaggerated version of the problems in his own leadership: he was "too strong, too central, so that people who did not need to, began to lean on me, to use me as a crutch."[173]

Chavez had once predicted that his strongest colleagues would inevitably become his enemies.[174] It was as if he both recognized and denied his own paranoia. He got Gil Padilla and Marshall Ganz to "game" Eliseo Medina, accusing him of trying to usurp the presidency—an allegation that reflected Chavez's awareness that Medina was the best candidate to inherit the leadership. Then Jerry Cohen and Dolores Huerta "gamed" Padilla, long Chavez's closest comrade, with whom he had "shared rooms, cigarettes and picket duty" for years; Chavez forced him to resign. When some tried to resist by "Gaming" Chavez himself, it proved disastrous because it "proved" that they were his "enemies."[175]

Divide-and-conquer worked. By undermining solidarity, the Game prevented a collective challenge to Chavez from emerging. Anyone remaining had to accept purging others.[176] Some even fed Chavez's paranoia by informing on others.[177] The followers disagreed individually, complained individually, and allowed themselves to be dismissed individually. Padilla was particularly self-critical. "I stood there in silence," he recalled of a meeting in which Chavez attacked Vera Cruz. "They treated him like dirt."[178] When a UFW organizer was raped by a farmworker, UFW women met to discuss the problem; their caucus was immediately denounced and their leader fired, with Ganz as one of her "judges." As Bardacke put it, Ganz acted as Grand Inquisitor, only to be denounced and driven out later. Revisiting this episode later, Ganz admitted, "Yes, we were all part of it, caught up in the management-by-purging approach." And he repeated Padilla's own acceptance of responsibility: "And we let him. Because we needed him."[179]

The staff's terror of losing Chavez—and with him their union—arose in part from their history of failed unionizing attempts. Their anxiety was fortified by journalistic coverage that always foregrounded Chavez, and only Chavez, which made doing without him seem unthinkable. They also felt that deserting this man who had given his life to the farmworkers' cause would be shamefully, unpardonably ungrateful. However unconsciously, they needed his love and respect. Soon almost all the UFW's original team and the most effective organizers were gone.

336 / SEVEN SOCIAL MOVEMENTS

Except for Dolores Huerta. She argued with Chavez often, and he even cursed at her, but she was now in a relationship with Cesar's brother Richard, with whom she had four children, so it would have been difficult for her to leave and impossible for Chavez to purge her. Her activism has continued through further decades. So has her courage: during a peaceful protest in 1988, she was severely beaten by San Francisco police officer Frank Achim; she emerged with broken bones and required emergency surgery to remove her spleen. It didn't stop her. At age ninety-three, she continues to devote her skills and energy to farmworkers and other social justice causes.* She remains, deservedly, a heroine.

CESAR CHAVEZ was one of the greatest leaders of the twentieth century. Through his organizing genius, tactical mastery, patience, hard work and self-sacrifice on behalf of farmworkers he created a movement that improved their lives and offered their children a better future, while inspiring others across the country to work for social justice. He inspired the Chicana/o and Mexican American civil rights movement, demonstrated the power of a consumer boycott, and furthered environmental campaigns against dangerous pesticides. He nurtured and trained activists, many of whom continued in progressive causes. He made brilliant use of religiosity—a Christianity of humility, a Christianity for the humble.

After several decades of stellar leadership, his anxieties undermined the movement he had worked so hard to build. His very strengths did it, as in a Greek tragedy. While his charismatic religiosity inspired farmworkers, it also made their deference to him take on a spiritual dimension. He used Mexican traditions to great effect but marginalized non-Mexican leaders, notably Filipinos, further thwarting the development of a loyal opposition. By making himself seem indispensable, he discouraged his followers' independent initiatives. Chavez began to see

* Huerta has received countless awards. She invented the now-ubiquitous slogan *Sí, se puede,* "Yes we can." She has been the subject of many *corridos,* murals, and films but not, surprisingly, a full biography.

himself as indispensable, and his fears of betrayal became so manic that he drove his best organizers out of the movement.

The UFW's second tier of leadership, its followership, also bears responsibility for that descent. Capable leaders became Chavez's henchmen. As farmworker and then political journalist Frank Bardacke recognized, the union weakened not because Chavez went crazy but because his followers did not demand a democratic structure. Instead they tolerated his misleadership, paralyzed by their indebtedness to him, by their fears of losing him and of being exiled from a movement that had been the core of their lives. Those fears made some of them willing to scapegoat others, even those they knew were trustworthy. The press contributed to the followers' passivity, by sanctifying Chavez, presenting the UFW as his creation, representing the farmworkers only as sufferers and the movement as only Mexican. Margo Okazawa-Rey, an organizer with long experience (we will meet her again in chapter 7), identifies what we might call the occupational hazards of charismatic leadership: it is "difficult to ascertain where a leader's asserted dominance ends and members' acquiescence begins."

These failures flowed in part from the conditions and constraints of the movement. Consider another movement with an extraordinary leader, the Montgomery bus boycott. Martin Luther King, Jr., could not and did not try to micromanage the boycott. Though he became an astute strategist later, during the boycott he was a religious leader, money-raiser, and morale-builder. Lay men and women of the Black working class and the small Black middle class did the planning and the work.

Farmworkers had few of these advantages. They had no middle class with disposable time but depended entirely on long, exhausting hours of low-wage work in the fields. They worked outdoors and could not count on churches as spaces for morale-building. A relatively small team had to coordinate the union movement across thousands of miles, relying on a small central office. Farmworkers faced an opposition ultimately more powerful than that facing Montgomery's boycotters. Montgomery Blacks faced attacks from police, government, and organizations defending white supremacy, while the farmworkers faced the big growers, their mercenaries, and the state and national politicians who backed them. The power of this opposition required Chavez to use every strength he could muster—his words, his prayers, his fasts—to maintain the morale of his constituents. He bore the double responsibility for inspiring the movement and developing its strategies and tactics. He carried the whole movement on his back. Martin Luther King, Jr., did not.

Social movements ultimately depend on relations between leadership and followership. Scholar Charles Payne in his study of the civil rights movement distinguished between mobilizers and organizers: between those who articulate the movement's ideals and those who plan strategy and tactics; between those who address a large public, including members of the movement and the larger public, and those who interact with members personally. Montgomery African Americans created an effective synergy between mobilizers and organizers. Cesar Chavez tried to be both.

The UFW has weakened radically over the decades. In early 2023 its members numbered about 5,500, meaning that less than 2 percent of California's 400,000 farmworkers are unionized—a statistical zero.[180] Election sites were often situated on grower property, and as a result, growers could intimidate workers by noting or even photographing who voted. Then in 2021 the U.S. Supreme Court ruled that growers had the right to bar union activity on their property. A small, bittersweet victory, a new California law allowing farmworkers to vote in union elections by mail, has not compensated for these losses.[181]

7

CONSCIOUSNESS-RAISING
AS ACTIVISM

Intersectionality in Practice

Combahee River Collective leading a women's march protesting police inaction in relation to eleven murders of women.

> In its early stages a group fosters intimacy and trust which frees women to discuss their fears and problems.... [then] we add from our own histories to arrive at an understanding of other social conditions of women ... [then] analyzing the reasons for the causes of the oppression of women.
>
> —PAMELA ALLEN, "FREE SPACE," 1970

> Of all the nasty outcomes predicted for women's libera-
> tion . . . none was more alarming, from a feminist point of
> view, than the suggestion that women would eventually
> become just like men. . . . We need a kind of feminism that
> aims not just to assimilate into the institutions that men have
> created over the centuries, but to infiltrate and subvert them.
> —BARBARA EHRENREICH

> This focusing upon our own oppression is embodied in the
> concept of identity politics. We believe that the most pro-
> found and potentially most radical politics come directly out
> of our own identity, as opposed to working to end somebody
> else's oppression.
> —COMBAHEE RIVER COLLECTIVE STATEMENT, 1977

Extending from the late 1960s through the 1970s, the women's
liberation movement, sometimes called second-wave feminism,
was the largest social movement in U.S. history. It consisted of
thousands of independent local groups, but nevertheless its participants
understood themselves as part of a single social movement. Arising out
of the civil rights and anti–Vietnam War movements, it took up such a
range of causes—from sports to world peace, from sex to job discrimination, from law to movies—that there can be no definitive list.* This
diversity was part of the genius of the movement, because it left women
free to create projects appropriate to Americans of every race, religion,
and locale.

That movement engendered an influential political concept known
as *intersectionality*, a concept that has traveled across the world. Coined

---

* Many scholars have defined the New Left ideologically, focusing on theoretical
statements. That definition privileges a predominantly white, middle-class, and
male-led movement located in universities. Along with others, I see the American
New Left as a related group of social movements beginning in the 1950s with civil
rights, extending through anti-imperialism and socialist feminism, and continuing
in, for example, environmentalism.

by distinguished Black feminist legal scholar Kimberlé Crenshaw in 1988, the term characterized how various forms of inequality, exploitation, and discrimination interacted and reinforced each other. While the term has generated a large body of feminist *theory*, this chapter focuses on intersectionality in *practice*, about which very little has been written. The protagonists in this chapter are two Boston-area socialist-feminist organizations: Bread and Roses, an organization of several hundred mainly white middle-class women, begun in 1969, and the Combahee River Collective, a group of about a dozen mainly African American lesbians, both middle class and working class, begun in the early 1970s.

The term *intersectionality* arose in response to an infuriating legal ruling. Kimberlé Crenshaw, Patricia Williams, Mari Matsuda, and other legal scholars of color were developing arguments that could force the law to respond adequately to cases where both race and gender discrimination were involved. An outrageous, obtuse federal district court ruling, *DeGraffenreid v. General Motors* (1976), dismissed a complaint that African American women had been denied access to better jobs because, the court found, there was no race discrimination (since black men were not barred from better jobs) and no sex discrimination (since white women were not barred from better jobs). Treating sex discrimination and race discrimination as two separate wrongs—Angela Davis recalled once being asked, "Are you Black or are you a woman?"—the ruling left women of color without the standing to challenge the discrimination against them.[1]

The intersectionality concept, then, arose from African American women's experience.[2] But even before the term existed, efforts to practice it characterized the socialist-feminist stream within the women's movement. Socialist feminism was an ideal, not an ideology or a political system, conceived as a democratic, civil libertarian, egalitarian political, social, and economic order. Its proponents campaigned against racism and homophobia and for policies that would benefit poor and working-class women in particular, such as subsidized child care, health care, equal wages, and equal educational opportunity. They championed free speech, reproductive rights, environmental justice, public health, and more. They fought violence against women and people of color. Refusing to focus exclusively on "women's issues," they argued to make women's needs and desires central to all policies, including foreign policy.

Between 1969 and 1975, seventeen socialist-feminist organizations arose, mainly in large cities but also in several smaller ones, such as Lexington and San Jose. This stream of feminism has been little recognized, even ignored, in most accounts of the women's liberation movement. It produced few manifestos.[3] Its ideas are better induced from what they did than from what they wrote—with one exception: the 1977 Combahee River Collective statement, arguably the most influential articulation of intersectionality to emerge.[4]

The feminist movement faced a unique obstacle: for many women and men, discrimination against women was invisible, taken for granted, just as the air we breathe is invisible. So ending it first required making it visible. Doing that was known as consciousness-raising. In small groups both intimate and political, women explored experiences and grievances, learning from each other. Their meetings were simultaneously pleasurable and maddening, as women recalled discrimination, insults, harassment, and even assaults. (Some "women's libbers" joked that they needed consciousness *lowering*, because these realizations were painful.) The pleasures came from an existing gendered pattern: women's propensity for friendships with other women. Consciousness-raising groups thus formalized and politicized traditional female behavior, then connected their personal stories to social structures—economic, political, social, familial. Despite their outrage as they uncovered the myriad aspects of male dominance, the dominant mood was exhilaration, because a better world came to seem possible.

Unsurprisingly, most consciousness-raising groups brought together women of similar race and age, often even religion and social class. In other words, they were usually as segregated as the nation. That segregation, and the greater visibility of white feminism, led many scholars to the mistaken impression that second-wave feminism was a white movement that women of color joined later; and relatedly that consciousness-raising was a white middle-class phenomenon, with women of color, notably African Americans, taking it up later.[5] This chapter will show that this chronology is mistaken.

The leading published accounts of women's liberation also mistakenly describe it as "divorcing" male-dominated movements such as civil rights and opposition to the Vietnam War. On the contrary, women's liberation groups remained actively involved in those causes. They did, however, distinguish themselves from several older activist streams. They criticized the *Old* Left, that is, the Communist Party, for its hierarchical leadership and its treatment of sexism as a minor, subsidiary issue. The few small 1970s Marxist-Leninist groups tended to treat male dominance as a product of capitalism; some even imagined that it would automatically end if capitalism were abolished.[6] (This perspective led Barbara Ehrenreich to call them "mechanical Marxists.")[7] Socialist feminists also rejected an approach known as "radical feminist," which viewed male dominance as the original and most important form of inequality; that perspective paralleled the Marxists' view of capitalism, in what the historian Deborah King has called "monism," the tendency to treat a single factor as the source of a problem. While socialist feminists respected liberal feminism, exemplified by the National Organization for Women, they also saw it as limited, because its focus on sex discrimination in the economy and polity neglected other realms of male domination, in culture, education, health, and sexuality, to name but a few.

Socialist feminists absorbed two ideals from the New Left. From Students for a Democratic Society (SDS), a student organization focused mainly on protesting the Vietnam War, they took on "participatory democracy" as a goal. A phrase first used by Tom Hayden in a 1962 manifesto, *The Port Huron Statement*, it identified the principle that a democratic society could be created only by democratic means, in which members not only voted on decisions but participated in formulating strategies and tactics.[8] The New Left also tried to practice a "prefigurative" mode of organizing. Its goal was to make an organization's internal relations model the ideal society it hoped to build, committing itself to creating a compassionate and supportive community. To socialist feminists, these goals meant rejecting the top-down, authoritarian, and macho leadership they had seen in the male-dominated SDS. These were high ideals, difficult to put into practice. In women's liberation organizations, the commitment to participatory democracy created at times an exaggerated recoil against formal leadership.[9] Similarly, the emphasis on the prefigurative mode sometimes allowed responding to each other's emotional needs to erode efficient decision making. Nevertheless, attempts to practice these ideals, however imperfect, produced organizations that provided support and warmth to their members.

THE MOTHER of women's liberation was the civil rights movement. It produced an analogy between racism and sexism used by both Black and white women to illuminate how gender operated.* The analogy was limited and overused, however, because people of color suffered different, greater, and more violent subjugation than did white women. As a result, the analogy contributed to a view, common in the 1970s among African Americans, especially Black nationalists, that "feminism" was a white thing—or worse, a movement that weakened the civil rights cause by dividing men and women.[10]

Nevertheless, by offering a virtual master class in the structures and operations of racism, civil rights opened a path to a *structural* analysis of sexism, understanding it as a matter not of prejudice but of social, economic and political institutions. Among civil rights organizations, SNCC influenced socialist feminism most directly. The youngest and most democratic civil rights group, it nurtured the confidence and leadership skills of many women. Nevertheless, SNCC women were sometimes shunted into background work—taking minutes, cleaning the office, cooking for the groups. Many social movements arise from the clash of raised aspirations with continued subordination, of expectations raised and then frustrated. This clash was experienced particularly sharply by women.

SNCC women conducted a first protest against sexism in 1964, a "strike for equality" in the Atlanta headquarters. Occupying SNCC leader James Forman's office, they called for ending the practice of assigning the least interesting tasks, notably clerical work, to women. Ruby Doris Robinson, one of the most respected of SNCC leaders, sat holding a sign reading "No more work till justice comes to the Atlanta

---

* The analogy had long roots: in the nineteenth century, exposure to the conditions of enslaved people led women's rights advocates—most of whom were also abolitionists—to a recognition of how male dominance constrained women's freedom.

office." This was a woman who had endured thirty days in a South Carolina jail.* She would replace Forman as executive secretary, a sign of the respect she commanded.[11] Not all SNCC women joined this first protest, because some of them already had major leadership responsibilities, because the solidarity and mutual affection in SNCC often overrode women's complaints, and because no one wanted to weaken SNCC.

One extraordinary woman pushed the protest further: Frances Beal, an early pioneer of second-wave Black feminism.[12] A child of Communist parents, she grew up in a CP community and attended its summer camps, so when she moved to Paris at nineteen in 1959, she was open to radical ideas. They came to her from a group responsible for the anti-colonialist magazine *Présence Africaine*. Through it she met activists from Vietnam, Chile, Angola, and especially Algeria, where an anti-colonial revolution was nearing victory. She met distinguished African American expats, such as Richard Wright. She helped bring Malcolm X to Paris in 1965, a time when he was influencing Black consciousness across the globe. When her daughter Anne was born, she benefited from French medical care, childcare, even weeks of paid vacation; France showed her how a welfare state could improve the lives of the working class, especially women and children.

Returning to the United States in 1966, Beal soon connected with SNCC, assuming responsibility for its new international affairs commission. Despite her extensive experience, she had been diffident about articulating her political ideas until she encountered feminism: "It . . . liberated the rest of me to be able . . . to say I have some real political thoughts of my own."[13] She got a job with the National Council of Negro Women (NCNW), a distinguished successor to the historic National Association of Colored Women,† editing its newsletter. This put her in a potentially awkward position, because her boss, Dorothy

---

* Robinson died of leukemia at twenty-four. Many of her comrades thought her cancer was a direct result of the terrible conditions she endured in jail.

† Before that position she had headed the Phyllis Wheatley branch of the District of Columbia YWCA—then a segregated institution. Surely she knew of Jane Hunter and the Cleveland Phillis Wheatley House, discussed in chapter 1. The NACW, founded in 1896, was the first Black civil rights organization in the United States, predating the NAACP, which is usually labeled the pioneer—a small error reflecting the lower status of women.

Height, head of the NCNW from 1958 to 1990, was "old school" and more conservative than Beal. They nevertheless developed a mutually respectful, even fond relationship.*

When Beal heard about the 1964 SNCC women's protest, she immediately thought, These were women who would not bow to Alabama state troopers, so why should they bow to the patriarchal ideas of some SNCC men? But relations within SNCC complicated Black women's relation to feminism. They were often treated as neutral, without gender, and some noted that Ruby Doris Robinson was able to lead because she was regarded as one of the boys.[14] This degendering of African American women, they understood, was the reverse face of many SNCC men's preference for dating white women—a practice that created considerable resentment.[15] Casey Hayden and Mary King, both white, distributed a memo listing eleven examples of discrimination against women in SNCC. Fearing rejection, they did not sign the memo, but everyone knew who had written it, and none of SNCC's Black women offered support.[16] The memo's title, "Sex and Caste," reflected their vivid awareness of sexism as part of an interlocking system of discrimination, in an early suggestion of intersectionality.

Meanwhile a wave of Black nationalism was encouraging macho posturing and disdain for women among SNCC men. Some of them were repeating the Nation of Islam's prescription that Black women should stand behind their men, bear many children, and devote themselves to family (a truly delusional wish, given the high proportion of African American women who had to earn and the many who had to support children without men's help). "Behind," of course, meant both supporting the man and remaining subordinate to him. Beal was comfortable with "Black power," a slogan for empowerment, because it stood for releasing Blacks from "the standards of the dominant white culture." In Black nationalism, by contrast, she charged that manhood

---

* Many Black women activists were outraged that although Height was the long-term leader of a major civil rights organization, the National Council of Colored Women, she was not allowed to speak at the great 1963 March on Washington. In response to this insult, a hastily planned "Tribute to Women" introduced Rosa Parks, Daisy Bates, Diane Nash, and Gloria Richardson but did not ask them to speak or walk with VIPs at the front of the march.

"replaced . . . racial justice" as the goal.[17] So as the women's allegations of sexism grew more frequent, it may have been because SNCC men were behaving worse.

Beal soon gathered some SNCC women to discuss their complaints—that is, to engage in consciousness-raising.[18] Beal and Gwen Patton, who had been student body president at Tuskegee and led a voting rights march to the state capitol, wrote a critique of the sexism in Eldridge Cleaver's influential *Soul on Ice*, which some SNCC men were promoting.[19] (Not all, however; James Forman and Bob Moses were consistently supportive of women.) Beal noted sardonically that Black nationalists were adopting a white *Ladies' Home Journal* model of how women should behave, thinly disguised by fantasies about "African queens."[20] Gwen Patton—whose grandparents had been active in the Montgomery bus boycott—pointed out that "all these people running around in these dashikis . . . I don't understand what kind of African history they been reading. . . . All these big time kings . . . are the same kings that sold us into slavery."[21]

Surrounding the complaints and criticisms, however, were the pleasures of the women's discussion group. Here is Fran Beal: "I mean, we used to stay up half the night talking about freedom, liberation, freedom, you know, all these ideas and it was natural—that in a sense freedom was in the air. And all this talk—it's like Sojourner [Truth] says, 'What's all this talk about Freedom?' . . . And then, when people began talking about men should do this and . . . women should do that, we said, 'Now, wait a minute. This sounds familiar' [laughter]."[22]

Out of these conversations came Beal's influential article "Double Jeopardy," published in 1969 but circulated beforehand in a SNCC consciousness-raising group, the Black Women's Liberation Committee.[23] An early formulation of intersectionality, it characterized how racism and sexism affected Black women neither as separate problems nor as separate categories but as parts of a gestalt.[24]

SIMULTANEOUSLY ANOTHER African American feminist was organizing: psychotherapist Patricia Murphy Robinson, who incorporated mental health issues into an analysis of capitalism and patriarchy. Coming from a prominent Black family, she had Old Left roots, resembling Beal in this respect. Her father was the publisher of the *Baltimore Afro-American*, the longest-running African American newspaper, founded in 1892, and a member of the national board of Planned Parenthood. The Murphys also had Communist Party connections—Paul Robeson and W. E. B. Du Bois were family friends—and an internationalist orientation.[25] An admirer and friend of Malcolm X, Robinson, after his death, helped create a group to support his wife and children.[26] (Robyn Spencer's video about Robinson, *Pat! A Revolutionary Black Molecule*, appeared in 2002.)

In 1960 Robinson began working for Planned Parenthood in Mt. Vernon and New Rochelle, neighboring towns just north of New York City,* visiting and talking with poor African American women in their homes. She began by listening, as organizers of "9 to 5" would do a decade later. Like Margaret Sanger a half century earlier, she saw how lack of access to birth control kept women overworked, in ill health, and unable to function as active citizens.[27] She organized a small Black women's group that became even more outspoken than Beal's—calling itself, defiantly, Poor Black Women.[28] While they criticized white feminists who appeared oblivious to their race privilege, they also criticized "bourgie [bourgeois] . . . educated Black women." Fearless in their criticism of Black men, the group denounced "jive-male oppressive power" in a 1968 pamphlet.[29] But unlike the doctrinaire Marxist-Leninists, they defended working with middle-class women, writing that

> *one does not . . . keep himself to one class, but you learn to be flexible, that is to say that the poor may have different ways of doing and teaching, much of which can benefit the middle class. In this way we can all grow together and understand each other more, and together we can do what has to be done.*[30]

Their agenda was capacious. Inspired by Harlem's Black Women Enraged, created by renowned actress Ruby Dee, they protested the

---

* Many African Americans fleeing the South had settled in these towns, creating two of the earliest free Black communities in the United States.

Marching for equal treatment of women in jobs and education and for abortion rights, 1970.

Vietnam War by picketing an army recruiting office, conducted a rent strike to protest abysmal housing, and created a Saturday afternoon Freedom School for kids.[31] This brought them support from the Old Left publication *Freedomways*, the leading Black political, cultural, and theoretical journal of the time. (Esther Cooper Jackson and Dorothy Burnham of the Communist Party were among its founders, and its writers included Alice Childress, Louise Moore, Lorraine Hansberry, and Alice Walker.)

Together with kids in their freedom school, in 1973 Poor Black Women published *Lessons from the Damned.** It included an essay by four sixteen-

---

* Its introduction explained that it was "written by a large number of poor and petit-bourgeois black people—the damned—poor students, poor unemployed young year-old girls calling for a "new type of family" in which men would love women like they love themselves and mothers would put children first.[32] These essays began circulating in feminist circles, and several years later the Combahee River Collective read and discussed them. They were particularly furious at Black nationalists who condemned birth control and instructed women to produce many as babies as possible to build the Black "nation,"[33] as well as the nationalists' claim that an alleged "Black matriarchy" was "castrating" Black men.[34] (The scholar Rhonda Williams has pointed out the "ruthless power" of the word *matriarch* in silencing Black women.) Black nationalists were complaining that Black women were "popping those [birth-control] pills into her mouth and telling her husband and lover what she thought," Robinson noted.[35] Their support for birth control arose from a child-centered perspective, aiming at better mothering and healthier children. "We poor women have known that you cannot move the men, so we have given ourselves to the children."[36] In a vision picked up a few years later by the multiracial Committee for Abortion Rights and Against Sterilization Abuse (CARASA), the group defined reproductive rights expansively, to include safe childbearing, providing children with a decent standard of living and education, and ending coercive sterilization. They were envisaging what is today called reproductive justice, defined by Loretta Ross, founder of Sister Song, the Women of Color Reproductive Justice Collective, as "making visible the web of apparently disparate policies that form a totalizing containment system."[37] In other words, intersectionality.

MEANWHILE, BACK in New York City, after SNCC disbanded, its Black Women's Liberation Committee renamed itself the Black Women's Alliance. Soon Puerto Rican women activists asked to join. Despite some initial resistance from those who preferred limiting the organization to African Americans, on the grounds that their history was unique, the group opened to all women of color. (Fran Beal argued that

---

women and men (the street bloods), workers in low-paying dead-end jobs, and women welfare recipients. . . . This book may be the first time that poor and petit-bourgeois black people have described the full reality of our oppression and our struggle."

"the complexities of intersecting oppressions are more resilient than the distinctions"—another early formulation of intersectionality.)[38] Then called the Third World Women's Alliance (TWWA), signaling their identification with the peoples of the global south, they saw themselves as subjects of an internal colonization imposed by the same forces that created external colonization.[39] Its newsletter, *Triple Jeopardy*, extended Beal's earlier "double jeopardy" by adding class to race and sex. The membership grew to several hundred, while the newsletter reached 1,400, including 150 copies sent to women in prison.[40]

The TWWA was uncomfortable with the label "feminist." Two women's experiences can illustrate why. In a march organized by NOW, one of its leaders criticized Fran Beal for carrying a sign in defense of the African American activist intellectual Angela Davis, who had been indicted for kidnapping, conspiracy, and murder.* The NOW woman said that this case had nothing to do with women's liberation, to which Beal replied, "It has nothing to do with the kind of liberation you're talking about but . . . everything to do with the kind of liberation we're talking about." Elizabeth "Betita" Martinez, a Chicana member of SNCC, encountered the same attitude in a small women's group in New York City, where she was often the only woman of color. At a meeting on the day Martin Luther King, Jr., was assassinated, she could think of nothing else, but the others wanted to continue with the previously planned topic. She was shocked and angry; "this is just too white for me. . . . I'm outta here!" She never went back.[41]

Other women of color felt the same. Referring to the history of light-skinned Blacks "passing," Cellestine Ware wrote, "Joining the women's liberation movement may seem at this time like a re-entry into the old farce of pretending to be white."[42] Looking back on this, Barbara Smith of the Combahee River Collective remembered thinking that these white feminists "were *perfectly* crazy"—what did they have to complain about?[43] Despite refusing the "f" label, the TWWA, like Poor Black Women, raged at Black men who thought "that we must become

---

* Davis was accused of helping a 1970 attempt to free Black Panther George Jackson from Soledad prison through taking hostages in an armed attack on a courtroom; police killed all the conspirators. Davis was acquitted of all charges in 1972.

breeders and provide an army . . . that we had Kotex or pussy power."[44] As Barbara Smith put it several years later, "The brothers had in fact created a sex-based definition of 'Blackness' that served only them."

THE PATH bringing whites to women's liberation led from SNCC to SDS. By 1965 the anti–Vietnam War movement had saturated campuses, and some hundred thousand students joined SDS. It organized demonstrations and teach-ins at hundreds of universities, demanding an end to university complicity with the war. SDS sexism was greater than SNCC's: few women held leadership positions and instead found themselves doing clerical and housekeeping work, while men—intent on rejecting allegations of cowardice because of their opposition to the draft—debated, orated, and wrote, displaying their lofty theoretical fluency and competing to be the most radical. SDS president Todd Gitlin would later call Casey Hayden "a revered founding mother of SDS," but she spent a whole summer in an SDS office typing the mailing list onto stencils while the men discussed strategy. At an SDS New Year's Eve party, the women set up food and drink while the men kept debating till midnight.[45] Meanwhile, a "sexual revolution" culture authorized men to label women uptight and insufficiently radical if they rejected sexual invitations or harassment.

Casey Hayden and Mary King of SNCC once again opened a discussion of sexism with a memo they entitled "Sex and Caste." They distributed it to forty-four women "across the spectrum of progressive organizing"—a phrase that expressed their sense of an inclusive New Left. It detonated a small firestorm at an SDS convention in December 1965.[46] Loud hostility from SDS men only piqued women's interest, and a workshop to discuss the memo met repeatedly throughout the three-day conference. SDSer Marilyn Webb thought it was "first time we applied politics to ourselves . . . we saw ourselves colonized in the same way as Fanon has described the Algerians." She might have been channeling Fran Beal. A year and a half later at another SDS conference, women managed, despite "sexist catcalls," to win official approval of a report calling for shared housework and childcare as well as support for birth control and abortion. The report did not discuss SDS men's behavior,[47] however, and male disdain for women's grievances—or was it fear?—continued.

One episode was particularly galling: At a National Conference for a New Politics, women asked the group to endorse a statement about sex inequality, and the conference leadership agreed to bring it to the floor. But when the time came, the chair dismissed it on the grounds that "more important" issues needed attention. Two women walked to the podium to protest, and as men in the audience laughed, he patted one of them—Shulamith Firestone—on the head, saying, "Cool down, little girl." As one women remembered, "Rage . . . kept us going for at least three months."[48]

Afterward women's protests spread so fast that it becomes impossible to construct a chronology. As Toni Cade Bambara wrote, it seemed that "every organization you can name has . . . mutinous cadres of women getting salty about having to man the telephones or fix the coffee while the men wrote the position papers and decided on policy."[49]

At some point in 1967–68, women began speaking of a "women's liberation movement." The word *liberation* signals their identification with anticolonial struggles abroad, such as the Vietnamese National Liberation Front. It would be difficult to exaggerate the impact of the Vietnam War on young Americans. Some 2.2 million men were drafted. It was the first televised war. In the comfort of home, one could watch American tanks literally rolling over the small thatched houses of Vietnamese peasants, planes spreading herbicide to destroy rice paddies, napalm bombs falling, their jellied gas designed to stick to skin. Unlike any previous war, in this one the most powerful nation in the world invaded a small country whose "crime" was to have a Communist government in the North. My generation was horrified and guilt-ridden.

In Boston some SDS women decided to support the antiwar movement by doing draft counseling. But when they met with the Boston Draft Resistance Group to discuss what they could do, they were infuriated by its sexism—for example, men ignored women's suggestions until a man then suggested the same thing. As the group considered how to respond, they were surprised by how much they enjoyed discussing politics without men present, just as Beal's group had. "We had never felt so comfortable in meetings," Bread and Roses member Nancy Hawley recalled a few years later. She invited "a handful of women to dinner (on a night my husband was out of course). The flood broke loose. . . . For hours we talked . . . and left feeling high."[50]

SOCIAL MOVEMENTS do not always produce such highs, but they always create camaraderie, particularly when participants meet in small groups. We have seen it everywhere in this book—in the settlements, in KKK klaverns, in Townsend and unemployed groups. These relationships are not ancillary but central to how social movements work, especially for women participants who typically engage in conversations more personal than men's. Particularly intense conversations developed at an historic 1968 women's conference, hastily organized and publicized mainly through word of mouth. Some 250 women showed up, from twenty states and Canada. For many, the mere fact of attending was a step toward feminism: some had never traveled without husbands or boyfriends and had never discussed political questions with a group of women. It proved exhilarating: "talked most of the night," one woman wrote. They attended workshops on sex, capitalism, caste, and class, "cruising: or the rationalization of the pursuit of men," alternative lifestyles (they were thinking of communes, coops, support groups), women and their bodies, women writers, family, and children. An eleven-page single-spaced "conference summary" included scores of fragments of comments like these:

> We drove through storm to reach physical togetherness . . .
> Doubts . . . Do they really think and feel as we do?
> One could feel a new community forming. . . .
> Understanding her because it is also me she speaks of. . . .
> Man may not be, but Woman certainly is a social animal.[51]

In planning the conference, however, a painful discussion had identified a central problem for women's liberation—the overwhelming whiteness of the group. Everyone regretted it, everyone felt guilty about it. Some opposed moving forward without involving Black women, suggesting that they invite activists from welfare rights and civil rights lest they divide and weaken antiracist activism. They worried lest the conference turn into a debate about *whether* women should organize against male dominance, making it impossible to discuss *how* to do so.[52] They did not seem to register that inviting women of color only after an event had been planned was insulting and racist. In any case, no invitations to Black women's groups were sent.

The conference was not intended to produce formal resolutions or decisions.* Considerable anxiety appeared when discussion turned to creating an independent women's organization. Nevertheless, despite their negative experiences with some bombastic, competitive, cocky SDS leaders, they appropriated the participatory democracy ideal, reinterpreted as a female principle. Similarly appropriating the New Left ideal of prefigurative organizing—the principle that relations among activists should exemplify the society they hoped to create, that the end cannot justify the means, that undemocratic practices cannot create a democratic society—and reinterpreting it in female terms, it soon became clear.[53] (These ideals would produce both strengths and weaknesses in socialist-feminist organizations.)

Those active in male-dominated organizations worried that creating a separate women's organization would mean discounting their previous hard work, even betraying the New Left. (This fear paralleled the worry that feminism would divide antiracist organizing, but the stakes for African Americans were higher.) To participant Amy Kesselman, later a women's studies professor, creating a separate women's organization felt like "divorcing your husband."[54] In hindsight, separate wom-

---

* Only one question resulted in a decision. Leery of allowing media to cover the conference, since they expected that the discussion would include emotional, personal experiences, they decided that in speaking with the press, conference participants would discuss only larger issues of sex discrimination and would not comment on the conference itself or name any of those who attended. The latter prohibition reflected how risky women's liberation appeared to many participants. Hostility to the male-dominated press had intensified when *Ramparts* magazine's story on the women's movement featured on the cover a woman with a cleavage and no head! This principle foreshadowed Bread and Roses' later resistance to creating media stars, as was happening in New York City, or to allowing a single person to represent the movement.

en's liberation groups seem inevitable, but that was not how it looked to these women at this time.

IN THE Boston area in 1968, a dynamic newcomer, Roxanne Dunbar, gathered a different group of women into a small and short-lived feminist group.[55] For those who began Bread and Roses, it became a model for what not to do. The group consisted of some dozen women, all white but unusually diverse in social class: they included Betsy Warrior, a working-class woman who had escaped an abusive marriage and then, influenced by Dunbar, adopted a new name to honor Native American heroism; Dana Densmore, daughter of the Communist Party–influenced Donna Allen, a founder of Women Strike for Peace; and Abby Rockefeller, heir to one of the greatest fortunes in the country, who financed the group.[56]

The charismatic Dunbar advocated a radical feminist politics, labeling men the enemy, rejecting political collaboration with men, advocating celibacy, and promoting karate as a means of resisting male aggression. (Karate soon became a popular martial art in the women's liberation movement). She called her approach "female liberation" rather than women's liberation because, unwittingly anticipating later post-structuralist feminist theory, she "didn't believe that 'woman' was real; it was patriarchy's idol, a fantasy, an oppressive . . . prescription [intended] to force female people into a limited subservient role for the service and convenience of the . . . patriarchy."[57] The group adopted the name Cell 16, because Abby Rockefeller's address was 16 Lexington, and "cell" indicated that their hope was to proliferate more cells.*

Dunbar's style made her recruits more disciples than comrades and soon evoked criticism from some who were at first drawn to Cell 16. One recalled that Dunbar claimed to be "far ahead of others" and often ridiculed those who raised questions: "That's like saying we should all love one another . . . brotherhood and all that." "That's bullshit." At one meeting she proclaimed, according to the notes of someone present,

---

* They may not have known that *cell* was the nomenclature for chapters in the CP, although surely Dana Densmore's mother would have known this.

"I know what is necessary. I am going to tell you." Some disapproved of her attempt to exclude lesbians, but their main objection was that "Roxanne was making all the decisions. . . . We began to write Roxanne's lies in a notebook."[58] Though it collapsed rather quickly, Cell 16 had a mixed influence on Bread and Roses—positively in identifying how the "sexual revolution" could serve to strengthen male domination, negatively in intensifying hostility to leadership.[59]

Bread and Roses grew out of several open meetings to discuss women's liberation, which attracted two to three hundred women. Then a conference at Emmanuel College drew more than six hundred, despite taking place on Mothers' Day. As small consciousness-raising groups began forming, women eager to join were turned away because keeping the groups small seemed essential to exchanging personal experiences. But many women complained that it was hard to "get in" to the women's movement. So a few took an initiative: They placed a notice in the *Boston Phoenix*, the alternative weekly, inviting those interested in learning about the new movement and joining a consciousness-raising group to a Thursday-evening event in a coffeehouse.* Scores showed up. The notice was repeated, and the next Thursday even more arrived, and the next and the next. . . . Organizers could not keep up with demand, so setting up new consciousness-raising groups was a makeshift process— some came together by neighborhood, some by special interests.[60] Ultimately there would be at least twenty-three such groups in Bread and Roses, averaging ten people each.

Frequently, a woman interested in these orientation gatherings would ask if she could bring her husband or boyfriend. After all, he needed to understand women's grievances, didn't he? How could women change their relationships with men if men didn't participate? These were reasonable questions, and mixed-sex discussions

---

* The meeting was held at the Sgt. Brown Memorial Necktie Coffeehouse, and therein lies a story. The Boston Draft Resistance Group frequently went to induction centers and passed out antiwar leaflets urging "don't go." Once when the recruiters asked them to leave and they refused, pushing and shoving ensued. One protester grabbed a recruiter's necktie. It turned out not to be a standard necktie but one fastened to a flexible metal collar holding it in place, so it came off. The protesters kept it, and the group named the coffeehouse in honor of the event.

could be constructive. But having seen how often men dominated and women deferred in meetings, organizers said no. Moreover, it was unclear that women could talk freely about sex with men present— yet sex was a vital topic in an era when the vast majority of American women had limited or even false information about female sexual pleasure. Finally, in this era, women in heterosexual relationships did not often go out without their partners, especially not to evening events. Socializing with other women often took second place to socializing with men; it was normal for women to cancel a plan with a woman friend if a guy asked her for a date. So taking an independent step into an all-women's space seemed vital. To some, these introductory events could be threatening, and a number of women probably decided against attending or were turned away when they arrived with boyfriends. But the women-only rule turned out to be crucial, not only for consciousness-raising groups but for the larger women's movement.

Consciousness-raising led some women to political activism for the first time. But to think of consciousness-raising only as encouragement to activism is a misunderstanding, because consciousness-raising *is* activism, it *is* politics.* This is the meaning of the slogan "the personal is political." (That phrase is often misinterpreted, relying on a narrow definition of "political," while in this context it referred to any relations of power, however informal.)

Though influenced by civil rights, white feminism faced a unique obstacle. Civil rights organizers didn't need to convince African Americans that they were subjugated and deprived, but only to persuade them that protest could produce change. By contrast, the majority of women accepted their subordination to men as natural or even as ordained by God. Some denied the existence of sexism altogether, and some found

---

* Consciousness-raising groups were for many the central, even the only experience in the women's liberation movement. Many groups spawned by Bread and Roses continued independently, either uninterested in organizational matters or, possibly, uncomfortable with the "socialist" or intersectional part of its approach. This was by no means a failure: consciousness-raising changed women's aspirations and behavior, which in turn powered a movement for change even among women who did not identify as feminists.

their current social position not just tolerable but rewarding. Sexism was hard to see because it operated in countless realms of the culture and because it was often loved ones who practiced it. Precisely because of these hurdles, consciousness-raising was a brilliant tactic. Thousands of speeches and texts denouncing the gender system could never have equaled its impact.

Because the rules of gender were everywhere, nothing was irrelevant in consciousness-raising groups. Typically meeting weekly, women discussed childhood and parents, schools and jobs, sex and love, health and sports. A group might choose a theme for each meeting—for example, one group devoted a meeting to discuss fathers. Most groups established a rule that nothing said in a meeting could be repeated outside it. This mattered not only because women revealed intimacies but also because relationships are complicated, and women often expressed grievances and love about the same person. The guarantee of confidentiality meant that meetings could resemble heart-to-heart talks with a close friend. But through exchanging experiences, women enriched their understanding of how the gender system worked, how it affected different women's lives—and how women both resisted and defied it.

Women often spoke about their mothers, some with pride, some with sadness about the opportunities their mothers did not have. Noticing how their lives already differed from their mothers' lives built young feminists' confidence that they could create even greater change.

This confidence made consciousness-raising discussions optimistic. In general, social movements increase participants' optimism, and none did so more than feminist movements. Contrary to the charge that feminists concentrated on complaints and self-pity, consciousness-raising on the whole seemed to make participants happier. True, down the road they would suffer losses. But the positivity in these years was by far the dominant mood—and the reason feminism spread so quickly.

Women rarely missed a meeting, and they spoke of their sense of loss if a member was absent. Some experienced relief from the discovery that problems and insecurities once considered personal were actually widespread. Some felt pain—it was no fun to notice the slights and obstacles once unnoticed. But consciousness-raising created a positive feedback loop that mitigated pain: the small-group sociability afforded a pleasure that made confronting insults bearable, which then allowed continued exploration of these insults. Participants laughed a lot, at the ridiculousness of some aspects of sexism and at their own responses to it. Discussions were intoxicating. One Bread and Roses member felt "as though whatever stood in our way would be swept away . . . with the power of our . . . unanswerable truth."[61]

Some observers charged that consciousness-raising was merely therapy or emotional support—that is, not political. Cellestine Ware, soon to become an influential Black feminist, at first thought it could become mere "indulgence."[62] Others, especially those allied with Marxist-Leninist parties, thought it a dead end, distracting women from political activism. Some of these concerns arose from a puritanical notion of politics, a secular form of Cesar Chavez's insistence on sacrifice, as if enjoyment was a barrier to serious politics. While consciousness-raising often made women feel better about themselves, it was not therapy. As the New York feminist Carol Hanisch wrote, "Group therapy implies that we are sick and messed up, but the first function of the small group is to get rid of self blame. . . . Therapy means adjusting. We desire to change the objective conditions."[63]

In fact, consciousness-raising constituted a practicum in social analysis through collective self-education. "It seems impossible that adults have ever learned so much so fast," one Bread and Roses member remarked.[64] Rejecting the practice common to many Marxist groups of studying theory and then applying it to daily life, consciousness-raising involved examining evidence first. New York's Kathie Sarachild, author of the phrase "sisterhood is powerful," wrote, "We were in effect repeating the 17th century challenge of science to scholasticism." The sociologist Ann Popkin saw consciousness-raising as creating a "phenomenology of everyday life."[65] By uncovering the power relations embedded in personal life, consciousness-raising confirmed a Foucauldian challenge to an Old Left view of power as centralized, showing how it operated in multiple locations. Consciousness-raising also challenged classical liberal ideology about individualism by demonstrating that autonomous selves were formed socially.[66]

SOON THE proliferation of consciousness-raising groups led to a decision to bring them together into an umbrella organization.* They named it Bread and Roses, after a slogan that was used in a 1912 strike of textile workers, predominantly women. The slogan had signified the strikers' demand not only for higher wages but also for shorter hours so they would have more leisure time.[67] Choosing this name also reflected the group's commitment to a labor movement, to making social class a part of its intersectional politics. Bread and Roses' intersectional politics was enshrined in its founding statement of goals: abolishing male supremacy was number three; number one was ending imperialism, and number two was abolishing racism.

The large Bread and Roses meetings, which often brought news of women's activism elsewhere, could be both frustrating and exhilarating. Women typically arrived in high spirits. The sociologist Ann Popkin, both participant and expert observer, described how one meeting began:

> *Some of the women there are laughing and joking with each other in small groups. Some are catching up with each other's lives in groups of twos. Others are hugging or holding hand affectionately. A few people are reading leaflets or notes they've written to themselves. Some are arguing over a recent article. . . . Somewhere between 8 and 8:15 several women start suggesting that the meeting begin; it takes a while for this sentiment to waft across the room. Stragglers wander in, many of them quietly, recognizing their disruption, a few others playing kazoos, openly challenging . . . the order and schedule.*[68]

Guiding a large meeting through its agenda efficiently requires skill. The commitment to participatory democracy, however, led to fetishizing an equality that did not exist, which made training in those skills

---

* Bread and Roses was primarily an organization of consciousness-raising groups, though it also had members who did not belong to one.

seem unacceptable. For SNCC, tutelage was imperative because so many southern African Americans had been deprived of decent education.[69] Even those with extensive activist experience and sophisticated understanding of how power worked could not, for example, count on passing the voter registration tests that were designed to keep Black people disenfranchised—and that were not required of whites. Septima Clark (whom we met in chapter 5) had pioneered freedom schools for adults as well as children. This coaching had transformative power: successfully registering to vote, for example, built confidence, which in turn strengthened further activism. By contrast, the largely white, largely middle-class members of SDS and Bread and Roses may not have needed formal schooling, but they did need to learn skills in organizing, running meetings, and handling the press, for example, and they did not get it.

Bread and Roses never elected officers. Chairing meetings was rotated. The chairs often failed to keep discussions organized by asking speakers to stick to the current topic. People spoke out of turn. Reluctance to limit discussion allowed very small issues to take up too much time. People repeated what others had already said, "as though repetition would lead to eventual consensus," one member observed. Someone who volunteered to carry out a task at one meeting might not attend the next, so no one knew whether it had been accomplished. Meetings did not set adjournment times, thereby undoing, ironically, the participatory democracy that everyone cherished, since women with jobs and/ or children often had to leave, while those with fewer obligations could stay late into the evening. (One scholar-participant has called this an "extrusion mechanism," pushing out individuals with other commitments.)[70] This inefficiency reflected members' relative privilege—they did not need efficiency because, unlike, say, the Depression's desperate unemployed, they did not need material help.

Some women expected the meetings to have the texture of consciousness-raising groups or conversations with friends. The ethic of equal participation meant that women who felt left out might interject personal complaints; someone might say she was feeling uncomfortable with a discussion, and the group's effort to identify and correct what made her feel this way would halt progress through the agenda.

The sociologist Francesca Polletta, author of the best book on these issues—with the apt title *Freedom Is an Endless Meeting*—identified the problems with using friendship as the model for organizational relationships.[71] Some condemned theoretical discussion as a male style, while others complained that the meetings lacked it.[72] Disagreements made some participants anxious, while others criticized the fear of disagreement.

In the absence of elected officers, those with greater experience, confidence, and/or free time often functioned as unofficial leaders. Unsurprisingly, they often relied for advice on friends or those who shared previous activist experience, which could make others feel marginalized. Fear of a dominating leadership occasionally produced resentment of more assertive women, who became known as "heavies," referring to the greater weight given to their comments. Members responded to this problem in contradictory ways. Some complained that a few dominated discussions (these complaints were called "trashing"), while others heard the complaints as criticisms of women who did not act in a conventionally feminine manner. One member perceived that there was "too much trying to eliminate the inner circle by denying it existed instead of bringing it up front as the perfectly reasonable, inevitable structure that it was."[73] These were in part problems of size: what worked in a small consciousness-raising group did not work in a meeting of several hundred, where only a few could speak. (One might well conclude that large groups may need representative democracy rather than participatory democracy.)

Trying to make everyone comfortable actually made it harder for less confident women to participate.[74] The political scientist Jo Freeman called this effect the "tyranny of structurelessness"—rejecting formal rules of order actually made it more difficult to challenge leaders.[75] At worst, structurelessness "encouraged the very kind of individualistic nonresponsibility that it most condemned."[76]

Determined not to exclude, Bread and Roses did not formalize membership. Being open to all seemed imperative. Bread and Roses' only roster of "members" was a phone chain list, and in this era before computers, making additions to it meant retyping and re-reproducing it, so it was never up to date. With no organized initiation provided, newcomers could be bewildered or reopen a discussion about something previously decided, which further derailed meetings.

NEVERTHELESS, BREAD AND ROSES meetings were packed. Seventy percent of members said that they always or usually attended, even though they were usually held on Friday nights.[77] The meetings helped newcomers "find" the women's liberation movement. News of the organization's many activities made it easy to join in, and most projects welcomed new people. However inefficient, these untidy proceedings communicated the energy behind this new women's liberation movement. And the abundance of Bread and Roses projects evoked people's pride in what they had created and made them part of a mass movement.

The inefficiency of meetings was tolerable because Bread and Roses was less an organization than a nexus, a whirling core of social-movement energy. It was in practice a federation of autonomous projects that did not require official organizational authorization. Seventy-five percent of members were engaged in one or more of its projects.[78] These were by no means focused only on sexism. Consider, for example, the announcements at one meeting:

Request for volunteers to leaflet a restaurant to support fired
    waitresses
Meeting to discuss women's demands for the Revolutionary
    People's Constitutional Convention
Cars offering rides to a Harlem meeting to discuss Panther defense
    tactics will leave from Boston Black Panther Defense office
Puerto Rican Liberation Conference scheduled for Sept 26, 1970
Teach-in on the Middle East, 8 PM at MIT
Meeting at Bread and Roses office to discuss courses to be offered
    at the women's school
Sign up at office for skills classes
Help circulate petitions for abortion law repeal
Help circulate petitions for repeal of laws "regulating sexual
    relationships"[79]

Antipathy to bureaucracy empowered Bread and Roses members. Small groups could initiate activities easily and quickly. The project Free Wheel, with its slogan "Share Your Car with Other Women," aimed to reduce the number of cars on the streets, help women without access to cars, and advance women's safety by encouraging women drivers to pick up women. A small group descended on the editorial offices of Boston's main newspaper, the *Globe*, demanding an end to sexist advertising, a weekly column for women that did not focus on cooking and homemaking, and desegregation of want ads.* Another produced stickers protesting the use of sexy women's images to sell things. The stickers, which always included Bread and Roses' phone number, featured slogans like "Women Are Not Cars," "Women Are Not Cigarettes," and "Not With My Body You Don't!" Women hitchhikers carried these stickers to use whenever a tempting target appeared, pasting obnoxious ads on subways and elsewhere. When a movie theater advertised a skin flick by calling it a women's liberation film, twenty-five women trooped into the theater, forcing a thirty-minute pause in the showing. They denounced the claim that feminists supported the film, argued that porn "degraded and exploited" women, and conducted a discussion with audience members. Some complained, but others applauded and spoke supportively. When Paul Krassner—editor of *The Realist* and a hero to the "Yippie," sexual-freedom side of the New Left—offered as proof of his support for women's liberation that he had fucked five feminists, a group denounced him in the *Old Mole*, a biweekly Boston New Left, counterculture newspaper. The criticism clearly struck a nerve, because a group of well-known local hipsters—so well known that they needed only to sign with their first names—published a defense, in the Krassner spirit, with the usual complaint: feminists have no sense of humor.[80]

Bread and Roses women often grumbled that the disk jockeys at WBCN, Boston's countercultural radio station, often called women

---

* At the time, employment ads were separated by gender, with the understanding that women would not be considered for male jobs, most of which offered higher wages and status. The group's demands were met, although not immediately—the *Globe* did not want to admit being swayed by a group of angry women.

"chicks." Once when it made an appeal for volunteers for a local drug program, it ended with "And if you're a chick, they need typists," and that was the last straw. Comparing this sexism to racism, a common analogy at the time, the women produced a leaflet that asked, "Could a radio station get away with an ad that ran, 'And if you're black, we need janitors.'" Women were all the more determined to protest because they *needed* WBCN—it was a community resource, playing the rock music they loved, broadcasting news with a progressive slant, announcing concerts and other events. So a group walked into the station, presented the manager with eight baby chicks, and suggested that he learn to tell the difference between chickens and women. (Today this might be considered animal abuse.) The action was catchy enough that the *Boston Globe* covered it, bringing the action—and their new radio program—to a city-wide audience. Not just a stunt, it produced results: a weekly prime-time hour to broadcast a women's liberation program, which a Bread and Roses group produced.[81]

Two Bread and Roses projects yielded renowned permanent organizations. One was 9 to 5, which today is Local 925 of the Service Employees International Union (SEIU), with 1.9 million members.[82] Its irreverent spirit appeared in the 1980 Hollywood comedy *9 to 5*, in which three clericals carry out revenge against an egotistical, lying, harassing sexist boss. Starring Jane Fonda, comedian Lily Tomlin, and country-western star Dolly Parton, it became the twentieth highest-grossing comedy of the early 1980s.[83]

The organization's initiator Karen Nussbaum, would go on to a distinguished career: she would serve as president of the 925 union until 1993, then President Clinton appointed her to head the Women's Bureau of the U.S. Department of Labor. She would then head the Women's Department of the AFL-CIO and soon thereafter would found Working America, the community affiliate of the AFL-CIO, representing workers who do not have the option of union membership.* Nussbaum's background was fairly typical in Bread and Roses: the daughter of middle-class Jews with progressive politics, she first

---

* The unemployed movement of the 1930s (the subject of chapter 4) tried to get the AFL to let the unemployed join but was turned down.

became active in antiwar protests as a student at the University of Chicago. When college paled compared to the urgency of the anti–Vietnam War movement, she dropped out. In 1970 she went as a volunteer to Cuba with the Venceremos Brigade, a project of young New Leftists who tried to help the Cuban economy by harvesting sugarcane. Moving afterward to Boston, where the women's liberation movement was in full gallop, she was soon silk-screening posters, studying karate, setting up free classes for women in everything from auto mechanics to political theory, and picketing in support of striking waitresses at the popular Cronin's restaurant in Harvard Square.[84]

Nussbaum supported herself as a Harvard University clerical worker, which led to her life's work as a union organizer. 9 to 5 began with personal discussions with other clerical workers, often over lunch, listening to their grievances and sharing stories. This method is sometimes marked as female, but it is an approach often used by social movement organizers such as settlement founder Jane Edna Hunter (profiled in chapter 1) and Cesar Chavez (discussed in chapter 6). Just as Chavez was a farmworker reaching out to farmworkers, 9 to 5 organizers were clerical workers reaching out to clerical workers—a social movement approach that differed from conventional union organizing. What they learned from these lunches led to a program specific to clerical workers' experiences. They produced an "Office Workers Bill of Rights." It began with a call for respect, echoing the Black Montgomerians and California farmworkers who found disrespect and insults as infuriating as segregation and low wages. They also demanded a written job description—these were the days when women workers were routinely expected to run personal errands for bosses.[85]

The best known Bread and Roses spin-off was the Boston Women's Health Book Collective, publisher of dozens of women's health manuals, often known by the name of the first, *Our Bodies, Ourselves*. Like 9 to 5, it arose from listening to women.[86] At a 1969 workshop, women vented their frustrations with physicians, particularly ob/gyns, who disrespected, even infantilized female patients.[87] (Consider a standard medical practice of this time: when a physician diagnosed a woman's serious illness, he would first communicate it not to her but to her husband or other male relative, on the grounds that women were hysterical and would not respond 'constructively.) The collective assembled a list of woman-respecting doctors in the Boston area and found it very short. So they began doing research and making presentations on women's health issues. The eager response led them to write their first manual—a 194-page seventy-five-cent newsprint pamphlet published in 1970 by the New England Free Press, which regularly published Bread and Roses writings. A runaway best seller, it sold 250,000 copies in seventeen months.*

Today manuals that discuss sex are common, but in the 1970s they were scandalous. *Our Bodies, Ourselves* explained that the clitoris rather than the vagina is the source of women's sexual pleasure, and it published drawings and photographs of women's and men's sexual and reproductive organs, leading several libraries to ban the book.† Since then the collective has produced more than fourteen additional manuals on topics including body image, physical fitness, menopause, lesbianism, aging, AIDS, new reproductive technologies, and violence against women. Bread and Roses' socialist-feminist politics show particularly in critiques of the for-profit healthcare economy, pharmaceutical corporations' practice of bribing doctors to prescribe their drugs, and the economics of food production and sale that make healthy diet a class and race privilege. Now translated into some thirty-three languages, the books are prepared by women's groups in the various locales with technical and financial support from the collective. The translations are never word-for-word but are revised to meet the needs of women in particular cultures.[88] The books have not only helped fund women's

---

* Over the years the collective has produced multiple editions, including books on particular topics such as pregnancy and childbirth, menopause, and the health needs of teenagers and the elderly. Its blog features entries about HIV-AIDS, Native Americans and the Keystone Pipeline, gay pride and antidepressants and many more topics. Today the various manuals have sold approximately 4.5 million copies.

† Rochelle Ruthchild and Marla Erlien remember that Simon & Schuster wanted to put the book's discussion of lesbianism in a section on psychiatry, implying, however unconsciously, that homosexuality was a mental health problem. This was obviously a nonstarter. The collective responded by suggesting it go in a chapter on sexuality, but the writers vetoed that too, because they were discussing not only sexuality but lesbian communities, politics, harassment, and legal status. They insisted on a separate chapter on lesbianism and ultimately prevailed.

health activism internationally but have contributed to revolutionizing medical assumptions and practices.

SOCIAL MOVEMENTS tend to release erotic energy, and in women's movements that energy is often directed toward other women. A survey found that 5.6 percent of Bread and Roses members and former members came out as lesbians, and as many as 20 percent had romantic relations with other women without defining themselves as lesbians.[89] At the time, some liberal feminists preferred that lesbians keep quiet, fearing that openly gay women would stigmatize the whole women's movement.[90] A Bread and Roses group addressed these anxieties directly, presenting lectures and conducting workshops on homophobia. Incorporating lessons from antiracism organizers, workshop leaders assured straight women that no one would condemn their fears or naïve questions. This allowed participants to respond honestly to questions such as "What are your fantasies about lesbians?" "What are your fears of them?" "How would you feel about a lesbian doctor, nurse . . . college professor?"[91] One group visited psychiatrists at Cambridge City Hospital demanding that they stop trying to "convert" gays to heterosexuality, a common "therapeutic" technique at the time.[92]

Some feminist organizations experienced internal conflict on this issue, but this did not happen in Bread and Roses. A few lesbian members felt that their presence made straight women nervous. One member described a complex experience: "I probably never would have discovered my homosexuality without women's liberation. You have helped to create what you now despise or fear."[93] Another thought that many heterosexual members considered lesbians "super cool" and lesbian relationships prestigious.[94] When Sue Katz, now a noted lesbian feminist writer, helped organize a women's liberation group at Boston University, straight members felt excluded when lesbians in the groups began meeting separately.[95] But Bread and Roses lesbians denounced the radical feminist charge that women who partnered with men were traitors to the cause of feminism, and one Bread and Roses member pointed out that the charge had the perverse effect of making it difficult to hold discussions of heterosexual sexuality.[96]

Lesbians in the Bread and Roses network brought feminism into Boston's gay bars. At Jacques, a predominantly male bar—and a rumored mafia hangout—they managed to get a few nights a week informally designated as lesbian.* It wasn't easy: they had to struggle to get cleaner bathrooms, a woman bartender, and the right to choose what played on the jukebox. Lesbian regulars at the bar were at first uncomfortable with the feminist lesbians and their leaflets.[97] As one Bread and Roses member described it, the older crowd were "old-world dykes—hard-drinking, hard people . . . didn't give a hoot for feminism."[98] (*Dykes* had been a pejorative term until younger lesbians claimed it assertively and proudly.) Having faced considerable abuse because of their sexuality, they were tough and brave but also protective of their space, fearful of the backlash that feminists might bring. It didn't help that the newcomers were overwhelmingly white and middle class, while the bar's habitués included many working-class white and Black women.[99] They felt constrained when the feminists brought nonlesbian friends, who often danced in circles or alone, drank nonalcoholic beverages, and blurred the distinction between butches and "fems." But soon Jacques's regulars began to enjoy aspects of the feminist culture. When a Boston group ventured into the Aquarius, a gay bar in Lynn, Massachusetts, a working-class factory town, it wasn't long before nearly everyone was dancing together.[100]

Lesbians have been presented in feminist discourse mainly as objects of oppression, without recognizing their leadership in many social justice campaigns, not only those about sexuality.[101] Having had to face down these homophobic attacks made lesbians more comfortable than many heterosexuals with challenges to dominant political and cultural standards. Their leadership appeared vividly in Bread and Roses and continued for years after it folded as an organization.[102]

WHILE LESBIANISM created minor tensions, issues of race created unresolved guilt feelings. Throughout its existence, Bread and Roses worried about its whiteness. Like most women's liberation groups, it wanted to be multiracial, while most Black feminists wanted their own

---

* It would have been most unusual that a bar's customers were both gay and mafia.

spaces.[103] Though everyone was anti-racist, they often failed to see their racial obliviousness—someone called it "thinking as whites without thinking that you are thinking as whites."[104] I have to out myself as an example of this white thinking, expressed in a Bread and Roses pamphlet I wrote, pointing to the limitations of conventional nuclear families. The pamphlet suggested that nuclear families could remove people from ties and responsibilities to larger communities, narrow the social world of children, and encourage viewing problems as individual or familial rather than societal. The sociologist Wini Breines's critique of the pamphlet noted that my language represented family negatively: "harnessing women"; "chained women"—in other words, describing nuclear families as imprisoning.[105] (These criticisms contrasted with antifeminist charges that feminism was antifamily altogether.)

In retrospect, I am surprised that I so uncritically accepted this critique because my own family—like the majority of American families— was nothing like the hegemonic ideal. For most of American history, families supported by a male breadwinner alone were possible only for relatively privileged people; for most families, like the one I grew up in, a man's wage was not enough to pay the bills. Moreover, millions of nuclear family members, far from being disconnected to larger communities, were active in churches, schools, and community groups; in fact most were not really "nuclear" but included siblings, parents, grandparents, aunts, uncles, and other relatives who provided crucial support. The sociologist Benita Roth has pointed out that "the family" was the least oppressive institution African Americans faced and a source of strength in a racist society.[106] Maria Varela, a Chicana from SNCC, thought likewise: "For the Chicano woman battling for her people, the family . . . is a fortress against the genocidal forces in the outside world."[107]

Although Bread and Roses never became multiracial, it supported and worked on a variety of African American causes. It celebrated the Black Panthers' social service projects that were run, unsurprisingly, mainly by women.* It protested government persecution of the Black

---

* These included thirteen free medical clinics, including an important one in Boston, and the Free Breakfast for Children program that ultimately fed breakfast to ten thousand schoolchildren every morning.

Panther Party (BPP) and co-organized a large East Coast demonstration to support Panther Ericka Huggins, who was imprisoned in New Haven.[108] Inversely, at first Bread and Roses shared with the whole New Left an unwillingness to criticize the Panthers because of the repression and violence they suffered. That soon changed, and Bread and Roses women condemned the Panthers' militaristic strutting and violence. (Later evidence showed that much of the violence was carried out by FBI provocateurs.) A Bread and Roses statement pointed out that blanket support for the Panthers was a condescending product of whiteness: "We are just beginning to see that it is largely our own racism" that made them reluctant to criticize the BPP. "We cannot let the chauvinism and egotism of Panther chieftains stand for the Black people of America."[109] Still, the statement's authors did not sign it—an indication of the pressure not to criticize the BPP.

BREAD AND ROSES frequently joined the male-dominated New Left in protesting the Vietnam War, condemning U.S. foreign policy, and

Feminists demonstrating against U.S. intervention in Vietnam.

highlighting anticolonial movements. Whenever possible, it provided speakers at antiwar protests. Its newsletters included announcements like these: "Work group on women in the 3rd world is presenting a series of informal forums with guest speakers." "Celebrate Women in the African Liberation Struggle on International Women's Day . . . at the Cambridge YWCA." It organized a Mothers' Day Speak-out for Peace on the Boston Common featuring Reverend William Sloan Coffin, Bread and Roses' Marya Levenson, and the mother of a draft resister. Putting intersectionality into practice, it gathered a variety of organizations to co-sponsor International Women's Day demonstrations, including New England War Tax Resisters, Grass Roots International, the Disabled People's Liberation Front, Massachusetts Friends of Midwives, and many more.[110]

At the same time, it criticized some parts of the antiwar movement's obliviousness to class and race inequality. Its attempts to convince other antiwar groups to make connections between imperialism and patriarchy in their materials and speeches were unsuccessful. One experience illustrates: When a coalition of antiwar groups asked Bread and Roses "to bring 'our people'" to protests against MIT's military contracts, the organizers stipulated that no "extraneous" issues such as male dominance should be mentioned at the rallies. Bread and Roses refused to join.[111] It refused to support an October 1969 Days of Rage action organized by the macho, ultrarevolutionary Weathermen, because the Weathermen would not commit to nonviolence.[112] When the organizers of a 1969 national anti–Vietnam War moratorium called on university students and faculty to boycott classes, they did not think to reach out to other university workers. So Bread and Roses leafleted university clerical and maintenance workers, suggesting that they too should be entitled to stop work for a day, without losing wages, and some did.[113]

In the summer of 1969, a few Bread and Roses members participated in a particularly dramatic antiwar event: a meeting with women from the Vietnamese National Liberation Front on a Canadian farm (the Vietnamese women were not permitted to enter the United States).[114] The intense emotion in this encounter may be unfamiliar to readers who have never *seen* the television coverage—showing children burned with napalm, tanks literally rolling over small thatched houses, pes-

ticides sprayed on rice paddies—that incited the antiwar movement.*
Wracked with guilt, the women at the meeting no doubt expected to
meet victims who sought apologies. This was not the case.

Expert at presenting their cause, the Vietnamese women were patient
with ignorant and insensitive questions such as, "Can some of us adopt
Vietnamese children who have been orphaned?" One replied politely
that Vietnamese children who lost parents went to extended families
or homes provided by the Mother-Child Protection Society. Someone
asked, when women joined the fight (thousands of armed Vietnamese
women fought in both guerrilla and regular armies), "Did you have any
trouble with the men?" Trying to smother their amusement, the Vietnamese women exchanged looks, then said they would prefer to discuss
this at a later time. When they did, they were open about Vietnamese
men's sexism. One woman said she "had a lot of the same thoughts we
did . . . such as having to wash socks for the men . . . or how when there
was a political meeting the men would sit and discuss the issues and she
served tea." When they complained, she said, "the next time . . . a man
served tea." This response, suggesting a suspiciously easy overcoming
of men's privilege, may have been calculated to connect with American
feminists, whose concerns about sexism may well have seemed marginal to her group. But she then provided an example of Vietnamese
women's existential need to challenge male dominance:

> They formed a women's militia unit . . . to fight in units with men.
> When weapons were handed out the men were heard to say, "Oh no, now
> I will have to carry the woman and the gun." . . . The women [were]
> angry and they decided to form their own units. . . . They turned out to
> be crack shots, much better than the men . . . [and] far superior in recon-
> naissance and spying. . . . After about six months, she said, a represen-
> tative came from the men's unit to ask if they couldn't join the women.

Bread and Roses initiated one entirely illegal project, which required
something unusual in social movements: secrecy. The group had long

---

* As a result, the U.S. government banned any further TV coverage of military
engagements.

wanted to establish a women's center that could host meetings, a women's school, a library, and a place for women to drop in and connect with feminists. Scouting for a site, a member found a near-empty building at 888 Memorial Drive, Cambridge, a former knitting factory then owned by Harvard. The group developed a plan to occupy it. Organizers arranged for food, cleaning equipment, childcare, legal services, self-defense training, medical services, and large banners to explain what they were doing and why. Harvard's ownership was an advantage: Cambridge residents, especially in working-class neighborhoods like this one, resented the fact that Harvard refused to contribute to its surrounding communities, despite its huge endowment, elite student body, and tax-exempt status.

On March 6, 1971, several hundred women and some men joined what they thought was simply a march celebrating International Women's Day. Starting from the Boston Common, the group jeered as they walked past the Playboy Club, shouted greetings to women watching from windows in the Charles Street jail, crossed into Cambridge, and then, to the surprise of most participants, turned left onto Pearl Street and proceeded to the 888 building. (A documentary film about this event is entitled *Left on Pearl*.)[115] Before entering the building, everyone received a leaflet emphasizing that they should know the risks— "liberating a building is a groove BUT IT'S ALSO ILLEGAL"—and listing the possible criminal charges.[116] Scores of women occupied the building for ten days, calling on Harvard to donate it for a women's center and to contribute to building low-income housing in collaboration with residents from the largely Black neighborhood, known as Riverside. The organizers distributed a leaflet throughout the neighborhood explaining these goals.[117]

Most of the marchers could not stay in the building—they had jobs, kids, and other responsibilities—but they contributed in other ways. Radcliffe and Harvard students presented petitions in support of the occupation to Dean John Dunlop.[118] Donations of food, coats, and blankets poured in. Harvard tried to dislodge them by turning off the heat and electricity; the women were able to reconnect the electricity, though not the heat. The occupation generated extensive publicity, and more women arrived, even from other cities and states. The charismatic, entertainingly provocative lawyer Flo Kennedy came from New York City to show support. An information table by the front door explained the purpose of the occupation. The occupiers distributed invitations to neighborhood women and children, offering free classes in karate, auto mechanics, silk-screening, and games and crafts for children. The occupation took on a festival-like ambiance with music and dancing. The women inside savored being in a fastidiously well-organized women's household. Being women, they left the building cleaner than ever.

Leaders of the neighborhood campaign for affordable housing were suspicious at first, distrusting the motives of these white middle-class outsiders. Tensions relaxed when neighbors learned that the occupiers had pledged their support for the affordable housing demand. Cambridge city councilor Saundra Graham, an African American and president of the Riverside community's planning team, defended the occupation and its demands.[119]

After Harvard drove the occupiers out, police gave university attorneys their photographs, urging them to take legal action, but Harvard declined to press charges. The organizers found a house for a women's center, and Susan Storey Lyman, chair of Radcliffe College's board of trustees, donated $5,000 for a down payment. The Bread and Roses group raised the rest of the purchase price.[*]

Despite this win, in the long run the occupation reinforced the city's inequality. Harvard did not contribute to building affordable housing. An urban renewal project evacuated some of the neighborhood to make way for an apartment building, but it housed fewer people than those who had been driven out. In other words, middle-class, largely white women secured a victory, while working-class, largely African American residents did not. And when Black students took over a Harvard building a few months later, the university obtained an injunction the same day, while it had waited ten days before evicting these predominantly white women.

Still, over time women made the women's center a valuable resource for their neighbors, and today a majority of its users are low-income

---

[*] The fact that the gift came from an individual, while Radcliffe and Harvard did not contribute, may have resulted from their wish for deniability.

women of color. In its range, it resembles a settlement house. Providing common spaces for relaxation, conversation, and meetings, it has been a launching site for new projects, including a rape crisis center, a domestic violence shelter, and the Boston Community Cancer Project. It offers a variety of classes, such as ESL for Spanish speakers, a "Spanish-English Conversation Exchange," discussion groups for women over sixty-five and for sex workers, and a "fat liberation" group—and it can provide childcare for participants in these groups. Staffers provide help in finding homeless shelters, legal advice regarding abuse and assault, affordable medical care, LGBTQ resources, and more.[120]

Bread and Roses ended in 1971.* Its consciousness-raising groups and projects continued, and many former members—I have called them veterans, for want of a better word—remained politically active.

SOON A group of African American socialist feminists in Boston created a small collective, the Combahee River Collective, whose influence—not only national but global—would be vastly dispropor-tionate to its size. Its ancestors included Fran Beal, SNCC women, and the Third World Women's Alliance, but its mother was the National Black Feminist Organization (NBFO), founded by several Black editors at *Ms.* magazine. Among them, Margaret Sloan was key: a precocious activist from Chicago, she had joined CORE when she was fourteen, founded the Junior Catholic Inter-Racial Council at seventeen, became an award-winning public speaker while still in high school, and worked with the Southern Christian Leadership Conference under Martin Luther King, Jr.[121] Taking a job at *Ms.*, she joined with two others from *Ms.* staff to create the NBFO. Her partners were Jane Galvin-Lewis, who came from Dorothy Height's National Council of Negro Women (Fran Beal's former employer) and the inimitable, intrepid Flo Kennedy.

---

* In the next few years former Bread and Roses members tried twice to create another citywide group—first, the Boston Area Socialist Feminist Organization (BASFO), then the Boston Women's Union. Neither took off, largely because of changes in the New Left landscape: sectarian Marxist-Leninist parties tried to impose their ideol-ogy so as to create "vanguard" organizations. Their divisive influence exhausted and demoralized socialist-feminist organization-building impulses.

(An example of Kennedy's audacity: having been rejected by Columbia University Law School, she threatened to sue and got admitted.)

Sloan and Kennedy teamed up to speak on campuses about the need to challenge racism and sexism simultaneously. The positive response led Sloan to initiate meetings in New York City, intent on making Black women's experience central to a feminist agenda. Inaugurated in 1973, the NBFO went public with a press conference featuring prominent women including Congresswoman Shirley Chisholm, artist Faith Ringgold, writer Alice Walker, and Eleanor Holmes Norton, New York City's human rights commissioner (now congresswoman from the District of Columbia). When its first conference was announced for November 30 to December 2, 1973, *Ms.*'s telephones didn't stop ringing, with women asking, how can we join? Four hundred women came.[122] Clearly, many Black women did not see feminism as a white-only politics. Within a year, the NBFO had two thousand members and ten chapters across the country.[123]

Beverly Smith, who would become a core member of the Combahee River Collective, was then working at *Ms.* She had "stumbled," she said, on Cellestine Ware's book *Woman Power*—initially skeptical, by this time Ware had become an ardent feminist—"started leafing through it . . . immediately knew I was a feminist. I was like, 'Oh, that's what I am!'"[124] She soon recruited her twin sister Barbara. Born in Georgia in 1946, they were nine when their mother died, and they went to live with their grandmother and aunt in Cleveland. Both women were active "in every kind of club you can imagine," in their church and at the polls during elections.[125] Educating the girls was their top priority. As Barbara Smith recalled, "It was like, We go to work every day. You go to school. School is your job."[126] The girls went to separate colleges, Beverly to the University of Chicago and Barbara to Mount Holyoke, spending junior year at the New School for Social Research in New York.[127]

At the 1973 NBFO conference, Barbara Smith connected with women from Boston, and they decided to form an NBFO chapter there. The city had numerous Black women's organizations, but none were feminist; their members tended to see feminism as a white thing and feared it would reinforce racism's damage to Black masculine pride. At a 1967 Black Women's Convention in Boston, for example, most of the participants probably agreed with civil rights leader Ellen Jackson that women should "become second-class citizens to our men but first-class women to others."[128] Recalling how frightening it was then for a Black woman to declare herself a feminist, Barbara Smith spoke of the fear of being "kicked out of the race."[129]

Still, Smith found some Black feminists, many of them young lesbians like herself and her sister.[130] One was Demita Frazier, who became a major intellectual influence. She grew up in Chicago, where, like Margaret Sloan and Karen Nussbaum, she was a precocious radical. An anti–Vietnam War activist at fourteen, she quickly recognized the war's disproportionate cost to people of color and the connection between racism and imperialism. Feminism soon followed. In 1973 she and four other women pooled their money to buy a car and drove to Boston, with a plan to organize Black women around feminist issues.[131]

More inspiration came from Sharon Bourke, a founding member of the Institute of the Black World, a think-tank founded by stellar African diaspora intellectuals.[132] She brought Marxism and African-influenced anticolonialism to the group. Because she was forty, Barbara Smith remembered thinking, "Whoa, she's so old and she talks to me like . . . we're equals. I learned a huge amount from her."[133]

From its outset, Boston's NBFO practiced what is today known as intersectionality. Rejecting an exclusive focus on sexism, racism, or homophobia, they stepped onto a path of coalition with white feminist and anti-racist progressives. What might have been a leisurely pace of consciousness-raising and theorizing was soon disrupted by injustices that pushed them into action.

They first responded to an attack by anti-abortion campaigners on African American physician Kenneth Edelin, chief resident in obstetrics and gynecology at Boston City Hospital—which primarily served people without medical insurance, that is, poor people. In early 1973, before *Roe*, he had performed a legal abortion for a seventeen-year-old. The abortion necessitated a hysterotomy (a procedure that involves detaching a fetus from the placental wall, required when saline injections did not remove the fetus). Anti-abortion activists claimed that he had killed a baby—they typically call a fetus, even an embryo, a baby—

and got him charged with manslaughter. Unanimously supported by his hospital, he was nevertheless convicted in 1974 by an all-white jury of nine men and three women.[134] The case connected the NBFO women to Bread and Roses veterans. Immediately after the verdict, the two groups staged a demonstration defending Edelin that brought out fifteen hundred women.[135] In an early signal of her leadership skills, Barbara Smith spoke fluently at press conferences and rallies. They won the Edelin case: in December 1976 the Massachusetts Supreme Judicial Court overturned the verdict.

Meanwhile conflict about school desegregation exploded. Boston was an extremely segregated city, so when a federal judge ordered the schools to integrate, the only way to do that was to move children from one school district to another—via school buses. Claiming that "busing" was deleterious to children, anti-integrationists turned violent: mobs threw rocks and bricks into the buses, injuring eight children and a bus monitor, even shooting into the buses. One anti-busing man attacked and badly injured Black lawyer Ted Landsmark with, in bitter irony, a metal pole flying an American flag.[136]

The anti-abortion and anti-busing campaigns then merged into what we might call a conservative intersectionality. Dr. Edelin was perfect as a target because he joined the two issues.[137] Boston city councilor Louise Day Hicks, leader of the anti-busing crusade, sponsored a resolution calling on the state supreme court to declare abortion unconstitutional. Opportunistically, she charged that busing violated women's rights—that is, rights to "protect" their children. In beating back this initiative, Bread and Roses and NBFO women were developing their Left intersectionality, which soon extended beyond abortion rights and school integration into other social justice campaigns.

Several involved defending three women of color convicted of murder. Boston's Ella Ellison, a mother of four, was convicted of killing a policeman, without any evidence other than the word of two men who struck plea bargains in return for naming her. (Charges against her were dropped, but only after she spent four years in prison.) Joan Little,* an inmate in the Beaufort County, South Caro-

---

* Because she pronounced her name "Jo-an," it is often spelled Joann or Joanne.

lina, jail, killed a guard who raped her—using an ice pick that he had brought into her cell to terrify her into submitting. Because he was found naked below the waist, with semen on his legs, and with his shoes and pants outside the cell—he obviously had no fear that other guards might object—the prosecution had to claim that she had enticed him into sex in the hope of gaining favors. She was charged with first-degree murder. A national protest campaign made her the first woman to be acquitted of murder committed in defense against sexual assault. Inez García, a Caribbean American farmworker in Soledad, California, was raped in 1974 by two men in an alley. Devout and ashamed, she did not at first tell police she had been raped and was never tested for rape; instead she got her son's .22 rifle and shot and killed one of her attackers. Convicted of second-degree murder, her case sparked a furious feminist campaign, and in 1977 she was retried and acquitted, setting a precedent for what became known as the battered women defense.[138]

Taken together, these campaigns—Edelin, busing, Ella Ellison, Joan Little, and Inez García—solidified the Boston NBFO chapter but simultaneously intensified its discontent with what its members saw as the "bourgeois" politics of the national organization. It would do little for the poor, they felt.[139] They condemned its reliance on white foundation funding, its undemocratic structure, and its leadership by elite women. They also believed that the NBFO hid the lesbians among its members and declined to speak out on controversial matters.[140] Besides, the national NBFO brought no resources to the Boston chapter. It seemed "bent on parodying the hierarchy and power-mongering of mainstream organizations," Barbara Smith remarked angrily. She soon realized "how hungry we were for something that reflected our concerns." Demita Frazier said, bluntly, "We wanted to talk about radical economics."[141]

So the Boston group left the NBFO. It wasn't just a leap into the unknown; it felt like leaving a family. Among the thousands of Black women's organizations, they were abandoning the only feminist one. Nevertheless they went ahead, formalizing their group identity in 1977, naming themselves the Combahee River Collective. In the Combahee River raid of 1863, the heroic Harriet Tubman had led 150 Black soldiers and some 750 enslaved people from South Carolina's low country into freedom. They could of course have named themselves "Tubman," but I am inclined to agree with Duchess Harris that they wanted to identify with the courage of a group rather than an individual.[142] That they felt no obligation to choose a female name embodied their intersectional politics.

As IN Bread and Roses, Combahee's membership was fluid. Its core remained about a dozen, but many African American women who attended some meetings and participated in some of its activism often called themselves members, and the core group seems to have had no problem with this.[143] All the core members had activist experience. As Demita Frazier put it, they were refugees—from the white-male-dominated New Left, from Black nationalists,[144] and from white feminists, especially "man-hating white feminists" who did not appreciate their intersectional analysis. They were also mainly lesbians, an identity that was unacceptable not only to Black nationalists but to feminist groups who feared stigmatizing the whole women's movement. They felt "stranded," as writer Michele Wallace puts it,[145] which strengthened their bonds. They needed each other.

Almost all of the Combahee's members went on to distinguished careers promoting social justice, a pattern that reflects both the influence of Combahee and the ability and ambition of those attracted to it. Combahee was both beneficiary and nurturer of their ambition and intelligence. In every case, their future careers involved working for social justice.[146]

Gloria Hull, now Akasha Hull, grew up in a three-room shotgun house in Shreveport, Louisiana. Her parents had not finished elementary school, while she was the valedictorian of her (segregated) high school, graduated summa cum laude from Southern University in Baton Rouge, and earned a PhD in English literature at Purdue. She also played piano and sang in her church choir. Before long it was clear that she wanted to write literature more than literary criticism. She became a prominent poet, novelist, short story writer, and journalist with a strong interest in global cultures. In 1992 she added a first name, Akasha, a Sanskrit word for "light" or "illumination."

Sharon Page Ritchie grew up in Chicago and earned a degree in sociology at the University of Chicago. She arrived having already experienced homophobia—she was refused membership in her mother's Black sorority, Delta, for example. She soon deserted sociology and found her calling in the arts and worked in a wide range of media: film, photography, textile art, dance, and music. Today she works for the San Francisco Arts Commission.

Cecilia "Cessie" Alfonso, an Afro-Caribbean, also studied sociology at the University of Chicago. She became a nationally recognized expert in forensic social work and domestic violence, providing social work and psychosocial assessments to the clients of civil and criminal attorneys. Today Alfonso is repeatedly called on to serve as expert witness in trials concerning domestic violence, capital punishment, substance abuse, and the psychosexual analysis of serial rapists and killers.

Margo Okazawa-Rey, another Chicagoan, daughter of a Japanese mother and a Black GI, arrived in Boston having already been a member the Daughters of Bilitis, an early lesbian rights organization (founded in 1955, when identifying as homosexual carried major risks). A social work scholar, she became a distinguished academic and through her studies of the impact of war and militarization on women, she has connected with feminist scholars and activists throughout Africa and Asia.[147]

Mercedes Tompkins, who shared a house with Okazawa-Rey, hailed from Brooklyn and attended Hunter College. She became a national leader in the struggle against domestic violence. She served as executive director of Boston's Casa Myrna, a pioneering shelter begun in 1977; later she helped establish an innovative program for homeless women, Brookview House. She is featured in the film *A Moment in Her Story: Stories from the Boston Women's Movement* (2013).

Chirlane McCray, the wife of New York's former mayor Bill de Blasio, became a writer, she recalled, because it provided an escape from the harassment she experienced as the only Black student in her high school in Springfield, Massachusetts. Equally brave in combating homophobia, she explained that she came out as a lesbian in order "to dispel the myth that there are no gay Black people . . . my way of telling Black women across the country, 'You are not alone.'" She served as speechwriter for several New York City politicians, including former mayor David Dinkins and her husband.[148]

The collective comprised an extraordinary group of women, highly educated, prodigies who had engaged in protest activities from a young age. The coincidences that brought them together in Boston had long-term, influential consequences.

FORMING AN independent group was risky. Being a Black feminist was hard enough, and being a lesbian multiplied the difficulty. Although "the most serious deterrent to Black lesbian activity is the closet itself," Barbara Smith thought, the closet also offered protection. At the time most Black leaders labeled homosexuality inimical to African American culture, and even the more open-minded complained that activists should focus on "more important" issues.[149] Black women's antagonism to homosexuality was particularly painful. In 1978, after Smith spoke at a National Black Writers Conference, Afrocentric psychiatrist Frances Cress Welsing denounced her from the audience, saying that she pitied this woman who obviously had a "psychological problem." Not one Black women in the audience defended Smith, not even Audre Lorde or Sonia Sanchez, a sign of how embedded homophobia was at this time. Smith remembered it as a "literary lynching." As late as 2003, she felt that she was "still dealing with coming out in the Black community. . . . You never finish coming out."[150] "We were traitors to the race," Smith recalled.[151]

Though Combahee regularly worked in coalition with men, it was nevertheless subjected to accusations of man-hating. So were many women's liberation groups, but Combahee women understood that what they were doing required more courage than what was asked of white feminists. Nor was Combahee accepted by the "white lesbian/gay power establishment," as they described it. Barbara Smith thought it was presenting "our community as an affluent consumer group to win favor from the corporate mainstream."[152] They criticized its refusal to recognize and campaign against race and class inequality. They were appalled by separatist white radical feminist lesbian groups; one such group took their withdrawal from men so far that they did not allow women to bring sons over the age of five to their events.[153] Combahee provided a space of safety and comfort, in which being lesbian was a strength, empowering them to explore how sexuality intersected with other issues of social justice. The "collective was a lifeline," letting them ask "cheeky, unsettling questions."[154]

These questions generated a program of self-education. Intellectual and political descendants of the Third World Women's Alliance, influenced by anticolonialist intellectuals, Combahee members saw themselves as Third World women and their campaigns in the United States as comparable to those against U.S. imperialism abroad.[155] (In fact, by this time it was common for Black activists to call themselves Third World people.) They supplemented their reading through an organic process of investigation, "getting all sorts of data from Black women in the diaspora." As Combahee became known, Black women sought them out, and their experiences added to the "data."[156] Their research method—listening and then using what they learned to form their strategies—resembled Jane Edna Hunter's (chapter 1) in her campaign to build a settlement and Cesar Chavez's (chapter 6) in building a farmworker movement.

Combahee was developing an intersectional analysis. Like Fran Beal before them, they added social class to race, sex, and sexuality.[157] Several of them were "third-generation union babies," said Frazier; her "mother didn't even believe in voting, but she believed in the union." Moving toward a socialist politics seemed imperative, because, she concluded, they "had to have an economic analysis. . . . Whenever we would talk about . . . Black women's condition, it was always looking at the economics. . . . The fact that we were socialists was just because we wanted to have an inclusive notion about [the] array of factors that impact Black women's lives." As Barbara Smith put it, "One would expect Black feminism to be antiracist and opposed to sexism. Anticapitalism is what gives it the sharpness, the edge, the thoroughness, the revolutionary potential."[158]

Aiming to remedy the isolation they often felt by connecting to a larger community of Black feminists, Combahee organized a series of weekend retreats.[159] The more activist they were, the more they longed for space and time to study and talk. Seven retreats took place between 1977 and 1980. Some of them were organized by women in other locations, but all required considerable advance planning—finding a location and convenient weekend, assembling publications that would be of interest, creating an agenda. As news of Combahee and the retreats spread, attendance grew. Many participants were writers: Cheryl Clarke, Lorraine Bethel, Audre Lorde, and Linda Powell were asked to bring their writings for discussion. For one retreat, the organizers asked participants to bring an object that told something about themselves— signifying Combahee's conviction that theory can emerge in many forms. The network created by the retreats continued long after the end of Combahee.

Retreat discussions typically united experience, politics, and theory. One focused on "What events in black women's lives make lesbianism 'circumstantially impossible' for many of us?"—such as "poverty, self-hatred, community hostility."[160] These places of safety, Combahee member Linda Powell noted, allowed room for disagreement among Black feminists, which they deemed essential.[161] Over time the agendas moved toward culture, from scholarship to music groups to poetry. One retreat focused on novels, including Toni Cade Bambara's *Gorilla, My Love*, and Toni Morrison's first two novels, *The Bluest Eye* and *Sula*.[162] Serious discussion also yielded time for relaxing and enjoying being together. The retreats were "perfectly serious and perfectly frivolous" at the same time. Participants often slept on floors in sleeping bags. Some flirted. Smith recalled that "the menus really got insane. . . . Like on Sunday morning we wouldn't just have waffles, we'd have three kinds of waffles." In the evenings, writers read their work. Terri Clark was in a band called Hysteria and played for them all; Sharon Page Ritchie did belly dancing, "from another people-of-color female tradition"—she still does belly dancing today—and displayed her exquisite handmade clothing.

Romantic couplings and uncouplings within Combahee produced some jealousies. This is not unusual. Hull-House women, for example, competed for closeness to Jane Addams. The sociologist Francesca Polletta has found that hurt feelings are particularly common in friendship-based organizations. In a large organization like Bread and Roses, those involved could avoid each other, but Combahee members could not. As Barbara Smith put it, "Sometimes, the feelings and the lines between friendship and attraction and love and, you know, possession . . . just kick things . . . into a really very turmoil-filled space."[163]

Class differences also created tension. Some members resented those with elite educations and their penchant for discussing social theory. Demita Frazier acknowledged the problem, noting that discussing class differences among African Americans was "almost a taboo." But she refused to disavow Combahee's intellectual discussions. Barbara Smith, often a target of this resentment, found it painful, but she insisted that grabbing "an education out of a system that prefers you not get one" could only be a positive for African Americans. As the Combahee statement put it, "Although our economic position is still at the very bottom . . . a handful of us have been able to gain certain tools . . . in education and employment which potentially enable us to more effectively fight our oppression."[164]

Class issues overlapped with leadership issues. Disgusted with "the hierarchy and power-mongering" she had seen in NBFO, Barbara Smith determined to reject the "careerism that has undermined other movements."[165] But Combahee members knew that the group had an informal leadership—the trio of Barbara and Beverly Smith and Demita Frazier. Besides their particularly strong speaking and writing ability, they could also devote more time to the organization, while other members with demanding jobs had less disposable time. Gradually Boston's progressive activists came to recognize Barbara Smith as the leader; anyone who wanted to contact Combahee reached out to her first.* This generated criticism. Margo Okazawa-Rey pointed out that issues came to the meetings only after they had been "filtered" by Barbara Smith, and she questioned calling their organization a collective. Still, Okazawa-Rey had a discerning and judicious view of the problem (one equally applicable to the United Farm Workers): "It was hard to know to what extent we kind of acquiesced to her influence and to what extent she really was domineering."[166]

. . .

---

* Smith's leadership continued long after Combahee dissolved; she went on to an extraordinary career as a writer, editor, and publisher. Elected to the Albany, New York, City Council in 2005 and 2009, she has led several Albany city campaigns against guns, for equal educational opportunity. Today she remains a national leading voice in intersectional feminism.

ONE PROOF that those with more skills could use them democratically was a 1977 manifesto—known as the Combahee River Collective
Statement—written by the Smiths and Demita Frazier. It has become a
political classic, and its influence continues today, forty-six years later.
An early articulation of intersectionality, no other document of the
women's liberation movement has become so influential and ubiquitous.

One of its phrases—"identity politics"—has been misunderstood
and denounced by critics who call it divisive, an obstacle to building
a broad social movement. As one leftist scholar argued, "The identity
politics that fueled women's liberation counter-posed the fight against
one's own oppression [with] the oppression of others."[167] Thus "identity
politics" in this understanding is politically selfish. By that definition,
Combahee would have been a paradigm example of narrowness, as it
consisted mainly of African American feminist lesbians.[168]

In fact, Combahee's "identity politics" meant something entirely
different: that democratic movements must arise from participants'
experience and from their awareness of their social position.[169] The
statement "reflects all the ways that we were trying to understand the
world," Margo Okazawa-Rey remembered.[170] This meant rejecting
white middle-class feminists' notion of a "sisterhood" as well as Black
nationalists' claim to speak for the race. To the charge that feminism
weakens Black solidarity, Combahee argued the opposite—that fear
of feminism had been an obstacle to developing Black political power.
(In later writings, Combahee would criticize Black anti-Semitism as
well.)[171] Combahee's identity politics also rejected the Marxist-Leninist
concept of "false consciousness," which assumes that organizers,
guided by their doctrine, know better than organizees what is in their
interest. To Combahee, useful social theory arose not from doctrine but
from the evidence of people's lives.

The "identity" discussed in the Combahee statement was always
complex. A person is not a Black *and* a woman *and* a lesbian; she is a
product not of addition but of fusion.* In Barbara Smith's words, "We

---

* This understanding reminds us that "intersectionality," like all metaphors, is limited; when visualized, it suggests many separate roads intersecting, preserving each
category—like race and sex—as distinct.

have a right as people who are not just female, who are not solely Black, who are not just lesbians, who are not just working class. . . . We are people who embody all these identities, and we have a right to build and define political theory and practice based upon that reality." Demita Frazier: "We stand at the intersection"—note this foreshadowing of the term *intersectionality*—"where our identities are indivisible. . . . We are as Black women truly and completely intact in our paradox."[172] (In this sense, a person's "identity" itself could be said, metaphorically, to be a coalition.)[173] Accepting this complexity was also a matter of survival. Being asked to locate oneself or others in discrete categories led to "feelings of craziness." Frazier again: "We in ourselves, in our very bodies, represented [an] emerging understanding of the complexity of the politics."[174]

This sense of identity politics did not mean standing alone; for Combahee, identity politics was not an alternative to but an enabling condition of coalitions. The Combahee River Collective was not only a master practitioner of coalitions but *depended* on coalition.[175] As the musician-activist Bernice Johnson Reagon pointed out, "You don't go into coalition because you just *like* it." Nor do you do it out of expediency. You do it out of need, to augment your strength, of course, but also because it is crucial to a democratic movement. Coalitions involve relationships with groups with whom you don't have 100 percent agreement, so they carry risks. Reagon added, "Most of the time you feel threatened . . . and if you don't you're not really doing no coalescing."[176]

COMBAHEE WOMEN had been working with Bread and Roses people for some time.* Bread and Roses "had it out on the table," Barbara Smith recalled, "that . . . race and class were important oppressions to be integrated into an analysis. . . . [They] understood that you could

---

* In the early 1970s Bread and Roses veterans tried twice to create another organization—first, the Boston Area Socialist Feminist Organization (BASFO), then the Boston Women's Union. Neither took off, largely because of changes in the leftist landscape: sectarian Marxist-Leninist parties tried to impose their ideology and to create "vanguard" organizations.

not really deal with sexism . . . if you didn't look at capitalism and also at racism."[177] Their coalitions were mutual: Boston's white socialist feminists joined Combahee initiatives, and Combahee joined white initiatives.[178] This is not to say that the Bread and Roses women were free of racism or racial obliviousness, but they tried to do better. Luckily, Combahee was not demanding perfection. Combahee did not consider it useful to focus primarily on criticizing white feminism; doing that seemed to treat white racism as ineradicable and to ignore what coalitions could achieve.[179]

Influenced by the New York Puerto Rican activist Dr. Helen Rodríguez-Trías, a pediatrician and president of the American Public Health Association, Boston's socialist feminists created a chapter of the Committee to End Sterilization Abuse. (It was later expanded and renamed the Committee for Abortion Rights and Against Sterilization Abuse.) CESA argued that reproductive freedom must include the right to have healthy children—a right that depended on the health and welfare of pregnant women, mothers, and children. At the time, a eugenics-influenced, coercive program of sterilizing women who were labeled inferior, sometimes done during childbirth and without the woman's knowledge, was disproportionately targeting women of color, especially Native Americans. This was closely related to the coercive population control policies that were then being imposed on Third World countries, sometimes with methods that carried considerable health risks. Population control programs often bribed women to accept sterilization, with payments large enough to be significant for poor women.[180]

With support from some Bread and Roses veterans, Combahee pulled off a stunning victory at the 1977 International Women's Year conference in Houston, sponsored by the U.S. government. Louise Day Hicks—leader of anti-school-integration and anti-abortion-rights campaigns, active in getting Edelin prosecuted—led an effort to pack the Boston delegation with conservative women. Organizing to counter that threat, Boston's socialist feminists brought enough women to a meeting that would choose delegates, and they got a number of their allies elected. Naming themselves the Lucy Parsons Brigade, after the Afro-Mexican anarchist labor organizer of the late nineteenth century, they wrote and printed 25,000 copies of a pamphlet to be circulated at

Billie Jean King, Susan B. Anthony II, Bella Abzug, and Betty Friedan at the First National Women's Conference, Houston, 1977. Athletes Sylvia Ortiz, Peggy Kokernot, and Michelle Cearcy carrying a torch being relayed from Seneca Falls, New York—location of the first women's movement conference, 1848.

the conference. Once in Houston, Barbara Smith worked with other delegates to join both lesbian and Black caucuses, and in doing so she expanded Combahee's networks nationally. Campaigning not only for a strong reproductive rights resolution, the group—with some trepidation, given widespread homophobia among Blacks as well as whites—also sought support, particularly from Black women, for a lesbian rights plank in its platform. Barbara Smith recalled doing a "pretty traditional form of party politicking," lobbying almost every state delegation. To their surprise, the plank won by a landslide, producing "jubilation like you could not believe"—not only because of the success but also because so many Black delegates had supported them.[181]

A year later the rape conviction of an innocent Black man generated a similar coalition. A white woman had been raped in the basement of a commercial building. She could not describe her assailant beyond saying that he was slender and Black and had a beard. When police asked if any Blacks worked in the building, a representative of the building's tenants named Willie Sanders, reporting that he was an extremely reliable employee and had recently earned a raise. During January 1979, three more rapes of white women took place in the same neighborhood, producing loud demands for action, so the police arrested Sanders. No victim identified him until after his picture appeared in the media. Then the police managed to get him identified by creating a lineup in which Sanders was the only slender bearded Black man, even telling one victim that her rapist was either number one or number three. But while Sanders was in jail, unable to pay a $50,000 bail, two similar rapes took place.[182] Combahee led a campaign to expose the frame-up, and the large coalition they created—including the Massachusetts Legislative Black Caucus, Bread and Roses veterans, Black community organizations, six ministers, Black and white, and the predominantly white Take Back the Night organizers—signaled the increasing citywide respect for Combahee. As Mercedes Tompkins put it, "People looked to Combahee for anchoring." If Combahee supported an initiative, "it almost gave them a rubber stamp [reading,] 'Combahee was involved in this.'"[183] Sanders was finally acquitted in 1980. The Sanders case provides an example of how intersectional feminist politics differed from that of many other feminists: the feminist newsletter *Off Our Backs* published an essay that said, "I could not side with a man in a rape case,"[184] a view that revealed a chasm between white trust in the police and Black people's deep distrust.

Overlapping with the rape cases came a rash of lethal violence: the murders of twelve women, eleven of them Black, in the Roxbury and Dorchester neighborhoods of Boston. In contrast to the response to crimes against white women, the killings were virtually ignored by the police and the media, except for the African American *Bay State Banner*, until the victims numbered six.[185] The police also maligned the victims, suggesting that some of them had ties to the "underworld." Black women in Roxbury and Dorchester were terrified but also angry that the police were doing little to find the perpetrators. Combahee women were outraged not only by the murders but also by the fact that African American leaders were treating the crimes only as racist, not as violence against women. Black male leaders created patrols to protect "their" women and advised women to stay home except with a male escort. In other words, the issue threatened to force a choice between antiracist

and antisexist politics—like the case that gave rise to Kimberlé Crenshaw's formulation of intersectionality. That choice discursively erased
women of color, an ugly reminder of phrases like "Blacks and women."[186]
Infuriated, Combahee produced a remarkable leaflet, headlined "Six
Black Women, Why Did They Die?" and ultimately distributed thirty
thousand copies. In a brilliant move, as the number of killings grew,
they reprinted the leaflet, each time crossing out the previous number
and inserting the latest number—a powerful visual message.[187]

Combahee initiated a community coalition demanding action,
thereby establishing itself as a force in the Black community, even in
the city as a whole. The Bread and Roses network formed the Support Group for Women's Safety, aiding the campaign with babysitting,
transportation, leaflets and bulk mailings, media contact, and a pamphlet that compiled the media coverage of the murders. They formed
the Bessie Smith Memorial Production Company, which organized
fundraising events, notably a Women's Freedom Stride, an activity
designed to include a maximum number of participants: you could do
a two-mile run, a six-mile run, a two-mile walk, or a six-mile walk.
Men participated in these events, many wearing T-shirts with the slogan ANOTHER MAN AGAINST VIOLENCE AGAINST WOMEN. The coalitions
formed in response to these murders were unprecedented in Boston.[188]

This coalition soon entered electoral politics, supporting the char-

Leaflets marking the increase in murders of African American women.

ismatic African American mayoral candidate Mel King. A longtime community activist, as director of Boston's Urban League King had led campaigns for better schools, human services, and employment opportunities for people of color. He became a prominent city figure while leading a protest against urban renewal programs that evicted residents and demolished housing without building new affordable housing. The protesters—supported by Celtics basketball legend Bill Russell—built a tent city on the razed site, occupied it for three days, and won the promise of a new, affordable housing complex. In honor of the protest, it was named Tent City.[189]

King's political career began in 1972, when he was elected to the state legislature, where he served for eleven years. In 1983 he ran for mayor. His platform was a model of intersectionality, and his campaign reassembled the earlier antiracist, pro-abortion-rights coalitions that had been built by Combahee and Bread and Roses. Though they no longer existed as organizations, their networks continued strong, and they began doing traditional electioneering; they registered twenty thousand new voters, manufactured buttons and posters, knocked on doors, conducted press conferences. The outcome was historic: King tied with the Irish Democrat Ray Flynn in a nonpartisan primary, an astonishing outcome in a city with a relatively small African American population and a long history of racism. He then won 35 percent of the final vote to Flynn's 65 percent—again a remarkable showing. Perhaps equally important, the election was not acrimonious, in part because King's popularity required Flynn to treat him with respect. King's strong showing pushed Flynn's mayoral administration toward more progressive policies.[190] Mel King died in March 2023 at age ninety-four. His memorial service became a major, citywide tribute.*

The King campaign demonstrated once again that Bread and Roses and the Combahee River Collective must be understood less as organizations than as hubs and networks of activism. True, organizations

---

* The service was attended by Massachusetts governor Maura Healey, former governor Deval Patrick, U.S. senators Elizabeth Warren and Ed Markey, Attorney General Andrea Campbell, U.S. representative Ayanna Pressley, Mayor Michele Wu, and former mayor Ray Flynn.

help build social movements—they connect people and facilitate sharing information and ideas. Also true, Boston's socialist feminists would have preferred more organizational longevity. But the robust, continuing networks of activists are reminders that social movements need not have organizations to make an impact.[191]

CONSCIOUSNESS-RAISING—the process of sharing personal experiences in order to identify the social structures that shape those experiences—has been fundamental to many social movements. But none used consciousness-raising as a foundational strategy as much as women's liberation did. Because male dominance was so ubiquitous as to seem "natural," one had to learn that it was a social creation. Because it was often invisible, it had to be made visible. Consciousness-raising was a method of unlearning as well as learning. It was also a form of research; through sharing experiences, women learned how inequalities work, and they developed tactics to challenge them. Furthermore, consciousness-raising bolstered optimism, a bottom-line necessity for social movements. In both Bread and Roses and the Combahee River Collective, optimism that discrimination and injustice could be defeated not only supported protests and projects but also sent many of their members into lifelong social justice careers.

Consciousness-raising's impact was multiplied by its context. Second-wave feminism arose from the civil rights and antiwar movements, and those earlier movements led socialist feminists—the heirs of those movements—to emphasize how sexism interacts with other forms of injustice, especially racism, imperialism, and economic inequality. Without this context, the insights of consciousness-raising would have been more limited and less consequential. Interaction among forms of injustice is now called intersectionality, but before the term was created, both Bread and Roses and Combahee made it the basis of their activism. The term arose from Black women's experience. It traveled through SNCC, the Third World Women's Alliance, and the NBFO into women's liberation organizations, particularly those of the socialist-feminist stream. Today many social movements, such as #MeToo, Black Lives Matter, 350.org, and Pride at Work, and slogans such as "No Human Is Illegal" and "Code Pink," express intersectional understandings of how different causes relate, whether or not they use the term.

Intersectionality has become a concept used around the world, but in some cases it has become a label empty of strategic meaning.[192] My undergraduate students often understand the term as a prescription for diversity; by this definition, any group including people of various races and sexes is intersectional. That can be mere tokenism. Endorsing diversity without attending to unequal power relations creates the impression that different groups operate with equal power. It can also slide into essentialism, suggesting that all members of a particular group—usually a nondominant group—will have the same opinions.* Focusing only on diversity draws attention away from the task of identifying who benefits from these inequalities.[193] These usages of the concept, which one might call "intersectionality lite," have drained it of democratic and strategic content.

Two other principles important to socialist feminists came from civil rights and other New Left movements. Participatory democracy is one. It has been an especially challenging goal to achieve, especially in large organizations. There the attempt to practice participatory democracy led to rejecting formal leadership and organizational procedures that might have extended the life of the organizations. Bread and Roses' inability to keep a phone chain up to date was a small symptom of the difficulty of maintaining a large organization, let alone involving every member in important decisions. Unable to face these difficulties, Bread and Roses attempted to create participatory equality by simply declaring it. It offered lessons in karate, auto mechanics, silk screening, political theory, women's history, and more, but not in organizational or leadership skills. Luckily Bread and Roses was decentralized, and its small groups created a whirlwind of projects. Combahee also chose not to formalize leadership, but that had different consequences in a small

---

* In a recent speak-out by students of color at NYU, I was shocked to hear how often professors called on students of color to represent their group—turning to a black student and asking, What do African Americans think about this? or to a student in hijab, asking, What do Muslims think?

group. At its meetings, everyone could speak and participate in devising strategies and tactics. True, its informal leadership engendered internal tensions. But its small size made for full discussions and decisive responses to injustices, thereby offering leadership to a wide-ranging set of campaigns.

The prefigurative ideal was similarly unrealistic. In women's organizations, it led to hopes that members would relate as friends, forming a community characterized by kindness, gentleness, and mutual support. Making friendship the model for organizational relationships often derailed efficient work toward goals, as the sociologist Francesca Polletta pointed out. Moreover the friendship model was not only impossible but could undermine solidarity; the closer the friendships in an organization, the more they can produce jealousies and resentments. Because of its smaller size, Combahee was better able to mix friendship with organizational relationships, but even there inequalities—notably of class—produced resentments.

Women's liberation organizations interpreted these ideals as particularly female. On average, women have more friends, rely more on friends, and reveal more to friends than men do. On average, women also dislike conflict more than men do. These generalizations about gendered differences are, at best, only averages; they fit some women and some men but not others, and the proliferation of newly recognized gendered identities, such as queer and trans, further disrupts simple generalizations. Nevertheless, the women's liberation movement tended to disparage behaviors it considered male. Their experience of male leadership in the New Left led to an exaggerated corrective: deferring to individual expressions of emotional discomfort slowed meetings and detoured agendas.

But inefficient meetings did not diminish the activist energy emanating from Bread and Roses and, later, the coalitions spearheaded by the Combahee River Collective. The shortcomings of *organizations* do not necessarily weaken *social movements*. Boston's socialist-feminist organizations were short-lived, but their ideas continue to be influential even today. The women's liberation movement's achievements are so ubiquitous that several generations now take them for granted—to the extent that younger generations of women are surprised and shocked when they learn about the many laws and practices that constricted women's lives a half century ago. The fact that these achievements are under attack should not keep us from celebrating what was accomplished—and understanding that these gains were produced by a social movement.

EPILOGUE

The Genius and Mystery of Social Movements

S ocial movements are always imperfect, as is evident in this book. But how could they be otherwise? Though some give rise to organizations with all their trappings, such as elected officers, membership lists, and *Robert's Rules of Order*, social movements are not identical with organizations. They may create rituals, they may establish orderly decision-making procedures, but they are often unruly, sometimes turbulent, even intolerant. They are precious nonetheless. No form of political activity has done more than progressive social movements to make democracy inclusive and participatory—to make American democracy democratic.

In making social movements work, the pleasure they offer members is fundamental, a feature not widely recognized or studied. Large or small, social movements thrive only when they are enjoyable as well as purposeful. Because activists may be motivated by anger, often understandably so, social movements can appear to outsiders as dour, repressive, no fun. This is a misunderstanding. Pleasure is not a de-politicizing or trivializing of their cause.

Much of that pleasure comes from feeling part of a community. Although social movements occasionally reach across a nation, even the globe, they typically depend on person-to-person contact. (Whether social media can substitute is an open question.) Few newcomers will show up at a meeting without a personal connection that makes them comfortable in a new space among strangers. Small groups within social movements make solidarity personal, often yielding life-long friendships. Mass demonstrations and rallies are social in another way, because being among dozens or hundreds or thousands of oth-

399

ers with shared beliefs can be heartening, even thrilling. Social movements grow through a positive feedback loop, in what has been called a bandwagon effect.

No matter how angry they appear, social movements usually arise out of optimism, or at least a degree of it. Grievances and sufferings do not produce social movements unless remedies appear possible. It is optimism that makes social movements contagious. The optimism lifts the spirits of the joiners and reinforces their positive emotions, even heightens them, through the feeling of solidarity.

Often associated with labor movements, the word *solidarity* connotes membership in a community, as well as unity in goals, better than any other. Social movements cultivate solidarity both formally, through meetings and rituals, and informally, as participants share work and relaxation. Some build their solidarity through excluding or even vilifying others, as the Ku Klux Klan did, but many build cohesion without doing that. The camaraderie that members experience can model and encourage a broader solidarity. While for most people, if they are lucky, family is the earliest and strongest site of belonging, social movements require people to imagine and nurture a wider range of ties and to consider the welfare of strangers.

Social movement experience, then, changes participants themselves. Through the Townsend movement, for example, elderly people shed identities as passive and dependent and forged identities as active, capable, even modern. The unemployed movement undid the self-blaming of the Depression's victims, relieving guilt and helping them slough off identities as failures. Although few social movements endure for long, these personality changes can be lasting, sometimes permanent. The grape boycott turned farmworkers who had never lived in cities, let alone spoken publicly, into assertive representatives of their movement, capable of speaking to strangers with confidence. Many boycott participants went on to constructive and rewarding futures that would have been unlikely, even inconceivable, beforehand. Such personal changes can affect others. The Montgomery bus boycott built confidence and self-esteem not only in its participants but also in the millions of African Americans who learned about it and went on to create a national civil rights movement a few years later. These legacies spread not only over time but also through larger populations. The women's liberation movement changed not only women but also men and children and stimulated gay and queer movements.

Even the most democratic movements, however, sometimes reproduce the difficulties of democratic government. Winston Churchill remarked wryly that democracy is the worst form of government except for all the others. Neither democracy nor solidarity is easily created. Few movements are free of internal tensions and partisan passions. Disagreement can lead to conflict, leadership can promote jealousy, unequal contributions can stir resentment. Movements may implode from internal conflicts, succumb to their opponents, or both. Such problems worsen when they fail to achieve their goals, leaving participants discouraged, sometimes bitter, seeking targets to blame. Not all social movements support democracy, equality, or freedom, of course. The 1920s northern Ku Klux Klan and the 1930s fascists sought to undermine those values. Moreover, social movement successes are rarely secure. Even the achievements of a movement as massive as civil rights and women's liberation can be insecure, as is evident today in attempts to undercut its gains. Social movements are risky, but the risks are worth taking.

While measuring social movements' impact was not the goal of this book, some of it is readily apparent in these narratives. The settlements won public health legislation. The Townsend and unemployed movements created near-irresistible pressure that led to old-age pensions and unemployment compensation. The KKK spread and intensified bigotry, then shepherded through Congress a racist immigration law that lasted for forty years. The Montgomery bus boycott won a Supreme Court ruling against segregation that demonstrated to future civil rights activists the power of solidarity and direct action. The farmworkers' movement built a labor union that radically improved their wages and working conditions. The women's liberation movement compelled the passage of laws against discrimination and elected the politicians who got them passed. Proof of a social movement's impact can be seen in the size and vigor of its opposition, which can reverse some of the victories. There are no guarantees.

Mysteries remain about social movements. We can analyze what draws people in, what ideas resonate with preexisting hopes and dreams, what new ideas make sense, and what makes some leaders charismatic and responsive. Important as these analyses can be, they rarely account for, let alone predict, the rise of social movements. Some seem to arrive so suddenly that they can seem meteoric. Others develop over years. Either way, they always bring surprises. Like their members, social movements are unpredictable, even inexplicable.

In the 1960s and '70s, some American New Leftists disparaged electoral politics, pointing to its many limitations—the near impossibility of third-party success, the overrepresentation of rural areas, the gerrymandering, the inordinate amount of legislators' time spent on raising money and the concomitant power of big donors—and argued for focusing exclusively on social movements. Most of these constraints on democratic elections remain today. But social movements and elections are not and have never been alternatives. Local as well as national movements have affected, even swayed elections. They have brought voters to the polls, offered political education, developed reform proposals, and nurtured candidates who support them. Every social movement in this book tried to influence elections. Today, among many threats to essential democratic values and programs—safeguarding health and welfare, the environment, free speech, bodily autonomy, the right to asylum and to fact-based education, to name just a few—nothing is more dangerous than attempts to limit the right to vote. These threats create a circular problem, a conundrum: voters who cannot vote cannot defend voting rights. The defense of democracy will continue to need social movements.

ACKNOWLEDGMENTS

UNTIL NOW almost all of my writing has been based on archives, and I was often telling a story previously unknown. This book rests almost entirely on the work of others. If I were to list all the scholars who made this book possible, the list might be as long as one of these chapters because I relied on different people and different scholarship for each chapter.

My gratitude and indebtedness goes out to all the hundreds who have participated in progressive social movements and to those who sought to learn from them. I would like particularly to recognize the many farmworkers and those who worked on their behalf, whose essays are posted on the Farmworker Movement Documentation Project website.

I am most indebted to those who have discussed the issues in this book with me:

Ros Baxandall   Allen Hunter
Leslie Cagan   Judith Walzer Leavitt
Nancy Cott   Elaine Tyler May
Barbara Ehrenreich   Rochelle Ruthchild
Marla Erlien   Gay Seidman
Sara Evans

I want to thank those who read and commented on sections of this book, including:

Felice Batlan   Demita Frazier
Leslie Cagan   Allen Hunter

Rosie Hunter

Temma Kaplan

Judith Walzer Leavitt

Eliseo Medina

Ruth Milkman

Judy Norsigian

Rochelle Ruthchild

Barbara Smith

Many others generously allowed me to interview them, some at length, some only briefly. They include:

Diane Balzer

Fran Beal

Trude Bennett

Libby Bouvier

Leslie Cagan

Maren Lockwood Carden

Margaret Cerullo

Cheryl Clarke

Kimberlé Crenshaw

Margery Davies

Marla Erlien

Tess Ewing

Johanna Fernandez

Demita Frazier

Duchess Harris

Eliseo Medina

Amy Merrill

Ruth Milkman

Karen Nussbaum

Margo Okazawa-Rey

Frances Fox Piven

Loretta Ross

Rochelle Ruthchild

Ellen Schrecker

Barbara Smith

Robyn Spencer

Laura Tillem

Sheli Wortis

Some left archives that were of great value:

Fran Ansley

Gene Bishop

Kathleen Blee

Wini Breines

Leslie Cagan

Hazel Carby

Tia Cross

Virginia Durr

Tess Ewing

J. Craig Jenkins

Philip Jenkins

Adrienne Lash Jones

Marya Levenson

Nancy Osterud

Ann Popkin

Loretta Ross

Rochelle Ruthchild

Jean Tepperman

Betsy Warrior

Thanks also to those who answered my questions:

Heather Booth

Amy Kesselman

Judy Norsigian

Kathryn Kish Sklar

Meredith Tax

Jeanne Theoharis

Mercedes Tompkins

Judy Ullman

Martin Zwick

The endnotes for each chapter provide the names of hundreds of scholars whose work I depended on, and they are too numerous to list here. But I want to thank here those whose work was particularly influential to my interpretations. They include

Edwin Amenta

Frank Bardacke

Felice Batlan

Kathleen Blee

Wini Breines

Pamela Brooks

Steve Burg

Anna Carastathis

Dorothy Sue Cobble

Nancy Cott

Kimberlé Crenshaw

Kathy Davis

John D'Emilio

Mark Engler and Paul Engler

Richard Evans

Sara Evans

Tess Ewing

Lori Flores

Joseph Fronczak

Marshall Ganz

Matt Garcia

Glenda Gilmore

Chad Goldberg

Robert Alan Goldberg

Beverly Guy-Sheftall

Duchess Harris

Lashawn Harris

Shannon Jackson

Robin D. G. Kelley

Alice Kessler-Harris

Elisabeth Lasch-Quinn

Judith Walzer Leavitt

Nancy MacLean

Jane Mansbridge

Erik S. McDuffie

Danielle McGuire

Ana Minian

Mark Naison

Annelise Orleck

Miriam Pawel

Charles Payne

Frances Fox Piven

Tony Platt

Francesca Polletta

Ann Popkin

Belinda Robnett

Margaret Eleanor Rose	Kimberly Springer
Kris Rosenthal	Eleanor K. Stebner
Loretta Ross	Randi Storch
Benita Roth	Richard Steven Street
Kathryn Kish Sklar	Jeanne Theoharis
Barbara Smith	Stephen Ward
Robyn Spencer	Keeanga Yamahtta-Taylor

Several scholars whose work was valuable to me are no longer alive but I want to recognize them anyway:

Glen Jeansonne	Roy Rosenzweig
James J. Lorence	Donald Warren

I am grateful to the staff of the Schlesinger Library. I had to work there during the covid epidemic when the library was short-staffed and they worked to give me the help I needed nevertheless.

I am particularly indebted to many Norton people whose support—and patience—were vital. I especially want to thank Steve Attardo, Haley Bracken, Jessica Friedman, Kathleen Karcher, Kadiatou Keita, Anna Oler, Don Rifkin, and Luke Swann.

Above all, the editor extraordinaire Bob Weil has been helping me become a better writer for decades. My agent, Charlotte Sheedy, has been with me for more than half a century, taking me on before I had published a single thing. I am indebted to both of them for their invaluable advice and support for the ethical and political values that underlie this book. Even if I never write another word, they will remain with me in many ways.

NOTES

Abbreviations

Abbott Papers	Grace Abbott Papers, University of Chicago
Addams Papers	Jane Addams Memorial Collection, Special Collections, Richard J. Daley Library, University of Illinois at Chicago
Benjamin Papers	Herbert Benjamin Papers, LOC
Bouvier Papers	Libby Bouvier Private Collection
CES Records	Records of the Committee on Economic Security, Records of the Social Security Administration, NARA
CU	Columbia University, New York
FMDP	Farmworker Movement Documentation Project, University of California at San Diego, https://libraries.ucsd.edu/farmworkermovement/
Hopkins Papers	Harry L. Hopkins Papers, Franklin D. Roosevelt Presidential Library and Museum, Hyde Park, N.Y.
LOC	Library of Congress
King Papers	Martin Luther King, Jr., Papers, Stanford University
McWilliams Papers	Carey McWilliams Papers, Library Special Collections, University of California at Los Angeles
MSRC	Moorland Spingarn Research Center, Howard University, Washington, D.C.
NARA	National Archives and Records Administration
SL	Schlesinger Library, Radcliffe Institute for Advanced Study, Cambridge, Mass.

VF	Voices of Feminism Oral History Project, Sophia Smith Collection of Women's History, Smith College, Northampton, Mass.
Welga Archive	Welga Digital Archive, Bulosan Center for Filipino Studies, University of California at Davis, https://welgadigitalarchive.omeka.net/
Witte Papers	Edwin Witte Papers, Wisconsin Historical Society, Madison

Introduction

1. Others attribute that point to psychoanalyst Theodor Reik, *Curiosities of the Self: Illusions We Have About Ourselves* (New York: Farrar, Straus & Giroux, 1965), 133.

1. Creating Free Spaces

1. Biographical material on Hunter is taken from Adrienne Lash Jones, *Jane Edna Hunter: A Case Study of Black Leadership, 1910–1950* (Brooklyn, NY: Carlson, 1990).
2. Allen Davis, *Spearheads for Reform: The Social Settlements and the Progressive Movement, 1890–1914* (New Brunswick, NJ: Rutgers University Press, 1985), 12.
3. Kevin Hetherington, "Identity Formation, Space and Social Centrality," *Theory, Culture and Society* 13, no. 4 (1996): 38–39.
4. Thomas Lee Philpott, *The Slum and the Ghetto: Immigrants, Blacks, and Reformers in Chicago, 1880–1930* (Belmont, CA: Wadsworth, 1991), 22; Michael Rose, "The Secular Faith of the Socialist Settlements," in *Settlements, Social Change and Community Action*, ed. Ruth Gilchrist and Tony Jeffs (London: Jessica Kingsley, 2001), 25; John P. Rousmaniere, "Cultural Hybrid in the Slums: The College Woman and the Settlement House, 1889–1894," *American Quarterly* 22, no. 1 (Spring 1970): 47.
5. Jane Addams, "Social Control," *Crisis* 1, no. 3 (1911): 22–23; Steven J. Diner, "Chicago Social Workers and Blacks in the Progressive Era," *Social Service Review* 44, no. 4 (1970): 398. For the New Left attitude toward social control, treating social control and altruism as in tension with each other, see Howard Jacob Karger, *The Sentinels of Order: A Study of Social Control and the Minneapolis Settlement House Movement, 1915–1950* (Lanham, MD: University Press of America, 1987), 35. Karger writes (at 71, 138) that settlement social control in the Progressive era "was not typically punitive" but became more "strident" in the 1920s.
6. Dorothy Ross, "Gendered Social Knowledge: Domestic Discourse, Jane Addams, and the Possibilities of Social Science," in *Gender and American Social Science*, ed. Helene Silverberg (Princeton, NJ: Princeton University Press, 1998), 240.
7. Jane Addams, *Democracy and Social Ethics* (New York: Macmillan, 1902), 19–20; Shannon Jackson, *Lines of Activity: Performance, Historiography, Hull-house Domesticity* (Ann Arbor: University of Michigan Press, 2000), 60.
8. Vida Scudder, "Early Days in Denison House," 1937, in Reel 1, Folder 1, Denison House Records, SL; Victoria Bissell Brown, *The Education of Jane Addams* (Philadelphia: University of Pennsylvania Press, 2004), 212–23. If Addams did not see this at first, Ellen Starr did.
9. Jane Addams, *Twenty Years at Hull-House* (New York: Phillips, 1913), 92–93.
10. Edith Abbott, "A Sister's Memories" (1952), in *The Grace Abbott Reader*, ed. John Sorensen with Judith Sealander (Lincoln: University of Nebraska Press, 2008), 6.

11. *Chicago Tribune*, March 1889, cited in Sharon Haar, "Location, Location, Location: Gender and the Archaeology of Urban Settlement," *Journal of Architectural Education* 55, no. 3 (2002): 151. Starr is quoted in Jackson, *Lines of Activity*, 47. Overall information on budget and fundraising is from Kathryn Kish Sklar, "Who Funded Hull-house?" in *Lady Bountiful Revisited: Women, Philanthropy and Power*, ed. K. D. McCarthy (New Brunswick, NJ: Rutgers University Press, 1990).

12. Addams to McCormick, February 8, 1895, in *Selected Papers of Jane Addams*, vol. 3, at https://muse.jhu.edu/chapter/2296371; "Art for Poor People: Formal Opening of Hull-house," *Chicago Herald*, June 21, 1891.

13. Eleanor J. Stebner, *The Women of Hull House: A Study in Spirituality, Vocation and Friendship* (Albany: State University of New York Press, 1997), 167–75.

14. Louise de Koven Bowen, *Growing Up with a City* (New York: Macmillan, 1926), 82. Bowen went on to become a reformer herself, not just a funder, and one particularly concerned with settlements' neglect of African Americans; see her "The Colored People of Chicago," *Survey* 31, no. 5 (November 1, 1913): 117–20.

15. James Weber Linn, *Jane Addams: A Biography* (New York: D. Appleton-Century, 1935), 127; Margaret Tims, *Jane Addams of Hull House: A Centenary Study* (New York: Macmillan, 1961), 51.

16. Hilda Satt Polacheck, *I Came a Stranger: The Story of a Hull-house Girl* (Urbana: University of Illinois Press, 1989), 100.

17. Living in cottages accustomed women to living collectively and to making decisions independently of their elders. Rousmaniere, "Cultural Hybrid," 64.

18. Kathryn Kish Sklar, "Hull-House in the 1890s: A Community of Women Reformers," *Signs* 10, no. 4 (1985): 660; Rousmaniere, "Cultural Hybrid," 53; Stebner, *Women of Hull-House*, 5.

19. Jackson, *Lines of Activity*, 174ff. Addams was well aware of her desire to dominate and be admired; already in 1889 she quoted, from Robert Browning, in a letter, "There's power in me, and will to dominate / Which I must exercise, they hurt me else." Brown, *Education of Addams*, 211. What was most remarkable in Addams's personality is not just the will to dominate but the willpower to keep it under control.

20. Mina Carson, *Settlement Folk: Social Thought and the American Settlement Movement, 1885–1930* (Chicago: University of Chicago Press, 1990), 88–89.

21. Addams, *Twenty Years*, 149–50.

22. Guy Szuberla, "Three Chicago Settlements: Their Architectural Form and Social Meaning," *Journal of the Illinois State Historical Society* 70, no. 2 (1977): 123.

23. Rousmaniere, "Cultural Hybrid," 61. Hull-House architecture is discussed in Szuberla, "Three Chicago Settlements."

24. Brown, *Education of Addams*, 220; Mary Ann Stankiewicz, "Art at Hull-House, 1889–1901: Jane Addams and Ellen Gates Starr," *Woman's Art Journal* 10, no. 1 (1989): 35–39.

25. Addams, *Twenty Years*, 94.

26. Carson, *Settlement Folk*, 60.

27. Jackson, *Lines of Activity*, 155, 167.

28. This achievement becomes all the more impressive when compared to Hull-House's later years, when the Octagon Room on its south side became an adulatory memorial for Jane Addams. Mary Lynn McCree Bryan, the first "curator" of the renovated Hull-House, criticized its antiseptic quality: the gracious home had lost its vibrant messiness, its "dingy disarray." Erin Cunningham, "Interiors, Histories, and the Preservation of Chicago's Hull-House Settlement," *Buildings and Landscapes: Journal of the Vernacular Architecture Forum* 23, no. 2 (2016): 61–62.

29. Ross, "Gendered Social Knowledge," 241.
30. Polacheck, *I Came a Stranger*, 89.
31. Louise De Koven Bowen quoted in Stebner, *Women of Hull-House*, 160. Historians and biographers have of course discussed the nature of Addams's relationship with, first, Ellen Starr and second, Mary Rozet Smith. Addams and Smith seem to have kept separate bedrooms; this may have been an accommodation to propriety but could have provided Addams a space of refuge from the many demands on her. In one mention of bedroom assignments, Addams added "of course, Mary and I slept together." Quoted in Brown, *Education of Addams*, 254. Some would assert that Addams was a lesbian, an anachronism since the concept did not exist at the time. We can never know the full nature of these relationships, inasmuch as it was common for women, including married women living with their husbands, to share beds. We do know that these women, and many other unmarried and supposedly single women, considered each other life partners and cared deeply about and for each other.
32. Louise W. Knight, *Citizen: Jane Addams and the Struggle for Democracy* (Chicago: University of Chicago Press, 2008), 74; Alexandra Fair, "'The Mind Has to Catch Up on Sex': Sexual Norms and Sex Education in the Hull-House," *Paedagogica Historica* 54, no. 3 (2018): 251–52; Jane Addams, *A New Conscience and an Ancient Evil* (New York: Macmillan, 1912), 105, 169, 208–11. Addams is quoted in Carson, *Settlement Folk*, 113.
33. Diane C. Haslett, "Hull-House and the Birth Control Movement: An Untold Story," *Affilia* 12, no. 3 (1997): 261–77. Interestingly, Haslett points out that Hamilton and Yarros explicitly rejected eugenic arguments, unlike Margaret Sanger. Fair, "'Mind Has to Catch Up,'" 257–58.
34. Dorothea Moore, "A Day at Hull House," *American Journal of Sociology* 2, no. 5 (March 1897): 636.
35. Abbott, "Hull-house Days," 5.
36. Moore, "Day at Hull House," 636.
37. Sklar, "Hull-House in 1890s," 664.
38. Material on Kelley is from Kathryn Kish Sklar, *Florence Kelley and the Nation's Work: The Rise of Women's Political Culture, 1830–1900* (New Haven, CT: Yale University Press, 1997).
39. Kelley knew Caro Lloyd, Henry's sister, from European connections. Sklar, *Kelley and Nation's Work*, 179, 225.
40. Jackson, *Lines of Activity*, 165.
41. Moore, "Day at Hull House," 636.
42. Shannon Jackson, "Toward a Queer Social Welfare Studies: Unsettling Jane Addams," in *Jane Addams and the Practice of Democracy*, ed. Marilyn Fischer, Carol Nackenoff, and Wendy Chmielewski (Urbana: University of Illinois Press, 2009), 153.
43. "Charles J. Hull House, Dining Room Wing, Written Historical and Descriptive Data," Historic American Buildings Survey, U.S. National Park Service, LOC no. HABS ILL-1110A, at http://lcweb2.loc.gov/pnp/habshaer/il/il0400/il0410/data/il0410data.pdf, accessed September 26, 2013.
44. Carson, *Settlement Folk*, 89.
45. Linn, *Addams: Biography*, 119.
46. Jackson, *Lines of Activity*, 194. It's interesting that Beatrice Webb's "higgledy-piggledy" and "queer" prefigured twenty-first-century meanings of *queer*.
47. Kathryn Kish Sklar, "How Did Changes in the Built Environment at Hull-House

Reflect the Settlement's Interaction with Its Neighbors, 1889–1912?" *Women and Social Movements in the United States, 1600–2000* 8, no. 4 (2004).

48. Felice Batlan, "Law and the Fabric of the Everyday: The Settlement Houses, Sociological Jurisprudence, and the Gendering of Urban Legal Culture," *Southern California Interdisciplinary Law Journal* 15 (2006): 246. A vivid example of listening: Hull-House resident Alice Hamilton was unusually credentialed, with medical and postgraduate science degrees, but her pioneering public health research also included "shoe leather epidemiology." When she investigated miners' "consumption," the owners blamed it on "germs," but she listened to the miners, followed the cases of illness, and concluded that they were right—the cause was silicosis from the dust in the mines. Linda Gordon, *The Great Arizona Orphan Abduction* (Cambridge, MA: Harvard University Press, 1999), 217–18.

49. In this academically ambitious generation, nearly one-third of women earning college degrees between 1868 and 1898 went on to do graduate work, and many earned doctorates. However, of nine women who earned doctorates in the social sciences during the University of Chicago's first fifteen years, none obtained a faculty appointment, while two-thirds of the male PhDs did. Linda Gordon, "Social Insurance and Public Assistance: The Influence of Gender in Welfare Thought in the United States," *American Historical Review* 97, no. 1 (1992): 19–54.

50. Sklar, "Hull-House in 1890s"; Linda Gordon, *Pitied But Not Entitled: Single Mothers and the History of Welfare* (Cambridge, MA: Harvard University Press, 1994), 168–74; Robert A. Woods and Albert J. Kennedy, *The Settlement Horizon* (New York: Russell Sage Foundation, 1922), 59; Joyce E. Williams and Vicky M. MacLean, *Settlement Sociology in the Progressive Years: Faith, Science, and Reform* (Leiden: Brill, 2015).

51. In the language of the time, Agnes Sinclair Holbrook wrote that "merely to state symptoms . . . would be idle; but to state symptoms in order to ascertain the nature of disease, and apply. . . its cure, is not only scientific, but in the highest sense humanitarian." Residents of Hull-House, *Hull-House Maps and Papers* (New York: Thomas Y. Crowell, 1895), 14.

52. Sklar, "Hull-House in 1890s," 670.

53. Kelley to Ely, June 21, 1894, in Florence Kelley, *The Selected Letters of Florence Kelley, 1869–1931*, ed. Kathryn Kish Sklar and Beverly Wilson Palmer (Urbana: University of Illinois Press, 2009), 73–74.

54. Florence Kelley, "I Go to Work," in Kelley, *Notes of Sixty Years: The Autobiography of Florence Kelley*, ed. Kathryn Kish Sklar (Chicago: Charles H. Kerr, 1986), 77–89.

55. Kathryn Kish Sklar, "Hull-house Maps and Papers: Social Science as Women's Work in the 1890s," in *Gender and American Social Science: The Formative Years*, ed. Helene Silverberg (Princeton, NJ: Princeton University Press, 1998).

56. Nicholas Kelley, "Early Days at Hull-house," *Social Service Review* 28, no. 4 (1954): 424–29. Residents, *Hull-House Maps and Papers*, used the same color scheme that Booth used. When the publisher complained about the cost, Addams and Kelley decided to waive their royalties. Christina E. Dando, *Women and Cartography in the Progressive Era* (London: Taylor & Francis, 2017), 129, 131.

57. N. Kelley, "Early Days"; Woods and Kennedy, *Settlement Horizon*, 237. An analysis of the contribution of this publication and the many other Hull-House surveys to social geography is in Dando, *Women and Cartography*, chap. 4.

58. Du Bois, like Hull-House's female residents, was denied an academic position even while doing cutting-edge scholarship. Hull-House's own Isabel Eaton worked with him on his research. Mary Jo Deegan, "W.E.B. Du Bois and the Women of Hull-

house, 1895–1899," *American Sociologist* 19, no. 4 (1988): 301–11. See also Joyce E. Williams and Vicky M. MacLean, "Settlement Sociology in the Progressive Years. Faith, Science, and Reform," *Studies in Critical Social Sciences Series* (Boston: Brill, 2015).

59. Florence Kelley, testimony before U.S. Industrial Commission, 1899, quoted in Susan Roth Breitzer, "Uneasy Alliances: Hull-house, the Garment Workers Strikes, and the Jews of Chicago," *Indiana Magazine of History* 106, no. 1 (2010): 45.

60. W. O. Atwater and A. P. Bryant, with the cooperation of Jane Addams and Caroline L. Hunt, *Dietary Studies in Chicago in 1895 and 1896* (Washington, DC: U.S. Department of Agriculture, 1898).

61. Sklar, *Kelley and Nation's Work*, 223; Kelley, "I Go to Work."

62. Heather M. Capitanio, "Denison House: Women's Use of Space in the Boston Settlement" (MA thesis, University of Massachusetts at Boston, 2010).

63. Moore, "Day at Hull House," 629.

64. Hull-House weekly programs, January–March 1891, doc. 7, Addams Papers.

65. Some Italian neighbors hesitated to participate in Hull-House activities because their priests disapproved. Florence Scala and Teresa Campo are quoted in Johanna Katherine Murphy, "Social Saints in the City: Race, Space and Religion in Chicago Women's Settlement" (MA thesis, Portland State University, 2020), 91–92.

66. Hull-House weekly programs, January–March 1891, doc. 7, Addams Papers.

67. Stephanie J. Jass, "Recipes for Reform: Americanization and Foodways in Chicago Settlement Houses, 1890–1920" (PhD diss., Western Michigan State University, 2004), 188.

68. Shannon Jackson, *Lines of Activity: Performance, Historiography, Hull-House Domesticity* (Ann Arbor: University of Michigan Press, 2000).

69. Addams, *Twenty Years*, 79.

70. Addams, *Twenty Years*, 78.

71. Jass, "Recipes for Reform," 213.

72. Polacheck, *I Came a Stranger*, 169.

73. Kelley, *Notes of Sixty Years*, 77.

74. Jackson, *Lines of Activity*, 60.

75. Sklar, "How Did Changes."

76. Jackson, *Lines of Activity*, 67–68.

77. Woods and Kennedy, *Settlement Horizon*, 67.

78. Polacheck, *I Came a Stranger*, 77.

79. Eliza P. Whitcombe, "The Jane Club of Hull-House," *American Journal of Nursing* 2, no. 2 (1901): 86–88; Knight, *Citizen*, 247. Today a Los Angeles co-working space for mothers calls itself the Jane Club.

80. Breitzer, "Uneasy Alliances." Kelley grew steadily more impatient with the "futility of palliative work" and soon left to head the National Consumers League, where she lent her support to labor unions. See Sklar, *Kelley and Nation's Work*, 1:163.

81. The four organized at Hull-House were shirtmakers' and cloakmakers' unions, the Dorcas Federal Labor Union, and the Chicago Women's Trade Union League. Woods and Kennedy, *Settlement Horizon*, 170; Davis, *Spearheads for Reform*, 120. Grace Abbott would later become head of the child labor division of the U.S. Children's Bureau, the first federal welfare agency.

82. *Hull House: A Social Settlement* (Chicago, n.p., February 1, 1894). Louise Knight suggests that Addams actively sought cooperation with Kenney; Knight, *Citizen*, 211.

83. Other Chicago settlements also supported labor struggles. During the massive 1904

stockyards strike of twenty thousand workers, Chicago's settlements became meeting spaces for labor leaders and middle-class supporters. As the historian Allen Davis writes, "From the dedicated band that gathered each evening for dinner [at the University of Chicago Settlement, next door to union headquarters,] came a flow of articles, editorials, novels and speeches" supporting the workers. Davis, *Spearheads for Reform*, 117.

84. Sklar, "How Did Changes."

85. Stankiewicz, "Art at Hull-House," 36. Hull-House's "Americanization" efforts were not directed exclusively toward high culture. When the immigrant Hilda Polacheck visited Hull-House in 1900, after a day of work in a shirtwaist factory, Addams greeted her and took her to the Labor Museum. Mary Hill, the museum "curator," observing that Polacheck was a garment worker, asked if she wanted to learn to weave something "typically American." She brought her materials, and soon "I was weaving a small Navaho-style blanket." Polacheck, *I Came a Stranger*, 64.

86. Polacheck, *I Came a Stranger*, 101.

87. "Art for Poor People: Formal Opening of Hull-house," *Chicago Herald*, June 21, 1891.

88. "Art for Poor People."

89. Rivkah Shpak-Lisak, *Pluralism and Progressives: Hull-House and the New Immigrants, 1890–1919* (Chicago: University of Chicago Press, 1989), 82.

90. *Hull-House: A Social Settlement.*

91. Addams, *Twenty Years*, 80.

92. The phrase is in a scrapbook in Slide 20, Reel 1, Denison House Records, SL, quoted in Lilli Thorne, "'Who Kindly Greet Me Home': Queer and Gendered Spaces in Settlement Houses, 1890–1930" (BA thesis, Simmons University, 2020), 9. Addams criticized the public schools' exclusive focus on teaching English to immigrant children because they "become ashamed of their parents"; quoted in Murphy, "Social Saints," 79. Hull-House did less outreach to Jews. On only two occasions up to 1913 did it ever sponsor a Jewish cultural event. There may have been some anti-Semitism here, including the view that Jews lacked a history of high culture. Davis, *Spearheads for Reform*, 163.

93. Breitzer, "Uneasy Alliances," 40–70; Sarah Henry Lederman, "Settlement Houses in the United States," in *Shalvi/Hyman Encyclopedia of Jewish Women*, at https://jwa.org/encyclopedia/article/settlement-houses-in-united-states; Shpak-Lisak, *Pluralism and Progressives*, 80.

94. Woods and Kennedy, *Settlement Horizon*, 211.

95. *Hull-House Year Book, 1906–1907.* Hull-House was less successful in attracting adult men, a problem common to all settlements. Davis, *Spearheads for Reform*, 88.

96. Woods and Kennedy, *Settlement Horizon*, 53.

97. Jackson, *Lines of Activity*, 68.

98. Jackson, *Lines of Activity*, 156.

99. The house is discussed at "Three More Degrees of Interior Decoration," Downeast Dilettante, July 3, 2011, http://thedowneastdilettante.blogspot.com/2011/03/three-more-degrees-and-were-done.html.

100. "The Brandeis Brief—In Its Entirety," Louis D. Brandeis School of Law Library, at http://www.law.louisville.edu/library/collections/brandeis/node/235.

101. Gordon, *Pitied But Not Entitled.*

102. *Hull-House: A Social Settlement.*

103. Hull-House's record regarding African Americans is mixed, and the scholarship about it includes both great praise and sharp criticism. Rima Lunin Schultz is

mainly critical in her "Hull-House and 'Jim Crow,'" in *Eleanor Smith's Hull-House Songs*, ed. Graham Cassano, Rima Lunin Schultz, and Jessica Payette (Leiden: Brill, 2019), 265, 268, 271; while Deegan offers mainly praise, "Du Bois and Women," 37 and passim.

104. Steven J. Diner, "Chicago Social Workers and Blacks in the Progressive Era," *Social Service Review* 44, no. 4 (1970): 399.

105. Deegan, "Du Bois and Women," 37, 40, 52.

106. Elisabeth Lasch-Quinn, *Black Neighbors: Race and the Limits of Reform in the American Settlement House Movement, 1890–1945* (Chapel Hill: University of North Carolina Press, 1993), introduction and chap. 1.

107. Karger, *Sentinels of Order*, 108–10.

108. Jane Addams, "Social Control," *Crisis* 1, no. 3 (1911): 22–23. Addams's belief was shared by several major African American scholars of her time and later, such as Du Bois. Franklin Frazier considered a deformed Black family structure partly responsible for Black poverty and "vice."

109. *U.S. Census Reports, 1890–1960*.

110. Lasch-Quinn, *Black Neighbors*, 24; Judith Trolander, *Settlement Houses and the Great Depression* (Detroit: Wayne State University Press, 1975), 137–40.

111. Schultz, "Hull-House and 'Jim Crow,'" 270.

112. Louise De Koven Bowen, who criticized Hull-House for its inattention to African Americans, was by no means free of racist assumptions herself, commenting, for example, that "the Black man 'does not resent social ostracism.'" Quoted in Lasch-Quinn, *Black Neighbors*, 16.

113. Louise W. Knight, "Harriett Alleyne Rice," in *Women Building Chicago, 1790–1990: A Biographical Dictionary*, ed. Rima Lunin Schultz and Adele Hast (Bloomington: Indiana University Press, 2001), 740–42; Stacy Lynn, "Dr. Harriet Rice: First Black Resident at Hull-House," Jane Addams Papers Project, at https://janeaddams.ramapo.edu/2021/08/dr-harriet-rice-first-black-resident-at-hull-house/. The story of her conflict with Hull-House is also told in Knight, *Citizen*, 289, 336, 387–88; Schultz, "Hull-House and 'Jim Crow,'" 273–74; Stebner, *Women of Hull-House*, 118, 220n75.

114. Iris Carlton-LaNey, "The Career of Birdye Henrietta Haynes, a Pioneer Settlement Worker," *Social Service Review* 68, no. 2 (1994): 254–73. I have been unable to find any further information about Boaz. In a similar case, Gertrude Brown, head of the Phyllis Wheatley House in Minneapolis, was forced out for her resistance to the white-dominated board, which stripped her of authority to hire and fire staff—and this was in 1936. Karger, *Sentinels of Order*, 116–18.

115. In Chicago, for example, between 1900 and 1910, nearly half of the six thousand African American women migrants became servants, while two-thirds of all Chicago's employed Black women were servants or laundresses. Carlton-LaNey, "Career of Birdye," 262.

116. Black settlements appeared in Atlanta, Boston, Chicago, Kansas City, Little Rock, Newark, New York, and Hampton, Virginia—in some cases before more well-known white ones. Ralph E. Luker, "Missions, Institutional Churches, and Settlement Houses: The Black Experience, 1885–1910," *Journal of Negro History* 69, nos. 3–4 (1984): 102; Stephanie J. Shaw, "Black Club Women and the Creation of the National Association of Colored Women," *Journal of Women's History* 3, no. 2 (1991): 18; Ruth Hutchinson Crocker, *Social Work and Social Order: The Settlement Movement in Two Industrial Cities, 1889–1930* (Urbana: University of Illinois Press, 1992), 214; Toby

Berman-Rossi and Irving Miller, "African-Americans and the Settlements During the Late Nineteenth and Early Twentieth Centuries," *Social Work with Groups* 17, no. 3 (1994): 77–95.

117. Steve Kramer, "Uplifting Our 'Downtrodden Sisterhood': Victoria Earle Matthews and New York City's White Rose Mission, 1897–1907," *Journal of African American History* 91, no. 3 (2006): 243; Flora Barnett Cash, "Radicals or Realists: African American Women and the Settlement House Spirit in New York City," *Afro-Americans in New York Life and History* 15, no. 1 (1991).

118. Anne Meis Knupfer, " 'If You Can't Push, Pull. If You Can't Pull, Please Get Out of the Way': The Phyllis Wheatley Club and Home in Chicago, 1896–1920," *Journal of Negro History* 82, no. 2 (Spring 1977): 225; Kimberley Phillips, " 'But It Is a Fine Place to Make Money': Migration and African-American Families in Cleveland, 1915–1929," *Journal of Social History* 30, no. 2 (1996): 400.

119. Kramer, "Uplifting." An influential white advocate for such women, the well-meaning but racist Progressive Frances Kellor, wrote of "green helpless negro woman brought up here from the South—on promises of 'easy work, lots of money and good times.' " Frances A. Kellor, "Southern Colored Girls in the North: The Problem of Their Protection," *Charities* 15 (March 18, 1905): 584–85. Kellor organized the Association for the Protection of Negro Women in 1905.

120. Sarah Deutsch, *Women and the City: Gender, Space and Power in Boston, 1870–1940* (New York: Oxford, 2000), 11.

121. Sophonisba Breckinridge and Edith Abbott, *The Delinquent Child and the Home: A Study of the Delinquent Wards of the Juvenile Court of Chicago* (New York: Russell Sage Foundation, 1912); Laura S. Abrams, "Guardians of Virtue: The Social Reformers and the 'Girl Problem,' 1890–1920," *Social Service Review* 74, no. 3 (2000): 436–52; Knupfer, " 'If You Can't Push,' " 222, 225–26; Iris Carlton-LaNey and Vanessa Hodges, "African American Reformers' Mission: Caring for Our Girls and Women," *Feminist Inquiry in Social Work* 19, no. 3 (2004): 264; Marian J. Morton, *And Sin No More: Social Policy and Unwed Mothers in Cleveland, 1855–1990* (Columbus: Ohio State University Press, 1993), 1; Cash, "Radicals or Realists"; Kellor, "Southern Colored Girls in the North," 584–85.

122. Matthews's address to the 1898 Hampton Negro Conference is quoted in Kramer, "Uplifting," 243.

123. Kramer, "Uplifting," 244.

124. Vanessa H. May, *Unprotected Labor: Household Workers, Politics, and Middle-class Reform in New York, 1870–1940* (Chapel Hill: University of North Carolina Press, 2011), 90–91.

125. Walter R. Chivers, "Neighborhood Union: An Effort of Community Organization," *Opportunity*, June 1925, 178–79; Luker, "Missions, Institutional Churches," 104.

126. The Black population of Cleveland quadrupled between 1870 and 1910, constituting only 1.5 percent of the city's total. In 1930 the number of Black migrants still showed: 72,000, of whom 80 percent had been born elsewhere. Cleveland ranked third in the country in the rate of increase in the African American population. R. H. Bishop, Jr., to Mrs. B. A. Spanye, in Jane Edna Hunter, *A Nickel and a Prayer* (1941; reprint Morgantown: West Virginia University Press, 2011), 173.

127. Daphne Spain, "Safe Havens for Cleveland's Virtuous Women, 1868–1928," *Journal of Planning History* 3, no. 4 (2004): 272; Dorothy Salem, *To Better Our World: Black Women in Organized Reform, 1890–1920* (Brooklyn, NY: Carlson, 1990), 134.

128. William W. Giffin, *African Americans and the Color Line in Ohio, 1915–1930* (Colum-

bus: Ohio State University Press, 2005), 56–57; David A. Gerber, *Black Ohio and the Color Line, 1860–1915* (Urbana: University of Illinois Press, 1976), 389. Black YMCAs were built in Cincinnati and Columbus but not in Cleveland.

129. Gerber, *Black Ohio*, 158–65.

130. Samuel P. Orth, *A History of Cleveland, Ohio* (Cleveland: S.J. Clarke, 1910), 1:119; Margaret Spratt, "To Be Separate or One: The Issue of Race in the History of the Pittsburgh and Cleveland YWCAs, 1920–1946," in *Men and Women Adrift: The YMCA and the YWCA in the City*, ed. Nina Mjagkij and Margaret Spratt (New York: NYU Press, 1997), 198; Kenneth Kusmer, *A Ghetto Takes Shape: Black Cleveland, 1870–1930* (Urbana: University of Illinois Press, 1976), 10.

131. Kusmer, *Ghetto Takes Shape*, 44, 61; Gerber, *Black Ohio*, 260–63; Jones, *Hunter*, 80; Giffin, *African Americans in Ohio*, 140.

132. "Colored Girls in Cleveland," *Crisis*, December 1929, 411. They were "women adrift," confronting the problems that Joanne Meyerowitz wrote about in her *Women Adrift: Independent Wage Earners in Chicago 1880–1930* (Chicago: University of Chicago Press, 1988).

133. Addams, *New Conscience*, 225.

134. Hunter, *Nickel and Prayer*, 67–68. A Dudley House settlement resident called dance halls, saloon, and variety shows "the strong forces of evil"; Capitanio, "Denison House," 100.

135. Hazel V. Carby, "Policing the Black Woman's Body in an Urban Context," *Critical Inquiry* 18, no. 4 (1992): 738–55; Spain, "Safe Havens," 272.

136. "Colored Girls in Cleveland," *Crisis*, December 1929, 411. See also William H. Jones, *Recreation and Amusement Among Negroes in Washington, D.C.* (Westport, CT: Negro Universities Press, 1927), 122; Judith Wiesenfeld, "The Harlem YWCA and the Secular City, 1904–1945," *Journal of Women's History* 6, no. 3 (1994): 67.

137. Jane Addams, *Spirit of Youth and the City Streets* (New York: Macmillan, 1909), 14.

138. Robert Woods, head of a Boston settlement, believed that Blacks had "a natural tendency to immorality"; Deutsch, *Women and the City*, 86. One of the worst racial slurs, among many that were sickening, was the claim that it was impossible to rape a Black woman because she was always willing.

139. So did Lugenia Burns Hope in her Atlanta settlement, Neighborhood House; Lasch-Quinn, *Black Neighbors*, 123.

140. Felice Batlan has called this "methodology of participation . . . knowledge grounded in understanding, empathy, participation and investigation," in Batlan, "Law and the Fabric," 245.

141. Hunter, *Nickel and Prayer*, 84.

142. Cornel West defines the prophetic tradition as a mode of thought and action consisting of "protracted and principled struggles against forms of personal despair, intellectual dogmatism and socioeconomic oppression that foster communities of hope. . . . The distinctive features of prophetic activity are Pascalian leaps of faith in the capacity of human beings to transform their circumstances, engage in . . . analyses and practices of social freedom." Cornel West, "The Prophetic Tradition in Afro-America," *Drew Gateway* 55, nos. 2–3 (Winter 1984–Spring 1985): 97–108.

143. Hunter, *Nickel and Prayer*, 83.

144. Matthew 5:16.

145. Regennia N. Williams, "'Race Women' and Reform: Cleveland, Ohio, 1900–1940," at https://www.ohioacademyofhistory.org/wp-content/uploads/2013/04/2002Williams.pdf. Victoria Matthews was also described as "forceful" and "decided"; Kramer, "Uplifting," 256.

146. Salem, *To Better Our World*, 136. Decades later its editor, Harry C. Smith, continued to condemn the Phillis Wheatley Home; Kusmer, *Ghetto Takes Shape*, 148–50.

147. Jones, *Hunter*, chap. 3. African Americans had been creating YWCA branches since 1870, but they were treated as auxiliaries, not as part of the national organization. In 1910 the national board of the YWCA resolved that "in certain cities . . . if the colored population is sufficiently large and able to support its own work, an association called the Colored Young Women's Christian Association shall be formed." Adrienne Lash Jones, "Struggle Among Saints: African American Women and the YWCA, 1870–1920," in Mjagkij and Spratt, eds., *Men and Women Adrift*, 169. This remained YWCA policy until 1946, and it was at times enforced even by the token Black women who held national positions. Sponsorship typically meant control, and the YW subordinated the Black settlements it supported to white authority. Wiesenfeld, "Harlem YWCA," 62–78; Carlton-LaNey, "Career of Birdye," 254–73; Spain, "Safe Havens," 223; Jones, "Struggle Among Saints," 169. Karger finds this true in Minneapolis's Phyllis Wheatley House, *Sentinels of Order*, 114–16. In at least one instance, a white group that could not dominate the Black settlement tried to crush it; Kramer, "Uplifting," 259.

148. The insult was newsworthy enough that the *Crisis* editorialized in their support: "They have declared that in principle the YWCA has no right to discriminate and that, therefore, they would not consent to a separate YWCA based on race and color." And yet the same *Crisis* article referred to the Phillis Wheatley Home as symbolizing "the generosity of American white folk." "Colored Girls in Cleveland," *Crisis*, December 1929, 411. See also Spratt, "To Be Separate or One," 199; Elizabeth Clark-Lewis, "'First You Helped Each Other': African American Women and Migration, 1900–1940," in *Black Women's History at the Intersection of Knowledge and Power*, ed. Rosalyn Terborg-Penn and Janice Sumler-Edmond (Acton, MA: Tapestry Press, 2000), 121–23; Carlton-LaNey and Hodges, "Reformers' Mission," 258–60, 266; Knupfer, "'If You Can't Push,'" 223; Carby, "Policing," 746. The Black sociologist E. Franklin Frazier criticized middle-class Blacks' reluctance to challenge the status quo; Tony Platt and Susan Chandler, "Constant Struggle: E. Franklin Frazier and Black Social Work in the 1920s," *Social Work* 33, no. 4 (1988): 295.

149. Editorial, *Cleveland Gazette*, January 21, 1911, quoted in Jones, *Hunter*, 47.

150. Frances R. Bartholomew, "A Northern Social Settlement for Negroes," *Southern Workman* 32, no. 2 (1903): 100.

151. Sarah Collins Fernandis, "Neighborhood Interpretations of a Social Settlement," *Southern Workman* 35, no. 1 (1906): 47.

152. Virginia R. Boynton, "Contested Terrain: The Struggle Over Gender Norms for Black Working-class Women in Cleveland's Phillis Wheatley Association, 1920–1950," *Ohio History*, no. 103 (Winter–Spring 1994): 14.

153. Quotations from Hunter, *Nickel and Prayer*, 127, and Boynton, "Contested Terrain," 14.

154. Knupfer, "'If You Can't Push,'" 223, 227; Phillips, "'But It Is a Fine Place,'" 396; Wiesenfeld, "Harlem YWCA," 67.

155. Salem, *To Better Our World*, 139–40; Spratt, "To Be Separate or One," 199.

156. Hunter, *Nickel and Prayer*, 90–91.

157. Hunter, *Nickel and Prayer*, app. A, 164.

158. Hunter, *Nickel and Prayer*, 90–91.

159. The political clout of these Black elites persuaded even Booker T. Washington not to endorse Hunter's project in its early years. George A. Myers to Booker T. Washington, July 20, 1914, in Hunter, *Nickel and Prayer*, 165. Harry C. Smith, founder of

Cleveland's Black newspaper the *Gazette*, never reconciled to the Phillis Wheatley Home; Kusmer, *Ghetto Takes Shape*, 148–50.

160. Giffin, *African Americans in Ohio*, 57.
161. Salem, *To Better Our World*, 140; Jones, *Hunter*, 53–54.
162. Jones, *Hunter*, 53; Spain, "Safe Havens," 273.
163. Board members paid dues of five dollars on joining and five dollars per year after that. Nonvoting "associate members" could join for just one dollar per year, after which they "gained the 'privilege' of promoting the organization, raising money, and participating in the activities" of the home. Salem, *To Better Our World*, 139.
164. Salem, *To Better Our World*, 138–39.
165. "Colored Girls in Cleveland," *Crisis*, December 1929, 411.
166. Salem, *To Better Our World*, 139–40.
167. Sadie Iola Daniels, *Women Builders* (Washington, DC: Associated Publishers, 1931).
168. Spain, "Safe Havens," 282.
169. Phillis Wheatley annual reports, in Spain, "Safe Havens"; "Colored Girls in Cleveland," *Crisis*, December 1929, 411–12. I have not been able to discover the difference in accommodations indicated by this wide range in price (from $39 to $98 in 2015 dollars).
170. Spain, "Safe Havens."
171. Matthews's White Rose Mission also taught "manners," and the Phillis Wheatley Home probably did so too; Kramer, "Uplifting," 252.
172. Annual reports cited in Spain, "Safe Havens," 285; Lasch-Quinn, *Black Neighbors*, 132–33.
173. "Colored Girls in Cleveland," *Crisis*, December 1929, 412; Daniels, *Women Builders*, 181; Spain, "Safe Havens," 270, 283.
174. Lasch-Quinn, *Black Neighbors*, 133; Morton, *And Sin No More*, 95–96.
175. Jones, "Struggle Among Saints," 179.
176. Boynton, "Contested Terrain," 17.
177. Hunter, *Nickel and Prayer*, 128–29.
178. Jones, *Hunter*, 116.
179. Lasch-Quinn, *Black Neighbors*, 133; Morton, *And Sin No More*, 95–96; Hunter, *Nickel and Prayer*, 123, 129.
180. Boynton, "Contested Terrain," 11.
181. Phillis Wheatley Home Board of Trustees minutes, October 9, 1928, quoted in Boynton, "Contested Terrain," 12.
182. Boynton, "Contested Terrain," 11.
183. Tera Hunter, *To "Joy My Freedom": Southern Black Women's Lives and Labors After the Civil War* (Cambridge, MA: Harvard University Press, 1998).
184. Jones, "Struggle Among Saints," 113; Boynton, "Contested Terrain," 14.
185. Hunter, *To "Joy My Freedom."*
186. Boynton, "Contested Terrain," 13, 17, 20.
187. Boynton, "Contested Terrain," 17–18.
188. Boynton, "Contested Terrain," 19.
189. Carby, "Policing," 742, 744, 746; Jones, "Struggle Among Saints."
190. "Colored Girls in Cleveland," *Crisis*, December 1929, 412. Carby's critique may be anachronistic, as she contrasts Hunter's regime to the cutting-edge, radical culture of Harlem in the 1920s.
191. Quoted in Rousmaniere, "Cultural Hybrid," 61.
192. In a sign of their distance from their clients, Hull-House women considered male-

headed families to be best for others even as they rejected marriage and often motherhood for themselves. Gordon, *Pitied But Not Entitled*.

2. From Ku Klux Klan to American Fascists, 1920s–1930s

1. *Congressional Record* 159, no. 108, S5951.
2. Albin Krebs, "Charles Coughlin, 30's 'Radio Priest'" (obituary), *New York Times*, October 28, 1979.
3. For a brief discussion of the synergy between electoral and social movement strategies, see Elisabeth Clemens, "Why We Should Rethink the Distinction Between 'Institutional' and 'Contentious' Politics," *Public Seminar*, March 30, 2022.
4. The southern Klan, by contrast, did not at first see any reason to expand into the North. An Alabama Kleagle responded to an organizer for the second Klan, "We don't need a Klan any more in this town. . . . We never did have any Catholics or Jews to be afraid of." "How I Put Over the Klan: 'Col.' William Joseph Simmons Tells His Story to William G. Shepherd," *Collier's*, July 14, 1928, 5.
5. While the KKK focused on Catholics as a key threat, for today's bigots Catholics are among the desirables. Contemporary promoters of the replacement threat might include the Florida state senator Dennis Baxley, who said that "when you get a birth rate less than two percent, that society is disappearing. And it's being replaced by folks that come behind them and immigrate, don't wish to assimilate into that society and they do believe in having children [and to] exterminate." Or Brian Babin, a Texas congressman: "They want to replace the American electorate with a Third World electorate that will be on welfare, public assistance, put them on a path to citizenship and amnesty, and franchise them with the vote, and they will have a permanent majority." These comments are drawn from the Global Project Against Hate and Extremism, at https://globalextremism.org/the-great-replacement/.
6. On the Know Nothings, see Tyler Anbinder, *Nativism and Slavery: The Northern Know Nothings and the Politics of the 1850s* (New York: Oxford University Press, 1992). To "gather facts" about what immigrant groups were desirable, nativist leaders constructed a multiple-choice questionnaire, which they sent to men whose opinions they valued, that is, those listed in *Who's Who*, Harvard Medical School graduates, prominent white southerners, and labor union officials such as Samuel Gompers (an ardent restrictionist). Unsurprisingly, the highly ranked were wealthy northern Europeans. Daniel Okrent, *The Guarded Gate: Bigotry, Eugenics, and the Law that Kept Two Generations of Jews, Italians, and Other European Immigrants Out of America* (New York: Scribner, 2019), 136, 237. As the Klan peaked in the mid-1920s, the Princeton psychologist Carl Campbell Brigham concluded that "Nordics" were superior even to "Alpine" or "Mediterranean" Europeans in his *A Study of American Intelligence* (Princeton, NJ: Princeton University Press, 1923). Using data supplied by Francis Amasa Walker, who ran the censuses of 1870 and 1880, Madison Grant then popularized the eugenic and anti-immigrant views of these elite scholars in his *The Passing of the Great Race* (New York: Charles Scribner's Sons, 1916), 104.
7. In the 1920s, chapters on eugenics appeared in most biology textbooks, and distinguished university professors promoted it. Okrent, *Guarded Gate*, 36, 237; Samuel P. Huntington, *Who Are We? The Challenges to America's Identity* (New York: Simon & Schuster, 2004).
8. Ben F. Johnson, *John Barleycorn Must Die: The War Against Drink in Arkansas* (Fayetteville: University of Arkansas Press, 2005).

9. Shawn Lay, "Imperial Outpost on the Border: El Paso's Frontier Klan No. 100," in *The Invisible Empire in the West: Toward a New Historical Appraisal of the Ku Klux Klan of the 1920s*, ed. Shawn Lay (Champaign: University of Illinois Press, 2004), 74; Glenn Michael Zuber, "'Onward Christian Klansmen!' War, Religious Conflict, and the Rise of the Second Ku Klux Klan, 1912–1928" (PhD diss., Indiana University, 2004), 284; Newell G. Bringhurst, "The Ku Klux Klan in a Central California Community: Tulare County During the 1920s and 1930s," *Southern California Quarterly* 82, no. 4 (2000): 376.

10. The first quotation is from Robert A. Goldberg, "The KKK in Madison, 1922–1927," *Wisconsin Magazine of History* 58, no. 1 (1974): 33. The second is from Mark Paul Richard, "'This Is Not a Catholic Nation': The KKK Confronts Franco-Americans in Maine," *New England Quarterly* 82, no. 2 (2009): 289. The third is from Kathleen M. Blee, *Inside Organized Racism: Women in the Hate Movement* (Berkeley: University of California Press, 2002), 130. Decades later sociologist Blee interviewed former Klanswomen and found that they still saw the Klan as an ordinary club; Kathleen M. Blee, "Evidence, Empathy, and Ethics: Lessons from Oral Histories of the Klan," *Journal of American History* 80, no. 2 (1993): 596–606.

11. There was considerable overlap in membership, but the 1920s DAR focused more on Americanizing than on excluding immigrants. It also focused more on fear of Communism than did the Klan. Carol Medlicott, "One Social Milieu, Paradoxical Responses: A Geographical Re-Examination of the Ku Klux Klan and the Daughters of the American Revolution in the Early Twentieth Century," in *Spaces of Hate: Geographies of Hate, Discrimination, and Intolerance in the United States*, ed. Colin Flint (London: Routledge, 2003).

12. *Congressional Record*, 159, no. 108 (July 25, 2013), S5951.

13. Blee, *Women of the Klan*, 87. Many more examples are in Linda Gordon, *The Second Coming of the KKK: The Ku Klux Klan of the 1920s and the American Political Tradition* (New York: Liveright, 2017), 46–49.

14. One Klan sympathizer told a journalist that even if it was a forgery, its message—that Jews were plotting to take over the world—was accurate. John L. Spivak, "Plotting the American Pogroms," *New Masses*, October 9, 1934, 10.

15. R. H. Sawyer, *The Truth About the Invisible Empire* (Portland, OR, 1922).

16. Frank Bohn, "Ku Klux Klan Interpreted," *American Journal of Sociology* 30, no. 4 (1925): 388. These allegations recall stories about white women kidnapped by Native Americans.

17. Tom Rice, "Protecting Protestantism: The Ku Klux Klan vs. the Motion Picture Industry," *Film History* 20, no. 4 (2008): 370–71, 374; Melissa Ooten, *Race, Gender and Film Censorship in Virginia, 1922–1965* (Boulder, CO: Lexington Books, 2015), 90; Tom Rice, "'The True Story of the Ku Klux Klan': Defining the Klan Through Film," *Journal of American Studies* 42, no. 3, (2008): 75.

18. Llewellyn Nelson, "The Ku Klux Klan for Boredom," *New Republic*, January 14, 1925, 196–98; Alva W. Taylor, "What the Klan Did in Indiana," *New Republic*, November 16, 1927, 330–32; John Grierson, untitled review, *American Journal of Sociology* 31, no. 1 (1925): 114–15; Bohn, "Ku Klux Klan Interpreted"; Frank Tannenbaum, *Darker Phases of the South* (New York: 1924); Kenneth T. Jackson, *The Ku Klux Klan in the City, 1915–1930* (Chicago: Ivan R. Dee, 1967), xiii; Wyn Craig Wade, *The Fiery Cross: The Ku Klux Klan in America* (New York: Simon & Schuster, 1987), 140; John Moffat Mecklin, *The Ku Klux Klan: A Study of the American Mind* (New York: Harcourt Brace, 1924).

19. Francis Butler Simkins, *A History of the South* (New York: Knopf, 1963), 545–46.

20. Malcolm M. Willey, untitled review, *American Journal of Sociology* 28, no. 3 (November 1922): 353–54; Arnold S. Rice, *The Ku Klux Klan in American Politics* (New York: Haskell House, 1972); William Peirce Randel, *The Ku Klux Klan: a Century of Infamy* (New York: Chilton, 1965); James M. Jasper, "Constructing Indignation: Anger Dynamics in Protest Movements," *Emotion Review* 6, no. 3 (2014): 208.

21. Charles C. Alexander, *The Ku Klux Klan in the Southwest* (Norman: University of Oklahoma Press, 1965); Jackson, *Klan in the City.* The critics' view that Klanspeople were poor and poorly educated finds echoes today, when some assume that right-wing populists represent the white working class. The median annual income of a Trump voter in 2016 was $72,000, while supporters of Hillary Clinton and Bernie Sanders earned $61,000. Nate Silver, "The Mythology of Trump's Working-Class Support," at fivethirtyeight.com/features/the-mythology-of-trumps-working-class support/

22. Robert D. Johnston, *The Radical Middle Class: Populist Democracy and the Question of Capitalism in Progressive Era Portland, Oregon* (Princeton, NJ: Princeton University Press, 2006).

23. For a fuller discussion of the costumes, see Alison Kinney, *Hood: Object Lessons* (London: Bloomsbury, 2016).

24. The author was Henry P. Fry, an ex-Kleagle and active Mason. Randel, *Ku Klux Klan*, 191; Miguel Hernandez, *The Ku Klux Klan and Freemasonry in 1920s America* (London: Routledge, 2019), 104.

25. George Lewis, "'An Amorphous Code': The Ku Klux Klan and Un-Americanism, 1915–1945," *Journal of American Studies* 47, no. 4 (2013): 976.

26. U.S. House of Representatives, 67th Congress, Committee on Rules, *Hearings on the Ku Klux Klan* (Washington, DC: GPO, 1921). William G. Shepherd claims that Georgia congressman William David "Wee Willie" Upshaw, who had been elected in 1919 with Klan votes, called for hearings *because* he figured that the publicity would help the Klan. Shepherd, "Ku Klux Koin," *Collier's*, July 21, 1928.

27. Felix Harcourt, *Ku Klux Kulture: America and the Klan in the 1920s* (Chicago: University of Chicago Press, 2017), 100; Charles Alexander, "Kleagles and Cash: The Ku Klux Klan as a Business Organization, 1915–1930," *Business History Review* 39, no. 3 (1965): 354.

28. Maxim Simcovitch, "The Impact of Griffith's 'Birth of a Nation' on the Modern Ku Klux Klan," *Journal of Popular Film* 1, no. 1 (1972): 45–54. Simcovitch makes the film largely responsible for the revival of the Klan, an exaggeration. Wilson is quoted in William Keylor, "The Long-Forgotten Racial Attitudes and Policies of Woodrow Wilson," *Professor Voices: Commentary, Insight and Analysis* (Boston University website), March 4, 2013.

29. The Kleagles functioned as traveling salesmen who sold products on commission. In other words, Klan membership was a commodity. The commission system was not unprecedented, as some fraternal orders also used it. Some southern members loyal to the first Klan charged that recruitment by commission was bringing in mere profit-seekers, who were not sufficiently motivated by defense of white supremacy. Mississippi senator LeRoy Percy criticized these unprincipled profiteers in the *Atlantic Monthly*, July 1922, 130, quoted in Hernandez, *Klan and Freemasonry*, 95–96, 99.

30. Randel, *Ku Klux Klan*, 193; Rice, *Klan in American Politics*, 18–19; Wade, *Fiery Cross*, 193; Craig Fox, *Everyday Klansfolk: White Protestant Life and the KKK in 1920s Michigan* (East Lansing: Michigan State University Press, 2011), chap. 1; Alexander, "Kleagles and Cash," 361. For a fuller discussion of the costumes, see Kinney, *Hood.*

31. Alexander, "Kleagles and Cash," 360; Ronald G. Fryer, Jr., and Steven D. Levitt,

"Hatred and Profits: Getting Under the Hood of the Ku Klux Klan," Working Paper No. 13417, National Bureau of Economic Research, September 2007, 11; Thomas M. Conroy, "The Ku Klux Klan and the American Clergy," *Ecclesiastical Review* 70 (1924): 50; Jackson, *Klan in the City*, 212.

32. Ben M. Bogard, *Ku Klux Klan Exposed* (1922), quoted in Hernandez, *Klan and Freemasonry*, 106.

33. Johnston, *Radical Middle Class*, 237; Hernandez, *Klan and Freemasonry*, 105–6; Blee, *Women of the Klan*, 2. The Klan thus contributed to a contemporary American usage in which part of the working class became middle class in common discourse, while others were labeled simply poor. Gordon, *Second Coming*, chap. 10.

34. Simmons told a reporter, "All of us at 'the Palace' used to take a drink. . . . Even when the Klan was fighting bootleggers, I asked. 'Why yes, that was a matter for each individual Klan.'" Simmons, "How I Put Over the Klan," 6.

35. "Jersey Organization Demands Expulsion of Two National Heads," *New York Times* September 21, 1921.

36. Winfield Jones, *Knights of the Ku Klux Klan* (New York: Tocsin, 1941), 141; Henry Fry, *The Modern Ku Klux Klan* (Boston: Small, Maynard, 1922), 31–32; Shepherd, "Ku Klux Koin," 9; Hernandez *Klan and Freemasonry*, 110.

37. Edgar Allen Booth, *The Mad Mullah of America* (Columbus, OH: B. Ellison, 1927), 39; Jones, *Knights of the Klan*, 142.

38. William D. Jenkins, *Steel Valley Klan: The Ku Klux Klan in Ohio's Mahoning Valley* (Kent, OH: Kent State University Press, 1990), 7; Richard K. Tucker, *The Dragon and the Cross: The Rise and Fall of the Ku Klux Klan in Middle America* (Hamden, CT: Archon Books, 1991), 93–94.

39. Zuber, "Onward," 162.

40. The following is based on a description of the Kokomo Klan rally of July 4, 1923, in Norman F. Weaver, "The Knights of the Ku Klux Klan in Wisconsin, Indiana, Ohio and Michigan" (PhD diss., University of Wisconsin, 1954), 157–58.

41. Linton Weeks, "When the KKK Was Mainstream," NPR, March 19, 2015.

42. Quoted in Fox, *Everyday Klansfolk*, 195; William Vance Trollinger, Jr., "The University of Dayton, the Ku Klux Klan, and Catholic Universities and Colleges in the 1920s," *American Catholic Studies* 124, no. 1 (Spring 2013): 8. The Klan's airplane stunts prefigured those of the fascists, particularly one made famous by Italian fascist pilot Italo Balbo; he led a squadron of daredevil seaplanes from Rome to Chicago, arriving at the 1933 World's Fair (commemorating the city's founding in 1833) to a cheering crowd of thousands. Curtis Black, "Behind Fascist Balbo Monument," *Chicago Reporter*, August 22, 2017, at https://www.chicagoreporter.com/behind-fascist-balbo-monument-a-history-of-multiracial-resistance/.

43. See the chapter on KKK women's activism, including a defense of applying the label *feminist*, in Gordon, *Second Coming*.

44. *Fiery Cross*, 1923, quoted in Blee, *Women of the Klan*, 24.

45. WKKK, *Women of America*, pamphlet, author's collection, 7.

46. My interpretation of secrecy was influenced by Allen Hunter, who directed me to Georg Simmel, "The Sociology of Secrecy and of Secret Societies," *American Journal of Sociology* 11, no. 4 (1906): 441–98.

47. Material on KKK rituals is from Florida Realm, Knights of the Ku Klux Klan, "The Seven Symbols of the Klan," author's collection. A fuller summary of Klavern ritual is in Gordon, *Second Coming*.

48. The Cyclops, sometimes spelled *cuclops* or *kuclops*, may have come from the

Illuminati—anti-Catholic societies formed in the eighteenth century—whose single all-seeing eye originally signaled opposition to obscurantism and superstition. Other derived from enemy sources: a Klan motto—*Non Silba Sed Anthar*, "Not for Self but for Others"—mixed Latin and Gothic, typical of its pastiche. Years were counted in Roman numerals and dated from the founding of the first Klan, so that AD 1922 became AK LVI.

49. Blee, *Women of the Klan*, 38. The songs included "Battle Hymn of the Republic" and "The Star-Spangled Banner" on the patriotic side, and "Whiter than Snow," "In the Cross of Christ I Glory," and "Blest Be the Tie that Bind" on the religious side. WKKK, *Musiklan* (Little Rock, n.d.), author's collection.

50. KKK choreography is further analyzed in Linda Gordon, "Visual Demagoguery" (unpub. ms., American Studies Association conference, 2019).

51. Francesca Polletta, *Freedom Is an Endless Meeting: Democracy in American Social Movements* (Chicago: University of Chicago Press, 2012), 224.

52. When performed by soldiers, unison movement leads them to see potential enemies as less threatening—and by consequence, themselves as more powerful. Jorina von Zimmermann et al., "The Choreography of Group Affiliation," *Topics in Cognitive Science*, no. 10 (2018): 80–94; Wray Herbert, "All Together Now: The Universal Appeal of Moving in Unison," *Scientific American*, April 1, 2009.

53. Jeffrey T. Schnapp, "Fascinating Fascism," *Journal of Contemporary History* 32, no. 2 (1996): 237.

54. The KKK's notion of "true America" resembles Benedict Anderson's notion of an imagined nation in his *Imagined Communities: Reflections on the Origins and Spread of Nationalism* (London: Verso, 1983).

55. In a 1922 Chicago event, 4,650 initiates joined; in Dayton in 1923, 7,000; in Farmingdale, New Jersey, 1,700; in Oakland, California, 500. Jackson, *Klan in the City*, 97; Trollinger, "University of Dayton," 7–8; Chris Rhomberg, "White Nativism and Urban Politics: The 1920s Ku Klux Klan in Oakland, California," *Journal of American Ethnic History* 17, no. 2 (1998): 46; *Matawan Journal*, August 31, 1923.

56. Susan Sontag, "Fascinating Fascism," *New York Review of Books*, February 6, 1975.

57. A former Kleagle from New York, speaking at the congressional investigation, described the KKK's purpose as to create a body that would all vote one way and thus "gain control" by putting "their own men in office." Lewis, "Amorphous Code," 978.

58. Zuber, "Onward," 227–28; James H. Madison, "The Klan's Enemies Step Up, Slowly," *Indiana Magazine of History*, no. 116 (2020): 114.

59. Goldberg, "KKK in Madison," 38; Alma White, *The Ku Klux Klan in Prophecy* (Zarephath, NJ: Good Citizen, 1925), 121–22; Rory McVeigh, "Structural Incentives for Conservative Mobilization: Power Devaluation and the Rise of the Ku Klux Klan, 1915–1925," *Social Forces* 77, no. 4 (1999): 2; William Loren Katz, *The Invisible Empire: The Ku Klux Klan Impact on History* (Washington, DC: Open Hand, 1987), 99. The Southern Poverty Law Center has counted twelve Klansmen serving as governors.

60. Wade, *Fiery Cross*, 196–97; Glenn Feldman, *Politics, Society and the Klan in Alabama, 1915–1949* (Tuscaloosa: University of Alabama Press, 1999), 24.

61. Tucker, *Dragon and Cross*, 54; Kristofer Allerfeldt, "Jayhawker Fraternities: Masons, Klansmen, and Kansas in the 1920s," *Journal of American Studies* 46, no. 4 (2012): 1042.

62. The Klan's ability to intimidate—and support—politicians resembles that of the NRA today.

63. *Chicago Daily Tribune*, October 24, 1924, quoted in Tara McAndrew, "The History of the KKK in American Politics," *JSTOR Daily*, January 25, 2017.

64. William Toll, "Progress and Piety: The Ku Klux Klan and Social Change in Tillamook, Oregon," *Pacific Northwest Quarterly* 69, no. 2 (1978): 79; McLain, "Unmasking the Oregon Klansman"; Michael W. Schuyler, "The Ku Klux Klan in Nebraska, 1920-1930," *Nebraska History* 66 (1985): 252.

65. The first KKK had been a major force in Indiana, which made it fertile ground for the second, which claimed 445 new recruits as of July 1922, peaking at 9,580 a year later; Leonard J. Moore, *Citizen Klansmen: The Ku Klux Klan in Indiana* (Chapel Hill: University of North Carolina, 1991), 17.

66. Weaver, "Knights of the Klan," 308–11; Tucker, *Dragon and Cross*, 103, 116.

67. Ron E. Smith, "The Klan's Retribution Against an Indiana Editor," *Indiana Magazine of History* 106, no. 4 (2010): 381–400.

68. Quoted in Rhomberg, "White Nativism," 44.

69. Barr and other Klanswomen are discussed at length in Gordon, *Second Coming*, chap. 7. Barr is profiled in Dwight W. Hoover, "From Quaker to Klan 'Kluckeress,'" *Indiana Magazine of History* 87, no. 2 (1991): 171–95; and by Stephen J. Taylor, "A Ku Klux Quaker?" *Historic Indianapolis*, September 28, 2015.

70. Blee, *Women of the Klan*, 115, 150; Allerfeldt, "Jayhawker," 1048.

71. In an attempt to make the ban constitutional, the Klan proposed banning all private schools, promoting such bills as nonprejudicial. But that fooled neither Klan supporters, who understood it as a weapon against Catholics, nor Klan opponents. The Klan did succeed in getting a Columbus Day holiday eliminated. Weaver, "Knights of the Klan," 165–7; Hatle and Vaillancourt, "One School, One Language," 367. Seeing the "Little Red Schoolhouse" float used in a Klan parade, one ten-year-old Catholic boy understood it perfectly: "it was a body blow," he recalled. Testimony of a "Klan Victim" from North Judson, Indiana, author's collection.

72. "Court Invalidates Oregon School Law," *New York Times*, April 1, 1924.

73. M. P. Holsinger, "The Oregon School Bill Controversy, 1922–1925," *Pacific Historical Review* 37, no. 3 (1968): 336; Lawrence J. Saalfeld, *Forces of Prejudice in Oregon, 1920–1925* (Portland, OR: Archdiocesan Historical Commission, 1974), 72; Goldberg, "KKK in Madison," 36.

74. Klan bills required that lessons include the creation story and the expulsion from Eden. Often it was entirely open about this agenda: "One of our purposes is to try to get the Bible back into the schools," said Oregon Klan minister Reuben H. Sawyer, quoted in Jackson, *Klan in the City*, 205; Kelly J. Baker, *Gospel According to the Klan: The Ku Klux Klan's Appeal to Protestant America, 1915–1930* (Lawrence: University Press of Kansas, 2011); Eckard V. Toy, "Robe and Gown: The Ku Klux Klan in Eugene, Oregon, During the 1920s," in *The Invisible Empire in the West: Toward a New Historical Appraisal of the Ku Klux Klan of the 1920s*, ed. Shawn Lay (Urbana: University of Illinois Press, 1992, 2004), 160ff.

75. "Poorly Restricted Immigration Is One of the Greatest Perils Confronting America," *Imperial Night-Hawk*, August 29, 1923.

76. Hiram Wesley Evans, "The Klan's Fight for Americanism," *North American Review* 223, no. 830 (March–May 1926): 42.

77. Kristofer Allerfeldt, "'And We Got Here First': Albert Johnson, National Origins and Self-Interest in the Immigration Debate of the 1920s," *Journal of Contemporary History* 45, no. 1 (2010): 22; Aaron Goings, "Albert Johnson," at https://www.historylink.org/File/8721.

78. Mae M. Ngai, *Impossible Subjects: Illegal Aliens and the Making of Modern America* (Princeton, NJ: Princeton University Press), 48, 288n97; Doug Blair, "The 1920 Anti-Japanese Crusade and Congressional Hearings," Seattle Civil Rights and Labor History Project, 2006, depts.washington.edu/civilr/Japanese_restriction.htm.

79. Adam Hochschild, 'Obstruction of Injustice," *New Yorker*, November 11, 2019. Emma Goldman was in this group of deportees and actually exchanged barbs with Hoover.

80. A survey of newspaper coverage of the Johnson-Reed Act found that the only criticisms came from the African American *Chicago Defender*. A cartoon shows a white California landowner—threatened by the efficient Japanese small farmers—throwing a brick that bounces off the head of a Japanese man and strikes the head of an African American; the caption reads, "Perhaps it wasn't intended for us, but—" Bradley J. Hamm, "Newspaper Justification for the 1924 Exclusion of Japanese Immigrants," *American Journalism* 16, no. 3 (1999): 58.

81. Tyler C. Cline, "'A Dragon, Bog-Spawned, Is Now Stretched o'er This Land': Nativism and the Rise of Patriotic-Protestantism in the Northeastern Borderlands During the 1920s and 1930s" (MA thesis, University of Maine, 2017), 12.

82. Malcolm X with Alex Haley, *The Autobiography of Malcolm X* (New York: Grove Press, 1965), chap. 1.

83. Clark, "Bigot Disclosed," 155.

84. Neill, *Fiery Crosses*, 30.

85. Jenkins, *Steel Valley Klan*, 26; Jerry Wallace, "The Ku Klux Klan Comes to Kowley Kounty, Kansas: Its Public Face, 1921–22," in *Celebrate Winfield History 2012* (Winfield, KS: Cowley County Historical Society, 2012), 11.

86. Hernandez, *Klan and Freemasonry*, 138; Hunt, "Fundamentalist–Ku Klux Klan Alliance," 86. When implicated in violence, the KKK often charged that criminal "aliens" seeking to smear the organization masqueraded in white robes, or that the accusations came from the Catholic-controlled press; David Norberg, "Ku Klux Klan in the Valley: A 1920s Phenomena [*sic*]," *White River Journal* (January 2004), White River Valley Museum, http://www.wrvmuseum.org/journal/journal_0104.htm.

87. Shawn Lay, *Hooded Knights on the Niagara: The KKK in Buffalo, New York* (New York: NYU Press, 1995), 71, 74; David M. Chalmers, *Hooded Americanism: The History of the Ku Klux Klan* (Durham, NC: Duke University Press, 1987), 213; Dana M. Caldemeyer, "Conditional Conservatism: Evansville, Indiana's Embrace of the Ku Klux Klan," *Ohio Valley History* 11, no. 4 (2011): 6; John Zerzan, "Rank-and-File Radicalism Within the KKK of the 1920s," *Anarchy* 37 (Summer 1993), 48–53.

88. Malcolm Clark, Jr., "The Bigot Disclosed: 90 Years of Nativism," *Oregon Historical Quarterly* 75, no. 2 (1974): 154–58.

89. Goldberg, "KKK in Madison," 34, 36, 40–41. On the role of women in supporting or even fomenting vigilantism, see Linda Gordon, *The Great Arizona Orphan Abduction* (New York: W. W. Norton, 1999).

90. Christopher N. Cocoltchos, "The Invisible Empire and the Search for the Orderly Community: The Ku Klux Klan in Anaheim, California," in *The Invisible Empire in the West: Toward a New Historical Appraisal of the Ku Klux Klan of the 1920s*, ed. Shawn Lay (Urbana: University of Illinois Press, 1992, 2004), 112, 114; Tucker, *Dragon and Cross*, 83.

91. A contemporary observer wrote that "night-riding" was "the great attraction . . . that renders the greatest personal satisfaction." *Outlook*, January 30, 1924, 184, quoted in Charles Easton Rothwell, "The Ku Klux Klan in the State of Oregon" (BA the-

sis, Reed College, 1924), 56; Evans, "Klan's Fight for Americanism," 18; Goldberg, "KKK in Madison," 38.

92. David A. Horowitz, "Order, Solidarity, and Vigilance: The Ku Klux Klan in La Grande, Oregon," in Lay, ed., *Invisible Empire*, 190.

93. Saalfeld, *Forces of Prejudice in Oregon*, 23; Jeffrey M. LaLande, "Beneath the Hooded Robe: Newspapermen, Local Politics, and the Ku Klux Klan in Jackson County, Oregon, 1921–1923," *Pacific Northwest Quarterly* 83, no. 2 (1992): 42–52.

94. University KKK fraternities of the 1920s are only just beginning to be discovered, but they were present at Harvard and at the Universities of Illinois, Nebraska, Virginia, Washington, Wisconsin, and many others. On the Klan at the University of Wisconsin, see Stephen Kantrowitz and Floyd Rose, "Report to the Chancellor on the Ku Klux Klan at the University of Wisconsin–Madison," April 4, 2018, https://news.wisc.edu/content/uploads/2018/04/Study-Group-final-for-print-April-18.pdf.

95. Timothy Messer-Kruse, "The Campus Klan of the University of Wisconsin: Tacit and Active Support for the Ku Klux Klan in a Culture of Intolerance," *Wisconsin Magazine of History* 77, no. 1 (1993): 4; Goldberg, "KKK in Madison," 31–44. Klan enemies also used these gendered insults: an anti-Klan newspaper called their robes "nightgowns"; Madison, "Klan's Enemies," 100.

96. Richard, " 'Not a Catholic Nation,' " 301.

97. Wallace, "Klan Comes to Kowley Kounty," 13–14; LaLande, "Beneath the Hooded Robe"; Eckard Vance Toy, "The Ku Klux Klan in Oregon: Its Character and Program" (MA thesis, University of Oregon, 1959), 70–73; Max Price, "The Oregon Ku Klux Klan: A Failed Attempt at Creating a Homogeneous State" (unpub. ms., Pacific University, 2011), 25.

98. Larry O'Dell, "Ku Klux Klan," in *Encyclopedia of Oklahoma History and Culture*, OKHistory.org; Allerfeldt, "Jayhawker," 1049.

99. "The Twenties in Contemporary Commentary: The Ku Klux Klan," National Humanities Center, n.d., http://americainclass.org/sources/becomingmodern/divisions/text1/colcommentaryklan.pdf.

100. Alfred L. Brophy, "Norms, Law, and Reparations: The Case of the Ku Klux Klan in 1920s Oklahoma," *Harvard BlackLetter Law Journal* 20 (2004): 37.

101. Gordon, *Second Coming*, 104–6.

102. As a result, native-born miners deserted the previously strong United Mine Workers and the Socialist Party—a major shift in local politics. Caldemeyer, "Conditional Conservatism," 8, 12–13, 17, 19; Goldberg, "KKK in Madison," 38. In one Indiana UMW local, 80 percent of members were Klansmen, 50 to 75 percent in others; Zerzan, "Rank-and-File Radicalism."

103. The fullest discussion of KKK relations to labor unions is Thomas R. Pegram's "The Ku Klux Klan, Labor, and the White Working Class during the 1920s," *Journal of the Gilded Age and Progressive Era*, no. 17 (2018): 375. When some AFL leaders sought to denounce the Klan, many of their members refused to go along; Benjamin Schmack, "Denouncing the Hooded Order: Radicalism, Identity and Dissent in the UMWA," *American Studies* 57, no. 4 (2019): 61. The distinguished Progressive journalists William Allen White and Emanuel Haldeman-Julius charged that employers sometimes financed the Klan's attacks on labor; James N. Leiker, "The Klan in the Coal Mines: The End of Kansas's Reform Era in the 1920s," *Western Historical Quarterly*, no. 48 (Autumn 2017): 288, 293–97.

104. Erasmo Gamboa, "Chicanos in the Northwest: A Historical Perspective," Chicano Studies Institutes paper (Summer 1971); Clark, "Bigot Disclosed; Jim Gen-

try, *In the Middle and On the Edge* (Twin Falls: College of Southern Idaho, 2003); Thomas H. Heuterman, *The Burning Horse: The Japanese-American Experience in the Yakima Valley* (Cheney: Eastern Washington University Press, 1995), 95–108; Linda Tamura, *The Hood River Issei: An Oral History of Japanese Settlers in Oregon's Hood River Valley* (Champaign: University of Illinois Press, 1993), 88ff; William Toll, "Black Families and Migration to a Multiracial Society: Portland, Oregon, 1900–1924," *Journal of American Ethnic History* 17, no. 3 (1998): 40, 57; Ngai, *Impossible Subjects*, 40, 46–47.

105. In fact, Asians were not undercutting white wages; rather, employers established dual wage rates, with white men earning more for the same work and accessing preferable jobs denied to Asians. The Klan and its supporters also accused Filipinos of sexual immorality: almost all single men, Filipinos frequented bars and dance halls where they patronized prostitutes and even dated white women. Richard Baldoz, "Valorizing Racial Boundaries: Hegemony and Conflict in the Racialization of Filipino Migrant Labour in the United States," *Ethnic and Racial Studies* 27, no. 6 (2004): 975.

106. Blair, "1920 Anti-Japanese Crusade."

107. Yakima Valley vigilantes compared their activity to those who sought to bring law and order in the California Gold Rush; Donald W. Meyers, "Union Members, Farmers Battle at Congdon Orchards," *Yakima Herald-Republic*, September 6, 2022. Asian farmers and farmworkers gained unexpected support from Yakama Indians, who considered their nation exempt from these restrictions and leased land to Japanese farmers, which of course escalated hostility to these Native Americans. One newspaper headlined "YAKIMA VALLEY IN JAP WAR." Thomas H. Heuterman, "'We Have the Same Rights as Other Citizens': Coverage of Yakima Valley Japanese Americans in the Missing Decades of the 1920s and 1930s," *Journalism History* 14, no. 4 (1987): 94; Heuterman, *Burning Horse*, 95–108; Ngai, *Impossible Subjects*, 105ff., 114; Gamboa, "Chicanos in the Northwest"; Trevor Griffey, "The Ku Klux Klan and Vigilante Culture in the Yakima Valley," Seattle Civil Rights and Labor History Project, http://depts.washington.edu/civilr/kkk_yakima.htm; Baldoz, "Valorizing," 980; Gordon, *Second Coming*, 145–47. These attacks foreshadowed the internment of 120,000 Japanese Americans during World War II. The role of racism is evident: German and Italian Americans were interned in much smaller numbers, although German American support for the Nazi regime was much greater than Japanese American support for the fascist regime in Japan. Moreover, interning European Americans was based on a review of each individual, in contrast to the mass internment of every Japanese American on the West Coast and Hawaii. True, the KKK was not solely responsible for the hysteria, but its decade-long drumbeat of bigotry influenced many white Americans.

108. Benjamin Herzl Avin, "The Ku Klux Klan, 1915–1925: A Study in Religious Intolerance" (PhD. diss., Georgetown University, 1952), 226–27; Bringhurst, "Klux in Central California," 369; V. Wayne Kenaston, Jr., quoted in Carlos M. Larralde and Richard Griswold del Castillo, "San Diego's Ku Klux Klan, 1920–1980," *San Diego Historical Society Quarterly* 46, nos. 2–3 (2000); William D. Carrigan and Clive Webb, *Forgotten Dead: Mob Violence Against Mexicans in the United States, 1848–1928* (New York: Oxford University Press, 2013), 148, 150.

109. To the best of my knowledge, the only study focused on resistance to the 1920s northern Klan is David J. Goldberg, "Unmasking the Ku Klux Klan: The Northern Movement Against the KKK, 1920–1925," *Journal of American Ethnic History* 15, no. 4 (1996): 32–48.

110. In Dayton, Catholic university leaders did not bother to call the police because they

knew the police would take no action; Trollinger, "University of Dayton," 7. The Dayton Klan alleged that the university's ROTC was training a clandestine Catholic army; Paola Flores, "Kluxing on Kampus, 1910–1933," *Ideals*, February 18, 2019; Todd Tucker, *Notre Dame vs. the Klan: How the Fighting Irish Defeated the Ku Klux Klan* (Chicago: Loyola Press, 2004); Madison, "Klan's Enemies," 102; Jenkins, *Steel Valley Klan.*

111. Douglas Flamming, *Bound for Freedom: Black Los Angeles in Jim Crow America* (Berkeley: University of California Press, 2005), 211.

112. The New Jersey Klan put on eighty-one public events in 1923–24 including three thousand initiations and at least nine cross burnings; "Klan in New Jersey Initiates 3,000," *Imperial Night-Hawk*, July 16, 1924. When a KKK automobile parade marched past Princeton, some eight hundred students poured out of the campus, stalled the parade, and ripped off some white hoods.

113. One historian concluded that opponents were more violent than the Klan; Goldberg, "Unmasking the Klan," 42.

114. David Renton makes this argument in his *Fascism: History and Theory* (London: Pluto Press, 2020).

115. *Reform Advocate*, June 27, 1935, discussed the Klan's use of the march to stop its decline. "40,000 Klansmen Parade in Washington," *New York Times*, August 9, 1925, put the number of marchers at forty thousand. Quotations are from several newspaper reports gathered in Gonzalo Pacanins, "When the Klan Descended on Washington," *Boundary Stones*, December 11, 2019.

116. "40,000 Klansmen Parade in Washington," *New York Times*, August 9, 1925, put the number of spectators at 200,000.

117. My description of the march path is indebted to Sarah Leavitt. See also Pacanins, "When the Klan Descended."

118. Pacanins, "When the Klan Descended."

119. Zuber, "Onward," 362.

120. For example, Minutes, in Horowitz, *Inside the Klavern*, 34, 44, 143, 146. Imperial Wizard Hiram Evans attempted to stanch the bleeding from Fox's crime by calling it a "personal affair."

121. Allen Safianow, "The Klan Comes to Tipton," *Indiana Magazine of History* 95, no. 3 (1999): 226; Alva W. Taylor, "What the Klan Did in Indiana," *New Republic*, November 16, 1927, 330–32.

122. Always one of the least disciplined of Klan leaders, Stephenson provided an irresistible subject for journalists and writers. His first biography appeared just a few years after his trial, in 1927. Material about him comes from Booth, *Mad Mullah*; Taylor, "What the Klan Did"; M. William Lutholtz, *Grand Dragon: D. C. Stephenson and the Ku Klux Klan in Indiana* (West Lafayette, IN: Purdue University Press, 1991); Karen Abbott, "'Murder Wasn't Very Pretty': The Rise and Fall of D. C. Stephenson," *Smithsonian Magazine*, August 12, 2012; Doug Linder, "The D. C. Stephenson Trial: An Account," Famous-Trials.com, n.d.

123. "Hold Sex-Klansman on Assault Charge," *New York Times*, April 4, 1925. NBC produced a two-part TV miniseries, *Cross of Fire*, on the event, broadcast November 5, 1989.

124. Attorney Donald G. Hughes to Atlanta Klan headquarters, August 20, 1923, quoted in Marion Monteval, *The Klan Inside-Out* (Claremore, OK: Monarch, 1924), 113; Zuber, "Onward," 364.

125. Joseph Fronczak, *Everything Is Possible: Antifascism and the Left in the Age of Fascism* (New Haven, CT: Yale University Press, 2023), 26–29, 46, 57, 89.

126. In some localities, the process was reversed, and fascist groups revitalized the Klan. Some merely reprinted and distributed Klan literature. Sarah Churchwell, "The Return of American Fascism," *New Statesman*, September 2, 2020; John Roy Carlson, *Under Cover: My Four Years in the Nazi Underworld of America* (Philadelphia: Blakiston, 1943), 152, 291, 312, 336, 392, 402, 504, 520; Philip Jenkins, *Hoods and Shirts: The Extreme Right in Pennsylvania, 1925–1950* (Chapel Hill: University of North Carolina Press, 2000), chap. 5, 114; Leonard Dinnerstein, *Antisemitism in America* (New York: Oxford University Press, 1991), 112; Richard Bak, "The Dark Days of the Black Legion," *Hour Detroit*, February 23, 2009.

127. Benjamin Stolberg, "Vigilantism, 1937," *Nation*, August 14, 1937.

128. Salaina Catalano, in "When It Happened Here: Michigan and the Transnational Development of American Fascism, 1920–1945," *Michigan Historical Review* 46, no. 1 (2020), categorizes the fascist groups by type: anti-labor organizing, anti-Communist, and immigrant/veterans, though of course these types are overlapping. The more upper-class America First Committee, established in 1940 with Charles Lindbergh as its major spokesman, claimed 800,000 members; it was not explicitly fascist but added anti–Semitism to its isolationism and focused on preventing war against the Nazi regime. It should not be confused with the America First *Party*, founded by Gerald L. K. Smith in 1943, or with the America First *Movement*, an organization of women's groups that incorporated defense of "family values" into its patriotism, defined in a manner similar to that of Phyllis Schlafly's 1970s Stop ERA organization. Both were isolationist and vehemently anti–New Deal, but the women's organization did not make anti–Semitism central to its ideology or activism. On America First, see Laura McEnaney, "He-Men and Christian Mothers: The America First Movement and the Gendered Meanings of Patriotism and Isolationism," *Diplomatic History* 18, no. 1 (1994): 47–57; Thomas Milan Konda, *Conspiracies of Conspiracies: How Delusions Have Overrun America* (Chicago: University of Chicago Press, 2019), 76; Leland V. Bell, "The Failure of Nazism in America: The German American Bund," *Political Science Quarterly* 85, no. 1 (1970): 591–93, 569–70, 589; Jenkins, *Hoods and Shirts*, chap. 5, 114; George Morris, *The Black Legion Rides* (New York: Workers Library, 1936); Joachim Remak, "Friends of the New Germany: The Bund and German-American Relations," *Journal of Modern History* 29, no. 1 (1957): 39; Rick Perlstein, "I Thought I Understood the American Right. Trump Proved Me Wrong," *New York Times*, April 11, 2017; Krishnadev Calamur, "A Short History of 'America First,'" *Atlantic*, January 21, 2017; Simon Wendt, "Defenders of Patriotism or Mothers of Fascism? The Daughters of the American Revolution, Antiradicalism, and Un-Americanism in the Interwar Period," *Journal of American Studies* 47, no. 4 (2013): 963.

129. Frederick Marksman, "These Are the 10 Cities in Ohio with the Most KKK Members," RoadSnacks.net, June 22, 2016.

130. "22 Black Legion Men Indicted for Plotting Coup," *American Jewish World*, August 28, 1936; Peter H. Amman, "A 'Dog in the Nighttime' Problem: American Fascism in the 1930s," *History Teacher* 19, no. 4 (1986): 567; Carlson, *Under Cover*, 285.

131. Joseph Fronczak, "The Fascist Game: Transnational Political Transmission and the Genesis of the U.S. Modern Right," *Journal of American History* 12 (2018): 567–68.

132. John L. Spivak, "Who Backs the Black Legion?" *New Masses*, June 9, 1936; Konda, *Conspiracies*, 76.

133. I have been unable to find the origin or meaning of *Lixto*. The first quotation is from Peter H. Amman, "Vigilante Fascism: The Black Legion as an American Hybrid," *Comparative Studies in Society and History* 25, no. 3 (1983): 496. The second is from

"22 Black Legion Men Indicted for Plotting Coup," *American Jewish World*, August 28, 1936. See also Morris, *Black Legion Rides*; Amman, "'Dog in Nighttime,'" 566; Andrew G. Palella, "The Black Legion: J. Edgar Hoover and Fascism in Depression Era," *Journal for the Study of Radicalism* 12, no. 2 (2018): 81; Catalano, "When It Happened Here," 46–47; Palella, "Black Legion," 83; Tom Stanton, *Terror in the City of Champions: Murder, Baseball, and the Secret Society That Shocked Depression-era Detroit* (Guilford, CT: Rowman & Littlefield, 2016), 156.

134. Frank B. Wanat, "The Silver Shirts: A Venture in Frustrated Fascism" (MA thesis, Youngstown State University, 1974), 46, 55.

135. Wanat, "Silver Shirts," 12; Eckard V. Toy, "Silver Shirts in the Northwest: Politics, Prophecies, and Personalities in the 1930s," *Pacific Northwest Quarterly* 80, no. 4 (1989): 142; Nick Centrella, "Rifles and Rhetoric: Paramilitary Anti-Semitism in the New Deal Era" (honors thesis, Boston College, 2015), 64–66, quotations at 56, 66.

136. Portland's police established a Red Squad whose leader, a Silver Shirt, opined that "if it were not for the Communist Party, there would be no Fascist or Nazi scare." Shane Burley and Alexander Reid Ross, "From Nativism to White Power: Mid-Twentieth-Century White Supremacist Movements in Oregon," *Oregon Historical Quarterly* 120, no. 4 (2019): 570–72.

137. Zachary shared Pelley's taste for the supernatural: he had a "clauradient" ear that received God's voice and messages "via the Psychic Eadio [*sic*], from Great Souls who graduated out of this Three-Dimensional world." Wanat, "Silver Shirts," 37–38. See also Bradley W. Hart, *Hitler's American Friends: The Third Reich's Supporters in the United States* (New York: St. Martin's Press, 2018), 64 and chap. 2 passim.

138. "The Franklin Prophecy," sometimes called "The Franklin Forgery," is an anti-Semitic speech falsely attributed to Benjamin Franklin, warning of the supposed dangers of admitting Jews to the nascent United States. The speech was purportedly transcribed by Charles Cotesworth Pinckney during the Constitutional Convention of 1787, but it was unknown before its appearance in 1934 in the Silver Legion's magazine *Liberation*. No evidence exists for the document's authenticity, and some of Pelley's claims have actively been disproven. Scott D. Seligman, "The Franklin Prophecy," *Tablet*, August 4, 2021. The Silver Legion also used "black psy war," forging and distributing forged leaflets ostensibly from the Communist Party that threatened violence, just as the Klan had distributed threats allegedly from the Catholic hierarchy.

139. Wanat, "Silver Shirts," 21, 43, 49; Suzanne G. Ledeboer, "The Man Who Would Be Hitler: William Dudley Pelley and the Silver Legion," *California History* 65, no. 2 (1986): 129; Burley and Ross, "Nativism to White Power," 567–68.

140. Konda, *Conspiracies*, 78. With an opportunism born of growing world fascism, Pelley asked a Chehalis, Washington, leader to give him the names of "key Japs" he could ask for financial support on the ground that "my destiny is peculiarly wound up with Nippon's." Yet he instructed a Silver organizer in the Northwest to "stress the economic situation . . . avoid mention of Jew." Quoted in Toy, "Silver Shirts," 143–44.

141. Shane Burley and Alexander Reid Ross, "Fascism, Anti-Semitism, and the Roots of Oregon's White Power Movement," *Journal of Social Justice* 9 (2019): 7; Burley and Ross, "From Nativism to White Power," 570. In theory, women were welcome in the Silver Legion, but I could find no information about their role or whether they were armed.

142. Centrella, "Rifles and Rhetoric," 56; Toy, "Silver Shirts," passim; Donald Warren, *Radio Priest: Charles Coughlin the Father of Hate Radio* (New York: Free Press,

1996), 131. Pelley's *New Liberator* issue of June 1931 is quoted in "The Repercussions of Hitlerism in the United States," at http://www.ajcarchives.org/ajc_data/files/thr-ss3.pdf.

143. Wanat, "Silver Shirts," 41–42; Centrella, "Rifles and Rhetoric," 70–71; Ledeboer, "Man Who Would Be Hitler." On murders disguised as suicides, see "Detroit Anti-Semitic Night Riders Linked to Scores of Unsolved Murders," *Sentinel*, May 28, 1936. The typhoid plot was reported in "Another 'Black Legion' Plot," *B'nai Brith Messenger*, August 21, 1936, 4; Bak, "Dark Days"; Amman, "Vigilante Fascism"; Catalano, "When It Happened Here," 46–47; Morris, *Black Legion Rides*; Warren, *Radio Priest*, 131.

144. Some corporate leaders actually planned a coup, later known as the "Business Plot." The American Liberty League, founded in 1934 by big-business men and right-wing politicians furious at FDR's New Deal proposals, approached Marine General Smedley Butler with a plan: if he would lead some 500,000 veterans to overthrow the president, they would contribute $30 million (equivalent to $56 million in 2020) and supply weapons from Remington Arms. General Butler reported their venture to the FBI, which told FDR. When it became public, all those involved denied it, but the House committee investigating un-American activities concluded that it "might have been placed in execution when and if the financial backers deemed it expedient." The most recent source is Sally Denton, *The Plots Against the President: FDR, A Nation in Crisis, and the Rise of the American Right* (London: Bloomsbury, 2012).

145. Stolberg, "Vigilantism, 1937."

146. The legions functioned as a "counterrevolutionary vanguard against . . . the surge of labor militancy"; Fronczak, "Fascist Game," 576. On the legions' strikebreaking in Pennsylvania, see Philip Jenkins, "'It Can't Happen Here': Fascism and Right-wing Extremism in Pennsylvania, 1933–1942," *Journal of Mid-Atlantic Studies* 62, no. 1 (1995): 38. On Silver and Black Legion cooperation, see *B'nai Brith Messenger*, June 19, 1936, reporting on the Dickstein investigation. *The Nation* called the Black Legion a "brainchild" of industrialists, as reported in *American Jewish World*, June 12, 1936.

147. Quoted in Centrella, "Rifles and Rhetoric," 66.

148. His was an informed estimate: a grand jury indicted twenty-nine Detroit police for murder. *American Jewish World*, June 12, 1936; "Vigilantes Exposed in Cleveland," *Reform Advocate* (Chicago), August 13, 1937; Stanton, *Terror in the City*, 184–86 and passim. Among those killed by Legionnaires was George Marchuk, a member of the Unemployed Councils discussed in chapter 4, and AFL organizer John Bielak.

149. "Vigilantes Exposed in Cleveland," *Reform Advocate*, August 13, 1937.

150. Some reports blamed Blacks, others Silvers, quite possibly because they joined forces in their attacks on labor organizing. *American Jewish World*, June 12, 1936. Silver and Black cooperation was reported in *B'nai Brith Messenger*, June 19, 1936, from the Dickstein investigation.

151. Both quotations from Fronczak, "Fascist Game," 572.

152. *Sentinel*, January 21, 1937. On Silver and Black Legion cooperation see *B'nai Brith Messenger*, June 19, 1936, reporting on the findings of Dickstein investigation. Pelley himself was eventually convicted of financial fraud, taking in well over $100,000 between 1931 and 1934. Sentenced to five years with a suspended sentence, he continued disseminating anti-Semitic material, but without much of a following, until 1942, when he was sentenced to fifteen years for violating the Espionage Act. Wanat, "Silver Shirts," 46, 55.

153. Centrella, "Rifles and Rhetoric," 65.
154. Catalano, "When It Happened Here," 47; Bak, "Dark Days"; John L Spivak, "Who Backs the Black Legion?" *New Masses*, June 9, 1936; Dorothy Roberts, "Old Anti-Semites in New Clothes," *New Masses*, October 23, 1945, 6–9; Palella "Black Legion," 81, 95–96; Stanton, *Terror in the City*, 224.
155. *American Jewish World*, September 25, 1936; *Sentinel*, June 25, 1936.
156. Stanton, *Terror in the City*, 123–25; Gene Fein, "For Christ and Country: The Anti-Semitic Anticommunism of Christian Front Street Meetings in New York City," *US Catholic Historian* 22, no. 4 (2004): 50. The Christian Front had "the greatest potential to become a genuine mass movement," according to Jenkins, "'It Can't Happen,'" 44.
157. In line with his earlier Populist leanings, Coughlin had pressed FDR to nationalize the banking system and provide for the free coinage of silver. He was infuriated by the president's lack of interest in his suggestion. Quotations are from Warren, *Radio Priest*, 18, 42–43; Dinnerstein, *Antisemitism*, 115. Coughlin also claimed that the Klan had sought a court injunction to stop the construction of his church, the Shrine of the Little Flower, but Warren found no evidence that this claim was true. Other scholars took Coughlin at his word, including Hart, *Hitler's American Friends*, 72–73.
158. James Wechsler, "The Coughlin Terror," *Nation*, June 22, 1939. Coughlin may have harped on Communism more when hoping to avoid criticism for his anti-Semitism, but he explicitly recruited men who "will not fear to be called 'anti-Semitic'"; quoted in Catalano, "When It Happened Here," 54; Warren, *Radio Priest*, 134. Some Christian Fronters denied that they were anti-Semitic, even as they trafficked in scurrilous name-calling and absurd claims, as "they are specialists in rape"; quoted in Fein, "For Christ and Country," 46. Christian Front's newsletter once claimed that a photograph of FDR hung prominently in Moscow; Fein, "For Christ and Country," 44.
159. Fein, "For Christ and Country," 50; Warren, *Radio Priest*, 139. The evangelical Protestant minister Gerald Winrod of Kansas claimed that the president was descended from Rosenbergs, Rosenbaums, Roosenvelts, Rosenblums, and Rosenthals; Dinnerstein, *Antisemitism*, 109, 116–17. Shortly after the 1938 *Kristallnacht*, a massive pogrom against German Jews, he made one of his most poisonous broadcasts, blaming the Bolshevik revolution on Jews, citing "data" from counterfeit documents disseminated by the Nazis—e.g., that 24 of 25 members of the Soviet Politburo and 56 of the 59 members of the Soviet Communist leadership were Jews. One distinguished priest pointed out, probably correctly, that the Third Reich was financing Coughlin's publications. Warren, *Radio Priest*, 233.
160. Albin Krebs, "Charles Coughlin, 30's 'Radio Priest'" (obituary), *New York Times*, October 28, 1979.
161. Warren, *Radio Priest*, 188; Jenkins, *Hoods and Shirts*, 177; *American Jewish World*, August 18, 1939; Fein, "For Christ and Country," 48; Victor C. Ferkiss, "Populist Influences on American Fascism," *Western Political Quarterly* 10, no. 2 (1957): 363; Ezra Pound, *America, Roosevelt, and the Causes of the Present War*, pamphlet (London: Peter Russell, 1951).
162. Charles E. Coughlin, *I Take My Stand*, broadcast of January 21, 1940, pamphlet from Royal Oak, Michigan; Alson J. Smith, *The "Christian Front,"* pamphlet (American League for Peace and Democracy, 1939), 19.
163. These clubs were organized from the ranks of Coughlin's earlier Social Justice clubs. Warren, *Radio Priest*, 188–89, quotation at 189.
164. Jenkins, *Hoods and Shirts*, 167, 178; Carlson, *Under Cover*, 91. Different reports on

the Christian Front inevitably provide different numbers for its size, audiences, and appearances. Stephen Peabody, "The 'Christian Front,'" *New Masses*, August 22, 1939, 12–14; James Wechsler, "The Coughlin Terror," *Nation*, June 22, 1939; Sam Marcy, "Fascist 'Christian Mobilizers' Open Drive in New York City," *Socialist Appeal* 4, no. 21 (May 25, 1940), 4.

165. Warren, *Radio Priest*, 145–47; Wechsler, "Coughlin Terror," 92, 95–96; Centrella, "Rifles and Rhetoric"; *New York Times*, February 13, 1940; Smith, "'Christian Front.'" Defensively, the police commission announced, "We know that a number of our men joined the Christian Front and when they did join they thought they were going to combat Communism. When they found out this was not the truth, they immediately resigned." *Sentinel*, February 15, 1940.

166. While some Boston Catholic leaders protested, the police and political leaders—including Massachusetts governor Leverett Saltonstall and Boston mayor Maurice Tobin—shrugged off complaints for fear of losing Irish Catholic votes; Stephen H. Norwood, "Marauding Youth and the Christian Front: Antisemitic Violence in Boston and New York During World War II," *American Jewish History* 91, no. 2 (2001): 233–67; Charles R. Gallagher, *Nazis of Copley Square: The Forgotten History of the Christian Front* (Cambridge, MA: Harvard University Press, 2021); H. Bayor, "Klans, Coughlinites and Aryan Nations: Patterns of American Anti-Semitism in the Twentieth Century," *American Jewish History* 76 no. 2 (1986): 194; Carlson, *Under Cover*, 455.

167. Dinnerstein, *Antisemitism*, 115, 121; Jenkins, *Hoods and Shirts*, 168. The Union Party's 1936 presidential campaign, supported by Coughlin (see chapter 3), got more votes in Boston than any other city. See also Jenny Goldstein, "Transcending Boundaries: Boston's Catholics and Jews, 1929–1965" (senior thesis, Brandeis University, 2001). The Christian Front claimed, with ludicrous exaggeration, to have 1 to 5 million members; Fein, "For Christ and Country," 50.

168. Norman Thomas, *What's Behind the "Christian Front"?* pamphlet, revised text of speech, (New York: Socialist Party, 1939), 9.

169. Goldstein, "Transcending Boundaries," chap. 2; Fein, "For Christ and Country," 41. The historian Stephen Norwood also concluded that the Christian Front undertook a campaign of beatings and slashings that were veritable pogroms; Norwood, "Marauding Youth," 233–67. At one point a group of Jewish boys were beaten in a police station.

170. *B'nai Brith Messenger*, September 15 and 22, 1939; Rick Perlstein, "I Thought I Understood the American Right. Trump Proved Me Wrong," *New York Times*, April 11, 2017; Smith, *"Christian Front,"* 15; Warren, *Radio Priest*, 191–92; Jenkins, *Hoods and Shirts*, 168; Carlson, *Under Cover*, 63, 75, 77, 82, 88, 101, 239, quotation at 101.

171. One case of censorship created a major controversy when the Queens College president, supported by the Queens borough president, disinvited German Jewish antifascist playwright Ernst Toller who had been scheduled to lecture. Lisa Marie Anderson, "Speech in a Low Dishonest Decade," *Wilson Quarterly* (Winter 2020).

172. *Sentinel*, June 6, 1940.

173. Stolberg, "Vigilantism, 1937."

174. Elizabeth Kirkpatrick Dilling, *The Red Network—A Who's Who and Handbook of Radicalism for Patriots* (Chicago, 1934); McEnaney, "He-Men and Christian Mothers," 47–57.

175. Bund *Yearbook* quoted in Susan Canedy, "America's Nazis: The German American Bund" (PhD diss., Texas A&M University, 1987), 101.

176. *Life*, March 7, 1938, 11; Ryan Shaffer, "Long Island Nazis: a Local Synthesis of Transnational Politics," *Long Island History Journal* 21, no. 2 (1010); *B'nai Brith Messenger*, June 19, 1931.

177. Quoted in Jenkins, *Hoods and Shirts*, 150, and in Arnie Bernstein, *Swastika Nation: Fritz Kuhn and the Rise and Fall of the German-American Bund* (New York: St. Martin's Press, 2013), 182. Leaders analogized the American colonies' fight against British colonialism to the struggle against Jewish communism; Canedy, "America's Nazis," 112.

178. Many newspapers saw it that way, using the terms *Bund* and *Nazis* interchangeably. Minna Thrall, "'What For Is Democracy?': The German American Bund in the American Press, 1936–1941," *Voces Novae* 12, no. 7 (2020): 8.

179. Ronald W. Johnson, "The German-American Bund and Nazi Germany, 1936–1941," *Studies in History and Society* 6, no. 2 (Spring 1975): 31–45. Unsurprisingly, Gerald L. K. Smith (discussed in chapter 3) credited Ford with teaching him the connection between Communism and the Jews: "The day came when I embraced the research of Mr. Ford . . . and became courageous enough and honest enough and informed enough to use the words: 'Communism is Jewish.'" "The Cross and Flag: In Memory of Gerald L. K. Smith," www.thecrossandflag.com, 7.

180. The records of the German foreign office provide reams of evidence of its support for the Bund. Francis MacDonnell, *Insidious Foes: The Axis Fifth Column and the American Home Front* (New York: Oxford University Press, 1995), 42–43; Sander A. Diamond, *The Nazi Movement in the United States, 1924–1941* (Ithaca, NY: Cornell University Press, 1974), 113–23; Bernstein, *Swastika Nation*, 29, 111.

181. John L. Spivak, "Plotting the American Pogroms, 1: The Organization of Anti-Semitism Here," *New Masses*, October 2, 1934; "Colonel Edwin Emerson Denies He Is Official Spokesman for the Nazi Party in America," Jewish Telegraph Agency, December 3, 1933.

182. Arthur L. Smith, Jr., "The DAI and the German-American Bund," in *The Deutschtum of Nazi Germany and the United States* (The Hague: Martinus Nijhoff, 1965). This book contains many more examples of Nazi German aid to the Bund.

183. Smith, "DAI and the Bund," 70, 84, 95, 96, 99, quotation at 95; Diamond, *Nazi Movement in United States*, 192; Bell, "Failure of Nazism," 591–93; Remak, "Friends of the New Germany," 39; Martha Glaser, "The German-American Bund in New Jersey," *New Jersey History* 92, no. 1 (1974): 38. Kuhn, who had served in the German Army during World War I, earning the Iron Cross, liked to dress in a Nazi uniform, including the tall black boots. He was not only unreliable but also corrupt: in late 1939 he was sentenced to 2½ to 5 years for grand larceny and forgery. He had used funds raised for the Bund for personal items, including gifts to his mistress; Shaffer, "Long Island Nazis"; Cameron Wolf, "Fritz Kuhn's Nazi America: Kuhn's Growth and Destruction of the German American Bund in the 1930s" (BA thesis, University of Kansas, 2019), 7–8, 13, 25; Jenkins, *Hoods and Shirts*, 155.

184. Jenkins, *Hoods and Shirts*, 141.

185. Canedy, "America's Nazis," 75.

186. Scott D. Abrams, "'By Any Means Necessary': The League for Human Rights Against Nazism and Domestic Fascism" (MA thesis, Kent State University, 2012), 28; Bell, "Failure of Nazism."

187. Jenkins, *Hoods and Shirts*, 146; Smith, "DAI and the Bund," 93, 95, 103, and chap. 4 passim; Bell, "Failure of Nazism," 591. There are many more examples of Nazi German aid to the Bund in this book.

188. Smith, "DAI and the Bund," 107.

189. Smith, "DAI and the Bund," 81.

190. Canedy, "America's Nazis," 89–92.

191. Bernstein, *Swastika Nation*, 51; Thrall, "'What For,'" 14, 17; Bell, "Failure of Nazism," 589, 591, 593; Jim Bredemus, "American Bund: The Failure of American Nazism," *Traces*, n.d, https://tinyurl.com/k9m2883j; Remak, "Friends of the New Germany"; Glaser, "Bund in New Jersey," 38; Ledeboer, "Man Who Would Be Hitler"; Warren, *Radio Priest*, 180; Jenkins, *Hoods and Shirts*, 137.

192. Diamond, *Nazi Movement in United States*, 228–29; Shaffer, "Long Island Nazis." Bund camps were sometimes used by other fascist groups, notably the Christian Front, for which it may have charged rent; Jenkins, "'It Can't Happen,'" 46. While Nazi Germany used the Bund when doing so was in their interest, and provided propaganda materials, it never funded the Bund. *Bundesleiter* Kuhn created puppet corporations that legally owned the campgrounds; Hart, *Hitler's American Friends*, 23, 35nn. For a short time Camp Siegfried included a small community of family homes, with Adolf Hitler Street its main drive. Bell, "Failure of Nazism," 590, 592; Jenkins, *Hoods and Shirts*, 145; Glaser, "Bund in New Jersey," 40; Julia Reischel, "Windham Was Home to Nazi Summer Camp in 1937," WatershedPost.com.

193. Diamond, *Nazi Movement in United States*, 242.

194. Full text in Diamond, *Nazi Movement in United States*, 242–43.

195. Some recently discovered film footage of this event can be seen at YouTube.

196. Wolf, "Fritz Kuhn's Nazi America," 3; Hart, *Hitler's American Friends*, 44; Shaffer, "Long Island Nazis."

197. Speeches in "Free America," quoted in Bernstein, *Swastika Nation*, 182.

198. Bernstein, *Swastika Nation*, 184, 187, and 188, and chaps. 21 and 22 passim.

199. The 100,000 estimate came from the police: Bernstein, *Swastika Nation*, 180. Canedy, "America's Nazis," 163; Hart, *Hitler's American Friends*, 44; Diane Bernard, "The Night Thousands of Nazis Packed Madison Square Garden," *Washington Post*, December 9, 2018.

200. It took the police a long time to figure out where the voice was coming from. Arnie Bernstein, interview by Jake Offenhartz, *Gothamist*, January 23, 2019, at https://gothamist.com/news/they-didnt-just-go-away-historian-talks-about-nycs-1939-nazi-rally.

201. Bernstein, *Swastika Nation*, 188–91; Sarah Kate Kramer, "When Nazis Took Manhattan," *All Things Considered*, NPR, February 22, 2019.

202. Seabury was an upper-class Progressive; Holmes was more to the left, a founding member of both the NAACP and the ACLU. Samuel Anthes, "Publicly Deliberative Drama: The 1934 Mock Trial of Adolf Hitler for 'Crimes against Civilization,'" *American Journal of Legal History* 42, no. 4 (1998): 391–410.

203. Although condemning labor unions was not their major theme, Bund leaders did describe unions as a tool of "Jewish-International moneyed interests." Quoted in Bernstein, *Swastika Nation*, 184.

204. Scott D. Abrams, "'By Any Means Necessary': The League for Human Rights Against Nazism and Domestic Fascism" (MA thesis, Kent State University, 2012); Haskel Lookstein, *Were We Our Brothers' Keepers? The Public Response of American Jews to the Holocaust* (New York: Hartmore House, 1985). Quotations are from *B'nai Brith Messenger*, September 15 and November 10, 1939.

205. Smith, "'Christian Front,'" 19; Warren, *Radio Priest*, 219.

206. Glaser, "Bund in New Jersey," 35, 42, 47.

207. Kristallnacht, literally "night of glass," was a massive pogrom in November 1938. It extended throughout Germany and Austria, as well as German-occupied parts of Czechoslovakia. Organized by the Nazi Party's *Sturmabteilung* (SA) paramilitary, rioters demolished over seven thousand Jewish businesses and 267 synagogues, and imprisoned at least thirty thousand who were then sent to concentration camps. Martin Gilbert, *Kristallnacht: Prelude to Disaster* (New York: Harper & Row, 2006). The Bund newspaper justified it on November 17 and 24; Canedy, "America's Nazis," 174.
208. Bak, "Dark Days."
209. Bayor, "Klans, Coughlinites," 186.
210. Bernstein interview by Offenhartz.
211. Centrella, "Rifles and Rhetoric," 65–66; Glaser, "Bund in New Jersey," 35.
212. So did Chicago "thug" Jacob Rubenstein, who then moved to Dallas and changed his name . . . to Jack Ruby! Lansky, Siegel, and Cohen were approached by high-up figures in the Jewish community, according to Lansky, and were asked to put an army together. They had so many volunteers that they had to run training camps on how to beat up Nazis. Bernstein interview by Offenhartz.
213. Its full name was the House Special Committee on Un-American Activities Authorized to Investigate Nazi Propaganda and Certain Other Propaganda Activities. It was chaired by Democratic congressmen John William McCormack of Massachusetts and Samuel Dickstein of New York. It collected testimony filling 4,300 pages. (The Bund called Dickstein "the ghetto Representative in Congress"; Glaser, "Bund in New Jersey," 38.) One source claims that Dies was a Klansman; Carlson, *Under Cover*, 288; Wolf, "Fritz Kuhn's Nazi America," 19.
214. The German ambassador to the United States, who was also the brother-in-law of von Ribbentrop, is quoted in Diamond, *Nazi Movement in United States*, 289.
215. *B'nai Brith Messenger*, October 6, 1939; James Wechsler, "The Coughlin Terror," *Nation*, June 22, 1939.
216. *Sentinel*, June 4, 1936.
217. The phrase is from Richard Steigmann-Gall, "Star-spangled Fascism: American Interwar Political Extremism in Comparative Perspective," *Social History* 2017, 42, no. 1 (2017): 98.
218. Umberto Eco, "Ur-Fascism," *New York Review of Books*, June 22, 1995; Robert Paxton, "The Five Stages of Fascism," *Journal of Modern History* 70, no. 1 (1998): 12. The historian Peter E. Gordon, "Why Historical Analogy Matters," *New York Review of Books*, January 7, 2020, differs somewhat, defending the use of the fascism label in relation to today's white nationalism, arguing that refusing the label has "merely inverted the idea of American exceptionalism."
219. Jason Stanley, *How Fascism Works: The Politics of Us and Them* (New York: Random House, 2018), makes a similar argument and applies the label to post-Reconstruction Klan terrorism, Nazi Germany, and the Bharatiya Janata Party in India, among other phenomena.
220. The classic articulation of the cluster-concept notion was in Wittgenstein's *Philosophical Investigations*. I listed some of the features one might consider fascist in Linda Gordon, "Populism and Fascism: Lessons from the 1920s, Ku Klux Klan," in *Destroying Democracy: Neoliberal Capitalism and the Rise of Authoritarian Politics*, ed. Michelle Williams and Vishwas Satgar (Johannesburg, South Africa: Johannesburg University Press, 2021).
221. Williams first used this phrase in his 1954 *A Preface to Film*, then elaborated it in his later books, *The Long Revolution* and *Marxism and Literature*. He used *structure*

as a concept to suggest the material reality of culture but employed the term *feeling* to distinguish it from worldview or ideology: "We are talking about . . . impulse, restraint, and tone; specifically affective elements of consciousness and relationships: not feeling against thought, but thought as felt and feeling as thought: practical consciousness of a present kind, in a living and interrelating continuity. We are then defining these elements as a 'structure': as a set, with specific, internal relations, at once interlocking and in tension." Williams, *Marxism and Literature* (Oxford: Oxford University Press, 1977), 132.

222. Dorothy Roberts, "Feuds Among the Fascists," *New Masses*, November 20, 1945, 12.

223. Helen Thomas, *Watchdogs of Democracy?: The Waning Washington Press Corps and How It Has Failed the Public* (New York: Scribner, 2007), 172.

224. Stanton, *Terror in the City*, 246.

225. Jason Stanley, "Donald Trump Has Normalized Fascism," Portside.org, December 24, 2021.

3. Trustees of the Nation

1. *Jackson Daily News*, June 20, 1935.

2. Francis Townsend, *New Horizons: An Autobiography*, ed. Jesse George Murray (Chicago: J.L. Stewart, 1943).

3. Among recent scholars, only sociologist Edwin Amenta has published a full-length study of Townsend: *When Movements Matter: The Townsend Plan and the Rise of Social Security* (Princeton, NJ: Princeton University Press, 2006). It focused not on Townsend as a social movement but on its influence. Amenta also wrote or co-wrote many articles on this subject.

4. *San Diego Sun*, May 29 and June 3, 1934, quoted in Paul David Lucas, "The Townsend Movement in San Diego County, 1934–1939" (MA thesis, San Diego State College, 1967), 13.

5. Townsend, *New Horizons*, 78.

6. Under "self-improvement" they listed lectures, theater, music, books, magazines, and travel. *Townsend Weekly*, March 4, 1935.

7. Townsend, *New Horizons*; Jackson K. Putnam, *Old-Age Politics in California: From Richardson to Reagan* (Stanford, CA: Stanford University Press, 1970), 50.

8. In 1940, OARP was reincorporated under a new name, the Townsend National Recovery Plan, and then the Townsend Plan in 1953. A Townsend Foundation appeared in 1938, incorporated in Delaware, but it appeared to be merely a front for bringing in more revenue. Arthur Carlyle O'Byrne, "The Political Significance of the Townsend Movement in California, 1934–1950" (MA thesis, University of Southern California, 1935), 61–64.

9. Luther Whiteman and Samuel L. Lewis, *Glory Roads: The Psychological State of California* (New York: Thomas Y. Crowell, 1936), 74.

10. *San Diego Sun*, September 15, 1934, and January 31, 1935, and *Coronado Journal*, May 31, 1934, quoted in Lucas, "Townsend Movement"; Abraham Holtzman, *The Townsend Movement: A Political Study* (New York: Bookman Associates, 1963), 56; O'Byrne, "Political Significance," 124–30; Whiteman and Lewis, *Glory Roads*, 71, 84–85; Marwood Harris, "The Townsend Movement in Portland, Oregon" (BA thesis, Reed College, 1987), 3, 14.

11. Harris, "Townsend in Portland," 10–11, 29.

12. Whiteman and Lewis, *Glory Roads*, 71, 84–85; Harris, "Townsend in Portland," 3, 14.

13. Townsend later added a 2 percent tax on inheritances and gifts. This and other negative consequences of the plan are discussed in Larry DeWitt, "The Townsend Plan's Pension Scheme," Social Security Administration, December 2001, at https://www.ssa.gov/history/townsendproblems.html.

14. Harry M. Thompson, *A Common Sense Analysis of the Townsend Plan* (Kansas City, MO: Harry M. Thompson, 1936), 86.

15. No doubt the requirement that the pension could not be saved would have required a giant administrative staff, but that proviso was supported by distinguished economists, such as Irving Fisher of Yale; Holtzman, *Townsend Movement*, 42.

16. Harris, "Townsend in Portland," 3, 14; Thompson, *Common Sense Analysis*, 14; Lenore K. Bartlett, "The Attack on the Townsend Plan," *Social Work Today*, May 1936, 12.

17. *San Diego Sun*, May 29 and June 3, 1934, quoted in Lucas, "Townsend Movement," 13.

18. Francis Townsend, speech of April 22, 1935, at https://www.ssa.gov/history/towns8.html.

19. Townsend, *New Horizons*, 138.

20. Morgan J. Dorman, *Age Before Booty* (New York: G.P. Putnam's Sons, 1936), 20–21, 28.

21. Linda Gordon and Nancy Fraser, "A Genealogy of 'Dependency': Tracing a Keyword of the US Welfare State," 19, no. 2 *Signs* (1994): 309–36.

22. Kevin Starr, *Endangered Dreams: The Great Depression in California* (New York: Oxford University Press, 1996), 133–34.

23. In California, a pension recipient had to be a fifteen–year resident; eligibility began at seventy; the amount of aid was needs-tested. Any property the recipient owned, such as a home, had to be bequeathed to the state. Current residents of poorhouses were ineligible. And there was no guarantee of a pension if the county ran out of money. Putnam, *Old-Age Politics*, 22–23 and chap. 2 passim.

24. Amenta, *When Movements Matter*, 64.

25. Similar cutbacks affected the 5 percent of the labor force that had private pensions, and as of 1932, only 140,000 of the country's elders actually received any pensions. Daniel Béland and Jacob S. Hacker, "Ideas, Private Institutions, and American Welfare State 'Exceptionalism': The Case of Health and Old-Age Insurance," *International Journal of Social Welfare* 13, no. 1 (2004): 49.

26. Keynes was not well known in the United States at this time, although a few Harvard professors were circulating his ideas. Harris, "Townsend in Portland," 19.

27. Gordon, *Pitied But Not Entitled*.

28. The eminent historian William Leuchtenburg appraised Social Security in *Franklin D. Roosevelt and the New Deal* (New York: Harper & Row, 1963), 105: "In no other welfare system in the world did the state shirk all responsibility for old-age indigency and insist that funds be taken out of the current earnings of workers. By relying on regressive taxation and withdrawing vast sums to build up reserves, the act did untold economic mischief. The law denied coverage to numerous classes of workers, including those who needed security most: notably farm laborers and domestics."

29. Arthur Schlesinger, Jr., *The Politics of Upheaval* (Boston: Houghton Mifflin, 1988), 36.

30. Daniel J. B. Mitchell, "Mitchell's Musings" (blog), UCLA Anderson School of Management, September 2, 2017.

31. Quoted in Bartlett, "Attack," 11.

32. Francis E. Townsend, "Recovery with Security," *Forum*, May 1936, 284; Harris, "Townsend in Portland," 32; Putnam, *Old-Age Politics*, 45. At one point Dr. Townsend

sided with chain stores that were protesting a proposal to tax them; Winston Moore and Marian Moore, *Out of the Frying Pan* (Los Angeles: DeVorss, 1939), 23.

33. In at least one state, Oregon, Townsend membership overlapped considerably with that of the KKK a decade earlier. For example, Walter Pierce, who as Oregon governor in the 1920s had supported the Klan, became a Townsend supporter. Harris, "Townsend in Portland," 60–61.

34. Francis Townsend to Long Beach *Press Telegram*, October 21, 1933, published in J. D. Gaydowski, "Eight Letters to the Editor: The Genesis of the Townsend National Recovery Plan," *Southern California Quarterly* 52, no. 4 (1970): 370.

35. The quotation is from Putnam, *Old-Age Politics*, 54. Holtzman also recognized this fusion of left and right, in *Townsend Movement*, 43–45;

36. *New York Times*, November 5, 1939, clipping in Box 23, Witte Papers; Gertrude Schaffner Goldberg, "A Decade of Dissent: The New Deal and Popular Movements," in *When Government Helped: Learning from the Successes and Failures of the New Deal*, ed. Sheila D. Collins and Gertrude Schaffner Goldberg (New York: Oxford University Press, 2014), 103.

37. Holtzman estimated 2.2 million in 1936, in *Townsend Movement*, 49, and summarized other estimates, 48. So did Gaston V. Rimlinger, *Welfare Policy and Industrialization in Europe and America* (New York: John Wiley & Sons, 1971), 201–2. For other estimates, see Amenta, *When Movements Matter*, 58; O'Byrne, *Political Significance*, 51–53; Brent Ranalli, "Historical Precedents for Basic Income Advocacy: The Townsend Movement" (July 2015), 4, at http://www.usbig.net/papers/Ranalli%20 2015%20Townsend%20Movement%20version%204-25-17.pdf.

38. Peter B. Bulkley, "Townsendism as an Eastern and Urban Phenomenon: Chautauqua County, New York, as a Case Study," *New York History* 55, no. 2 (1974): 193.

39. Quoted in Steven B. Burg, "The Gray Crusade: The Townsend Movement, Old Age Politics, and the Development of Social Security" (PhD diss., University of Wisconsin, 1999), 244. To the best of my knowledge, Burg's is the only study of a Townsend *chapter* and thus the only truly grassroots study of the movement. Steve was my graduate student, and I am extremely grateful to be able to use his material.

40. Bulkley, "Townsendism," 194; Burg, "Gray Crusade," 245.

41. Abraham Holtzman thought the number of African Americans in the movement was small because they had no "experience in independent political action." His racism was probably not atypical of Townsenders. Holtzman, *Townsend Movement*, 48, 55.

42. In 1930, of California's 5.7 million residents, approximately 415,000 were of "Hispanic" origin, 81,000 were African American, and 169,000 of Asian origin. Data from Campbell Gibson and Kay Jung, "Historical Census Statistics on Population Totals by Race . . . ," U.S. Census Bureau, Population Division, Working Paper no. 56, 37, at https://census.gov/content/dam/Census/library/working-papers/2002/demo/POP -twps0056.pdf.

43. Although many younger people supported the plan, the organization had little success in recruiting younger members; Amenta, *When Movements Matter*, 118. Townsend's style of socializing probably seemed too staid and old-fashioned to younger people.

44. Burg, "Gray Crusade," 239.

45. Edwin Amenta and Yvonne Zylan, "It Happened Here: Political Opportunity the New Institutionalism, and the Townsend Movement," *American Sociological Review* 56, no. 2 (1991): 262–65.

46. *Jackson* (MS) *Daily News*, June 20, 1935, quoted in John Simkin, "Francis Townsend," n.d., Spartacus-Educational.com.

47. Townsend, *New Horizons*, 163. A copy of the call and instructions for this mass rally is in Box 33, Witte Papers.
48. A copy of Townsend's call for these events is in Box 70, Witte Papers.
49. Harris, "Townsend in Portland," 44–49; U.S. Congress, House of Representatives, *Hearings Before the Select Committee Investigating Old-Age Pension Organizations* (Washington, DC: GPO, 1936), I, 55.
50. Bruce Mason, "The Townsend Movement," *Southwestern Social Science Quarterly* 35, no. 1 (1954): 40; O'Byrne, *Political Significance*, 55–60.
51. *San Diego Sun*, September 15, 1934, and January 31, 1935, and *Coronado Journal*, May 31, 1934, quoted in Lucas, "Townsend Movement," 10–11 and 18; Holtzman, *Townsend Movement*, 56.
52. Clements divided the country into regions and appointed "managers" for each. These managers were allegedly earning as much as $2,500 a month (about $42,000 today). Harris, "Townsend in Portland," 2.
53. Amenta, *When Movements Matter*, 141.
54. Burg "Gray Crusade," 108–9.
55. *Townsend National Weekly*, July 22, 1935, quoted in "Old Age: Townsendites Have to Hang Out SRO Sign at Chicago," *Newsweek*, November 2, 1935, 13.
56. Burg, "Gray Crusade," 109; Amenta, *When Movements Matter*, 53; Bartlett, "Attack," 11; O'Byrne, *Political Significance*, 54; Mason, "Townsend Movement," 44. A study of the Oregon Townsend movement reported that members were asked for an initial fee of twenty-five cents and dues of ten cents per week; Harris, "Townsend in Portland," 27. On these inconsistencies, see J. Michael Carter, "Jerry W. Carter and the Townsend Movement in Florida, 1936–1940" (MA thesis, Samford University, 1973), 16.
57. Burg "Gray Crusade," 109
58. Mason, "Townsend Movement," 43.
59. Burg "Gray Crusade," 110–14.
60. At that time income was still growing, $350,000 in the last quarter of 1935. Harris, "Townsend in Portland," 30; "Old Age: Townsendites Have to Hang Out SRO Sign at Chicago," *Newsweek*, November 2 and December 2, 1935.
61. "Old Age," *Newsweek*; Mason, "Townsend Movement," 39, 41; Townsend, *New Horizons*, 152–53; American Institute for Economic Research, *Research Reports Weekly Bulletin*, April 6, 1936, 33; Richard L. Neuberger, "The Townsend Plan Exposed," *Nation* 141, no. 3664 (October 30, 1935): 505; "Old Age," *Newsweek*, November 2, 1935, 13; Amenta and Zylan, "It Happened Here," 255; Lucas, "Townsend Movement," chap. 5. For an example of Peterson's work in favor of Townsend earlier in the year, see his letter to *New Republic*, January 23, 1935, 305–6.
62. Burg, "Gray Crusade," 90–91. Clements earned, in 2017 dollar equivalents, an estimated $160,000 a year and Townsend about $115,000—not bad considering the Depression economy. In a sign of his discomfort about doing so well from his cause, Dr. Townsend later wrote defensively, "I determined to scrape by as cheaply as I could and take no more than barest living expenses out of receipts. When, a year later, I was able to start my own [*sic*] newspaper, I started drawing a salary. . . . I never have taken any money except expenses—and they do not run very high at my age and with my frugal tastes." Townsend, *New Horizons*, 152.
63. Putnam, *Old-Age Politics*, 61.
64. Letter of October 28, 1933. We will see the importance of this requirement again in chapter 6.

65. Burg, "Gray Crusade," 251–52; Herbert Harris, "Dr. Townsend's Marching Soldiers," *Current History* 43 (1936): 456.
66. Burg, "Gray Crusade," 253.
67. Harris, "Townsend in Portland," 28.
68. Burg, "Gray Crusade," 257.
69. Hadley Cantril, an academic psychologist who argued the irrationality of social movements, meant this contemptuously in his *The Psychology of Social Movements* (New York: J. Wiley & Sons, 1941), 186.
70. Mason, "Townsend Movement," 43; Schlesinger, *Politics of Upheaval*, 33.
71. Gordon, *Second Coming*, 90–91.
72. Mason, "Townsend Movement," 36–47, esp. 47.
73. Leuchtenburg, *Roosevelt and New Deal*, 105.
74. Mason, "Townsend Movement," 44; Kelly Loe and Richard L. Neuberger, "The Townsend Plan and Its Astonishing Growth," *Harper's*, March 1936, 433.
75. Burg, "Gray Crusade," 254.
76. Burg "Gray Crusade," 220.
77. Burg "Gray Crusade," 261–62.
78. Burg "Gray Crusade," 267–68.
79. Again, because we have no membership lists, we don't have a count of members' sexes.
80. Burg, "Gray Crusade," 243; Harris, "Townsend in Portland," 25–27. The historian of women Gerda Lerner found that an organization's or a profession's decline in status correlates with higher positions for women. The pattern is so common that it became known in her community as "Gerda's law."
81. The quilt can be seen at "A Townsend Plan Quilt," University of Arizona, http://www.cs.arizona.edu/~gmt/roots/tquilt.html.
82. Burg, "Gray Crusade," 240–43; Harris, "Townsend in Portland," 25–27, 51.
83. Burg "Gray Crusade," 258
84. Harris, "Townsend in Portland," 24–27.
85. Burg, "Gray Crusade," 243; Harris, "Townsend in Portland," 25–27.
86. Whiteman and Lewis, *Glory Roads*, 98–103.
87. Burg, "Gray Crusade," 268.
88. Harris, "Townsend in Portland," 28
89. O'Byrne, *Political Significance*, 124–30.
90. Harris, "Townsend in Portland," 29.
91. Harris, "Townsend in Portland," 30, 2.
92. Herbert Harris, "Marching Soldiers," 457.
93. Harris, "Townsend in Portland," 29–30, 41–49, 66; U.S. Congress, House of Representatives, *Hearings Before the Select Committee Investigating Old-Age Pension Organizations* (Washington, DC: GPO, 1936), 1:55.
94. O'Byrne, *Political Significance*, 55–60.
95. Goldberg, "Decade of Dissent," 105; Amenta and Zylan, "It Happened Here," 256; Luke Norris, "The Workers' Constitution," *Fordham Law Review* 87, no. 4 (2019): 1485.
96. Amenta, *When Movements Matter*, 112.
97. A chart with these figures is in O'Byrne, *Political Significance*, 140; disavowals on 152. Unfortunately there is no study of political success in other states.
98. Putnam, *Old-Age Politics*, 40.
99. *San Francisco Chronicle*, February 14, 1935; *Los Angeles Times*, February 23, 1935; *New York Times*, December 3, 1934, quoted in John Dennis Moynihan, "The Radical

Press Views the Townsend Movement" (MA thesis, San Jose State College, 1969), 19, 21. Moynihan offers many more quotations from press attacks on Townsend. The *Newsweek* story, "Plan for Old Age Pensions Outlined," was on the cover of the January 26, 1935, issue.

100. Mason, "Townsend Movement," 46.
101. Witte to Marianne Sakman, December 7, 1935, in Boxes 33, 70, and 234, Social Security Correspondence, Witte Papers; Box 57, CES Records.
102. Letter to James Farley, Postmaster General, September 7, 1934, in Box 56, CES Records. The letter referred also to a previous post office investigation of the National Old Age Pension Association.
103. O'Byrne, *Political Significance*, 139. Committees holding hearings included the Senate Finance Committee in 1935, the House Select Committee Investigating Old-Age Pensions (called the Bell Committee) in 1936, the House Ways and Means Committee Social Security Hearings in 1939, and the Senate Special Committee to Investigate Old-Age Pension Systems in 1941.
104. Twentieth Century Fund, Committee on Old Age Security, *The Townsend Crusade: An Impartial Review of the Townsend Movement and the Probable Effects of the Townsend Plan* (New York: Twentieth Century Fund, 1936); Neuberger, "Townsend Plan Exposed," 505–7; Moynihan, "Radical Press Views," chap. 7.
105. Bartlett, "Attack," 11; William Graebner, "The Golden Age Clubs," *Social Service Review* 57, no. 3 (1983): 416–28.
106. David Lasser, *Old-Age Security, $60 at 60*, a pamphlet reproducing Lasser's testimony to the House Ways and Means Committee on March 2, 1939, c. 1940. "Unhealthy channels" was probably a reference to the Communist Party.
107. Holtzman, *Townsend Movement*, 28; Moynihan, "Radical Press Views," 38, 41. I am not sure what specific criticism led to calling it a "hoax."
108. Harry W. Laidler, "The Townsend Plan: A Critical Analysis," *American Socialist Monthly* 5, no. 1 (1935): 12–16.
109. Eugene Vasilew, "Norman Thomas at the Townsend Convention of 1936," *Speech Monographs* 24, no. 4 (1957): figures at 234, quotation at 238.
110. The Lundeen bill, introduced by Ernest Lundeen, Minnesota congressman of the Farmer-Labor Party, was also supported by the Communist Party in its Popular Front period; see Gordon, *Pitied But Not Entitled*, 236–41. *Western Worker* April 27, 1936, 3. *Daily Worker*, November 21, 1934, is quoted in Moynihan, "Radical Press Views," 60–61.
111. *San Diego Sun*, May 29, 1934, is quoted in Lucas, "Townsend Movement," 9.
112. Frank Peterson, "Concerning the Townsend Plan," *New Republic*, January 23, 1935, 305–6.
113. Thompson, *Common Sense Analysis*, 84.
114. Daniel J. B. Mitchell, *Pensions, Politics and the Elderly: Historical Social Movements and Their Lessons for Our Aging Society* (Armonk, NY: M.E. Sharpe, 2000), 87–88.
115. Townsend, "Recovery with Security," 283.
116. Frances Perkins, *The Roosevelt I Knew* (New York: Viking, 1946), 294.
117. Townsend, "Recovery with Security," 283. The House Ways and Means Hearings went equally badly for Townsend.
118. O'Byrne, *Political Significance*, 139–43; Mitchell, *Pensions*, chap. 4, and his blog, "Mitchell's Musings," September 2, 2017.
119. Aware of this problem, Edwin Witte argued that the Social Security bill should expand the Old Age Assistance Program (a then small program that could help some

of the majority of Americans who were excluded from Social Security old-age pensions); Witte to Harry Hopkins, February 26, 1935, in Box 57, CES Records.

120. Bruce Mason, "The Townsend Movement," *Southwestern Social Science Quarterly* 35, no. 1 (1954): 36–47; Hearings before the Senate Finance Committee on HR 7260, passim; Mitchell, *Pensions*, 83–85.

121. Holtzman, *Townsend Movement*, 153; Mitchell, *Pensions*, chap. 4.

122. Holtzman, *Townsend Movement*, 44.

123. Unsigned letter to U.S. Children's Bureau, August 20, 1935, Box 573, 10-17-1, Children's Bureau Archives, NARA.

124. Quotations in Harris, "Townsend in Portland," 22–23.

125. Emily C. Hammond, "Citizens' Pensions—An American Plan," *New York Herald Tribune* September 30, 1950, clipping in Box 234, Witte Papers.

126. Francis Townsend to Long Beach *Press Telegram*, October 21, 1933, in Gaydowski, "Eight Letters," 371.

127. Quoted in Burg, "Gray Crusade," 187.

128. Townsend's letters of February 20, 1934, January 6, 1934, December 13, 1933, October 28 1933, September 30, 1933, collected in Gaydowski, "Eight Letters," 365–82.

129. When socialist writer Upton Sinclair's introduced his 1934 "End Poverty in California" campaign, calling for government appropriation of factories and farms idled by the Depression and reviving them by hiring the unemployed, Townsend denounced it angrily; Putnam, *Old-Age Politics*, 89. The Left also denounced this plan, arguing that it would amount to forced labor: "Upton Sinclair's Threat," *New Masses*, September 11, 1934, 6.

130. Somewhat puritanical, he labeled unmarried and unemployed men a threat to law and order; they might fall into a "cigarette-smoking, whiskey-drinking, road-side petting hell of idleness"; Burg, "Gray Crusade," 186.

131. Harris, "Townsend in Portland," 15, 21.

132. Schlesinger, *Politics of Upheaval*, 33. That judgment was reflected in Schlesinger's labeling them not as middle class but as lower middle class.

133. He detested the policies of Franklin Roosevelt. Nicholas Roosevelt, "Evangelical Economics," *Forum*, May 1936, 287.

134. Graebner, "Golden Age Clubs," 418.

135. Townsend, *New Horizons*, 148.

136. *Modern Crusader*, June 13, 1934, quoted in Burg, "Gray Crusade," 201.

137. "Old Age Revolving Pensions: A Proposed National Plan 'Youth for Work Age for Leisure,'" *Long Beach Press-Gazette*, September 30, 1933; "The Townsend Plan's Pension Scheme," Research Note no. 17, https://www.ssa.gov/history/townsendproblems.html; Holtzman, *Townsend Movement*, 46.

138. Nancy Fraser and Linda Gordon, "A Genealogy of Dependency: Tracing a Keyword of the US Welfare State," *Signs* 19, no. 2 (1994): 309–36.

139. Frank A. Pinner, Paul Jacobs, and Philip Selznick, *Old Age and Political Behavior: A Case Study* (Los Angeles: University of California Press, 1959), 69.

140. Pinner, Jacobs, and Selznick, *Old Age*, 89.

141. Thompson, *Common Sense Analysis*, 92–93.

142. *Old Age Revolving Pensions: A National Plan* (1934), 5.

143. *Townsend Weekly* quoted in Putnam, *Old-Age Politics*, 55.

144. Goldberg, "Decade of Dissent," 106. Mencken is quoted in Glen Jeansonne, *Gerald L. K. Smith: Minister of Hate* (Baton Rouge: Louisiana State University Press, 1997), 48.

145. Raymond Gram Swing quoted in Brinkley, *Voices of Protest*, 226; Warren, *Radio Priest*, 88–89.

146. Quoted in Watkins, *The Hungry Years: American in an Age of Crisis, 1929–1939* (New York: Henry Holt, 1999), 252; Jeansonne, *Minister of Hate*.

147. Jeansonne, *Minister of Hate*, 51; Amenta, *When Movements Matter*, 148, 156.

148. Edward C. Blackorby, "William Lemke: Agrarian Radical and Union Party Presidential Candidate," *Mississippi Valley Historical Review* 49, no. 1 (1962): 78. The first Frazier-Lemke Act was overturned by the Supreme Court—one of many of its resistance to New Deal measures. Renamed as the Farm Mortgage Moratorium Act, it was passed again later and was this time upheld by the Court, but the Roosevelt administration opposed it.

149. Blackorby, "William Lemke," 122; Vasilew, "Norman Thomas," 242; Brinkley, *Voices of Protest*, 255–56. They called it a "Union" party to recognize that it was a coalition of autonomous movements and organizations.

150. David Owen Powell, "The Union Party of 1936" (PhD diss., Ohio State University, 1962), 120–21.

151. Jeansonne, *Minister of Hate*, 53–54. The lack of good polling data at the time was also a factor: The *New York Times* had written of the National Union Party that "the movement threatens to embarrass both parties. . . . Politicians in Washington are worried."

152. Graebner, "Golden Age Clubs," 416, 423; Blackorby, "William Lemke," 67–84; Norman Thomas, "Roosevelt Faces Re-election," *American Socialist Monthly* 5, no. 1 (1936): 4–5; David Ramsey, "Roosevelt and the Democratic Platform," *Communist* 15 (August 1936): 708.

153. Harris, "Townsend in Portland," 39–41, 45–46.

154. Harris, "Townsend in Portland," 29–30, 41–49, 66; U.S. Congress, House of Representatives, *Hearings Before the Select Committee Investigating Old-Age Pension Organizations* (Washington, DC: GPO, 1936), 1:55.

155. Harris, "Townsend in Portland," 66.

156. Perkins, *Roosevelt*, 10, 278–79. The story of FDR's about-face and quotations are in Norris, "Workers' Constitution," 1486–88. Other politicians agreed. Illinois senator Paul Douglas observed that Townsend elicited support for Social Security from "quarters which would have been unaffected by more soberly drafted proposals . . . the widespread support [for Townsend] probably did weaken the die-hard opposition to the security bill." Paul H. Douglas, *Social Security in the United States* (New York: McGraw-Hill, 1936), 69–74, quotation at 73. Frank Bane of the Social Security Board recalled, thirty years later, that "we had two great allies that were helping us put Social Security legislation through. Those two were a gentleman by the name of Dr. Townsend, and the second one by the name of Huey Long." "The Reminiscences of Frank Bane," 1963, 24, in Oral History Collection, CU. The economist Broadus Mitchell wrote that Townsend "took the curse off social security legislation." Broadus Mitchell, *Social Security in the United States* (New York, 1947), 307; Mitchell, "Mitchell's Musings," September 2, 2017.

157. Passing Social Security depended on having votes from southern Democrats. For one example of their views, the *Jackson* (MS) *Daily News* wrote "The average Mississippian can't imagine himself chipping in to pay pensions for able-bodied Negroes to sit around in idleness on front galleries, supporting all their kinfolks on pensions, while cotton and corn crops are crying for workers to get them out of the grass." Quoted in John Simkin, "Francis Townsend," Spartacus-Educational.com, January 2020.

158. This new identity illustrates, by contrast, one of the weaknesses in the Depression-era unemployed movement discussed in chapter 4: an identity as unemployed, even a political, activist identity, was never asserted proudly, never fully escaped stigma—on the contrary, the unemployed sought to reject that identity as quickly and permanently as possible.

159. Charles Ernst as late as 1938 hoped that the Townsend clubs would spark a campaign for expanding Social Security to a "wider eligibility"; *Survey Midmonthly* 74, no. 5 (1938): 144.

160. Charles R. Morris, *The AARP: America's Most Powerful Lobby and the Clash of Generations* (New York: Crown, 1996).

161. The size of that shift shows in 2018 statistics. Eleven percent of the federal budget went to the elderly as compared to 3 percent for children; the federal government spends seven times as much on the elderly as on children. Even if you add in state spending on children, the elderly still receive 3.2 times as much. Figures drawn from Michael Collins, "Report: The Federal Government Is Spending Less on Children and More on the Elderly," *USA Today*, June 7, 2018; Julia B. Isaacs, "How Much Do We Spend on Children and the Elderly?," Brookings, November 2009; and Ben Leubsdorf, "The Federal Government Spends a Lot More on the Elderly Than on Children. Should It?" *Wall Street Journal*, March 2, 2018. However, as of 2019, "pension generosity did not drain resources from children," according to Teresa Ghilarducci in "Making Old People Work: Three False Assumptions Supporting the 'Working-Longer' Consensus" (conference paper, September 26, 2019, author's collection).

4. Shareholders in Relief

1. Nathaniel Weyl, "Organizing Hunger," *New Republic*, December 14, 1932, 119.

2. Rose Chernin, "Organizing the Unemployed in the Bronx in the 1930s," History IsaWeapon.com, n.d.

3. Horace Cayton, "The Black Bugs," *Nation*, September 9, 1931, 255.

4. John Garraty, *The Great Depression* (Garden City, NY: Anchor Press, 1987), chap. 1; David Hoskins, "Recalling the Great Depression's Eviction Struggles," *Workers' World*, February 14, 2008; Lee J. Alston, "Farm Foreclosures in the United States During the Interwar Period," *Journal of Economic History* 43, no. 4 (1983): 886; Andrew Richards, "Mobilizing the Powerless: Collective Protest Action of the Unemployed in the Interwar Period," Estudio Working Paper 2002, 18, 20.

5. Michael R. McBrearty, "Fighting Evictions—The 1930s and Now," MROnline.org, September 2, 2020.

6. Washington, D.C., alone had ten thousand "hidden" unemployed and homeless women in 1932. See Elaine S. Abelson, "'Women Who Have No Men to Work for Them': Gender and Homelessness in the Great Depression, 1930–1934," *Feminist Studies* 29, no. 1 (2003): 112; Erroll Lincoln Uys, "The Boxcar Boys and Girls," Erroluys.com, 2021.

7. Studies of the 1930s Depression found considerable "quiet resignation," "apathy and despair," "hopelessness and inertia, even blaming themselves among the unemployed, particularly among men"; quoted in Richards, "Mobilizing the Powerless," 3, 11, 31. The most influential scholarly view of the unemployed as apathetic was the study of an Austrian town by Marie Jahoda, Paul F. Lazarsfeld, and Hans Zeisel, *Marienthal: The Sociography of an Unemployed Community* (Chicago: Aldine, 1971).

Similar findings can be found in several articles in Matthias Reiss and Matt Perry, eds., *Unemployment and Protest: New Perspectives on Two Centuries of Contention* (Oxford: Oxford University Press, 2011); C. Wright Bakke, *The Unemployed Man: A Social Study* (New York: E. P. Dutton, 1934); Bernard Sternsher, "Victims of the Great Depression: Self-Blame/Non-Self-Blame, Radicalism, and Pre-1929 Experiences," *Social Science History* 1, no. 2 (1977): 137–77; Richard Croucher, "The History of Unemployed Movements," *Labour History Review* 73, no. 1 (2008): passim.

8. Roy Rosenzweig was for long the only historian studying the unemployed movement, and his three articles are frequently cited. He estimated that the unemployed movement at most included 5 percent of the unemployed at any one time, in "'Socialism in Our Time': The Socialist Party and the Unemployed, 1929–1936," *Labor History* 20, no. 4 (1979): 495.

9. The first quotation is from Steve Nelson, James R. Barrett, and Rob Ruck, *Steve Nelson: American Radical* (Pittsburgh: Pittsburgh University Press, 1981), 76, 163; the second is from Randi Storch, *Red Chicago: American Communism at its Grassroots, 1928–1935* (Urbana: University of Illinois Press, 2007), 117.

10. Co-ops have a long history, especially if we include cooperative ventures that did not use that label. Recently they had become an economic structure used widely: the United States has 29,000 cooperative businesses with millions of members and a thriving sector of worker cooperatives. Andrew Bibby, "The State of the Co-operative Nation," *Guardian*, March 6, 2012; "US Worker Cooperatives; A State of the Sector," Democracy at Work Institute, n.d.

11. Celine Kuklowsky, "The Great Depression and Self-Help Coops," DRPop.org, May 28, 2015; Abdurrahman Pasha, "The Self-Help Cooperative Movement in Los Angeles, 1931–1940" (PhD diss., University of Oregon, 2014); Jonathan Rowe, "Depression-Era Coops a Model for Today," May 6, 2006, reprinted as "What History Books Left Out About Depression Era Co-ops," *Yes! Magazine*, September 14, 2018.

12. Arthur Hillman, *The Unemployed Citizens' League of Seattle* (Seattle: University of Washington Press, 1934), 193. One estimate held that one-third of Seattle's 144,000 voters were UCL members, cited in Irving Bernstein, *The Lean Years: A History of the American Worker, 1920–1933* (New York: Da Capo Press, 1960), 417.

13. Hillman, *Unemployed Citizens' League*, 202; Gordon Black, "Organizing the Unemployed: The Early 1930s," and Summer Kelly, "Self-Help Activists: The Seattle Branches of the Unemployed Citizen's League," both at depts.washington.edu/depress/UCL.

14. The UCL did, however, prevent the city from imposing a discriminatory wage rate in these jobs, and in the first half of 1932, eighty thousand men received relief payments. Hillman, *Unemployed Citizens' League*, 202; Weyl, "Organizing Hunger," 117–20.

15. William H. Mullins, "Self-Help in Seattle, 1931–32," *Pacific Northwest Quarterly* 72, no. 1 (1981): 11–19.

16. Mullins, "Self-Help in Seattle," 11–19; Black, "Organizing the Unemployed." No one has studied the records of this Seattle experiment so we don't know how fairly, cleanly, or creatively the UCL administrated help to the unemployed.

17. Weyl, "Organizing Hunger," 119. One may see an analogy in today's calls to defund the police.

18. Bernstein, *Lean Years*, 416. Prefigurative politics will be discussed more fully in chapter 7.

19. Helen Seymour, "The Organized Unemployed" (MS thesis, University of Chicago, 1937), 59.

20. People who had previously experienced stable employment and were new to poverty could resist, while those who had long been poor could not. Hillman, *Unemployed Citizens' League*, 197.

21. Nancy Fraser and Linda Gordon, "A Genealogy of 'Dependency': Tracing a Keyword of the US Welfare State," *Signs* 19, no. 2 (1994): 309–36.

22. Mordecai Ezekiel, *Jobs for All Through Industrial Expansion* (New York: Knopf, 1939), 240.

23. Roy Rosenzweig, "Organizing the Unemployed: The Early Years of the Great Depression, 1929–1933," *Radical America* 10, no. 4 (1976): 39; Richards, "Mobilizing the Powerless," 25.

24. *Lumpen* literally means "ragged." This term, coined by Marx and Engels in the 1840s, referred to an underclass rabble incapable of developing into a working class. Van Gosse, "'To Organize in Every Neighborhood, in Every Home': The Gender Politics of American Communists Between the Wars," *Radical History Review* 50 (1991): 109–41.

25. Mark Naison, *Communists in Harlem During the Depression* (New York: Grove Press, 1983), 35–36; Daniel J. Leab, "'United We Eat': The Creation and Organization of the Unemployed Councils in 1930," *Labor History* 8, no. 3 (1967): 300–15.

26. Rosenzweig, "Organizing the Unemployed," 49. Trotskyist Communists, although hostile to the Comintern, were no more respectful, calling cooperatives "the planned economy of garbage picking." Quoted in Len Myers and Chis Knox, "Organizing the Unemployed in the Great Depression," *Workers Vanguard* 73, July 18, 1975.

27. The CP charged that Seattle's UCL and other governments that provided social welfare were variants of fascism because they stood in the way of a dictatorship of the proletariat. Examples of this CP approach appear in Mark Naison, "Harlem Communists and the Politics of Black Protest," in *Community Organization for Urban Social Change*, ed. Robert Fisher and Peter Romanofsky (Westport, CT: Greenwood Press, 1981), 89–126.

28. Bernstein, *Lean Years*, 426–47.

29. Franklin Folsom, *Impatient Armies of the Poor: The Story of Collective Action of the Unemployed, 1808–1942* (Niwot: University Press of Colorado, 1991), 214, 234; Benjamin Papers, LOC.

30. Bert Cochran, *Labor and Communism: The Conflict that Shaped American Unions* (Princeton, NJ: Princeton University Press, 1977), 79. Membership figures are from Seymour Martin Lipset, "Roosevelt and the Protest of the 1930s," *Minnesota Law Review* 68 (1984): 275.

31. Danny Lucia, "The Unemployed Movements of the 1930s: Bringing Misery Out of Hiding," *International Socialist Review* 71 (May 2010).

32. James J. Lorence, *Organizing the Unemployed: Community and Union Activists in the Industrial Heartland* (Albany: State University of New York Press, 1996), 31, 77, 79.

33. John R. Stockham, "An Analysis of the Organizational Structure, Aims, and Tactics of the Workers' Alliance of America in Franklin County an Cuyahoga County, Ohio, and in Hennepin County, Minnesota; and of the Federal Workers Section of the General Drivers Union, Local 544, in Hennepin County, Minnesota" (MA thesis, Ohio State University, 1938), 9–10.

34. Cochran, *Labor and Communism*, 79.

35. Demonstrators included an estimated 50,000 in Boston and Chicago, 30,000 in Philadelphia, 25,000 in Cleveland, 20,000 in Pittsburgh; Folsom, *Impatient Armies*, 255; Lorence, *Organizing*, 23–25; Frances Fox Piven and Richard Cloward, *Poor People's Movements: Why They Succeed, How They Fail* (New York: Pantheon, 1977), 45–46,

50–52; Paul D'Amato, "The Communist Party and Black Liberation in the 1930s," *International Socialist Review* 103 (Winter 2016–17).

36. "35,000 Jammed in Square," *New York Times*, March 7, 1930; Piven and Cloward, *Poor People's Movements*, 51; David Carpenter, "The Communist Party—Leader of the Struggle of the Unemployed," *Political Affairs* 29 (1930): 85. Critics of the CP, including people of the Left such as Dorothy Day of the Catholic Worker movement, accused the organizers of demonstrations like this of seeking "drama, even melodrama"; she also blamed the CP for making demonstrators vulnerable to police violence. She conceded, however, that many participants responded with greater respect for CP and Council members: "They sure have got gumption." Dorothy Day, "Hunger Marchers in Washington," *Commonweal* 43 (December 24, 1932): 277–79.

37. Christopher C. Wright, "Down But Not Out: The Unemployed in Chicago during the Great Depression" (PhD diss., University of Illinois at Chicago, 2017), 478. One example of the CP's undemocratic report, an unnamed writer begins a report on an early strike of relief workers in Minnesota, "The Party decided for a strike . . ." in *Party Organizer*, July 1933, 22.

38. Harold D. Lasswell and Dorothy Blumenstock, *World Revolutionary Propaganda: A Chicago Study* (1939; reprint Plainview, NY: Books for Libraries Press, 1970), 74.

39. Steve Valocchi, "External Resources and the Unemployed Councils of the 1930s: Evaluating Six Propositions from Social Movement Theory," *Sociological Forum* 8, no. 3 (1993): 462; Black, "Organizing the Unemployed."

40. Henry W. Francis, report to Harry Hopkins, November 18, 1934; Louisa Wilson to Hopkins, November 17, 1934, and November 30, 1934, in Boxes 66 and 67, FERA-WPA Field Reports, Hopkins Papers; "The CPUSA and the Unemployed Movement of the 1930s," speech at the third congress of the Marxist-Leninist Party USA, Marxists.org.

41. Robin D. G. Kelley, *Hammer and Hoe: Alabama Communists During the Great Depression* (Chapel Hill: University of North Carolina Press, 1990), chap. 5. That Jews and Blacks shared those cultures did not always guarantee easy collaboration. Harlem's Jewish store owners were not always respectful of African Americans.

42. Annelise Orleck, "'We Are That Mythical Thing Called the Public': Militant Housewives During the Great Depression," in *U.S. Women in Struggle: A Feminist Studies Anthology*, ed. Claire Goldberg Moses and Heidi Hartmann (Urbana: University of Illinois Press, 1995), 199, quotation at 159.

43. Rosemary Feurer, "The Nutpickers' Union, 1933–34: Crossing the Boundaries of Community and Workplace," in *We Are All Leaders: The Alternative Unionism of the Early 1930s*, ed. Staughton Lynd (Champaign: University of Illinois Press, 1996), 35–36; Meredith Tax, "Women's Councils in the 1930s" (unpub. ms., author's collection); Naison, "Harlem Communists," 149.

44. Lashawn Harris, "Running with the Reds: African American Women and the Communist Party During the Great Depression," *Journal of American History* 94, no. 1 (2009): 27; Naison, "Harlem Communists," 149; Tax, "Women's Councils." Orleck, "'That Mythical Thing,'" 201, cites a claim that 4,500 butchers were boycotted, probably an exaggerated number.

45. Erik McDuffie, *Sojourning for Freedom: Black Women, American Communism and the Making of Black Left Feminism* (Durham, NC: Duke University Press, 2011), 79.

46. McDuffie, *Sojourning for Freedom*, 8; Naison, "Harlem Communists," 279, quotation at 77.

47. Frank B. Wilderson III, *Afropessimism* (New York: Liveright, 2020); Mark I. Solo-

mon, *The Cry Was Unity: Communism and African Americans, 1917–1936* (Jackson: University Press of Mississippi, 1998), 139–40, 16; Naison, *Communists in Harlem*, 13, 34, 43, 46–9, 69, 264, 280–81.

48. While the Roosevelt administration created a moratorium on foreclosures on farm mortgages, it did not create a moratorium on evictions from housing.

49. In Harlem, resistance to evictions dated back to the 1929 Harlem Tenants League and would eventually produce an organization fighting for rent control during World War II. Mark Naison, "From Eviction Resistance to Rent Control: Tenant Activism in the Great Depression," in *The Tenant Movement in New York City, 1904–1984*, ed. Ronald Lawson (New Brunswick, NJ: Rutgers University Press, 1986), 99–101.

50. Tax, "Women's Councils," 16A; Orleck, " 'That Mythical Thing,' " 149.

51. At one such event, thirty-five speakers held forth, pledging support from a variety of organizations local and national. Mark Naison, "Fighting Evictions During the Great Depression," *International Socialist Review* 81 (January 2012).

52. Folsom, *Impatient Armies*, 269; Mark Naison, "Foreclosure Defense in the Bronx," *n+1*, April 12, 2012, 11; Wright, "Down But Not Out," 462, counted 185,794 evictions in New York City in the eight months before June 30, 1932, of which 77,000 were successfully resisted.

53. Naison, "Fighting Evictions," covers both evictions and rent strikes.

54. Nelson, Barrett, and Ruck, *Nelson*, 163.

55. Robert Fisher, *Let the People Decide: Neighborhood Organizing in America* (New York: Twayne, 1994), 44; Naison, "Fighting Evictions."

56. Piven and Cloward, *Poor People's Movements*, 57

57. Wayne Parish to Harry Hopkins, November 11, 1934, and Edward J. Webster to Hopkins, reports dated October 25 through November 14, 1934, and December 8, 1934, in Box 67, Hopkins Papers.

58. James S. Allen, *Organizing in the Depression South: A Communist's Memoir* (Minneapolis: MEP Publications, 2001), 49, 51. This use of the KKK was not uncommon and indicates the degree to which it functioned effectively as part of government.

59. Mary Stanton, *Red Black White: The Alabama Communist Party, 1930–1950* (Athens: University of Georgia Press, 2019), 20.

60. Allen, *Organizing*, 49, 51, quotation at 55.

61. An extraordinary and widely respected strategist and organizer, Hudson wrote a memoir, *Black Worker in the Deep South: A Personal Record* (New York: International Publishers, 1972). He was also the subject of study by the historian Nell Painter, *The Narrative of Hosea Hudson: The Life and Times of a Black Radical* (New York: W. W. Norton, 1994).

62. Lucia, "Unemployed Movements."

63. Angelo Herndon, "You Cannot Kill the Working Class" (1937), Historyisaweapon.com.

64. James John Lorence, *The Unemployed People's Movement: Leftists, Liberals, and Labor in Georgia, 1929–1941* (Atlanta: University of Georgia Press, 2009), 134–35, 139; Harris, "Running with Reds," 21.

65. Charles Payne, *I've Got the Light of Freedom* (Urbana: University of Illinois Press, 1994).

66. Robert Korstad, *Civil Rights Unionism: Tobacco Workers and the Struggle for Democracy in the Mid-Twentieth-Century South* (Chapel Hill: University of North Carolina Press, 2003), 125.

67. Robert P. Ingalls, "Antiradical Violence in Birmingham During the 1930s," *Journal of Southern History* 47, no. 4 (1981): 521.

68. Hudson, *Black Worker in the Deep South*, 51–52.

69. Karen Ferguson, *Black Politics in New Deal Atlanta* (Chapel Hill: University of North Carolina Press, 2002), 160–62.

70. Glenda Gilmore, *Defying Dixie: The Radical Roots of Civil Rights* (New York: W. W. Norton, 2008), 109. The Black Shirt application form is pictured in this book.

71. Len De Caux, *Labor Radical: From the Wobblies to the CIO* (Boston: Beacon Press, 1971), 162; Harold R. Kerbo and Richard A. Shaffer, "Lower Class Insurgency and the Political Process: The Response of the U.S. Unemployed, 1890–1940," *Social Problems* 39, no. 2 (1992): 150. From 1929 to 1934, the CP organized or participated in over two hundred demonstrations in Chicago; Lasswell and Blumenstock, *World Revolutionary Propaganda*, 172–73.

72. Estimating the size of any of the unemployed groups is an exercise in guesswork, wide open to the bias of whoever is doing the estimating. The Chicago Leagues soon claimed 67 locals and 25,000 members, a size approximately equivalent to that of the CP councils. Ohio claimed 187 locals and 100,000 members; Pennsylvania claimed 50 locals with 70,000 members. Robert S. Asher, "The Jobless Help Themselves: A Lesson from Chicago," *New Republic*, September 28, 1932, 168–69; Folsom, *Impatient Armies*, 341–42; Weyl, "Organizing Hunger," 120; Piven and Cloward, *Poor People's Movements*, 72; Helen Seymour, *When Clients Organize* (Chicago: American Public Welfare Association, 1937).

73. Mauritz A. Hallgren, "Help Wanted—for Chicago," *Nation*, May 11, 1932, 534–35; Mauritz A. Hallgren, *Seeds of Revolt: A Study of American Life and the Temper of the American People During the Depression* (New York: Knopf, 1933), 123–27; Asher, "Jobless Help Themselves," 168.

74. I have not been able to find an ethnic breakdown of SP members. But in the Chicago CP, half of members were foreign-born, 15 percent were Russian, 10 percent other Slavs, and 22 percent Jews; Storch, *Red Chicago*, 40; Wright, "Down But Not Out," 459, 462, 474.

75. Gary Roth, *Marxism in a Lost Century: A Biography of Paul Mattick* (Chicago: Haymarket Books, 2015), 42, 97; Storch, *Red Chicago*, 112–13; Wright, "Down But Not Out," 457, 474–75.

76. Eleanor Nora Kahn, "Organizations of Unemployed Workers as a Factor in the American Labor Movement" (MA thesis, University of Wisconsin, 1934), 79.

77. Kahn, "Organizations of Unemployed Workers," 44–45, 79.

78. Kahn, "Organizations of Unemployed Workers," 42–43.

79. Weyl, "Organizing Hunger," 120; Asher, "Jobless Help Themselves," 168–69.

80. Piven and Cloward, *Poor People's Movements*, 67.

81. Lasswell and Blumenstock, *World Revolutionary Propaganda*, 73–74; Wright, "Down But Not Out," 462–66, 473, 477.

82. Storch, *Red Chicago*, 114–15; Lizabeth Cohen, *Workers Make a New Deal: Industrial Workers in Chicago, 1919–1939* (Cambridge: Cambridge University Press, 1990), chap. 6, found that these demonstrations contributed to Americanizing immigrants.

83. Cohen, *Workers Make*, 263.

84. Sally M. Miller, "The Socialist Party and the Negro, 1901–1920," *Journal of Negro History* 56, no. 3 (1971): 220–29.

85. Lucia, "Unemployed Movements," The CP's commitment to fight race discrimination continued into the declining years of the New Deal; for example, Rayford Logan, "The Negro and the New Deal," *Social Work Today* 6, no. 9 (1939): 7.

86. Erik S. McDuffie, "'They Shall Not Die': The Movement to Free the Scottsboro

Boys" (unpub. ms., author's collection, 2000), 7; Robin D. G. Kelley, *Race Rebels: Culture, Politics, and the Black Working Class* (New York: Free Press, 1994).

87. Wright, "Down But Not Out," 472; quotation from Storch, *Red Chicago*, 115.

88. Storch, *Red Chicago*, 99–100, 111–13; Folsom, *Impatient Armies*, 268.

89. In 1934 African Americans made up 21 percent of all unemployed activists in Chicago. Cohen, *Workers Make*, 266. These figures also reflect the fact that 40 percent of Chicago Blacks were relying on relief; Melissa Ford, "Suppose They Are Communists! The Unemployed Councils and the 1933 Chicago Sopkin Dressmakers' Strike," *American Communist History* 16, nos. 1–2 (2017): 47.

90. George Edmund Haynes, *Communists Are Bidding for Negro Loyalty*, pamphlet reprinted from *Southern Workman*, April 1933, 3, 9. W. E. B. Du Bois also harbored skepticism about CP efforts in 1930, though he would soon revise this view.

91. Storch, *Red Chicago*, 118; Ford, "Suppose," 51; Wright, "Down But Not Out," 470–71. The huge success of Gold's somewhat autobiographical novel, *Jews Without Money*, had made him an influential cultural leader in the CP.

92. Christine Ellis, "People Who Cannot Be Bought," introduction to *Rank and File: Personal Histories by Working-class Organizers*, ed. Alice Lynd and Staughton Lynd (New York: Monthly Review Press, 1973), 18–19.

93. Nelson, Barrett, and Ruck, *Nelson*, 75–76.

94. Wright, "Down But Not Out," 494, quotation at 462. On repairs, see Gertrude Springer, "Shock Troops to the Rescue," *Survey*, January 1933, 9–11.

95. They considered themselves a club; Ford, "Suppose," 51. I have been unable to determine why they were called "bugs." One disdainful scholar referred to them as "seedy colored people"; Bernstein, *Lean Years*, 428.

96. Horace Cayton, "The Black Bugs," *Nation*, September 9, 1931, 255.

97. Lasswell and Blumenstock, *World Revolutionary Propaganda*, 204.

98. Hallgren, *Seeds*, 129, 176; Storch, *Red Chicago*, 99–101, 115, 119; Folsom, *Impatient Armies*, 268; Wright, "Down But Not Out," 460.

99. Jeff Singleton, *The American Dole: Unemployment Relief and the Welfare State in the Great Depression* (Westport, CT: Greenwood, 2000), 80–81.

100. Hallgren, "Help Wanted," 535. Personal note: Humboldt Park is next to where I grew up.

101. Weyl, "Organizing Hunger," 118; Cohen, *Workers Make*, 264; Folsom, *Impatient Armies*, 268; Singleton, *American Dole*, 82; Asher, "Jobless Help Themselves," 169; Piven and Cloward, *Poor People's Movements*, 59–60, 67; Storch, *Red Chicago*, 122–23; Wright, "Down But Not Out," 483.

102. Jo Ann Ooiman Robinson, *Abraham Went Out: A Biography of A. J. Muste* (Philadelphia: Temple University Press, 1981), 35. Muste's saying would have been a good response to the snide academic's comment on the Socialist League meeting.

103. Among Brookwood's progressive aspects was its commitment to African American workers, unlike the AFL. Charles F. Howlett, "Brookwood Labor College: Voice of Support for Black Workers," *Negro History Bulletin* 45, no. 2 (1982): 38–39. The CPLA's original plan was to reform the AFL but from within, not by organizing competing unions as the CP was doing.

104. The charge appeared in the pamphlet *The Little Brothers of the Big Labor Fakers* (New York: Trade Union Unity League, 1931).

105. A. J. Muste, "My Experience in Labor and Radical Struggles," in *As We Saw the Thirties*, ed. Rita James Simon (Urbana: University of Illinois Press, 1967), 133.

106. Roy Rosenzweig, "Radicals and the Jobless: The Musteites and the Unemployed

Leagues, 1932–1936," *Labor History* 16, no. 1 (1975): 60; A. J. Muste, "The Columbus Convention of Unemployed—An Analysis," *Labor Action* 1, no. 8 (July 15, 1933): 3–4.

107. Wade, *Fiery Cross*, 258–59.

108. A. J. Muste, "The Challenge to Progressives," in *The American Labor Year Book, 1930* (Rand School of Social Science, 1930), 90.

109. Leilah Danielson, *American Gandhi: A. J. Muste and the History of Radicalism in the Twentieth Century* (Philadelphia: University of Pennsylvania Press, 2014), passim.

110. Stockham, "Analysis of the Organizational Structure," 10; Rosenzweig, "Organizing the Unemployed," 49–50.

111. Rosenzweig, "Radicals and the Jobless"; Folsom, *Impatient Armies*, chap. 28; Stockham, "Analysis of the Organizational Structure."

112. These lists and reports are in the Hickok folder, Box 67, Hopkins Papers.

113. Danielson, *American Gandhi*, 184–86. By then Muste had folded his CPLA/NUL into the American Workers Party, an attempt to unite the unemployed and the employed.

114. Danielson, *American Gandhi*, 184–86.

115. Robinson, *Abraham Went Out*, 54–59; Danielson, *American Gandhi*, chaps. 6 and 7.

116. The councils trained members in public speaking; the Chicago Leagues set up a library and a "Workers' Training School." Roy Rosenzweig, "'Socialism in Our Time': The Socialist Party and the Unemployed, 1929–1936," *Labor History* 20, no. 4 (1979): 486–509.

117. Martha Gellhorn observed this personally in Camden, New Jersey, in her report to Hopkins April 25, 1935, Box 101, Hopkins Papers; Lasswell and Blumenstock, *World Revolutionary Propaganda*, 170.

118. Rose Chernin, "Organizing the Unemployed in the Bronx in the 1930s" (1949), HistoryIsaWeapon.com.

119. Doug McAdam, *Political Process and the Development of Black Insurgency, 1930–1970* (Chicago: University of Chicago Press, 1982), 51.

120. Scholars noted that psychological depression was greatest among men; Bakke, *Unemployed Man*; George Tselos, "Self-Help and Sauerkraut: The Organized Unemployed, Inc. of Minneapolis," *Minnesota History* 45, no. 8 (1977): 312; Piven and Cloward, *Poor People's Movements*, 56.

121. Wright, "Down But Not Out," 474–76; McDuffie, *Sojourning for Freedom*, 84.

122. Naison, "Fighting Evictions."

123. Anecdotes from Wright, "Down But Not Out," 476, and recollection of Mrs. Willye Jeffries in Studs Terkel, *Hard Times: An Illustrated Oral History of the Great Depression* (New York: Pantheon, 1970), 456–62.

124. Lorence, *Organizing*, 117.

125. Lorence, *Organizing*, 117.

126. Robinson, *Abraham Went Out*, 50.

127. McDuffie, *Sojourning for Freedom*, 84–89

128. McDuffie, *Sojourning for Freedom*, 84.

129. Storch, *Red Chicago*, 125, 220. CP women published a feminist critique a few years later, notably Mary Inman's 1940 *In Woman's Defense*, a sign that some discontent with sexism and gender conventionality was already simmering in the 1930s CP.

130. During the Depression, an estimated 2 million men roved the country in search of work; in 1932 alone, the Southern Pacific Railroad ejected 683,457 "hoboes" from its trains. Wright, "Down But Not Out," 477; Folsom, *Impatient Armies*, 311; Piven and Cloward, *Poor People's Movements*, 48; Stockham, "Analysis of the Organizational Structure," 42ff.

131. Quoted in Linda Gordon, "Harry Hopkins Brings Relief," in *Days of Destiny: Crossroads in American History*, ed. James M. McPherson and Alan Brinkley (New York: Agincourt Press for the Society of American Historians, 2001), 284.

132. Disregarding Comintern policy, the councils excluded TUUL members from a demonstration. Randi Storch, "'The Realities of the Situation': Revolutionary Discipline and Everyday Political Life in Chicago's Communist Party, 1928–1935," *Labor: Studies in Working-class History of the Americas* 1, no. 3 (2004); Storch, *Red Chicago*, 124–25. Northwestern states' Communists had sent delegates to the Socialist Party convention asking for a united front; Seth Goodkind, "The *Voice of Action*: A Paper for Workers and the Disenfranchised," Great Depression in Washington State, 2009, at https://depts.washington.edu/depress/voice_of_action.shtml. In Georgia, the CP-dominated sharecroppers' union sought alliance with the better-known SP-dominated STFU; the Highlander Center did manage to bring some SP and CP people together; Lorence, *Unemployed People's Movement*, 139, 141; Feurer, "Nutpickers' Union," 40.

133. Joining European Popular Front members, 2,800 Americans fought in Spain against the fascist coup.

134. The Comintern's acceptance of a Popular Front strategy led to a rapid expansion of the American CP. Its membership doubled between 1934 and 1938, and by 1943 the proportion of women members jumped from 10 to 50 percent—a direct result of CP involvement in community organizations. Storch, *Red Chicago*, 217–19; Rosalyn Baxandall, "The Question Seldom Asked: Women and the CPUSA," in *New Studies in the Politics and Culture of U.S. Communism*, ed. Michael E. Brown et al. (New York: Monthly Review Press, 1993), 156.

135. Several previous attempts to federate the unemployed groups failed due to sectarian hostility between the CP and the CPLA; Wright, "Down But Not Out," 498. In some regions the Alliance was represented by local groups, such as Washington State's Commonwealth Federation.

136. Chad Alan Goldberg, "Contesting the Status of Relief Workers during the New Deal," *Social Science History* 29, no. 3 (2005): 342, 358.

137. Proceedings, Illinois Workers Alliance; Chad Alan Goldberg, "Haunted by the Spectre of Communism: Collective Identity and Resource Mobilization in the Demise of the Workers Alliance of America," *Theory and Society*, no. 32 (2003): 755; Seymour "Organized Unemployed," 44. Lorence puts the membership at 400,000 in only eighteen states in *A Hard Journey: The Life of Don West* (Urbana: University of Illinois Press, 2007), 67; Richards, "Mobilizing the Powerless," 29.

138. "David Lasser, An American Spaceflight Pioneer," NTRS.NASA.gov. In 1930 Lasser founded the American Interplanetary Society, the first organization to promote space travel. (It ultimately became the American Institute of Aeronautics and Astronautics.)

139. Lasser's interest in space connected with his socialist politics: space exploration, he believed, could become a cooperative international project as a way of uniting "mankind." Utopian in both areas of interest, he ended his book by recalling Giordano Bruno, martyred "for believing in the plurality of worlds." Space exploration would not only create a better life on earth through science—verifying or destroying current theories of atoms, of bacteria and disease, of plant and animal life—but would also help humans seeking "the meaning of life." Arthur C. Clarke, introduction to David Lasser, *The Conquest of Space* (1931; reprint Burlington, Ont.: Apogee Books, 2002), 154–55.

140. Newsletter, Box 101, Hopkins Papers.

141. Workers Alliance of Cook County, Illinois, Bulletin no. 56, September 14, 1936, quoted in Seymour, "Organized Unemployed," 79.

142. Proceedings, Illinois Workers Alliance.

143. Lasswell and Blumenstock, *World Revolutionary Propaganda*, 171. Other examples of social workers' taking the side of clients include Mary Siegel, "Worker and Client Join Hands," *Social Work Today* 3, no. 4 (1936): 18; and Charlotte Carr, executive director of New York City's Home Relief Bureau, who defended the right of relief workers to unionize; "Charlotte Carr Is Needed in the Front Ranks," *Social Work Today*, December 1938, 18.

144. Edgar Hare, Jr., "Behind the Pressure Group," *Survey*, April 1935, 101–2, quoted in Seymour, "Organized Unemployed," 69.

145. Lorence, *Organizing*, 213, 232, offers an example of getting supervisors fired.

146. Lorence, *Hard Journey*, 68–69; Lorence, "Teacher and Learner: Don West and the Democratic Classroom," *Georgia Historical Quarterly* 90, no. 3 (2006): 418–41.

147. Lorence, *Organizing*, 212–13. This story suggests the importance of more local studies.

148. "Walker Off Tonight to Fight for Mooney," *New York Times*, November 20, 1931. It was of course not only Communists who had these concerns: the government photographer Dorothea Lange went to San Quentin to photograph Mooney, and New York's mayor visited Mooney's sister to express solidarity.

149. Dorothy Sue Cobble and Michael Merrill, "Occupy Wall Street Theater Is a Jab at Political Paralysis," NJ.com, December 18, 2011; Seymour, "Organized Unemployed," 100–1; "Unemployed Councils, Eviction Riots, and the New Deal," EconomicPopulist.org, July 1, 2009.

150. Mark Engler and Paul Engler, *This Is an Uprising: How Nonviolent Revolt is Shaping the Twenty-first Century* (New York: Nation Books, 2016), 145. The sociologist Frances Fox Piven has also argued this perspective.

151. Singleton, *American Dole*, 175–76. New Yorkers were particularly often denied WPA jobs when a 1937 amendment to an appropriation bill made ineligible aliens who were not yet in the process of becoming citizens. Several earlier, smaller jobs programs, notably the Civil Works Administration, which employed 4.3 million on 180,000 projects but lasted only five months, made no dent in the unemployment rate; Jeannette Gabriel, "'Natural Love for a Good Thing': The Unemployed Workers' Movement's Struggle for a Government Jobs Programme, 1931–1942" (unpub. ms., author's collection, n.d.), 119.

152. Between 1.5 and 3 million were WPA workers at any one time, constituting between 16 and 31 percent of the unemployed. Theodore E. Whiting and T. J. Woofter, Jr., *Summary of Relief and Federal Work Program Statistics, 1933–1940* (Washington, DC: GPO, 1941), 46–48.

153. The membership of the progressive bloc, initiated by New York City mayor Fiorello LaGuardia when he was a congressman, varied between nine and nineteen representatives, depending on the issues. The liberal bloc consisted of approximately forty-five representatives, including Lyndon Johnson and Maury Maverick.

154. James J. Lorence, *Gerald J. Boileau and the Progressive-Farmer-Labor Alliance* (Columbia: University of Missouri Press, 1994), 173–80.

155. Gertrude Springer, "Relief in November 1938," *Survey Midmonthly* 74, no. 11 (November 1938): 339, 341.

156. The WPA wage schedule was problematic. Wage rates, ranging from nineteen to ninety-four dollars a month, were categorized by region of the country (four catego-

ries, with southern workers earning least and New England and mid-Atlantic workers most); by population size (five categories ranging from cities with over 100,000 residents to areas with under five thousand); and by skill level. These categories were arbitrary and unworkable. A worker might live just outside the limits of a large city, for example, but nevertheless have to function within the city's more expensive economy. The skill categories to which jobs were assigned were arbitrary and/or biased, yet those categories determined wage rates. Several cities that were assigned to low-wage regions, such as Louisville, Kentucky, had to be transferred into higher-wage region once someone—possibly an Alliance representative—actually examined the cost of living there.

157. Lorence, *Organizing*, 213

158. Examples of employer complaint letters can be found in Entry 17, Box 2366, Record Group 16, NARA.

159. John E. Miller, "Progressivism and the New Deal: The Wisconsin Works Bill of 1935," *Wisconsin Magazine of History* 62, no. 1 (1978): 32. Before this agreement, the WPA had paid "security" wages, based on the minimum that could, in theory, support survival.

160. Williams, originally a social worker, served as assistant federal relief administrator under Hopkins. In World War II he headed the Lend-Lease program, providing aid to U.S. allies. He will reappear in chapter 5, on the Montgomery bus boycott; Senator James O. Eastland of Mississippi would condemn him as a Communist. In the early 1960s, Alabama governor George Wallace would take up the fight, using a 1957 photograph that showed Rev. Dr. Martin Luther King, Jr., and Williams seated side by side.

161. Lorence, *Organizing*, 129; Gabriel, "'Natural Love for a Good Thing,'" 136.

162. Sixty-five percent of the strikes concerned wages and hours. The only full-length book about the Workers Alliance, Lorence's study of its activities in Michigan, documents so many strikes that the total of 288 (from Seymour, "Organized Unemployed," table 2, 94) seems likely to be a great underestimate; Lorence, *Organizing*, 115–16. See also Edwin Amenta and Drew Halfmann, "Who Voted with Hopkins? Institutional Politics and the WPA," *Journal of Policy History* 13, no. 2 (2001): 263. Notably, a nationwide strike in January 1937 produced significant wage and hour gains; Gabriel, "'Natural Love for a Good Thing,'" 136.

163. Singleton, *American Dole*, 153.

164. A few CIO unions considered including the unemployed, but that plan was never realized. The UAW tried first to co-opt the unemployed groups by creating an unemployed "auxiliary" to the union, but then it decided it could do better by creating its own unemployed group, which began to poach Alliance members. The United Electrical Workers allowed the unemployed to remain bona-fide members for five cents a month, instead of the standard one dollar, and fought for their entitlement to relief. The Trotskyist-led Teamsters in Minneapolis created a special "federal" section for the unemployed, who were excused from paying dues. The Steel Workers helped laid-off members obtain relief. In Minneapolis–St. Paul, when 162 WPA workers were arrested for striking, the Central Labor Council pledged its Labor Temple as bond to get them out on bail; Hermann Erickson, "WPA Strikes and Trials of 1939," *Minnesota History* 42 (1971), 209. On the UAW, see Lorence, *Organizing*, 11–14, 290–92. Some union leaders recognized that the Alliance functioned as a training ground for leaders, which led some organizers to leave the unemployed movement for union jobs; Lorence, *Organizing*, 14, 220; Croucher, "History of Unemployed Movements," 6.

165. Chad Alan Goldberg, *Citizens and Paupers: Relief, Rights and Race from the Freedmen's Bureau to Workfare* (Chicago: University of Chicago Press, 2008), 124.
166. WPA chief Harry Hopkins sent out a handful of journalists to survey the attitudes of those receiving relief. This comment is from Martha Gellhorn, report from North Carolina, November 13, 1934, Box 66, Hopkins Papers.
167. Few historians have paid adequate attention to this deficiency. The exception is the Scottish historian William Ranulf Brock in *Welfare, Democracy and the New Deal* (Cambridge: Cambridge University Press, 1988).
168. Bakke, *Unemployed Man.*
169. Linda Gordon, "Shareholders in Relief: The Political Culture of Relief and Public Jobs in the Depression," Russell Sage Foundation Working Paper No. 135 (1998).
170. Charles F. Ernst, "Clients Aren't What They Used to Be," *Survey Midmonthly* 74, no. 5 (1938): 142.
171. Poll findings varied but not significantly. Hadley Cantril, ed., *Public Opinion, 1935–1946* (Princeton, NJ: Princeton University Press, 1951), 696, 893ff.; Jodie T. Allen, "How a Different America Responded to the Great Depression," Pew Research Center, December 14, 2010. These views remained as war grew nearer: a 1942 Roper poll found that 25 percent thought "some form of socialism would be a good thing," while 40 percent thought it a bad thing. The Gallup samples were heavily male, relatively well off, and overwhelmingly white. The sociologist Seymour Martin Lipset found that the results showed a sharp class divide: the "less affluent strata" were more favorable toward these social democratic politics. Lipset, "Roosevelt and 1930s Protest," 278.
172. Wayne W. Parish to Hopkins, November 11 and December 1, 1934, Box 65–66, Hopkins Papers; McClure to Hopkins, quoted in Brock, *Welfare, Democracy,* 264; Lorena Hickok, *One-Third of a Nation: Lorena Hickok Reports of the Great Depression* (Urbana: University of Illinois Press, 1981), 122.
173. Charles F. Ernst, "Clients Aren't What They Used to Be," *Survey Midmonthly* 74, no. 5 (1938): 142–45.
174. Gordon, "Shareholders in Relief."
175. Hickok, *One-third,* 193; Wilson to Hopkins, November 30, 1934, and Gellhorn to Hopkins, Box 66, Hopkins Papers.
176. Mrs. C. A. VerNooy to FDR and to Frances Perkins, March 2, 1933, Box 462, Records of the Children's Bureau, NARA; J. E. Perkins to Alfred E. Smith, April 1, 1935, in Folder 94, Box 119-7, WPA Collection, MSRC; I. H. Smith to Hopkins, February March 34, Folder 1, Box 119-1, MSRC.
177. Alfred E. Smith Papers, MSRC. Other stories of dramatic protest appear in Painter, *Narrative of Hudson*; and Robin D. G. Kelley, "The Black Poor and the Politics of Opposition in a New South City, 1929–1970," in *The "Underclass" Debate,* ed. Michael Katz (Princeton, NJ: Princeton University Press, 1993), 293–333. Of course, many complainants were not unemployed workers but sharecroppers who had been poor, undernourished, without education for their children for decades before the Depression. For many of them, the dole was more money than they had ever seen before. They too were making demands of the federal government.
178. Political letter-writers are usually elites: typically 40 to 46 percent come from the wealthy, 26 to 34 percent from the prosperous, 7 to 9 percent from the poor. But 46 percent of FDR's 1934 correspondents were laborers. Leila A. Sussman, *Dear F.D.R.: A Study of Political Letter Writing* (Totowa, NJ: Bedminster Press, 1963), 135–42.
179. Landon Storrs, *The Second Red Scare and the Unmaking of the New Deal Left* (Princeton, NJ: Princeton University Press, 2013).

180. Goldberg, "Haunted by the Spectre," 750–51. On Lasser, see Frank A. Warren, *An Alternative Vision: The Socialist Party in the 1930s* (Bloomington: Indiana University Press, 1974), 114, 149.
181. Goldberg, "Decade of Dissent," 88.

5. Leadership and Followership

1. Raymond Arsenault, "The Montgomery Bus Boycott and American Politics," in *Dixie Redux: Essays in Honor of Sheldon Hackney*, ed. Raymond Arsenault and Orville Vernon Burton (Montgomery, AL: New South Books, 2013), 308.
2. L. D. Reddick, "The Bus Boycott in Montgomery," in *The Walking City: The Montgomery Bus Boycott, 1955–1956*, ed. David J. Garrow (Brooklyn, NY: Carlson, 1989), 70; Thomas J. Gilliam, "The Montgomery Bus Boycott, 1955–1956," in Garrow, *Walking City*, 197; Preston Valien, "The Montgomery Bus Protest as a Social Movement," in Garrow, *Walking City*, 89.
3. Jeanne Theoharis, *The Rebellious Life of Mrs. Rosa Parks* (Boston: Beacon Press, 2013), 83–84, suggests that constructing Rosa Parks as a shy, simple, tired woman who just sat down because she was tired resulted in part from an effort to counteract the red-baiting used against activists.
4. This story is beautifully told in Danielle L. McGuire, *At the Dark End of the Street: Black Women, Rape, and Resistance—A New History of the Civil Rights Movement from Rosa Parks to the Rise of Black Power* (New York: Knopf, 2010).
5. Theoharis, *Rebellious Life*, 92.
6. For documentation, see Doron Shultziner, "The Social-Psychological Origins of the Montgomery Bus Boycott: Social Interaction and Humiliation in the Emergence of Social Movements," *Mobilization* 18, no. 2 (2013): 117–42. Even a white businessman understood this, maintaining that "the desire for change in seating would never have come about if the bus had treated Negro passengers with respect." James J. Bailey quoted in Shultziner, "Social-Psychological Origins," 139n37. But Bailey's comment also represented the view of Montgomery white elites that "men in the lowest income level" were to blame, "the type of men who do nothing but drink and talk about the 'niggers' for recreation"; Dave Norris quoted in Shultziner, "Social-Psychological Origins," 134.
7. She also saw the practice of reserving seats for whites, even when empty, as the "ultimate humiliation." Jo Ann Gibson Robinson, *The Montgomery Bus Boycott and the Women Who Started It: The Memoir of Jo Ann Gibson Robinson*, ed. David J. Garrow (Knoxville: University of Tennessee Press, 1987), 16, 35, and 43.
8. Mary Fair Burks, "Trailblazers: Women in the Montgomery Bus Boycott," in *Women in the Civil Rights Movement: Trailblazers and Torchbearers, 1941–1965*, ed. Vicki L. Crawford Jacqueline Anne Rouse, and Barbara Woods (Bloomington: Indiana University Press, 1990), 78.
9. Darlene Clark Hine, "Rape and the Inner Lives of Black Women in the Middle West," *Signs* 14, no. 4 (1989): 912–20.
10. McGuire, *At the Dark End*, 12, 40–42, 58–61, 64, 70–71.
11. Montgomery's White Baptist churches numbered seven in 1930 and twenty by 1952. Pentecostal congregations grew to 40 percent of the white churches. David R. Goldfield, *Black, White, and Southern: Race Relations and Southern Culture 1940 to the Present* (Baton Rouge: Louisiana State University Press, 1990), 95.
12. J. Mills Thornton III, "Challenge and Response in the Montgomery Bus Boycott of 1955–1956," in Garrow, *Walking City*, 323–37, 364; Rebecca Retzlaff, "Desegregation

of City Parks and the Civil Rights Movement: The Case of Oak Park in Montgomery, Alabama," *Journal of Urban History* 47, no. 4 (2019): 1–38; Lamont H. Yeakey, "The Montgomery, Alabama, Bus Boycott" (PhD diss., Columbia University, 1979), 174; Goldfield, *Black, White, and Southern*, 47, 93.

13. The two cases were *Sweatt v. Painter* and *McLaurin v. Oklahoma State Regents*.
14. Virginia Foster Durr, *Outside the Magic Circle*, ed. Hollinger F. Barnard (Tuscaloosa: University of Alabama Press, 1985), 274. Although *Brown* repudiated *Plessy v Ferguson*, it did not necessarily apply to segregated bus seating since separate facilities were not involved.
15. Yeakey, "Montgomery Boycott," 139–41; John A. Salmond, *A Southern Rebel: The Life and Times of Aubrey Willis Williams, 1890–1965* (Chapel Hill: University of North Carolina Press, 1983), 199.
16. Theoharis, *Rebellious Life*, 50.
17. Ralph David Abernathy, *And the Walls Came Tumbling Down* (New York: Harper & Row, 1989), 34.
18. Rosa Parks with Jim Haskins, *Rosa Parks: My Story* (New York: Dial Books, 1992), 79; the quotation is from Rosa Parks et al., "Mrs. Rosa Parks Reports on Montgomery, Ala., Bus Protest," recorded from Highlander Folk School Planning Conference on Public School Integration, March 3–4, 1956, Crmvet.org.
19. Pamela E. Brooks, *Boycotts, Buses and Passes: Black Women's Resistance in the U.S. South and South Africa* (Amherst: University of Massachusetts Press, 2008), 119.
20. Steven M. Millner, "The Montgomery Bus Boycott: A Case Study in the Emergence and Career of a Social Movement," in Garrow, *Walking City*, 521. Many Black Montgomerians shared this view; see Theoharis, *Rebellious Life*, 79.
21. Virginia Durr to Clark Foreman and Corliss Lamont, February 24, 1956, in Virginia Foster Durr, *Freedom Writer: Letters from the Civil Rights Years*, ed. Patricia Sullivan (New York: Routledge, 2003).
22. Thornton, "Challenge and Response," in Garrow, *Walking City*, 353.
23. Everett Carll Ladd, Jr., *Negro Political Leadership in the South* (Ithaca, NY: Cornell University Press, 1966), 128.
24. Robinson, *Montgomery Bus Boycott*, 20; David J. Garrow, *Bearing the Cross: Martin Luther King, Jr., and the Southern Christian Leadership Conference* (New York: William Morrow, 1986), 15.
25. Burks, "Trailblazers," 72.
26. Mary Stanton, *Journey Toward Justice: Juliette Hampton Morgan and the Montgomery Bus Boycott* (Athens: University of Georgia Press, 2006), 153.
27. Fred Gray, *Bus Ride to Justice: Changing the System by the System: The Life and Works of Fred Gray* (Montgomery, AL: Black Belt Press, 1994), 45. The quotation is from Lewis V. Baldwin and Aprille V. Woodson, *Freedom Is Never Free: A Biographical Portrait of Edgar Daniel Nixon* (Atlanta: Office of Minority Affairs, 1992), 37.
28. Marissa Chappell, Jenny Hutchinson, and Brian Ward, "'Dress Modestly, Neatly . . . As If You Were Going to Church': Respectability, Class and Gender in the Montgomery Bus Boycott and the Early Civil Rights Movement," in *Gender and the Civil Rights Movement*, ed. Peter J. Ling and Sharon Montieth (New Brunswick, NJ: Rutgers University Press, 2004), 75 and passim.
29. Payne, *I've Got the Light of Freedom*.
30. Gwen Bell quoted in Brooks, *Boycotts, Buses*, 108.
31. Brooks, *Boycotts, Buses*, 131, 149, 162, quotation at 12.
32. Despite this insult, the WPC regularly invited LWV members to its meetings. Ber-

nice McNair Barnett, "Black Women's Collectivist Movement Organizations: Their Struggles During the 'Doldrums,'" in *Identity Politics in the Women's Movement*, ed. Barbara Ryan (New York: NYU Press, 2001), 207; Millner, "Montgomery Bus Boycott," in Garrow, *Walking City*, 521.

33. This was the judgment of Stewart Burns, editor of *Papers of Martin Luther King, Jr. Birth of a New Age, December 1955–December 1956* (Berkeley: University of California Press, 2020), 7.

34. Barnett, "Black Women's Collectivist," 207–8.

35. Unnamed WPC members quoted in Barnett, "Black Women's Collectivist," 208–10, at 208. In fact, Robinson *was* fired a few years later, in 1960, after a state committee "investigated" her. Moreover, the WPC systematically destroyed its records in an attempt to protect its members from retaliation, as did the MIA.

36. Burks, "Trailblazers," 74, 76.

37. Brooks, *Boycotts, Buses*, 162.

38. Unnamed WPC member, quoted in Barnett, "Black Women's Collectivist," 206. (If they thought that working-class women could not organize such a project, Georgia Gilmore would prove otherwise, as we will see below.)

39. MIA newsletter 1, no. 2 (June 23, 1956), in Stewart Burns, ed., *Daybreak of Freedom: The Montgomery Bus Boycott* (Chapel Hill: University of North Carolina Press, 1997), 279.

40. Robinson, *Montgomery Bus Boycott*, 28; Abernathy, *Walls*, 143; Baldwin and Woodson, *Freedom Is Never Free*, 29; John White, "'Nixon Was the One': Edgar Daniel Nixon, the MIA and the Montgomery Bus Boycott," in *The Making of MLK and the Civil Rights Movement*, ed. Brian Ward and Tony Badger (New York: NYU Press, 1996), 50.

41. Jack Santino, *Miles of Smiles, Years of Struggle: Stories of Black Pullman Porters* (Urbana: University of Illinois Press, 1991), 38, 55; Nixon, November 10, 1976, quoted in Yeakey, "Montgomery Boycott," 113–14.

42. Nixon himself tried to register for ten years before succeeding. Baldwin and Woodson, *Freedom Is Never Free*, 33; White, "Nixon," 45–47.

43. Baldwin and Woodson, *Freedom Is Never Free*, 35.

44. Parks, *My Story*, 80, 95, 129, 134.

45. Gray, *Bus Ride to Justice*, 28; Baldwin and Woodson, *Freedom Is Never Free*, 37.

46. Whites inadvertently encouraged that collaboration. "The whites have forced the Montgomery Negro to recognize . . . that they are Negroes first and then domestics, doctors' wives, scholars or lawyers second." J. E. Pierce quoted in Williams and Greenhaw, *Thunder of Angels*, 233.

47. White, "Nixon," 28. On interclass cooperation, see Barnett, "Black Women's Collectivist," 212.

48. Gilliam, "Montgomery Bus Boycott," in Garrow, *Walking City*, 220.

49. Baldwin and Woodson, *Freedom Is Never Free*, 49.

50. Engler and Engler, *This Is an Uprising*, 183; Paul Hendrickson, "The Ladies Before Rosa: Let Us Now Praise Unfamous Women," *Rhetoric and Public Affairs* 8, no. 2 (2005): 287; SEIU, *Our Life and Times* (March–April 2005): 10; McGuire, *At the Dark End*, 75. White press accounts made her out to have been violent, which was not the case. Chappell, Hutchinson, and Ward, "'Dress Modestly,'" 85; Robinson, *Montgomery Bus Boycott*, 38–39. Perhaps unsurprisingly, Colvin's ancestors had a history of resistance, and she herself had attended NAACP meetings, seen Rosa Parks in action, and thought she was a stronger complainant: Parks, *My Story*, 111; Theo-

haris, *Rebellious Life*, 78–79. Just as Rosa Parks was constructed as a political innocent, a sympathetic white observer did the same about Colvin, marveling that "this
child had had no teaching about civil rights or Americanism—this is what makes life
so amazing"; Virginia Durr, oral history, 263–64, Virginia Foster Durr Papers, SL.

51. The first quotation is from McGuire, *At the Dark End*, 71; the second, from Virginia
Durr, is in Paula Giddings, *When and Where I Enter: The Impact of Black Women on
Race and Sex in America* (New York: Bantam, 1985), 263.

52. Yeakey, "Montgomery Boycott," 271.

53. Robinson is quoted in Taylor Branch, *Parting the Waters: America in the King Years,
1954–63* (New York: Simon & Schuster, 1988), 123; Hendrickson, "Ladies Before
Rosa," 287; Baldwin and Woodson, *Freedom Is Never Free*, 49.

54. Rachel Devlin, *A Girl Stands at the Door: The Generation of Young Women Who
Desegregated American Schools* (New York: Basic Books, 2018).

55. Hendrickson, "Ladies Before Rosa," 289.

56. Nathan Heller, "Out of Action: Do Protests Work?" *New Yorker*, August 21, 2007, 75.

57. Engler and Engler, *This Is an Uprising*, 181, 185.

58. Martin Luther King himself contributed to this image in his references to her.
Engler and Engler, *This Is an Uprising*, 181, 185; King, "The Montgomery Boycott,"
speech at Holt Baptist Church, December 5, 1955; Chappell, Hutchinson, and Ward,
"'Dress Modestly,'" 86–89; Branch, *Parting the Waters*, 120.

59. Kirt H. Wilson, "Interpreting the Discursive Field of the Montgomery Bus Boycott:
Martin Luther King Jr.'s Holt Street Address," *Rhetoric and Public Affairs* 8, no. 2
(2005): 314.

60. The role of class bridgers is examined in Belinda Robnett, "African American
Women in the Civil Rights Movement, 1954–1965: Gender, Leadership, and Micro-
mobilization," *American Journal of Sociology* 101, no. 6 (1996): 1661–93; Chappell,
Hutchinson, and Ward, "'Dress Modestly,'" 87; Erna Dungee Allen, interview by
Steven M. Millner, in Garrow, *Walking City*, 76; Theoharis, *Rebellious Life*, 72. Virginia Durr described the Montgomery Industrial School for Girls this way: "these
old maid Yankee schoolteachers came down here and started a school . . . for the
freedwomen. These schoolteachers would come down every winter and . . . go back
to New England in the summer. . . . But it was a very fine school. . . . The leaders of
the Southern civil rights movement came out of these schools." Durr oral history,
262, Durr Papers, SL.

61. Theoharis concludes that leaders consciously or unconsciously "obscured" Parks's
years of activism in order to make her the symbolic figure they needed; *Rebellious
Life*, 83; Dungee Allen interview by Millner in Garrow, *Walking City*.

62. Recy Taylor's story is told in Theoharis, *Rebellious Life*, 16; J. Mills Thornton III,
*Dividing Lines: Municipal Politics and the Struggle for Civil Rights in Montgomery,
Birmingham, and Selma* (Tuscaloosa: University of Alabama, 2002), 27; L. McGuire,
At the Dark End.

63. Theoharis, *Rebellious Life*, 66.

64. The FBI opened a file on the Durrs in 1934. That file alleged that Virginia joined
the Communist Party, a dubious claim based on what we know of her, but she was
a member of organizations the FBI labeled CP fronts, such as the National Committee to Abolish the Poll Tax. In 1954 both Durrs were called to a McCarthyist
hearing, chaired by Mississippi senator James O. Eastland, under the aegis of the
Internal Security Sub-Committee. John A. Salmond, "'The Great Southern Com-
mie Hunt': Aubrey Williams, the Southern Conference Educational Fund, and the

Internal Security Subcommittee," *South Atlantic Quarterly* 77, no. 4 (1978): 433–52. Clifford Durr defended victims of McCarthyism and later became president of the left-wing National Lawyers Guild. And even at the peak of the McCarthyist anti-Communist hysteria, Virginia Durr would not disavow her Communist friends. John A. Salmond, *The Conscience of a Lawyer: Clifford J. Durr and American Civil Liberties, 1899–1975* (Tuscaloosa: University of Alabama Press, 1990).

65. Brooks, *Boycotts, Buses*, 182; Durr oral history, 272, Durr Papers, SL.

66. The phrase is from SNCC activist Dorothy Zellner in "They Stood Up," *Jewish Currents*, May 2006.

67. Durr oral history, 257–59, Durr Papers, SL.

68. Gray, *Bus Ride to Justice*, 48. Gray attended law school at Case Western Reserve, as the University of Alabama law school would not admit Blacks.

69. "The Press: Something Thrown In," *Time*, November 21, 1949.

70. Williams, in turn, credited Nixon with galvanizing Montgomery Blacks into action. Nixon quoted in Salmond, *A Southern Rebel: The Life and Times of Aubrey Willis Williams, 1890–1965* (Chapel Hill: University of North Carolina Press, 1983), 252.

71. Stanton, *Journey Toward Justice*, 138, 174.

72. Williams and Greenhaw, *Thunder of Angels*, 137.

73. When he was offered the position in Montgomery, Graetz had been warned against activism by the Lutheran hierarchy. He promised to be "just" a pastor, a promise he could not keep. He had been in town only six months before the boycott began. Rosa Parks was among those who helped clean up the Graetz house. Amy Harris delivered a set of new dishes to them, saying that "when they bombed the Graetzes, they bombed us." Robert S. Graetz, *A White Preacher's Memoir: The Montgomery Bus Boycott* (1991; reprint Black Belt Press, 1999), 45, 139, 141–42, 146–48; McGuire, *At the Dark End*, 185.

74. Parks, *My Story*, 95–96.

75. Durr oral history, 265, Durr Papers, SL; Parks, *My Story*, 101.

76. Stanton, *Journey Toward Justice*, 167–68; Thornton, *Dividing Lines*, 40; Durr, *Outside the Magic Circle*, 278; Brooks, *Boycotts, Buses*, 183.

77. One of the charges against Highlander was "that the flat roof was built that way so helicopters from Russia could come in," Septima Clark remembered in *Ready from Within: A First Person Narrative*, ed. Cynthia Stokes Brown (Africa WorldPress, 1990), 55.

78. Parks, *My Story*, 116.

79. Beulah C. Johnson to F. D. Patterson of the Phelps-Stokes Fund, which had funded her visit, July 27, 1955, quoted in Aimee L. Horton, "An Analysis of Selected Programs for the Training of Civil Rights and Community Leaders in the South," author's collection.

80. Clark remembered that when Parks arrived she seemed extremely shy and rarely spoke, so she was shocked when she heard about Parks's defiance on the bus. Clark, *Ready from Within*, 32–34.

81. Everything here on Parks, unless otherwise cited, is from Theoharis, *Rebellious Life*. The quotation, as recalled by Septima Clark, is on 41.

82. Long before her story became recounted universally, she was using it on behalf of other civil rights campaigns. Parks et al., "Mrs. Rosa Parks Reports."

83. Durr oral history, 267, Durr Papers, SL; Brooks, *Boycotts, Buses*, 124–28, 131–32.

84. As the boycott developed, however, Raymond Parks was consistently supportive; while his wife was working nonstop for the boycott, he and her mother were at home

receiving the seemingly endless threats and abusive phone calls. Theoharis, *Rebellious Life*, 75–77, 101–2.

85. Carr and Allen are profiled in Millner, "Montgomery Bus Boycott," in Garrow, *Walking City*; Carr is quoted in Barnett, "Black Women's Collectivist," 212.

86. Santino, *Miles of Smiles*, 53; Branch, *Parting the Waters*, 131.

87. Robinson, *Montgomery Bus Boycott*, 46–52; McGuire, *At the Dark End*, 80.

88. Robinson, *Montgomery Bus Boycott*, 45–46.

89. Burks, "Trailblazers," 82–83.

90. Brooks, *Boycotts, Buses*, 193. For several decades after the boycott, both journalists and scholars disregarded not only Robinson's and the WPC's initiative but also the continuing work of scores of women. Robinson's memoir did not appear until thirty years later. In his foreword, David Garrow admits that at first he thought her manuscript not a credible candidate for publication. He characterizes her in stereotypical terms—"kind," "friendly," and in need of encouragement. He came to support her manuscript on the condition that she add "personally compelling stories about her own feelings," hardly a demand he would have made to, say, E. D. Nixon. Garrow, foreword to Robinson, *Montgomery Bus Boycott*, ix–xv; Burg, "Gray Crusade," 90–92.

91. Trenholm was shocked to learn of the outrageous abuse of Black bus passengers because he never rode buses. Luckily, Robinson was a friend of his wife, Portia Trenholm, a pianist who taught music at the college. Robinson kept her apprised of the boycott's progress, assuming that this information would be relayed to the president. Trenholm refused to accept the firings but was then summoned by a state legislative committee. There "he was treated like a boy . . . supporters who witnessed his humiliation could hardly bear to remain through the cross-examination." Abernathy, *Walls*, 164; Burks, "Trailblazers," 75. Similarly, more than thirty faculty at the University of Alabama were fired for supporting the enrollment of Autherine Lucy; Stanton, *Journey Toward Justice*, 179.

92. Theoharis, *Rebellious Life*, 80–81.

93. Baldwin and Woodson, *Freedom Is Never Free*, 1.

94. Quoted in Garrow, *Bearing the Cross*, 20. As Nixon put it, "So many ministers accept a handout, and then they owe their soul," quoted in McGuire, *At the Dark End*, 84; and "He had not been there long enough for the city fathers to put their hand on him," quoted in Juan Williams, *Eyes on the Prize: America's Civil Rights Years, 1954–1965* (New York: Penguin, 1988), 73.

95. Parks, *My Story*, 136; Gary J. Dorrien, *Breaking White Supremacy: Martin Luther King, Jr. and the Black Social Gospel* (New Haven, CT: Yale University Press, 2018), 287.

96. Johnnie Carr in Garrow, *Walking City*, 529.

97. Abernathy generously explained King's hesitation by pointing to his very recent arrival and Montgomery and the fact that he had a newborn daughter; Garrow, *Bearing the Cross*, 17. At first King, like many others, conceived of a boycott as an economic struggle only—"suggestive of merely an economic squeeze devoid of a positive value." Williams and Greenhaw, *Thunder of Angels*, 252.

98. Nixon described this conversation in slightly different words in different interviews, though always with the same message: Santino, *Miles of Smiles*, 54; Millner, "Montgomery Bus Boycott," in Garrow, *Walking City*, 454; White, "Nixon," 50.

99. Alan Johnson, "Self-Emancipation and Leadership: The Case of Martin Luther King," in *Leadership and Social Movements*, ed. Colin Barker, Alan Johnson, and Michael Lavalette (Manchester: Manchester University Press, 2001), 103.

100. White, "Nixon," 52.
101. Garrow, *Bearing the Cross*, 625.
102. Millner, "Montgomery Bus Boycott," in Garrow, *Walking City*, 454.
103. Abernathy, *Walls*, 17; Yeakey, "Montgomery Boycott," 108, 323.
104. C. Eric Lincoln and Lawrence H. Mamiya, *The Black Church in the African American Experience* (Durham, NC: Duke University Press, 1990). 101, 121, 209.
105. Lincoln and Mamiya, *Black Church*, 115–16.
106. Sara M. Evans and Harry C. Boyte, *Free Spaces: The Sources of Democratic Change in America* (New York: Harper & Row, 1986).
107. Robinson, *Montgomery Bus Boycott*, 56.
108. Robinson, *Montgomery Bus Boycott*, 64.
109. Millner, "Montgomery Bus Boycott," in Garrow, *Walking City*, 522.
110. Brooks, *Boycotts, Buses*, 195.
111. Abernathy, *Walls*, 140.
112. Durr oral history, 269, Durr Papers, SL.
113. Theoharis, *Rebellious Life*, 82.
114. Martin Luther King, Jr., *Stride Toward Freedom: The Montgomery Story* (New York: Harper & Bros., 1958), 53.
115. Yeakey, "Montgomery Boycott," 307.
116. Abernathy, *Walls*, 126. King, *Stride*, 32; Abernathy quoted in Yeakey, "Montgomery Boycott," 286–88; Norman W. Walton, "The Walking City: The Montgomery Bus Boycott," in Garrow, *Walking City*, 37.
117. Parks, *My Story*, 135.
118. Durr oral history, 270, Durr Papers, SL. Nixon's wisdom in supporting King did not prevent him from feeling, later, that King got the "glory" that he didn't get; Durr oral history, 273–74. Some accounts claim that Rufus Lewis disliked Nixon and acted to prevent him from becoming the lead: Yeakey, "Montgomery Boycott," 328. Whether or not that is true, Nixon quickly apprehended that King had the charisma and energy to be the right man; Theoharis, *Rebellious Life*, 81.
119. Garrow, *Bearing the Cross*, 53, quotation at 54.
120. Thornton, "Challenge and Response," in Garrow, *Walking City*, 347; Yeakey, "Montgomery Boycott," 313.
121. Abernathy, *Walls*, 123; Parks, *My Story*, 137. Holt Street Baptist church was built in 1913 on the corner of South Holt and Bullock streets. Its congregation was born in 1909 as Bethel Baptist Church.
122. Nixon's statements, not recorded, have been rendered differently by different scholars. This version quoted in Belinda Robnett, *How Long? How Long? African American Women in the Struggle for Civil Rights* (New York: Oxford University Press, 1997), 62; others are in King, *Stride*, 43; Theoharis, *Rebellious Life*, 90.
123. B. J. Simms, in Garrow, *Walking City*, 577; Abernathy quoted in Yeakey, "Montgomery Boycott," 315; Nixon quoted in Yeakey, "Montgomery Boycott," 329; Nixon quoted in White, "Nixon," 51; Gilliam, "Montgomery Bus Boycott," in Garrow, *Walking City*, 217.
124. McGuire, *At the Dark End*, 87; Theoharis, *Rebellious Life*, 93, 104. Rosa Parks, ever accommodating, explains this slightly differently, saying she "didn't feel any particular need to speak"; Parks, *My Story*, 139.
125. Theoharis, *Rebellious Life*, 93, 83.
126. Supporters of compromise were stuck in part because municipal officers and the bus company blamed their intransigence on each other. Ladd, *Negro Political Leadership*, 136; Valien, "Montgomery Bus Protest," 123.

127. Catsam, "'Onward March,'" 151.

128. Minutes of executive board meeting, January 30, 1956, in Burns, *Daybreak of Freedom*, 129.

129. Bayard Rustin pointed out the silence of "white liberalism" in "Report on Montgomery," March 1956, in Burns, *Daybreak of Freedom*, 208.

130. From the *Alabama Journal*, January 8, 1956, quoted in Gilliam, "Montgomery Bus Boycott," in Garrow, *Walking City*, 257.

131. Thornton, "Challenge and Response," in Garrow, *Walking City*, 357–58, 91; Stephanie Misaki Whiting, "A Symbolic Interactionist Analysis of the Montgomery Bus Boycott: Society as a Communicative Process" (MA thesis, University of Wisconsin at Stevens Point, 1987), gives the date as February 11 (128). See also Theoharis, *Rebellious Life*, 107. As Rosa Parks put it, "White people were getting angrier and angrier"; Parks, *My Story*, 146; Graetz, *White Preacher's Memoir*, 114.

132. Thornton, "Challenge and Response," in Garrow, *Walking City*, 354; Theoharis, *Rebellious Life*, 106.

133. Thornton, *Dividing Lines*, 93; Henry Hampton and Steve Fayer, *Voices of Freedom: An Oral History of the Civil Rights Movement from the 1950s Through the 1980s* (New York: Bantam Books, 1991), 31.

134. The crew were Rosa Parks, Euretta Adair, Maude Ballou, Erna Dungee, and Jo Ann Robinson. McGuire, *At the Dark End*, 100.

135. Burns, *Daybreak of Freedom*, 4.

136. King, *Stride*, 124, 135–36; Theoharis, *Rebellious Life*, 108; Parks, *My Story*, 147; Dorrien, *Breaking White Supremacy*, 292.

137. John D'Emilio, *Lost Prophet: The Life and Times of Bayard Rustin* (Chicago: University of Chicago Press, 2003), 226.

138. Recent scholarship has punctured the myth that all civil rights activists were fully committed to nonviolence. See Payne, *I've Got the Light of Freedom*; Emilye J. Crosby, "'This nonviolent stuff ain't no good. It'll get ya killed': Teaching About Self-Defense in the African-American Freedom Struggle," in *Teaching the Civil Rights Movement: Freedom's Bittersweet Song*, ed. Julie Buckner Armstrong et al. (New York: Routledge, 2002); Lance Hill, *The Deacons for Defense: Armed Resistance and the Civil Rights Movement* (Chapel Hill: University of North Carolina Press, 2004); Timothy Tyson, *Radio Free Dixie: Robert F. Williams and the Roots of Black Power* (Chapel Hill: University of North Carolina Press, 2009); Charles E. Cobb, Jr., *This Nonviolent Stuff'll Get You Killed: How Guns Made the Civil Rights Movement Possible* (Durham, NC: Duke University Press, 2015).

139. Rustin remembered that when journalist William Worthy came to report on the boycott in February 1956, he was about to sit down when Rustin cried, "Wait . . . couple of guns in that chair. You don't want to shoot yourself." Bayard Rustin, "Montgomery Diary," in Burns, *Daybreak of Freedom*, 169. On shots at a bus, see Donnie Williams with Wayne Greenhaw, *The Thunder of Angels: The Montgomery Bus Boycott and the People Who Broke the Back of Jim Crow* (Chicago: Lawrence Hill, 2006), 115.

140. Abernathy, *Walls*, 161.

141. Nixon quoted in Williams and Greenhaw, *Thunder of Angels*, 243.

142. Anonymous domestic worker, interviewed by Willie Lee, January 27, 1956, in Burns, *Daybreak of Freedom*, 125.

143. Clay Risen, "Lucille Times" (obituary), *New York Times*, August 23, 2021.

144. Henry Louis Gates, Jr., "Who Designed the March on Washington," *The African Americans: Many Rivers to Cross*, PBS, n.d.

145. Bayard Rustin, "Montgomery Diary," February 26, 1956, in Burns, *Daybreak of Freedom*, 169, and in D'Emilio, *Lost Prophet*, 227, 230. Also see John D'Emilio, "Homophobia and the Trajectory of Postwar American Radicalism," in *Modern American Queer History*, ed. Allida M. Black (Philadelphia: Temple University Press, 2001).

146. Rustin ghost-wrote King's first published article, in *Liberation*, April 1956; D'Emilio, *Lost Prophet*, chap. 11. That King understood and relied on Rustin's advice points favorably to King's capacity to respect and trust a gay man.

147. Jeff Woods, *Black Struggle, Red Scare: Segregation and Anti-Communism in the South, 1948–1968* (Baton Rouge: Louisiana State University Press, 2004); Arsenault, "Bus Boycott and American Politics," 311, 348. Reverend Graetz sometimes tried to engage these callers in discussion, but calling him a Communist usually ended the possibility; Graetz, *White Preacher's Memoir*, 76–77. Even Rosa Parks was "a trained Communist Party (CPUSA) activist," a charge repeated even today; see Henry Makow, "'Red' Rosa Parks: Fabricating An American Icon," Rense.com, November 5, 2005. Red-baiting had destroyed the Workers Alliance (discussed in chapter 4).

148. FBI agents invented lies, or repeated WCC lies, notably that the boycotters beat up anyone riding a bus and had stocked up on arms. Hoover would soon develop an obsessive hatred for Martin Luther King, spying on his every move and attempting to discredit him with allegations of extramarital affairs for the rest of his life. Branch, *Parting the Waters*, 181; Arsenault, "Bus Boycott and American Politics," 340–41. Adam Clayton Powell, Jr., neatly reversed these allegations, calling the prosecution of the boycotters "another ghastly victory for communism." Arsenault, "Bus Boycott and American Politics," 346.

149. Edgar N. French, "Beginnings of a New Age," in Garrow, *Walking City*, 182.

150. Whiting, "Symbolic Interactionist Analysis," 111–12.

151. Donald T. Ferron, a Fisk University researcher who was often in Montgomery, in Burns, *Daybreak of Freedom*, 121; Robinson, *Montgomery Bus Boycott*, 117–18; Millner, "Montgomery Bus Boycott," in Garrow, *Walking City*, 476–77; Branch, *Parting the Waters*, 155–57.

152. Millner, "Montgomery Bus Boycott," in Garrow, *Walking City*, 476.

153. Millner, "Montgomery Bus Boycott," in Garrow, *Walking City*, 478.

154. Simms in Garrow, *Walking City*, 577–78. Sims claimed that after he took over the transport operation from Rufus Lewis, he put a stop to this behavior through rigorous accounting,

155. Millner wrote that Nixon resigned from leadership over this issue, but Nixon's own words were more guarded: "I disagreed with how the records were kept. And I thought that King's were somehow remiss. I wanted to protect my 'open book' reputation." Nixon quoted in Millner, "Montgomery Bus Boycott," in Garrow, *Walking City*, 496, 550. For other discussion of this issue, see Walton, "Walking City," in Garrow, *Walking City*, 24–26.

156. Reconsidering the allegations twenty years later, Johnnie Carr offered a judicious appraisal: "Now there may have been some money spent unwisely, but I don't think no money was spent any other way. Now anybody with any sense at all knows that you will make mistakes and blunders and things." Millner, "Montgomery Bus Boycott," in Garrow, *Walking City*, 530.

157. Allen, *Organizing*, 523; Walton, "Walking City," in Garrow, *Walking City*, 25–26. Note that "fool" had a more derogatory meaning in African American speech at the time than it might appear today.

158. Walton, "Walking City," in Garrow, *Walking City*, 24–25; Gilliam, "Montgomery Bus Boycott," in Garrow, *Walking City*, 255. King later insisted that the alleged agreement was a hoax; *Stride*, 107.

159. The plaintiffs were five women (none of them Rosa Parks) chosen because of the particularly intense outrage at the abuse of women, and the fact that men would likely lose their jobs and thus endanger their families. Robinson, *Montgomery Bus Boycott*, 136. The five were Aurelia S. Browder, Susie McDonald, Mary Louise Smith, Jeanatta Reese, and Claudette Colvin, who had been previously rejected as the subject of a suit because she was then a pregnant teenager. Threats frightened Reese and she withdrew, so the plaintiffs in the case that reached the U.S. District Court for the Middle District of Alabama numbered only four; the case was *Browder v. Gayle*, 142 F.Supp. 707 (1956).

160. Gray, *Bus Ride to Justice*. On the importance of a having a Black lawyer, see Valien, "Montgomery Bus Protest," 97; Leonard S. Rubinowitz, "The Courage of Civil Rights Lawyers: Fred Gray and His Colleagues," *Case Western Reserve Law Review* 67, no. 4 (2017): 1227–49, and David J. Garrow, "In Honor of Fred Gray: The Meaning of Montgomery," *Case Western Reserve Law Review* 67, no. 4 (2017): 1045–53.

161. Rufus Lewis, interview by Millner, in Garrow, *Walking City*, 540.

162. Abernathy, *Walls*, 155, 160.

163. Donald T. Ferron, "Report on MIA Mass Meeting, February 1956," in Burns, *Daybreak of Freedom*, 173; Georgia Gilmore, interview for *Eyes on the Prize*, Blackside Films, February 17, 1986, at https://tinyurl.com/3xnvhvk8; Theoharis, *Rebellious Life*, 104.

164. Willie Mae Lee, a Fisk University researcher in Montgomery, notes on a mass meeting. January 1956, in Burns, *Daybreak of Freedom*, 130–31. Abernathy pointed out that at the first mass meeting the first hymn was "What a Fellowship, What a Joy Divine," chosen because it was without "revolutionary overtones" so it could be sung publicly without fear; Abernathy, *Walls*, 150–51; Wilson, "Interpreting," 317.

165. I am indebted to Martin Zwick for helping me to interpret this passage as Montgomery's Blacks might have done. African American Protestant services tend to make greater use of the Old Testament that do white services. Other African American favorites include Isaiah 40 and 53, Joshua 24, and of course Exodus.

166. Garrow, *Bearing the Cross*, 53, quotation at 54.

167. Johnson, "Self-emancipation and Leadership," 103.

168. Durr oral history, 274, Durr Papers, SL.

169. Reddick, "Bus Boycott," 75; Lewis interview by Millner in Garrow, *Walking City*, 541.

170. Howell Raines, *My Soul Is Rested: Movement Days in the Deep South Remembered* (New York: Penguin, 1983), 54.

171. Bertha Howard Abernathy, Hazel Gregory, S. S. Seay, A. W. Wilson, and Garrick Hardy quoted in Yeakey, "Montgomery Boycott," 357–59; Abernathy, *Walls*, 153.

172. Abernathy, *Walls*, 157–59.

173. Allen, *Organizing*, 524.

174. Parks, *My Story*, 143–44. There was a particular need for shoes, she explained, because walking to and from work wore them out quickly.

175. Gilliam, "Montgomery Bus Boycott," in Garrow, *Walking City*, 229; Arsenault, "Bus Boycott and American Politics," 327–28.

176. The MIA was technically a membership organization, with dues of one dollar, or fifty cents for "youth." But no one had to pay, and as in all social movement organizations, many took no decision-making responsibility. Gilliam, "Montgomery Bus Boycott,"

in Garrow, *Walking City*, 229; Baldwin and Woodson, *Freedom Is Never Free*, 55; Rustin in Burns, *Daybreak of Freedom*, 209; Christopher Coleman, Laurence D. Nee, and Leonard S. Rubinowitz, "Social Movements and Social-Change Litigation: Synergy in the Montgomery Bus Protest," *Law and Social Inquiry* 30, no. 4, (2005): 663–736, n69; Raines, *My Soul Is Rested*, 55–56. Though Nixon was described as uneducated by Montgomery's ministers and middle class, he was obviously capable of effective speech-making at least to a labor audience.

177. Millner, "Montgomery Bus Boycott," in Garrow, *Walking City*, 491.
178. King, recommendations to MIA executive board, in Burns, *Daybreak of Freedom*, 268.
179. Georgia Gilmore's activism continued well after the boycott. In 1957 her son Mark was arrested and beaten by two white police officers while taking a shortcut through whites-only Oak Park. Gilmore sued (in *Gilmore v. City of Montgomery*, 1959*)*, charging that excluding Blacks was unconstitutional according to the Fourteenth Amendment. The court ruled against the city—which responded by closing the public parks altogether. The case was relitigated in 1971, because the city was allowing private schools and the YMCA sole use of public parks and recreational facilities. This time Gilmore won. See the entry for "Georgia Gilmore" in Wikipedia.
180. Brooks, *Boycotts, Buses*, 194.
181. On the Club from Nowhere, see Coleman, Nee, and Rubinowitz, "Social Movements and Synergy"; McGuire, *At the Dark End*, 96.
182. Gilmore in *Eye on the Prize*; Robinson, *Montgomery Bus Boycott*, 71–72; McGuire, *At the Dark End*, 97.
183. One example is the anonymous domestic worker interviewed by Willie M. Lee, January 27, 1956, in Burns, *Daybreak of Freedom*, 231.
184. Yeakey, "Montgomery Boycott," 307.
185. Rustin diary, February 24, 1956, in Burns, *Daybreak of Freedom*, 167.
186. Theoharis, *Rebellious Life*, 95; Yeakey, "Montgomery Boycott," 307, 388.
187. Lynne Olson, *Freedom's Daughters: The Unsung Heroines of the Civil Rights Movement from 1830 to 1970* (New York: Simon & Schuster, 2001), 117.
188. Durr oral history, 290, Durr Papers, SL; Graetz, *White Preacher's Memoir*, 58, 68, 74.
189. Mayor Gayle pleaded, "The Negroes are laughing at white people behind their backs"; Williams and Greenhaw, *Thunder of Angels*, 119. Durr is quoted in Hampton and Fayer, *Voices of Freedom*, 27.
190. Chappell, Hutchinson, and Ward, "'Dress Modestly,'" 87.
191. Rustin diary, in Burns, *Daybreak of Freedom*, 167; Yeakey, "Montgomery Boycott," 388.
192. To support the campaign for voter registration, Rosa Parks wrote, Lewis allowed only registered voters to go into the nightclub, but I have been unable to find other sources for this claim. Parks, *My Story*, 136.
193. Lewis had even set up a committee to support Claudette Colvin after her arrest. Gilliam, "Montgomery Bus Boycott," in Garrow, *Walking City*, 203, 215, 218, 220; Yeakey, "Montgomery Boycott," 94–98, 319–20, 383–84; Rufus Lewis in Millner, "Montgomery Bus Boycott," in Garrow, *Walking City*, 537–43; transcript of proceedings in *Browder v. Gayle* in Burns, *Daybreak of Freedom*, 77.
194. Walton, "Walking City," in Garrow, *Walking City*, 28.
195. Gilliam, "Montgomery Bus Boycott," in Garrow, *Walking City*, 224–25, 229, 540. The ridership estimate is from Whiting, "Symbolic Interactionist Analysis," 145.
196. Yeakey, "Montgomery Boycott," 377–78.
197. Durr oral history, 285, Durr Papers, SL; Gilliam, "Montgomery Bus Boycott," in Garrow, *Walking City*, 227.

198. Yeakey, "Montgomery Boycott," has a whole chapter on the transportation system. I have relied on his information except where otherwise cited. Other authors, such as Whiting, "Symbolic Interactionist Analysis," give slightly different numbers.
199. Abernathy, *Walls*, 135.
200. Anonymous domestic worker, interviewed by Willie M. Lee, January 24, 1956, in Burns, *Daybreak of Freedom*, 119.
201. Hampton and Fayer, *Voices of Freedom*, 30–31; McGuire, *At the Dark End*, 98.
202. Accounts of the number arrested vary between 93 and 123.
203. It is not clear how many of them did so spontaneously and how many were organized to do so by the MIA leadership. French, "Beginnings of a New Age," in Garrow, *Walking City*, 180–81; Millner, "Montgomery Bus Boycott," in Garrow, *Walking City*, 484.
204. Sims quoted in Millner, "Montgomery Bus Boycott," in Garrow, *Walking City*, 485.
205. Durr oral history, 287, Durr Papers, SL.
206. Theoharis, *Rebellious Life*, 113.
207. Abernathy, *Walls*, 161.
208. Simms in Garrow, *Walking City*, 579.
209. Clifford Durr in Durr oral history, 271, Durr Papers, SL.
210. Rustin to King, December 23, 1956, in Burns, *Daybreak of Freedom*, 329–30.
211. One effort was laughable: a proposal to create a separate whites-only bus line. No bus company could have survived without women Black riders. Parks, *My Story*, 159.
212. Anthony G. Windau, "Practicing What You Preach: The Untold Story of Rev. Robert S. Graetz Jr. in the Montgomery Bus Boycott" (unpub. ms., University of Wisconsin at Eau Claire, 2018), 25–26; Graetz, *White Preacher's Memoir*, 139; Branch, *Parting the Waters*, 198–202.
213. MIA code of conduct, in Burns, *Daybreak of Freedom*, 326–27; Robert L. Cannon (from the Fellowship of Reconciliation) to Hassler and Smiley, October 3, 1956, in Burns, *Daybreak of Freedom*, 293; Whiting, "Symbolic Interactionist Analysis."
214. In later years, Nixon resented, understandably, not being given the credit he deserved.
215. Engler and Engler, *This Is an Uprising*, 121.
216. Rustin to King, December 23, 1956 in Burns, *Daybreak of Freedom*, 329.
217. French, "Beginnings of a New Age," in Garrow, *Walking City*, 33.
218. Chappell, Hutchinson, and Ward, "'Dress Modestly,'" 89.
219. Robnett, "African American Women," 1667, 1671.
220. Among her efforts to raise funds for Parks, she proposed to Myles Horton of Highlander the establishment of a Voters Service Bureau. It would be housed in Fred Gray's law office, with Parks in charge for salary of thirty-five dollars a week; Durr to Horton, November 5, 1956, in Burns, *Daybreak of Freedom*, 298. Even after the Parkses moved to Detroit and she received many honors, she got no significant help from King or the Montgomery elite. It was only Congressman John Conyers who came through, hiring her in his Detroit office. Theoharis, *Rebellious Life*, 118–21, 162–64.
221. Theoharis, *Rebellious Life*, chaps. 5–7, quoting Abernathy on 141; Theoharis to the author, August 12, 2021. Rosa and Raymond Parks moved to Detroit, where her brother lived, and there she continued to be a civil rights leader.
222. Whatever his resentment, he never doubted King's genius and bravery. In one letter to King he wrote that "when you choosed [*sic*] to serve time than to pay a fine was the most courageous stand. . . . Because of your courage in face of known danger I want to commend you for your stand for the people of color all over the world." At the same

time, in praising King, he was claiming a certain authority, claiming that his opinion mattered. Nixon to King, September 9, 1958, MLKP-MBU, King Papers.

223. Santino, *Miles of Smiles*, 55.

224. Anonymous, "Sit-in Mythology, II," 10, Folder 16, Box 230, Surveys and Studies 1944–1969, Amistad Research Center.

225. Branch, *Parting the Waters*, 825.

226. Johnson, "Self-Emancipation and Leadership," 101.

227. Beulah Johnson quoted in Parks et al., "Mrs. Rosa Parks Reports," 5.

6. Leadership and Followership Continued

1. Marshall Ganz, "Not the Cesar Chavez I Knew," *Nation*, April 1, 2014.

2. "Social movement unionism" is a concept often used with little clarity. But there are numerous examples of it, past and present, including the community support for the sit-down strikes we saw in chapter 4; today's UNITE HERE, Justice for Janitors, and more. One definition fits the farmworkers' struggle: "the way activists mobilised working-class communities outside the confining framework of authoritarian industrial relations legislation, in support of demands that went beyond factory grievances." Gay Seidman, "Social Movement Unionism: From Description to Exhortation," *South African Review of Sociology* 42, no. 3 (2011): 94–102.

3. Cesar Chavez, speech at Solidarity House to UAW, April 1, 1967, in Richard J. Jensen and John C. Hammerback, *The Words of César Chávez* (College Station: Texas A&M University Press, 2002), 24; Eliseo Medina, interview by the author, December 6, 2021. Medina's union is the Service Employees International Union.

4. Frank Bardacke, *Trampling Out the Vintage: Cesar Chavez and the Two Souls of the United Farm Workers* (New York: Verso, 2012); Matt Garcia, *From the Jaws of Victory: The Triumph and Tragedy of Cesar Chavez and the Farm Worker Movement* (Berkeley: University of California Press, 2012); Miriam Pawel, *A Union of Their Dreams: Power, Hope and Struggle in Cesar Chavez's Farm Worker Movement* (New York: Bloomsbury Press, 2009); and Miriam Pawel, *The Crusades of Cesar Chavez: A Biography* (New York: Bloomsbury Press, 2014). See also Matt Garcia, "A Response to My Critics," Mattgarcia.org.

5. Pawel, *Crusades*, 431.

6. Andrew J. Yawn, "On This Day, January 30: The Rev. Martin Luther King Jr.'s Montgomery House Bombed," *Montgomery Advertiser*, January 30, 2017.

7. Medina interview by the author.

8. Pawel, *Crusades*, chap. 15, quotation at 160.

9. David Bacon, "What Cesar Chavez Movie Missed," *In These Times*, May 22, 2014. Filipino unions were targeted in the anti-Communist hysteria of the 1950s—more than thirty union members were arrested and threatened with deportation. Even the conservative Filipino businessman, Andy Imutan, resented the erasure of Filipino contributions; David Bacon, "How Filipino Migrants Gave the Grape Strike Its Radical Politics," *Dollars & Sense*, May–June 2018, https://www.dollarsandsense.org/archives/2018/0518bacon.html; "Andy Imutan Correspondence to Patty Enrado," Welga Archive.

10. The *latifundia* remark is from Cesar Chavez, speech at interfaith gathering of clergy and labor, New York, 1968, in Jensen and Hammerback, *Words of Chávez*, 31. The second is from Carey McWilliams, *Factories in the Field: The Story of Migratory Farm Labor in California* (Boston: Little, Brown, 1939).

11. Albert Croutch, "Housing Migratory Agricultural Laborers in California" (MA thesis, University of California, 1948), 7, table 3; State Relief Administration of California, "Migratory Labor in California," mimeographed report, 1936, 8. The DiGiorgio grape fields used about eleven hundred workers in December and 5,200 in July; Alexander Morin, *The Organizability of Farm Labor in the United States* (Cambridge, MA: Harvard University Press, 1952), 43.

12. Discrimination against Filipinos had worsened in the twentieth century. In 1925 a U.S. Supreme Court decision barred those of Asian descent from citizenship. Anti-miscegenation laws barred them from marrying whites. A 1934 law set a quota on Filipino immigration of 50 per year. Philip Vera Cruz, *The Original Writings of Philip Vera Cruz*, ed. Sid Amores Valledor (n.p.: Dog Ear, 2006), 85–86. As Eliseo Medina described it, "We lived in different worlds—the Latino world, the Filipino world, the African American world and the Caucasian world," quoted in Bacon, "What Chavez Movie Missed."

13. Medina interview by the author.

14. Data from Bureau of Labor Statistics, reported in Melissa Montalvo and Nigel Duara, "In Familiar Refrain," Calmatters.org, January 20, 2022.

15. Rey Huerta and Paul Carrillo. This and all further references consisting solely of personal names refer to testimony documents of farmworkers or UFW staff archived at FMDP. Cletus E. Daniel, *Bitter Harvest: A History of California Farmworkers, 1870–1941* (Ithaca, NY: School of Industrial and Labor Relations, 1981), 179; Carey McWilliams, "The Great Exception," typescript, 3, in Box 14, McWilliams Papers (this manuscript was apparently part of a draft for his 1949 book of the same title); McWilliams in "What Should America Do for the 'Joads'?" *Town Meeting*, March 11, 1940, 15.

16. A California state agency reported Filipinos averaging higher wages, but other evidence shows that they were typically poorer than Mexican farmworkers. The discrepancy may have arisen because Filipinos were almost all single men, lacking other family members' wage contributions. Workers in the San Joaquin (aka Central) Valley area earned most, those near Sacramento and in the south the least. State of California, Advisory Committee on Farm Labor Research, *The California Farm Labor Force: A Profile* (Sacramento: California State Press, 1969), 22, 59; Marc-Tizoc González, "Critical Ethnic Legal Histories: Unearthing the Interracial Justice of Filipino American Agricultural Labor Organizing," *University of California Irvine Law Review* 3, no. 4 (2013): 1039 n138.

17. Jerry Brown testimony, in Jerry Barry Brown, "The United Farm Workers Grape Strike and Boycott, 1965–1970: An Evaluation of the Culture of Poverty Theory" (PhD diss., Cornell University, 1972), 164–65.

18. Douglas L. Murray, "The Abolition of *El Cortito*, the Short-handled Hoe: A Case Study in Social Conflict and State Policy in California Agriculture," *Social Problems* 30, no. 1 (1982): 26–39, quotations at 28, 34.

19. Between 1930 and 1948, three-quarters of all agricultural strikes were in California; Morin, *Organizability*, 14–15.

20. Richard Steven Street, "The Battle of Salinas," *Journal of the West* 26, no. 1 (1984): 41. The Salinas Valley today produces 61 percent of leaf lettuce, 57 percent of celery, 56 percent of head lettuce, 48 percent of broccoli, and 28 percent of strawberries grown in the United States. One indicator of the relative weakness of the UFW today is that only 34 percent of Salinas farmworkers are "food secure," that is, can count on having enough healthy food. Because lettuce grows low on the ground, the

labor of farmworkers was responsible for many wrecked backs in relatively young men. Claire Chang, "Food Insecurity: In the 'Salad Bowl of America,'" *Yale Global Health Review*, December 21, 2016.

21. Supported by Catholic priests, they denounced *The Grapes of Wrath* as a "black, infernal creation of a twisted, distorted mind." Their organization, American Federation of Farmers—an entirely false identification since none of them did farm work—hired "journalists" to shill for the company with stories of happy field workers, and it even went so far as to commission a book called *Plums of Plenty*. Eric Johnson, "John Steinbeck, Despised and Dismissed . . ," *Monterey County Weekly*, August 5, 2004.

22. Larry Salomon, "Filipinos Build a Movement for Justice in the Asparagus Fields," *Third Force* 2, no. 4, October 31, 1994; Matt Meier and Feliciano Ribera, *Mexican Americans/American Mexicans: From Conquistadors to Chicanos* (New York: Hill & Wang, 1993), 142–43; F. Arturo Rosales, *Dictionary of Latino Civil Rights History* (Houston: Arte Publico, 2006), 109. Mexicans established some forty unions in California and an umbrella group, El Confederación de Uniones de Campesinos y Obreros Mexicanos, modeled on a similar federation in Mexico; it came to include five thousand members in California.

23. Dick Meister and Anne Loftis, *A Long Time Coming: The Struggle to Unionize America's Farm Workers* (New York: Macmillan, 1977), 30. Oddly enough, a different book by Loftis offers slightly different figures: twenty-five strikes, of which twenty-one won wage raises. Anne Loftis, *Witnesses to the Struggle: Imaging the 1930s California Labor Movement* (Reno: University of Nevada Press, 1998), 10; Stuart Marshall Jamieson, *Labor Unionism in American Agriculture* (Washington, DC: U.S. Bureau of Labor Statistics), 87. Farmworker organizing efforts had been frequent for at least sixty-five years before Chavez began his organizing, beginning with Indian, Chinese, and Japanese workers in the late nineteenth century. The notorious Wheatland "riot" of 1913, spearheaded by the IWW, had united at least twenty-seven different nationalities, despite the grower's policy of keeping different ethnic groups isolated from each other. Other leftists worked to organize in the 1930s. In the 1940s the National Farm Labor Union had organized strikes in the Central Valley. None succeeded, suffering from ethnic distrust, hostility from evangelical churches, and lack of outside support. Edward J. Walsh, "Mobilization Theory vis-à-vis a Mobilization Process: The Case of the United Farm Workers' Movement," *Research in Social Movements, Conflicts and Change* 1 (1978): 159–63; John Gregory Dunne, *Delano: The Story of the California Grape Strike* (New York: Farrar, Straus & Giroux, 1967), 108; Theo Majka, "Poor People's Movements and Farm Labor Insurgency," *Crime, Law and Social Change* 4, no. 3 (1980): 283–308.

24. McWilliams, *Factories in Field*, 230–53; Herbert Klein and Carey McWilliams, "Cold Terror in California," *Nation*, July 24, 1934.

25. Cesar Chavez, eulogy for Fred Ross, October 17, 1992, in Jensen and Hammerback, *Words of Chávez*, 175; Fred Ross, *Conquering Goliath: Cesar Chavez at the Beginning* (El Taller Gráfico Press, 1992). Ross's son Fred Jr. became a full-time organizer for the UFW in 1970, the year of a historic mass strike in the California lettuce fields.

26. Eduardo Bonnin, *Cursillos in Christianity: The How and the Why* (Dallas: National Cursillo Center, 1981).

27. Walsh, "Mobilization Theory," 164. Today's *cursillo* credo argues, "If the Catholic Church is not today the dominant dynamic social force, it is because Catholic

scholars have taken the dynamite of the Church, have wrapped it up in nice phrase-ology, placed it in an hermetic container and sat on the lid. It is about time to blow the lid off so the Catholic Church may again become the dominant social dynamic force." National Secretariat, "The Cursillo Movement—What Is It?" Jolietcursillo.org; "Resources for Every Parish," RENEW International, Renewintl.org.

28. Cesar Chavez, "The Organizer's Tale," *Ramparts*, July 1966.
29. Many organizers, including Malcolm X, used house meetings in recruiting.
30. Vera Cruz, *Original Writings*, 36–37.
31. He called this a "chain letter effect." Chavez, "Organizer's Tale"; LeRoy Chatfield, *To Serve the People: My Life Organizing with Cesar Chavez and the Poor* (Albuquerque: University of New Mexico Press, 2019); Chavez, speech to California SNCC, Fresno, November 1965, in Jensen and Hammerback, *Words of Chávez*, 10–14.
32. Chavez, "Organizer's Tale"; Chatfield, *To Serve the People*, 73.
33. Olga Idriss Davis, "'I Rose and Found My Voice': Claiming 'Voice' in the Rhetoric of Ida B. Wells," in *Black Women's Intellectual Traditions: Speaking Their Minds*, ed. Kristin Waters and Carol B. Conaway (Burlington: University of Vermont Press, 2007), 321. Marshall Ganz, who went on to become a theorist of social movement organizing, explains that telling a personal history is a revealing of oneself that demonstrates trust in others—and thereby earns their trust in the organizer. Marshall Ganz, "Organizing Notes: People, Power, and Change," Leadingchangenetwork.org, Spring 2018.
34. Richard Rodriguez, "Saint Cesar of Delano," *Wilson Quarterly* (Winter 2010): 16.
35. Chavez, speech to California SNCC meeting, Fresno, November 1965, in Jensen and Hammerback, *Words of Chávez*, 10–14. He also concluded that the CSO was focusing less on the poor and more on helping members to become middle class. This was consistent with his continuing contempt for those who sought to make money and with his religious emphasis on sacrifice; Miriam Pawel, "A Self-Inflicted Wound: Cesar Chavez and the Paradox of the United Farm Workers," *International Labor and Working-Class History*, no. 83 (Spring 2013): 155.
36. Chatfield, *To Serve the People*, 50, 52, 73. By its second year of existence, the FWA had enough income—about $13,000 per year from dues—to pay Chavez sixty-five dollars a week. It was not much for a family with seven children that often provided for other farmworker children as well.
37. Mark Day, *Forty Acres: Cesar Chavez and the Farm Workers* (New York: Praeger, 1971), 58. Disaffection with church conservatism lay behind some of the Mexican conversions to Protestantism.
38. Marco G. Prouty, *Cesar Chavez, the Catholic Bishops, and the Farmworkers' Struggle for Social Justice* (Tucson: University of Arizona Press, 2008); Alan J. Watt, *Farm Workers and the Churches: The Movement in California and Texas* (Laredo: Texas A&M International University Press, 2010).
39. Margaret Eleanor Rose, "Women in the UFW: A Study of Chicana and Mexicana Participation in a Labor Union, 1950–1980" (PhD diss., UCLA, 1988), 326; Bardacke, *Trampling Out the Vintage*, 115.
40. Jessica Govea.
41. Francesca Polletta, *Freedom Is an Endless Meeting: Democracy in American Social Movements* (Chicago: University of Chicago Press, 2002), 74–76.
42. Jacques E. Levy, *Cesar Chavez: Autobiography of La Causa* (Minneapolis: University of Minnesota Press, 2007), 537.
43. Pawel, *Crusades*, 95; Garcia, *Jaws of Victory*, 31. Chavez himself reported a drop to

twelve dues-payers; Chavez, impromptu speech to church people, La Paz, October 4, 1971, in Jensen and Hammerback, *Words of Chávez*, 68.

44. Pawel, *Crusades*, 48.
45. Maria Saludado Magaña; Alberto Escalante; Doug Adair, "El Malcriado 1964–1979: Analysis," FMDP.
46. By 1970 the credit union had loaned $281,308 to 1,264 members; Margaret Eleanor Rose, "Women in the UFW: A Study of Chicana and Mexicana Participation in a Labor Union, 1950–1980" (PhD diss., UCLA, 1988), 147. See also Brown, "United Farm Workers Grape Strike," 259.
47. Alfredo Vazquez; Margaret Murphy; Marc Sapir; Barbara Macri-Ortiz; Tina Solinas; Ida Cousino; Helen Serda.
48. Brown, "United Farm Workers Grape Strike," 259–60.
49. Alfredo Acosta Figueroa; Jessica Govea; Helen Serda; Obdulia "Abby" Flores Rivera; Elizabeth Hernandez; Maria Fuentes.
50. Alberto Escalante; Chatfield, *To Serve the People*, 57; Bardacke, *Trampling Out the Vintage*, 343–44, 554.
51. Bardacke, *Trampling Out the Vintage*, 54–56; Gilbert Padilla.
52. Francisco Garcia. Visiting a labor camp in Tulare County, where workers lived in appalling conditions in condemned facilities, Padilla organized a successful rent strike of the three hundred residents that stopped a threatened rent increase. This victory sent more farmworkers to the FWA, looking for more gains. Lauren Araiza, "Complicating the Beloved Community: The SNCC and the NFWA," in *The Struggle in Black and Brown: African American and Mexican American Relations during the Civil Rights Era*, ed. Brian D. Behnken (Lincoln: University of Nebraska Press, 2011), 82.
53. Eliseo Medina, in *Hope Dies Last: Keeping the Faith in Difficult Times*, ed. Studs Terkel (New York: New Press, 2003), 125.
54. Bardacke, *Trampling Out the Vintage*, 249–51, quotation at 251; Pawel, *Union*, passim. Medina became international secretary-treasurer of the powerful Service Employees International Union (SEIU), leading its campaign for progressive immigration policy. In 2013 he was one of the leaders of the Fast for Families movement and fasted for twenty-two days on the National Mall in support of immigration reform. He was identified as one of the "Top 50 Most Powerful Latino Leaders."
55. Lori Flores, "The Neglected Heroines of 'César Chávez'" (review of the film *César Chávez: An American Hero*), Colorlines.com, March 31, 2014.
56. Rick Baldoz, "Valorizing Racial Boundaries: Hegemony and Conflict in the Racialization of Filipino Migrant Labour in the United States," *Ethnic and Racial Studies* 27, no. 6 (2004): 972.
57. Itliong had been influenced by Filipino farmworker Carlos Bulosan's 1946 autobiographical novel, *America Is in the Heart*. The FBI had denounced it as un-American because of its focus on workers' struggles." The Salinas strike yielded a thirty-cent-per-hour wage increase and six improvements in working conditions. Howard A. DeWitt, "The Filipino Labor Union: The Salinas Lettuce Strike of 1934," *Amerasia Journal* 5, no. 2 (1978): 1–21. The 1948 Stockton strike failed when growers evicted farmworkers from their camps and police arrested strikers and charged them with felonies. See "Asparagus Strike Pickets Face Felony Charges," *Fresno Bee / Republican*, May 9, 1948, 1.
58. González, "Critical Ethnic Legal Histories," 1044. Material on Itliong and Vera Cruz is from Vera Cruz, *Original Writings*. Dawn Mabalon is quoted in Bacon, "What Chavez Movie Missed."

59. After the meeting, the group adjourned to a local bar to drink beer and play pool. Ganz recalled, "Cesar was quite a pool player and so was Stokely and I think they surprised each other." Araiza, "Complicating," 86.

60. Chavez referred to her working in the fields "a few hours every day," but her hours were six a.m. to one p.m.; Margaret Rose, "Cesar Chavez and Dolores Huerta" (2002), in *A Dolores Huerta Reader*, ed. Mario T. Garcia (Albuquerque: University of New Mexico Press, 2008), 39; Pawel, *Crusades*, 83.

61. Chatfield, *To Serve the People*, 69.

62. Maxine Baca Zinn, "Political Familialism: Toward Sex Role Equality in Chicano Families," *Aztlan* 6, no. 1 (1975): 13–26.

63. Pawel, *Crusades*, 147; Ida Cousino.

64. Virginia Hirsch (sister of Helen Chavez) quoted in Bardacke, *Trampling Out the Vintage*, 117. Background on Helen Chavez is from Rose, "Women in UFW," chap. 3.

65. "Margaret Murphy. Ana Raquel Minian, "'Indiscriminate and Shameless Sex': The Strategic Use of Sexuality by the United Farm Workers," *American Quarterly* 65, no. 1 (2013): 63–90; Garcia, *Jaws of Victory*, 34.

66. Aggie Rose Chavez compared her experience to that of the woman protagonist in the film *Salt of the Earth*. Aggie Rose Chavez.

67. "Jessica Govea; Maria Saludado Magaña; Maria Rifo; Aggie Rose Chavez; Barbara Macri-Ortiz; Rudy Ahumada.

68. Pawel, *Crusades*, 146.

69. This story is from Bill Esher, in Bardacke, *Trampling Out the Vintage*, 134–40.

70. FWA leaders have differing memories of Chavez's timeline. Marshall Ganz says it was two years in Ganz, "Resources and Resourcefulness: Strategic Capacity in the Unionization of California Agriculture, 1959–1966," *American Journal of Sociology* 105, no. 4 (2000): 1030. Brown, "United Farm Workers Grape Strike," 124, says five to ten years.

71. David Bacon, "How Filipino Migrants Gave the Grape Strike Its Radical Politics," *Dollars & Sense*, May–June 2018. In 1930 Watsonville an organized a mob of some five hundred whites shot at and beat Filipinos, enraged that some white "girls" were employed in a Filipino Club. The mob almost set fire to a large house where many Filipinos lived, until finally police and firemen held them off. *San Francisco Chronicle*, January 23, 1930.

72. LeRoy Chatfield recounted a meeting with AFL-CIO at which one of its attorneys lectured the farmworker group as if they knew nothing about labor law, and "ordered Larry [Itliong] around as if he were a rebellious teenager and spoke to him in the most condescending manner possible. Larry said nothing." Chatfield, *To Serve the People*, 65.

73. Chatfield, *To Serve the People*, 63.

74. Those voting were about 80 percent Filipino, with smaller numbers of Mexicans and other nationalities. Andrew Imutan. See also Andy Imutan to Patty Enrado, October 25, 2004, Welga Archive.

75. Bardacke, *Trampling Out the Vintage*, 156.

76. Doug Adair, "Commentary: 'From the Jaws of Victory,'" FMDP.

77. Ganz, "Resources and Resourcefulness," 1032.

78. Adrian Cruz, "Racialized Fields: Asians, Mexicans, and the Farm Labor Struggle in California" (PhD diss., University of Illinois at Urbana-Champaign, 2009), 94. "It's ironic," Philip Vera Cruz wrote, "that probably the most important thing Larry [Itliong] ever did to help the UFW was just keeping his mouth shut and not voicing

some of his deepest feelings. . . . Few people . . . recognize how difficult a decision that was for Larry." Vera Cruz, *Original Writings*, 40; see also González, "Critical Ethnic Legal Histories," 1051–52.

79. Vera Cruz, *Original Writings*, 94; Philip Vera Cruz oral history transcript, Interview 2, March 21, 1978, Welga Archive.
80. Obdulia "Abby" Flores Rivera.
81. Garcia, *Jaws of Victory*, 10.
82. Suṣan Ferris and Ricardo Sandoval, *The Fight in the Fields: Cesar Chavez and the Farmworkers Movement* (New York: Harcourt Brace, 1997), 86–123.
83. Robert Gordon, "Poisons in the Fields: The UFW, Pesticides, and environmental Politics," *Pacific Historical Review* 68, no. 1 (1999): 52, 63; Adair, "El Malcriado 1964–1970"; Gordon, "Poisons in Fields," 52; Laura Pulido and Devon Peña, "Environmentalism and Positionality: The Early Pesticide Campaign of the United Farm Workers' Organizing Committee, 1965–71," *Race, Gender and Class* 6, no. 1, pt. 2 (1998): 33–50.
84. Lauren Araiza, *To March for Others: The Black Freedom Struggle and the United Farm Workers* (Philadelphia: University of Pennsylvania Press, 2013) 125; Garcia, *Jaws of Victory*, 115.
85. Jennifer Gordon, "Law, Lawyers, and Labor: The United Farm Workers' Legal Strategy in the 1960s and 1970s and the Role of Law in Union Organizing Today," *University of Pennsylvania Journal of Business Law* 8, no. 1 (2005): 33–40, quotation at 39.
86. Eugene Nelson, Jr., "Huelga: New Goals for Labor," *Nation*, June 5, 1967, 724–25. Chavez was uncomfortable with King's increasing anti–Vietnam War positions, fearing that it would spread a movement too thin, while King was suspicious of labor unions due to their long history of racism. Gordon Keith Mantler, *Power to the Poor: Black-Brown Coalition and the Fight for Economic Justice, 1960–1974* (Chapel Hill: University of North Carolina Press, 2013), 44, 47. Marshall Ganz recalls that in December 1965 a small delegation from SNCC—including Stokely Carmichael, Cleveland Sellers, and Ralph Featherstone—came to the Delano office to discuss how SNCC could help. SNCC's major contributions to the UFW did not last, however. Most of the help SNCC provided came from whites, and its decision to expel "whites" deprived the UFW of valuable activists. Ironically, Mexican American SNCC members María Varela and Elizabeth Martínez were made to understand that they were included in "whites." Araiza, "Complicating," 85, 96–97.
87. Medina and Brooks quoted in Araiza, "Complicating," 84.
88. Vera Cruz, *Original Writings*, 93; Pawel, "Self-Inflicted Wound," 156; Obdulia "Abby" Flores Rivera; Ida Cousino.
89. "Rey Huerta. Chatfield, *To Serve the People*, 124; Pawel, *Union*, 185.
90. To Oscar Mondragon, this was a joke; he usually earned $150 a week in the fields. Many strikers lost their homes, cars, furniture, and TV sets, and the stress undermined marriages, Rudy Ahumada recalled. Oscar Mondragon and Rudy Ahumada. Before the union, workers had taken up collections to cover the losses of co-workers who did this work, but the UFW constitution prohibited that. Pawel, *Union*, 145.
91. He was able to do organizing sometime later, when the Migrant Ministry paid him a salary; Jose Guadalupe Murguia.
92. J. Craig Jenkins and Charles Perrow, "Insurgency of the Powerless: Farm Worker Movements (1946–1972)," *American Sociological Review* 42, no. 2 (1977): 252.
93. Miriam Pawel, "Decisions of Long Ago Shape the Union Today," *Los Angeles*

Times, January 10, 2006; Jennifer Gordon, "A Movement in the Wage of a New Law: The United Farm Workers and the California Agricultural Labor Relations Act," *Fordham Law Legal Studies Research Paper* No. 86 (2005).
94. Pawel, *Crusades*, 149; Pawel, "Self-Inflicted Wound," 157.
95. Pawel, *Crusades*, 202; Pawel, "Self-Inflicted Wound," 156.
96. Medina interview by the author.
97. Pawel, *Union*, 86–89, 185; Richard Baldwin Cook, "As Deceivers Yet True," FMDP; Medina interview by the author.
98. The following discussion of the hiring halls is taken from Pawel, *Union*, 84–89, 182, 185; Pawel, *Crusades*, 249–50, 279; Bardacke, *Trampling Out the Vintage*, 396–403; Barbara Macri-Ortiz.
99. The union also sometimes used the hiring halls to coerce workers to skip work and join a rally or a picket line by threatening them with loss of seniority if they refused. Vera Cruz, *Original Writings*, 75–76; Dorothy Fujita Rony, "Coalitions, Race, and Labor: Rereading Philip Vera Cruz," *Journal of Asian American Studies* 3, no. 2 (2000): 139–62; Cruz, "Racialized Fields," 145; Pawel, *Crusades*, 249–50, 253; Adair, "Commentary"; *The Delano Manongs: Forgotten Heroes of the United Farm Workers Movement*, dir. Marissa Aroy, 2014, Digital File.
100. Bardacke, *Trampling Out the Vintage*, 31.
101. Vera Cruz, *Original Writings*. See also "An Interview with Philip Vera Cruz Spring 1971," *Asia Pacific: Perspectives*, May 15, 2006, 61–63.
102. Rony, "Coalitions," 145; Garcia, *Jaws of Victory*, 122.
103. Gil Padilla, interview by Dawn Mabalon and Robyn Rodriguez, n.d., Welga Archive; Cruz, "Racialized Fields," 122; Garcia, *Jaws of Victory*, 139; Baldoz, "Valorizing Racial Boundaries," 975. Some Filipino leaders also disapproved of their compatriots' leisure activities. Philip Vera Cruz criticized those who frequented bars, card rooms and pool halls, strutted around, perhaps filling a "shirt pocket with those long fat cigars" in order "to feel and look important." Harsher yet, he condemned Filipino community leaders who live on those enterprises. Philip Vera Cruz, "Sour Grapes: Symbols of Oppression," *Gidra*, November 1976, 302–4.
104. Isao Fujimoto, interview by Robyn Rodriguez, February 13, 2015, Welga Archive.
105. Norma De Leon, "Philip Vera Cruz Resigns from UFW," *Ang Katipunan* 4, no. 15 (September 15–30, 1977): 5, 7, 9.
106. Rony, "Coalitions," 147; Fujimoto interview by Rodriguez.
107. Adair, "El Malcriado 1964–1970," FMDP; Brown, "United Farm Workers Grape Strike," 262–65.
108. Ferris and Sandoval, *Fight in the Fields*, 83; Brown, "United Farm Workers Grape Strike," 262–65.
109. Chavez in Jensen and Hammerback, *Words of Chávez*, 15. Rodriguez likened it to a medieval religious procession in "Saint Cesar of Delano," 17.
110. The march is covered by many authors, but a good short description is in Ferris and Sandoval, *Fight in the Fields*, 117–23.
111. On Chavez's statements on including all groups, see for example, his impromptu speech in Austin, February 6, 1971, in Jensen and Hammerback, *Words of Chávez*, 57. The text of "The Plan of Delano" is at FMDP. It was SNCC volunteers who suggested a march: it was part of the African American civil rights pool of tactics but not something customary among farmworker activists, according to Araiza, "Complicating," 89–90. Chavez claimed that "in every religious orientated culture 'the pilgrimage' has had a place," which is not the case; Chavez letter, March 1966, in Jensen and Hammerback, *Words of Chávez*, 15.

112. Juanita Brown; Antonia Maria Saludado; Maria Saludado Magaña.
113. Bardacke, *Trampling Out the Vintage*, 214, 302; Obdulia "Abby" Flores Rivera; Prouty, *Chavez, Catholic Bishops*, 24. It is revealing that Huerta called opposition to the religiosity "bigotry"; Levy, *Chavez: Autobiography*, 277.
114. Obdulia "Abby" Flores Rivera; Levy, *Chavez: Autobiography*, 277.
115. Epifanio Camacho, *The Autobiography of a Communist: Communists Are Made, Not Born*, Kindle book, loc. 40; Bardacke, *Trampling Out the Vintage*, 214; Chatfield, *To Serve the People*, 132.
116. Bacon, "How Filipino Migrants."
117. Quoted in Cruz, "Racialized Fields," 118.
118. Vera Cruz, *Original Writings*, 37–38; González, "Critical Ethnic Legal Histories," 1051; Rony, "Coalitions," 139–62.
119. Quoted in Cruz, "Racialized Fields," 111.
120. Eugene Nelson, *Huelga: The First Hundred Days of the Great Delano Grape Strike* (Delano, CA: Farm Worker Press, 1966), 86.
121. "UFWOC's Assistant Director Resigns," *Bakersfield Californian*, October 25, 1971; Vera Cruz, *Original Writings*, 75–76; Rony, "Coalitions," 148; Benji Chang, "Larry Itliong and the Pilipino Farm Workers," in *Asian Americans: An Encyclopedia of Social, Cultural, and Political History* (Santa Barbara: ABC-CLIO, 2013), 577–78; Marc-Tizoc González, "Critical Ethnic Legal Histories: Unearthing the Interracial Justice of Filipino American Agricultural Labor Organizing," *University of California Irvine Law Review* 3, no. 4 (2013): 991n138; Adrian Cruz, "Racialized Fields: Asians, Mexicans, and the Farm Labor Struggle in California" (PhD diss., University of Illinois, 2009), 145.
122. Mae N. Ngai, *Impossible Subjects: Illegal Aliens and the Making of America* (Princeton, NJ: Princeton University Press, 2004), 159.
123. Frank Bardacke, "The UFW and the Undocumented," *Internal Labor and Working-class History*, no. 83 (Spring 2013): 162.
124. Cesar Chavez, speech to a union gathering in Los Angeles, June 1974, in Jensen and Hammerback, *Words of Chávez*, 85; Bardacke, "UFW and Undocumented," 166.
125. Bardacke, *Trampling Out the Vintage*, 488.
126. To be fair, we must note that starting in 1960, AWOC members had been assaulting braceros; Ngai, *Impossible Subjects*, 164.
127. Bardacke, "UFW and the Undocumented"; Bardacke, *Trampling Out the Vintage*, chap. 24; Pawel, *Crusades*, 288–95, 313–14, 419–20, 456; Garcia, *Jaws of Victory*, 149. David G. Gutiérrez interprets this as consistent with Chavez's insistence, since his earliest days of organizing farmworkers, that "the union's energies needed to be expended exclusively on . . . American citizens" and that the undocumented would always constitute an obstacle to unions; Gutiérrez, *Walls and Mirrors: Mexican Americans, Mexican Immigrants, and the Politics of Ethnicity* (Berkeley: University of California Press, 1995), 197.
128. Obdulia "Abby" Flores Rivera.
129. Nelson, *Huelga*, 74, 86; Pawel, *Union*, 25; Dolores Huerta.
130. Barbara Macri-Ortiz; Walsh, "Mobilization Theory," 166. For another example of red-baiting the UFW, see Gary Allen, *The Grapes: Communist Wrath in Delano*, pamphlet (n.p., 1966), at Farmworkermovement.org. As in the civil rights movement, red-baiting was a tactic, but it also reflected the assumption that white people were manipulating gullible people of color.
131. Pawel, *Union*, 108.
132. UFW staff believed that the FBI and the CIA helped in the cover-up; Walsh,

"Mobilization Theory," 166. For another example of red-baiting the UFW, see Allen, "Grapes: Communist Wrath," n.p.

133. See *El Malcriado* no. 21, FMDP. This still goes on: see "Migrant Farmworkers Repeatedly Sprayed with Pesticides in Illinois Sue Pioneer Hi-Bred and Pesticide Applicators," Legal Aid Chicago, at https://legalaidchicago.org/newsroom/migrant -farmworkers-repeatedly-sprayed-with-pesticides-in-illinois-sue-pioneer-hi-bred -and-pesticide-applicators; "Pesticides in the Fields," Walter Reuther Library, at https://reuther.wayne.edu/ex/exhibits/fw/pesticide.html; Dolores Huerta and Jerry Cohen, "Statement of United Farm Workers Organizing Committee, AFL-CIO, November 21, 1969, at https://tinyurl.com/pr2ffwfj.

134. Nelson, "Huelga," 9, 55, 69, 81; Pawel, *Crusades*, 133–34, 269–71; Pawel, *Union*, 108; "UFW Martyrs," UFW.org., April 3, 2017; Ganz, "Not the Chavez I Knew."

135. This was why those leading the picketers would not put Camacho in charge. He later joined the "revolutionary" Progressive Labor Party. Camacho, *Autobiography of a Communist*, 39, 57–59; Alfredo Acosta Figueroa; Doug Adair; Bacon, "What Chavez Movie Missed." LeRoy Chatfield thought that every farmworker "experimented at some point with 'violence' or at least considered the possibility of using it if they thought it might force the growers to recognize the union"; Chatfield, *To Serve the People*, 101.

136. Oscar Mondragon and Gil Padilla were tried for these activities, and Mondragon served eleven months in jail. Ferris and Sandoval, *Fight in the Fields*, 140; Bardacke, *Trampling Out the Vintage*, 448–49; Tina Solinas; Oscar Mondragon.

137. Bardacke, *Trampling Out the Vintage*, 448–49; Camacho, *Autobiography of a Communist*, 57; Pawel, *Crusades*, 158; Pawel, *Union*, 109; Reyes quoted in Bardacke, *Trampling Out the Vintage*, 287.

138. The first quotation is from Cesar Chavez to E. L. Bara, Jr., president, California Grape and Tree Fruit League, 1969, in Jensen and Hammerback, *Words of Chávez*, 34; the second is from Levy, *Chavez: Autobiography*, 196.

139. Cesar Chavez, speech ending fast, March 10, 1968, in Jensen and Hammerback, *Words of Chávez*, 167; Pawel, *Union*, chap. 4, quotations at 46–47 and 90.

140. Ferris and Sandoval, *Fight in the Fields*, 141.

141. At least one member of his team thought the fast was also a tactic to avoid charges that he was responsible for the vandalism; Ganz, "Not the Chavez I Knew." Chavez was already an experienced faster, having previously experimented with two unpublicized fasts; Pawel, *Crusades*, 166.

142. This support was not totally selfless, because Kennedy expected and got significant support from the union. Cesar Chavez spoke for Kennedy in every county that had a significant Mexican population and organized massive voter registration drives. Steven W. Bender, *One Night in America: Robert Kennedy, Cesar Chavez, and the Dream of Dignity* (Boulder, CO: Paradigm Publishers, 2008), chap. 4; Cesar Chavez, speech ending fast, March 10, 1968, in Jensen and Hammerback, *Words of Chávez*, 166.

143. Gordon, "Law, Lawyers and Labor," 22–24; Randy Shaw, *Beyond the Fields: Cesar Chavez, the UFW, and the Struggle for Justice in the 21st Century* (Berkeley: University of California Press, 2008), 87–89; Luis D. León, "Cesar Chavez in American Religious Politics: Mapping the New Global Spiritual Line," *American Quarterly* 59, no. 3 (2007): 873; Pawel, *Union*, 40ff.

144. Chatfield, *To Serve the People*, 106; Doug Adair and Dawn Mabalon in Bacon, "What Chavez Movie Missed"; Pawel, *Crusades*, 158–64.

145. The idea came from the civil rights movement: Reverend Jim Drake was familiar

both with the Harlem "don't shop where you can't work" boycotts and with the origin of the term, an Irish rent strike by peasants against landowner Charles Boycott in the late nineteenth century. Araiza, "Complicating," 88; Bardacke, *Trampling Out the Vintage*, 168. At first it was directed only at Giumarra Vineyards, one of the largest grape producers in California. The growers recognized John Giumarra as their general in their war against the UFW. He tried duplicity, packing his nonunion grapes in boxes with other growers' labels. This left the UFW no choice but to extend the boycott to all grapes, which simplified the message. They no longer had to ask shoppers to check the label on grape boxes; rather they could ask them not to buy grapes at all.

146. Wayne Moquin, ed., *A Documentary History of the Mexican Americans* (New York: Praeger, 1971), 363–65.

147. Pawel, *Union*, 33.

148. The story of the New York City boycott told here is indebted to Sarah Stern, " 'We Cast Our Lot with the Farm Workers': Organization, Mobilization and Meaning in the United Farm Workers' Grape Boycott in New York City, 1967–70" (BA thesis, New York University, 2013); Pawel, *Union*, 61–62; Garcia *Jaws of Victory*, 65–66, 77; Araiza, *To March*, 102. On the variety of boycott organizers' work, see the recollections of J. M. "Pancho" Botello, Paul Carrillo, Ed Chiera, Graciela Cisneros, Jessie De La Cruz, Hope Lopez Fierro, Jessica Govea, Maria Saludado Magaña, Jose Guadalupe Murguia, Hijinio Rangel, Virginia (Jones) Rodriguez, in FMDP.

149. Pawel, *Union*, 7–8, 31–34; Maria Saludado Magaña.

150. Pawel, *Union*, 166, 258–59.

151. The older, establishment African American organizations were not unanimously supportive. At first the Urban League and the national NAACP hedged, worried that direct action would drain resources from their litigation. Reverend Leon Sullivan of the Philadelphia NAACP executive board even condemned the boycott, and King's SCLC held back, quite possibly because it received substantial contributions from the Teamsters. But ultimately all these organizations championed the boycott in some fashion. Black support came earliest and strongest in California, where African Americans were acutely aware of racism against Mexican Americans. Boycott leader Esperanza Fierro Lopez fasted in front of a Philadelphia A&P—the one grocery chain that insisted on continuing to buy grapes—and got a positive response from Black customers but not from Black elites. Araiza, "Complicating," 71–72, 89; Araiza, *To March*, 109 and chaps. 3–4, passim; Mantler, *Power to the Poor*, 44.

152. Eliseo Medina, interview by the author, December 6, 2021.

153. Brown, "United Farm Workers Grape Strike," 204–7; Pawel, *Union*, 31–34.

154. Garcia, *Jaws of Victory*, 76–78; Matt Garcia, "A Moveable Feast: The UFW Grape Boycott and Farm Worker Justice," *International Labor and Working-Class History*, no. 83 (Spring 2013): 146–53, at 152; Harris poll cited in Majka, "Poor People's Movements," 304; Prouty, *Chavez, Catholic Bishops*, 60. The London story is from a UFW member quoted in Adair, "What Chavez Movie Missed."

155. This description is from a contract with Sunharvest, a subsidiary of United Brands, which became a pattern for later contracts. It appears on Miriam Pawel's website Unionoftheirdreams.com, offering links to primary sources; Majka, "Poor People's Movements," 306; Rony, "Coalitions," 145.

156. Obdulia "Abby" Flores Rivera.

157. Pawel, *Union*, 166, 258–59.

158. Medina interview by the author.

159. Medina interview by the author.
160. Tina Solinas; Obdulia "Abby" Flores Rivera; Terry (Vasquez) Scott.
161. Chatfield, *To Serve the People*, 156.
162. The first quotation is from Pawel, *Union*, 185; the second is from Cook, "As Deceivers." Pawel, *Crusades*, 232; Levy, *Autobiography of La Causa*, 197.
163. Pawel, *Crusades*, 283; Rudy Ahumada.
164. One example: Jack Quigley became business manager in 1972 and found that no one had kept proper books since Rudy Ahumada left in 1971, so he set up a record-keeping system and quarterly budgets. But Chavez charged that Quigley had "usurped too much power" and got rid of him. Bardacke, *Trampling Out the Vintage*, 458–59; Pawel, *Crusades*, 278–79. An earlier experience of LeRoy Chatfield foreshadowed this practice. When the UFW was battling California Proposition 22, which would have prohibited consumer-led boycotts, regulated the timing of strikes, and banned collective bargaining on safety issues, Chavez "explained" that if they lost the vote, Chatfield would have to accept the blame. Chatfield, *To Serve the People*, 166.
165. Pawel, *Crusades*, 426.
166. Bardacke, *Trampling Out the Vintage*, 541. Dederich's *New York Times* obituary referred to "accounts of violence and the insistence by Mr. Dederich on forced vasectomies for men in Synanon, mandatory abortions for women, and the divorce of more than 230 of its married couples who were to switch to other partners." Lawrence Van Gelder, "Charles Dederich, 83, Synanon Founder, Dies," *New York Times*, March 4, 1997. By the 1970s, Synanon had been charged with more than eighty beatings and one murder and had been the subject of exposés in the national media. See Wikipedia entry on Synanon.
167. The board was created at the UFW's first constitutional convention in 1973, though Chavez was at best lukewarm about what he labeled "so-called democracy"; Pawel, *Crusades*, 273.
168. The practice is one of a number of attack therapies that aim to "tear down the patient's defenses by extreme verbal or physical measures." Donald A. Eisner, *The Death of Psychotherapy* (Westport, CT: Praeger/Greenwood, 2000), 45. Most psychologists have adjudged these "therapies" harmful to participants.
169. The first quotation is from in Pawel, *Union*, 56; the second is from Gilbert Padilla, in Bardacke, *Trampling Out the Vintage*, 542.
170. Pawel, *Union*, 214; Garcia, *Jaws of Victory*, 221–23. In another instance, he accused a plumber who had come to do some construction work of being a spy, then tried to confiscate his truck, with all his tools. When Liza Hirsch, a law student whom Chavez had mentored, argued that the plumber should have his truck, he denounced her as a Communist and fired her too. Pawel, *Crusades*, 344–46.
171. Pawel, *Union*, 344–45.
172. "People inside the union are really intimidated . . . afraid to express themselves," Vera Cruz said. Leon, "Vera Cruz Resigns"; Pawel, *Crusades*, 204, Padilla quoted on 431.
173. Kimberly Springer, *Living the Revolution: Black Feminist Organizing, 1968–1980* (Durham, NC: Duke University Press, 2006), 160.
174. Pawel, *Crusades*, 273.
175. Pawel, *Crusades*, 386–88, quotation at 431; Gilbert Padilla; Bardacke, *Trampling Out the Vintage*, chap. 26.
176. Cook, "As Deceivers," FMDP.
177. For example, Dolores Huerta informed on volunteers Donna Haber and Eliezer

Risco (a pro-Castro Cuban) and farmworker/staffer Ida Cousino, telling Chavez that they had attended a party of the *People's World*, a Communist West Coast newspaper. Bardacke, *Trampling Out the Vintage*, 264–65.

178. According to Padilla, Vera Cruz was usually silent in meetings but regularly took notes, and Chavez came to believe that he was planning to write a book denouncing him. Gilbert Padilla.

179. The first quotation is from Bardacke, *Trampling Out the Vintage*, 568; the second is from Pawel, *Crusades*, 431.

180. Kurtis Lee and Liliana Michelena, "Can the United Farm Workers Rise Again?" *New York Times*, March 12, 2023.

181. Kurtis Lee, "Newsom Signs California Bill to Ease Farmworker Union Voting," *New York Times*, September 29, 2022.

7. Consciousness-Raising as Activism

1. Simon Hattenstone, "Angela Davis on the Power of Protest: 'We Can't Do Anything Without Optimism,'" *Guardian*, March 5, 2022. The case, *DeGraffenreid v. General Motors Assembly Div.*, 413 F.Supp. 142 (1976), can be found at https://www.leagle.com/decision/1976555413fsupp1421520.xml. Kimberlé Crenshaw, "Race, Reform and Retrenchment: Transformation and Legitimation in Anti-Discrimination Law," *Harvard Law Review* 101 (1988): 1331; Crenshaw, "Intersectionality: The Double Bind of Race and Gender," *Perspectives: A Newsletter For and About Women Lawyers* 12, no. 1 (2003–4).

2. Several Black scholars have called the intersectionality concept "the intellectual property of Black feminism." Samantha Pinto and Jennifer C. Nash, "Then and Now: Women of Color Originalism and the Anthological Impulse in Women's and Gender Studies," *Feminist Studies* 48, no. 1 (2022): 79–101. Precisely because it has been so influential, Ann duCille has warned that intersectionality can become a "sacred object," valued for its celebrity, in "The Occult of Black Womanhood: Critical Demeanor and Black Feminist Studies," *Signs* 19, no. 3 (1994): 591–629.

3. The Chicago Women's Liberation Union's did produce such a statement in 1972: "Socialist Feminism—A Strategy for the Women's Liberation Movement."

4. One scholar found the statement reprinted thirty-two times in various books and articles between 1979 and 2019; Kayla M. Bloodgood, "Multiple Archives, Multiple Futures: Reexamining the Socialism of the Combahee River Collective Statement" (MA thesis, Duke University, April 2020), appendix.

5. These mistakes were identified and corrected in Springer, *Living the Revolution*, 3, and in Benita Roth, *Separate Roads to Feminism: Black, Chicana, and Movements in American's Second Wave* (Cambridge: Cambridge University Press, 2004), 8.

6. Socialist feminists rejected the assumption that Marxist theory could provide a formula or strategy for a more just and democratic society. Bread and Roses was one of several socialist feminist organizations attacked by doctrinaire Marxist-Leninist parties in attempts to impose their doctrine and discipline on the women's liberation movement. A good discussion of this difference can be found in Rosemarie Tong and Tina Fernandes Botts, *Feminist Thought*, 5th ed. (New York: Taylor & Francis, 2017), chap. 3. Although one scholar mistakenly calls the distinction between Marxist and socialist feminisms "fuzzy"—Ashley Bohrer, "Intersectionality and Marxism: A Critical Historiography," *Historical Materialism* 26, no. 2 (2018): 47—those active in women's liberation in the 1970s thought the distinction quite sharp. Since then

Marxist feminism has become far more capacious and complex in its understanding of inequality and exploitation.

7. Barbara Ehrenreich, "What Is Socialist Feminism?" *Win Magazine*, June 3, 1976.

8. Linda Gordon, "Participatory Democracy from SNCC Through Port Huron to Women's Liberation to Occupy," in *Inspiring Participatory Democracy*, ed. Tom Hayden (Boulder, CO: Paradigm, 2012), 103–26.

9. One critic called it a somewhat mystical notion, as if an organizer's role were mainly to help members of a group express themselves until reaching consensus or a majority decision. The best discussion of how New Leftists tried to practice participatory democracy is in Francesca Polletta, *Freedom Is an Endless Meeting: Democracy in American Social Movements* (Chicago: University of Chicago Press, 2002), chap. 4.

10. Cellestine Ware, "The Relationship of Black Women to the Women's Liberation Movement," in *Radical Feminism: a Documentary Reader*, ed. Barbara A. Crow (New York: NYU Press, 2000), 98–112.

11. Judy Richardson, "Womanpower and SNCC," *Massachusetts Review* 52, no. 2 (2011): 183–84; Cynthia Griggs Fleming, "Black Women Activists and the SNCC: The Case of Ruby Doris Smith Robinson," *Irish Journal of American Studies* 3 (1993): 34. Mary King, however, writes that Ruby Doris Smith Robinson was unsympathetic to women's grievances: Mary King, *Freedom Song: A Personal Story of the 1960s Civil Rights Movement* (New York: Morrow, 1987), 453–54.

12. Frances Beal, interview by Loretta J. Ross, March 18, 2005, Box 7, VF.

13. Stephen Ward, "The Third World Women's Alliance: Black Feminist Radicalism and Black Power Politics," in *The Black Power Movement: Rethinking the Civil Rights–Black Power Era*, ed. Peniel Joseph (New York: Routledge, 2006), 125. Beal soon saw that the CP's economic determinism blinded it to sexism; McDuffie, *Sojourning for Freedom*, 209. Still, Beal may well have encountered discussions of Black women's particular exploitation by 1930s Black Communists Esther Cooper Jackson, Claudia Jones, and Louise Thompson Patterson. Anna Carastathis, in *Intersectionality: Origins, Contestations, Horizons* (Lincoln: University of Nebraska Press, 2016), 31–33, describes these women as "subversively deploying a Marxist-Leninist conceptual arsenal" in these interventions.

14. SNCC member Cynthia Washington is quoted in Ruth Rosen, *The World Split Open: How the Modern Women's Movement Changed America* (New York: Penguin, 2000), 105; Fleming, "Black Women Activists," 34; Kristin Anderson-Bricker, "'Triple Jeopardy': Black Women and the Growth of Feminist Consciousness in SNCC, 1964–1975," in *Still Lifting, Still Climbing: Contemporary African American Women's Activism*, ed. Kimberly Springer (New York: NYU Press, 1999), 55.

15. Sara M. Evans, *Personal Politics: The Roots of Women's Liberation in the Civil Rights Movement and the New Left* (New York: Knopf, 1979), 78–82.

16. For example, Black staff member Cynthia Washington, who directed a Mississippi organizing project, thought the sit-in made no sense; "Cynthia Washington," SNCCdigital.org; Harold L. Smith, "Casey Hayden: Gender and the Origins of SNCC, SDS, and the Women's Liberation Movement," in *Texas Women: Their Histories, Their Lives*, ed. Elizabeth Hayes Turner et al. (Athens: University of Georgia Press, 2015), 378; King, *Freedom Song*, 450; Anderson-Bricker, "Triple Jeopardy," 55; Harold L. Smith, "Casey Hayden: Gender and the Origins of SNCC, SDS, and the Women's Liberation Movement," in Elizabeth Hayes Turner et al., *Texas Women*, 159.

17. Beal quoted in Carol Giardina, *Freedom for Women: Forging the Women's Liberation Movement, 1953–1970* (Gainesville: University Press of Florida, 2010), 101–2.

18. Johnnetta Betsch Cole and Beverly Guy-Sheftall, *Gender Talk: The Struggle for Women's Equality in African American Communities* (New York: One World, 2003), 6; Beverly Guy-Sheftall, "Sisters in Struggle: A Belated Response," in *The Feminist Memoir Project: Voices from Women's Liberation*, ed. Rachel Blau DuPlessis and Ann Snitow (New York: Three Rivers Press, 1998), 487–88; Springer, *Living the Revolution*, 118–22. Still, Barbara Smith saw a "time lag"—that Black feminism was in an earlier stage of development than white feminism; Winifred Breines, *The Trouble Between Us: An Uneasy History of White and Black Women in the Feminist Movement* (New York: Oxford University Press, 2006), 134.

19. Written by Eldridge Cleaver, a founder of the Black Panthers, while in jail—hence the phrase "on ice"—it argued that American Blacks had been colonized. It was an early expression of conceiving of the American struggle against racism as part of global anti-colonialism. Barbara Smith of the Combahee River Collective remembers that she couldn't finish reading the book, disturbed particularly by its homophobic attack on James Baldwin. Smith to author, March 3, 2022.

20. Frances Beal, "Double Jeopardy," in *Liberation Now: Writings from the Women's Liberation Movement* (New York: Dell, 1971), 185–97.

21. Ward, "Third World Women's Alliance," 129. It was an "oppositional strategy that both counters racism and constructs conservative utopian images of African-American life," according to E. Frances White, "Africa on My Mind: Gender, Counter Discourse, and African-American Nationalism," *Journal of Women's History* 2, no. 1 (Spring 1990): 77.

22. Beal interview by Ross.

23. Stanford professor Clay Carson, a historian of SNCC, considered this committee the only successful SNCC project after 1968. Ariane Vani Kannan, "The TWWA: History, Geopolitics and Form" (PhD diss., Syracuse University, 2018), 56; Springer, *Living the Revolution*, 116–17; Ward, "Third World Women's Alliance," 127–29; Ula Taylor, "The Historical Evolution of Black Feminist Theory and Praxis," *Journal of Black Studies* 29, no. 2 (1998): 245. On SNCC's identification with anti-colonial struggles, see Dan Berger, "SNCC's Unruly Internationalism," *Boston Review*, November 16, 2021.

24. In fact there are many not-yet-explored or -discovered early formulations of intersectionality *avant la lettre*, particularly by Black feminist or womanist activists. For example, Shirley Chisholm is discussed in Anastasia Curwood, "Black Feminism on Capitol Hill: Shirley Chisholm and Movement Politics, 1968–1984," *Meridians: Feminism, Race, Transnationalism* 13, no. 1 (2015): 204–32; Pauli Murray, notably in Pauli Murray and Mary O. Eastwood, "Jane Crow and the Law: Sex Discrimination and Title VII," *George Washington Law Review* 34, no. 2 (1965): 232–56; Benita Roth, *Separate Roads to Feminism: Black, Chicana, and White Feminist Movements in America's Second Wave* (Cambridge: Cambridge University Press, 2003), 87.

25. My discussion of Patricia Robinson is indebted to Robyn Spencer, who is working on her biography. Rhonda Y. Williams, *Concrete Dreams: The Search for Black Power in the 20th Century* (New York: Routledge, 2015), 109–10; Roth, *Separate Roads*, 87.

26. John Henrik Clarke, A. Peter Bailey, and Earl Grant, *Malcolm X: The Man and His Times* (1969; reprint Trenton, NJ: Africa World Press, 1990).

27. Thirty years later many Black women still lacked access to birth control. A 1991 National Council of Negro Women study found that 58 percent of Black women over eighteen never used birth control but only 1 percent wanted to get pregnant and only

2 percent said they did not know how to use birth control. Loretta Ross, "Reproductive Justice as Intersectional Feminist Activism," *Souls* 19, no. 3 (2017): 296.

28. A Poor Black Woman statement of September 11, 1968, can be found in Rosalyn Baxandall and Linda Gordon, eds., *Dear Sisters: Dispatches from the Women's Liberation Movement* (New York: Basic Books, 2000).

29. Recording of a Poor Black Women meeting quoted in Giardina, *Freedom for Women*, 126. The "bourgeois" label came to be applied critically to the National Organization for Women, founded in 1966, by women's liberation people, white and Black alike. It was wrong in at least one important respect—NOW included some influential labor union leaders, hardly "bourgie." This arrogant attitude reflected a youthful disdain for their elders—NOW women were on average a generation older than women's liberation women.

30. Joyce Holt, Rita Van Lew, and Priscilla Leake to Margaret Benston (a white Canadian feminist theorist), November 4, 1968, author's collection. Robinson had also been something of a counselor to some white New York City feminists and always supported coalitions with white feminists; Roth, *Separate Roads*, 95.

31. M. Rivka Polatnick, "Diversity in Women's Liberation Ideology: How a Black and a White Group of the 1960s Viewed Motherhood," *Signs* 21, no. 3 (1996): 687–88; Giardina, *Freedom for Women*, 135.

32. Two of their leaflets—"Poor Black Women" and "A Historical and Critical Essay for Black Women"—are reproduced in Baxandall and Gordon, *Dear Sisters*, 93–95 and 135. The work of the group is described in Rosalyn Baxandall, "Re-Visioning the Women's Liberation Movement's Narrative: Early Second Wave African American Feminists," *Feminist Studies* 27, no. 1 (2001): 234–38; and Polatnick, "Diversity," 679–706. Polatnick answers the allegation that the middle-class Robinson was the author of these views at 688n20. The Combahee River Collective would later read and discuss *Lessons from the Damned*.

33. In defying the Black nationalists, the group was reclaiming an older history of African American support for contraception, even abortion. "Not all women are intended for mothers," announced the nineteenth-century Black newspaper the *Women's Era*. In the 1920s, Du Bois and the NAACP endorsed birth control and in the 1930s and '40s Black newspapers denounced bans on birth control and the arrests of abortionists.

34. The reference to a Black "nation" recalled the Comintern's opportunist support for a Black nation (discussed in chapter 4). The reference to "matriarchy" mirrored, ironically, the 1965 Moynihan Report, which blamed Black "matriarchy" for Black poverty. The report, "The Negro Family: The Case for National Action," 1965, can be found at Daniel Geary, "The Moynihan Report: An Annotated Edition," *Atlantic*, September 14, 2015.

35. Patricia Robinson, "Revolt of the Black Women," in n.a., *Lessons from the Damned: Class Struggle in the Black Community* (Ojai, CA: Times Change Press, 1973), 7; Loretta J. Ross, "A Simple Human Right: The History of Black Women and Abortion," *On the Issues* (Spring 1994); see also Roth, *Separate Roads*, 92–93; Giardina, *Freedom for Women*, 166–67; Williams, *Concrete Dreams*, 241–44.

36. Joyce Holt, Rita Van Lew, and Priscilla Leake to Margaret Benston, November 4, 1968, author's collection.

37. A group of twelve Black women working on reproductive health and rights coined the phrase "reproductive justice" at a 1994 conference; Ross, "Reproductive Justice," 290–91.

38. Springer, *Living the Revolution*, 48. Springer uses the term *polyvocal* at 115.

39. Beal interview by Ross, 45; Linda Burnham, interview by Loretta J. Ross, March 18, 2005, Box 12, VF; Voichita Nachescu, "Becoming the Feminist Subject: Consciousness Raising Groups in Second-wave Feminism" (PhD diss., State University at Buffalo, 2006), 165; Alethia Jones, Virginia Eubanks, and Barbara Smith, eds., *Ain't Gonna Let Nobody Turn Me Around: Forty Years of Movement Building with Barbara Smith* (Albany: SUNY Press, 2014), 57. Cherríe Moraga has pointed out that the "*idea* of Third World feminism has proved . . . much easier between the covers of a book than between real live women." Moraga, "Refugees of a World on Fire," foreword to *This Bridge Called My Back: Writings for Radical Women of Color*, 2nd ed. (New York: Kitchen Table: Women of Color Press, 1983), xiv.

40. Julie R. Enszer and Agatha Beins, "Inter- and Transnational Feminist Theory and Practice in *Triple Jeopardy* and *Conditions*," *Women's Studies* 47, no. 1 (2018): 27.

41. Beal's account has been described by many: Ward, "Third World Women's Alliance," 141; Taylor, "Historical Evolution," 246; Springer, *Living the Revolution*, 89. Martinez's story is from Betita Martinez, interview by Loretta J. Ross, March 3 and August 6, 2006, Box 30, VF. Martinez is featured in Dorothy Sue Cobble, Linda Gordon, and Astrid Henry, *Feminism Unfinished: A Short, Surprising History of American Women's Movements* (New York: Liveright, 2014), chap. 2.

42. Cellestine Ware, "The Relationship of Black Women to the Women's Liberation Movement," in *Radical Feminism: A Documentary Reader*, ed. Barbara A. Crow (New York: NYU Press, 2000), 100. A 1970 set of letters to *Essence* magazine complained that "white chicks" had no right to "comment on our male-female situation," Cambridge Women's Center newsletter 5 , no. 16, Cambridge Women's Center Records, SL.

43. Kimberly Springer, "Black Feminist Organizations and the Emergence of Interstitial Politics," in *Modern American Queer History*, ed. Allida Mae Black (Philadelphia: Temple University Press, 2001), 185.

44. The TWWA could not escape adopting a defensive position, as in its statement "Is a Third World Women's Group Divisive to the National Liberation Struggle?" Third World Women's Alliance, "Women in the Struggle," in *Radical Feminism: A Documentary Reader*, ed. Barbara A. Crow (New York: NYU Press, 2000), 461.

45. Wesley C. Hogan, *Many Minds, One Heart: SNCC's Dream for a New America* (Chapel Hill: University of North Carolina Press, 2007), 112; Smith, "Casey Hayden, 368, 370.

46. King, *Freedom Song*, 457–59 and appendix 3. Addressees included SNCC, SDS, the NSA, the Student Peace Union, and the Northern Student Movement. Smith, "Casey Hayden," 382. In 1966 the statement was published in the New Left magazine *Liberation*.

47. Giardina, *Freedom for Women*, 95–97, 127.

48. The first quotation is from Jo Freeman in *The Feminist Memoir Project: Voices from Women's Liberation*, ed. Rachel Blau DuPlessis and Ann Snitow (New York: Three Rivers Press, 1998), 180; the second is from Giardina, *Freedom for Women*, 129–30.

49. Toni Cade Bambara, "On the Issue of Roles," in *The Black Woman: An Anthology*, ed. Toni Cade Bambara (York and Scarborough, Ont.: Mentor Books, 1970), 107.

50. A remembrance of these early days in the form of a letter to "sisters" by Nancy Hawley, October 8, 1970, in Folder 2.39, Popkin Papers, SL.

51. This description of the conference, unless otherwise cited, is from last folder, Box 1, Marya Randall Levenson Papers, SL.

52. A full transcript of this discussion appears in Alice Echols, *Daring to Be Bad:*

Radical Feminism in America 1967–1975 (Minneapolis: University of Minnesota Press, 1989), app. A.

53. Casey Hayden defined the prefigurative as "to act now as they wanted the world to be." Hogan, *Many Minds, One Heart*, 110–11. Organizers-writers Mark Engler and Paul Engler discuss prefigurative modes of organizing in *This Is an Uprising*, 272–76; they consider it opposed to strategic politics; I imagine that what is prefigurative can also be strategic.

54. Some scholars have labeled those who favored autonomy "feminists" and the others "politicos." That distinction is extremely misleading—the "feminists" were also "politicos," committed to political action. The differences were often more emotional than ideological. Kesselman quoted in Ashley Eberle, "Breaking With Our Brothers: The Source and Structure of Chicago Women's Liberation in 1960s Activism," *Western Illinois Historical Review* 1 (Spring 2009): 68.

55. Coming from a poor sharecropper family, Dunbar was briefly married into the upper-middle class and for a time hid her background out of shame. She later became an important advocate for Indigenous rights and opponent of U.S. support for the Contras in Nicaragua. See Dunbar-Ortiz, *Red Dirt: Growing Up Okie* (New York: Verso, 1997); Dunbar-Ortiz, *Outlaw Woman: A Memoir of the War Years* (San Francisco: City Lights Books, 2002); Dunbar-Ortiz, *Blood on the Border: Memoir of the Contra War* (Boston: South End Press, 2005); and Dunbar-Ortiz, *An Indigenous Peoples' History of the United States* (Boston: Beacon, 2014).

56. Ann Hunter Popkin, "Bread and Roses: An Early Moment in the Development of Socialist-Feminism" (PhD diss., Brandeis University, 1978), 44–45.

57. Dana Densmore, paper presented at the conference "A Revolutionary Moment: Women's Liberation in the Late 1960s and Early 1970s," Boston University, March 27–29, 2014.

58. The first quotation is from Folder 6.8, Maren Lockwood Carden Papers, SL; the second is from Folder 1.8, Rochelle Goldberg Ruthchild Papers, SL, and related material in Folder 1.13, SL. Many of the quotations from Dunbar came from the accounts of those opposed to Cell 16, so they must be understood as opinionated. As the organization imploded, a bitter struggle over the group's resources arose, between Abby Rockefeller and others remaining loyal to Cell 16, and those who defected and joined the Trotskyist Socialist Workers Party and its offshoot, the Young Socialist Alliance; Cindy Jaquith of SWP/YSA to Comrades, December 14, 1970, author's collection. Dunbar's paranoia and insistence on authority is reminiscent of the worst years of Cesar Chavez's leadership (see chapter 6).

59. After Cell 16 imploded, a dissident group seized control of its publication, *No More Fun and Games* (a title that seems to imply that enjoyment cannot be part of a feminist movement). The group continued to publish it for several years with a far more open and diverse editorial policy. The group is discussed in Kristine M. Rosenthal, "Women in Transition: An Ethnography of a Women's Liberation Organization as a Case Study of Personal and Cultural Change" (D.Ed. thesis, Harvard School of Education, 1972), 47ff.

60. Many of the groups formed at these meetings brought together women with little in common, so many of them dissolved, their members forming new groups with greater commonality. The consciousness-raising groups of women who had belonged to male-dominated New Left groups tended to be more cohesive. Popkin, "Bread and Roses," 101; Cellestine Ware, *Woman Power: The Movement for Women's Liberation* (New York: Tower, 1970), 116.

61. Judith Herman quoted in Popkin "Bread and Roses," 59.

62. Ware, *Woman Power*, 111. Her first name was originally Celestine, but she later spelled it Cellestine.
63. Susan Brownmiller, "Sisterhood Is Powerful," *New York Times*, March 15, 1970.
64. Popkin, "Bread and Roses," 98.
65. Sarachild quoted in Redstockings, *Feminist Revolution* (New Paltz, NY: Redstockings, 1975), 145; Popkin, "Bread and Roses," 57.
66. Carmen Sirianni, "Learning Pluralism: Democracy and Diversity in Feminist Organizations," *Nomos* 35 (1993): 287; Jane Mansbridge, "Feminism and Democratic Community," *Nomos* 35 (1993): 339–95.
67. The phrase appeared first in a poem of that name by James Oppenheim, published in *American Magazine* in December 1911. It was first applied to the strike in a labor anthology, *The Cry for Justice: An Anthology of the Literature of Social Protest*, ed. Upton Sinclair (Philadelphia: John C. Winston, 1915).
68. Popkin, "Bread and Roses," 125–26.
69. Jim Foreman, "Don't Shut Me Out! Some Thoughts on How to Move a Group of People from One Point to Another" (unpub. ms., author's collection, n.d.).
70. Joan Cassell, *A Group Called Women: Sisterhood and Symbolism in the Feminist Movement* (New York: David McKay, 1977), 143.
71. Polletta, *Endless Meeting*, 21, 154, 166.
72. Popkin, "Bread and Roses," 129.
73. Popkin, "Bread and Roses," 129.
74. Popkin, "Bread and Roses," 150. The fear of leadership showed in Bread and Roses' policy never to provide an individual speaker, insisting that two or even three people take turns presenting; Trude Bennett, interview by the author, June 2020. The policy did, however, make the talks more theatrical, like a public reading of a dramatic text.
75. The phrase and its now widely accepted analysis come from the political scientist Jo Freeman's *The Politics of Women's Liberation: A Case Study of an Emerging Social Movement and its Relation to the Policy Process* (New York: David McCay, 1975). However, as Ann Popkin notes, Freeman treated structurelessness as a "technical flaw" rather than as a political problem; Popkin "Bread and Roses," 143.
76. Polletta, *Endless Meeting*, 21, 154, 166; quotation from Sirianni at 293.
77. Popkin, "Bread and Roses," 124.
78. Popkin, "Bread and Roses," 114.
79. Mimeographed agenda for a late September 1970 meeting of the whole, author's collection; calendar at Folder 1.12, Ruthchild Papers, SL. Members did not need authorization to use the Bread and Roses name.
80. Danny, Bill, Henry, Marty and others, "Dissenting Opinion," n.d., in Folder 4, Fran Ansley Papers, SL.
81. Leaflet in Box 1, Bouvier Papers; Bread and Roses leaflet "On WBCN—The American Revolution Stereo Radio Station," *Boston Globe*, February 14, 1970, 3.
82. A fuller discussion of *9 to 5* is in Cobble, Gordon, and Henry, *Feminism Unfinished*, chap. 2.
83. Rank on gross for *9 to 5*, Box Office Mojo, http://boxofficemojo.com/movies/?id=9to5.htm. The 2021 documentary film *9 to 5: The Story of a Movement*, dir. Julia Reichert and Steven Bognar, is available on PBS video.
84. The eight waitresses rebelled when they asked for a raise and were refused with the words "Well, you're only women." Karen Nussbaum, interview by Kathleen Banks Nutter, December 18–19, 2003, Box 37, VF.
85. Desire for respect and personal dignity is often a primary motivation for work-

ers' activism. The social movement and labor organizing theorist Marshall Ganz addresses this point in "Leading Change: Leadership, Organization, and Social Movements," in *Handbook of Leadership Theory and Practice: A Harvard Business School Centennial Colloquium*, ed. Nitin Nohria and Rakesh Khurana (Boston: Harvard Business Press, 2010). See also Linda Gordon, *The Great Arizona Orphan Abduction* (Cambridge, MA: Harvard University Press, 2001), chaps. 2 and 6, on the importance of respectful treatment for miners.

86. A fuller discussion of the health book collection is in Cobble, Gordon, and Henry, *Feminism Unfinished*, chap. 2.

87. The collective learned that women were terrified of vaginal exams and hesitated to consult gynecologists, thus putting their health at risk; Nancy Shaw, "Working on Women" (mimeographed report, April 28, 1969, author's collection).

88. Kathy Davis, *The Making of Our Bodies Ourselves: How Feminism Travels Across Borders* (Durham, NC: Duke University Press, 2007).

89. Popkin, "Bread and Roses," 182.

90. One infamous statement—Betty Friedan's complaint that a "lavender menace" would scare off women and make it harder to build a broad movement—has been mistakenly taken as representative. In fact, her statement did not represent the views of her organization, and she soon disavowed it, in response to an angry reaction from a broad range of feminists.

91. "Gay Women in the Women's Movement," mimeographed one-page handout, author's collection.

92. Tess Ewing, interview by the author.

93. Mary Damon letter, Spring 1970, in Box 1, Bouvier Papers; Rochelle Ruthchild, interviews by the author.

94. Laura Tillem, interview by the author, March 1, 2020; Ann Popkin, "The Social Experience of Bread and Roses: Building a Community and Creating a Culture," in *Women, Class, and the Feminist Imagination: A Socialist Feminist Reader*, ed. Karen V. Hansen and Ilene J. Philipson (Philadelphia: Temple University Press, 1990), 195.

95. Sue Katz, interview by the author. Their feelings of exclusion were exacerbated by the fact that the lesbians were at the home of Mary Daly, a prominent lesbian radical feminist philosopher and theologian who taught, paradoxically, at the Jesuit Boston College—at the time the students were all male. In 1968 the college tried to fire her but backed down because of protests from the students! She was eventually forced out because once Boston College became co-ed, she began refusing to admit male students to some of her classes.

96. A much-circulated 1970 statement by the New York group Woman-Identified Woman argued that lesbianism is the highest form of feminism; Baxandall and Gordon, *Dear Sisters*, 107–9. But that statement is often taken out of context: it was a response to Friedan's fear that lesbian presence could stigmatize the women's movement; Ruthchild interview by the author.

97. The old-timers at Jacques did not use the word *lesbian* but instead *butch* and *femme*. Some of the older customers belonged to the Daughters of Bilitis, but that then-homophile organization was not yet engaged in open protest. In 1974 lesbians opened the Saints bar, and one Bread and Roses member recalled the "comfort level" she felt there. Libby Bouvier, Leslie Cagan, Marla Erlien, and Sue Katz, interviews by the author.

98. Folder 4.8, Carden Papers, SL; Susan Krieger, *The Mirror Dance* (Philadelphia: Temple University Press, 1983), chap. 11; Judith Ezekiel, *Feminism in the Heartland* (Columbus: Ohio State University Press, 2002), 53–54.

99. Amy Hoffman, "Boston in the 1970s: Is There a Lesbian Community? And if There Is, Who is in it?" *Journal of Lesbian Studies* 18, no. 2 (2014): 139.
100. One woman recalled that "someone spoke of the expedition as an 'action.' . . . I didn't think it was an action, I thought it was fun. But . . . I guess it was both." "Good Time Girls Go Bar Hunting," *Hysteria*, February 5, 1971.
101. Claire Bond Potter, "Not in Conflict, But in Coalition: Imagining Lesbians at the Center of the Second Wave," in *The Legacy of Second-Wave Feminism in American Politics*, ed. Angie Maxwell and Todd Shields (New York: Palgrave Macmillan, 2017), 205–30. For an examination of the leading role of lesbians in Buffalo's industrial labor unions, see Elizabeth Lapovsky Kennedy and Madeline D. Davis, *Boots of Leather, Slippers of Gold: The History of a Lesbian Community* (New York: Routledge, 1993). Lesbians influenced how New Left women dressed. One outside observer commented that it was "difficult to distinguish lesbian feminists from 'straight' women, since both groups might wear jeans or overalls, work boots or sneakers, and no cosmetics," an appearance still unusual in the late 1960s; Cassell, *Group Called Women*, 83. See also Breines, *Trouble Between Us*, 104–6.
102. Lesbians were disproportionately often shop stewards and other leaders in labor union struggles; Kennedy and Davis.
103. Breines, *Trouble Between Us*, 148; Elizabeth Lapovsky Kennedy, "Socialist Feminism: What Difference Did It Make to the History of Women's Studies?" *Feminist Studies* 34, no. 3 (2008): 504. This difference paralleled that between straights, who wanted to work with lesbians, and lesbians, who felt a need for their own spaces. But the race differences in preference were harder to act on, given the fundamental class and race inequality in the society as a whole.
104. Granted, this failure was worse in liberal and radical feminist circles. Numerous Black feminists have noted that socialist feminists worked harder to divest themselves of racist assumptions. One such statement is in Barbara Smith, interview by Loretta J. Ross, May 7–8, 2003, VF.
105. Wini Breines presents a powerful critique of this thinking in *Trouble Between Us*, 89–92 and 229nn33–34.
106. Roth, *Separate Roads*, 102–5; Benita Roth, "The Making of the Vanguard Center: Black Feminist Emergence in the 1960s and 1970s," in *Still Lifting, Still Climbing: Contemporary African American Women's Activism*, ed. Kimberly Springer (New York: NYU Press, 1999), 77.
107. Elizabeth Sutherland, "Colonized Women: The Chicana," in *Liberation Now! Writings from the Women's Liberation Movement* (New York: Dell, 1971), 198.
108. When her husband was murdered, Ericka Huggins came to New Haven with her three-month-old baby. Charged with conspiracy, she spent two years in prison there, her baby in the care of others, before the charges were dropped. The charges were so evidently false that in the jury's deliberation, one juror—a white woman—was so incensed that she "picked up a chair [apparently threatening to throw it] and shouted, 'Let these defendants go. You know you don't have any evidence. . . Why are we trying these people?'" Quoted in Mary Phillips, "The Power of the First-Person Narrative: Ericka Huggins and the Black Panther Party," *Women's Studies Quarterly* 43, nos. 3–4 (2015): 33. The rally had the serendipitous effect of connecting Bread and Roses women with other East Coast feminists, a connection that produced a series of retreats that influenced socialist feminist thinking. At least one, in New York City, is still going as I write.
109. A statement by three Bread and Roses women, n.d., in Folder 2.39, Popkin Papers, SL; Breines, *Trouble Between Us*, 111.

110. Fourth fat folder, Fran Ansley Papers, SL; Bread and Roses newsletters May 19 and July 1, 1970, and flyer, March 4, prob. 1970, in Bouvier Papers; IWD call in Cambridge Women's Center Papers, 1, no. 2, SL.

111. Tepperman report in Folder 1.4, Nancy Grey Osterud Papers, SL.

112. The Weatherman group named itself after Bob Dylan's line "You don't need a weatherman to know the way the wind blows." One of its leaflets announced that participants were "willing to die in battle." Weatherman's Mark Rudd insisted that "we don't want to be part of a sissy movement." When Bread and Roses responded that the plan would produce a bloodbath, Weatherman Eric Mann responded, "There are good bloodbaths and bad bloodbaths." Quotations from Meredith Tax and Cynthia Michel, "An Open Letter to the Boston Movement," n.d., author's collection; Popkin, "Bread and Roses," 66–67.

113. "Memo to Office Workers," mimeographed leaflet, n.d., Folder 22.7, Popkin Additional Papers, SL. Over one hundred secretaries at MIT received permission to participate but I was unable to find out if this happened on other campuses.

114. Vietnamese women leaders had asked two antiwar groups—Women's Strike for Peace and the Canadian Voice of Women—to arrange a meeting with "the North American Women's Liberation Movement." My account of this meeting, including quotations, is from Ellin Hirst, report to Bread and Roses, in Folder 2.39, Popkin Papers, SL. Patricia Robinson and members of the Poor Black Women group attended along with several Bread and Roses members; n.a., *Lessons from Damned*, 96; Giardina, *Freedom for Women*, 108.

115. *Left on Pearl: Women Take Over 888 Memorial Drive, Cambridge*, dir. Susan Rivo, 2016, a documentary film about this occupation, is available for rental at Leftonpearl.com

116. Capital letters in the original. Potential charges included trespass, disorderly conduct, "wanton injury to personal property"—even "assault and battery on a police officer," behavior that was extremely unlikely but it was common knowledge that police might claim to have been attacked. The leaflet, headed "We thought it would be a good idea to tell people," is in Folder 22.7, Popkin Papers, SL.

117. "We thought it would be a good idea to tell people a little of the history behind this struggle," mimeographed leaflet, Folder 22.7, Popkin Additional Papers, SL.

118. "Rally—Tuesday March 9, 12 noon, Holyoke Center, in support of Liberated Women's Center," leaflet, author's collection; Daphne Spain, "Women's Rights and Gendered Spaces in 1970s Boston," *Frontiers* 32, no. 1 (2011): 166–67.

119. Breines, *Trouble Between Us*, 102. Today a public school in the area is named for Graham. On Harvard's behavior, see Spain, "Women's Rights," 166.

120. Most ambitiously it initiated a drop-in program, supported by a $100,000 grant from the Cummings Foundation, which offered a range of resources and help, including a community kitchen stocked with nutritious foods, toiletries, bus and subway passes; access to computers with staff assistance to those who need it; a resource database with information on health, legal, housing, and other services; and a lending library. For more, visit the website Cambridgewomenscenter.org.

121. The SCLC arose from the Montgomery bus boycott victory; see chapter 5.

122. The story of the origins of NBFO is from Beverly Davis, "To Seize the Moment: A Perspective on the National Black Feminist Organization," *Sage* 5, no. 2 (1988): 43–47. As is often the case, estimates of the attendance vary: Taylor, "Historical Evolution," 248, puts it at 250.

123. Roth, *Separate Roads*, 108.

124. Keeanga-Yamahtta Taylor, *How We Get Free: Black Feminism and the Combahee*

River Collective (Chicago: Haymarket Books, 2017), 115. She had, however, intersected with some early feminists at university—looking back, she described them as "proto-feminists."

125. Payne, *I've Got the Light of Freedom*, found that that many of SNCC activists had previously worked in community causes not typically considered political, such as church work. The same was true of farmworker activists (discussed in chapter 6).

126. Barbara Smith, *The Truth That Never Hurts: Writings on Race, Gender, and Freedom* (New Brunswick, NJ: Rutgers University Press, 2000), 179; Taylor, *How We Get Free*, 75; Barbara Smith interview by Ross, 6.

127. Both had been activists starting in high school. Barbara remembers participating in an anti-Vietnam war march to the UN in 1967, hearing Martin Luther King, Jr., speak against the war, and being "on the streets" of Chicago at the 1968 Democratic Party convention where the police rioted and attacked demonstrators. Smith, *Truth Never Hurts;* Taylor, *How We Get Free*, 86.

128. The convention was covered in the new Black newspaper, founded in 1965, the *Bay State Banner*, September 14, 1967.

129. The first quotation is from Barbara Smith in the introduction to *Home Girls*, xlii; the second is from Jane Mansbridge and Barbara Smith, "How Did Feminism Get to Be All White?" *American Prospect*, March 13, 2000, 33.

130. First Barbara Smith returned briefly to New York City—for a job at the *National Enquirer*! There she participated in a consciousness-raising group, in which she was the only nonwhite woman, an experience that must have confirmed her view of the need for a Black group.

131. Taylor, *How We Get Free*, 130.

132. They included the Trotskyist Marxist writer C.L.R. James, the Caribbean historian Walter Rodney, the radical academics John Henrik Clarke and Julius Lester, and the Jamaican-Cuban novelist and postcolonial theorist Sylvia Wynter. Originally a project of the Martin Luther King, Jr., Center for Nonviolent Social Change, it became an independent organization in 1969. Committed to both scholarship and advocacy, it focused on the struggle for racial equality as well as African American self-determination and self-understanding.

133. The first quotation is from Smith interview by Ross, 51; the second is from Springer, "Interstitial," 187; Springer, *Living the Revolution*, 59–60.

134. "Boston Abortion Witchhunt Convicts Black Doctor," *Black Panther*, March 8, 1975, 10, 24. The story became a cause célèbre, covered by media throughout the country.) The Edelin case is featured in a medical ethics textbook: Gregory E. Pence, *Medical Ethics: Accounts of Ground-Breaking Cases* (New York: McGraw-Hill, 2011). Constructing the fetus not only as a baby but as a person capable of decision making, one juror explained bizarrely, "That baby should have had the chance to prove his own viability. . . . There is only one person that can make that decision, and that is the baby."

135. Sara Dubow, *Ourselves Unborn: A History of the Fetus in Modern America* (New York: Oxford University Press, 2011), 99. Along with the Massachusetts Organization to Repeal Abortion Laws and Planned Parenthood of Massachusetts, the NAACP and Boston City Hospital medical staff raised the money for Edelin's legal costs.

136. The assailant, Joseph Rakes, was tried, convicted, and sentenced, but the sentence was suspended. The use of a flagpole as weapon was seen again in January 2021 in the Far Right mob that invaded the U.S. Capitol.

137. Two prominent amendments to the same 1975 HEW appropriations bill also merged

the issues: it prohibited the use of federal funds for court-ordered desegregation bus- ing and abortion services or referrals. Conservative William Safire, President Nixon's speechwriter, also joined the two causes. Jennifer Donnally, "The Edelin Man- slaughter Trial and the Anti-Abortion Movement," *Massachusetts Historical Review* 20 (2018): 19; Dubow, *Ourselves Unborn*, chap. 3 passim; Gillian Frank, "The Colour of the Unborn: Anti-Abortion and Anti-Bussing Politics in Michigan, United States, 1967–1973," *Gender and History* 26, no. 2 (2014): 351–78.

138. Regarding Inez García, whose case is less well known than the other, see Bax- andall and Gordon, *Dear Sisters*, 201–3.

139. Fran Beal, "Slave of a Slave No More: Black Women in Struggle," *Black Scholar* 6, no. 6 (1975): 9. Beal similarly objected to the NBFO because it was not "talking about changing the power balance." Barbara Smith thought that "in some of its aspirations and its perspectives, [it] wanted to be like NOW. . . . broad, maybe electorally focused, not . . . by any means radical or Left"; quoted in Taylor, *How We Get Free*, 53.

140. Springer, *Living the Revolution*, 66–70, 83–85, 135–37, quotation at 73; Smith inter- view by Ross, 55; Smith in Taylor, *How We Get Free*, 55. In fact, the NBFO's funding was tenuous: it had no access to the economic resources of comparable white orga- nizations such as NOW and WEAL. And there were competing loyalties, between NOW and *Ms.* magazine. The quarrels reached enmity so great that some NBFO groups withheld NBFO records from other groups. Davis, "To Seize the Moment"; Springer, *Living the Revolution*, 85.

141. Smith interview by Ross, 49; Frazier quoted in Harris, "Running with Reds," 15. Springer, *Living the Revolution*, 51; Roth *Separate Roads*, 106–12.

142. Harris, "Running with Reds," 10.

143. Barbara Smith noted that others sometimes described themselves as members—no doubt because the Combahee River Collective was so widely respected—and the core group chose not to correct their claims; Smith to author.

144. Barbara Smith remembered that they chose to make the cover graphic of her book *Home Girls* African as a visual way of countering the nationalist view that they were "not a part of the race because we are not heterosexual . . . and therefore we are not Black." She discussed this in Jaimee A. Swift, "Where Would Black Feminism Be Today If It Wasn't for Barbara Smith?" BlackWomenRadicals.com, n.d.

145. Taylor, *How We Get Free*, 22.

146. The same pattern—careers that contributed to social justice—may have character- ized Bread and Roses members as well, but it is hard to trace because of their num- bers. Moreover, their distinguished careers may be less surprising because they so often came from relatively privileged backgrounds. By contrast, Combahee members faced the triple "jeopardy," as Fran Beal labeled it, faced by working-class African American lesbians.

147. Her many publications include " 'Nation-izing' Coalition and Solidarity Politics for US Anti-militarist Feminists," *Social Justice* (2020); *Beyond Heroes and Holidays: A Practical Guide to K-12 Multicultural, Anti-Racist Education and Staff Development* (1998); and "Children of GI Town: The Invisible Legacy of Militarized Prostitution," *Asian Journal of Women's Studies* (1997). A fellowship in her name at the Claremont Colleges is one of her many awards.

148. Chirlane McCray in *Essence Magazine*, June 2013. Born to working-class parents in Springfield, McCray's family moved to Longmeadow, Massachusetts, becoming the second Black family in the area, defying some white residents' petitions demand- ing that they leave. She denounced the racism she experienced in a column for the

school newspaper and soon became a professional writer, using her skills to support several progressive New York City politicians. She became an editor, journalist, activist, and poet. She entered New York City politics as a speechwriter for Mayor David Dinkins.

149. Some straight women ultimately left the group because of discomfort in being associated with lesbians, though that split overlapped with class and political differences. Taylor, *How We Get Free*, 25; Mansbridge and Smith, "How Did Feminism."

150. Smith interview by Ross, 63 and 64, further discussion at 60–65, 91–95.

151. Smith, *Truth Never Hurts*, 171; Kevin Gosztola, "Authors of Combahee River Statement," Shadowproof.com, July 10, 2017.

152. Barbara Smith, "Why I Left the Mainstream Queer Rights Movement," *New York Times*, June 19, 2019.

153. Smith, "Why I Left."

154. Jones, Eubanks, and Smith, *Ain't Gonna Let Nobody*, 57; Danica London Potts, "Barbara Smith Is Still One of Feminism's Most Essential Voices," *Shondaland*, February 15, 2018.

155. Jones, Eubanks, and Smith, *Ain't Gonna Let Nobody*, 57; Gosztola, "Authors of Statement."

156. Taylor, *How We Get Free*, 128.

157. Today's intersectionality discourse still often omits class. Linda Gordon, " 'Intersectionality,' Socialist Feminism, and Contemporary Activism: Musings by a Second-Wave Socialist Feminist," *Gender and History* 20, no. 2 (2016): 340–57.

158. The quotation from Frazier is in Taylor, *How We Get Free*, 127, 130–31; the one from Smith is in Taylor, *How We Get Free*, 69.

159. This discussion of the retreats uses material from Barbara Smith, email to author; Harris, "Running with Reds," 20–24; Smith interview by Ross, 67; Springer, *Living the Revolution*, 107ff; Taylor, *How We Get Free*, 56–59. For a detailed summary of the retreats, see Saraellen Strongman, "The Sisterhood: Black Women, Black Feminism, and the Women's Liberation Movement" (PhD diss., University of Pennsylvania, 2018).

160. Springer, *Living the Revolution*, 107–8, quotation at 108.

161. Springer, *Living the Revolution*, 107–11. Powell became a singer, songwriter, and actor with New York's Women's Experimental Theater.

162. Barbara Smith had proposed an anthology on Black women's studies to the Modern Language Association's Commission on the Status of Women in the Profession; she and Gloria Hull had already begun to work on the anthology, *All the Women Are White, All the Blacks Are Men, But Some of Us Are Brave: Black Women's Studies* (New York: Feminist Press, 1982). Only a few of its contributors had attended Combahee's retreats.

163. Smith interview by Ross, 67; Strongman, "Sisterhood," 267–68.

164. Springer, *Living the Revolution*, 128–29; Frazier quoted in Breines, *Trouble Between Us*, 130–31.

165. Springer, *Living the Revolution*, 73.

166. Springer, "Interstitial," 192; Okazawa-Rey interview by the author.

167. Eli Zaretsky, "Rethinking the Split Between Feminists and the Left," in *Public Seminar*, October 11, 2013.

168. Kwame Anthony Appiah and Henry Louis Gates, Jr., have pointed to what they call a paradox: that identity politics can be either the most conservative or the most radical of strategies: "conservative, because the idea that identities are largely

derived from natural characteristics" reinforces an essentialist view of identity; "radical, because [of] the idea of embracing stigma and turning it into the basis of political agency." Appiah and Gates, eds., *Identities* (Chicago: University of Chicago Press, 1995). Barbara Smith has charged critics with commodifying "identity politics"; Jones, Eubanks, and Smith, *Ain't Gonna Let Nobody*, 55.

169. Identity politics was a "contemporary term for what has long been a political theoretical practice"—organizing on the basis of one's own oppression; Diane L. Fowlkes, "A Writing Spider Tries Again: From Separatist to Coalitional Identity Politics," in *Identity Politics in the Women's Movement*, ed. Barbara Ryan (New York: NYU Press, 2001), 279. Some criticisms of identity politics mistakenly see it as essentialist, as if it assumed that identities are fixed. Combahee and most feminists consider identity socially constructed.

170. Roth, *Separate Roads*, 122.

171. Barbara Smith, ed., *Home Girls: A Black Feminist Anthology* (Kitchen Table/Woman of Color Press, 1983), xliii–xlv. Elly Bulkin, Minnie Bruce Pratt, and Barbara Smith, eds., *Yours in Struggle: Three Feminist Perspectives on Anti-Semitism and Racism* (Brooklyn, NY: Long Haul Press, 1984). One male scholar agreed: "Trump's "unparalleled racism tells us . . . about . . . our failure to interrogate and challenge patriarchy in the Black community." Luke Harris, speaking at "Under the Blacklight," African American Policy Forum, episode 18, October 28, 2020.

172. Taylor, *How We Get Free*, 127

173. Kimberlé Crenshaw, "Mapping the Margins: Intersectionality, Identity Politics, and Violence Against Women of Color," *Stanford Law Review* 43, no. 6 (1991): 299. On identity as coalition, see Carastathis, *Intersectionality*, 7.

174. Taylor, *How We Get Free*, 127.

175. The Combahee statement was itself a product of collaboration. Demita Frazier recalls working on it at the Cambridge Women's Center, the product of Bread and Roses activism; Taylor, *How We Get Free*, 123. Zillah Eisenstein solicited the essay for her collection *Capitalist Patriarchy and the Case for Socialist Feminism* (New York: Monthly Review Press, 1979), a white socialist-feminist collection of essays published by a white Marxist press. Unremarkably for the time, all the other articles were by whites, a fact that signified many white feminists' ignorance of Black feminist work.

176. Bernice Johnson Reagon, "Coalition Politics: Turning the Century," in Smith, *Home Girls*, 356.

177. Roth, *Separate Roads*, 123; Smith quoted in Taylor, *How We Get Free*, 43 and 50.

178. Taylor, *How We Get Free*, 107.

179. Audre Lorde was among the Black feminists who insisted that they should not focus on educating white women; Strongman, "Sisterhood," 257.

180. Unlike feminist reproductive rights principles, which saw birth control as a personal decision and often a means of empowering women, population control sought to "cure" poverty not by redistributing wealth but by reducing the size of subject population. Linda Gordon, *Woman's Body, Woman's Right: A Social History of Birth Control in America* (New York: Penguin, 1976); the revised second edition of this book is *The Moral Property of Women: A History of Birth Control Politics in America* (Urbana: University of Illinois Press, 1990).

181. Smith interview by Ross, 83–88.

182. Doreen L. Cook, "The Case of Willie Sanders," in *Collage* (Boston University) 2, no. 1 (October 1, 1979); WGBH audio report on the case, transcript, n.d.; Charles Ray Johnson, "Commonwealth vs. Willie Sanders," *Black Scholar*, January–

February 1980, 82. The Boston police were far less diverse than other city forces in the 1970s—only 3.5 percent were people of color. See C. J. Chivers, "From Court Order to Reality: A Diverse Boston Police Force," *New York Times*, April 4, 2001.

183. Springer, *Living the Revolution*, 146. Barbara Smith considered this "the most dynamic organizing" they had done; Swift, "Where Would Black Feminism Be Today." The coalition included Green Light in Dorchester, a safe house program for abused women; City Life, a left community organization in Jamaica Plain; Women Against Violence Against Women, a chapter of a national organization; Crisis, a Black women's group focused on the killings; and several other predominantly Black organizations. Combahee asked its white collaborators not to attend these meetings, in order to make sure that the primary initiative came from African Americans.

184. Aimee Sands, "Rape and Racism in Boston: An Open Letter to White Feminists," *Off Our Backs*, January 1981, 16–17.

185. "A Climate of Fear in Boston," *Boston Globe*, May 9, 1979, 18. Identifications of the murdered women can be found in the Wikipedia entry for "Roxbury Murders."

186. The title of a Combahee-inspired book highlights the sexist-racist assumption behind this phrase: *All the Women Are White, All the Blacks Are Men, But Some of Us Are Brave: Black Women's Studies.*

187. Combahee organized a large protest demonstration, carrying a banner reading "3rd World Women. We cannot live without our lives" (thus considering American Blacks part of the Third World). Swift, "Where Would Black Feminism Be?" Combahee used the occasion of its fifth retreat, held in Cambridge in July 1979, to raise funds by organizing poetry readings; Strongman, "Sisterhood," 270. The killings were part of the inspiration for Audre Lorde's poem "Need: A Chorale for Black Woman Voices."

188. Breines, *Trouble Between Us*, 158–69; Folder 11.19, Tia Cross Papers, SL.

189. Jim Vrabel, *A People's History of the New Boston* (Amherst: University of Massachusetts Press, 2014), chap. 21; "April 27, 1968: Activists Erect Tent City in Boston," MassMoments.org.

190. "Three in Tight Race for Boston Mayor," *New York Times*, October 2, 1983; "The Campaign That Changed Boston—1983," *Dorchester Reporter*, May 15, 2013; Vrabel, *People's History of New Boston*, chap. 21.

191. Scores of Black women scholars and activists inherited Combahee's mantle, so to speak. Kitchen Table Press, inspired by a 1980 conversation between Barbara Smith and Audre Lord, published writings by women of color for some twenty years. Its name was meant to communicate that it was a press run by "women who cannot rely on inheritances of other benefits of class privilege"; Barbara Smith, "A Press of Our Own," *Frontiers* 10, no. 3 (1989): 11. Smith was saddened by the press's demise; Smith interview by Ross, 76. National organizations that could be considered direct descendants include African American Women in Defense of Ourselves (the group that formed to block Clarence Thomas's appointment to the Supreme Court and to support Anita Hill), the Black Radical Congress, Black Lives Matter, the Black Youth Project 100, Black Women Radicals, the Black Women's Studies Association, the Audre Lorde Project, Me Too, Say Her Name, the Black Alliance for Just Immigration, the Ella Baker Center for Human Rights, the African American Policy Forum, and the Massachusetts Women of Color Coalition. Strongman, "Sisterhood," 273, discusses the press.

192. Numerous scholars have pointed out that *intersectionality* has become a buzzword emptied of implications for social justice movements; they include Kathy Davis, Les-

lie McCall, Jennifer Nash, and more. These critiques are summarized in Carastathis, *Intersectionality*, 1–3.

193. This understanding of intersectionality repeats the limitations of an earlier concept much used by feminists, "difference," of which I have been equally critical; Linda Gordon, "On Difference," *Genders* 10 (1991): 91–111; Gordon, "'Intersectionality,' Socialist Feminism." See also Sirma Bilge, "Intersectionality Undone: Saving Intersectionality from Feminism Intersectionality Studies," *Du Bois Review* 10, no. 2 (2013): 405–24; Sara Salem, "Intersectionality and Its Discontents: Intersectionality as Traveling Theory," *European Journal of Women's Studies* 25, no. 4 (2016): 1–16.

INDEX

Page numbers in *italics* refer to illustrations.
Page numbers after 406 refer to endnotes.

veterans of, 389*n*, 390, 392
women's center in Cambridge, 376–77
Brecht, Bertolt, 181
Breckinridge, Sophonisba, 46, 49, 143
Brown v. Board of Education, 236, 243,
244, 247, 248, 260
Budenz, Louis, 210
Burg, Steven, 154, 156–57, 160
Burks, Mary, 235, 239, 252

Camacho, Epifanio, 306–7, 309, 319–20,
323
capitalism
Bread and Roses and, 390
Combahee River Collective and, 385
focus on immediate survival and, 214–15
Kelley's socialism and, 29, 36
Ku Klux Klan and, 7
male dominance and, 343
Townsend movement and, 145, 168
unemployed movement and, 3
Carby, Hazel, 70–71
Carr, Johnnie, 244–45, 246, 250, 253–54,
256
Catholic hierarchy
Mexican farmworkers and, 106, 320
supporting Franco, 119
threatened by Department of Justice,
129
Catholics. *See also* Chavez, Cesar; Coughlin, Charles
anti-fascist groups of, 128
Mexican farmworkers, 317–20, *318*
opposed by the Klan, 2, 76–77, 80,
82–84, 86–87, 96, 98, 104–5, 424
welcomed by fascist groups, 77
Cayton, Horace, 205
Cell 16, 356–57, 486
Chaplin, Charlie, 84
Chautauquas, 159–60
Chavez, Cesar, 3–4, 6, 7, 9, *283. See also*
United Farm Workers (UFW)
building a community organization,
295–96
campaign against undocumented workers, 321
Catholicism of, 292, 313, 314, 318, 336
compared to King, 284, 287, 337–38, 475

condoning vandalism, 323–24
co-opted into running a union, 309–10
discouraging independent initiatives,
336–37
disintegrating leadership of, 332
as extraordinary organizer, 283, 284
as a farm worker, 291, 294
fasts of, 286, 287, 312, 318, 320, 324–
25, 338, 478
fear of losing him, 334–35, 337
few leaders willing to challenge him,
319–20
followers sharing responsibility for
downfall, 286, 287
forcing workers out of UFW, 330
as great leader, 336
imagined spiritual community of, 331
impatient with running a union, 314
insistent on making all decisions, 314
labor union as ultimate goal, 296, 297
learning from organizers, 291–92
mentoring a group of followers/lead-
ers, 285–86
move to Delano, 294–95
move to La Paz, 331–32
organizing method of, 292–94
paying all staff equally, 312–14, 315
purging most capable staff, 334–35,
336
purging those he considered disloyal,
285
sacrifice emphasized by, 287–88, 312–
14, 319, 324, 332
slide into paranoia and delusion, 284,
285–86, 332–35
social movement unionism and, 285, 286
spiritual vision undermining his work,
285–86
starting the FWA, 294–97
as tragic figure, 286, 336
women in organizing plans, 295–96, 305
working around Catholic clergy, 295
Chavez, Helen, 294, 303–4, 305, 331
Chavez, Manuel, 321, 323
Chavez, Richard, 301, 312, 336
Christian Front. *See also* Coughlin, Charles
allied with Klan's anti-Semitism, 118
Catholics worried about, 128

Freedom Singers, 279–80
free ridership, 214, 279
free spaces, 63, 255, 339
Friedan, Betty, 488
Fröbel, Friedrich, 34

Game, played by Synanon, 334–35
Ganz, Marshall, 302–3, 311, 319, 333, 335, 472
Garcia, Inez, 381
Garvey, Marcus, 101
German American Bund, 113, 121–28
anti-Semitism of, 78*n*, 124
decline of, 129–30
family activities of, 121, 124–26
glorifying fascist violence, 131
Kristallnacht and, 128
marching in Nazi uniforms, 75, 125–26
Nazi Party and, 122–24
opponents of, 127–28
rally in Madison Square Garden, 126–28, *126*, 129
Gilmore, Georgia, 270–71, 467
Goldmark, Josephine and Pauline, 41
Govea, Jessica, 295–96, 298, 327
Graetz, Robert, 247–48, 264, 272, 461
Gramsci, Antonio, 132
grape boycott, 325–31, 479
losses attributable to, 330–31
Grapes of Wrath, The. See Steinbeck, John
Gray, Fred, 238, 242*n*, 247, 249*n*, 266, 468
Great Migration, 13, 47

Hamilton, Alice, 17*n*, 20, 41, 411
Hart, Sarah, 36*n*
Haynes, George Edmund, 203
Height, Dorothy, 345–46, 377
Herndon, Angelo, 197, 203, 250*n*
Hicks, Louise Day, 380
Highlander Center, 246, 248–49, 263, 281, 461, 468
Hill, Joe, 227*n*
homeless in 1930s, 180, 188. *See also* eviction resistance
homophobia, 341, 369, 370, 383–84, 391
Hoover, J. Edgar, 99, 117, 206, 263, 465
Hoovervilles, 183

Hopkins, Harry, 215, 221, 224–25
Hudson, Hosea, 196, 198
Huerta, Dolores, 300–302, *300*, 304, 305, 318, 319, 331, 335–36
Hughes, Langston, 282
Hull, Gloria (Akasha), 382
Hull-House, 2, 6, 12. *See also* Addams, Jane
achievements and failures of, 46–47
application procedures for, 24–25
becoming city block of buildings, 20–21
both home and community center, 21, 22
coffeehouse at, 32–33
conversation in, 24
decor of, 21–22
expert social scientists in, 28, 411
food rejected by neighbors, 32–33
governmental and institutional positions and, 40–41, *41*
gymnasium for boys, 34–35
high culture for the poor, 37–38
male-headed families and, 418–19
maternalist stance of, 42–43
men staying at, 22, 28–29
neighbors invited into, 31
neighbors' own desires and, 38, 39
nursery for neighborhood children, 33–34
Phillis Wheatley Home compared to, 72–74
political action and, 43
quantitative social research in, 28, 29–31
queer domesticity of, 22–24
as "queer" home for privileged women, 17
range of activities offered at, 31–32, 412
rearrangements of time and space, 26, 39–40
resources of privileged women and, 19
risky meetings and lectures at, 36–37
rules and rituals of, 20, 22
same-sex liaisons in, 23–24
shocked by neighborhood inhabitants, 29, 53–54

Social Security and, 143
survey of, 38
Kennedy, Flo, 377–78
Kennedy, Robert F., 286, 324
Kenney, Mary, 36
Keynesian economics, 143, 167
Keyser, Mary, 21
King, Coretta, 257, 261, 324
King, Martin Luther, Jr., 3, 6
  agreeing to support boycott, 254–55,
    462
  arrest of, 276, *276*, 277
  arriving in Montgomery, 237–38, 240,
    253–54
  in Birmingham campaign, 282
  bombings of his home, 261, 266, 278,
    287
  Chavez compared to, 284, 287, 337–38,
    475
  Hunter's religiosity and, 56
  on the law, 231
  as leader of MIA, 257, 259
  Margaret Sloan and, 377
  nonviolence and, 259, 261–62, 263, 278
  not helping Rosa Parks, 468
  raising money as a speaker, 270
  on self-changing in a movement, 282
  spiritual and rhetorical brilliance of,
    268
  supporting Chavez's fast, 324
Krassner, Paul, 365
Kristallnacht, 128, 432, 436
Kuhn, Fritz, 123–24, 128, 434
Ku Klux Klan
  four avatars of, 76*n*
  Montgomery bus boycott and, 260–61,
    277–78
  southern origin of, 6, 76
  unemployed organizers in the South
    and, 196
Ku Klux Klan, northern, 2, 6
  African American victims of, 101–2,
    104
  aggressive masculinity, 103–4
  asking little of most members, 95
  commission system in, 421
  compared to fascist groups, 131–34
  corruption in, 7, 89–90, 110–12

costumes of, 87–88
cross burnings by, *75*, 94, 105, 110, 118
declining membership, 110–12
denounced by Coughlin, 118
diversity rejected by, 82, 92, 94, 131
electoral and legislative work of, 76–77,
  90, 95–101, 132, 133
emotions shared with fascists, 131–32,
  436–37
entirely mainstream, 82
family entertainment events, 90–91,
  110–11
fascist groups as reorientation of,
  112–14
fascists too extreme for, 130
identifying friendly stores, 89
mainly lower middle class, white collar, 85
march on Washington, D.C., 108–10,
  109
mass outdoor rallies, 94–95, 110–11
media empire of, 80, 83, 90, 108
mistaken 1920s critics of, 84–86
Muste appealing to some of, 208
"naturalization" of "aliens," 94, 96,
  97, 110
normalizing bigotry, 134
opposition to, 106–8
organized activities of, 81–82
primarily nonviolent, 76, 132
recruitment techniques, 86–87, 90, 95
secret mystic rituals of, 92–94, 103, 110
selling paraphernalia, 87–88
size of, 76*n*
sociability in, 132
targeting Jewish businesses, 89
Townsend movement compared to,
  146–48, 150–52, 156, 160, 162, 169,
  439
trying to "cleanse" schools, 98
upward mobility for members, 88–89
vigilantism of, 101–3, 114
violent actions by, 90, 104–6
white Americans largely sharing beliefs
  of, 77, 108
as white evangelical revival, 80
women in, 76, 82, 91–92, 97–98, 103,
  109, 132